THE WONDER THAT WAS INDIA

1200–1700

Volume Two

A survey of the history and culture of the Indian sub-continent from the coming of the Muslims to the British conquest

S. A. A. RIZVI

PICADOR INDIA

First published in the UK 1987 by Sidgwick & Jackson, London
First published in India 2019 by Picador India
This edition published 2022 by Picador India
an imprint of Pan Macmillan Publishing India Private Limited
707 Kailash Building
26 K. G. Marg, New Delhi 110001
www.panmacmillan.co.in

Pan Macmillan, The Smithson, 6 Briset Street, Farringdon, London EC1M 5NR
Associated companies throughout the world
www.panmacmillan.com

ISBN 978-93-89109-35-1

7

Typeset in Times New Roman by R. Ajith Kumar, New Delhi
Printed in India by Repro India Limited

FSC
www.fsc.org
MIX
Paper | Supporting responsible forestry
FSC® C047271

CONTENTS

ILLUSTRATIONS

PLATES

IMPORTANT DATES

c. 571	Birth of the Prophet Muhammad
622	*Hijra* (emigration) of the Prophet from Mecca to Medina
630	The Prophet conquered Mecca
632	The Death of the Prophet
632–4	Abū Bakr, the first caliph
634–44	’Umar, the second caliph
644–56	’Usmān, the third caliph
656–61	’Alī, the fourth caliph
661–749	The Umayyads
680	The martyrdom of Imām Husayn
705–715	Caliph al-Walīd
712	Conquest of Sind by Muhammad bin Qāsim
749–1258	The ’Abbāsids
998–1030	Mahmūd of Ghaznī
1150–1	Sack of Ghaznī by Ghūrīd ’Alā ‘u‘d-Dīn Jahān-sūz
1178	Defeat of Mu’izzu‘d-Dīn Muhammad bin Sām at Anhilwāra
c. 1185–1205	Lakshmana Sena’s rule in Bengal
1191	Defeat of Mu’izzu‘d-Dīn Muhammad bin Sām at the first battle of Tarā’in by Prithvīrāja Chauhān
1192	Second battle of Tarā‘in, defeat of Prithvīrāja Chauhān
1192–3	Delhi seized by Qutbu’d-Dīn Aybak
1200	Conquest of Bihār and Bengal by Ikhtiyāru‘d-Dīn Bakhtiyār Khaljī
1206	Death of Mu’izzu‘d-Dīn Muhammad bin Sām

Ilbarī Turks: 1206–90

1210	Death of Qutbu‘d-Dīn Aybak
1221	Chingīz chases Jalālu‘d-Dīn Mingburnū
1227	Chingīz died
1235	Death of Khwāja Qutbu‘d-Dīn Bakhtiyār Kākī
1236	Death of Sultan lltutmish
	Death of Khwāja Mu’inu‘d-Dīn at Ajmīr
1236–40	Raziyya
1246–66	Nāsiru‘d-Dīn Mahmūd Shāh
1265	Death of Bābā Farid
1266–87	Ghiyāsu‘d-Dīn Balban

Khaljīs: 1290–1320

1290–6	Jalalu‘d-Dīn Fīrūz Shāh II
1294	Devagirī invaded by ’Alā ‘u‘d-Dīn
1296–1316	’Alā ‘u‘d-Dīn Muhammad Shāh
1297	Conquest of Gujarāt
1303	Capture of Chitor
1306–7	Expedition of Devagirī
1309–10	Malik Kāfūr’s invasion of Wārangal
1310–11	Kāfūr’s invasion of Dvārasmudra near Bangalore
1316	Death of ’Alā ‘u‘d-Dīn Khaljī
1316–20	Qutbu‘d-Dīn Mubārak Shāh

Tughluqs: 1320–1414

1320–5	Ghiyāsu‘d-Dīn Tughluq Shāh
1325	Death of Shaykh Nizāmu‘d-Dīn Awliyā‘
	Death of Amīr Khusraw
1325–51	Ghiyāsu‘d-Dīn Muhammad Shāh I
1327	Deogiri, renamed Daulatābād, made the second capital
1330–2	Token currency
1332	Arrival of Ibn Battūta in India
1340–1	Investiture from the ’Abbāsid Caliph
1341–3	New code (*Asālīb*)
1342	Ibn Battūta sent as ambassador to China
1347	Foundation of the Bahmanī kingdom
1351–88	Fīrūz Shāh III
1353–4	Fīrūz’s first Bengal expedition
1356	Death of Shaykh Nasīru‘d-Dīn Chirāgh-i Dihli
1359	Fīrūz’s second Bengal expedition
1365–6	Fīrūz’s Thatta expedition
1367	Aśoka’s pillars transplanted
1370	Death of Khān-i Jahān I
1376	Levy of *jizya* on the brāhmans
1388–1414	Successors of Fīrūz
1398	Tīmūr seized Delhi
1399	Tīmūr re-crossed the Indus

The Sayyids: 1414–51

Provincial Kingdoms

1336–1576	The Bengālī Sultans
1346–1589	The Sultans of Kashmīr
1391–1583	The Sultans of Gujarāt
1394–1479	The Sultans of Jaunpūr
1401–1531	The Sultans of Mālwa
1347–1527	The Bahmanīds

1422	Death of Khwāja Gīsū Darāz
1370–1601	The Fārūqī Sultans of Khāndesh.

The Lodīs: 1451–1526

1451–89	Bahlūl Lodī
1469	Birth of Gurū Nānak
1489–1517	Sikandar Lodī
1505	Death of Kabīr
1517–26	Ibrāhīm Lodī

Early Mughals: 1526–1707

1526–30	Zahīru'd-Dīn Muhammad Bābur
1530–40	Humāyūn's first reign
1539	Gurū Nānak's death

The Sūrs: 1540–55

1540–5	Sher Shāh Sūr
1542	Birth of Akbar at Amarkot in Sind
1545–54	Islam Shāh
1555	Humāyūn's second reign
1556–1605	Jalālu'd-Dīn Akbar
1560	Fall of Bayram Khān
1562	Akbar's first pilgrimage to Ajmīr
	Akbar's marriage to Raja Bhār Mal's daughter at Sāmbher
	Abolition of enslavement in war
1563	Remission of tax on Hindu pilgrim centres
1564	Abolition of *jizya*
1565	Founding of Agra fort
1568	Fall of Chitor
1569	Birth of Prince Salīm, order given to build Sīkrī palaces
1571	Akbar at Fathpūr-Sīkrī supervising construction work
1572	Gujarāt Campaign
1573	Akbar's lightning raid on Gujarāt
1574	Mullā Badā'ūnī and Abu'l Fazl presented at court
1575	Building of the 'Ibadat Khāna
1578	Fortress of Kumbhalmīr seized
1579	The *Mahzar*
	First Jesuit mission left Goa
1580–1	Bihār and Bengal rebellions suppressed
1585	Death of Mīrzā Muhammad Hakīm at Kabul and Akbar's departure for the north-west frontier
1586	Annexation of Kashmīr
1590–1	Conquest of Sind
1591–2	Second Jesuit mission

1592	The millennial year of *Hijra*, millenial coins issued
1595	Surrender of Qandahār
	Arrival of third Jesuit mission at Lahore
1598	Death of ’Abdu‘llāh Khān Uzbek of Transoxiana
	Akbar’s return to Agra
1599	Akbar left Agra to command the Deccan expedition
1600	Rebellion of Prince Salīm
	Fall of Ahmadnagar
1601	Asīrgarh seized
	Akbar’s return to Agra
1602	Murder of Abu‘l-Fazl
1603	Death of Khwāja Bāqi Bi‘llāh
1605	Death of Akbar
1605–27	Nūru‘d-Dīn Jahāngīr
1606	Prince Khusraw’s revolt
	Shaykh Nizām Thāneswarī’s banishment
	Gurū Arjan’s execution
1610	Qāzī Nūru‘llāh Shustarī flogged to death
1611	Jahāngīr marries Nūr Jahān
1619–20	Mujaddid imprisoned
1622	Mujaddid released
	Qandahār seized by Shāh ’Abbās
1624	Mujaddid’s death
1626	Mahabat Khān’s *coup de main* – foiled by Nūr Jahān
1627	Death of Jahāngīr
1628–58	Shihābu‘d-Dīn Shāhjahān
1631	Death of Mumtāz Mahal
1635	Death of Miyān Mīr
1638	Qandahār surrendered by the Irānian governor, ’Alī Mardān Khān
1642	Death of Shaykh ’Abdu‘l-Haqq Muhaddis Dihlawi
1648	Shāhjahānabād founded
	Qandahār recaptured by Irānians
1657	Shāhjahān’s serious illness
1658	Aurangzīb defeats Dārā Shukoh at Sāmūgarh
1658–1707	Aurangzīb
1659	Dārā Shukoh executed
1660–1	Execution of Sarmad
1661	Death of Mullā Shāh
1663	Death of Mīr Jumla
1664	Shivājī’s first sack of Sūrat
1665	Customs duties on Hindus doubled
	Jai Singh’s victories over Shivājī
1666	Death of Shāhjahān in captivity at Agra
	Shivājī presented to Aurangzīb at Agra, escapes from Agra

1667	Shivājī's second sack of Sūrat
1674	Aurangzīb leaves for Hasan Abdāl to suppress Afghān uprisings
1675	Execution of Gurū Tegh Bahādur
	Aurangzīb returns from Hasan Abdāl
1678	Jaswant Singh's death at Jamrūd
1679	*Jizya* re-imposed on Hindus
	War against Mārwār
1680	Death of Shivājī
1680	Rebellion of Prince Akbar foiled
	Aurangzīb leaves Ajmīr for the Deccan
1686	Bījāpūr seized by Aurangzīb
1687	Golkonda seized by Aurangzīb
1689	Shivājī's son, Shambhājī, and his family taken captive, Shambhājī executed
	Rājārām, the Marātha king, makes Jinjī his centre for operations against the Mughals
1698	Zu'lfaqār Khān seizes Jinjī
1700	Rājarām dies, Tārā Bā'i rules as queen mother
1707	Aurangzīb's death

Later Mughals: 1707–1857

1707–12	Shāh 'Alam I, Bahādur Shāh
1713–19	Farrukhsiyar
1719–48	Nasīru'd-Dīn Muhammad Shāh
1729	Death of Shāh Kalīmu'llāh Jahānābādī
1739	Nādir Shāh sacks Delhi
1757	Clive's victory at Plassey
1757–58	Ahmad Shāh Durranī declared Emperor of Delhi, Delhi and Mathura plundered
1761	Ahmad Shāh Durranī crushes Marāthā power at Panipat, Delhi plundered by the Afghāns
1762	Death of Shāh Walīu'llāh
1773	Death of Ahmad Shāh Durrānī
1785	Mawlānā Fakhru'd-Dīn's death
1799	Tīpū died defending Seringāpatam
1803	Shāh 'Alam II (1760–1806) surrenders Delhi to the British
1824	Death of Shāh 'Abdu'l-'Azīz
1831	Defeat and death of Sayyid Ahmad Shāhid and Shāh Isma'īl at Bālākot
1837–57	Sirāju'd-Dīn Bahādur Shāh Zafar, the last Mughal emperor

LIST OF MAPS

NOTE ON PRONUNCIATION

Every Indian language has a complex phonetic system and contains phonemes which to the average speaker of English seem almost exactly the same, but to the Indian ear are completely different. Only after long practice can the hearing be trained to recognize these differences, or the vocal organs to pronounce them accurately. The scripts of Indian languages reproduce these sounds, but they can be expressed in Roman script only by means of numerous diacritical marks below or above the letters. It is assumed that most the readers of this book will not be students of Indian languages, and therefore a simplified system of alliteration has been used, which gives some idea of the approximate sound.

Words in classical languages are transliterated according to the simplified system mentioned above. Place-names in general follow the present-day official spellings of the governments of the countries of South Asia, as given in Bartholomew's *World Travel Map*, India, Pakistan, and Ceylon, 1970. Proper names of nineteenth- and twentieth-century Indians are given in the spelling which they themselves favoured. Diacritical marks have been placed over the long vowels in such names, in order to give some ideas of the correct pronunciation. Exceptions are made only in the case of a very few Anglicized words, like Calcutta and Bombay.

Only three letters with diacritical marks are normally used: *ā*, *ī*, and *ū*. These distinguish long from short vowels. In most Indian languages *e* and *o* are always long, and therefore do not need diacritics.

Vowels

a short is pronounced like *u* in 'hut', never like *a* in 'hat'. Bengali speakers usually pronounce it like a short *o* as in 'hot'.

ā long, as in 'calm'.

e approximately as the vowel in 'same', but closer to the long *e* in French or German.

i as in 'pin'. The word 'Sikh', incidentally, should sound approximately like English 'sick'. The pronunciation like 'seek' seems to have been adopted by some Englishmen in India for this very reason, in order to avoid depressing overtones in the name of a tough, vigorous people.

ī as in 'machine'.

o approximately as in 'so'. Close to the long *o* in French or German.

u as in 'bull', never as in 'but'. 'Punjāb', however, is an Anglicized spelling, and is more accurately written 'Panjāb'. In the case of this word we have deviated from our rule about using the accepted spelling, in order to avoid the pronunciation 'Poonjab', which one sometimes hears from speakers who are doing their best to be correct. The first syllable is like the English 'pun'.

ū as in 'boot'.

Consonants

Most of the Hindī consonants are pronounced roughly as in English, but special care should be taken of the aspirated consonants *kh*, *gh*, *chh*, *jh*, *th*, *dh*, *ph*, and *bh.* These are exactly like their unaspirated counterparts, *k*, *g*, *ch*, *j*, *t*, *d*, *p*, and *b*, but with a stronger emission of breath.

Urdu has imported several sounds from Arabic and Persian. Many speakers are inclined to pronounce words in these languages according to the Indian phonetic system, but educated Muslims attempt to pronounce them correctly.* The Arabic alphabet indicates several shades of pronunciation which cannot be expressed in simple Roman script; for example, *t* represents two different Persian letters, *s* three letters, and *z* four letters. In works intended for specialist readers such consonants are indicated by diacritical marks; this seemed unnecessary in this work. The vowels, *a*, *e*, *i*, *o*, and *u*, are pronounced roughly as mentioned above.

Consonants are to be pronounced approximately as in English, with the following exceptions: *kh* sounds like the Scottish 'loch' or German 'buch'; *gh* is pronounced like the French *r; q* is a deep guttural unknown in most European languages, pronounced like *k* but with the back of the throat wider open as though swallowing. The sign ' represents a distinct letter known as *ain* in Arabic and Persian. It is known to phoneticians as a 'glottal stop'; a similar sound occurs in some dialects in English, as in the eastern English and 'cockney' pronunciation of 'bottle', where the *t* is not heard, but a momentary suppression of breath and a slight swallowing movement of the throat takes place. The raised comma ' represents the Arabic *hamza*, which is not strictly a letter. It normally occurs between vowels and indicates that they form separate syllables, but the swallowing sound between is much less noticeable.

*Adapted from A. L. Basham (ed.), *A Cultural History of India*, Oxford, 1975, pp. xvi, xvii.

INTRODUCTION, WITH A REVIEW OF SOURCES

INDIA and China have the oldest cultural traditions in the world. India has enjoyed over 4,000 years of civilization, and every period of its history has contributed something to present-day life. The most significant characteristic of Indian civilization, as it evolved through the ages, is its unity in diversity. *The Wonder That Was India*, first published in 1954, now called Volume I, deals with the ancient civilization of India. It was stated there that the ancient civilization of India differed from those of Egypt, Mesopotamia, and Greece in that its traditions have been preserved without a break to the present day.* Muslim rule in India, which was firmly established in the thirteenth century and flourished until the beginning of the eighteenth century, and is now the subject of the present volume, did not destroy the ancient culture of India, as did the onslaughts of the Muslims in Persia.

> Under the rule of some of the Delhi sultans of the Middle Ages there was persecution, and we read of temples being razed to the ground and brāhmans put to death for practising their devotions in public; but in general the Muslims were reasonably tolerant, and at all times Hindu chiefs continued to rule in outlying parts of India, paying tribute to their Muslim overlords. Conversions to Islam were numerous, though only in a few regions were the majority of Indians persuaded to embrace the new faith. Hindus in those parts of India dominated by Muslims often accepted the situation as normal. In such conditions mutual influence was inevitable. Hindus began to learn Persian, the official language of their Muslim rulers, and Persian words found their way into the vernaculars. Well-to-do Hindu families often adopted the system of 'strict parda' from the Muslims, and made their womenfolk veil their faces in public. The surviving Hindu kings borrowed new military techniques from the Muslims, learnt to employ cavalry with greater effect, and to use heavier armour and new types of weapon. One great religious teacher of medieval India, Kabīr (1425–1505), a poor weaver of Banāras, taught the brotherhood of Hindu and Muslim alike in the fatherhood of God, and opposed idolatry and caste practices, declaring that God was equally to be found in temple and mosque. Later, Nānak (1469–1539), a teacher of the Panjāb, taught the same doctrine with even greater force, and founded a new faith, that of the Sikhs, designed to incorporate all that was best of both Hinduism and Islam.

*A. L. Basham, *The Wonder That Was India*, London, 1954. p. 4.

Nevertheless, the Muslim invasions, and the enforced contact with new ideas, did not have the fertilizing effect upon Hindu culture which might have been expected. Hinduism was already very conservative when the lieutenants of Muhammad of Ghūr conquered the Ganges Valley. In the Middle Ages, for every tolerant and progressive teacher there must have been hundreds of orthodox brāhmans, who looked upon themselves as the preservers of the immemorial Aryan Dharma against the barbarians who overran the holy land of Bhāratavarsa. Under their influence the complex rules of the Hindu way of life became if anything stricter and more rigidly applied.

In the sixteenth and seventeenth centuries the Mughal emperors unified practically the whole of North India and much of the Deccan, and built up an empire such as had not been seen since the days of the Guptas. The Mughal period was one of great splendour, which has left its mark on India in the form of many lovely buildings, wherein Islamic and Hindu motifs often blended in a perfect unity. The Tāj Mahal at Agra, the Mughal capital, is of course the most famous memorial of the times. Akbar (1556–1605), the contemporary of Queen Elizabeth I and the first of the four great Mughal emperors, fully realised that the Empire could stand only on a basis of complete toleration. All religious tests and disabilities were abolished, including the hated poll-tax on unbelievers. Rājput princes and other Hindus were given high offices of state, without conversion to Islam, and inter-communal marriages were encouraged by the example of the Emperor himself. If the policy of the greatest of India's Muslim rulers had been continued by his successors, her history might have been very different.

The great-grandson of Akbar, Aurangzīb (1658–1707), reversed the policy of toleration. Restrictions were placed on the free practice of Hindu rites, and preferment at court was confined to orthodox Muslims; later the tax on non-Muslims was reimposed. After nearly a century of equality this was bitterly resented by many Hindus, especially by the chiefs, many of whom had loyally served the earlier Mughals. The main resistance came from the Western Deccan, where, around Poona, the Marāthā chief, Śivājī (1627–80) laid the foundations of a new Hindu empire. At about the same time the Sikhs of the Panjāb, incensed at the new policy and the persecution of their leaders, reformed their faith, and were welded into a closely knit martial brotherhood. When the aged Aurangzīb died, the Mughal Empire was virtually at an end.

Politically the eighteenth century was one of Hindu revival. Though the Marāthā successors to Śīvaji could not build up a large, closely knit empire, their horsemen ranged far and wide over India, levying tribute from local chiefs, Hindu and Muslim alike. In the Panjāb towards the end of the century the Sikhs built an important kingdom, and almost everywhere Islam was on the defensive. But there was still no real cultural revival in Hinduism. Śīvājī, a brilliant leader, a just ruler, and a statesman of consummate craft, was conservative in his outlook, and appeared to his contemporaries rather as a restorer of the old than as a builder of the new. Unlike Akbar, he had no fresh vision of a state transcending religious differences, though he learnt much from the Mughals in statecraft and military science and respected the faith of his adversaries. The Marāthās did not encourage reforms in Hindu society, and the India of the eighteenth century was if anything more conservative than it had been in the days of the first Muslim invasions.

It was through the influence of Europe that revival came. Early in the sixteenth century the Portuguese founded the first European trading stations and settlements. They were followed by the Dutch, British, Danes, and French, and throughout the seventeenth century the number of European 'factories' increased. In the eighteenth century, with the break-up of the Mughal Empire, the Europeans began to take a greater interest in local politics, and, by the early nineteenth century, the British East India Company had virtually pushed out its rivals and dominated most of the subcontinent. The comparative ease with which the British established their supremacy is a measure of the political decadence of India at the time. By the middle of the nineteenth century the whole of India was either directly ruled by Britain, or governed indirectly through petty princes with local autonomy. A new conqueror had come, a conqueror far more alien to the Hindu than the Muslims had been, with an aggressive culture and immense technical superiority.*

The unique character of Muslim culture in India calls for separate treatment. The continuity it displays with the ancient culture discussed in *The Wonder That Was India*, Volume I, prompted us to name this work, *The Wonder That Was India*, Volume II.

This book concentrates mainly on the period between the thirteenth and seventeenth centuries. The first three chapters, dealing with the political history of the Arabs, Turks, Afghāns, and Mughals, do not comprise a catalogue of invasions, rebellions, and conquests, but analyse the currents and cross-currents of the social, economic, and cultural changes in the country. This was the period when India's contact with the vast, external, Muslim world deepened and urban society developed. Nevertheless, despite the introduction of the political and economic institutions which the Muslims in Irān and Central Asia had evolved, the dominance of the Hindu money-lender at the urban level, and the Rājpūt chieftains in rural areas, remained intact.

Although the struggle to regain political power was confined to the scions of former princely Rājpūt families, the Turkic ruling dynasties were also torn by internecine wars, to the extent that, in the fifteenth century, India was again fragmented into innumerable independent dynasties. It was Akbar who founded a strong Mughal empire, but the conceptual framework of his kingship was radically different. It was therefore important to analyse the theories of kingship, together with the military and administrative institutions of both the sultans and the Mughals, and this is done in Chapter 4.

*Ibid., pp. 479–81.

Chapter 5, on social and economic conditions, discusses the interaction between Hindus and Muslims and the forces that created Muslim social and economic groups equivalent to Hindu classes and castes. Nevertheless, both the Delhi sultans and the Mughals, in the interest of their own stability, did not concentrate solely on collecting taxes but paid due attention to agriculture and commerce. From the sixteenth century the introduction of European factories opened new trade opportunities and accelerated the growth of indigo and textile production. Although no improvement was made in manufacturing techniques, the individual skill of the artisans and craftsmen was refined.

The Muslims strictly adhered to their religious doctrines, but the analysis of the philosophical movements, sūfī ideologies, and sectarian divisions discussed in Chapter 6, highlights their distinctive features and characteristics. Chapter 7, devoted to the arts, goes a long way to show that Muslim symbols in architecture, painting, and music were predominantly influenced by ancient Indian motifs. Indeed, the *lacunae* in literary sources regarding the life and culture of this period may be filled by a study of its monuments and paintings.

SOURCES

The sources used for this volume are varied and enormous. Broadly they can be divided into four categories: archaeological, artistic, numismatic, and literary.

At one time Indian archaeology was confined mainly to unearthing India's remote past: prehistory and proto-history. In recent decades, however, archaeologists have diverted their attention to discovering the sites of medieval towns, villages, caravanserais, and roads. The scientific restoration of dilapidated monuments has highlighted previously unknown engineering and artistic techniques in this period. The archaeological survey departments in New Delhi and the states publish survey reports and journals. These are very useful sources of information for our study of the monuments of medieval times. Some universities and individual scholars have also published reports on surveys of different sites.

Not only do medieval paintings and artefacts reveal the artistic talents of the medieval painters and craftsmen, but they illuminate the social and economic history of the times. Museums in London, Dublin, Paris, Berlin, New York, Boston, Washington, Calcutta, New Delhi, Lahore, Kārāchi, and Dacca, the Khudā Bakhsh Library of Patna, the Razā Library of Rāmpūr, and the Sir Sālār Jang Museum of Hyderābād comprise some of the important art repositories. Many of these institutions have published catalogues describing their rare exhibits.

The coins preserved in the museums in the Indian subcontinent, Europe, and North America are a most important source for the study of currency systems, trade, and commerce. They are also helpful in correcting dates of political events. Many museums have published catalogues listing their collections. The *Journal of the Numismatic Society of India* and journals published by other numismatic societies in the subcontinent also contain articles on the hoards of coins discovered from time to time. A unique treatise on medieval Indian coins was written by

Thakkura Pherū, son of Chandra, the Master of the Mint during 'Alā 'u'd-Dīn Khaljī's reign (1296–1316). Entitled *Drārya-Par'iksha* (*An Examination of Coins*), it is written in Apabhramsa and deals with the technique of purifying gold, silver, mixed metals, and alloys. The work also discusses the weight and value of coins struck in different parts of India, including those minted under Sultan 'Alā 'u'd-Dīn Khaljī and his successor, Qutbu'd-Dīn Mubārāk Shāh.

Literary sources remain the most important source of information, however. Original *farmāns* (imperial decrees), notes, orders, and the correspondence of some rulers and their dignitaries have been discovered. Various manuals on polity, administration, law, and warfare, and diplomatic letters written from the reign of the Ghaznavids to the end of Mughal rule have survived; but the political chronicles are the most significant category of source material for our study. They are usually in Persian, but some are written in Arabic or in the local Indian dialects. They are generally compiled under the patronage of the central or provincial governments, but independent scholars also wrote a considerable number. Although the official chroniclers had access to their patrons' archives, some of the scholars who compiled historical works independently could draw upon documents in the possession of state dignitaries and other scholars.

British Interest in Muslim History

Some valuable bibliographical works were written in Arabic, but no such attempts were made in the realm of Persian scholarship. Their economic and political interests led the British to discover and translate Muslim histories of India, in a process which went through three phases. The first was analysis of the principal features of Muslim rule to discover the reasons for its decline. The pioneer in this field was James Fraser (1713–54). He resided in Sūrat in India from 1730 to 1740 and from 1742 to 1748. He wrote a history of Nādir Shāh of Irān, who had invaded India in 1739, and collected Persian, Sanskrit, and Zend manuscripts, taking them to England when he retired. After his death they were bought for the Radcliffe Library at Oxford and are now in the Bodleian Library. At Fraser's instigation, his teacher, Shaykh Muhammad Murād, compiled a history of Aurangzīb and his successors up to 1738, to serve as a background study for Fraser's history of Nādir Shāh. The only copy of Shaykh Muhammad Murād's history appears to be an autograph in the Bodleian Library. It examines the history of the period objectively and critically.

After the establishment of East India Company rule in Bengal, the need to increase European competence in Persian became paramount. William Jones (1746–94) published a Persian grammar in order to promote the study of Persian among the servants of the East India Company. In addition, 150 copies of John Richardson's *Dictionary of Persian, Arabic and English*, published in 1777, were subscribed by the Company. Similar encouragement was given to Major Davy, the Persian secretary to the Governor-General, Warren Hastings (1774–85), who translated into English *Institutes, Political and Military written... by the great*

Timour... first translated into Persian by Abu Taulib Alhusseini, and thence into English with notes... A preface and indices were compiled by J. White, and the work was published at Oxford in 1783. Although modern research questions the authenticity of the original by Timūr, who invaded India in 1398–9, British authorities relied heavily upon it for their analysis of the institutions of the great conqueror.

The most popular general history of the Muslim rulers of India was written by Muhammad Qāsim Hindū Shāh Astarābādī, known as Firishta (d. after 1609–10). He held senior positions under the Deccan sultans of Ahmadnagar and Bījāpūr. In 1606–7 he wrote a history of the Delhi sultans, the Mughals, and the provincial kingdoms of fifteenth- and sixteenth-century India, entitled *Gulshan-i Ibrāhīmī*, popularly known as *Tārīkh-i Firishta.* The importance of this work stimulated Alexander Dow (d. 1779), who had entered the service of the East India Company in 1760, to translate extracts into English. These were published in London in 1768, in two volumes, and a second edition came out in 1770–1. Dow also translated extracts from other Persian chronicles dealing with the reigns of Aurangzīb and his successors. John Briggs (d. 1875) published his new translation of the *Tārīkh-i Firishta* in London in 1829. Although Briggs's translation is also inaccurate, scholars who cannot read Persian still draw heavily upon it.

The *Siyaru 'l-muta'akhkhīrin*, by Nawwab Ghulam Husayn Khān Tabataba'i (d. after 1815), was translated into English by Raymond, or Hajji Mustata (d. 1791). Tabataba'i had served both the Mughals and the British. His *Siyaru'l-muta'akhkhīrin* was completed in 1781. It is a detailed history of eighteenth-century India and deals at great length with the fall of the Mughal empire and the conquests of the East India Company.

Warren Hastings encouraged Francis Gladwin (d. 1813), of the Bengal army, to study oriental literature, and Gladwin produced an abridged translation of the first three volumes of the *Ā'īn-i Akbarī*, or *The Institutes of Akbar's Reign*, by Akbar's secretary, Abu'l-Fazl (d. 1602). Hastings instigated the translation of the Muslim law book, the *Hidāya*, into English. Charles Hamilton (d. 1792) completed it in 1791. It became the basis of the East India Company's judicial system for Muslims.

In 1782 Robert Orme (d. 1801), an official historian of the East India Company and the author of the British military transactions in India, published *Historical Fragments of the Mogul Empire, of the Morattoes, and of the English Concerns in Indostan from the year 1659.* His knowledge of Persian was not perfect; nevertheless his work is of value in that it examines the Mughal and Marāthā institutions from a British point of view.

The growing preoccupation of the East India Company with conquering and consolidating its rule all over India prompted British intellectuals to examine and analyse the history and institutions of the Marāthās and other independent princes of India. In 1784 Jonathon Scott (d. 1829), Persian secretary to Warren Hastings, helped his master to found the Asiatic Society of Bengal. Two years later he published a general history of the Deccan and the fall of the Mughal empire, comprising abridged translations of the *Tārīkh-i Firishta*, the *Siyaru'l-*

muta'akhkhīrin, and other contemporary eighteenth-century works.

By the nineteenth century the establishment of British rule over the entire subcontinent was a foregone conclusion, and the East India Company had embarked upon a policy of Anglicizing the Indian administration. The need to understand Mughal institutions as such no longer remained. The interest of European intellectuals in Indian history deepened, and they entered the second epoch of scholarship, characterized by the authentic translation of texts. John Leyden (d. 1811) and William Erskine (d. 1852) translated the Persian translation of Bābur's memoirs into English. Major C. Stewart (d. 1837) translated the memoirs of Humāyūn's reign (1530–40, 1555) by Mihtar Jauhar, a ewer-bearer to the Emperor. Erskine's deep study of the sources on the reigns of Bābur and Humāyūn enabled him to write authoritatively his *History of India under Bābur and Humāyūn.* After his death this work was edited and published by his son in London in 1854.

Henry George Raverty (b. 1825) joined the East India Company's 3rd Bombay Infantry in 1843 and retired in 1864. He took part in the siege of Multān, in the Panjāb campaign of 1849–50, and in the first North-West Frontier expedition in 1850 against tribes on the Swāt border; and he served as assistant commissioner in the Panjāb from 1852 to 1859. Raverty had achieved a very high degree of competence in Pashto and Persian. His knowledge of the history and problems of the Panjāb, North-West Frontier Provinces, Afghānistan, and eastern Irān was profound. He wrote a number of historical works and brought his vast understanding of the region to bear on the footnotes to the *Tabaqāt-i Nāsirī*, a general history of the Muslim ruling dynasties of the world written by Minhāj Abū 'Umar 'Usmān bin Sirāj Jūzjānī (b. 1193). This work deals at length with the rise of the Turkic dynasties, gives an authoritative account of the Turkic conquest of India, and brings the history of the Delhi sultans down to 1260. Major Raverty collated all the available manuscripts of the *Tabaqāt-i Nāsirī* before undertaking the translation.

In 1841 Mountstuart Elphinstone (1779–1859), who played an important role in liquidating Marāthā power, published *The History of India.* It examines the Persian sources intensively and marshals facts to substantiate the liberality of the Muslim rulers in India.

The most comprehensive collection of Persian and Arabic sources was, however, made by Henry Miers Elliot (d. 1853). His principle objective was to remind Hindus of the atrocity of the Muslim rulers as contrasted with the blessings of the rule of the East India Company. In 1849 he brought out the first volume of his *Bibliographical Index to the Historians of Muhammedan India;* the remaining three volumes that he wrote were never published. The first volume listed 231 works, of which 31 general histories were discussed. Translations of short extracts from each of these works were also given. Some short Persian excerpts were included.

In 1853 Elliot died, leaving behind a massive collection of manuscripts and translations of extracts from the sources. These were later acquired by the British Museum. Elliot's official position had enabled him to obtain manuscripts easily from the Indian landlords, and Indian scholars collaborated with him in explaining and translating the texts. Before his death Elliot had changed his earlier plan and had decided to publish a thirteen-volume history of India under Muslim rule. After his death, John Dowson (d. 1881), a professor of Hindustānī at University College, London, edited Elliot's papers and, adding new material and notes to them, published *The History of India as Told by its Own Historians* (*the Muhammadan Period*) in eight volumes. Beginning with accounts of India in Arab geographical works and travelogues, Dowson's work gives extracts from 154 historical works to the end of the eighteenth century. Each of these excerpts is preceded by a note on the author and the salient features of the work. Despite inaccuracies in the translation, Elliot and Dowson's *History of India* was, and is still, drawn upon by scholars who do not know Persian or have no access to original works. Finding modern scholars misled by the inaccurate translations of Elliot and Dowson, S. H. Hodivala published a critical commentary on their *History of India*, in two massive volumes, correcting their mistakes on the basis of more authentic manuscripts and printed works.

By the end of the nineteenth century the third epoch of British scholarship in Indian history had commenced. It was marked by more accurate translations, and the stage was set for the production of analytical and scholarly monographs by both British and Indian scholars. Henry Ferdinand Blochmann (d. 1878), philological secretary to the Asiatic Society of Bengal, translated the first volume of the *Ā'īn-i Akbarī*, with extensive notes on Akbar's dignitaries. H. S. Jarrett, an assistant secretary to the Legislative Department of the Government of India from 1870 to 1894, translated the second and third volumes of the *Ā'īn-i Akbarī*. All the volumes were published in Calcutta between 1860 and 1894. The translation of the official history of Akbar's reign, the *Akbar-nāma* of Abu'l-Fazl, by H. Beveridge, was published in Calcutta between 1897 and 1921. The first volume of the *Muntakhabu 't-tawārīkh* by Mullā 'Abdu'l-Qādir Badā'ūnī, an inveterate enemy of Akbar's reforms, was translated by G. S. A. Ranking and was published in Calcutta during 1895–9; the second volume, translated by W. H. Lowe, was published in Calcutta in 1884–8, and the third, translated by T. W. Haig, saw the light of day at Calcutta between 1899 and 1925. Between 1909 and 1914 the *Tuzuk-i Jahāngīrī* (the memoirs of the Emperor Jahāngīr, 1605–27) was translated by A. Rogers and edited by H. Beveridge. It was published in London during 1909–14. In 1905 the *Bābur-nāma* (the memoirs of Bābur, b. 1483, d. 1530), written in Chaghatay Turki and reproduced in facsimile from a manuscript belonging to Sir Sālār Jang of Hyderābād, was published in the Gibb Memorial Series at Leyden and London. The English translation, by A. S. Beveridge, was published in London in 1921.

In the twentieth century more Persian chronicles were critically edited, and some were translated into English. *Persian Literature, A Bio-Bibliographical Sūrvey*, Volume I, Part I, by C. A. Storey, first published in London between 1927 and 1939, comprises a detailed description of the manuscripts, editions, and translations of Persian historical works. The second part of Volume I discusses biographical works. Volume II deals with works on mathematics, weights and measures, astronomy, astrology, geography, encyclopædias, arts, crafts, and science. Volume III, which is not yet complete, discusses lexicography, grammar, prosody, and poetics.

Muslim Travellers and Ambassadors

The Muslim travellers, geographers, merchants, adventurers, pilgrims, fortune-hunters, and ambassadors who visited India from the eighth century onwards have left very valuable accounts of items the political historian did not consider worth describing. Some are a mixture of cultural, social, and economic information. They were generally written in Arabic but some were in Persian.

Arab merchants had traded with India before the rise of Islam, but their accounts, if any, do not survive. After the conquest of Syria, Egypt, and Irān, the Arabs opened a sea route through their newly founded port of Basra, and the old route via Egypt was abandoned. Some travellers kept their own diaries, while others provided information to geographers who wrote valuable accounts of India. The first travel diary to attract attention was written by Sulaymān Tājir (the merchant), who flourished around 851. It is entitled *Akhbāru's-Sind wa'l-Hind.*

The most important travelogue on India was written by the Moorish traveller Ibn Batūtta, who was born in Tangier in 1304 and left his country in 1325 to embark on his ambitious travel project. Journeying through Egypt, Syria, Arabia, Irān, Irāq, Turkey, and Transoxiana, he arrived in the Indus Valley on 12 September 1333. He left Delhi in 1342 as an ambassador of Sultan Muhammad bin Tughluq (1325–51) and, travelling by the western coast of India, the Maldives (twice), Ceylon, Bengal, Assam, and Sumātra, he reached the Chinese port of Zaytūn. It is not certain that he visited Peking. He returned to his homeland via Sumātra, Malabar, the Persian Gulf, Iraq, and Syria, completing his travels in December 1353. He finished dictating his *Rihla* (*The Travelogue*) in December 1357. The European edition of the work, with French translation by C. Defrémery and B. R. Sanguinetti, published in Paris in four volumes between 1853 and 1859, is still regarded as the most authentic edition, although many new ones have come out since then. Subsequently it was translated into many languages. The English version by H. A. R. Gibb, entitled *The Travels of Ibn Battūta*, is the best.

The geographer and historian al-Mas'ūdī (d. 956) spent his whole life travelling and wrote two works in several volumes. Of these him in *Murūju'z-zahab*, reveals them to be monumental works. In the *Murūju'z-zahab* he surpasses his predecessors' perspicacity concerning the Islamic world and gives a most accurate account of India. The text, with French translation by Barbier de Meynard and Pavet de Courteille, was published in Paris in nine volumes. Sharīf al-Idrīsī (d. 1165) wrote his *Kitāb Nuzhat al-mushtāq* on the orders of Roger II, the Norman king of Sicily; consequently it is also known as *Kitāb Rujar* (*The Book of Roger*). It is based both on Greek works and on those of Arab geographers and astronomers, but provides many new insights into the manners and customs of India.

The Arabs in Sind and the neighbouring Hindu princes of the Gurjara-Pratihāra dynasty were at war with each other. Unlike them, the southern princes, the Ballahras (Vallabh-rajas) of the Raśtrakūta dynasty (who in turn were fighting the northern Hindu princes) encouraged Arab merchants and travellers to settle in their territories. Consequently there are few works by Arabs on north or central India, most being on the south.

A most comprehensive and authoritative description of Indian religions, beliefs, and social customs was given by al-Bīrūni (d. after 1086) of Khwarazm (*Alberuni's India* in E. Sachaus's English translation, London, 1887). Al-Bīrūni did not travel much in India, but he wrote his *magnum opus* on the basis of translations from the Sanskrit classics and oral information which he obtained from brāhman scholars who, like him, had been taken captive.

An encyclopaedic work on the geography, history, and social and economic condition of all the Islamic countries of the fourteenth century was written by Shihābu'd-Dīn al-'Umarī (d. 1348) of Damascus. His work, entitled *Masālik al-absār fī mamālik al-amsār*, is in twenty-two volumes. His description of India, like that of other countries, is based on the accounts of contemporary merchants and travellers. 'Umarī's masterly selection of the material he obtained has made this work indispensable for students of fourteenth-century India. On the basis of 'Umarī's work, the Egyptian scholar al-Qalaqashandī (d. 1418) wrote his monumental *Subhu'l-A'sha*, published in Egypt in fourteen volumes. An English translation of the chapters on India from both works was made by Otto Spies.

In 1441 Kamālu'd-Dīn 'Abdu'r-Razzāq was sent on a political mission to south India by Timūr's son, Shāh Rukh (1405–47). There he visited the Zamorin of Calicut and the King of Vijayanagara, returning to Hirat in 1444. His historical work, entitled *Matla'-i Sa'dain* in Persian, gives a detailed account of his travels. A. Galland translated this into French, but it was not published; the manuscript is in the Bibliothèque Nationale, Paris. Excerpts giving an account of these travels were translated into English by William Chambers and published in the *Asiatic Miscellany, Volume I*, Calcutta, 1785. R. H. Major re-edited the work, and the Hakluyt Society published it in London in 1859. Russian translations were also published.

European Travellers

In Europe after the ninth century Venice began to emerge as a trade centre. Marco Polo (1254–1324), who left Venice on his travels in 1271, took Europe by storm with his account of commercial, religious, and social conditions in the East, particularly in India. He was followed by a series of adventurers and missionaries.

The narratives of the stream of travellers who poured into India go a long way to making the history of urban growth in India from the fifteenth to the seventeenth centuries reliable and perspicacious. In 1419 Nicolo de' Conti, a Venetian, set out from Damascus upon his travels in the East, returning to his native city in 1444. He dictated his adventures to the secretary to Pope Eugene IV, and his account of the Hindu kingdom of Vijayanagara, and its wars with the Muslim Bahmanīd kingdom of the Deccan, is of considerable importance. In 1468 Athanasius Nikitin, a Russian, left his native town of Tver. He travelled through Irān and Central Asia, arrived at Gujarāt, and stayed for four years at Bidar, which he calls 'Beuṛuk'. Nikitin vividly describes the Bahmanī kingdom. His account of Vijayanagara, which he did not visit, is based on second-hand evidence.

During the fifteenth and sixteenth centuries innumerable Portuguese travellers visited India. The most important work to have resulted is *A Description of the Coasts of East Africa and Malabar in the Beginning of the Sixteenth Century*, by Duarte Barbosa. It is said to have been written by the voyager Magellan. Both visited India in the early days of Portuguese rule. Magellan returned to Europe in 1512, and Barbosa five years later. Some scholars ascribe this work to several authors. Be that as it may, it reflects acute observation and analysis.

Fifteenth- and early sixteenth-century travellers mainly visited Gujarāt, the west coast, the Deccan, and Bengal. The number of books on exploration and travelogues by Europeans mushroomed, as did the visitors, due to Akbar's interest in the religion and culture of different parts of the world and the commercial ramifications of the Portuguese, Dutch, English, and French. It is impossible even to list all these works; only those which made a real contribution to the history of the period are mentioned.

In 1579 a group of three priests set out from Goa: Father Rudolph Acquaviva, newly ordained and aflame with zeal for a martyrdom he was later to meet, Father Monserrate, and Father Francis Henriquez, who was to act as interpreter. The mission was involved in religious debates; it was allowed to build a chapel, and discussed theological points privately with the Emperor. Akbar admitted an interest in Christianity but he was more interested in philosophy and the sciences. The Fathers were filled with frustration when they failed to convert him to their religion. In April 1582 Akbar allowed Father Monserrate to accompany an embassy which he proposed to send to Philip II, King of Spain and Portugal, but it never left the shores of India. Father Monserrate wrote the *Commentarius* in Latin to keep his seniors in touch with the situation. It provides illuminating details about Fathpūr-Sīkrī, which was not yet complete, and describes court life and the customs and manners of the people. The letters written by the Fathers to Goa discuss their own reactions to the interest shown by Akbar and his favourites in Christianity.

In 1591 a second mission arrived at Akbar's request, but, finding a strong court faction opposed to Christianity, the Fathers returned to Goa. In May 1595 the third Jesuit mission arrived at Akbar's court in Lahore. After Akbar's death, Father Jerome Xavier of the third mission continued to live at court for the first twelve years of Jahāngīr's reign (1605–27). Unlike his father, Jahāngīr was not an ardent seeker of truth. During his reign the Jesuit mission assumed to all intents and purposes the character of a political agency.

The letters of Father Xavier are the main source for the study of the third Jesuit mission. The *Histoire* of Father Pierre du Jarric (1566–1617) describes the sixteenth-century Jesuit missions. *The Relations* by Father Fernao Guerreiro deals with Jesuit activity in the seventeenth century. *Akbar and the Jesuits* and *Jahāngīr and the Jesuits*, translated into English by G. H. Payne, comprise valuable notes from original letters and secondary sources and are very useful for studies of the Jesuit missions at the courts of Akbar and Jahāngīr.

The *Itinerario de las missiones del India Oriental*, by Sebastian Manrique, an Augustine friary who, around 1612, was sent by the Portuguese with other missionaries to propagate Christianity in Bengal, merits special attention for its richness of narrative and acuteness of observation. For thirteen years Manrique travelled widely. He visited Chittagong, Arakan, Agra, Lahore, Multān, Bhakkar, and Thatta and even met such high dignitaries at Jahāngīr's court as the Emperor's brother-in-law, Āsaf Khan. He comments on all aspects of contemporary life.

The European travellers who visited India from the end of the sixteenth to the eighteenth centuries were motivated by commercial interests. Their works are written to explore trade potential in India, and they describe the towns and villages critically. The contrast between the extravagance and luxury of the emperors, their household, and dignitaries and the dismal poverty in the villages bewildered them. They tend to exaggerate both extremes; nevertheless, their narratives are indispensable for the study of the social and economic history of sixteenth- and seventeenth-century India.

The pioneer among the English travellers to India was Ralph Fitch (1583–91). He sailed from London with a small party in February 1583. At Hurmuz (Ormuz) they were arrested and sent to Goa. The English Jesuit Father Thomas Stephens (1579–1619) and some other officials intervened on their behalf, and they were released on bail. In April 1584 Fitch and the jeweller, Leeds, escaped to Bījāpūr. From there they moved to Golkonda, seeking. and procuring jewels. From Golkonda they made their way through Ujjain and Agra to Akbar's court at Fathpūr-Sīkrī. Leeds entered Akbar's service. Fitch, however, travelled extensively in India from Agra to Bengal, and voyaged to Pegu in Malacca, before returning home via Goa and Hurmuz. He landed in London at the end of April 1591.*

Ralph Fitch's accounts discuss the apparently inexhaustible possibilities of trade with India and Hurmuz. Fitch pays glowing tribute to the prosperity of Bījāpūr and praises the diamonds from Golkonda. He says: 'Agra and Fatepore are two very great cities, either of them much greater than London and very populous.' At Prage (Prayaga, near Allahabad) the sight of naked beggars disgusted Fitch. He gives a detailed description of idol worship in Banāras, and remarks that cloth, particularly for turbans, was produced there in large quantities. He describes the technique of gold-mining at Patna, and the cotton and sugar trades in the town. There he also saw a Muslim saint whom he described as a 'lasie lubber', although the people 'were much given to such prating and dissembling hypocrites'.

Nearly twenty years after the visit of Ralph Fitch and his companions, John Mildenhall or Midnall (1599–1606), a self-styled ambassador from Queen Elizabeth to Akbar, visited India twice. In a letter dated 3 October 1606 he gave

* W. Foster (ed.), *Early Travels in India, 1583–1619,* London, 1921, pp. 1–8.

an account of the trade concessions he had obtained from Akbar despite Jesuit intrigue. Modern scholarship has, however, rejected his claims. The real battle for trade concessions from the Mughal emperors commenced after the establishment of the East India Company in 1600. In August 1607 Captain William Hawkins (1608–13) landed at Sūrat, but Portuguese hostility made life difficult for Hawkins and his colleague, William Finch. Leaving Finch to look after the goods at Sūrat, Hawkins made his way to Agra, arriving in the middle of 1609. Jahāngīr received him graciously and listened attentively as King James's letter was read to him by a Jesuit priest. Hawkins's fluency in Turkish prompted Jahāngīr to invite him to stay at court as a resident ambassador. He gave him the rank of 400 horse, 'a post in the imperial service that was nominally worth over three thousand pounds a year sterling'. Hawkins's repeated attempts to obtain a royal *farmān* (edict) for trade concessions were, however, unsuccessful. We receive from his narrative a full account of Jahāngīr's temperament and propensities. He describes the hierarchy of imperial officials, known as *mansabdārs*, the income and expenditure of the Mughal emperors, and the magnificence of their court.

William Finch (1608–11), who was left at Sūrat by Hawkins, arrived at Agra in April 1610. He travelled to Bayāna, and around the Panjāb, but his enterprise, when buying indigo involved him in considerable difficulties. Even his superiors became suspicious of him. He left for London but died *en route* at Baghdad. He had carefully maintained his diary, which gives a detailed description of the towns he visited and the people and curiosities he observed. Historically, his journal is more important than Hawkins's narratives.

Until 1612, the year Hawkins sailed away from Sūrat, the prospects for English trade in India were bleak. Captain Thomas Best, who arrived at Sūrat in September 1612, obtained a spectacular victory over the Portuguese fleet off Swally. The Mughals of Gujarāt were impressed and decided to enter into trade negotiations with the English and the court at Agra. Early in 1613 a royal *farmān* was obtained from the Emperor. Nicholas Withington (1612–16), who had learnt Arabic in Morocco, was sent to Agra. He then went to Ahmadābād to assist in the purchase of indigo. His adventurous career in Cambay and Thatta in Sind began from that time. He escaped death in Sind only to be incarcerated in Ajmīr. He failed to convince the Sūrat factors of his innocence and was forced to sail for England in February 1617. Withington's journal describes his vicissitudes at length, but also provides a lively account of Sind, the *banians* (Hindu merchants) and the Baluchis.

The most interesting character among the seventeenth-century English to write about India was Thomas Coryat (1612–17), a courtier of James I. In October 1612 he left on his Eastern journey; intending to write a book about his observations. He was neither a merchant nor a sailor. Travelling through Constantinople, Syria, and Irān, he arrived at Agra via Multān, Lahore, and Delhi. From Agra he visited Ajmīr in order to call on the Emperor. Sir Thomas Roe, who will soon be discussed, avoided his company in the interests of British trade, for Coryat frequently offended Muslims by his indiscreet remarks about Islam, though no one harmed him. Coryat travelled widely in northern India and visited even the Hindu pilgrimage centres of Haridvār and Jwalamukhī in north-east Panjāb. He spoke both Hindustani and Persian fluently. The common people called him a half-witted English fakir. He died at Sūrat in December 1617.

Coryat's eccentricity coloured his cynical observations, but they are very informative. Unfortunately for us, his detailed descriptions of his Indian tours have not survived; his letters, though few, are very valuable historical documents. Like all other contemporary travellers, Coryat was baffied by the extremes in Jahāngīr's character. He describes his cruelties and his compassion. To him Jahāngīr was a true patron of the poor, who readily conversed with them and offered them gifts.

Coryat's friend Edward Terry (1616–19) joined Sir Thomas Roe at Ujjain in February 1617 and served as his chaplain. He accompanied Roe to Mandu and from there to Ahmadābād. In September 1618 he left India. His account owes something to Coryat, to the gossips of the ambassador's suite and to the Sūrat merchants, but his own observations play no mean role.

Terry's narrative describes the Mughal empire, the most remarkable examples of art and nature it contained, the people of India, their habits and diet, women, language, learning, arts, riding, games, markets, arms, valour, mosques, and Hindu and Muslim rites and ceremonies. It gives an interesting account of potato and tobacco cultivation. Terry was impressed by Indian gunpowder, but was critical of 'lesser gunnes made for footmen who are somewhat long in taking their ayme, but come as neere the marke as any I ever saw'.*

The growing intrigues against the East India Company by the Portuguese, in the wake of their declining commercial and economic influence, prompted the Company's directors to urge King James to send Sir Thomas Roe as a special plenipotentiary to Jahāngīr's court. Leaving England in February 1613, Roe arrived at Ajmīr on 23 December 1613 and presented his credentials to the Emperor. Roe ceaselessly tried to persuade Jahāngīr to enter into some kind of trade agreement with the English. He travelled with the Emperor as far as Ahmadābād, until finally, at his request, the Emperor allowed him to return home, giving him a letter for King James. Although Roe had failed to obtain a formal treaty, he secured substantially improved terms, under which the English factory at Sūrat was maintained, and various branches opened. In February 1619 Roe left India.

Throughout his stay, Roe had tried to restore English prestige, which had been eroded by the disorderly behaviour of English officials. In his *journal* and correspondence Roe gives vivid descriptions of the magnificent Mughal court and the Naw Rūz (New Year's Day) festivities. The Emperor's birthday weighing ceremony is given in minute detail. The *Journal* also discusses the influential Empress, Nūr Jahān, and the indifference displayed by her brother, Āsaf Khān, towards the British. Roe also refers to Jahāngīr's insatiable appetite for gifts and European novelties, as well as his extremes of character.

Among the stream of seventeenth-century European visitors to India,

*Ibid., p. 314.

Francisco Pelsaert (1620–7) of Antwerp, a factor with the Dutch East India Company, deserves special mention. He worked in Agra from 1620 to 1627. His *Remonstrantie*, written in 1626, highlights the flourishing trade at Sūrat, Ahmadābād, Cambay, Broach, Burhānpūr, Agra, Lahore, Multān, and Srīnagar. Muslims and their sectarian beliefs and festivals are described at considerable length. John de Laet was permitted to draw upon the *Remonstrantie*, which he summarized in his *De Imperio Magni Mogulis*, published at Leyden in 1631.

A traveller who visited India to enrich his knowledge of the world was John Albert de Mandeslo, a German who landed at Sūrat in 1638. He gathered his information mostly from secondary sources and left India after only a short stay. Other notable European travellers were the Frenchmen Tavernier, Thévenot, Bernier, and Chardin. During his first voyage in 1631 Tavernier stopped at Irān. On his second voyage he visited India briefly in 1640–1. In 1645 he came again and stayed for three years. In 1664 he made his sixth and last voyage and landed in India for the fourth time, carrying £30,000 worth of stock. In 1665 he had an audience with Aurangzīb. He also met Bernier, with whom he travelled to Bengal. In 1667 he sailed for Bandar 'Abbās. The publication of *Six Voyages*, the story of his travels, made him famous, but Thévenot and Bernier ignored him, while Chardin and Careri abused him. Tavernier did not retaliate.

Tavernier's historical accounts are not original. Like Bernier he did not examine facts in the light of historical or social philosophy, but he described what he saw vividly, from the Tāj Mahal to the caravanserais. Most valuable are his notes on cotton cloth, indigo, cinnamon, and jewels, particularly diamonds.

Jean de Thévenot landed at Sūrat in January 1666. He travelled through Ahmadābād and Cambay, and across the Deccan peninsula through Burhānpūr, Aurangabad, and Golkonda, visiting the rock-cut temples of Ellora. He was the first European to describe them; his notes on commerce and industry are welded into history. In the autumn of 1667 he left for Irān and died in a small town there.

François Bernier was a French physician and philosopher, who arrived in India in 1656 and stayed for twelve years. Dānishmand Khān (d. 1670), one of Aurangzīb's leading nobles, was his patron, and Bernier referred to him as 'my *Nawwāb* or *Agah*'. Bernier translated for Dānishmand Khān the medical works of European scientists such as William Harvey (1578–1657), Jean Pecquet (1622–74), and Pierre Gassendi (1592–1655), and the works of the great philosopher René Descartes (1596–1650). Unlike other travellers, Bernier had a good perception of the Mughal administration, but his prejudices clouded his conclusions.

Niccolao Manucci ran away from his native city, Venice, at the age of fourteen in 1653 and three years later arrived at Sūrat. Although he was only sixteen years old, he obtained work as an artilleryman in the army of Dārā Shukoh, whose succession to his father Shāhjahān (1628–58) was challenged by his three brothers. Manucci accompanied Dara to Multān and Bhakkar but, after Dara's execution by Aurangzīb in 1659, he worked on different occasions as a quack doctor, an artillery captain, an ambassador, and finally a foreign correspondent and interpreter for his English masters. He died at Madras in 1717. His adventurous career and diverse experiences made his *Storia do Magar*, written in a mixture of Italian, French, and Portuguese and translated into English, a mine of information on seventeenth-century India.

John Fryer, an English traveller who was in Irān and India during the nine years ending in 1681, vividly describes Bombay and Sūrat. What has made his narratives indispensable to the Mughal historian is his analysis of the circumstances of Shivājī's rise and the problems of Bījāpūr.

Gemelli Careri, an Italian, was familiar with Thévenot's works. Landing at Daman, he visited the Mughal camp at Galgala to the south of the ruins of Bījāpūr in 1695. Although the Marāthās had been subdued, their guerrilla raids posed a threat to the unwieldy Mughal camp. Careri was admitted to the court of the ageing Emperor, now verging on his eightieth year. His remarks on the Emperor's military organization and administration are important.

The Dutch travellers Wouter Shouten and Nicholas de Graaf, and the Englishman Sir William Hedges, an East India Company agent in Bengal from 1681 to 1688, discuss the Mughal administration in Bengal and European commercial activity. Many other Europeans, including missionaries, merchants, and travellers, also wrote about seventeenth- and eighteenth-century India, usefully supplementing the Persian chronicles.

Mystical Literature

Modern works in Islam in the Indian subcontinent have not made adequate use of sūfī literature in analysing the political, social, and economic history of medieval India. The enormous collection of this literature, largely in Persian, may conveniently be divided into the following categories:

(1) Treatises written by sūfīs on the theory and practice of sūfīsm
(2) Letters written by sūfīs.
(3) Discourses by sūfī leaders called *malfūzāt.*
(4) Biographical dictionaries of the sūfī orders.
(5) Collections of sūfī poetry.

The Hindī devotional literature was composed in the local dialects and throws considerable light on the religious movements and the manners and customs of the people. Only a few of the works by sūfīs and Hindu sages have been translated. Sūfi works have been discussed, however, in the introductions to Volumes I and II of *A History of Sūfism in India*, by S. A. A. Rizvi.

Other significant works in different categories are mentioned in the bibliography.

I

THE ARABS AND THE TURKS

EARLY ISLAM

ISLAM literally means 'submission'. It calls for the total surrender of the whole self to God. Those who give their heart and mind to God's will are Muslims. The Qur'ān says:

> Say (O Muslims): We believe in Allah and that which is revealed unto us and that which was revealed unto Abraham, and Ishmael, and Isaac, and Jacob, and the tribes, and that which Moses and Jesus received, and that which the Prophets received from their Lord. We make no distinction between any of them, and unto Him we have surrendered.[1]

Islam's birthplace and spiritual centre is Mecca in the north-western part of the Arabian Peninsula. Although Mecca is only a city in a rocky and infertile valley, its location at the intersection of busy commercial routes had made it, in the sixth century, exceedingly affluent. There was a brisk circulation of capital in Mecca, and even the humblest citizen could invest in the caravan trade. Usury at 100 per cent interest and speculation, mainly concerning exchange rates, were rampant there. The rich Meccans owned huge capital, and even the small shopkeepers, brokers, and traders were wealthy. The commercial importance of Mecca was enhanced by the annual pilgrimage to the cube-like sanctuary called Ka'ba, whose deities were worshipped by both tribesmen and town-dwellers. The ninth day of the last month of the lunar year was kept for pilgrimage, and the first, eleventh, and twelfth months of each year formed the period of holy truce when all tribal wars were abandoned.

The summer resort of the Meccan aristocracy was Ta'if, famous for its fruit, roses, honey, and wine. Some three hundred miles north of Mecca was Yasrib, later known as Medina, which was rich in agriculture and oases. The wealthy Judaized clans of Arabia had settled in Medina and half a dozen villages near by. About 542–3 the non-Jewish Aws and Khazraj tribes of al-Yemen also migrated to Medina.

It was the Bedouins, however, who dominated the north-western part of the Arabian Peninsula. Their culture was predominant even in the main towns, and babies born in the cities were brought up in the tribal environment. The Arab's most prized possession was his language.

Muhammad, the founder of Islam, was descended from the dominant Quraysh tribe of Mecca. His father, 'Abdu'llāh, died before his birth; his mother, Amina, took her last breath some seven years later. Muhammad was brought up by his uncle Abū Talīb and was known as a young man for his integrity and trustworthiness in all matters. When he was about twenty-five years old, he married his employer, a wealthy widow of forty called Khadīja. Wealth and comfort did not, however, change his life. He identified himself with the downtrodden section of society and saw their suffering as his own. Muhammad often retired to.the nearby Hira cave and stayed there for several days, meditating on God. Whilst he was there he became conscious of a voice commanding: 'Read: In the name of the Lord who createth.' This revelation was identified as Muhammad's first call to the Prophethood. The night of that day was named 'the night of power' (*laylat al-qadr*). The voice came more frequently, sometimes like 'the reverberations of bells', and later identified itself as belonging to the archangel Gabriel. Muhammad was convinced that he was the messenger (*rasul*) of Allah, and a 'warner'. His wife, Khadīja, and his cousin 'Alī became his earliest followers, although some of his friends also accepted him as the Prophet. The divine revelations he received, emphasizing monotheism, social equality, and justice, were anathema to most of the wealthy Meccans, who determined to persecute him and his followers. In 615 Muhammad permitted a group of his disciples to migrate to the Christian Negus of Ethiopia. Four years later Abū Talīb died, followed in 619 by Khadīja. Three years after this Muhammad migrated to Medina at the request of the Khazraj and Aws tribes, arriving on 24 September 622. Seventeen years later his emigration was made the starting-point of the Muslim *hijra* (immigration) era, when the date was changed to 16 July 622 to make it compatible with the first day of the first month of the Muslim lunar calendar. Muhammad's Meccan followers moved to Medina in due course. The immigrants were known as *mūhajirs.* The other inhabitants of Medina, except the Jews, who welcomed the immigrants were known as *ansārs* or 'the helpers'. Muhammad's influence stopped the existing feuds and rivalries between the people of Medina and forged a remarkable Islamic brotherhood between the *ansārs* and *mūhajirs.*

In Mecca the Prophet prayed facing in the direction of Jerusalem in order to distinguish his prayers from those of the pagan Arabs, who faced the Ka'ba. The Muslims were permitted to eat most foods prepared by the People of the Book (Jews and Christians) and to marry their women. They were, however, prohibited from eating pork and any animal which had died naturally, had been sacrificed to idols, had had its neck wrung, or had not been slaughtered in accordance with Jewish law. Although the Jewish books promised a Messiah, they would not accept anyone who was not a Jew as Messiah. They were appalled when Muhammad recited the Qur'ānic verses stating that the Jews had falsified their scriptures and that their divine revelations pertained only to a particular age. He also declared that the Christians had likewise departed from their scripture. The Jews were completely alienated, however, when early in 624, acting upon God's commands, he ordered his followers to pray facing the ancient sanctuary of Ka'ba. They also resented Muhammad's repeated condemnation of usury and hoarding.

When the caravans from Mecca passed through Medina, the travellers jeered and taunted the *muhājirs* as cowards for fleeing from Mecca. The Muslims were eventually forced to defend themselves. The first major trial of strength took place in March 624 at Badr Hunayn, a small town south-west of Medina. The Meccans were defeated but they avenged their humiliation the following year at Uhud near Mecca. In 627 Meccans, Bedouins, and some Ethiopian mercenaries jointly attacked Medina. On the suggestion of his Irānian companion Salman, the Prophet had a ditch dug around Medina to save it from immediate assault, while 'Alī's fierce sorties disheartened the invaders, and they withdrew. Next year the people of Mecca were forced to make a truce with Muhammad in order to prevent him from conquering their city. In 629 Muhammad defeated the Jews at their formidable Khaybar fort and seized their oases north of Medina. Towards the end of 630 Muhammad triumphantly entered Mecca with his followers. He died in June 632, after complaining of having a severe headache.

After Muhammad's death the *muhājirs* and *ansārs* at Medina, who believed that Muhammad had not nominated any successor, elected Abū Bakr as caliph (Arabic *khalīf* = 'successor'), but a number of the Prophet's companions and the members of the Prophet's Hashimite clan, who considered that the Prophet had nominated his cousin and son-in-law 'Alī as his heir, dissociated themselves with these proceedings. They were known as 'partisans' or Shī'as of 'Alī. After several decades the first group, who had no specific title, became known as Sunnīs. Abu Bakr (632–4) named 'Umar ai Khattab as his successors. Under 'Umar, the Byzantine territories of Syria, Palestine, and Egypt and the Sasanid countries of Irān and Iraq were conquered.

The defeated nations were offered three choices: acceptance of Islam, payment of poll-tax (*jizya*), or total destruction. Since the institution of poll-tax already existed in the Byzantine and Sasanian empire, it was easily accepted by the subject nations. The Zoroastrians were also given the status of the people of the revealed books, as afforded to the Jews and Christians. The Meccan idols had never been worshipped in these regions, so the Muslim condemnation of idolatry did not cause any religious crisis in the early stages of expansion. The Arab conquerors were either merchants or tribesmen; they had no interest in agriculture, and the farms were left with their original owners. For administrative purposes the revenue of large areas was placed under the control of military commanders. According to 'Umar's decrees, Arabs were even forbidden to settle on the land; they garrisoned the frontier forts and extended the boundaries of their empire from these points. The *dihqāns* (chieftains) in Iraq and Irān, who controlled land assessment and the payment of *kharāj* (land tax), enforced law and order and revenue collection in village communities in accordance with their ancient laws and practices.[2] They became the link between the Arab commanders and the cultivators. 'Umar then started *diwān* (literally a revenue register of pre-Islamic Irān) to record revenue collections and the payment of stipends to the Arab chiefs, and founded the Muslim treasury or *baytu'l-Māl.* The conversion of the local population to Islam was a complex and long-drawn-out process. The immediate problems were defence and administration, not Islamicization.

In 644 'Umar was assassinated by one of his Irānian slaves. 'Usmān (644–56), one of the Prophet's senior companions, was elected caliph by a council of six members who had been nominated by 'Umar. The first six years of 'Usman's reign were peaceful, but civil war broke out in the second half. 'Usman had made his relations governors of various provinces; their despotism forced the people to rebel. The dissidents advanced on Medina to force 'Usman to dismiss them. The first to arrive were the Egyptians who besieged 'Usman's house and then killed him.

Subsequently, on the invitation of the Medina elite, 'Alī (656–61) accepted the caliphate in order to save the community from disintegration. Muhammad's wife, 'A'isha, who had initially opposed 'Usman's government, now changed her mind and became leader of 'Alī's enemies, who were demanding immediate vengeance for 'Usman's blood. An army of about 10,000 men under 'A'isha marched against 'Alī, and six months after 'Usman's assassination a fierce battle was fought near Basra. 'A'isha was defeated and sent back to Medina. 'Alī now moved the capital from Medina to Kufa in Irāq. Mu'āwiya, the governor of Syria, who was related to 'Usman, refused to submit to 'Alī and gave battle near Baghdad. When Mu'āwiya's soldiers realized they were losing the fight, they raised the Qur'ān on their spears to force 'Alī to make arbitration on the basis of the Qur'ān. Some of 'Alī's followers disapproved of this arbitration and deserted him. Later they also fought 'Alī but were defeated. They were called the Khawārij (singular Khariji). 'Alī was assassinated by a Khariji while at prayers in the mosque in Kufa, and Mu'āwiya renewed his attempts to seize the caliphate by military force. 'Alī's son, Hasan, who had been chosen as his father's successor by the people of Kūfa, abdicated to avoid bloodshed, and Mu'āwiya became caliph.

Mu'āwiya made Damascus his capital and reduced Mecca and Medina to purely spiritual centres of Islam. Some years before his death, Mu'āwiya made his son, Yazīd, who was notorious for his dissipation, his successor. This constituted a major departure from the earlier tradition of election. Hasan's brother, Husayn, and other leading Muslims opposed Yazīd's succession. After Mu'āwiya's death, Yazīd tried to force Husayn to accept him as caliph, but Husayn refused. Instead he moved to Kufa at the invitation of the leading Muslims there who wished to make him their leader. A strong force sent by Yazīd's governor in Kūfa intercepted Husayn and his followers at Karbalā in Iraq. On 10 October 680 they killed Husayn and his followers. The tragic circumstances of Husayn's martyrdom spread a wave of hatred against Yazīd, and 'revenge' became the battle-cry of many anti-Umayyad movements. In 750 the Umayyads (the ruling dynasty founded by Mu'āwiya) were overthrown by the 'Abbāsids (750–1258), who had secretly built up their strength among the anti-Umayyad sections of the Irānian and Arab population. The 'Abbāsids were descended from the Prophet's uncle, 'Abbās, and this gave their rule a certain legitimacy. Although the Umayyads and the 'Abbasids were called caliphs, they were hereditary monarchs, like the Irānian and Byzantine emperors preceding them. The first four rulers following the Prophet are known as Rāshidūn or 'rightly guided caliphs'.

INSTITUTIONS

According to the Qur'ān, its divine revelations superseded all previous disclosures in the Torah, the Psalms, and the Gospel, brought by Moses, David, and Jesus. The name 'Qur'ān' ('the Book') occurs in the Book itself. The verses in the Qur'ān were revealed during the twenty-three years of Muhammad's Prophetic mission in Mecca and Medina. Its verses and chapters were arranged by Muhammad, and the entire Qur'ān was written down and memorized during his lifetime. It is divided into 114 chapters and contains 6,360 verses.

The principal objective of the Qur'ān is to guide humanity to lead an ethical life and to emphasize the fact that only the spiritual force should be dominant. It does not, however, advocate any compulsion in religion. It envisages war but only 'to stop religious persecution and to protect houses of worship'. It speaks of life after death as a continuation of earthly life. Monogamy is preferable, but in special circumstances four wives can be taken at the same time. In contrast to the laws of Hinduism, females are entitled to a share in their father's and husband's property. They are not forbidden to leave their homes, but they must be modest in their dress and demeanour. The Qur'ān also provides rules for male behaviour and for social, economic, and political ethics.

The Qur'ān is supplemented by the Sunna, or practices of Muhammad, which were transmitted in the form of short narratives called *hadīs* (statements or traditions). Although there is no controversy over the Qur'ān, the Sunnī and Shī'ī *hadīs* differ in both content and methodology. The most authentic collection of Sunnī *hadīs* was made by Muhammad bin Ismā'īl al-Bukhāri (810–70). His work, known as the *Sahīh* (*Authentic*), contains 2,762 statements, each preceded by the chain of its transmitters. They were selected from a mass of 600,000 traditions. This shows the enormous number of false statements current in Bukhāri's time and the difficulties he faced. Another authentic compilation is that of his contemporary, Muslim ibn al-Hajjāj. Together with four other accepted selections, the Sunnī works of *hadīs* are collectively known as the six canonical books.

The Shī'ī works of *hadīs* contain the sayings of 'Alī and his descendants, known as imāms, besides those of the Prophet. According to the Shī'īs, the imāms were the custodians of Muhammad's knowledge, both esoteric and exoteric, so their narratives embody true Prophetic traditions. There are four works of Shī'ī *hadīs;* the earliest, by Muhammad ibn Ya'qūb al-Kulaynī (d. 940), is the most important.

LAW

In the Qur'ān and *harfis*, law and religion exist side by side. All works of Muslim law deal with fundamental religious duties such as prayers, the payment of *zakāt* (one-fortieth of annual savings given to the needy and to travellers), fasting in the month of Ramazan, pilgrimage to Mecca (which should be performed at least once in a lifetime), and *jihād* (holy war). The caliphs who followed the Prophet tried to solve the problems confronting them in the light of the Qur'ānic injunctions and the precedents set by the Prophet. Their successors, the Umayyad governors, delegated their power to an army of officials. Among these were the *qāzīs* or Islamic judges, who used their own discretion or 'sound opinion' (*ra'y*), drawing upon the Qur'ān, other religious norms, and the legal concepts of the conquered territories as far as they were compatible with Islamic ideals. Their main concern was to consolidate the Islamic way of life mainly through *ijtihād* (individual reasoning or reasoning by analogy). Their efforts made Medina, Kāfa, and Damascus the early centres of islamic jurisprudence (*fiqh*). This included the regulations relating to prayers and rituals (*'ibādāt*), civil and legal obligations (*mu'āmalāt*), and punishments (*'uqābāt*).

The oldest corpus of Islamic law is *al-Muwatta* by Mālik ibn Anas (*c.* 715–95) of Medina. It comprises some 1,700 juridical traditions, based on consensus of opinion (*ijmā'*) among those who were believed to be best acquainted with the spirit of the Prophet's decisions. Mālik's followers were known as the Mālikites.

From the main body of the ancient law schools of Kāfa and Basra grew the Hanafiyya or the Hanafi *mazhab* (school of religious law) of Abā Hanīfa (699–767). He is said to have been brought as a slave from Kabul to Kāfa, where he was set free by a member of an Arabian tribe. Abu Hanīfa did not himself write any books on law, but the works of his disciples Abū Yūsuf (d. 798) and al-Shaybānī (d. 805), embodying their master's views, form the basic structure of Hanafi law. Besides personal judgement and conclusion by analogy, Abu Hanīfa insisted upon the right of 'preference' (*istihsān*). This meant departure from analogy on grounds of equity. Mālik's pupil, Muhammad ibn Idrīs al-Shāfī'ī (767–820), who worked mainly in Baghdād and Cairo, carved out a middle-of-the-road system between the Mālikī and Hanafī schools, while al-Shāfī'ī's pupil Ahmad bin Hanbal (780–855), the founder of the fourth school of *fiqh* known as the Hanābila, was a formidable champion of puritanism.

The works of the founders of the four schools of jurisprudence and their disciples and successors form the major corpus of the Sunnī schools of law. After Ahmad bin Hanbal's death, an agreement developed among all four schools that all essential legal questions had finally been settled and that future jurists should abide by the laws propounded by them. This decision is known as 'the closing of the door of *ijtihād'*. The unquestioning acceptance of the doctrine of any of the four schools is known as *taqlīd* or imitation; the jurists of subsequent centuries were therefore *muqallids* (imitators).

By the time Mālik and Abu Hanīfa had risen to eminence, Imām Muhammad Bāqir (677–733) and Imām Ja'far al-Sādiq (702–65), the fifth and sixth Shī'ī imāms, who lived in Medina, had worked out the legal system which the Shī'īs follow. It embodies the principles which, as 'Alī's direct descendants, they inherited from the Prophet Muhammad.

The 'Abbāsid caliphs gave the Hanafiyya school of jurisprudence official status, and it held supreme authority in all the kingdoms as far as eastern Irān, Transoxiana, Turkey, and India. The *qāzīs* and scholars at the 'Abbāsid courts and under the Irānian and Delhi sultanate composed a large number of handbooks dealing with the application of Hanafiyya law. These are largely collections of *fatwas* (legal decisions) of earlier *qāzīs* who were mainly concerned to answer questions relating to their respective environments. The most impressive collection of Hanafiyya *fatwas* is the *Fatāwa al-'Ālamgīriyya* compiled by a board of Indian *'ulamā'* (religious scholars, singular *'ālim*), appointed by the Mughal Emperor Aurangzīb.

THE ARAB CONQUEST OF SIND

Since time immemorial, commercial relations existed between Arabia and the western coastal regions of India. Even before the advent of Islam, the Arabs had acquired a monopoly of the sea trade in several Indian ports and had established settlements there. After the Islamicization of the Arabian Peninsula, these communities built mosques, recited congregational prayers, and converted some of the indigenous people to Islam. Their children naturally were brought up as Muslims. The rulers, in the interest of trade and according to the tolerant traditions of India, took no exception to their religious activities, and relations between them remained cordial. The Muslim community at Malabar, called *moplahs* (from *mapilla*, meaning a bridegroom or child), developed from the matrimonial alliances between the Arabs and the local population.

Pirates posed a potent threat to the Arab sea trade. In 636 the governor of Bahrayn and 'Ummān sent an expedition to Thana, near modern Bombay. Other Arab expeditions left also for the ports of Broach and Dābol. The second caliph, 'Umar, did not favour sea wars, but the raids through Makrān (Baluchistān), captured during his reign, continued. Legends wrongly assert that Muhammad bin Qasim's invasion of Sind in the early eighth century was initially a punitive expedition.[3] It was, in fact, part of the forward policy of the Umayyad governor of Iraq, Hajjāj bin Yusuf (694–714), to annex the region from Sind to Transoxiana.

Sind was then ruled by Raja Dāhir. He was the son of a usurper, the brāhman Chach, who had overthrown Buddhist rule, although their influence was still strong in the territory. In 712 Muhammad bin Qāsim, the young nephew and son-in-law of Hajjāj, marched at the head of a strong army through Shiraz (Irān) and Makran. *Ballistae*, one of which required five hundred trained men to operate it, were sent by sea to join the main army at Debal, an inland commercial port near modern Karāchī. Dāhir's garrison, entrenched in the stone fortification at Debal, offered stiff resistance, but the bombardment with rocks by the *ballistae* forced them to capitulate. Early in 712 Nīrūn, south of modern Hyderābād, was seized. Sehwān, a commercial centre, surrendered without resistance. Although the Jāts of the lower Sind fought fiercely, they too were defeated. The Arab onward march, however, was balked near a tributary of the Indus by an epidemic of scurvy among the troops and disease in the horses. Hajjāj sent both reinforcements and medicines. A hotly contested battle was fought by Dāhir, near Brahmanābād (north of Hyderābād) in June 712, but he was defeated and killed. Muhammad bin Qāsim took Brahmanābād, married Dāhir's widow, Rānī Lādī, and became the master of lower Sind. In October he marched against the capital, Aror (near modern Rohrī), held by the Raja's son, and seized it. Conquering upper Sind early in 713, Muhammad bin Qāsim proceeded towards Multān. The garrison there resisted but finally surrendered.

Muhammad bin Qasim sent one-fifth of the booty (*ghanīma*) to the Caliph's treasury. The rest, according to early Islamic practices, was distributed among the army. The *Chach-nāma* details the administrative regulations Muhammad introduced into Brahmanābād. According to the author, the artisans, merchants, and common people were left alone, but all the captured soldiers were beheaded. Those civilians who had not become Muslims were then divided into three categories for the imposition of poll-tax (*jizya*). The men in the highest income brackets paid 48 *dirhams*[4] of silver per head, the middle income groups 24 *dirhams*, and the lowest class 12 *dirhams.* Tribute was fixed according to their resources on all chieftains who had surrendered. A census of merchants, artisans, and farmers was taken. The number of common people was about 10,000. Because the merchants and artisans had already lost much of their property through looting, it was decided that all classes should pay a tax (*māl*) of 12 silver *dirhams.*[5] Village chiefs (*dihqāns*) and headmen (*rā'is*) were appointed to collect it from the townspeople and villagers, and were offered a small salary.[6] The Brāhmans, encouraged at the favour shown by Muhammad to the headmen, urged him to restore their own former position and status also. Muhammad granted their request. The brāhmans then visited the outlying villages, and at their persuasion the community leaders in the countryside also submitted to the Arabs and promised to pay taxes. An order was received from Hajjāj that, since the people of Sind had accepted the status of protected subjects (*zimmī*), no interference should be made in their lives and property. They should be permitted to worship freely in their own temples and should also be allowed to build new ones.[7] The brāhmans were permitted to collect their customary fees from the merchants, Hindu chiefs (*thākurās*), and common Hindus; the 3 per cent share of government revenue which they had previously received was also reinstated. Even the harsh and discriminatory treatment which the brāhmans had meted out to the Jāt tribe was not changed. The Jāts were not allowed to put on comfortable clothes and wore rough black blankets; their chiefs were forbidden to ride horses. They were treated as brutes.[8]

Muhammad bin' Qasim's victory over Sind was decisive and spectacular. It was due mainly to his better and more advanced military methods. His co-ordination of sea and ground forces was remarkably successful. Dāhir's defence of his forts was feeble, and the princes and chieftains under him had no personal interest in holding them. Moreover, he remained entrenched at Brahamanābād and did not take the opportunity to strike first when Muhammad's troops and horses were prostrated by sickness at the Indus tributary. Some of Dāhir's generals were disloyal, but the importance of the betrayal of the brāhman cause by the Buddhists, whom the brāhmans had previously replaced as rulers cannot be over-emphasized as a factor in their defeat.

Muhammad bin Qasim's lightning raids in rebellious areas, his far-sighted handling of the local chieftains, and his conciliation of the brāhmans helped him consolidate his power without much difficulty. The military governors he appointed in the forts and the Arab garrisons under them were also considerate and capable. Hajjāj's death in June 714, followed next year by that of his patron, Caliph Walīd (705–15), led to the recall of Muhammad bin Qāsim. The new Caliph put him in chains, and he died in prison in Irāq. The administration in Sind broke down.

When the Umayyad Caliph 'Umar bin 'Abdu'l-'Azīz (717–20) came to power he embarked upon a policy of converting the Hindu princes to Islam. Dāhir's son, Jaisinha, embraced Islam, but then recanted and fell fighting on the battlefield. Some Hindu chieftains also became Muslims. In 724 Junayd took over the governorship of Sind. He subdued the rebellions there and embarked on a series of raids in Kathiāwār and Ujjain. Junayd's incursions beyond Sind, however, failed, and he was recalled in 740. Only strong governors could rule Sind effectively and attempt, even if unsuccessfully, to extend their boundaries. Other governors became too involved in crushing local rebellions and combating the intrigues among Arab chiefs and Indian converts to contemplate further conquests. In 731 the Arabs founded a town on the river Indus named Mahfūza, to garrison their troops. Six years later they built their capital, Mansūra. In 854 'Umar bin 'Abdu'l-'Aziz Hibbārī established an hereditary Arab government in Sind, and the 'Abbāsids of Baghdād were regarded as caliphs in name only. In 977 the Ismā'īlīs, who owed allegiance to the Fātimid caliphs of Egypt,[9] seized Multān by a *coup d'état* and eight years later took Sind from the Hibbārī family.

Historians do not attach much importance to Arab rule in Sind, but it was remarkable in many ways. It strengthened Arab trade on the west coast of India and encouraged more Arabs to make new settlements on the east coast and even in South-East Asia. The Arabs rapidly assimilated local customs and manners. They adjusted Arab tribal life to the Sindī tribal pattern. In 886 the Qur'ān was translated into Sindī on the request of a Hindu chief. Arab historians who visited the region in the tenth century noted that the urban population spoke both Arabic and Sanskrit. The cultural interchange was most productive. The Kūfa leather workers trained the Makrān and Sind tanners in the art of tanning leather with dates. This improved the finish of indigenous leather products and made them softer. Sind shoes now fetched a high price and were regarded as a luxury item in the caliph's territories. Sind breeds of camel were also upgraded, and the demand for them rose in neighbouring countries.[10] On the other hand, Sanskrit works on astronomy, medicine, ethics, and administration were introduced by the Sindī intellectuals to the translation bureau at the 'Abbāsid court. The contribution by Sindī scholars to the development of Islamic sciences such as *hadīs* and *fiqh* is also impressive.

THE GHAZNAVIDS

Contemporaneous with the conquest of Sind were the Arab victories over the eastern Turks of Transoxiana by Hajjāj's equally enterprising general Qutayba bin Muslim. In the north Qutayba's armies reached Shāsh (Tāshkend) and in the south-east they penetrated deep into Kāshghar, at that time part of the Chinese empire. Arab governors were appointed to administer the conquered provinces. When the Umayyad Caliph Sulaymān (715–17) assumed power, Qutayba (like Muhammad bin Qāsim) was disgraced, but he rebelled against his recall. He was eventually killed by his own army in 715. Proselytization in Transoxiana was more successful than in Sind. The spearhead of the proselytization movement were the sūfi mystics, while the *dihqāns*, hereditary aristocratic landholders who lived in fortified castles, responded to the call of Islam enthusiastically. The revenues remitted to the caliphate from this region were enormous, but from the ninth century their most valued contribution was the supply of Turkic slaves. Armed Turkic slaves supplanted not only the Irānians but also the Arab contingents as bodyguards and crack troops. They were loyal to none but their masters and were transferred by them like any other chattel.

From the ninth century onwards, certain enterprising leaders, backed by the Turkic slaves, began to carve out independent ruling dynasties in the eastern regions of the caliphate, paying only nominal obedience to the 'Abbāsid caliphs. In Khurāsān (the eastern province of Irān) and Transoxiana, Sāmān-Khuda, a *dihqān* in the Balkh district who had been converted to Islam, founded the Sāmānid dynasty, which ruled from 819 to 1005. Under them, Alptigīn, a Turkic slave, rose to the rank of commander-in-chief of the guard (*hājibu'l-hujjāb*) and, in the reign of the Samanid 'Abdu'l-Malik I (954–61), became the governor of Khurāsān. When he was dismissed by 'Abdu'l-Malik's successor, he withdrew to Balkh, where he defeated the Sāmānid army in 963. He then made a dash to Ghaznī on the periphery of the Sāmānid kingdom and vanquished Abū 'Alī Lawīk, or Anūk, said to be a brother-in-law of the Hindu Shāhī ruler of the region, Kābul Shāh.

Alptigīn died in 963. Three short-lived rulers followed him. In 977, however, Alptigīn's slave and son-in-law, Subuktigīn, seized power. In the first two years of his reign he conquered the regions around Ghaznī and then turned his attention to the Hindu Shāhis. The latter ruled the territory from Lamghān to the river Chenāb and from the hills of southern Kashmīr to the frontier kingdom of Multān. Their capital was Waihind or Hund. In 986–7 their king, Jayapāla, in retaliation for an earlier incursion by Subuktigīn into his territory, marched upon Ghaznī, but was defeated by Subuktigīn. Jayapāla made peace, promising to pay a huge indemnity, but later he repudiated his word. Then, joined by a number of other Hindu rajas, he again marched on Ghaznī, but was once more badly defeated between Lamghān and Peshāwar. Subuktigīn died in 997, nominating his younger son, Ismā'īl, as his successor. Subuktigīn's elder son, Mahmūd, refused to accept his father's decision and ascended the throne after defeating Ismā'īl in battle. Two years later Mahmūd crushed the Sāmānid army and seized the commercially rich and agriculturally fertile region of Khurāsān. The 'Abbasid Caliph al-Qādir (991–1031), whose succession to the throne had been threatened by the Sāmānids, out of gratitude bestowed on Mahmūd the title Yamīnu'd-Dawla wa Amīnu'l-Mulk (Right-hand of the Empire and Trustee of the Nation). Mahmūd next conquered the dynasties which had been subject to the Samanids. His conquest of Khwārazm, Sīstān, and Ghūr made him the most formidable power in eastern Irān and Transoxiana. Mahmūd is, however, more famous for his Indian conquests, which commenced in September 1000, when he captured some forts near Lamghān. His earlier invasions of the territory of the Hindu Shāhis and their supporters, as well as that of the Ismā'īlīs of Multān, were designed to clear a way into the rich Gangetic plains. In 1001 he fought a fierce battle against Jayapāla near Peshāwar and defeated him. Returning to the Panjāb, Jayapala died and was succeeded by his son, Ānandapala. Towards the end of 1005 the Sultan seized Bhatinda, which guarded the passage from the north-west into the rich Ganges valley. Its raja was defeated, but the Sultan's army also suffered heavy losses on the return journey.[11]

A serious obstacle to the Sultan's entry into the Gangetic plain was Abu'l Fath bin Dāwud, the Ismā'īlī ruler of Multān. He had entered into alliances with both Subuktigīn and Mahmūd, but his relations with Anandapala were also friendly. In 1006, in order to complete his mopping-up operations, Mahmūd therefore marched on Multān via Peshāwar. Adandapala tried to stop him but was swept away. Dāwud fled from Multān; the Ismā'īlīs were slaughtered, and their mosques desecrated. Only the Sunnīs were spared. Mahmūd returned to Ghaznī after installing Sukhapāla, Jayapala's Islamicized grandson, on the Multān throne. The Sultan's prolonged involvement in the Khurāsān wars, however prompted Sukhapāla to rebel. Mahmūd therefore hastened back to Multān, captured Sukhapāla, and executed him in January 1008.[12] Meanwhile Ānandapāla had collected a vast army of neighbouring rajas. Mahmūd then crossed the Indus and defeated Ānandapāla in the plain opposite Waihind in January 1009. The rajas fled to Nagarkot temple near Kangra, with Mahmūd at their heels. Nagarkot surrendered, and the vast booty from the vaults of its temple fell into Mahmūd's hands. Ānandapāla, however, escaped. After the Sultan's return to Ghaznī, Ānandāpala re-established his kingdom on the northern spur of the Salt range, commanding the main route into the Gangetic *doāb*, with Nandana as his capital. Shortly afterwards he died and was succeeded by his son Trilochanapāla.[13]

Mahmūd's repeated invasions over the Panjāb as far as Kashmīr and eastern Rājasthān destroyed Rājpūt resistance. Kashmīr itself was saved by its difficult terrain.[14] Nevertheless Mahmūd's way into the Gangetic *doāb* was now clear. In September 1018 he penetrated into the east of Delhi and conquered Baran (Bulandshahr), while Mahaban (Mathurā) surrendered. The beauty of the Hindu architecture in Mathurā impressed the Sultan, but his hatred of idols prevented him from sparing any temples.[15] He collected a vast amount of booty. At the end of December 1018 the Sultan seized Kanauj. On his return he conquered various forts in quick succession. Besides a huge quantity of gold, the booty he acquired included 55,000 slaves and 350 elephants.

From 1019 to 1023 Kālinjar was Mahmūd's target. Deeper raids into eastern India were of no use to his mission of plunder, and in October 1025 he set out at the head of 30,000 regular cavalry and a vast army of volunteers on his famous expedition to Somnāth on the coast of Kāthiāwār (now again known by its ancient name, Saurāshtra). Elaborate arrangements were made for the journey through the inhospital desert of Jaisalmīr and Anhilwāra. Bhūdeva, the Chalākya raja of Anhilwāra, offered no resistance.[16] At Mundhīr, near Anhilwāra (modern Patan in the Ahmadābād district of Gujarāt), some 20,000 Hindus made a strong stand but were finally routed. Early in January 1026 the Sultan was positioned before the Somnāth fortress on the sea-shore. The garrison made desperate assaults on the invaders but were unable to withstand their deadly showers of arrows. About 50,000 devotees laid down their lives in vain to save their deity's honour. The idol was smashed, and the booty obtained amounted to 20,000,000 *dinars*, each of which contained 64.8 grains of gold.[17] After staying there for a fortnight, Mahmūd took a westerly route through Kacch and Sind in order to avoid a confrontation with the vengeful Hindu rajas from the neighbouring states. The Ismā'īlī ruler of Mansūra fled, but the Hindu tribes harassed the returning army and inflicted heavy losses on them. In April 1026 the Sultan arrived in Ghaznī. That same year Bhimapāla, who had succeeded his father Trilochanapāla in 1021–2, died and the Hindu Shāhi dynasty came to an end. Mahmūd's Somnath victory made him a legendary hero in Islamic history.[18] He died on 30 April 1030.[19]

Mahmūd's conquests extended from Iraq and the Caspian Sea to the river Ganges, from the Aral Sea and Transoxiana to Sind and the Rājasthān deserts. His actual rule in India, however, was confined to the Panjāb and parts of Sind. His eastern empire comprised northern Baluchistān, Sistān, Khurāsān, and Transoxiana. In 1023 his standing army consisted of 54,000 cavalry and 1,300 elephants but during wartime contingents from the vassal princes, volunteers, and local militia also joined his forces. The military backbone was the corps of Turkic slaves who were paid and maintained by the state.[2] The booty from the rich Irānian provinces and the Indian campaigns, however, did not always cover the cost of Mahmūd's military expeditions. The ruinous imposts he levied on Khurāsān led to the desertion of agricultural areas; irrigation works fell into decay, and some even ceased to exist.[21]

Mahmūd had assumed the role of defender of Sunni orthodoxy; he boasted of annihilating the Ismā'īlī sect and ruthlessly plundered Hindu temples. He did not, however, hesitate to employ the Hindus in his multiracial Muslim army. They served under their own commander, called the *sālār-i Hindūyān.* The anonymous history of Sīstān contains complaints of the ruthless massacre of Muslims and Christians by Mahmūd's pagan Indian troops.[22]

Mahmūd was passionately fond of erecting magnificent palaces, mosques, seminaries, and gardens. They were built largely on the proceeds of his Indian campaigns, but their maintenance often fell on the local people, who were hard put to bear the cost. The Sultan's love of ostentation and desire for historical immortality made him extremely generous to those poets who composed glowing panegyrics on him. Scientists, however, such as Abu Rayhān al-Bīrunī (d. after 1086), who was taken captive after the fall of Khwārazmshāh in 1017, were given little encouragement. Even Firdawsi, who completed his great Persian epic, the *Shāh-nama*, in 1010, was not adequately rewarded. The philosopher Avicenna (Ibn Sīna) wisely never came near Mahmūd. Despite his faults, Mahmūd's personal judgements, firm will, far-sightedness, and moral courage were striking. None of his contemporaries in Irān, Transoxiana, or India could match his talents.

His successor's stars were not in the ascendant. The Seljūqs, a branch of the Oghuz Turkic people belonging to the steppes north of the Caspian and Aral seas,[23] seized Khurāsān and Khwārazm from Mahmūd's son Mas'ūd I (1031–41) after defeating him on the steppes of Dandanaqān in May 1040.[24]

During the latter part of the reign of the Ghaznavid Yaminu'd-Dawla Bahrām Shāh, who ruled from 1118 to 1152, the rulers of the Ghūr hill region between Hīrāt and Kābul became very powerful. The region had previously been conquered by Mahmūd of Ghaznī, and the population converted to Islam. After the rise of the Seljūqs, however, the Ghurs accepted Seljūq authority. 'Alā 'u'd-Dīn Husayn (d. 1161), who came to power there in 1149, fought a battle against the Ghaznavid Bahrām Shāh, near Tiginābād (Qandahār). The Ghur infantry, with their walls of protective shields, defeated the Ghaznavid army, which relied mainly on elephants. Bahrām fled to the Panjāb. 'Alā 'u'd-Dīn entered Ghaznī and gave it over to a horrendous seven-day orgy of plundering and destruction which earned him the title of Jahān-Sūz (Burner of the World). The corpses of all the Ghaznavid rulers, except for Mahmūd, Mas'ūd, and Ibrāhīm, were exhumed and burnt. The towns between Ghaznī and Ghur were also destroyed with revolting barbarism. In 1152 Bahrām was succeeded by Khusraw Shāh, but the Ghūrīd reduced his rule to Lahore, where he died in 1160. His successor, Khusraw Malik (1160–86), was the last ruler of the Ghaznavid dynasty, which the Ghūrīd finally extinguished in 1186.

The Ghaznavid rule in the Panjāb lasted much longer than in Khurāsān and was not subject to the vicissitudes of Ghaznī. It was free from external invasions for at least 150 years. The governors generally belonged to the Ghaznavid royal house. The sources do not discuss the administrative framework of Ghaznavid Panjāb, but it probably did not differ greatly from that of the Sāmānid provinces or at least from the Ghaznavid administration in Khurāsān, which is mentioned in passing in the contemporary sources. After the fall of Khurāsān the most important source of Ghaznavid revenue was the Panjāb. The urban economic life of the Hindu Shāhī dynasty seems to have boosted the Ghaznavid financial system. Lahore became more prosperous as an entrepôt for the goods and merchandise from Irān and the northern Indian plains. Muslim merchants settled in several Indian towns because of the Hindu desire to promote trade and commerce. The development of Lahore, which is reflected in both contemporary poetry and sūfi works, could not have taken place without the import of argicultural products from the Panjāb villages. There the counterparts of the Irānian *dihqāns* (the hereditary aristocracy in the villages) were the Indian hereditary village chiefs or *thākurās*. Those *thākurās* who possessed strong fortresses were crushed by the

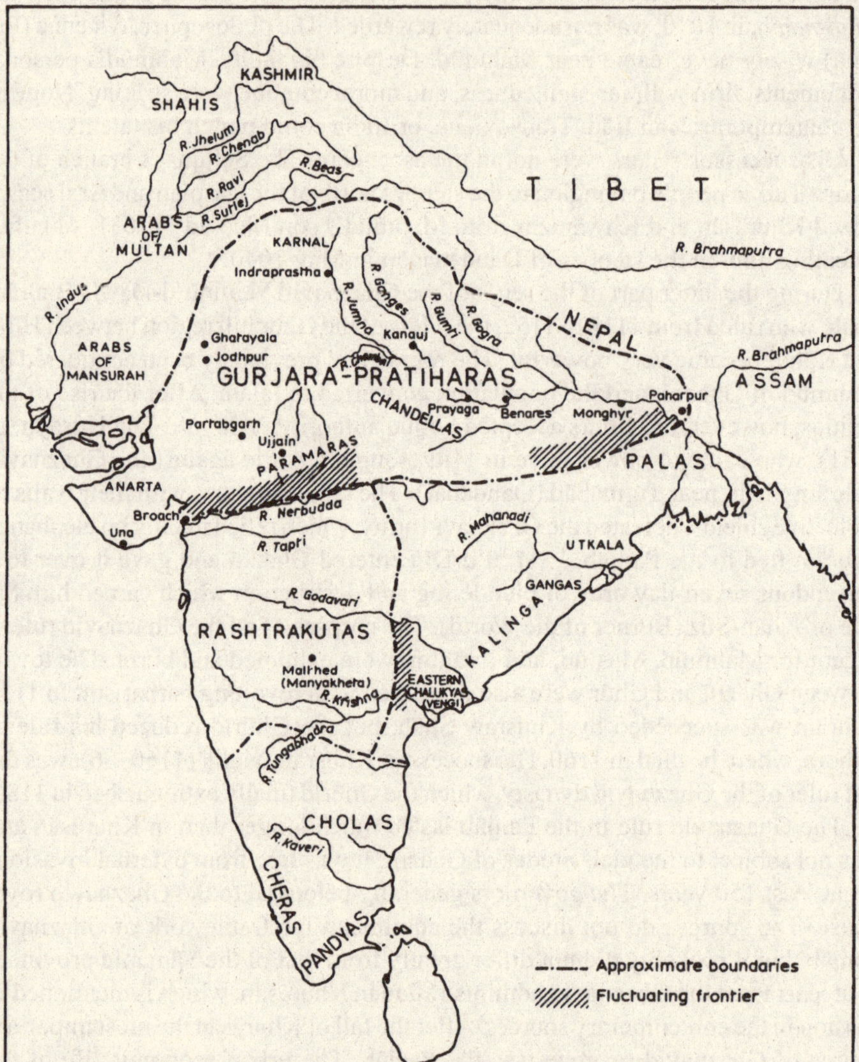

India at the close of the ninth century

Ghaznavids and forced to pay tribute, while the more docile chiefs seem to have acted as intermediaries between the state and the farmers. Following Arab and Irānian custom, the Ghaznavids changed neither the pattern of land ownership nor the rural economy, except in the villages near Lahore. The Hindu money-lending class, known as the Sāhs and the Multānīs in thirteenth- and fourteenth-century literature, also carried on their business without any interference from their Muslim rulers. In fact the Multānīs and Sāhs were no different from the Jews in the time of the later 'Abbasids, on whom the commercial prosperity of the caliphate and its Irānian provinces depended.

Although Mahmūd was a puritanically orthodox Sunni, the Hindus continued to enjoy *zimmī* (protected subject) status. Initially the Ismā'īlīs were defeated but they were not completely crushed, and the political instability in Ghaznī allowed their rule to be revived. The Panjāb became increasingly important, and sūfīs from the Ghaznī region and other areas moved there. Abu'l-Fazl Muhammad bin al-Hasan Khattalī, a disciple of Husrī (d. 981–2) of the school of Junayd,[25] ordered his disciple Shaykh Hasan Zinjānī to move to the Panjāb. Khattali later asked his young disciple 'Alī bin 'Usmān Hujwīrī to follow Zinjānī. Before Hujwīrī's death, the sūfī traditions, as we shall show in Chapter 6, were firmly rooted in India.

Among the Persian poets, Mas'ūd ar-Rūnī (d. *c.* 1091) lived in Lahore. The opinion held by some scholars that Rūnī's rival Mas'ūd Sa'd Salmān compiled a collection of his own (Salmān's) Hindawī (Hindī) verses is rightly contested by many, but on the basis of Salman's surviving Persian lyrics, he can undoubtedly be called the founder of the Indo-Persian style of poetry.

THE GHŪRĪDS

'Ala'u'd-Dīn Jahān Sūz's conquests made the Ghurid empire very extensive, but it reached its zenith under two brothers: Shamsu'd-Din (later Ghiyasu'd-Dīn) Muhammad (1163–1203) and Shihabu'd-Dīn (later Mu'izzu'd-Dīn) Muhammad (1173–1206). Ghiyasu'd-Dīn concentrated on expanding westwards to prevent the Khwarazm-Shāhs, or Khāns of Khīva on the lower Oxus, from moving into Khurāsān. Mu'izzu'd-Dīn, whose capital was in Ghanzi, followed Mahmūd's tradition of invading India. His army consisted mainly of Turkic and Tājik (Persian-speaking Turks) slaves, although it included horsemen of other racial groups.

Finding the Ismā'īlīs a threat to his power in the east, Mu'izzu'd-Din seized Multān in 1175 and dispersed them. Then he conquered Uch. In 1178 he invaded Anhilvāra or Patan, the capital of the Vaghela raja of Gujarāt, Mūlaraja II. A battle was fought near Mount Abu, and the raja's army, which outnumbered the Turks, won the day. The invaders fled through the inhospitable deserts in a miserable condition and endured considerable hardship. Mu'izzu'd-Dīn thereupon decided to give up Mahmūd's plans of invasion through Sind and Multan. The Panjāb offered better prospects. In 1179 he seized Peshawar. Two years later he invaded Lahore. The Ghaznavid ruler there, Khusraw Malik, made peace. In 1182 Mu'izzu'd-Dīn conquered Debal and made the Sūmra rulers of lower Sind his vassals. After a three-year lull Mu'izzu'd-Din invaded Lahore again and, after ravaging the surrounding countryside, occupied the strategic fort of Siālkot. The deposed Khusraw Malik made an alliance with the Khokkhars, a Hindu tribe from the Salt Range[26] but was unable to recapture Sialkot. Mu'izzu'd-Dīn invaded Lahore for the third time in 1186, captured Khusraw Malik by perfidy, and sent him to the Balarwan fort in Ghurjistān, where he was killed in 1192. With his death the Ghaznavid dynasty came to an end.

Multān, Lahore, and Sind now became part of the Ghurid empire. After consolidating his conquests, Mu'izzu'd-Dīn seized Tabarhinda (Bhatinda) in 1189. Prithvirāja Chāhamāna (Chauhāna), who ruled the area from Ajmīr to Delhi, Sirhind (in Patiala), and Hisār, in a bid to contain Mu'izzu'd-Dīn, marched out at the head of a large army. Other rajas also joined him. The battle took place at Tarā'in, eighty miles from Delhi, in 1190. The Rājpūt thrust broke both Mu'izzu'd-Dīn's left and right wings. The Sultan himself was about to fall when a Khaljī soldier sprang upon Mu'izzu'd-Dīn's horse and, holding him in his arms, rushed after the fleeing Ghurid army. Prithvīrāja recaptured Tabarhinda but did not pursue the invaders further.

Next year, after more elaborate preparations, Mu'izzu'd-Dīn marched towards Bhatinda, seized the fort, and again pitched his camp at Tarā'in. About 150 chieftains joined Prithvīrāja's army, which was several times larger than Mu'izzu'd-Dīn's force. The Sultan divided his troops into five divisions. Four of these consisted of mounted archers, who were ordered to attack the flanks and if possible the rear of the enemy, avoiding hand-to-hand conflict. When the enemy pressed too closely they were to feign flight. From early morning to the afternoon this force attacked continuously, exhausting the cumbrous Rājpūt army. Then Mu'izzu'd-Dīn charged the enemy at the head of 12,000 fresh troopers with drawn swords and lances. The Rājpūts were routed. About 100,000 Hindu soldiers died, including the brave Tomar prince of Delhi, Govindarāja. In his predicament Prithvīrāja alighted from his elephant, mounted a horse, and fled, but he was overtaken near the town of Sarsutī. Hasan Nizāmi's account states that Prithvīrāja was taken prisoner to Ajmīr, where he ruled for some years as a Ghurid vassal;[27] this is corroborated by numismatic evidence. Later he was executed for treason, but his son was appointed to succeed him. Another Tomar prince, Govindarāja's son, was appointed as the Ghurid's vassal in Delhi. The conquered local chiefs, called *rā'is*, submitted, agreeing to pay tribute and land tax (*mālguzārī*). A military station was established at Indraprastha. The Turks captured Hānsī, Kuhrām, and Sarsutī and placed them too under Turkic garrisons. Ajmīr was also assaulted and taken. On his return from Ajmīr, the Sultan besieged Delhi again, and Govindarāja's son agreed to resume paying tribute.

The victory of Tarā'in was a watershed in Indian history. It marked the beginning of Turkic rule in India proper. Previously this had been confined to the Panjāb and Sind. Mu'izzu'd-Dīn subsequently withdrew to Ghaznī, leaving his trusted general Qutbu'd-Dīn Aybak to consolidate their gains and make further annexations. Aybak then seized Delhi, deposing Govindarāja's son, who had rebelled yet again. In 1193 Mu'izzu'd-Din summoned Aybak to Ghaznī, possibly to draw up plans for future Indian conquests.[28]

After his return Aybak seized Kol ('Alīgarh). While he was busy suppressing various Rājpūt uprisings, Mu'izzu'd-Dīn left Ghaznī for Delhi, where Aybak later joined him. Although Jai Chand, the Gāhadavāla raja of Kanauj and Banāras, had not assisted his rival Prithvīrāja in attempting to overthrow the Turkic army, Mu'izzu'd-Dīn and Aybak marched against him. He was killed and his army was defeated in 1194 in the battle of Chandawār, between Kanauj and Etāwa on the Jamuna. The victorious Ghurid army marched on to Banāras (Varanasi) and Asnī. The Gāhadavāl's treasury was plundered. Four years later Kanauj was also captured. The Sultan then returned to Ghaznī. Aybak crushed a rebellion at Kol and finally brought Ajmīr under his control. Replacing Prithvīrāja's son with a Turkic governor, he gave him Ranthambhor instead.[29]

In 1195–6 Mu'izzu'd-Dīn again marched from Ghaznī and, defeating the Jādon Bhattī Rājpūts, seized Bayāna. The Sultan made Malik Bahā'u'd-Dīn Tughril governor of the region. Bahā'u'd-Dīn encouraged Indian and Khurāsān merchants to settle there and also to improve agriculture. He founded a new fort-town named Sultan-kot, near Bayāna. Before leaving the region Mu'izzu'd-Dīn had made the raja of Gwālior a tributary, but Bahā'u'd-Dīn, in obedience to the Sultan's orders, posted troops around Gwālior. Before his death around 1200, Gwālior's defences had been considerably weakened.[30]

Ajmīr rebelled again in 1195–6. Aybak, who had hastened to crush the uprising, was defeated and forced to withdraw to Ajmīr fort. The timely arrival of a Ghaznī contingent, however, turned the tables on the Rājpūts. Aybak next marched on Anhilwāra, whose Chālūkya ruler had made common cause with the dissident Ajmīr raja. The battle took place on the Abu mountain, where Aybak's mobility and shock tactics crowned him with success. The victory yielded considerable booty, but Anhilwāra itself was not annexed until 1240.[31]

Aybak seized Badā'ūn from a Rāśtrakūta Rājpūt in 1197–8. He also raided Malwa. In 1202–3 Aybak besieged Kālinjar, the capital of the Chandela king, in Bundelkhand. The siege was protracted, but when the invaders cut off the water supply the garrison surrendered. Kālinjar, Mahoba, and Khajuraho were also conquered.[32]

By 1200 Turkic military outposts had been set up and fort commandants appointed from Banāras to the Panjāb and from Gwālior to Anhilwāra. Neither Mu'izzu'd-Dīn nor Aybak had any plans to penetrate Bihār and Bengal. These areas were conquered by Ikhtiyāru'd-Dīn Muhammad bin Bakhtiyār, who belonged to the Khaljī Turkic tribe of Ghūr. Finding little encouragement from the muster master at Ghaznī and later at Delhi because of his humble origins, Bakhtiyār proceeded to Badā'ūn. He showed promise there and at Avadh, and was awarded an *iqta'* near Chunar.[33] His successful incursions into Bihār, east of the river Karmanasa, encouraged other Turkic soldiers to join him. He conquered regions as far as the Buddhist university of Odantapurī, Bihār, where he slaughtered the Buddhist monks and seized the town. He then visited Aybak in March 1203 at Badā'ūn and obtained permission to attempt further conquests.

Passing through the Jhārkhand jungles in the south of Bihār in 1204–5, Bakhtiyār rushed to Nadia or Navadvip, one of the two capitals of Lakshmana Sena, the King of Bengal. His army was unable to keep up with him, and, according to the *Tabaqāt-i Nāsiri*, only eighteen horsemen were with him when he forcibly entered the palace. Lakshmana Sena, who is reported to have just sat down to his midday meal, fled through a postern door to the eastern region of his kingdom, where he ruled for some years. The story of the eighteen horseman conquering Bengal is hotly disputed by Bengali authors, but it is not unlikely that Bakhtiyār's lightning raid with a small force under him struck such a terror in the king's heart as to make him fly without resistance. Bakhtiyār plundered Nadia and acquired immense booty.

Retreating northwards, Bakhtiyār took up his quarters in the Sena's western capital, Lakhnautī or Lakshmanavatī, near the present site of Gaur. He established another outpost at Lakhanor or Nagar in the Bīrbhūm district, thereby connecting Bihār with Orissa. To the north-east an outpost was established at Devakot near Dinājapūr. His spectacular conquests prompted him to seize Karmapattan (possibly Kumrīkotah in Bhūtān) and Tibet. The enterprise was designed to ensure the supply of horses from that region. At the head of 10,000 horsemen, Bakhtiyār followed the Brahmaputra and, ignoring the advice of the Raja of Kāmrūp not to proceed beyond his territory, reached Karmapattan. The subsequent news of the arrival of an army of 50,000 men from the mountains of Tibet disheartened Bakhtiyār's troops. He retreated to Kāmrup, where the local forces made short work of his soldiers. He himself with great difficulty reached Devakot. Bedridden as a result of his hardships, Bakhtiyār was assassinated by one of his own commanders.[34]

Meanwhile, Ghiyasu'd-Dīn had died at Hirāt in 1202–3. In 1204 Mu'izzu'd-Din was defeated at Andhuī on the Oxus by the allies of the Khwārazm rulers and, except for Hirāt, lost the whole of Khurāsān. The news of the disaster encouraged the Gakkhar tribes of the Panjāb to regain control over the Lahore-Ghaznī route. Mu'izzu'd-Dīn, joined by Aybak, crushed their uprising and then marched to Lahore. After a short stay there, he sent Aybak to Delhi and himself returned to Ghaznī. On 15 March 1206 he was assassinated by a Gakkhar at Damyak on the bank of the Jhelam (near modern Sohawa).[35]

The motives for Mu'izzu'd-Dīn's conquests were no different from those of Mahmūd of Ghaznī. Both were in need of plunder from India to maintain their slave armies and to attract the wandering bands of Islamicized mercenaries known as *ghāzīs* to their forces. The Islamicization of India was not their main objective, although some tribal leaders, such as the Gakkhars, were encouraged to embrace Islam. The exaggerated accounts of Muslim historians and poets of the slaughter of infidels in the spreading of Islam are designed to give a religious colour to wars which were basically waged for political domination and plunder. Mu'izzu'd-Din's achievements were more permanent than those of Mahmūd. Before his death, the strategic centres of India from Ghaznī to the borders of Assam had been conquered and the forts efficiently garrisoned.

The factors surrounding the Turkic victory are highly controversial. Hindu historians such as A. L. Srivastava divide 'causes of our defeat' under two headings. Under general causes, Srivastava says: 'lack of political unity and proper organisation and capable leadership must, therefore, remain the most important general cause of our helplessness and defeat'. As regards the particular causes, he says: 'Our rulers did not care to find loop-holes in the organisation of their common enemy.'[36] Srivastava's comments seek to impose modern nationalist sentiments on twelfth- and thirteenth-century India; but such sentiments did not exist in India until the nineteenth century. On the other hand, according to modern Muslim scholars, such as Muhammad Habīb and K. A. Nizāmi:

> The real cause of the defeat of the Indians lay in their social system and the invidious caste distinctions, which rendered the whole military organization rickety and weak. Caste taboos and discriminations killed all sense of unity – social or political. Even religion was the monopoly of a particular section, and the majority of the Indian people were never allowed a glimpse of the inside of a high caste Indian temple. Thus for the bulk of the Indian people there was hardly anything which could evoke patriotic responses in them when face to face with the Ghūrīd invader.[37]

This theory also presupposes the existence of modern patriotic feelings or religious solidarity in other parts of the world, when even in Muslim-dominated regions they did not exist. Nizāmi has himself quoted the great poet Sa'dī, who wrote: 'the lashkarī [professional soldier] fought for the wages he got; he did not fight for king, country or religion'.[38] The same was true of India, and Indian caste taboos cannot be blamed for the Rājpūt defeat. India was then ruled by Rājpūt rulers who were proud of their ancient Kshatriya blood, reckless swordsmanship, and chivalric sense of honour. Their political and social systems were feudal. They fought for the safety of their own boundaries and constantly feuded with their neighbours. The Panjāb, Multān, and Sind, ruled by the Muslims from the eighth century onwards, did not concern them. It was not until 1150 that Vasāla Deva (Vigraharāja III) of Ajmīr, who had seized Delhi from the Tomars, was prompted also to take Hānsī from the Ghaznavids. The time was then ripe to wipe out the tottering Ghaznavid kingdom of the Panjāb. Neither Mūlarāja of Anhilwāra, who defeated Mu'izzu'd-Dīn in 1178, nor Prithvīrāja had the good sense to pursue and attempt to annihilate the Ghūrīd invaders after delivering a crushing defeat on them. The two major defeats of Mu'izzu'd-Dīn show that Rājpūt military strength was quite formidable; their fault lay in their adherence to fighting a defensive war and their inability to take full advantage of a victory. The ponderous war machinery of the Rājpūts with their slow-moving elephants was no match for the mobility and lightning attacks of the Central Asian Turkic guerrilla warriors. Separated from their homes by long distances and committed to obtaining victory for their own enrichment, the Turkic troopers fought with vigour and desperation. No such personal stake was involved for the Rājpūts. Political independence and nationalism in the twentieth-century sense meant nothing to the twelfth-century Hindus and Muslims. Nevertheless, as we shall see, the resistance of the Hindu, in order to save his hearth and home, was unending.

THE ILBARĪ TURKS

Mu'izzu'd-Dīn had no sons. According to the *Tabaqāt-i Nāsirī*, he had bought a large number of slaves but he did not nominate any particular one as his successor.[39] The most prominent slave was Tāju'd-Dīn Yilduz, whose daughters were married to Aybak and Qabācha. Yilduz was therefore recognised as the ruler of Ghaznī and, although the Indian territories had been conquered and consolidated by Aybak, Yilduz considered them his dependencies. Aybak consequently moved from Delhi to Lahore and proclaimed himself the independent ruler of the Indian territories. Yilduz thereupon invaded the Panjāb but was defeated, and Aybak seized Ghaznī. When Yilduz reappeared before Ghaznī, however, Aybak fled to Lahore. There he remained, busily consolidating his administration, until his death in 1210 following a fall from a horse during a polo game. Aybak was a far-sighted military commander and had tactfully controlled the heterogeneous racial groups of soldiers who hailed from Khurāsān, Ghār, Khalj, and India. He is also remembered for his munificence.[40]

Arām Shāh, who succeeded his father Aybak, was a weakling. Meanwhile, Qābacha had consolidated his rule in Multān, Uch, Bhakkar, and Sehwān and had extended his kingdom as far as Lahore. Another contestant in the struggle for power was lltutmish, who had been bought as a slave by Aybak in Delhi and had become his son-in-law. He commenced his career as a *sar-jāndār* (head of the royal bodyguard) and controlled the prized *iqtā'* of Badā'ūn. Iltutmish seized Delhi without much difficulty, defeating Ārām Shāh, whose supporters quickly surrendered. Since he belonged to the Ilbarī tribe, his successors up to 1290 are known as the Ilbarī Turks. They are also called *ghulām* or *mamlūk* rulers, both of which terms mean 'slaves'.

Iltutmish devoted the first ten years of his reign to securing his throne from rivals. He acted with considerable caution and patience. When Yilduz marched on Lahore and occupied the greater part of the Panjāb, Iltutmish turned the ensuing war between Qabācha and Yilduz to his advantage. In 1215 Yilduz was driven out of Ghaznī by Khwārazm Shāh and took refuge in Lahore. His claim to overlordship there precipitated a war against Iltutmish, who was well prepared. On the battlefield of Tarā'in, Iltutmish defeated Yilduz and sent him captive to Badā'ūn, where he was beheaded. Iltutmish then restored Lahore to Qabācha, but two years later marched against him. Qabācha fled to Mansura, and Iltutmish followed and defeated him.[41]

Chingīz Khān (b. 1167), the founder of the Mongol world empire, had meanwhile become supremely powerful. In the summer of 1215 the Mongols captured Peking and five years later conquered Transoxiana. In 1221 the last Khwārazm ruler, Jalalu'd-Dīn Mingburnu (1220–31), defeated a Mongol force in the Ghaznī region. Chingīz rushed with lightning speed to avenge the defeat and chased Jalalu'd-Dīn as far as the Indus. Jalalu'd-Dīn retreated to the upper Sind Sagar *doāb* in the western Panjāb and there married the daughter of a local Khokkhar chief. Qabācha's rule over Sind Sagar *doāb* ended. Jalalu'd-Dīn reached Lahore but could not persuade Iltutmish to send reinforcements. Fortunately for Iltutmish and Jalalu'd-Dīn, Chingīz turned back at the Indus and resumed the route he had been following. Jalalu'd-Dīn also left India in 1224, but, until Chingīz's death in August 1227.[42] Iltutmish did not interfere with Qabācha, who remained a buffer between the Mongols and his own kingdom.

In 1228 Iltutmish ordered his governor in Lahore to invade Multān while he himself marched on Uch. Qabācha fled to the inland fortress of Bhakkar on the lower Indus. Uch was taken after a three-month siege. The vigorous assault on Bhakkar frightened Qabācha, and he was drowned crossing the Indus while fleeing for safety. Multān and Sind were thus annexed to the Delhi sultanate.

After Chingīz's departure from the Indus, Iltutmish reasserted his control over the district of Bihār south of the Ganges. In 1225 Husāmu'd-Dīn 'Iwaz Khaljī, who had established an independent Bengal sultanate, submitted to him. As soon as Iltutmish's back was turned however, 'Iwaz again rebelled. The Sultan's son, Nāsiru'd-Dīn Mahmūd, thereupon swooped down from his base in Avadh on Lakhnautī and defeated and killed 'Iwaz. In Avadh siru'd-Dīn Mahmūd died in Lakhnauti in March or April 1229, and Bengal again rose in rebellion. This time Iltutmish suppressed it personally in 1229.[43]

The Sultan also effectively quashed the uprisings by the Rājasthān chiefs. In 1226 he recovered Ranthambhor; two years later the Chauhān chief of Jālor also agreed to pay tribute. Ajmīr and Sāmbhar were subsequently reoccupied, and Nāgaur reconquered. In 1231 Gwālior surrendered again; Malik Tā'isī, a slave of Mu'izzu'd-Dīn, was made its commander. Contingents from Kanauj and Mahāban were also placed at his disposal, and he seized areas from Kālinjar to Chanderī. In 1234–5 Iltutmish led an expedition against Mālwa and captured Bhilsa. The conquest of Ujjain was followed by the demolition of the ancient Mahā-kāl temple.[44]

Iltutmish's military expeditions in Badā'ūn, Kanauj, and Banarās completely undermined the local rajas' independence. Katihar (modern Rohekhand) was one of the few areas to offer stiff resistance before submitting. Iltutmish's son, Mahmūd, whom he had appointed governor of Avadh in 1226, however, met strong opposition from the local chief Brītū or Prīthū. According to Minhāj Sirāj, 120,000 Muslims were killed fighting Brītū. This number is exaggerated, but Hindu strength in the region remained undisputed.[45]

Sultan Iltutmish died on 30 April 1236. He was the greatest ruler of thirteenth-century India and a wise statesman. He transformed Mu'izzu'd-Dīn's Indian conquests into a cohesive hereditary monarchy. The receipt of the deed of investiture from the 'Abbāsid caliph in February 1229 gave legal status to Iltutmish's kingship. Iltutmish was welcoming and generous to the talented people, both Turkic and non-Turkic, driven from their homelands in Irān and

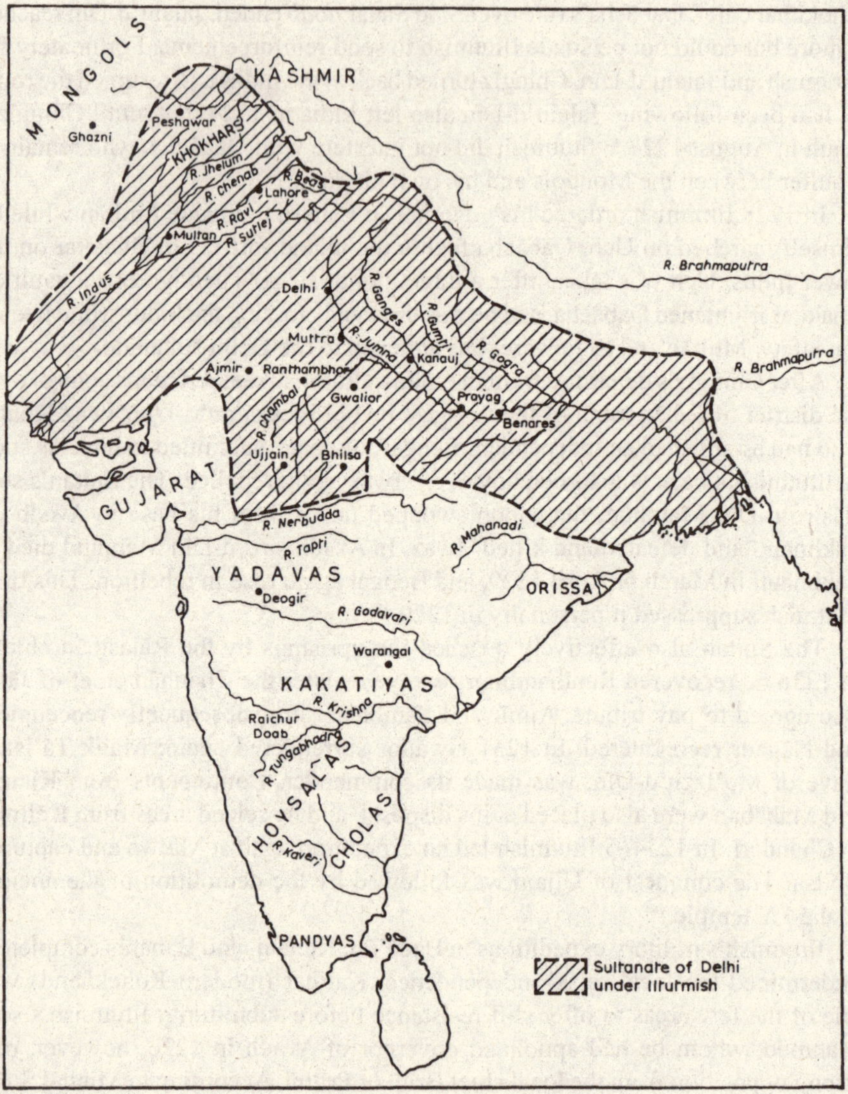

India in 1236

Central Asia by Chingīz Khān's invasions. They quickly became pillars of the central administration and many settled in the areas between Lahore and Avadh. The Turkic military commanders also supported the Delhi sultanate, as well as extending its boundaries. The land tax from the territorial units know as *iqtā's* was usually assigned to them. He appointed his own officials (*'āmils*) to collect revenue from the areas which had not been assigned as *iqtā's*. These were known as *khālisas*. He also assigned villages to troopers of his own central army. These too were known as *iqtā's*.

Iltutmish organized court etiquette on the Samanid and Ghaznavid patterns, which made special provision for the *'ulamā'* (scholars of Islamic theology) and sūfīs. According to sūfī anecdotes, Iltutmish's services to them in his youth were responsible for his subsequent rise to the throne.[46] Historically the stories are untenable; nevertheless the Sultan's relations with the contemporary sūfīs were based on respect, and they, in their turn, supported him, counterbalancing the *'ulamā'* pressure groups in the bureaucracy. Iltutmish had promoted his intelligent daughter Raziyya over his incompetent sons. In 1231 he appointed her his deputy in Delhi while he was away on his Gwālior expedition. His decision was not welcomed, and perhaps he himself finally doubted its wisdom.[47]

After Iltutmish's death, Shāh Turkān, the mother of Iltutmish's eldest surviving son, with the help of a section of the *'ulamā'* and the Turkic commanders, had her son crowned as Ruknu'd-Dīn Fīrūz. Turkān was an arch-intriguer but not an administrator. She unleashed a reign of terror and vengeance on her rival queens and their supporters, while Fīrūz sank into a life of licentiousness. Consequently the ruler of Ghaznī mounted an invasion of Sind.[48] Another son of Iltutmish rebelled in Avadh, and other *iqtā'* holders united to overthrow the new Sultan. Ruknu'd-Dīn Fīrūz marched out of the capital to suppress the rebellion. This gave Raziyya the opportunity to seize the throne. Fīrūz was imprisoned and put to death in November 1236. He had ruled for only some seven months.[49]

Minhaj Siraj, who was a distinguished *'alim* (singular of *'ulamā'*), comments: 'Raziyya was endowed with all the admirable attributes and qualifications necessary for kings; but, as she did not attain the destiny, in her creation, of being computed among men, of what advantage were all these excellent qualifications to her?'[50] Minhaj, however, was not hostile to her, and the other *'ulamā'* did not oppose her; but Nizāmu'l-Mulk Junaydi, Iltutmish's vizier, rebelled, winning many important Turkic noblemen to his side. Raziyya marched out of Delhi against the rebel group and succeeded, by negotiations, in breaking the coalition. Nizāmu'l-Mulk fled and died. Some important rebel leaders were killed. Raziyya then appointed Muhazzabu'd-Dīn, a Tājik, as deputy vizier and elevated many other Tājiks to high positions. Her subsequent appointment of Malik Jamālu'd-Dīn Yāqūt, an Ethiopian, as superintendent of the royal horses, aroused resentment in a majority of the already disgruntled Turkic commanders. Raziyya ignored their opposition and began to appear unveiled in public, wearing a short tunic and conical hat. The people of Delhi supported her, but hostility mounted among the *iqtā'* holders. In 1239–40 she crushed some of the rebellious *iqtā'* holders, but one of them, Altūnia, who held Bhatinda, killed Yaqut, took Raziyya prisoner, and had her incarcerated. The ruling party in Delhi ignored Altūnia and placed Iltutmish's third son, Bahrām, on the throne. Raziyya, exploiting the situation to her own advantage, married Altūnia. They marched against Delhi together, but their principal supporters now deserted them. They were both killed on 14 October 1240 by Hindu robbers.[51]

Raziyya ruled successfully for three and a half years. She combated intrigues competently, displayed a remarkable insight into military tactics, resourcefully implemented her independent decisions, and diplomatically reconciled the recalcitrant *iqta'* holders. Her chief merit was her ability to rise above the prejudices of her age. The romantic tragedy of this remarkable woman is something unique in the history of India.

Raziyya's fall made the clique of Turkic *maliks* (military commanders), and *amīrs* dominant in the government. Baranī calls them *chihalgānī*, or the 'family of forty', and they embarked on a scramble for supremacy.[52] They did not form any organized groups, however, and did not even number forty. Minhāj Sirāj gives the biographies of merely twenty-five of Iltutmish's leading *maliks*, who each struggled to dominate the government. They controlled various strategic forts, and their personal jealousies and rivalries destroyed them. They were able neither to raise one of their members to the throne nor to strengthen the royal power. The leading nobles who had placed Iltutmish's third son, Mu'izzu'd-Din Bahrām Shāh (1240–2) on the throne made him create the position of regent (*malik na'ib* or *na'ib-i mamlakat*).[53] The regent was intended to be the *de facto* ruler, the sultan merely a figurehead. Intrigue and chaos ran riot during the reigns of Bahrām Shāh and his successors. The palace ladies also formed factions, and the *'ulama'* too took the opportunity to fish in troubled waters.

In 1241 the Mongols crossed the Indus and reached the gates of Lahore. No help arrived from Delhi. The Mongols smashed the fort ramparts, and the governor fled. Although the citizens fought valiantly, and the Mongols suffered heavy losses, they eventually sacked the city and laid it waste. When they left, the Khokkhar tribesmen entered and plundered it mercilessly. Bahrām Shāh now attempted to assert his authority over the dominant Turkic chiefs but failed.[54] He was taken captive and in May 1242 put to death. Malik 'Izzu'd-Dīn Balban Kishlū Khān, a leading Turkic slave commander, tried to make himself sultan, but he lacked support, and was forced to accept the governorship of Nāgaur. 'Alā'u'd-Dīn Mas'ūd, son of Ruknu'd-Dīn Fīrūz, was eventually made king. Mas'ūd ruled from 1242 to 1246. Tughān Khān, who had been acknowledged as the governor of Lakhnauti by Raziyya, now proclaimed his independence and annexed Bihār and Avadh to his Bengal kingdom. The King of Jājnagar (Orissa) then invaded Bengal.[55] Meanwhile the Mongols had crossed the Indus and besieged Uch. An army under Balban, now governor of Nāgaur, was sent to Lahore, and the Mongols retreated to their own territory. After his return Balban and his supporters conspired with Nasīru'd-Dīn Mahmūd's mother, Malika-i Jahān, to overthrow Mas'ūd. Nasīru'd-Dīn was the eldest son of Iltutmish's son,

Nasīru'd-Dīn Mahmūd, who had died in Lakhnauti. Mas'ūd was deposed and thrown into prison, where he died.[56]

Sultan Nasīru'd-Dīn is wrongly described as a very God-fearing, pious, and amicable person. Born in 1229, he was not more than seventeen years old when he ascended the throne. He knew the fate of his predecessors and had no alternative but to leave the administration in Balban's hands. The sultanate was in a critical condition. The Mongols had devastated the country west of the river Jhelam, and no food was available in the Panjāb. In 1246–7 Balban mounted an expedition as far as the Salt Range to chastise the Khokkhars, who acted as guides to the Mongols. During the following two years he overran Kālinjar, Ranthambhor, and Mewāt.[57] In August 1249 the Sultan married Balban's daughter and made him the *na'ib-i mamlakat* (regent of the kingdom). He was also awarded the title Great Khān (Ulugh Khān), and all the important positions were given to his relations. Balban was now ruler in all but name.[58]

Before long, however, the Sultan grew resentful of Balban's power. In 1253 'Imadu'd-Dīn Rayhān, a Hindu convert, who was supported by both Indian Muslims and a section of Turks, managed to have Balban transferred to his *iqta'* of Nagaur. Balban's principal supporters were also dispersed and sent to distant *iqta's*. They were appalled at the rise of an Indian Muslim to power and assembled with their forces near Hansi for a trial of strength. The Sultan, accompanied by Rayhan, arrived with his army, but the Turk and Tājik leaders succeeded in persuading him to transfer Rayhan to Badā'ūn. In December 1254 Balban was reconciled to his son-in-law and returned to Delhi with the Sultan.[59]

Balban's efforts to assert the authority of the centre and to suppress rebellion were not successful. His repeated expeditions to Bengal failed to maintain Delhi's control over the region. Even Avadh did not remain loyal, and Bahrāich followed Avadh's example. Hasan Qarlugh, the Khwārazmī prince who had ruled Multān and Uch for some years, had been expelled earlier by Balban. Kishlu Khān, who had been made governor there, was forced to surrender Sind to Hulāgū Khān (1256–65), the founder of the Īl-Khānid Mongol dynasty of Irān. Jalālu'd-Dīn Mas'ūd, the Sultan's brother, fled from Hulāgū to the court of Mengū Khān of Qaraqorum, who ruled Mongolia and China. A strong Mongol contingent helped him to seize areas extending from the Salt Range to Lahore.[60] Mas'ūd, however, was not a competent ruler, and even Mongol help could not keep him on the throne. Sher Khān, the ambitious governor of Bhatinda, who was the Sultan's cousin, was ambivalent and alternately attended the courts. of Hulāgū and Mongke, the ruler of south Russia and Qipchāq. Balban, however, came to an understanding with Hulāgū, and the Mongol invasions were confined to the region beyond the Beas. In 1260 Hulāgū's emissary was received in Delhi with a flamboyant demonstration of the sultanate's military strength.[61] The *Tabaqāt-i Nāsirz* abruptly ends with the events of early 1260. Only 'Isāmī, who completed his *Futūhu's-Salātīn* in 1350–1, tells us that Balban poisoned Sultan Nāsiru'd-Dīn's drink. Some modern historians disbelieve 'Isāmi because of Balban's close family connections with the Sultan.[62] This is hardly a valid argument, for the murder of relations to gain throne and position was then the order of the day.

Balban was now proclaimed Sultan. His perception of the Delhi sultanate's problems was very realistic, and he solved them successfully. He knew that the real threat to the monarchy came from the Turkic nobles' intrigues and their scramble for power. He introduced rigorous court discipline, such as prostration before the king and kissing his feet, in order to reduce the nobles to abject servility. A picked body of fearsome soldiers with drawn swords protected the throne. The court was an austere assembly where jest and laughter were seldom heard. The Sultan was himself a paragon of severity and harshness. He persistently brought home to his sons and noblemen that the monarch was the vicegerent of God and next in sanctity only to the prophets. The Sultan was God's shadow on earth and the recipient of direct divine guidance. Only the most servile of noblemen and commanders survived; the rest were eliminated on flimsy pretexts. Malik Baqbaq, the governor of Badā'ūn, who had had one of his servants beaten to death, was publicly flogged. Haybat Khān, governor of Avadh, who had killed a man while drunk, was flogged and handed over to the victim's widow to dispose of as she wished. Malik Ītigīn Mū'ī Darāz (Amīn Khān), the governor of Avadh,when defeated by Tughril, the rebel governor of Bengal, was hanged at the gate of Avadh. Sher Khān, the ambitious governor of Bhatinda, was poisoned and died.[63] Only those junior Turkic officers who were servile to the Sultan were promoted to high positions.

Balban abandoned his earlier scheme of conquests. His military expeditions as a *nā'ib-i mamlakat* had convinced him that it was impossible to retain distant territories such as Gwālior, Mālwa, and Rājasthān, which had several times been conquered and lost. He instead gave top priority to restoring peace in the region surrounding Delhi.[64] In Nāsiru'd-Dīn's reign the constant Mewāti raids from the northern Alwar region into Delhi had made the people's lives miserable. Balban's repeated attacks on the Mewāti strongholds and villages stopped these incursions. Military posts, manned by Afghāns, were established in these regions, and the soldiers were given tax-free land.[65] The villages belonging to the rebels of the *doāb* were also destroyed, and the peasants were encouraged to settle down to a peaceful life. The Sultan twice marched on Avadh, killing the rebel leaders and devastating the villages. Strong forts were built at Kampil, Patiālī, and Bhojpūr, the principal rendezvous for robbers and strongholds of rebels. These forts were also garrisoned by Afghāns, who were given tax-free land in the neighbourhood to maintain themselves.[66]

Muslim families were encouraged to settle there. The rebels in Badā'ūn, Amroha (western Uttar Pradesh), and Katihar (modern Rohilkhand) were also killed. Dense forests were cut down and burnt; the roads too were cleared. Balban's regular hunting trips, in conjunction with the newly established military posts, kept the area from Delhi to Avadh reasonably peaceful. The roads became safe for travel, and trade and agriculture improved, leading to further urbanization.[67]

The Sultan reorganized the army. The loyal troops were sent to the central contingents. Expense was no consideration. A body of one thousand reckless soldiers, the counterpart of modern commandos, who had been recruited before Balban assumed royal power, always accompanied him.

The Sultan had every reason to be pleased with his success, but his own slave, Tughril, whom he had made governor of Bengal, gave him a rude shock by rebelling in about 1275. The Sultan sent Amīn Khān, governor of Avadh, to crush the rebellion, but he was defeated. Another army left Delhi but was also driven away by Tughril. In 1280–1 the Sultan went to Sunām and Sāmāna, which were ruled by his younger son, Bughrā Khān, and divided the territories into smaller *iqtā's* to prevent the rebellion of any more powerful governors. Taking Bughrā Khān with him, he proceeded to the *doāb*. There he made Fakhru'd-Dīn Kotwāl his regent (*nā'ib-ghaybat*). At Avadh some 200,000 infantry, archers, and local horsemen were added to the Delhi army. Before Balban reached Lakhnauti, Tughril had fled to the east, hoping that the Sultan would return to Delhi.[68] The octogenarian Sultan was, however, determined not to leave until he had destroyed Tughril. From Lakhnauti the Sultan hurried to Sunārgāon. The local ruler, Danujamādhava of the Deva dynasty, refused to help unless the Sultan showed his respect when he was introduced to the court. The Sultan sat down on his throne with a falcon on his hand. When the Raja appeared he stood up. The courtiers thought the Sultan was flying the falcon; the Raja believed that Balban was demonstrating his respect.[69] Tughril was ultimately captured by Balban's army and his severed head sent to the Sultan. The army's morale quickly rose. At Lakhnauti, Tughril's followers were impaled on a row of gibbets running for about two miles beside the road. Then, appointing Bughrā Khān governor of Bengal and urging him to take a lesson from the evil consequences of rebellion, the Sultan returned to Delhi after three years' absence.[70] The capital was safe in Fakhru'd-Dīn's hands and the frontier strongholds in the west were defended by the Sultan's brave elder son, Sultan Muhammad. The Chaghatay branch of the Mongols, ruling Transoxiana and eastern Turkistan, was locked in battle with the Il-Khānid branch which ruled Irān. Unfortunately for the Sultan, however, a Mongol army suddenly appeared in 1285, while Sultan Muhammad was busy fighting the local Sāmra rebels in Sind. Muhammad returned quickly and attacked the Mongols, but was killed in battle. It was a mortal blow to his father, Sultan Balban.

Not only had Muhammad been an excellent fighter but he was a great patron of poets and scholars. Famous poets like Amir Khusraw and Amir Hasan had in their early career been employed by him. Amir Khusraw was also taken captive by the Mongols and suffered considerable hardship at their hands.[71]

Balban summoned his younger son, Bughra Khān, to Delhi, but after two or three months he left for Lakhnauti. The Sultan hid his misery and unremittingly discharged his duties, although it is said that he wept throughout the night for his dead elder son. On his deathbed in 1287 Balban made Kaykhusraw, Sultan Muhammad's son, his successor; but when Balban was dead the powerful *kotwāl* of Delhi sent him to Multān and raised Kayqubād, Bughra Khān's son, to the throne.[72]

Kayqubād was about eighteen years old and had been brought up under strict discipline by his austere grandfather. Once upon the throne, which he had never dreamt of attaining, Kayqubād sank into an orgy of profligacy and debauchery. The Sultan's favourite, Malik Nizāmu'd-Dīn, nephew and son-in-law of Fakhru'd-Dīn *kotwāl*, became virtual ruler. He beheaded all the leading noblemen of Balban's reign who posed a threat to his dominance. Muhammad's son, Kaykhusraw, was also killed. Meanwhile in Lahore a Mongol army which had arrived in the vicinity was repulsed by the local commanders. Bughrā Khān subsequently proclaimed himself king in Bengal and wrote to his son Kayqubād advising him to pay more serious attention to his duties. Finding no change in his son's behaviour, he marched towards Delhi. The two armies met at Avadh (Ayodhya) in 1289. War between father and son was, however, averted by Bughrā Khān's fatherly kindness. Kayqubad listened respectfully to his father's wise counsel and, following his advice, transferred his favourite Nizāmu'd-Dīn to Multān.[73] But he was unable to give up his dissipated life-style, and the administration broke down. Before long he was struck with paralysis. A party of Turkic noblemen thereupon elevated Kayqubad's three-year-old son, Kayūmars, to the throne, but their rivals, the Khaljī *maliks*, who were more united, proved too powerful for them. They killed the Turkic commanders but kept Kayumars on the throne for a further three months. Kayqubad was killed in pitiable circumstances, his body thrown in the Jamuna.[74] The Ilbarī rule came to an end. In June 1290 Jalalu'd-Dīn Fīrūz became the first Khaljī sultan of Delhi.

THE KHALJĪS

Before the rise of the Mongols, the Khalj people had lived in western Turkistān and later in close proximity to the Afghān tribal lands of modern eastern Afghānistan. Their pure Turkic origin is disputed, because in the eleventh century they intermarried with the Pashto-speaking Ghalzay tribe of Afghāns and became pre-dominantly Afghān. Mahmūd of Ghaznī had recruited them for his army, but Mas'ūd of Ghaznī sent a punitive expedition against them. The Khalj tribe also fought in the Ghūrīd army. In the early thirteenth century they conquered Bengal.

At first the new Sultan, Jalalu'd-Dīn Khaljī, feared the formidable Ilbarī opposition, even though the principal Khaljī claimants to the throne had been killed. It took him some months to conciliate the Ilbarī supporters, to whom he showed a paternal and kindly attitude.[75] He gave all the high positions to his own sons, nephews, and brothers, but he did not ignore the Ilbarīs altogether, and Balban's nephew, Malik Chajjū, was made governor of Kara, where he soon rebelled. The Hindu chiefs with their infantry and archers joined Chajjū. The disbanded army recruited by Balban for his Bengal expeditions also swelled Chajjū's ranks, and they marched on Delhi to seize the throne. The Sultan sent an advance division, which defeated Chajjū at Rāmganga. The rebel leaders were taken captive, but the Sultan, to his relations' annoyance, acted magnanimously. Chajju was simply deprived of his governorship, which the Sultan bestowed upon his nephew and son-in-law, 'Alī Gurshāsp ('Ala'u'd-Dīn).[76]

The Sultan's magnanimity went so far that he was even merciful on a gang of thugs who were taken captive and brought to Delhi. They were merely banished to Bengal. His leniency was taken for weakness, and the disgruntled nobles began to hatch plots at their drinking parties to overthrow the old Sultan. Though news of these plots reached the Sultan, no action was taken against them either. The Sultan's near relations were shocked at his leniency, but he explained to their spokesman, Malik Ahmad Chap, that the sultanate was too weak to assert itself effectively. The best way out of the impasse was to govern the country with tolerance and mildness.[77]

In 1291–2 a Mongol invasion of the Dipālpūr-Multān region saw the Sultan leading his army against the invader. There his liberality so impressed a group of Mongols that they decided to embrace Islam and settle in Delhi.[78]

In 1292 the Sultan mounted an expedition against Ranthambhor, where the Chauhān rulers had already greatly expanded their domain. He conquered Jhā'in and destroyed the beautifully carved idol in its main temple. Ranthambhor was besieged, but, finding the siege was protracted, the Sultan abandoned it, comforting himself with the thought that the fort was not worth a single hair of a Muslim head.[79] It would seem also that the Sultan was informed of the conspiracies to kill him which were rampant in Delhi. He returned to the capital. Inquiries revealed that the arch-conspirator was the famous dervish Sīdī Māwla, who enjoyed a large following of both Khaljī nobles and Sultan Balban's friends. The evidence warranting his execution, however, was not conclusive. An ordeal by fire was rejected as un-Islamic by the *'ulamā'*. So, at the Sultan's instigation, a group of wandering dervishes called Haydarī Qalandars attacked Sidi with razors, and one of the royal princes arranged for him to be trampled to death. The severe dust-storm and famine which followed were attributed by the gullible Delhi populace to divine retribution.[80]

The most remarkable achievement of Jalālu'd-Dīn's reign was the invasion of the Yādava capital Devagiri by his nephew, 'Ala'u'd-Dīn, governor of Kara. Although 'Ala'u'd-Dīn's personal life was made miserable by the intrigues of his wife and mother-in-law against him, he was very ambitious. He recruited a large army at Kara and, towards the end of 1293, mounted an expedition against the region around Bhilsa. He collected an enormous amount of booty and sent some to the Sultan to win his favour. For the next two years 'Ala'u'd-Dīn made preparations for another expedition and withheld the revenue due to the capital. Then he assigned the administration of Kara to 'Alā'u'l-Mulk, uncle of the historian Baranī, and marched off through the comparatively unknown Elichpūr route. Near Devagiri some Yādavas, including two women leaders, fought gallantly against 'Ala'u'd-Dīn. The Raja's main army had left to fight under his son, Sinhana, against the Raja of Warangal. Ramadeva, although a seasoned warrior, was forced in their absence to sue for peace. Sinhana, the Raja's son, subsequently returned with the main army and, contrary to his father's advice, attacked 'Ala'u'd-Dīn. The Sultan divided his army into two and confronted Sinhana himself at the head of one column. The invaders were on the verge of defeat when their reserve column fell upon the Yādavas. Sinhana mistakenly took this for the arrival of the Sultan's main army. He panicked and fled. Enormous booty fell into 'Ala'u'd-Dīn's hands. The Raja agreed to pay a heavy tribute. When the news of 'Ala'u'd-Dīn's victory reached Delhi, the Sultan was advised to move to Chanderī, intercept 'Ala'u'd-Dīn's return journey, and seize the booty himself. The Sultan stopped at Gwālior, however, thereby enabling 'Ala'u'd-Dīn to reach Kara safely. Pretending to be sorry that he had invaded Devagiri without obtaining prior approval, 'Ala'u'd-Dīn succeeded in persuading his doting uncle to visit him at Kara by boat. When Jalālu'd-Dīn landed, 'Ala'u'd-Dīn prostrated himself at his uncle's feet. Then 'Ala'u'd-Dīn signalled the assassins who were awaiting his orders. They immediately killed the Sultan on the seventeenth day of the fasting month of Ramazān 695 (21 July 1296). 'Ala'u'd-Dīn was proclaimed king.[81]

In Delhi the Sultan's widow, Malika-i Jahān, proclaimed her youngest son king with the title of Ruknu'd-Dīn Ibrāhīm, passing over Arkalī Khān, the rightful heir, who was at Multān. Arkalī Khān and his supporters in Delhi waited passively. 'Ala'u'd-Dīn, who had left Kara, was emboldened to act and rushed to Delhi, scattering gold and silver coins among the people. Ruknu'd-Dīn fled to Multān. 'Ala'u'd-Dīn thereupon ascended the throne and promoted his supporters to high positions. An army sent to Multān took Arkalī Khān, Ruknu'd-Dīn, and their mother captive. The princes were beheaded in Delhi and their mother imprisoned. Jalālu'd-Dīn's other relations and adherents were also killed barbarously. In the second year of his reign 'Ala'u'd-Dīn wiped out those noblemen of the old regime who were still loyal to Jalālu'd-Dīn.[82]

The early years of the Sultan's reign were torn by successive Mongol invasions. Duwa (1291–1306), the ruler of the Chaghatāy Mongols of Transoxiana, was determined to acquire as much booty as possible to finance his fight against his Il-Khānid rivals of Irān. The first two invasions by the Mongol army were beaten back, but in 1297 the third invader, Qutlugh Khwāja, son of Duwa, reached Kīlī near Delhi. The Sultan's army was composed mainly of cavalry trained in repulsing Hindu troops, but the Sultan, throwing prudence overboard, recklessly tackled the invaders himself. Zafar Khān, the Sultan's indefatigable commander, fell fighting the enemy, but the Sultan won the day. The commander's death was a welcome relief to the Sultan and his brother, Ulugh Khān, who were jealous of his outstanding military reputation.[83] The Sultan reorganized the defence of his frontier strongholds and appointed Ghāzī Malik governor of Dīpālpūr. In 1303 the Mongol leader Targhī reached Sīrī but was then defeated. Two years later the Mongols marched as far as Amroha but were again beaten back. Their invasion in 1306 was stopped at the bank of the river Rāvī, when Ghāzī Malik, the warden of the marches, defended the frontiers stoutly.[84] On the other hand, no major invasions were launched by Duwa's successors.

'Ala'u'd-Dīn's success in Devagiri had convinced him of the inability of the distant Hindu kingdoms to defend themselves. Ignoring the conquest of Mālwa and Rājasthān, therefore, the Sultan sent an army in February 1299 under the command of his brothers Nusrat Khān and Ulugh Khān to conquer Gujarāt. Although it had been raided previously, it was never subdued. 'Ala'u'd-Dīn's army besieged Anhilwāra, the capital of Raja Karan Vaghela of Gujarāt. The Raja, who was taken by surprise, fled with his daughter to Devagiri. Kamlā Devi, the Raja's wife, was taken captive and sent to Delhi, where the Sultan married her. The temple of Somnath, which had been rebuilt, was again sacked. The victorious army plundered both the Hindu and Muslim merchants in Cambay. The Hindu eunuch Kāfūr Hazārdīnārī, whom the Sultan later made *malik nā'ib* (regent), was also taken from his master. The Sultan appointed his brother-in-law Alp Khān governor of Gujarāt. At Jālor the army returning from Gujarāt mutinied. The rising was crushed, and the mutineers' families in Delhi were brutally slaughtered.[85]

In 1299 Nusrat Khān and Ulugh Khān attacked Hamīr Deva of Ranthambhor, ostensibly for refusing to surrender a couple of converted Mongols who had taken shelter there. Nusrat Khān was killed directing the siege, and Hamīr Deva's sorties drove Ulugh Khān back to Jhā'in. It was only after the Sultan's arrival that the siege was brought to a successful conclusion.[86]

Baranī invites us to believe that 'Ala'u'd-Dīn's victories undermined his mental balance. He decided to found a new religion and surpass the Prophet Muhammad, but Baranī's uncle, 'Ala'u'l- Mulk, persuaded him to abandon this mad scheme. The anecdote hardly seems correct, but the Sultan was inordinately ambitious.[87] The number of rebellions by his nephews and trusted officers prompted the Sultan to take immediate steps to root out the traitors. An analysis by his trusted advisers of the causes of these rebellions convinced him that the general prosperity of his officials, intermarriages between the families of the grandees, inefficiency in the espionage system, and drinking liquor were the root causes of rebellion. 'Ala'u'd-Dīn therefore passed four ordinances. By the first he confiscated all grants of tax-free land and seized Muslim religious endowments. Secondly, the intelligence system was reorganized, and all secret transactions in the houses of the nobility were immediately reported to the Sultan. Thirdly, the Sultan himself abandoned drinking and enforced strict prohibition in Delhi. Later on, personal distilling for home consumption was tolerated, but the public sale of liquor and drugs was totally stopped. The fourth ordinance forbade social gatherings in noblemen's houses, and no senior officials were allowed to arrange marriages between members of their families without the Sultan's prior consent.[88]

These regulations were directed against the Muslim noblemen, but the village headmen known as *khūts* and *muqaddams*, who lived in those areas where the revenue was reserved for the Sultan's treasury, were also very rich. They were Hindus and paid no taxes. They frequently offered military help to the rebels. The Sultan's revenue regulations reduced this class to poverty and brought them down to the level of the ordinary peasants. The over-enthusiastic Baranī says that they were unable to buy horses or arms and could not afford to wear fine clothes. They were even deprived of the common luxury of chewing betel. So great was their poverty, according to Baranī, that their wives were forced to work as maidservants in the houses of their Muslim neighbours.[89]

The country's defence remained intact, but the Sultan could not realize his imperialistic ambitions without a well-equipped standing army. According to

Baranī, he fixed the annual salary for a trained armed soldier with one horse at 243 *tankas*,[90] with an additional 78 *tankas* for those who had two horses. Firishta says that he recruited 475,000 cavalrymen. In order to keep his army satisfied with their salary, the Sultan introduced strict price-control measures based on production costs. He also established separate shopping centres in Delhi for (1) grain, (2) cloth, sugar, dried fruits, herbs, butter, and oil, (3) horses, slaves, and cattle, and (4) miscellaneous commodities. The supply of grain was ensured by collecting tax in kind in the *doāb* and keeping it in the royal storehouses. Hoarding of grain was forbidden. Elsewhere the growers were ordered to sell their grain for cash in their fields at fixed prices and were not allowed to take any grain home for private sale. The market controller, the state intelligence officers, and the Sultan's secret agents each submitted independent reports on these shopping centres to the Sultan. Even a minor violation of the rules was not tolerated.

The shopping centre for cloth, known as the *sarā-i 'adl*, was established near one of the royal palaces on the inner side of the Badā'ūn gate. All goods, including foreign imports, were first taken there and their price fixed. Every merchant was registered with the commerce ministry and had to sign a bond guaranteeing a regular supply of the goods in which they traded. The Hindu Multānī merchants were advanced money by the treasury to import rare commodities for the *sarā-i 'adl.* Some prices were subsidized. Costly fabrics and luxury goods could be sold only to those who had obtained permits from the government.[91]

The brokers helped the government to fix the price of horses. The horses were divided into three categories. The best were sold for 100 to 120 *tankas*, the mediocre cost 80 to 90 *tankas*, and poor-quality animals could be bought for 60 to 70 *tankas.* Ponies were available at from 10 to 25 *tankas.* All dishonest brokers and unscrupulous horse merchants were deprived of their trading rights. The price of slaves and cattle was also fixed.[92]

The shopping centre for general commodities was under the direct control of the commerce ministry. 'Ala'u'd-Dīn's minister of commerce was also the superintendent of weights and measures and the controller of commercial transactions. He was assisted by superintendents for each commodity. Prices and weights and measures were checked by sending the children employed in the royal pigeon-house to buy petty articles.[93]

The prices fixed for the Delhi market were also applied in the provincial capitals and towns. It was in the army's interest that the Delhi regulations should be enforced at other places. The success of the system depended on fixing prices in relation to production costs, although other factors, such as the growing poverty of the nobles and fear of the Sultan's atrocities, ensured obedience. An anecdote narrated by the eminent sūfī Shaykh Nasīru'd-Dīn Mahmūd Chirāgh of Delhi some fifty years later to a gullible sūfī audience ascribed philanthropic motives to the Sultan's market regulations; but Baranī's analysis of 'Alá'u'd-Dīn's military motives,[94] reinforced by other medieval historians, is irrefutable.

The Sultan's army brought him success both against the Mongols and in his schemes of conquest. In 1302–3 he sent an army against Telingāna. The army marched through Bengal and Orissa and attacked Wārangal. The Kākatīya Raja Pratāparudra Deva, however, defeated the invaders, and the Sultan recalled his forces.[95]

At the end of January 1303 the Sultan himself marched against Chitor. The fort was formidable, the terrain mountainous. The Rājpūts fought valiantly, but finally the ruler, Raja Ratan Singh, submitted. The Sultan entered the fort at the end of August 1303. The Raja's family were not persecuted, but the village headmen were slaughtered. The fort's administration was handed over by the Sultan to his son Khizr Khān.[96] According to Rājpūt legends, the Sultan conquered Chitor in order to seize the beautiful Padminī, Rana Ratan Singh's wife. This story is first recounted by Malik Muhammad Jā'isī in his romantic Hindi poem *Padmāvat*, written in 1540. Certain sixteenth- and seventeenth-century historical works also relate this tale. It is probably based on the common stock of legends current in India from ancient times. Khizr Khān lacked sufficient forces to maintain his rule in the region; eight years later it was given to a friendly Rājpūt chief.

The Sultan's armies also conquered Ujjain, Māndū, Dhār, and Chanderī, and governors were appointed for these areas. Jālor was left under the control of its own Raja, but his boastful claims finally led the Sultan to annex his kingdom. 'Ala'u'd-Dīn himself marched against Mārwār, where the ruler stoutly defended his fort of Siwāna but ultimately submitted. The territory was left in his possession. The Sultan was satisfied with establishing his overlordship over the Rājpūt chiefs, since he wished essentially to ensure communications between Delhi and Gujarāt.

The Sultan's most memorable conquest was that of the Deccan and the far south, which were ruled by three important Hindu dynasties. The Kākatīyas of Wārangal ruled over eastern Deccan, while the Hoysalas of Dvārasamudra and the Pāndyas of Madurai, ruling the regions adjacent to Sri Lanka, had divided the rest of the peninsula between them. The coastal trade from Kollam (Quilon) to Nellore had made them extremely wealthy. Nevertheless they were all, including the Yādava rulers, engaged in internecine wars.

'Ala'u'd-Dīn did not annex their countries but fleeced their treasuries and forced them to pay annual tributes. In 1306–7 the Sultan commissioned Malik Kāfūr to reduce to submission Raja Rāmadeva, who had withheld his tribute. Early in 1307 Kāfūr marched through Dhār at the head of 30,000 horsemen. After a feeble resistance Rāmadeva surrendered. Kāfūr took him to Delhi, together with the enormous booty seized in Devagiri. The Sultan treated Rāmadeva generously. He gave him the title Rāi Rāyān (leading *ray* or ruler). Devagiri was restored to him, and Nausārī in Gujarāt was also given to him as a gift. Deval Devī, the daughter of Raja Karan and Kamlā Devi, who was being sent by her father to be married to Rāmadeva's son, Sinhana, fell accidentally into the hands of the Sultan's troops. They sent her to Delhi, where the Sultan married her to Prince Khizr Khān.[97]

In November 1309 Malik Kāfūr set out against Telingāna, where the Sultan's army had been defeated six years earlier. Marching rapidly, Kāfūr reached Wārangal, the capital of the Kākatīya kingdom of Raja Pratāparudra Deva II. The fort there was surrounded by two ramparts, each enclosed within a moat. The outer wall was built of impacted mud and the inner one of stone. The mud wall was so tough that the stones from the *ballista* rebounded like nuts from it; even spears could not penetrate it. Pratāprudra's army stood behind these strong defences. The invading army, however, heavily bombarded the outer ramparts with stones and, after several days, seized one of the outer mud wings. Penetration into the stone rampart was difficult, but finally the Raja surrendered. An enormous amount of gold, 20,000 highly bred horses, and one hundred elephants were taken as booty. As well as this, the Raja agreed to pay regular tribute. Leaving Wārangal in March 1310, the army returned to Delhi on 10 June 1310 and received a hero's welcome from the Sultan.[98]

After resting for about six months, Malik Kāfūr marched against the Hoysala kingdom of Dvārasamudra (Divaravalipura, near modern Bangalore), via Devagiri. The city was besieged on 26 February. Raja Vīra Ballāla III was taken by surprise and agreed to become the Sultan's vassal. Vast quantities of booty, including elephants, were seized.

Without losing any time, Malik Kāfūr marched against the Pāndya kingdom in the extreme south of the Deccan peninsula. Raja Vīra Pāndya fled, abandoning the capital, Madurai. Temples were plundered, palaces were sacked, and enormous quantities of gold, 512 elephants, and 5,000 horses were collected as booty. There is no contemporary evidence that Kāfūr reached the famous Hindu shrine of Rāmeshvaram on Pamban Island or built a mosque there. On 19 October 1311 Kāfūr was accorded a royal welcome by the Sultan in Delhi. He was given the title *malik nā'ib.* Kāfūr once again marched to Devagiri in 1313 to collect tribute from Rāmadeva's son, who had rebelled after his father's death. Kāfūr invaded Devagiri and subdued the new ruler. After a short stay he returned to Delhi.[99] Although the gold coins plundered from the Deccan stabilized the price controls enforced by 'Ala'u'd-Dīn, they also created a surplus in the capital.

The Sultan's health had rapidly deteriorated by 1315. Kalur, as *malik nā'ib*, seized the reins of government. He had the heir apparent, Khizr Khān, imprisoned in Gwālior fort and Alp Khān, the governor of Gujarāt, summoned to Delhi and put to death. Alp Khān's brother, who was governor of Jālor, was also killed. Thereupon Alp Khān's troops in Gujarāt rebelled, the Rānā of Chitor declared his independence, and Harapāla Deva of Devagiri drove the Turkic garrison from his territory. On 4 January 1316 'Ala'u'd-Dīn, the greatest Muslim conqueror to sit on the throne of Delhi, died, helplessly watching the disintegration of the kingdom he had built.

According to Baranī, 'Ala'u'd-Dīn was a tyrant who did not hesitate to adopt ruthless means to achieve his imperialistic and military ends. He was, however, inventive and original in devising new policies and administrative systems and formidable in implementing them. Although illiterate himself, he enjoyed the company of poets such as Amīr Khusraw and Amīr Hasan. His passion for immortality is reflected in his grandiose architectural monuments. At the end of his life he lost his remarkable power of independent decision and was unable to combat Malik Kāfūr's intrigues to seize power.[100]

Before 'Ala'u'd-Dīn's eyes were sealed in death, Malik Kāfūr had nominated Shihābu'd-Dīn, 'Ala'u'd-Dīn's six-year-old son by Rāmadava's daughter, Jhitā'ī, as ruler. Khizr Khān was blinded in Gwālior fort, as was his half-brother, Shādī Khān. Mubārāk Khān, another of 'Ala'u'd-Dīn's sons, who like Khizr Khān was about seventeen, was imprisoned but before he could be blinded, Malik Kāfūr was killed by 'Ala'u'd-Dīn's loyal bodyguards in order to save their late king's family from annihilation.

Mubārāk was released from prison. For some weeks he worked as regent for his brother, Shihābu'd-Dīn, but then he sent him back to prison in Gwālior, where his eyes were put out.[101] On 18 April, Mubārāk Shāh ascended the throne. Some 17,000 to 18,000 political prisoners from 'Ala'u'd-Dīn's reign were released. Grants to the *'ulamā'* were increased, villages earlier resumed to the *khālisa* were restored to their owners,[102] and 'Ala'u'd-Dīn's economic laws were abolished. Mubārāk Shāh could have ruled for many years without much problem but, although he was fond of pretty girls, he was also passionately homosexual. He fell deeply in love with two Islamicized Barādūs brothers, Hasan and Husāmu'd-Dīn. According to Amīr Khusraw, the Barādūs belonged to the Hindu military caste and had served as 'commandos' under the Hindu Ra'is.[103] Mubārāk Shāh gave Hasan the title Khusraw Khān and transferred Malik Kāfūr's *iqtā'* and army to him.

The first two years of the Sultan's reign were very successful. Peace was restored in Gujarāt. In 1319 Mubārak conquered Devagiri and, departing from his father's policy, made an Islamicized slave officer, Yaklakhī, governor there. Khusraw was sent to Wārangal, where he collected the arrears and obtained a bond guaranteeing regular tribute payments. The Sultan waited for him on the Deccan border. They returned to Delhi together. There, the discovery of a conspiracy to kill the Sultan so deeply alarmed him that he had all his brothers and near relations murdered. He then sent Khusraw to Devagiri again to suppress Yaklakhī's rebellion and to march against Ma'bar (the coastal area of what is now Tāmilnādu). Yaklakhī was taken captive and handed over to the imperial army. Khusraw's invasion of Ma'bar yielded little booty, and the army commanders would not co-operate with him. The unsuccessful army returned empty-handed, but the Sultan, who had grown impatient at his separation from Khusraw, was over-joyed to see him. At Khusraw's request about 10,000 Barādūs were recruited from Mālwa, Rājasthān, and Gujarāt to act as palace guards. They obtained full control over the Sultan's palace. On 9 July 1320 Khusraw killed Mubārak with the help of his Barādū chiefs and had himself proclaimed Sultan, assuming the title Nāsiru'd-Dīn.[104]

Baranī and, following him, other historians, including modern Muslim scholars, accuse Khusraw of introducing idolatry into the palace and insulting Islam and the Qur'ān, but this view is unfounded. A section of the leading Turkic nobles and commanders supported Khusraw enthusiastically. Only Ghāzī Malik, the governor of Dīpālpūr, and his son, Fakhru'd-Dīn Jauna, who was at that time in Delhi, were strongly opposed to him. Jauna managed to flee with the son of Bahrām Ayba, the governor of Uch, to Dīpālpūr. Ghāzī Malik wrote letters to the neighbouring Turkic commanders and noblemen at Delhi, but the majority remained loyal to Khusraw. Beside his own family and Bahrām Ayba, the Khokkhars and the Mewātīs were Ghāzī Malik's main supporters.

Khusraw sent an army to Sirsa to fight Ghāzī Malik. The Khokkhars in Ghāzī Malik's army broke Khusraw's ranks, and his soldiers fled in panic. In the second battle, however, Khusraw's mixed Hindu and Muslim army fought fiercely near Delhi and dispersed Ghāzī Malik's forces. While the victorious troops were looting the baggage they had captured, Ghāzī Malik reassembled his army and turned the tables on Khusraw Malik. Khusraw fled but was discovered lurking in a garden. He was brought before Ghāzī Malik and beheaded. In 'Ala'u'd-Dīn's palace Ghāzī Malik wept after seeing the scenes of the Khaljī family's destruction. After showing formal reluctance, Malik ascended the throne in September 1320 under the title of Sultan Ghiyāsu'd-Dīn Tughluq Shāh.

THE TUGHLUQ DYNASTY

Baranī correctly credits Ghiyāsu'd-Dīn Tughluq's reign with moderation. The Sultan recovered the treasure which Khusraw had squandered in buying support. This brought him into conflict with Shaykh Nizāmu'd-Dīn Awliya', the most influential sūfī in Delhi.[105] Like many other notable sūfīs, the Shaykh had been given money by Khusraw to pray for his success. The rest had kept the money safely, intending to return it to the next ruler if Khusraw lost, but the Shaykh, according to his custom, had distributed it among the needy townspeople and dervishes. Naturally he could not return it. He told the Sultan that the money belonged to the treasury of the Muslims and he had himself distributed it to poor Muslims. He had kept nothing for himself. The Sultan was not appeased.

The Sultan modified 'Ala'u'd-Dīn's revenue regulations so that they benefited both farmers and headmen without undermining treasury interests. His officials encouraged the farmers to extend cultivation and kept taxes down to a reasonable level. He was kind and affectionate to his subjects.

In 1321 he sent his heir apparent, Jauna Khān, who was given the title Ulugh Khān, to reassert Delhi's authority over the rebellious Pratāparudra Deva, the Kākatīya ruler of Wārangal. Ulugh Khān was not satisfied with imposing suzerainty and collecting tribute. He wished to annex the country. The Hindu garrison resolutely defended the fort. The villagers cut off all supplies to the army and destroyed postal centres. The siege was protracted, and news from Delhi ceased. The troops were struck with panic; wild rumours that the Sultan had died began to circulate in the imperial camp. Ulugh Khān was forced to raise the siege and marched to Devagiri, much harassed by the local chiefs. There he was reassured of the Sultan's safety.[106]

Ulugh Khān returned to Delhi. In 1323 the Prince marched out again to strengthen the communication line and postal centres to the south. Pratāparudra defended Wārangal for about five months, but then had to surrender. He was sent to Delhi and imprisoned, and Telingāna became part of the Delhi sultanate.

The Hindu officials there were retained, but Delhi's hold on Telinagāna was still precarious. On his way back to Delhi, Ulugh Khān invaded Jājnagar in Orissa and seized fifty elephants.[107]

During Ulugh Khān's absence in the Deccan, a Mongol invasion was repelled at Samānā, and a Gujarāt rebellion was suppressed. Bengal was torn by civil war between the various contenders for the throne. Appointing a council of regents, including Ulugh Khān, the Sultan himself marched against Bengal, where he was victorious. On his return from Bengal the Sultan attacked Raja Har Singh Deva of Tirhut (north Bihār). The Raja fled, and the Sultan, appointing a governor there, returned to Delhi. His son Ulugh Khān hastily built a temporary wooden pavilion in the Afghānpūr village near Tughluqābad, now New Delhi. He received his father and took him to the pavilion. After lunch the Sultan ordered that the elephants he had captured be paraded there. The wooden pavilion, however, was not strong enough to bear the vibrations caused by the elephant race and collapsed. Both the Sultan and his younger son were crushed to death. The story is described in detail by 'Isāmī[108] and Ibn Battūta.[109] Both accuse Ulugh Khān of parricide. Baranī is cryptic and laconic.[110] The fifteenth- and sixteenth-century Persian historians agreed with 'Isāmī and Ibn Battūta,[111] but some later writers consider Ulugh Khān to have been innocent. Modern scholars are also divided, but the delay in rescuing the Sultan does suggest Ulugh Khān's guilt. Also the fact that the pavilion collapsed at all, and that Ghiyās was killed, is suspicious. If it were really a light pavilion, it is surprising that its fall should have killed anyone. Baranī's ambiguity is quite understandable in the circumstances.

After Ghiyāsu'd-Dīn Tughluq's death in July 1325, Ulugh Khān succeeded his father under the title of Sultan Muhammad bin Tughluq. According to his contemporaries, his character was a heterogeneous combination of arrogance and piety, pride and humility, cruelty and kindness, generosity and greed. Historians were unable to assess his personality and left their readers confused. Of the three authors of this period, 'Isāmī was an avowed enemy of the Sultan; Ibn Battūta was continually amazed at his actions; and although Baranī basked in the sunshine of the Sultan's patronage, his ideal monarch was Muhammad's successor, Fīrūz. In fact neither Baranī nor Ibn Battūta took pains to examine all aspects of the Sultan's personality in the correct perspective.

Of all the Delhi sultans, Muhammad bin Tughluq was the only ruler who had received a comprehensive literary, religious, and philosophical education, as well as military training. He believed that the time was ripe to replace the local tributary chiefs with centrally appointed governors and *iqtā'* holders, but unfortunately for him there were not enough competent officials. Disappointed with the continuous rebellions by trusted officers such as Sayyids, Shaykhs, Afghāns, and Turkic governors, he promoted to high positions intelligent administrators whose ancestors had been vintners, barbers, cooks, gardeners, musicians, and weavers.[112] The offended nobles refused to co-operate with him. The Sultan had invited foreigners from all over the world to his court, but they did not understand Indian conditions and were of no real help to him.

After his accession the Sultan was confronted almost immediately by a Mongol invasion. The enemy camped near Meerut, before being repulsed. There were no more Mongol invasions during his reign. The Sultan's armies conquered Kalānaur and Peshāwar and transformed them into a bulwark against the Mongols.[113] In 1326–7 his cousin, Baha'u'd-Dīn Gurshāsp, governor of Sagar (near Gulbarga), rebelled. The imperial army defeated him and he fled. He was captured, and the Sultan had him flayed alive.

Gurshasp's rebellion prompted the Sultan to make the centrally located Devagiri his second capital. In 1327 he made extensive preparations for the transfer of his mother, the royal household, and the *'ulamā'* and sūfīs from Delhi to Devagiri, which he named Daulatābad. The Sultan intended to transform Daulatābad into the well-planned Muslim capital of the east. Meanwhile, Bahrām Kishlū Khān, the governor of Multan, rose against the Sultan. The Sultan marched from Devagiri to Delhi, defeating Bahrām at Abohar. At roughly the same time another rebellion by Ghiyāsu'd-Dīn Būrā, governor of Bengal, was also crushed.

In 1328–9 the Muslim upper classes and the *'ulamā'* and sūfīs were ordered to move to Daulatabad. Comfortably settled in Delhi's social and cultural life, however, they resisted the order. The Sultan considered the sūfīs' refusal to emigrate treasonable, for he believed that their prime duty was the spread of Islam.[114] The sūfīs, for their part, saw themselves as custodians of their ancestral traditions; staying in Delhi was essential for maintaining this. The Sultan enforced his orders relentlessly, causing great hardship to the Delhi populace. The cultural and social life of the capital's élite received a set-back, but no mass exodus, as described by some of the historians, ever took place. In fact, the two capitals flourished simultaneously.

In 1327–8 the Sultan had started building a new town in Delhi called Jahān Panāh, intending to unite the earlier townships within a single wall. The scheme was, however, too expensive to fully materialize.

The Sultan's order for the transfer of the Delhi élite to Devagiri coincided with his plans to extend his boundaries beyond Peshāwar in order to prevent further Mongol incursions. This project is described by Baranī as the Sultan's ambition to conquer Khurāsān and Irāq. A tent was pitched in Delhi to arouse enthusiasm among the people for *jihād* (religious war) against the Mongols, but the leading sūfīs refused to co-operate.[115] The Sultan nevertheless enlisted 37,000 men and spent vast sums purchasing war materials and making advances of one year's salary to the soldiers. Stiff opposition to the invasion forced the Sultan to abandon the project, however. He disbanded the army, thereby incurring great financial losses.[116]

In the early years of his reign the Sultan was informed that the Chinese were making incursions into the Himalayan kingdoms. In a bid to secure his northern frontiers he dispatched an army of 10,000 troops to the Kāngra region in order to annex it to his empire. The contemporary historians refer to it as the Qarāchil expedition. It seems to have taken place during 1329–30. After some initial victories in Kāngra, the imperial army pressed on to Tibet, where the local hillmen annihilated it.[117] This was a major catastrophe, for which the commander, who had exceeded the Sultan's orders to confine the invasion to Kāngra, was responsible. Nevertheless in 1337–8 Nagarkot was conquered and the Raja made tributary.[118]

In 1329–30 the Sultan introduced a token currency, which remained in circulation until 1331–2. Imitating the *chao*, or the paper money of Qubilay Khān (1260–94) of Mongolia and northern China, the Sultan issued bronze coins at par with the value of the silver *tanka* coins. The scheme was designed to fill the gap in the gold and silver reserves which had widened as a result of the two frontier expeditions and a shortage of silver. The goldsmiths, who were generally Hindus, began to forge the token coins on a large scale. Following Gresham's law, bronze coins replaced gold and silver ones completely. Land tax was paid in the token currency, and other commercial transactions also utilized it. Foreign merchants naturally stopped all business dealings with India. In order to combat the mounting economic chaos, the Sultan stopped the circulation of the token currency and was forced to pay genuine gold coins in exchange, even for the forged ones. According to Baranī, the heaps of bronze coins rose like mountains near Tughluqābād.[119] Despite the distressing loss of royal treasury suffered, it had no difficulty in honouring the Sultan's orders.

The Sultan had in 1328–9 inordinately increased the land tax on the *doāb* farmers. Additional cesses were also levied. Baranī says that the Hindus (farmers) set fire to their grain barns and drove their cattle from their houses. Baran (Bulandshahr), Baranī's home town, was the scene of a terrible uprising. The rebellion was ruthlessly crushed, but the Sultan himself laid waste large areas of land during the fighting. Grain became increasingly scarce. In March 1334, when Ibn Battūta reached Delhi, the *doāb* was prostrated with famine. The Sultan soon realized that adequate relief measures and the promotion of agricultural production were the only solution to the problem. He sold six months' supplies from the royal granary to the Delhi populace at cheap rates. Large sums were advanced to enable the cultivators to buy seed, to sink wells, and to extend cultivation. This was not state farming, as a modern historian claims,[120] but the traditional system of famine relief.

The rebellion of Sayyid Ahsan Shāh, the governor of Ma'bar, however, prompted the Sultan himself to leave the capital even though the famine had now assumed dreadful proportions. It spread to eastern Panjāb; human skins were cooked and sold in the bazaar, the people roasted and ate the limbs of corpses. At Bīdar many of the Sultan's army officers died of the bubonic plague which was raging there. The Sultan himself fell seriously ill. He was taken back on a litter to Daulatabad. The Ma'bar rebels remained undefeated, and Sayyid Ahsan Shāh founded the independent Madurai sultanate.[121] The Sultan appointed new governors to Daulatābād, Telingāna, and Bīdar. During his absence from the Deccan from January 1335 to July 1337 five rebellions broke out, only four of which were suppressed. The foundation of the Hindu Vijayanagara kingdom in 1336 and the subsequent independence of Wārangal and Kampilī were the most severe blows to the Sultan's prestige. His dreams of founding a central Delhi sultanate, controlling the whole of India, came to an end.

After his return to Delhi the Sultan stayed from the close of 1338 to the middle of 1341 at Svargadvārī near Kanauj, where supplies could be obtained from Karā and Avadh. Famine was still raging. Four different governors broke into revolt in succession. The most serious uprising was that of 'Aynu'l-Mulk Multānī, the governor of Avadh, Zafarābad, and Lucknow, in 1340, but he was finally defeated.[122]

Between 1338 and 1341 both eastern and western Bengal became independent. During his stay in Delhi the Sultan introduced new regulations to improve farming. An agriculture ministry called the Dīwān-i Amīr-i Koh was established to bring barren land under cultivation. Opportunists and adventurers signed written bonds promising to cultivate barren land. They were richly rewarded and given loans to farm with but they spent the money on personal needs – only a very small fraction of the fallow land was cultivated.[123]

Not only were the governors rebellious, but the *amīrān-i sada* (controllers of one hundred villages), who performed both military and civil duties, also revolted. Like the governors they did not belong to any organized factions but, like other Muslim leaders, they hated the Sultan for his ruthless persecution of his opponents and savage use of capital punishment. Cries of 'War against the tyrant!' were heard everywhere. The Sultan believed that the root cause of the widespread rebellion was the *amīrān-i sada.* He appointed his favourite, 'Aziz Khammār ('the Vintner'), governor of Mālwa, granting him absolute powers to crush the *amīrān-i sada.* 'Aziz executed some eighty of its members at Dhar. The Sultan's admiration and rewards for 'Aziz's atrocities extinguished all hope of survival in the *amīrān-i sada* from Daulatābād to Gujarāt. They felt that only rebellion could save them. As well as plundering the royal treasury, they seized all the merchandise in Dabhoī and Baroda. Then they moved to Cambay, set free a rebel officer – Taghī by name – and made him one of their leaders. 'Aziz Khammār hastened to quell the uprising but was killed.[124]

In January 1344 Sultan Muhammed left his capital to personally crush the *amīrān-i sada's* rebellion, ignoring his loyal commanders' advice. In Delhi he appointed a council of regents to control the administration. He marched to Broach and seized several centres of insurrection. In Daulatābād a number of competent *amīrān-i sada* had organized a formidable force. The Sultan raised a huge army, but the rebel ranks were reinforced by more leaders. The Sultan met the rebels at Daulatabad and defeated them, but they fled to Gulbarga and set up new headquarters there. The Sultan reorganized the Daulatābād administration, but Taghī's rebellion in Gujarāt impelled him to rush to that region. On his way to Anhilwāra he was informed that Hasan Kangū and other rebel leaders had defeated the army sent against them at Gulbarga and that, on 3 August 1347, Hasan Kangū had established an independent kingdom, known as Bahmanī, from the family name of its founder.[125] The Sultan's health was deteriorating rapidly; he was unable to stop the disintegration of the sultanate he had dreamt of centralizing. In an impassioned speech he told Baranī that wicked and evil-minded people had become predominant. Now, on the merest suspicion of rebellion or conspiracy, he relentlessly executed people. He added that he was determined to pursue his policy until either he himself perished or the people reformed and stopped rebelling. He strove to win support by distributing largess, but that too failed to win his subjects' hearts. His people were estranged from him and were his enemies. The Sultan was even prepared to abdicate, but his sense of prestige called him to crush all rebellion first.[126]

For three years the Sultan concentrated on chasing the elusive Taghī and reorganizing the provincial administration. Taghī took shelter with the Sumrās of Thatta. The Sultan therefore moved towards Thatta via Kathiāwār but on 20 March 1351 he died in a village *en route*. According to Badā'ūni, the sixteenth-century historian, death liberated the Sultan from his people and freed them from him.[127]

Two daughters had been born to the Sultan, although a subsequent surgical operation had made him sexually impotent. According to 'Isāmī, the Sultan wished to see the whole world heirless like himself. The Sultan had, however, paid great attention to the education of Fīrūz, the son of his uncle Rajab. Fīrūz's mother was the daughter of the Jāt chieftain Rāi Ranmal Bhattī of Dīpālpūr, but Fīrūz inherited neither Jāt tenacity nor Turkic ferocity. In private life Fīrūz continued to drink liquor on the sly, despite the remonstrances of such nobles as Tātār Khān. He was also passionately fond of music, which from the point of view of the Islamic orthodoxy was also a vice.

Sultan Muhammad had appointed Fīrūz a member of the council of regents. Before his death Muhammad summoned both Fīrūz and Shaykh Nasīru'd-Dīn Chirāgh-i Dihli,[128] the famous Chishtiyya sūfī of Delhi, to his camp. Following the Sultan's death, the Chaghatāy Mongols of Transoxiana, who had joined his army to suppress the rebellion, combined with the Sindī rebels to plunder the Sultan's camp, which was now in a state of turmoil and confusion. The *'ulamā'* and sūfīs who were members of Sultan Muhammad's retinue raised Fīrūz to the throne and silenced his rivals. They believed correctly that a regent ruling in a puppet's name usually made the worst despot. A mature and experienced man who would rule under their guidance was best suited to the time. Fīrūz was crowned on 23 March 1351. His accession did not mark the restoration of the principle of election[129] but was a triumph for the dominant clique of the religious classes and the bureaucracy.

The new Sultan led the army safely from Thatta to Delhi, paying his respects to the sūfī monasteries (*khānqāhs*) on the way, and showering gifts on them and on the *'ulamā'*. When Fīrūz arrived near Delhi the aged Khwāja-i Jahān, a member of the council of regents who had put a boy of six on the throne, calling him Muhammad's son, surrendered and begged for mercy. Fīrūz was only too willing to pardon him but acquiesced to the demand of the Khwāja's rivals to eliminate him. At the end of August 1351 the Sultan entered Delhi.

Fīrūz's long reign of thirty-seven years may be divided into two parts. The first period of about twenty years is marked by new legislation to restore peace and prosperity. The last seventeen years saw inanition and a precipitous decline in the strength and prosperity of the sultanate. Until he died in 1368–9 the unpretentious vizier Khān-i Jahān Maqbūl, an Islamicized Telingānī Hindu, successfully maintained the prestige of the Sultan and governed the country wisely.

Fīrūz set about reforming the administration. He sent the foreigners who had crowded Sultan Muhammad's court back to their own countries with rich rewards and gifts. The loans advanced by the previous administration for agricultural purposes were written off. Compensation was paid to the heirs of all those whom Sultan Muhammad had executed, and the letters of gratitude obtained from them were deposited in a box at the head of Sultan Muhammad's cenotaph. Pious Sunnīs were not executed for treason or crimes against the state, but unorthodox Sunnī leaders and Shī'īs were annihilated. Painstaking reforms were made in the assessment and collection of land taxes. Newly dug wells and irrigation canals improved cultivation, enabling the government to overcome the food shortage. Gardens and orchards were planted under state patronage. In the early years of Fīrūz's reign prices were high compared with those of 'Alā'u'd-Dīn's time but gradually they stabilized. The special tax on some twenty-eight items of urban trade and commerce deemed un-Islamic was abolished. The manufacturing centres (*kārkhānas*) were developed rapidly by the army of slaves recruited by Fīrūz, and the promotion of urbanization and the establishment of new towns made the artisans prosperous. Artisans' wages increased, to the dismay of those dependent upon charity and gifts. The Sultan ordered that jobs be created for the unemployed. Free hospitals were established, as was a marriage bureau offering assistance to poor Muslim parents in meeting wedding expenses for their daughters.[130]

The Sultan paid his army and civil officials by assigning the revenue from *iqtā's* to them. Only a small percentage of soldiers drew a cash salary. All positions were made hereditary, irrespective of competence. During his predecessor's reign the prestige of 'Alā'u'd-Dīn's once invincible army had vanished; under Fīrūz, manned by hereditary soldiers, it was reputed to be rotten to the core.

Fīrūz made little effort to regain lost territory. He led several feeble military expeditions to Bengal, Kāngra, and Sind but only to assert the tottering central authority. In November 1353 he marched against Bengal. The Ra'is of Gorakhpūr and Champāran paid their tribute, but the Raja of Tirhut angered the Sultan by refusing to accompany him on his expedition. In Bengal the rebel Hājjī Ilyās fled to the Ikdala mud fort near Pandua in the Mālda district. The Sultan was unable to capture the fort quickly and returned to Delhi in order to avoid the horrors of the Bengal monsoon. He reached Delhi in September 1354. Three years later Zafar Khān of Sonārgāon visited Delhi to seek the Sultan's help against Hājjī Ilyās. The Sultan bided his time and, after Ilyās's death in November 1358, invaded Bengal again. He had hoped to defeat Ilyās's successor, Sikandar, without much difficulty, but Sikandar also took refuge in the Ikdala fort. This time the Sultan succeeded in negotiating a peace settlement and persuaded Sikandar to accept his suzerainty. On his return to Delhi the Sultan decided to attack Raja Gajpati of Jājnagar in Orissa, who had allied himself with the rebellious Bengal sultans. Firāz seized Cuttack and destroyed the Jagannath temple at Purī. Gajpati surrendered, and the Sultan returned to Delhi in May or June 1361 accompanied by a booty of elephants.[131]

Fīrūz stayed in Delhi for four years. He then decided to invade the Deccan but wisely changed his mind and instead attacked Nagarkot in the Kāngra region. The Raja submitted and offered to pay tribute. The Sultan collected 1,300 Sanskrit manuscripts from the Jwālāmukhī and other temples. Some of these were translated into Persian.

The Sultan next marched to Thatta on the bank of the Indus in lower Sind. When the siege proved too protracted and epidemics had taken a heavy toll on his horses, Fīrūz moved to Gujarāt. The Sindī guides misled the army, which suffered severe hardships in the Rann of Kacch. At home, in the absence of news from the army, Khān-i Jahān had wisely maintained the peace. The Sultan ultimately reached Gujarāt and re-equipped the army with the money he had received from Delhi. Again he invaded Thatta and destroyed the Sindī crops. The food shortage in Sind forced its rulers, Jām Unnar and Sadru'd-Dīn Bānbhina, to surrender. Both were taken to Delhi. Bānbhina's brother and one of Jām's sons were made governors in Thatta. The Sultan returned with his army after two and a half years' absence, occasioning great rejoicing in Delhi.[132]

The last years of the Sultan's reign were marked by a precipitous decline in central political control. In 1377–8 a rebellion erupted in Etāwa. Another uprising in Katihar resulted in widespread destruction. The Sultan's eldest son, Fath Khān, had died in 1376. The new vizier, Khān-i Jahān II, enjoyed Fīrūz's confidence but he could not match his father's experience. In 1387 he was driven out of Delhi by the Sultan's son Prince Muhammad, who became vizier instead. Fīrūz abdicated in August 1387, crowning Prince Muhammad king. Two months later Fīrūz's slaves, numbering 100,000, who hated Muhammad, rebelled. Muhammad fled to the Sirmur hills. Fīrūz appointed his grandson, Tughluq Shāh II, son of Fath Khān, his heir. On 20 September 1388 Fīrūz died, aged eighty-two.

The process of installing a puppet king from the Tughluq family had already been started by factions of the nobility. After Fīrūz's death the sultanate grew even weaker. In 1394 an independent kingdom was carved out in Jaunpūr. The two important provinces of Mālwa and Gujarāt were also severed from the Delhi sultanate. Then Tīmūr arrived upon the scene, and his invasion sealed the fate of the Tughluq dynasty.

Tīmūr's family belonged to the Gorgān branch of the Barlās, a Turco-Mongol tribe. His father, Amīr Taraghay, was the governor of Kash in Transoxiana. Tīmūr was born on 8 April 1336. Struggling against heavy odds, he asserted his power in neighbouring areas. In 1363 he was wounded by an arrow while fighting in Sistan and was left permanently lame. He was known as Tīmūr Lang (Tīmūr the Lame). Later the name was Anglicized as Tamerlane. Seven years later he made himself ruler of Balkh. In 1392 he began his five years' campaign that resulted in the conquest of the Caspian provinces, Fārs, Armenia, Georgia, Mesopotamia, and south Russia.

In 1396-7 Tīmūr's grandson Pīr Muhammad quickly seized Uch and Dīpālpūr, but his siege of Multān was protracted. Tīmūr, who had set out on his Indian campaign from Samarqand in March 1398, overtook his grandson after Multān had at last surrendered. In September 1398 Tīmūr crossed the Indus. The Hindu

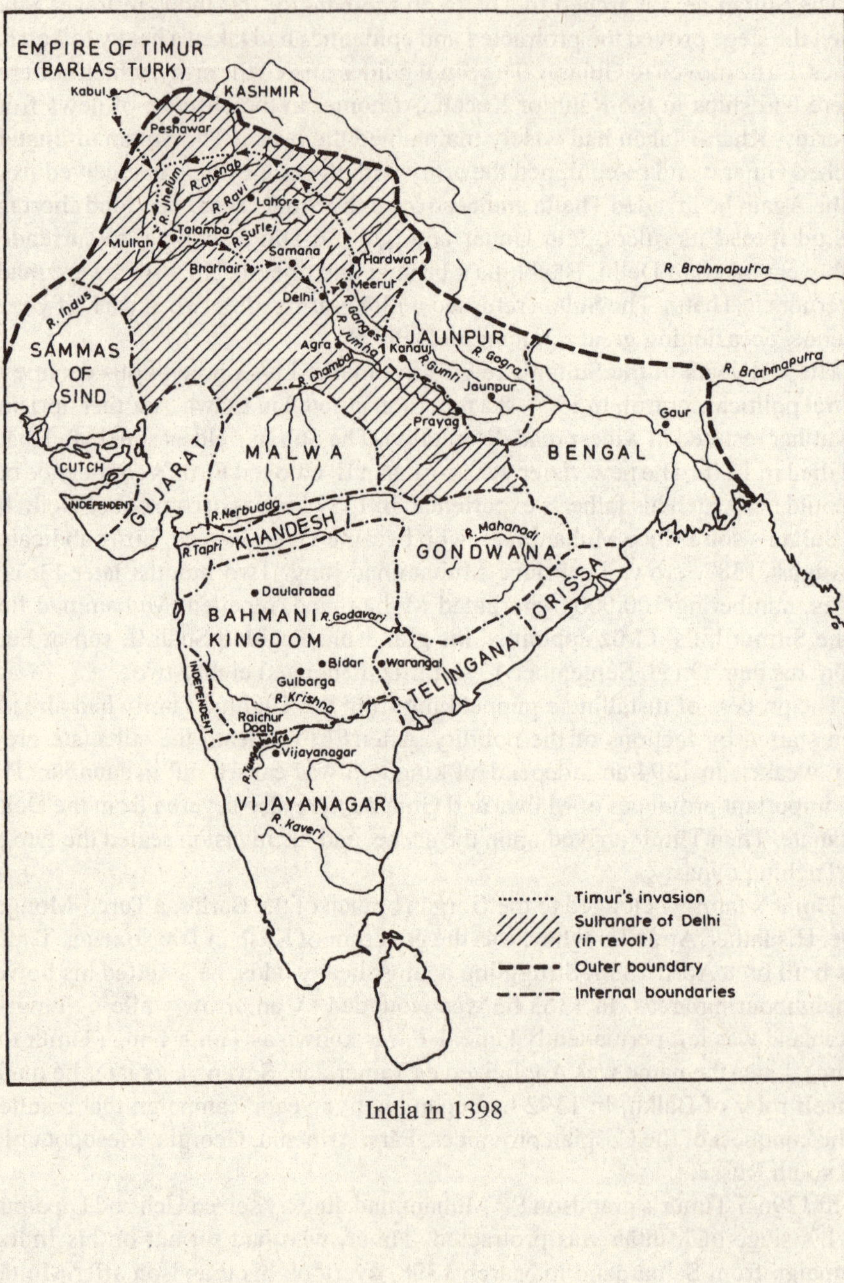

India in 1398

chiefs of the Salt Range gave him passage through their territory, and he met no serious obstacles in his Panjāb journey. Only the Rājpūt fort of Bhatnīr offered stiff resistance. The people of Fathābād, Kaythal, Sāmānā, and Pānīpat fled to Delhi. Tīmūr crossed the Jamuna near Delhi on 11 December. An army sent against him was easily routed, and the Delhi notables offered their allegiance. Nevertheless during the last three days of December 1398 Tīmūr's army sacked Delhi and indiscriminately massacred both Hindus and Muslims.[133] Early in January 1399, Tīmūr reached Meerut and plundered it. Travelling through Haridvār, Nagarkot, and Jammū, he crossed the Chenāb on 3 March. There he released large numbers of captives to facilitate his return journey. Skilled artisans, masons, and builders were still detained, however, in order to work on his Samarqand monuments. After devoting seven more years to his restless campaigns, Tīmūr died on 18 February 1405. He was buried in the tomb he had planned for his son in Samarqand. His Indian invasion was merely a plundering raid; according to his spurious *Autobiographical Memoirs*, his principal objective was to fight and pillage the infidels. His army, however, massacred and plundered both Hindus and Muslims. His invasion delivered the death blow to the Tughluq dynasty. Although Tīmūr's ancestors had embraced Islam, his invasion was considered no different from the earlier 'accursed', 'infidel', and 'satanic' Mongol invasions.[134]

THE SAYYIDS

Before his departure from India, Tīmūr had conferred Multān and Dīpālpūr on Khizr Khān, the son of Malik Sulaymān. These territories were already under Sulaymān's control, and after his death Khizr Khān ruled them. Tīmūr's confirmation enhanced Khizr Khān's prestige. Khizr's position was challenged by the adventurer Mallū Iqbāl, who rose to power in Delhi. He marched against Khizr Khān but was defeated near Ajodhan and killed in 1405. The kingless nobles of Delhi therefore invited Mahmūd Tughluq, Fīrūz's younger son, to reclaim his ancestral throne. The independent rulers of Gujarāt and Mālwa refused to help Mahmūd. Nevertheless, he ascended the throne but died in 1412. Thereupon Khizr Khān, who four years earlier had failed to capture Delhi, occupied it in June 1414.

It is said that the famous sūfī Makhdūm-i Jahāniyān had once referred to Khizr's father, Sulaymān, as 'Sayyid' (a descendant of the Prophet Muhammad);[135] this enabled him and his three successors to claim that lineage. Khizr tried to consolidate Delhi's control from Multān to Kanauj and from the foot of the Himalayas to the Mālwa frontier. The dominance of his son and successor, Mubārak Shāh (1421–33), however, was challenged by Jasrath, chief of the Khokkhar tribe, who ruled near Siālkot. Mubārak took the field personally, defeated the chief, and demolished some of his forts around Siālkot, but the Lahore *iqtā'dārs* failed to finish Jasrath off.

The Sultan's successful expeditions against Mewātis, Katihar, and the Gangetic *doāb* enabled him to collect revenue from that region, although Delhi's authority over their chiefs was precarious. In February 1434 the Sultan was assassinated by the dominant faction at his own court.

His adopted son, Muhammad Shāh (1434–43), was also unable to combat the intrigues among the leading nobles. In 1440 Mahmūd Khaljī of Mālwa invaded Delhi. The Sultan asked Bahlūl Lodī, the *iqtā'dār* of Sāmānā, to help him. Meanwhile, during Mahmūd's absence the Sultan of Gujarāt had invaded Māndū, the capital of Mālwa. Mahmūd therefore hastily made peace with Muhammad Shāh and returned to Mālwa. Bahlūl was rewarded with the *iqtā's* of Dīpālpūr and Lahore and was commissioned to crush Jasrath. Bahlūl, however, accepted Jasrath's offers of peace and instead seized territories extending up to Panipat. He was unable to capture Delhi, but the Sultan was reduced to the pitiable position of ruling a territory which extended merely forty miles around his capital.

After Sultan Muhammad Shāh's death, his son, Sultan 'Ala'u'd-Din 'Ālam Shāh (1443–76), came to the throne, but in 1447 he retired to Badā'ūn, which he had held earlier as an *iqtā'dār.* Bahlūl Lodī captured Delhi. Ālam Shāh did not contest Bāhlūl's usurpation and formally transferred the sovereignty of Delhi to him in 1451. He himself ruled over Badā'ūn and its neighbourhood until his death in 1476.

The Sayyids had ruled in name only, but the Lodīs revived the prestige of the Delhi sultanate. Nevertheless the distant provinces continued to be independent until one by one they were annexed by Akbar the Great to his empire.

II

THE INDEPENDENT RULING DYNASTIES

BENGAL

THE efforts of the Delhi sultans to assert their rule over all the conquered and annexed territories were unsuccessful except for a brief period during Sultan 'Ala'u'd-Dīn's Khaljī's reign. In Bengal submission to the Delhi sultans had been nominal from the time of its conquest by Bakhtiyār Khaljī to its complete independence. Sultan Ghiyasu'd-Dīn Tughluq of Delhi attempted to ensure the loyalty of Bengal by dividing it into three administrative divisions with capitals at Lakhnautī (North Bengal), Sonārgāon (East Bengal), and Satgāon (South Bengal), but his measures failed. His successor Muhammad bin Tughluq was unable to assert his authority over Fakhrū'd-Dīn Mubārak Shāh (1336–49) of Sonārgāon, who undauntedly assumed pretentious titles. In North Bengal, 'Ala'u'd-Dīn 'Alī Shāh (1339–45) declared himself independent and transferred his capital from Lakhnautī to Pandua. Bengal was finally united under one independent rule by 'Ala'u'd-Din's foster-brother, Shamsu'd-Dīn Ilyās Shāh (1345–58), and the Delhi Sultan, Fīrūz Shāh Tughluq, had no alternative but to make peace with him. Ilyās's reign is marked by the development of an impressive coinage system and the number of monuments erected. His successor, Sikandar Shāh (1358–90), also successfully defied Fīrūz's attempts to subdue him. Ghiyasu'd-Dīn A'zam Shāh (1390–1410), who followed Sikandar, established diplomatic and cultural relations with China, and the growth of the port of Chittagong stimulated the increase in trade with the Far East.

In 1415 Raja Ganesa of Dinājpur (Rājshāhi), originally a leading noble of the Ilyās Shāhi rulers, assumed royal power. Subsequently, at the request of the outraged Bengali *'ulamā'* and sūfīs, who repudiated a non-Muslim ruler, Ibrahim Shāh Sharqī neighbouring Muslim state of Jaunpūr invaded Bengal.[1] Peace was soon concluded, however, on the intercession of the leading Bengal sūfī Nūr Qutb-i'Ālam, and Ganesa's twelve-year-old son, Jādū, was converted to Islam and proclaimed king as Jalālu'd-Dīn. After Ibrāhim Sharqī had returned to Jaunpūr, Ganesa reappeared in Bengal and ruled in his son's name until he died in 1418. Upon his death in 1431, Jalālu'd-Dīn was succeeded by his son, Shamsu'd-Din Ahmad Shāh (1431–5). The Ilyās Shāhī dynasty was restored in 1437. The second Ilyās Shāhī ruler, Ruknu'd-Dīn Bārbak Shāh (1459–74), organized a militia of Ethiopian slaves and recruited Arab soldiers as his palace guards. One of these,

Ismā'īl Shāh, conquered Kāmrūp for his master. Bārbak's army also invaded regions as far north as Pūrnia district, and Bengal control over the Jessore-Khulna districts was strengthened. The Sultan is known as a patron of Bengali literature. The Chinese were deeply impressed by the wall of Pandua, the well-arranged bazaars, and the imposing royal palace.[2]

In 1487 the Ilyās Shāhī dynasty was overthrown by Sultan Shāhzāda Bārbak Shāh, the commander of the Ethiopian guards. Bengal was then ruled by Ethiopians until 1494. They were eventually deposed by an Arab, 'Ala'u'd-Dīn Husayn Shāh (1494–1519), who had risen to a high position in their service. After coming to the throne, Husayn replaced the Ethiopian soldiers and administrators with Bengali Hindus and Muslims. He was an indomitable warrior, and his generosity to both Hindus and Muslims has made him a legendary hero in Bengal. The rise of Sher Shāh Sūr ended the Husayn Shāhī dynasty of Bengal, but the state's prosperity under their rule amazed both Portuguese and Chinese visitors. Barbosa tells us of luxury and extravagance among the Muslim aristocracy in whose hands the country's wealth was concentrated. In the cities they lived in brick-built houses with flat roofs and flights of ornamented steps. Bathing-tanks were attached to their houses. Their cuisine was sumptuous. Men wore very thin, long, white garments reaching to their ankles, with cloth girdles under them and silk scarves over them. The poor went around stark naked.[3]

The principal feature of Husayn Shāhī rule in Bengal was a tendency towards unity among all classes of Hindus and Muslims. A genuine pride in Bengali culture and social values had emerged. The Muslim foreigners adopted Bengali customs, while the Hindus learned Persian to secure positions in the administration. This is reflected both in mystical works and in poetry. The movement towards cultural synthesis, however, had by no means eliminated all reactionary and revivalist tendencies.

ASSAM

On the eve of Bakhtiyār Khaljī's conquest, Assam was ruled by two important Hindu kingdoms. In the western region was the kingdom of Kāmātā, known as Kāmrūp in Persian chronicles. Its capital, on the Brahmaputra, was either Gauhātī or in its immediate neighbourhood. The other kingdom, Ahom, was in the north-east. There were also many independent chiefs, called *bhuyans*, who ruled small areas in the region.

At the end of the thirteenth century the Kamata kingdom became independent, but early in the fourteenth century the Bengal governors overran Mymensingh district and then, crossing the Brahmaputra, seized Sylhet (now in Bangladesh). Tippera and Chittagong were annexed as well. Later still Ilyās Shāh of Bengal also invaded Assam, and numismatic evidence shows his dominion over it. Husayn Shāh of Bengal subsequently annexed the whole of the Kāmātā kingdom as far as Barnadī. In 1515 the Koch tribe established its rule over Kāmarūpa. Mounting tensions between the King and his nobility during the 1570s forced him to divide the kingdom into two: Kooch Bihār and Kooch Hājo.

The Ahoms of north-eastern Assam consolidated their kingdom in the early thirteenth century. They were related to the Shans. Following Husayn Shāh's conquest of Kāmātā, his son Nusrat Shāh (1519–32) attempted to invade the upper Brahmaputra valley but was defeated. Four years later the Bengali sultans launched several naval attacks on the Ahoms but were repulsed. Then, in 1532, Nusrat Shāh was assassinated, and the Bengali attacks on Ahom ceased. Finally the great Ahom ruler Suhungmung (1497–1539) crushed the Nagas of the north-eastern hills and made the Ahom kingdom very powerful.[4]

TIRHUT

Tirhut (Mithila or Videha), bounded by the Himalayas on the north and the Kosī, Gandak, and Ganga on the east, west, and south, was also frequently attacked by the thirteenth-century Turks, but the Karnātaka kings of Mithila succeeded in retaining their independence. In 1324–5, however, the Delhi sultanate established its overlordship when Ghiyās'd-Dīn Tughluq conquered the Tirhut plains. His successor, Muhammad bin Tughluq, issued coins from Tirhut, now called Tughluqpūr, while Fīrūz claimed suzerainty but left it under its Hindu ruler. Ilyās Shāh of Bengal also invaded Tirhut and penetrated the interior of Nepal in 1349–50. Subsequently, Tirhut was constantly invaded – even Ibrāhim Shāh Sharqī of Jaunpūr conquered it – and a mosque was built at Darbhanga in 1402–3. Yet Tirhut maintained its internal autonomy despite frequent invasions by the Jaunpūr and Bengal sultans, until Nusrat Shāh of Bengal finally annexed it and appointed his brother-in-law governor of the province. As an island of Hindu culture, the small state of Tirhut preserved ancient Sanskrit works and patronized Sanskrit scholars.[5]

ORISSA

The independence of Orissa, the coastal plain between the Ganga and the Godāvarī, was also threatened in Ghiyasu'd-Din Tughluq's reign, while Fīrūz Tughluq's invasion saw the desecration of the famous Jagannāth temple at Puri. Bhānudeva III (1352–78) of Orissa submitted to Fīrūz, promising to send an annual tribute of elephants. Orissa's independence was equally endangered by the Sharqī kings of Jaunpūr, the Bahmanīds of the Deccan, the Reddīs of Kondavīdu (the region between the Krishna and the Godāvarī), and the Vijayanagara empire.

Kapilendra (*c.* 1434–67), the founder of the Gajapati dynasty of Orissa, defended his kingdom from both the Bahmanī and Vijayanagara incursions. Purushottama (1467–97), his successor, lost the southern half of the territory from the Godāvarī downwards. Under his successors the kingdom was gradually eroded. In 1568 it was annexed by the independent Afghān kingdom of Bengal.[6]

RĀJASTHĀN

Rājasthān (the homeland of the Hindu rajas) was the land occupied by the royal families called *rājpūts* (princes). It was composed of independent and semi-independent principalities which came into existence after their liberation from Khaljī and Tughluq domination. The most important of these were Mewār and Mārwār. Hammīr (1314–78) of the Sisodia branch of the Guhilaputras (Guhilots) was the liberator of the medieval state of Mewār which had been conquered by 'Ala'u'd-Dīn Khaljī. In the early fifteenth century the discovery of silver and lead greatly strengthened the kingdom's economy. A new system of weights and measures was introduced. Trade and commerce also increased. An artificial lake, now called Pichhola in modern Udaipur, was excavated, and pilgrims were given state funds to travel to Hindu religious centres.[7]

In the fifteenth century Rānā Kumbhakarana (1433–68) increased his army and built numerous forts to strengthen his defences. He took the petty Rājpūt states, which owed suzerainty to the Mālwa sultans, under his protection. In 1437 he defeated Mahmūd Khaljī and built a victory tower in Chitor.

Kumbha seized Nāgaur and gained many victories over his Rājpūt enemies. He also defended his territory from the incursions by Mālwa and Gujarāt on his eastern and western boundaries respectively.[8] Kumbha was also a poet, a man of letters, and a musician, writing commentaries on several Sanskrit works. He built many temples, and his architect Mandana composed a treatise on house building, iconography, and ornamentation.[9] The Jain community in his kingdom also erected several temples; the most famous are at Rangpūr, Sirohi, and Chitor.

Kumbha was followed by two weak rulers, and then the greatest ruler of the dynasty, Rānā Sānga (1508–28), ascended the throne. In 1518 Rānā Sānga gained a resounding victory over Sultan Mahmūd II of Mālwa, although the latter had obtained assistance from the Sultan of Gujarāt. Kālpī, Bhilsa, Ranthambhor, Sārangpūr, and Chanderī, belonging to Mālwa, were seized and assigned to chiefs who paid tribute to the Rānā. Three years later a Gujarāt army, which arrived at Īdar to overthrow the local Rājpūt chief and install his protege on the throne, was driven off by the Rānā and chased as far as Ahmadābād. Sultan Ibrāhịm Lodī's bid to annex Ranthambhor and Ajmīr to the Delhi sultanate led Rānā Sānga to make peace with the Sultan of Gujarāt and to persuade Bābur to invade Delhi.

The other leading Rājpūt state, Marwār, was ruled by the Rāthors. Its enterprising ruler, Rāo Chanda (1384–1423) seized Khattū, Didwāna, Sāmbhar, Nāgaur, and Ajmīr. One of his successors, Jodha (1438–89) was a restless warrior who greatly extended his principality. In 1459 he built Jodhpūr, naming it after himself, and later, Mandor fort.[10] Rānā Kumbha made an alliance with him, realistically fixing the Mewār and Mārwār boundaries.[11] The greatest Rāthor ruler was Māldeva (1532–62).

1. Jāmi‘ Masjid (Congregational Mosque), Delhi (p. 241)

2. Pietra Dura in the I'timadu'd-Dawla's tomb, Agra (p. 239)

3. Screen in the Diwān-i Khāss in the Red Fort, Delhi (p. 242)

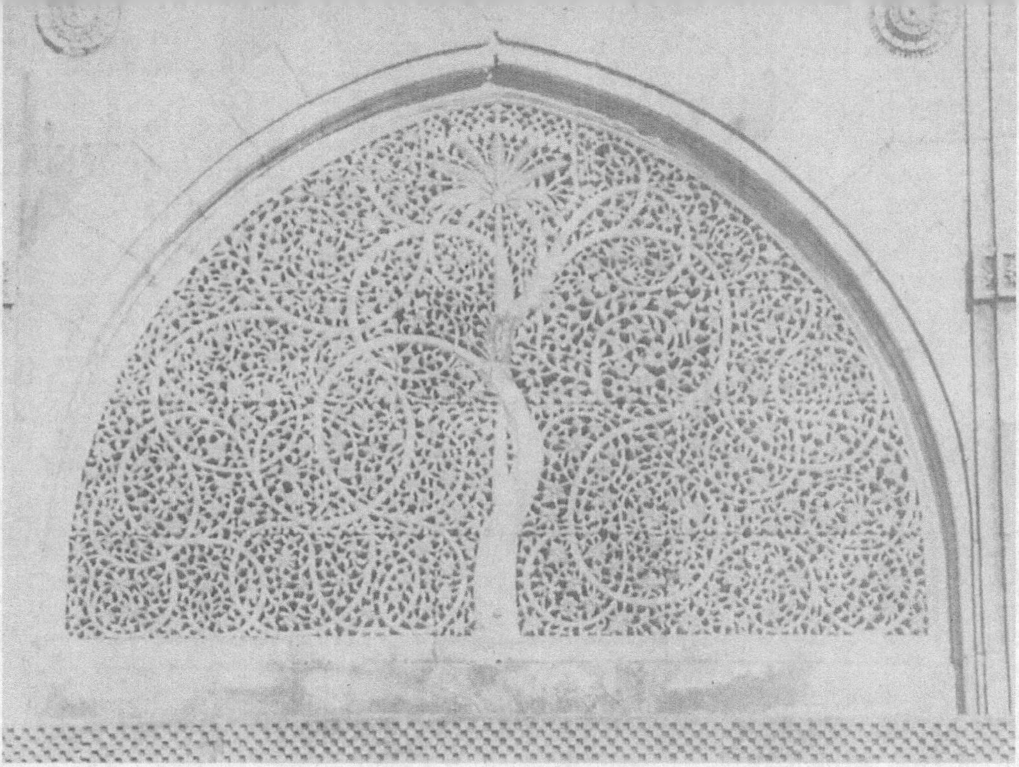

4. Screen of the Sidī Sayyid Mosque, Ahmadabad, Gujarat (p. 233)

5. The Panch Mahal, Fathpur-Sīkrī (p. 238)

6. The throne in the Dīwan-i Āmm, in the Red Fort (p. 241)

7. Jāmi' Masjid at Māndū pulpit with canopy (p. 232)

8. Sīkrī Mosque from the courtyard. The columns of Shaykh Salīm Chishtī's tomb may be seen in front (p. 237)

9. Sher Shāh's mosque in the old Ford, Delhi (p. 236)

10. Madrasa (college) of Mahmūd Gāwan in Bīdar (p. 241)

11. Shaykh Ruknu‘d-Dīn Multānī’s tomb at Multān (p. 229)

12. Māndū, Jahāz Mahal (p. 232)

13. Humāyūn's tomb in New Delhi (p. 236)

14. The interior of the Jodh Bāi's palace (p. 238)

KASHMĪR

Kashmīr was attacked even by Muhammad bin Qāsim, the conqueror of Sind, but neither he nor other Arab invaders succeeded in conquering it. Mahmūd of Ghaznī's attempt to capture Kashmīr also failed. In the thirteenth and fourteenth centuries, however, Muslim families began to move to the Kashmīr valley, where they obtained employment under its Hindu rulers. One of the settlers was Shāh Mīr, who arrived apparently from Swāt with his family in 1313. Seven years later the Mongol invaders callously slaughtered most of the Kashmīrī population and shook the foundations of Hindu rule. After the invaders had left the valley, Rinchana of the Ladākh ruling family, who served the commander-in-chief of Suhadeva, the Hindu ruler of Kashmīr, seized the throne. Because he was a Tibetan Buddhist, Rinchana did not get much co-operation from the local Hindu noblemen. The rising wave of Mongol conversions to Islam in Irān and Transoxiana seems eventually to have prompted him to become Muslim, although Shāh Mīr played an important part in this decision. The stories surrounding Rinchana's conversion may be dismissed as stock-in-trade legends attributed to innumerable conversions.[12] He adopted the name Sadru'd-Dīn. After his death in 1323, Hindu rule was re-established in Kashmīr. Nevertheless Shāh Mīr retained his influence and became very popular when his followers repulsed a second Mongol invasion. He won over the leading Hindu noblemen to his side; imprisoned the widow of the Hindu raja, Kota Rānī, whom he subsequently married; and became king in 1339 under the title Shamsu'd-Dīn. Thus the Shāh Mīr dynasty of Kashmīr was founded. He changed the Hindu feudal framework to the Turkic system based on assigning *iqtā's* which he gave to his loyal commanders, both Hindu and Muslim. Shamsu'd-Dīn fixed the land tax at 17 per cent on the gross produce and abolished a considerable number of imposts.[13]

Sixteen more members of the Shāh Mīr dynasty ruled Kashmīr between 1342 and 1561. One of them, 'Ala'u'd-Dīn (1343–54), transferred his capital from Indrakot to 'Ala'u'd-Dīn-pūr (Srīnagar). Sultan Shihābu'd-Dīn (1354–73) loved fighting. He conquered Pakhlī, invaded Gilgit, defeated the Kāshgharī Mongols, and penetrated Ladākh and then Nagarkot. Regions from Kishtwār to Jammū were also conquered by him.[14]

His successor, Sultan Qutbu'd-Dīn (1373–89), conquered Punch. During the reign of his son Sikandar (1389–1413), Tīmūr invaded India, but Sikandar was able to save Kashmīr by diplomatic negotiations with the invaders. Sikandar also sent a successful expedition against the ruler of Ohind. During his reign a considerable number of Muslims, who had been displaced by Tīmūr's invasions, migrated from Irān and Transoxiana to Srīnagar. Their presence led the Sultan to Persianize the administration and the life of the Kashmīrī Muslims. The process had already begun during his father's reign with the arrival of Mir Sayyid 'Alī Hamadānī and his followers. Sikandar's prime minister, Suha Bhatta, who had embraced Islam, strove to Islamicize the country with the efficiency of a new broom. The Kashmīrī brāhmans were dismissed from top positions. Important temples, including the famous sun-temple of Martand, were desecrated and destroyed. For the first time *jizya* was imposed on the Hindus. Before his death, however, conscious of the problems resulting from his persecution of the brāhmans, the Sultan 'fixed with some difficulty a limit to the advance of the great sea of *yavanas* (Muslims) and abolished *turushkādanda* (*jizya*)'.[15]

Sikandar's policy was completely reversed by his successor, Sultan Zaynu'l-'Ābidin (1420–70). He rebuilt some of the temples destroyed by Sikandar and encouraged the brāhmans who had left Kashmīr to return to their homeland and resume their former high positions. Islamicized Hindus were also permitted to revert to their ancestral faith. Cremation tax (Hindus burned their dead) was abolished, and cow slaughter (which was contrary to Hinduism) was prohibited. Even *sati* (the Hindu custom of burning widows on their husband's funeral pyre), which Sikandar had abolished, was permitted. Muslims who supported these policies were also treated generously by the Sultan, and many eminent Muslim scholars moved to Kashmīr from India and other Islamic countries. The wave of Islamicization which had been rising among the non-brāhman classes did not, however, subside.

The Sultan was a patron of education and learning. He founded Muslim schools in Srinagar, staffed them with famous scholars, and offered grants to students. He established a department to translate Sanskrit works into Persian and vice versa. The translation of the *Mahābbārata* and Kalhana's *Rājataranginī* into Persian was its most outstanding achievement. The Sultan was also interested in developing crafts. It would seem that paper had previously been imported into Kashmīr from Samarqand, but the Sultan sent his own artisans there to learn paper making and book binding. Before long, Kashmīr became an important centre for both these crafts. Under the Sultan's personal guidance, powder for fireworks was also manufactured in Kashmīr. Crafts such as stone polishing, stone cutting, bottle making, window cutting, and gold beating developed in Kashmīr because of Sultan Zaynu'l-'Ābidin's patronage.[16] The Sultan also fostered the development of agriculture; a number of new canals and tanks were dug, and dams were constructed. The Sultan appreciated the necessity of a strong army and stable government and forced regions such as Ladākh and Bāltistān to reacknowledge the suzerainty of the Kashmīr sultans.[17] Friendly relations were established with the Tīmūrīd rulers of Khurāsān and Transoxiana, the kings of Gīlīan and Egypt, and the sherifs of Mecca. Many independent Hindu and Muslim rulers also exchanged envoys with him.

The Kashmīris gave Sultan Zaynu'l-'Ābidin, the title Bad Shāh (the Great King), and he is still remembered by it. His successors were unable to match his achievements, although they were interested in promoting the social and cultural life of the region. Eventually the weaker rulers fell under the domination of adventurers. In 1540 Mīrzā Haydar Dughlāt, whose mother was the sister of Bābur's mother, captured Kashmīr with the help of disloyal Kashmīrīs. The Mirza began to rule in the name of Nāzuk Shāh of the Shāh Mīr dynasty. Although Haydar streamlined the administration and built many new monuments, he was unable to command the loyalty of the Kashmīrī upper classes and in October 1551 he was killed whilst quelling a rebellion. Three rulers of the Shāh Mīr family succeeded him, but in 1561 the Kashmīrī Chaks established a new dynasty and provided the next six rulers until 1588, when Akbar annexed Kashmīr to the Mughal empire.

JAUNPŪR

Among the dynasties founded by the governors appointed by Fīrūz Tughluq or his successors, a short-lived but brilliant line was that of the Sharqīs of Jaunpūr, north of Varanasi. It was founded by Malik Sarwar, a eunuch belonging to Sultan Fīrūz Tughluq. Malik Sarwar's remarkably rapid rise to power was due largely to the anarchy which followed Fīrūz's death. Fīrūz's younger son, Muhammad Shāh (1390–3) eventually conferred the title Sultanu'sh-Sharq (Ruler of the Eastern Kingdom) upon him and made him his vizier.[18] As a reward for his services he was in 1394 appointed governor of Jaunpūr, where he firmly crushed uprisings by the Hindu chiefs of Avadh and Bihār. The chiefs of Darbhanga, Muzaffarpūr, Champāran, and Tirhut acknowledged his overlordship. When Tīmūr left Delhi, Sarwar proclaimed himself the independent ruler of Jaunpūr. Before his death in November 1399 the western boundary of his kingdom had been extended to Kol (modern 'Alīgarh), Sambhal (Murādābād), and Rapri (Mainpurī district). His eastern borders now ran along Bihār and Tirhut.[19]

Although Sultānu'sh-Sharq was succeeded by his adopted son Malik Mubārak Qaranfal (1399–1401), it was his younger brother, Ibrahim Shāh Sharqi (1401–40) who made Jaunpūr a powerful kingdom. He made an alliance with Kīrtī Singh of Tirhut. When Tirhut was attacked by a Muslim adventurer, he sent his forces to help him and also attended his coronation. Then he invaded Bengal to remove the Hindu ruler Ganesa from the throne and annexed the petty independent sultanate of Kālpī to his kingdom. He invaded Delhi too, forcing the Sayyid sultan there, Muhammad Shāh (1435–46), to make peace with him and sealing the alliance with a marriage between his son and the Sultan's daughter.[20]

Ibrahim's son, Mahmūd Shāh Sharqī (1440–57), was also an ambitious ruler. In 1452 he captured Delhi but lost it through the treachery of his Afghān commander, Daryā Khān, who supported Delhi's first Afghān ruler, Bahlūl Lodī. Bahlūl Lodī (1451–89) consolidated the eastern boundaries of the Delhi sultanate from Etāwa to Shamsābād. In Jaunpūr, Mahmūd's successor, Muhammad, was deposed after a few months because of his excessive cruelty. The next ruler, Husayn Shāh Sharqī, made peace with Bahlūl, strengthened the army, and forced Orissa and Gwālior to submit to him.[21] In 1469 he invaded Delhi but was driven away before he could cross the Jamuna. In retaliation the Delhi Sultan Bahlūl, not content with Etāwa and Shamsābād as his eastern boundary, attacked Jaunpūr. Husayn Shāh had frittered away his resources in raising huge armies, but his three successive bids to defeat Bahlūl failed. In 1481–2 he sustained a crushing defeat near Kanauj. Bahlūl reached Jaunpār in a series of forced marches and seized it, issuing coins there in 1483–4.[22] Husayn made four more successive efforts to expel Bahlūl's governor from Jaunpūr, but Bahlūl defeated Husayn and forced him to seek refuge in Bihār. The Rājpūts, particularly the Bachgotīs, were Husayn's staunch supporters and helped him to establish his rule over an area between Chunār and Bihār. In 1494 he suffered another crushing defeat at the hands of Bahlūl's successor, Sultan Sikandar Lodī, near Banāras. Sikandar seized Bihār fort, while Husayn Shāh took refuge with Sultan 'Ala'u'd-Dīn Husayn Shāh (1493–1518) of Bengal. Sikandar stayed at Jaunpūr for six months, demolishing the Sharqī monuments in order to demonstrate his control of the district.[23] Only the mosques were spared. Husayn Shāh died in 1505.

The sultans of Jaunpūr were frequently helped by the Hindu chiefs against their Muslim opponents, particularly the Lodīs. The fall of the Sharqī kingdom was deemed a personal loss by these Hindu rulers. This short-lived kingdom surpassed others in helping the cause of cultural synthesis and social *rapprochement.*

MĀLWA

The kingdom of Mālwa was founded by Husayn Ghuri, whom Fīrūz Tughluq had made a noble, giving him the title Dilāwar Khān. In 1390–1 Fīrūz's son, Sultan Nāsiru'd-Dīn Muhammad, appointed Dilāwar governor of Mālwa. After Tīmūr's departure from India, Dilāwar proclaimed himself the independent ruler of Mālwa with his capital at Dhār.[24] His son, Alp Khān, reinforced the defences by completing the fortification of Māndū. Dilāwar maintained a conciliatory religious policy which made both Rājpūts and other Hindus friendly to him. He even settled Rājpūts in his newly acquired territory of Nīmar. Dilāwar extended his kingdom by snatching Saugar and Damoh from the Delhi sultanate and making the ruler of Chanderī accept his overlordship.

After his death in 1406–7 his son, Alp Khān, became the Sultan of Mālwa with the title Hūshang Shāh (1406–35). Almost immediately Sultan Muzaffar Shāh of Gujarāt invaded Mālwa, defeating Hūshang and taking him captive. Nusrat, Muzaffar's brother, who was appointed the governor of Mālwa, was unable to control it and returned to Gujarāt. Muzaffar intended to crush the popular uprising in Mālwa by force, but good sense prevailed and he restored the throne to Hūshang. Back in his kingdom, Hūshang transferred his capital to Māndū.[25] He then invaded Rāi Narsingh Kherla's kingdom in the southern part of Gondvāna in order to obtain military assistance and a supply of elephants.[26] Profiting from Hūshang's absence, Ahmad I of Gujarāt besieged Māndū, but Hūshang, eluding the invading army, returned to the city, forcing Ahmad to retreat. Hūshang then seized Gāgraun. His subsequent invasion of Gwālior, however, failed because Mubārāk Shāh of Delhi relieved the besieged fort. Hūshang ensured his popularity with the majority Hindu population by introducing a policy of religious toleration, although he also encouraged the *'ulamā'* and sūfīs to settle in Mandu. Many Rājpūts settled in his kingdom and served his army loyally. The Jains also supported him and proved an assest to the promotion of trade and commerce in Mālwa. Although constant wars against the rulers of Gujarāt, Jaunpūr, Delhi, and the Bahmanīds brought no material gains to his kingdom, they frustrated his neighbours' expansionist designs. Before his death in 1435 Hūshang also founded a new town, Hūshangābād, on the river Narbada.

His son and heir, Muhammad Shāh, was an ineffectual ruler and was deposed by one of his nobles, who ascended the throne in 1436, with the title Mahmūd Khaljī (1436–69). He crushed Ghurīd resistance and established the Khaljī dynasty. In 1442 he invaded Delhi, but Ahmad Shāh of Gujarāt's invasion of Mālwa forced him to make peace and return to Māndū. In 1443 Mahmād attacked Chitor but, finding the fort impregnable, retreated. The historians of Mālwa kingdom nevertheless claim victory for their ruler. Mahmūd next captured the Gagraun and Mandalgarh forts on the Mālwa border and later, in 1457, again marched against Chitor, once more unsuccessfully. His wars against the Sultan of Gujarāt were abortive, too, and he eventually concluded an agreement guaranteeing the integrity of their borders. The two rulers also divided Mewār between them into respective areas for future military operations. Thrice Mahmūd's efforts to seize parts of the Bahmanīd territory failed because the ruler received timely assistance from the Sultan of Gujarāt. Mahmūd was at length forced to make a treaty with the Bahmanīds, cementing good neighbourly relations.[27] Before his death in 1469 a realistic boundary had been established for Mālwa on its Gujarāt and Deccan borders.

Mahmūd was interested in all aspects of community life. He actively promoted the development of agriculture and trade, established centres of Islamic learning, and encouraged scholars from other parts of India to move to Māndū. The hospital he founded there was a large establishment with provision for free medicine.

The reign of Mahmūd's successor, Ghiyās Shāh (1469–1501), saw a period of peace and prosperity. In 1482 he marched to the assistance of Rāwal Jai Singh, the Raja of Champānīr, when he was invaded by the Sultan of Gujarāt. Realizing that he would actually have to fight the Sultan, however, he returned home on the pretext that the *'ulamā'* were opposed to him helping a Hindu ruler. [28] Ghiyās Shāh collected about 16,000 slave girls in his palace, including the daughters of many Hindu chieftains. An army of Ethiopians and Turkic slave girls was formed to act as guards. Another five hundred pretty girls were trained in state business, and a bazaar run by women was opened in the palace. Mahmūd quaintly combined his voluptuous desires with nightly prayers and vigils. He was easily duped by people pretending to be religious.[29] His elder son, 'Abdu'l Qādir Nāsir Shāh, whom he appointed his successor, had a very aggressive nature. He beheaded his younger brother and, although his father was still living, proclaimed himself king. Ghiyās abdicated, dying, possibly from poisoning, four months after surrendering the throne.[30]

Nāsir Shāh's despotic character and heavy drinking disgusted his nobles. His rule ended in 1510. His third son, who came to the throne as Mahmūd II (1511–31), appointed Medinī Rāi, the Rājpūt chief of Chanderī, as his vizier, in order to frustrate the intrigues of his Muslim noblemen. Medinī Rāi filled all the important positions with his own supporters. He also ordered that Muslim women be trained as dancing girls, in retaliation for Ghiyās's treatment of Hindu women. The Sultan ultimately grew to hate Medinī, and he escaped to Gujarāt. Early in January 1518 he returned with Sultan Muzaffar Shāh of Gujarāt, and captured Māndū. Leaving a supportive Gujarāt contingent, Muzaffar returned to his capital.[31] Medinī then seized Gagraun. Mahmūd besieged him but was defeated by Rānā Sānga, who rushed to relieve Māndū. Rānā Sānga captured the Sultan and took him to Chitor but when his wounds had healed the Rana sent him back to Māndū and restored him to his throne. Comparing Muzaffar's assistance to Mahmūd Khaljī with the Rānā's magnanimity, a Mughal historian gives the greater credit to the Rānā; for Muhammad had helped a refugee, while the Rānā had restored his kingdom to his captive enemy.[32] Muzaffar again sent a contingent to Mahmūd's assistance, but the Sultan grew suspicious of his intentions and sent the Gujarātīs back. Before long all the border region was taken from Mahmūd. Medīnī Rāi seized Chanderī, while his associate Silahdī occupied Bhilsa and Rāisen. Rānā Sānga invaded Mandasor. Harautī, Khichīwāra, and Satwās also became independent. Then Mahmūd offended the Sultan of Gujarāt by sheltering his rebellious brother. In March 1531 Bahādur Shāh of Gujarāt captured Māndū. Mahmūd and his sons were sent as captives to Champānīr but were killed on the way. For six years Mālwā remained under the control of Gujarāt but after Bahādur Shāh's death in 1537 it regained its independence.

Mālwa's new sultan was Mallū-Khān, who adopted the title Qādir Shāh. He was a far-sighted ruler, making peace with Silahdī's sons, who ruled over Rāisen, and improving relations with the Rājpūt chieftains. Sher Shāh, the Sūr ruler of Delhi, however, conquered Mālwa and installed Afghān governors there.

KHĀNDESH

The kingdom of Khāndesh, lying between the rivers Tāptī and Narbada, was not very large, but the need to maintain the balance of power between the Gujarāt, Mālwa, and Bahmanīd rulers ensured its independence. The kingdom's founder, Malik Raja or Raja Ahmad, had been assigned Thalnīr and Kuronda as an *iqtā'* by Fīrūz Tughluq in 1370. Raja Ahmad subdued the local chieftains and then became an independent ruler in 1382, making his capital Thalnīr. He unsuccessfully attempted to take Sultanpūr and Nandrbār from Gujarāt, and this area always remained a bone of contention between the two neighbouring kingdoms. He married his daughter to Hūshang, and his son married Dilāwar's daughter. This brought him two strong allies. Before his death in April 1399 he had succeeded in firmly consolidating the Khāndesh kingdom. He claimed descent from the Caliph 'Umar, whose title was Fārūq, and the dynasty was therefore known as the Fārūqi dynasty.[33]

Malik Raja's successor, Nasīr Khān, captured the impregnable fort of Asīrgarh by subterfuge. He built a new town by the river Tapti. Zaynu'd-Dīn, a disciple of the famous Chishtiyya sūfī Shaykh Burhānu'd-Dīn Gharib, suggested to Malik that the town should be named after his master, so Nasīr Khān called it Burhānpūr.

Nasīr was deeply devoted to Zaynu'd-Dīn, and the next town he founded was called Zaynābād after him. In 1417, reinforced by the Mālwa army, he invaded the eastern region of Gujarāt, but Sultan Ahmad Shād repulsed the attack and, following at the heels of the vanquished army, besieged Asīrgarh. Ultimately Nasīr concluded a peace treaty with Ahmad, who in turn recognized Nasīr's right to rule over Khāndesh. Nasīr died in 1437.[34] His successors, 'Ādil Khān (d. 1441) and Mubārāk Khān (d. 1457), accepted Gujarāt's overlordship. 'Ādil Khān (d. 1501) was more enterprising and several times invaded regions belonging to the rajas of Gondvāna and Jhārkhand and the Kol and Bhil tribes. Under 'Adil Khān's successor, Khāndesh was torn by dynastic rivalries which enabled Gujarāt to tighten its control over the country.

GUJARĀT

The independent kingdom of Gujarāt was founded by Zafar Khān, son of Sadhāran, a Jāt convert to Islam. Sadhāran's sister was married to Fīrūz Tughluq. Zafar Khān was appointed governor of Gujarāt in 1391, with the title Muzaffar Khān. Despite his advanced age, he firmly suppressed the rebellious Muslim noblemen and Hindu chieftains. He remained loyal to the Delhi sultanate, even after Tīmūr left India and anarchy prevailed there. In 1403–4 he was deposed by his son, Tātār Khān; but his uncle, Shams Khān Dandanī, then poisoned Tātār Khān, and Zafar was restored to the throne.[35] In 1407 Muzaffar declared his independence as Muzaffar Shāh. He died in 1411 and was succeeded by Shihābu'd-Dīn Ahmad Shāh (1411–42), the son of the dead Tātār Khān.[36]

Ahmad Shāh's rule of thirty-one years was a period of relentless warfare but also saw the consolidation of the Gujarāt sultanate. In 1416 he crushed a rebellious confederacy of Rājpūts, reinforced by Hūshang's army, in the north-west. Two years later Ahmad invaded Mālwa, bringing home to Hūshang that Mālwa was no match for Gujarāt. A truce was signed in 1419. Hūshang subsequently invaded Jājnagar to obtain more elephants. His absence prompted Sultan Ahmad to make forced marches to Mandu, but the garrison there stoutly defended the fort. Hūshang returned meanwhile and was defeated by Ahmad near Sārangpūr. Ahmad was still unable to capture Māndū fort, returning to Gujarāt in May 1423.[37]

After 1425 Gujarāt entered upon an era of intermittent warfare with the Rājpūt Raja of Īdar. Ahmad also exacted tribute from the Rājpūt chieftains of Champānīr, Dungarpur, Kota, and Būndī to help finance his campaigns and enhance his power. He died in 1442.

Muslim historians praise Ahmad for his devotion to sūfīs and for his determination to destroy idols.[38] He forced the Rājpūt chiefs to marry their daughters to him in order to make them outcastes in their own community, thereby ensuring their subservience to him. His Muslim nobles also pursued the same policy, and the interracial marriages gave rise to a mixed religious group in Gujarāt.[39] The soldiers in his army drew half their salary in cash from the royal treasury and half from land-tax assignments. To ensure his subjects' obedience and to prevent them uniting against him, half of the civil posts in each department went to the free-born Muslims and the other half to slaves.

Ahmad's successor, Muhammad Shāh (1442–51), was a mild ruler, as was the next Sultan, Qutbu'd-Dīn Ahmad Shāh II (1451–9). Fath Khān, who ascended the throne aged thirteen as Muhmūd Shāh (1459–1511), was the greatest Muslim ruler of Gujarāt. Soon after his coronation the ruler of Khāndesh sought his assistance in repelling an invasion by Muhmūd Khaljī of Mālwa. Despite his youth, Mahmūd's military exploits so impressed the Mālwa Sultan that he decided that no military solutions could be maintained while Gujarāt had such a strong ruler, and he ceased attacking the buffer state of Khāndesh.

In 1461 Mahmūd defeated the Muslim ruler of Jālor in south Rājasthān and made him his protege. He then seized the port of Daman on the west coast from its Hindu rulers. Initially, in 1466, he exacted tribute from the Yādava Prince of Girnār (Junāgarh) but four years later he annexed Girnār to his sultanate, thereby gaining control of the flourishing port of Verāval. Mahmūd founded a new town at the foot of the Girnār hills, Mustafābād, where he settled members of the Muslim religious classes and elite.[40]

He then fought the Sūmra, Soda, and Kahla tribes of the Kacch border who, although they had been Islamicized, still practised Hindu customs. After defeating them he sent some of their leaders to Mustafābād to learn the Sharī'a laws. In Sind his maternal grandfather, Jām Nizāmu'd-Dīn, ruled effectively because of his relationship to Mahmūd, which not only prevented the Gujarātis from attacking him but also deterred other potential invaders. In 1473, as a reprisal for a pirate attack on a Muslim merchant, Mahmūd sacked Dvārka, north-west of Kāthiāwār peninsula. After that he foiled an attempt to depose him by his nobles. Then he attacked Champānīr, which was surrendered by the Rājpūts in 1484 after two years of intense fighting, during which the Gujarātis bombarded the fort with mortars and rockets. Meanwhile the ruler of Khāndesh, having conquered Gondvāna, Garha, Mandala, Kolīs, and Bhīls, had become puffed up with his own importance. So, in 1498, the Sultan invaded Khāndesh and forced its ruler, 'Ādil Khān, to take an oath of loyalty to him.[41]

Mahmūd's supremacy was threatened only by the Portuguese. After the arrival of Vasco da Gama in Cālīcut in 1498, the Portuguese became a serious threat to the trade of Cambay and other Gujarāt ports. In the battle of Chaul in January 1508 the governor of Jūnāgarh and the Egyptian fleet sent by the Mamlūk Sultan were victorious, but the Egyptian and Gujarāti fleets were routed by the Portuguese in February 1509. Mahmūd realized that the Portuguese were invincible at sea and opened negotiations for peace with Governor Albuquerque. In November 1510 the Portuguese conquest of Goa, which belonged to the 'Ādil Shāhī ruler of Bījāpūr, so greatly enhanced Portuguese power that Mahmūd unconditionally released his Portuguese hostages, and the Egyptian-Gujarāt confederacy was broken.[42]

Mahmūd died in November 1511. According to the Italian adventurer Ludovico de Varthema, Mahmūd's beard reached his girdle, and he tied his inordinately long moustaches behind his head. According to Barbosa, he had been regularly fed on some poison since childhood, with the result that 'if a fly settled on his hand it fell dead'.[43] His ravenous hunger led him to consume enormous amounts of food. His title 'Begarha' was a constant reminder of both his conquest of the two forts, Jūnāgarh and Champānīr, and his moustaches, for the Gujarāti word *vegaro* means a bullock with sweeping horns.[44]

Mahmūd's successor, Muzaffar II (1511–26), was a gentle but active ruler. He refused to allow the Portuguese to build a fortress at Div; instead he strengthened its defences and foiled two successive Portuguese attempts to seize it. He also helped Mahmūd of Mālwa without any motives of personal gain. Although he loved music and patronized musicians, this did not conflict with his piety. His death in 1526 was followed by the brief reigns of two incompetent rulers. Then Bahādur Shāh (1526–37) ascended the throne. He was the last of the energetic Gujarāt rulers. Early in 1531 his navy, in collaboration with the Turkish fleet, defeated the Portuguese fleet which took shelter in Goa. Next, he annexed Mālwa to his kingdom and then arrested Silahdī, the ruler of Rāisen, Sārangpūr, and Bhilsa, when Silahdī visited the Sultan in his camp to conclude a treaty. Bahadur then seized Rāisen and gave it to a Lodī chief from Kālpī, whom the Emperor Humāyūn had expelled from his territory. In March 1535 the use of artillery belonging to the Turkish gunner Rūmī Khān made the Sultan master of Chitor. Rūmī Khān, however, disappointed at the Sultan's refusal to make him governor of Chitor, decided to betray him. The opportunity arose before long, when Humāyūn, in pursuit of Bahādur, reached Mandasor. Rūmī Khān urged the Sultan first to strengthen his defences and then to make short work of Humāyūn by using his superior artillery. The suggestion seemed reasonable, but Bahādur's loyal commanders rightly rejected it.[45] They believed that the victorious Gujarāti army's best interest lay in an immediate assault. Waiting around would only destroy their morale. While the defences were being strengthened, Humāyūn naturally seized the opportunity to cut off supplies to Bahādur's camp, and his army starved. Rūmī Khān deserted to Humāyūn at the end of April 1535, and Bahadur had no alternative but to retreat to Māndū. Chased by Humāyūn, Bahadur fled from Mandu to Champanīr. From there he sent extremely valuable presents to the Ottoman Sultan, Sulaymān the Magnificent (1520–66), in the unrealistic hope of obtaining his help. Humāyūn's pursuit was relentless; Bahādur had to flee to Cambay. There he burnt his fleet of one hundred warships in order to prevent them falling into Humāyūn's hands, and sailed to Div. In the despairing hope of obtaining assistance from the Portuguese, Bahādur granted them permission to erect a fort at Div, which he had until then refused.[46] Humāyūn conquered Champānīr and then Ahmadābād. He marched on to Div but then had to abandon the pursuit of Bahādur in order to deal with Sher Khān's threat to his throne. Bahādur took the opportunity to leave Div and, reassembling his army, regained his lost kingdom. Now regretting his concessions to the Portuguese, Bahādur marched to Gogha near Div, but was outwitted by the Portuguese and slain while returning from negotiations aboard their flagship. On 13 February 1537 he died. With his death the glory of the independent kingdom of Gujarāt vanished. Its extinction by Akbar was only a matter of time.

THE WESTERN COAST

Ibn Battūta, who visited the western coast of India in 1343–4, mentioned several Hindu principalities which ruled between Sandapār (Goa) and Quilon. A sizeable community of Muslim merchants lived there comfortably, and their Muslim ruler, Jamalu'd-Din Muhammad of Hinawr (Honovar), owed suzerainty to the Hindu Hoysala king. The Hindu King of Cālīcut was the most powerful ruler on the coast. He was called Sāmutiru in Malyālam, but Sāmurī (meaning Sea-King) by the Arabs and Zamorin by the Portuguese. The Arabs, who exercised a monopoly of the trade between Malabar and the Red Sea, enjoyed considerable respect at the Zamorin court.[47]

On 17 May 1498 Vasco da Gama, who had left Lisbon with three vessels on 8 July 1497, touched land eight miles north of Cālīcut. The Zamorin welcomed the Portuguese, but the Muslims were alarmed. They poisoned the Zamorin's mind against the Portuguese and convinced him that the newcomers were spies who would bring huge forces to conquer the country. Their prophecies were not groundless. The Portuguese had meanwhile discovered that the Hindu princes on the Malabar coast were jealous of each other and that the region, which depended for food on grain vessels from the Coromandel coast, was extremely sensitive to a sea blockade. Most importantly they had learned that the Indian and Arab ships could not withstand cyclones and typhoons and sailed from Gujarāt to Aden and Basra, from Bengal to Malacca, and from Malabār to Malacca, only at particular times of the year. By contrast, the Portuguese ships could hold the seas in all weathers, and their cannon could destroy Indian ships with the first volley.

Vasco da Gama returned to Lisbon in August 1499 with a cargo of spices collected at Cālīcut. In March 1500 the King of Portugal sent a larger fleet of thirteen vessels carrying l,200 men, under Pedro Alvarez Cabral, to destroy their Muslim enemies. Seven ships were lost on the way to Cālīcut, but the journey took only a few days more than six months. The Zamorin welcomed but did not help them. War then broke out between the Portuguese and Muslims. The Portuguese sank ten Muslim vessels and bombarded the town of Cālīcut for two days. Cabral then sailed to the neighbouring port of Cochin, where the Raja gave him full support against the Muslims. Cabral also sank the ship which the Zamorin had sent to punish the Portuguese. The rajas of Cannaniore and Quilon became Portuguese allies; Cochin, which was better suited to trade, was transformed into the Portuguese trading headquarters.[48]

The success of their first two expeditions prompted the Portuguese King to dispatch Vasco da Gama again in 1502, not only to destroy Arab trade but also to plant Christianity in India. Da Gama exerted considerable pressure on the Zamorin to expel all the Muslims from Cālīcut, but the Zamorin only partially complied with his demands. Da Gama then sank several Arab ships and tortured

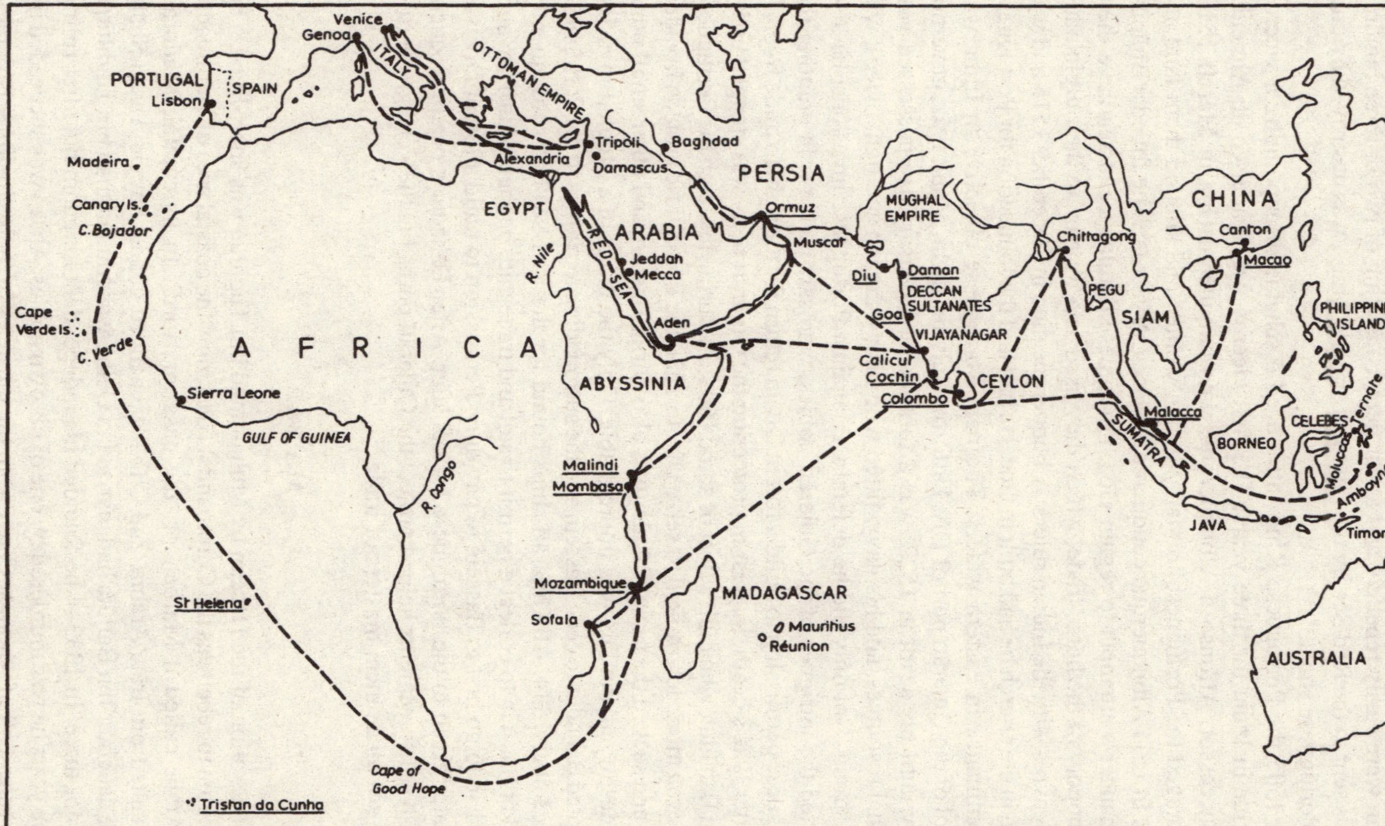

The Portuguese possessions in the East and the route to India

the innocent men and women he captured. The Zamorin's attempted invasions of Cochin were easily repelled, and a war fleet, consisting of two or three hundred vessels sent to the Red Sea by the Zamorin and the Arabs, was destroyed by only four Portuguese ships.[49]

In 1505 the Portuguese King introduced a scheme of appointing a viceroy to reside in India for three years. The first viceroy was Francisco de Almeida. His successor, Alfonso d'Albuquerque, who conquered Goa in March 1510, encouraged the Portuguese to marry Indian women and allotted them land and cattle. In 1511 Albuquerque conquered Malacca. A year later he foiled a Bījāpūrī commander's attempts to regain Goa. Portuguese dominance at sea gave them a monopoly of the horse trade, which they used as a weapon in their diplomatic manoeuvres with the Indian rulers. Albuquerque died in December 1515 and was buried in the church he had built in Goa. He had laid the foundation for Portuguese predominance in eastern waters. The next Portuguese objective in India was control of the Gujarāti port of Div. Unfortunately for them, Malik Iyāz, governor of Div until his death in 1522, was a formidable adversary. He possessed vast personal resources, and his navy, fitted with heavy cannon and light pieces, was quite strong. Not only did he defend Div against Portuguese invasions; he also thwarted the intrigues of the Gujarāti nobles, who saw no harm in granting the Portuguese permission to build a fort in Div in return for the right to trade freely.[50]

After Iyāz's death, interest in protecting the Gujarāti ports was stepped up by Sultan Bahādur, who built a fleet of some 160 sail. During his reign the Portuguese grew even more determined to seize Div. In 1530 the Portuguese armada invaded Sūrat and sacked the town. Rānder was also burnt, Bassein and other small ports were destroyed, but Div was impregnable. Only the threat of a Mughal invasion prompted Bahādur to cede Bassein and the surrounding territories to the Portuguese in December 1534. All Gujarātī ships bound for the Red Sea had subsequently to call at Bassein to collect a permit to sail and trade and, on their return voyage, again had to go first to Bassein to pay duty. Permission to build a fort at Div was also later given to the Portuguese by Bahādur. After Bahadur's death, frequent Turkish reinforcements helped protect the Gujarātī ports, but the Portuguese rule of the sea made them masters of trade.[51]

MA'BAR

The annexation of the Deccan by Muhammad bin Tughluq was short-lived. The first region to rebel was the Coromandel coast, now the coastal area of Tamilnadu. The Arabs called it Ma'bar, or 'the pass' or 'ford'. In its capital, Madurai, merchants from Irān, Arabia, and China exchanged goods. Sayyid Ahsan Shāh, whose daughter Ibn Battūta had married in Delhi, was Muhammad bin Tughluq's governor there. In 1333–4 he founded his independent kingdom but after ruling for five years he was murdered by one of his own nobles. Ahsan was succeeded by seven rulers, all of whom suffered from the intrigues of their Muslim aristocracy. The Hindus naturally took the opportunity to regain their independence. Ma'bar's fourth ruler, Ghiyasu'd-Dīn Muhammad Damghān Shāh (1340–5), like Ibn Battūta, was Sultan Ahsan Shāh's son-in-law. He was an energetic warrior who destroyed his enemies ruthlessly.

Around 1364 the short-lived sultanate lost the greater part of its territory. Only Madurai remained, and in 1377–8 the Vijayanagara ruler annexed it to his kingdom.[52]

THE BAHMANĪ KINGDOM

In Chapter I we outlined the circumstances that led Hasan Kangū to carve out the independent Bahmanī kingdom in 1347.[53] Hasan Kangū assumed the title 'Alā'u'd-Dīn Hasan Bahman Shāh. The court genealogists linked his ancestors with Bahman Isfandār, the Irānian king. The story that he was the servant of Gangū Brahmin[54] of Delhi is also mythical, because he was a nephew of 'Ala'u'd-Dīn Khaljī's famous general, Hizabru'd-Dīn Zafar Khān.

Hasan made Gulbarga in north Karnātaka his capital and subdued the pro-Tughluq and recalcitrant chiefs there. He captured Goa and occupied Dābol, making it his principal port on the Arabian Sea. His frontiers now extended as far as Bhongīr in northern Telingāna, so he divided the kingdom into four provinces; (1) Gulbarga with Raīchūr and Mudgal, (2) Daulatābād with Bīr, Junnār, and Chaul, (3) Berār with Mahūr, and (4) Bahmanī Telingāna with Indūr and Kaulās.

'Ala'u'd-Dīn's successor, Muhammad I (1358–75), consolidated the kingdom most effectively. In 1363 the Raja of Wārangal ceded Golkonda and its dependencies to the Sultan. The territory north of the river Tungabhadra had been a bone of contention between the rulers of these regions since ancient times. The Bahmanīs were Muslims, and the Vijayanagara ruler was Hindu. The historians of each kingdom give an exaggerated communal colour to the wars between them, but they are essentially political.

The Bahmanī Sultan took the field against Bukka and captured Mudgāl but could not hold it. He penetrated deep into Vijayanagara territory but was again unable to consolidate his gains, and the war dragged on for several more months. At length the weary Sultan sued for peace; neither side gained any territory, although both suffered terrible human losses.

After 'Ala'u'd-Dīn's death in 1375 five sultans ruled up to 1397. During this period the tensions among the Bahmanī population came to the fore. Immigrants such as Arabs, Turks, and Irānīs, who were known as the Āfāqis or Gharībs, were bitterly resented by the settlers from north India, the local Muslims, and the Habshīs, who were known collectively as the Dakhnīs. Hindu influence was rising in both cultural life and the government, and when Tājud-Din Fīrūz (1397–1422) ascended the throne he promoted Hindus to high office in order to offset any Āfāqi predominance – although he also resumed the war against Vijayanagara. Like his predecessors, he was unable to capture Vijayanagara but he forced Devarāya I to give him his daughter in marriage and to cede Bankapār fort as her dowry. In 1417 he again invaded the Vijayanagara kingdom but was defeated at Panagal

(Nalagonda). In his old age Fīrūz was forced to surrender the government to his brother, Khān-i Khānān, who defeated his supporters. He died in 1422.[55]

Ahmad I (1422–36) began his rule with a victory over the Raja of Wārangal in 1424. He then shifted his capital from Gulbarga to Bidar, situated on a plateau not far from Wārangal and Golkonda. He was more adventurous than his predecessors, soon defeating the chief of Māhūr and making it the northern outpost of his kingdom. In 1428 he made the ruler of Kherla his tributary chief and forced the ruler of Khāndesh to marry his daughter to his (Ahmad's) son 'Ala'u'd-Dīn.[56] The Bahmanīd army also advanced into Gujarāt territory but was repulsed at Nandurbar. The Bahmanī forces then seized Māhim near Bombay but soon lost it again. In retaliation the Gujarātīs captured the Bahmanī town of Thana. The fruitless war soon ended with a treaty between the two powers.

Although Ahmad's successor, 'Ala'u'd-Dīn (1436–58), was not as active as his father, he was also involved in wars against Vijayanagara, Khāndesh, and Mālwa. He had a fickle nature and first massacred the Āfāqis on Dakhinī allegations, then slaughtered the Dakhinīs when the Āfāqīs lodged counter-complaints. Towards the end of his life he took to heavy drinking and dissipation. 'Ala'u'd-Dīn's successor, Humāyūn Shāh (1458–61), appointed as prime minister an Irānian immigrant, Khwāja Mahmūd Gīlānī (Gāwān), who had arrived in the Deccan during his father's reign.[57] Mahmūd tried to persuade the Āfāqīs and Dakhinīs to channel their energies into state interests.

After Humāyūn's early death, Nizāmu'd-Dīn II, who was only eight years old, ascended the throne. His extreme youth made administration exceedingly difficult, since the members of the council of regency could not agree amongst themselves. In 1461–2 Mahmūd Khaljī of Mālwa invaded the Bahmanī kingdom, routed the defending army, and besieged Bīdar. The timely arrival of Mahmūd Begarh of Gujarāt at the head of 20,000 soldiers, however, forced Khaljī to retreat. A year later Khaljī again marched against the Deccan and besieged Daulatabad, but the news of Begarh's impending arrival forced him to withdraw once more.

In July 1463 Nizāmu'd-Dīn died. The new ruler, Shamsu'd-Dīn Muhammad (1463–82), was also only about nine years old. The council of regents continued to rule, but two years later one of its members, Khwāja-i Jāhān, died and then the second councillor, the Queen Mother, retired from politics. Mahmūd Gāwān was now the sole administrator of the Bahmanī kingdom. Ignoring the hatred between the Dakhinīs and the Āfāqīs, he gave the senior positions to the Dakhinis, and also brought the Hindu chiefs into the government, in order to establish a united Bahmanī kingdom. The Russian traveller, Athanasius Nikitin, who visited the Deccan from 1469 to 1474 under the Muslim name Khwaja Yusuf Khurāsānī, says:

> The Sultan (of Beder) is a little man, twenty years old, in the power of the nobles. Khorassanians rule the country and serve in war. There is a Khorassanian Boyar, Melik-Tuchar, who keeps an army of 200,000 men; Melik Khān keeps 100,000; Kharat Khān, 20,000, and many are the khans that keep 10,000 armed men. The Sultan goes out with 300,000 men of his

> own troops. The land is overstocked with people; but those in the country are very miserable, whilst the nobles are extremely opulent and delight in luxury. They are wont to be carried on their silver beds, preceded by some twenty chargers caparisoned in gold, and followed by 300 men on horseback and 500 on foot, and by horn-men, ten torchbearers and ten musicians.[58]

Mahmūd Khaljī's army penetrated the Bahmanī borders in 1466 but was repulsed. Next year the Bahmanī army seized Kherla in Mālwa. Mahmūd Gāwān then agreed to sign a treaty with the Mālwa Sultan, according to which Kherla was ceded to Mālwa and Berar went to the Deccan. Mahmūd Gawan's campaigns against the western coastal plains and the Konkan were a great success. He captured Rāmgarh in July 1470 and Khelna in January 1471. Making Kolhāpūr his headquarters, he squashed the guerrilla wars in the hills and seized several forts. The recapture of Goa in February 1472 was Gāwān's major victory, and three months later he returned to a hero's welcome in Bidar.[59] Daulatabad subsequently broke into revolt, but the governor, Yūsuf 'Adil, crushed the rebels. Meanwhile, at Vijayanagara's instigation, the chief of Belgām rebelled and besieged Goa. Mahmūd Gāwān's enemies urged the Sultan to lead the campaign himself, and, accompanied by Mahmūd Gāwān, he marched against Belgām and besieged the fort. Gāwān breached the walls by laying gunpowder mines, forcing the rebel chief to surrender.[60] The conquests during Shamsu'd-Dīn's reign extended the Bahmanīd's frontiers to Khāndesh in the north, Tungabhadra in the south, and Orissa in the north-east, and included Goa in the south-west.

Gāwān's administrative reforms weakened the power of the provincial governors, who had often intrigued against him and frequently rebelled. Eight provinces were carved out of the existing four districts, and certain areas in each of them were placed directly under the central administration, while their revenue was reserved for the state. The governors were allowed personal control over only one fortress in their territory; the remaining forts in their lands were surrendered to the commanders appointed by the central government. All the military commanders were paid partly in cash and partly by *iqtā'* assignments. *lqtā'* holders were directly accountable to the Sultan for revenue receipts and the payment of salaries to their levies. The land was measured, and revenue records were reorganized. Gāwān developed friendly relations with the Ottoman Sultan Muhammad II (1444–6, 1451–81), the conqueror of Constantinople. He wrote letters to the rulers of Gīlān, Irāq, and Egypt and corresponded with the rulers and ministers of Gujarāt, Jaunpūr, and Mālwa.

Mahmūd Gāwān built a college in Bidar which made the Deccan an important intellectual centre. Nevertheless, the curtailment of their power alienated the senior governors from him; in particular Nizāmu'l-Mulk, the governor of Rājamundrī, could not accept the truncation of Telingāna. The dissatisfied nobles bribed Gāwān's secretary to affix his master's seal to a sheet of blank paper. They then wrote on it a treasonable letter to the Raja of Orissa and showed it to the Sultan. Gāwān admitted that the seal was his but denied writing the letter. The Sultan, unconvinced by Gāwān's explanations, had him executed in April 1481. Many of Gāwān's friends were also beheaded.[61] Although the Sultan did not outlive Gāwān by more then twelve months, his subsequent inquiries revealed Gāwān's innocence.

THE FIVE DECCAN KINGDOMS

Shamsu'd-Dīn Muhammad Shāh's successor, Shihābu'd-Dīn Mahmūd, ruled from 1482 to 1518. During his reign the factional wars between the Dakhinīs and Āfāqīs assumed serious proportions. The central administration, which had been strengthened by Mahmūd Gawān, collapsed within a few years, and the governors became rebellious. In 1487 Fathu'llah 'Imadu'l-Mulk, then governor of Berār, became virtually independent, while Qāsim Barīd, the new prime minister, reduced the Sultan to a mere puppet. In 1490 Malik Ahmad Nizāmu'l-Mulk Bahri, governor of Ahmadnagar, founded the Nizām Shāhī kingdom and built Ahmadnagar as his capital. Yusuf 'Ādil Khān, the governor of Bījāpūr, proclaimed his independence in the same year. In 1491 Sultan Qulī of the Shī'ī Qarā Qoyūnlū tribe of Azerbayjān and Irāq, the governor of Telingāna, became virtually independent but in his own political interest never severed relations with Sultan Shihabu'd-Dīn. After Shihabu'd-Dīn's death, four sultans ascended the Bahmanīd throne between 1518 and 1526. The last one moved from Bīdar to Ahmadnagar, where he died in 1526. In 1538 the Bahmanī kingdom came to an end. The successors of the prime minister, Qāsim Barīd (d. 1504), consolidated their power, until 'Alī Barīd (1543–79), the first monarch of that dynasty, assumed royal power.

The above five kingdoms, which emerged in the wake of the extinction of the Bahmanīd kingdom, were not satisfied with the boundaries inherited from the Bahmanīd provincial divisions. They were constantly involved in wars both amongst themselves and against the neighbouring kingdoms. The situation was further exacerbated by the different backgrounds of the rulers of the three most powerful states; Ahmadnagar, Bijāpur, and Golkonda. Ahmad's father, Nizāmu'l-Mulk Hasan Bahrī of Ahmadnagar, was an Islamicized Hindu who had risen from a slave to a leading commander. On the other hand, the ancestors of the rulers of Bījāpūr and Golkonda were foreigners. From the very beginning of his reign Yūsuf 'Adil Shāh of Bīljāpūr declared Shī'īsm as the state religion. The Qutb Shāhīs were also Shī'īs. These sectarian and racial antagonisms aggravated the Āfāqī and Dakhinī feuds among the nobles in all three states.

Although the border disputes of the Deccan states were derived from their Bahmanīd origins, their attempts at aggrandizement at the expense of neighbouring states were influenced by both the scramble for more territory between the sultans and the court intrigues of the ambitious nobles. Two larger states generally combined against the third, and the smaller states sided with whoever offered the best safeguards to themselves. Matrimonial alliances were made between them to promote political interests, but sometimes instead of cementing friendship they bred enmity.

In Berar, 'Ala'u'd-Dīn 'Imad Shāh refused to surrender Pathrī, north of the river Godāvari, which was the hometown of Burhān Nizām Shāh's (1510–33) Hindu ancestors, even on favourable terms. Consequently Burhān seized it by force in 1518. Then in 1525 the rulers of Berār, Bīdar, and Ahmadnagar invaded Bījāpūr, but the mounted archers of Bījāpūr defeated them. Burhān Nizām was determined to retain Pathrī at all cost; he also took Māhūr from 'Imad Shāh and, aided by Barīd, ravaged Berār, which had formed an alliance with Khāndesh. The defeated rulers appealed to Bahadur Shāh of Gujarāt, who promptly invaded Ahmadnagar, and for at least three years Nizām Shāh owed suzerainty to Gujarāt.[62]

After Krishnadeva Raya's death, Ismā'īl 'Ādil Shāh of Bījāpūr (1510–34) recaptured Raichūr and Mudgal from Vijayanagara after a three-month siege. Then Sultan Qulī of Golkonda seized the interior districts north of Krishna and coastal areas as far north as Rājamundri on the Godāvari from Vijayanagara. After Ismā'īl's death, however, Achyuta Rāya of Vijayanagara regained Raichūr and Mudgal from Bījāpūr.

Around the early 1540s the political rivalries between Bijāpur and Ahmadnagar assumed a new dimension when their respective rulers changed their sectarian beliefs. The Shī'ī, Ibrahim 'Ādil Shāh (1535–58) of Bījāpūr, embraced the Sunni faith, while the Sunni, Burhan Nizām Shāh of Ahmadnagar, adopted Shī'īsm. Towards the end of 1542 Ibrahim recaptured Sholapur from Ahmadnagar. At Burhan Nizām Shāh's instigation an alliance was made between Ahmadnagar, Golkonda, and Vijayanagara against Bījāpūr. Invaded from three different directions, Ibrāhīm of Bijapur had to cede Sholāpūr to Ahmadnagar and make friends with Vijayanagara.

About 1545 Ibrāhīm unleashed a reign of terror and persecution upon his army officers, whom he suspected of treachery. His own son, Prince 'Abdu'llāh, took refuge with the Portuguese in Goa.[63] They refused to surrender him despite Ibrāhīm's persistent demands, but the Prince was forced in 1548 to relinquish his claim to Salsette and Bardez ports. Then in 1574 Murtāza Nīzam Shāh annexed Berār to his Ahmadnagar kingdom.

Meanwhile in Bījāpūr, Ibrāhīm's son and successor, 'Alī 'Adil Shāh (1558–80), adopted Shī'īsm and elevated the Ālāqīs to high positions. At about this time in Golkonda, Ibrāhīm Qutb Shāh (1550–80), who had succeeded Sultan Qulī Qutbu'l-Mulk, began to encourage the local Telugu culture. His policy of awarding land grants to brāhman and Hindu temples and not realizing *jizya* earned him the support of the neighbouring brāhman chiefs.[64]

'Alī 'Ādil Shāh of Bījāpūr now signed a treaty with Vijayanagara in order to recover Kalyānī and Sholāpūr from Husayn Nizām Shāh of Ahmadnagar (1553–65). During 1559–61 Bījāpūr and Vijayanagara were allied on one side, against Ahmadnagar on the other, sometimes supported by Berar, sometimes by Golkonda. This made Rāmarāja, regent of the Vijayanagara kingdom, sole arbiter of the Muslim principalities. In 1561 he proposed a humiliating treaty, which Husayn Nizām Shāh was forced to sign. It involved the restoration of Kalyānī to Alī'Ādil Shāh, who had earlier in 1558 requested Rāmarāja's aid in securing it, and also Husayn's personal submission before Rāmarāja. After complying with Rāmarāja's conditions, Husayn made one more effort to capture Kalyānī but was beaten off by the allies. Although 'Alī 'Ādil Shāh was the victor he was disgusted at Rāmarāja's game of playing one kingdom against the other, and at his suggestion hostilities ceased in 1563. Then 'Alī 'Adil Shāh had to cede Itgīr (Yādgīr) and Bāgalkot to Rāmarāja, while Ibrāhīm Qutb Shāh gave him Kovilkonda and Panagal district in return for Vijayanagara's previous assistance. Raichur *doāb* had already been secured by Rāmarāja. Vijayanagara's territorial expansion, brought about largely by their personal jealousies and feuds, alarmed the Muslim sultans. Husayn Nizām Shāh made an alliance with Ibrāhīm Qutb Shāh and then persuaded him to combine with him against Vijayanagara. Husayn strengthened the alliance by marrying his daughter, Chānd Bībī, to Prince 'Alī of Bījāpūr, while 'Alī's sister was married to Husayn's son. Sholāpūr fort, for which much blood had been shed from the very inception of the two kingdoms, was handed over to Bījāpūr as Chānd Bībī's dowry.[65] Later, Barīd Shāh also joined the confederacy. Next 'Alī 'Adil wrote asking Rāmarāja to return the districts ceded by Bījāpūr and Golkonda to their original owners. Rāmarāja refused, and the Muslim envoys of all principalities left Vijayanagara for home. On 24 December 1564 the combined armies of the four sultans encamped twenty-two miles north of the Krishna near Tālīkota. They crossed the only ford separating them from the Vijayanagara army, and on 23 February 1565 a fierce battle took place near Banīhattī. The sultans' armies were at first overwhelmed by Vijayanagara's numerical superiority, but then the artillery, under the Turk Rūmī Khān, broke Rāmarāja's attacks. Rāmarāja himself was picked up by a mahout on one of Nizām Shāh's war elephants and was executed. The victory was decisive. Vijayanagara was sacked and devasted by the sultans.[66]

Five months later, when the four sultans left Vijayanagara laden with massive booty, their feuds once again erupted with renewed vigour. In June 1566 Husayn Nizām Shāh died and was succeeded by Murtazā Nizām Shāh (1565–88). In 1570 Murtazā Nizām Shāh of Ahmadnagar and 'Ādil Shāh of Bījāpūr joined forces to expel the Portuguese from their coastal possessions. The Zamorin also joined them. They decided to attack the Portuguese simultaneously at each port. Murtazā Nizām Shāh invaded Chaul, and Goa was besieged by 'Ādil Shāh's army. The siege dragged on, but the Portuguese main fleet first defeated the Zamorin at Malabar and then besieged Dābol. Treachery and corruption were rampant in the 'Ādil Shāhi's camp, and at Chaul the Nizām Shāhīs lost 3,000 men in one day. Murtaza's minister, Chingīz Khān, entered into an offensive and defensive alliance with the Portuguese in order to save the kingdom from further loss. In 1571 'Ādil Shāh also concluded a treaty with the Portuguese, which was finalized four years later. 'Ādil Shāh was allowed to buy horses at Hurmuz and transport them through Goa without paying the Portuguese extra duty. The Portuguese Viceroy gave an undertaking neither to molest Bījāpūr ships sailing with the Portuguese *cartazas* (permits) nor to convert Bījāpūr subjects forcibly to Christianity.[67]

In April 1574 Murtazā Nizām seized Berār, but by this time the Mughal invasion from the north, which destroyed all the Muslim sultans of the Deccan, was imminent.

THE VIJAYANAGARA KINGDOM

In 1335 Sultan Muhammad bin Tughluq had marched to crush the rebellion by the Ma'bar Sultan, but a severe outbreak of plague in his camp forced him to return to Delhi. The Sultan's retreat encouraged Kapaya Nāyaka or Krishna Nāyaka of the coastal districts of Āndhra, who had already been acknowledged their leader by the influential Nayāka brāhmans of the region, to seize Wārangal. He assumed the title Andrades'adhis'vara (Supreme Lord of Andhra Countries), and Hindu domination was restored in coastal and central Andhra. The movement to overthrow Tughluq rule spread as far as the Krishna-Tungabhadra *doāb.* In Kampilī the people rose against the Tughluq governor, Malik Maqbūl, who fled for shelter to a fortress. Sultan Muhammad bin Tughluq therefore released the two Telugū chiefs Harihara and Bukka, the sons of Sangama, the ruler of Kampili, hoping they would restore the province to him. These brothers had originally served the Kākatīya King Pratāparudra but had fled to Kampilī after its capture by Ulugh Khān. When Kampilī was annexed to the Tughluq empire in 1327, they were imprisoned and taken to Delhi, where they later became Muslims. Sultan Muhammad now appointed Harihara his new governor in the Kampilī region. A modern scholar disputes their Islamicization, although, with slight variations, both Persian and Sanskrit sources reiterate the story. According to this authority, Sangama belonged to the Karnataka province, and his son, Harihara, was in the service of the Hoysala king, Ballāla III of Dvārasamudra. As one of the heads of the liberation movement, he overthrew Tughluq rule and founded the Vijayanagara kingdom in the mixed Kannada-Telegū speaking region.[68] These arguments are not conclusive, for Islamicized chiefs such as Sukhapāla, grandson of Jayapāla, had in the past been appointed governors only to recant later. Harihara founded his capital on the southern banks of the Tungabhadra and named it Vidyanagara after the famous Vedic scholar Vidyaranya, who was the *gurū* (mentor and teacher) of the two princes. The dynasty was known as the Sangama, after its founder. The empire was called Karnātaka Sāmrājya (the Karnātaka, or the 'Kannada-speaking country'). Vidyanagara or, as it was later more frequently called, Vijayanagara, was its capital. The Vijayanagara kingdom, extending from the Tungabhadra to the southern reaches of the Kaveri, lay within the declining Hoysala dominions, and the setting up of the new kingdom was more a threat to the Hoysalas than to the Muslims.

Harihara had four brothers who staunchly supported him in consolidating and extending his territory. In 1346 the Vijayanagara kingdom annexed the Hoysala principalities, which were now exhausted from their continuous wars against Madurai.[69]

Bukka I (1356–77), who succeeded his brother Harihara as king, patronized many Vedic pandits. During his reign Hindu society enjoyed a renaissance.

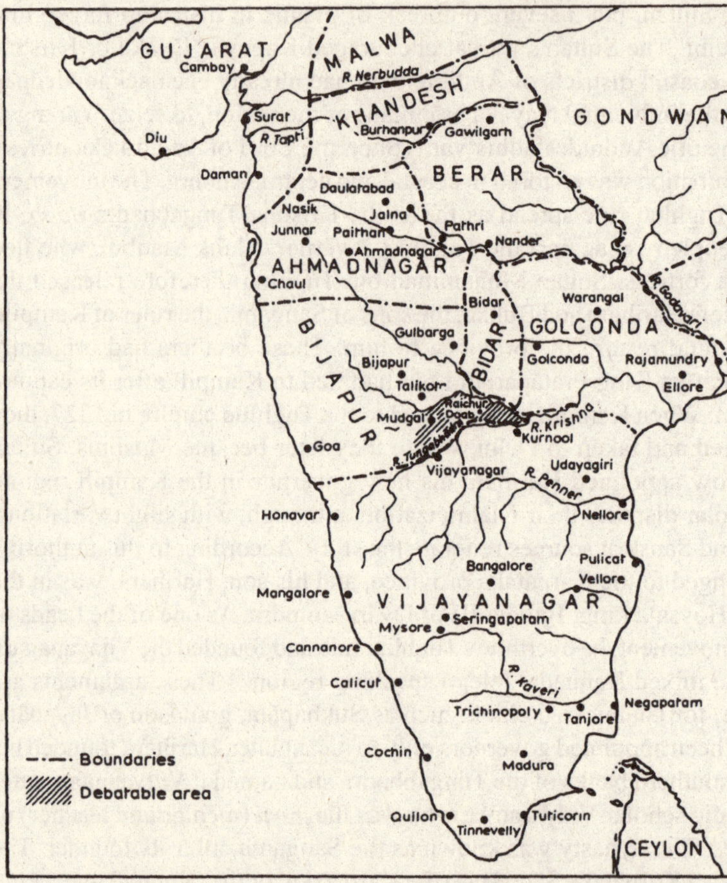

The Sultanates of the Deccan and the Hindu kingdom of Vijayanagar in the sixteenth century

Temples were rebuilt, and works on religion, philosophy, and law were written. Vaishnavas and Jainas were urged to reconcile their differences and live in amity.[70] Bukka meanwhile ordered his son, Kumāra Kampana, to exterminate the Ma'bar sultanate while he took the field against the Bahmanīds. Vijayanagara was still fighting them when the King died. The two brothers succeeded in rolling back the tide of Muslim aggression from the Bhima to the Indian Ocean.

During the reign of Bukka's son, Harihara II (1377–1404), Bahmanī rule lost its vigour, and Harihara's army seized Goa, Chaul, and Dābol on the northern Konkan from them. The Kenara, Karnātaka, Trichinopoly, and Kānchī regions were also captured. The income from the ports naturally made the principality affluent. The last years of Harihara's reign were very peaceful.

After his death his three sons fought a war of succession for two years. The winner, Devarāya I (1406–22), crowned himself king. The early years of his reign were, like those of his predecessors, devoted to wars against the Bahmanī sultans, and the countryside in both kingdoms was devastated. He later constructed a dam across the Tungabhadra in order to provide the city with canals and also dammed the Haridra river to irrigate the countryside.

Devarāya's two sons each ruled for a few months. They were succeeded by Devarāya II (1423–46), who waged constant but inconclusive wars against the Bahmanīds, although he succeeded in capturing Kerala. In 1443 'Abdu'r Razzaq, the ambassador of Tīmūr's son Shāh Rukh of Hirāt (1405–47), was given a warm welcome by Devarāya. The envoy was highly impressed with the capital and the personalities of Devarāya and his nobles.[71]

Devarāya was convinced that the reason for the Bahmanīds' continued military superiority, when he himself possessed immense resources in men and materials, was the quality of their archers and horses. To remedy these deficiencies, he recruited about 2,000 Muslim archers and gave them land-tax assignments. He also built a mosque in the city and had a copy of the Qur'ān placed before his throne on a richly carved desk, so that the Muslims could kiss it while performing the ceremony of obeisance in his presence.[72] His army now comprised 80,000 horse, 200,000 foot, 2,000 Muslim archers, and 6,000 Hindu archers.

After his death, the Sangama dynasty began to decline. Its last king, Virūpaksha II (1465–85), was a cruel ruler. In 1496 he slaughtered about 10,000 Muslims in Bhatkal as a reprisal for the sale of horses to the Bahmanī Sultan. He had no military skill and eventually lost Goa to the Bahmanīs.[73] When finally one of his nobles, Saluva Narasimha (1485–1506), overthrew him, the Sangama dynasty came to an end.

Narasimha was involved in wars against Bījāpūr, Bīdar, Madurai, and Srirangapattanam. He paid extravagant prices to Arab merchants to bring the best-quality stallions from Aden and Hurmuz. Shortly after his death, his commander's son, Vīra Narasimha, deposed his worthless son and heir and crowned himself king.

This new dynasty, called the Saluva, ruled from 1486 to 1570. Vira Narasimha spent his short reign crushing the rebel chieftains. His younger brother Krishna Devarāya (1509–29) was a great warrior, shrewd statesman, profound scholar, and generous patron of intellectuals. He was the greatest ruler of the Vijayanagara dynasty; some scholars assert that he was the greatest of the Indian rulers. Barbosa says: 'the King allows such freedom that every man may come and go and live according to his own creed without suffering any annoyance and without enquiring whether he is a Christian, Jew, Moor or Heathen. Great equity and justice is observed to all, not only by the ruler but by the people to one another.'[74]

Krishna Devarāya had only just ascended the throne when an envoy arrived from Albuquerque to seek his assistance against the Zamorin and to ask for the grant of a site to build a factory between Bhatkal and Mangalore. In return, Albuquerque promised to help Krishna reconquer Goa and to give him exclusive rights to import horses. By January 1510 Krishna had defeated Yūsuf 'Adil Shāh of Bījāpūr. Although the Portuguese had by then captured Goa without his help Krishna assured them that he would help them to keep it. In his own territories Krishna Devarāya defeated various rulers from the south and then delivered a crushing defeat on the Sultan of Bījāpūr, near Raichār.[75]

Krishna Devarāya was succeeded by his half-brother Achyuta Rāya (1530–42), but he was unable to control the political factions in his kingdom, who were engaged in a fierce power struggle. The neighbouring Muslim states seized the chance to exact vengeance. Semi-independent principalities were carved out of Madurai, Thanjavur, and Jinjī. After Achyuta's death, power fell into the hands of Rāmarāja, the son-in-law of Krishna Rāya. Achyuta's son, who was still a minor, ruled for a few months, but then Rāmarāja raised Krishna Devarāya's nephew, Sadāsiva (1543–70), to the throne. Ramaraja was a dynamic leader. His victories over Bījāpūr prompted him to take the offensive against the Muslim princes to offset their attacks on Vijayanagara. His diplomatic manoeuvrings aggravated the disagreements between the Ahmadnagar and Bījāpūr kingdoms, and he succeeded in negotiating a commercial treaty with the Portuguese which deprived Bījāpūr of its horse supply. Subsequently the Vijayanagara army, now allied with Ahmadnagar, defeated Bījāpūr in three successive battles.[76] Ahmadnagar annexed Kalyanī and Sholāpūr, while Vijayanagara took possession of Raichūr and Mudgal. Rāmarāja, however, was not a rigid statesman. As soon as the new ruler of Ahmadnagar invaded Bījāpūrī territory again in alliance with Golkonda, realizing the threat to himself, he rushed to the rescue of the Bījāpūrī Sultan. Ahmadnagar and Golkonda were forced to withdraw. Until 1564 Rāmarāja constantly changed sides in order to prevent a confederacy of the three powerful Deccan sultans. Early in 1565, however, a confederacy of Muslim princes in the Deccan delivered a death blow to the Vijayanagara kingdom at the battle of Bānīhattī (Tālīkota).[77] The Vijayanagara kingdom survived within a reduced boundary until 1664.

The emergence of the Vijayanagara kingdom, like the Muslim provincial dynasties, was facilitated by Muhammed bin Tughluq's bid to impose central control over the distant south. It did not mirror Hindu reaction to Muslim rule, although it did protect Hindu faith and culture and helped to preserve ancient Hindu ideals of kingship, law, and justice.

III

THE AFGHANS AND THE MUGHALS

THE LODĪS

THE inhabitants of the Sulaymān mountains to the west of the Indus were known as Afghāns. Expert horse-breeders, they often served in the army of the Turkic rulers, sometimes rising to the level of commander and even governor. In their own homeland their tribal rivalries were responsible for unceasing feuds, but as soldiers they were well disciplined. Of these the Lodī tribe was most prominent.

During Muhammad bin Tughluq's reign many leading Afghān tribal heads left their mountain home for Delhi. Some of them, under Malik Shāhū Lodī, the governor of Multān, later rebelled against Muhammad bin Tughluq. They were unsuccessful and many subsequently returned to their homeland, which Baranī calls Afghānistan (the land of the Afghāns).[1]

In Delhi, Khizr Khān, who later became the first Sayyid Sultan, appointed another Afghān, Malik Sultān Shāh Lodī, governor of Sirhind, giving him the title Islām Khān. He also promoted Malik Shāh's four brothers to high positions. One of them, Malik Kālā, had a son called Bahlūl. After his father's death Bahlūl was brought up by his uncle, Islām Khān, who not only married his daughter to him but, passing over his own sons, declared Bahlūl his successor. Islām Khān's sons, however, repudiated their father's will and combined to fight Bahlūl. They were defeated. The successful Bahlūl consolidated his position and then invaded Delhi twice but each time failed to conquer it. Finally, on 19 April 1451, he captured Delhi by a coup and ascended the throne. The Sayyid Sultan, 'Ala'u'd-Dīn, had already retired to Badā'ūn. The new ruler successfully crushed the Sharqī Sultan's bid to seize Delhi and subdued the Muslim Langāh, ruler of Multān, but his invasion of Mālwa failed. Although Bahlūl encouraged the Afghān tribesmen to migrate to India, he was cautious about awarding them positions and promotions. The senior offices were reserved for his loyal Afghān supporters, and the important governorships were given to the royal princes. Muslims of non-Afghān origin were given minor positions. Historians writing about Bahlūl during the reigns of Akbar and Jahāngīr try to show that his monarchy resembled a tribal confederation, but like his predecessors he was in fact a despot. Before his death at the age of eighty, the Lodī sultanate was firmly established from the Panjāb to the borders of Bihār.

The senior Afghān leaders usually favoured those of pure Afghān stock, but one of Bahlul's wives, who was a Hindu goldsmith's daughter, won their support for her son Nizām Khān. Nizām adopted the title Sultan Sikandar (1489–1517) when he ascended the throne. The Sultan crushed Husayn Shāh Sharqī of Jaunpūr, liquidated the Rājpūt uprisings in the neighbouring region, and forced the Raja of Tirhut to agree to pay tribute. Bihār was also seized, and the Sultan of Bengal signed a treaty with Sikandar. Dholpūr, a Gwālior dependency, was sacked. Gwālior itself was surrounded by a chain of forts built by the Tomar rulers. Its king, Raja Mān Singh (1486–1517), was popular with both Hindus and Muslims. Sikandar seized the small forts surrounding Gwālior one by one and cut off its food supply from Rājasthān. From 1506 to 1517 the Sultan devoted all his energies to capturing Gwālior, but his gains were not worth the energy he spent. Although in 1514 he captured Chanderi, Gwālior and Mālwa remained unconquered. He died in 1517.

Sikandar Lodī enhanced the prestige of the sultanate without alienating the Afghān nobility. *Iqtā's* were granted to the Afghāns, but the loyal Hindu chiefs were not neglected. Sikandar tightened the espionage system, and his leading nobles were shocked to find that even minor family incidents were reported to the Sultan. He also took a keen interest in the development of agriculture and regularly examined the price schedules for the markets. Persian histories enthusiastically relate stories of the Sultan's bigotry and zeal to destroy Hindu temples; nevertheless the Sultan and his nobles were deeply interested in Hindu culture and institutions.[2]

At the beginning of the reign of his son, Sultan Ibrāhīm Lodī (1517–26), the leading Afghān nobles again made strong efforts to undermine the Sultan's autocracy. They forced Ibrāhīm to make his younger brother Jalāl the independent ruler of the Jaunpūr region, formerly ruled by the Sharqīs. This unrealistic scheme of dual monarchy, however, was opposed by Ibrāhīm's favourite noble, Khān-i Jahān Lodī, who persuaded Ibrāhīm to change his mind. Jalāl refused to accept this reversal, and civil war broke out between the two brothers. Jalāl lost. He was imprisoned in the Hānsī fort and later beheaded. Meanwhile the civil war had provided Rāna Sanga of Mewār with the opportunity to make inroads into the Lodī territories as far as Bāyana near Agra. Ibrāhīm marched personally against Rāna Sanga, but the Afghān centrifugal tendencies enabled the Rāna to capture Chanderi.

The Sultan embarked upon building the superstructure of his power on the loyal nobles and the leaders of the younger generation, to whom he gave the senior commands once held by the old guards. The Sultan even sought support from the Indian Muslims. The persecution of the senior commanders from Sikandar's reign lit the fire of rebellion in Bihār. The Sultan summoned Dawlat Khān Lodī, who had governed the Panjāb for about twenty years, to help him. Instead of coming himself, however, and pretending to be ill, the Khān sent his son, Dilāwar Khān. Dilāwar Khān was alarmed at the persecution of the dismissed Afghān leaders and reported it to his father. Finding no other way out of the impasse, Dawlat Khān wrote to Bābur, the ruler of Kabul, asking him to save them from annihilation.[3]

BĀBUR AND HUMĀYŪN

Zahīru'd-Dīn Muhammad Bābur, the founder of the Mughal empire in India, was descended on his father's side in the fifth generation from Tīmúr and through his mother in the fifteenth degree from Chingīz Khān. Although popularly known as 'Mughals' or the descendants of Mongols, Tīmūr's descendants preferred to call themselves the Chaghatāyids, originating from Chingīz's second son, Chaghatāy, who ruled Transoxiana.

Bābur was born on 14 February 1484 and succeeded his father, 'Umar Shaykh Mirza, as ruler of Farghānā in June 1494. For twenty years Bābur endured severe hardship whilst attempting to gain command of the country between the Oxus and the Jaxartes which comprised the cultural and commercial centres of Samarqand and Bukhara. The people of Samarqand loved him, and initially his surprise invasion of the country in 1500 was successful; but in 1501 Shaybānī Khān Uzbek, a descendant of Chingīz Khān's eldest son, Jochī, rose to power in the region and defeated him. Although this reduced Bābur to a mere fugitive, in June 1504 he took Kabul from one of his uncles. Bābur pacified the Afghān tribes there and collected tribute from them with great tact and patience. He also married the daughter of a Yūsufza'i leader in order to strengthen his friendship with the tribe. In December 1510 Shāh Ismā'īl Safavī of Irān defeated and slew Shaybānī and sent his sister, who had been married to Shaybānī, to Bābur. In October 1511 Bābur seized Samarqand as Shāh Ismā'īl's vassal, promising to issue coins in the Shāh's name and to adopt the Shī'ī life-style. This made him unpopular in the predominantly orthodox Sunnī country. The Uzbeks, under Shāybanī's nephew 'Ubaydu'llāh Khān, subsequently rallied their forces, and after two years Bābur was forced to return to Kabul. There he acquired firearms with the help of Turkish gunners and strengthened his army.

Immediately after Bābur had settled in Kabul in 1504 he developed an interest in the conquest of India. In 1505 he had reconnoitred regions to the west of the river Indus, as far as Jamrūd, Kohāt, and Tarbīla. In 1519 he mounted his first invasion of India, seizing Bajaur by storm and imposing a ransom on its people. Next he sent an envoy to Ibrāhīm Lodī, asking him to surrender the west Panjāb region previously conquered by Tīmūr. Because this proposal would mean his loss of the Panjāb, the governor there, Dawlat Khān, stopped the envoy going further than Lahore. Bābur returned to Kabul again and in September of the same year invaded the Yūsufza'īs. In 1220 he mounted his third invasion of India and seized Siālkōt. For two years he was busy occupying Qandahār. Then in I523 Dawlat Khān's son, Dilāwar, and Bahlūl's younger son, 'Alam Khān, also visited Bābur to induce him to overthrow Ibrāhīm Lodī. In Delhi, getting an inkling of the conspiracy, Ibrāhīm Lodī sent an army against Lahore to nip the invasion in the bud. His forces seized Lahore, and Dawlat Khān took refuge in Multān. Bābur, who had left Kabul on his fourth Indian expedition, was meanwhile approaching Lahore and he in turn defeated Ibrāhīm's army. Lahore was sacked and burned. Then Bābur moved to Dīpālpūr where Dawlat Khān was waiting to obtain the Panjāb from him. His expectations were unrealistic, since Bābur had himself decided to seize Delhi and was not prepared to be merely Dawlat Khān's tool. Appointing a governor at Lahore, Bābur left for Kabul to organize reinforcements. After Bābur's departure, Dawlat Khān imprisoned his son, Dilāwar, who had disclosed his plans to Bābur, captured Sultanpur, and defeated 'Ālam Khān in Dīpālpūr. 'Ālam Khān fled to Kabul, but Bābur sent him back to Lahore with a body of troops and a letter to the Mughal commander there ordering him to help 'Ālam Khān.

Bābur left Kabul in October 1525 to conquer India. 'Ālam Khān had meanwhile laid siege to Delhi but was repulsed by Ibrāhīm's army. By this time Dawlat Khān had assembled an army of between 20,000 and 30,000 men in the Panjāb but early in January 1526 he surrendered to Bābur.

Ibrāhīm left Delhi to meet Bābur with an army of 100,000 cavalry and I,000 elephants. Bābur's army comprised about 10,000 troopers. He took up a position near Pānīpat, keeping the town and its suburbs on his right. Cannons mounted on wagons had been placed in front of his army. Between sets of wagons, tied together by strong rope, were gaps where small breastworks had been erected to deploy one or two hundred horsemen. On the left, and in other strategic areas, ditches had been dug. Bābur's cavalry, or 'flying flanks', was expert in making lightning attacks on the enemy's flanks and rear. Ibrāhīm's army depended on elephants and consisted of mercenaries. The battle took place on 21 April 1526. Bābur's flying flanks wheeled from right and left to attack the enemy's rear, showering Ibrāhīm's troops with arrows. Ibrāhīm sent reinforcements to the hard-pressed flanks. Groups from Bābur's right, left, and centre surrounded clusters of lndian troops, while the cannons discharged balls on them from the left-hand side. By the afternoon the Indian armies, which had no experience of these tactics, had been routed. Between 16,000 and 40,000 Indians were killed. Herd upon herd of elephants was captured. Besides an immense quantity of booty, Delhi and Agra fell into Bābur's hands.[4] At Agra the family of Gwālior's rulers presented the famous Koh-i Nūr diamond to Bābur's son, Humāyūn. Bābur was very generous in sharing the booty with his noblemen (called Begs) and soldiers. All the Kabul residents also received some money, and even the major Muslim towns in Central Asia and the holy cities of Mecca and Medina were not forgotten.

Bābur treated those Afghān leaders who submitted to him magnanimously. He assigned to his Mughal Begs the revenue of various areas between Delhi and Kanauj. Those territories which had not as yet surrendered were also assigned to the Begs, who subdued the recalcitrant Afghān leaders and brought the region under Mughal rule. Nevertheless it took a long time to restore confidence to the general populace, who took to flight at the sight of Mughal troops. A large number of Bābur's own Begs were unwilling to stay in India; they were interested only in war and plunder. Bābur settled down in Agra, preparing schemes for further conquests and supervising the casting of mortars. He spent his leisure hours organizing the laying out of gardens, digging of wells, and planting of fruit trees from Kabul in Indian soil. Nothing deterred him from noting down in his daily diary the observations he had started to record after ascending the throne.

The most formidable threat to the nascent Mughal empire was Rāna Sānga, the mighty ruler of Mewār, who dreamed of restoring the great empire of Prithvīrāja Chauhān. A large number of Rājpūt chiefs had joined him to fight the Mughals. Hasan Khān Mewāti had also formed an alliance with him to overthrow Bābur. Although the Rāna could not occupy land further than Chanderī, he much preferred to see the weak Ibrāhīm on the throne of Delhi and Agra than the formidable Bābur. The Rāna consequently made full preparations and marched to expel Bābur from India. Bābur moved towards Sīkrī, but his Begs were frightened by the Rāna's fame as an invincible warrior. The arrival of reinforcements from Kabul encouraged them, but then an astrologer's calculations predicting Bābur's defeat spread consternation in the Mughal army. Bābur, however, did not panic; in order to reassure his army of his confidence in Allah's support he renounced the wine forbidden by Islam, which until then he had enjoyed drinking with his friends. He also ordered that gold and silver wine vessels should be broken and the pieces distributed to the needy and the dervishes. He then reiterated his vow to remit transit dues called *tamgha* on Muslim merchandise.[5] Meanwhile, however, the regions between Kol and Kanauj had been reconquered by the Afghān leaders and the Mughal garrisons expelled.

On 17 March 1527 the final battle between the Mughals and the Rājpūts was fought at Kanwāh near Sīkrī. The Mughal gunners and matchlockmen took up their positions behind the carts, and wheeled tripods for the guns were arrayed in front of the army. The ropes joining the carts had been replaced by chains. The Rājpūt army, which outnumbered Bābur's army many times, made a determined attack on Bābur's extreme right. The Mughals retaliated fiercely, their guns playing havoc all around the enemy ranks. Wave after wave of Rājpūt troops stormed Bābur's right but could not smash the Mughal ranks. The Rājpūts then directed their pressure to the left but could not shake it. Then Bābur's cavalry besieged the Rājpūts from all sides and balked the Rājpūt counter-attacks. Before evening Bābur had gained a decisive victory. Innumerable leading Rājpūts, fighting with their proverbial chivalry, were killed. Bābur, who had from the outset declared the war against the Rājpūts to be *jihād* (holy war), assumed the title of Ghāzī (Islamic Hero).[6] The defeated Rāna Sānga died of poison at Kālpī towards the end of January 1528.

Kanwah victory secured Bābur's Indian throne, and he finally allowed those Begs who were reluctant to stay in India to return to Kabul. His son, Humāyūn, was ordered to control Kabul and Badakhshān. Bābur reached Chanderī in January 1528, but the news of the loss of Avadh, which he had already received, prevented him invading Rāisen, Bhilsa, and Sārangpūr. Instead he returned to Kanauj and marched as far as Baksar on the Ganges, driving his Afghān enemies deep into Bihār and Bengal. In Bengal, Nusrat Shāh sided with the defeated Afghāns and by the end of December 1528 they had organized a three-pronged drive against the Mughals in the region of Chunār, Banāras, and Ghazīpūr. Bābur marched personally against them in January 1529 and reached the borders of Bihār, but the ensuing rainy season made him return to Agra without engaging them in battle.

Bābur's son Humāyūn failed to regain Samarqand from the Uzbeks. Bābur therefore recalled Humāyūn from Badakhshān and gave it to his youngest son, Hindāl. At the end of June 1529 Humāyūn arrived at Agra. By now Bābur's health had been shattered by the long and strenuous campaigns he had fought and the hot Indian climate. In addition, he had substituted heavy doses of opium and other drugs for the liquor he had renounced. Bābur died on 26 December 1530. Several years later his dead body was taken to Kabul and buried in the terrace of a beautiful garden. According to his will no dome or other structure surmounted his grave, because the great lover of nature preferred exposure to snow and sun.

As a military leader Bābur had no equal in his day. His indomitable courage ensured the confidence of his commanders and troops. As a soldier he was dauntless, never giving way to panic or despair. Nothing could shake his belief in his own ultimate success with divine help. Bābur loved to call himself a *qalandar* (carefree dervish), and the prodigality of his nature and lavish rewards to his Begs and soldiers justified this claim. He was very creative, frequently introducing innovations when building monuments, laying out gardens and orchards, and casting new types of guns and matchlocks.[7] His martial and diplomatic strategies were always well calculated. The cold hand of death prevented a demonstration of his administrative abilities, but the fragmentary records available to us show his deep awareness of the problems inherent in governing the multicultural and multi-religious society of India. He remains unsurpassed as a writer of both poetry and prose in Chaghatāy-Turkī, his mother tongue; his memoirs frankly confess his own failures and are free from inhibitions. Always welcoming the company of scholars and poets, he enjoyed many erudite discussions with them. Bābur was a devoted follower of the famous Naqshbandiyya sūfī Khwāja 'Ubaydu'llah Ahrār (d. 1490), whose writings he loved, finding comfort in them for his body and spirit.[8] Sectarian enmities and quarrels were furthest from his mind. He was a lovable man who enjoyed excursions with his friends and happily braved storms, frost, and snow while out hunting. Bābur admired the Indian acrobats and was himself fond of wrestling and swimming. At wine-parties his joviality knew no bounds, and he drank without restraint. Liquor never prevented him from immediately carrying out any duty, however. Through his courage and many-sided genius the foundations of the Mughal empire were laid.

Bābur's eldest son, Humāyūn, was born on 6 March 1508. He had three half-brothers: Kāmrān, who was a year or two younger, 'Askarī (b. 1516), and Hindāl (b. January 1519). Humāyūn's throne was no bed of roses. Besides his brothers and his brother-in-law, Muhammad Zamān Mīrza, other Tīmūrīd princes and Afghān chiefs were a potent threat. Following the Turco-Mongol custom, Humāyūn divided the empire among his half-brothers, but they were dissatisfied with their portions. Kāmrān, who had received Kabul and Badakhshān, forcibly seized Lahore and the rest of the Panjāb. To avoid civil war, Humāyūn left them in Kāmrān's hands, thereby forfeiting not only extensive territories but also control of the military roads from Kabul to Delhi. Nevertheless, for the time being Kāmrān was satisfied and apparently grateful.

Humāyūn now turned his attention to the Afghān rebels east of Lucknow. Before he could attack them, however, he received the alarming news that Bahādur Shāh of Gujarāt, having consolidated his Mālwa conquests, was moving against the Mughal frontiers. Humāyūn hastily made a treaty with the rising Afghān leader Sher Khān Sūr, leaving him in full control of the area east of Banāras. Sher Khān thus gained a strong base from which to mount further operations against the Mughals.

In November 1534 Humāyūn marched towards Mālwa to crush Bahādur Shāh, who was besieging Chitor. Humāyūn moved slowly, reinforcing his army and countering the unexpected Afghān attack. The respite gained by Bahādur Shāh enabled him to storm Chitor and conquer it.[9]

Humāyūn seized Mandū. In July 1536, displaying remarkable heroism, he stormed Champanīr after four months' blockade. Then he occupied Ahmadābād. Had Humāyūn made Bahādur Shāh, who was a popular ruler, his vassal he would not have failed so miserably, but he instead appointed 'Askarī viceroy of Gujarāt. Humāyūn had only just left Ahmadābād in pursuit of Bahādur when he was forced to return by the alarming news of rebellions in the northern provinces. Once again Humāyūn moved slowly, this time in order to give the rebels time to surrender, and spent four to five months resting at Māndū. In Gujarāt, 'Askarī's lack of tact and inexperience alienated his nobles, who refused to support him. Bahādur marched to Ahmadābād, but Humāyūn took no prompt action to prevent Gujarāt being recaptured. 'Askarī fled to Champanīr and thence to Agra. In February 1537 Humāyūn reached Agra. Both Gujarāt and Mālwa had now passed out of Mughal control. The two years wasted by Humāyūn in his fruitless Gujarāt expeditions had made Sher Khān a formidable threat.

SHER KHAN (LATER SHER SHAH) SŪR

The early history of Sher Khān, whose original name was Farīd, is based on legends of the nostalgic Afghāns collected during Akbar's reign and is not dependable. Farīd's grandfather and father migrated from Roh and served several Afghān nobles at the courts of Bahlūl and Sikandar. Farīd was born in Bahlūl's reign. His early life in his father's polygamous home had been unhappy, but he acquired an excellent literary education at Jaunpūr through his own efforts. Farīd's career began with the administration of his father's *iqtā'* at Sahasrām in south Bihār. There he put his theoretical knowledge to practical use by establishing a clear understanding between the peasants and the village chiefs. Naturally the area prospered, to the great satisfaction of Farīd and his father, Hasan, but his stepmother's jealousy forced Farīd to seek another avenue of employment. He moved to the court of the Afghān ruler of Bihār, Sultan Muhammad Nūhānī, who gave him the title Sher Khān for his bravery. After Bābur's victory over Rāna Sānga, Sher Khān entered Mughal service and subsequently was rewarded with a grant of land. Nevertheless he deserted the Mughal camp at Chanderī with the conviction that the Mughals were not invincible and that his future lay in an independent career in eastern

India. Sher Khān did not, however, sever relations with the Mughals. He gained a hold over Bihār, and, when Humāyūn ascended the throne, his diplomacy and military talents made him the ruler of the region from Chunār to Patna. Humāyūn's treaty with Sher Khān in February 1533, allowing him to retain Chunār fort which controlled the road to Bihār and eastern India, was a great victory for the rising Afghān chief. During the next four years Sher Khān recruited a large number of Afghāns, many of whom had lost their jobs during the Mālwa war. Some important Afghān leaders also joined him. Sher Khān consolidated his hold over the region extending from Chunār to northern Bihār. At the end of February 1536 he appeared before the walls of Gaur in Bengal and obtained enormous sums in indemnity from its ruler, Mahmūd Shāh.[10]

Humāyūn, having just returned to Agra from Gujarāt, could not immediately march against Sher Khān but first spent some time organizing the administration. Then, at the end of July 1537, he left Agra on his eastern campaign and besieged Chunār in January 1538. The garrison resisted for five months, and it was only after the Turkish artillery commander, Rūmī Khān, constructed a mobile battery of boats which damaged the walls of the fort that the Afghāns surrendered. Sher Khān, who had again invaded Gaur in October 1537, returned meanwhile to Rohtas in Bihār and seized it from its Hindu raja by trickery. In April 1538 his Afghāns took Gaur. Humāyūn, who had already wasted considerable time besieging Chunār, now captured Banāras. There he learned of Sher Khān's Bengal conquests. He marched towards Patna and opened negotiations with Sher Khān, offering him undisputed rule in Chunār and Jaunpūr if he surrendered Rohtās and Bengal to the Emperor's representative. Sher Khān demanded Bengal too and asked Humāyūn to confine his rule to the area west of Jaunpūr. Shortly afterwards the Sultan of Bengal himself came to Humāyūn for aid. Humāyūn marched towards Gaur, but his progress was checked at the Garhī pass by Sher Khān's son, who had been commissioned to prevent the Mughal advance. In September 1538 Humāyūn reached Gaur and seized it without any opposition. The Emperor stayed there for three to four months, thereby giving Sher Khān opportunity to invade the region around Banāras. Humāyūn then sent his brother Hindāl to Tirhut and Pūrnea to collect supplies, but Hindāl went instead to Agra and declared himself king. Humāyūn next sent Shaykh Phūl, the famous Shattariyya sūfī, to arouse Hindāl's sense of obedience, but Hindāl callously killed him.[11] The Emperor now assembled his troops from the Bengal districts and hurriedly marched to Chausa, which divided Bihār from Banāras. There Sher Khān's war-weary army was sighted. For two months Sher Khān managed to keep Humāyūn inactive by exchanging peace messages. Then he marched off in full battle array, giving the impression that he was going to fight some far-distant Hindu raja. A subsequent week of mock-campaigns lulled the Mughals into a false sense of security. On 7 June 1539, before dawn, the Afghān army swooped down upon the Mughal camp, taking it completely by surprise. Almost the whole Mughal force was destroyed, and Humāyūn, falling from his saddle while fleeing across the Ganges on horseback, was forced to use an inflated skin offered him by a poor water-carrier.

The victorious Sher Khān gave the Mughal ladies safe conduct home. Then, at Banāras, he declared himself an independent king with the title Sher Shāh. His Afghān army easily reconquered Bengal.

After two years' absence Humāyūn returned with the remnants of his defeated army to Agra, where Kamran was awaiting him. 'Askarī, who had also managed to escape from Chausa, was there, as well as Hindāl, who was forced to promise his loyalty. Humāyūn made the water-carrier who had saved his life king for half a day in fulfilment of his promise. His nobles were utterly disgusted.

Mīrzā Kāmrān, who was thoroughly distressed at the Chausa debacle, offered to march against Sher Shāh with his fresh troops, but Humāyūn rejected the suggestion, since he was determined to avenge the defeat personally. Then Kāmrān fell ill and returned to Lahore, taking his army with him despite the Emperor's request that they stay behind to fight Sher Shāh. For seven months no concerted Mughal plan was made. In March 1540 Sher Shāh, now well prepared to make a final bid for the throne of India, moved towards Kanauj. Humāyūn, with about 40,000 well-armed soldiers and some 60,000 retainers, crossed the Ganges. The battle took place on 17 May 1540 near Kanauj. The Afghān army consisted of only 10,000 horsemen, but their flanking detachments, avoiding the Mughal artillery, drove the Mughal cavalry into the centre between the opposing forces, causing great panic. The Afghān's vigorous charges smashed first Humāyūn's left wing, then his right, and lastly the central Mughal army. Many Mughals were drowned fleeing across the Ganges. Hotly pursued by the Afghāns, Humāyūn reached Agra with great difficulty. From there he returned to Delhi on his way to Lahore. Kāmrān offered no help and refused him asylum in Kabul and Badakhshān, although he consented to take care of his brother's family. Kāmrān also tried to make peace with Sher Shāh but had to leave for Kabul because of the Afghān's determination to drive the Mughals out of India. Humāyūn left for Sind in order to make it a base for further operations to regain the throne. Thus began his fifteen-year exile.[12]

THE SŪR SULTANATE

The Sūr sultanate of Sher Shāh was short-lived but it was better planned and administered than the first Afghān Lodī empire. Sher Shāh was fifty-five or sixty when he ascended the throne; he ruled vigorously until his accidental death five years later. His first task was to ensure that the Mughals did not reconquer India.

After Humāyūn left Agra, Sher Shāh stayed there for only a fortnight. Then, marching through Delhi and Sirhind, he reached Lahore hot on the heels of the fleeing Mughals. From Lahore, Sher Shāh set out towards Bhīra, halting at Khushāb to dispatch detachments to chase the Mughal princes. He was now confronted with the more complex problem of controlling the hill ranges in the northern part of the Jhelam, Shāhpūr, and Miānwālī districts of the Panjāb, called the Salt Range. These hills were home to the turbulent Gūjar, Bhattī, and Khokhar tribes which had not been completely subdued by the Delhi sultans, mainly because of the Mongol raids in the region. Sher Shāh took the far-sighted step of constructing a formidable fort on the north-west of Jhelam town, which he named Rohtās, after the fort in Bihār.

Sher Shāh had just begun to concern himself with the problems of upper Sind and Multān when he received news that Khizr Khān, his governor in Bengal, had married the daughter of Mahmūd Shāh, the late Bengal ruler, and had usurped the prerogatives of an independent sovereign. Sher Shāh rushed to Gaur, reaching it in the rainy season of 1541, and imprisoned the governor. He next reorganized the administration and appointed Qāzī Fazīlat, a Muslim jurist, to co-ordinate the work of the divisional heads. To prevent future rebellion no governor was appointed.

On his return from Bengal, Sher Shāh seized Gwālior from Humāyūn's governor and brought Mālwa under his control. He appointed military commanders to strategic centres in the area.[13]

In the beginning of the rainy reason of 1542 Sher Shāh returned to Agra, where he learnt that Humāyūn was hovering on the Mārwār frontier. Māldeva, the ruler of Mārwār, had opened negotiations with Humāyūn to overthrow Sher Shāh, but the Afghān's conquest of Mālwa frightened him, and he retracted his undertaking to help Humāyūn.

Silahdī Pūrbiya Pūranmal of Chanderī, who like his father was accused of dishonouring Muslim women and training them to be dancing girls, was Sher Shāh's next target. Unable to capture Rāisen, Puranmal's stronghold, he seized it by perfidy. Sher Shāh's governors conquered Multān and ravaged the Balūch territories. Upper Sind, including ·the notable forts of Bhakkar and Sehwān, was also captured. Sher Shāh's conquests of Sind made Maldeva's western borders even more unsafe.

Towards the end of 1543 Sher Shāh marched towards Mārwār at the head of a very strong army, but Maldeva was still formidable in the Mount Abu region. The Emperor faked treacherous letters in the names of Māldeva's commanders and had them delivered to his camp. When he read them Māldeva was so panic-stricken that he fled, ignoring his loyal commanders' entreaties. The Rājpūt army nevertheless fought stubbornly. Sher Shāh was victorious but often remarked, referring to the barren Mārwār territories, that he had nearly lost the empire of Hindustān for a handful of millet.[14]

Sher Shāh's general, Khawās Khān, then seized Jodhpur while Sher Shāh himself captured Ajmīr and completely overran the Mount Abu region. After returning to Agra, a few months later he attacked the famous Rājasthān fort, Chitor, which was now weakened by internal feuds. It capitulated without much resistance. The Kacchwāha territory of Dhundhar (near modern Jaipūr) also surrendered. Sher Shāh's capture of the chain of forts from Mālwa to Mārwār was a unique achievement, but the Raja of Kālinjar, who sympathized with Humāyūn, was still defiant. Sher Shāh blockaded this fort but failed to storm it. The Rājpūts there fought back to back for seven months. Finally, however, when mines had been laid, a lofty tower for mounting a battery had been erected, and covered approaches were ready, the attack was launched. Lighted hand-grenades were thrown into the fort. One grenade suddenly struck the wall and, rebounding into a heap of hand-grenades, exploded. Immediately the whole ammunition dump blew up. Sher Shāh himself was very badly burned, and although the fort was stormed and the Rājpūts overpowered, he died, with his ambitions unrealized. Sher Shāh's rise to power, from the position of a petty *iqtā'* holder's neglected son to the throne of Delhi, was remarkable. He was not a military adventurer like so many conquerors in that age, but a far-sighted monarch with a clear vision of the prestige and responsibility of a ruler. He attracted a large number of new Afghān tribes to his service and handled the restless Afghān grandees firmly. He pacified the Salt Range and the inaccessible regions of Multān and Lahore by populating them with Afghān tribesmen. He had plans to set up other Afghān colonies in Rājasthān, Mālwa, and Bundelkhand, but death put an end to his schemes. He did not, however, make the blunder of annexing the whole of Rājasthān to his empire; instead some of the petty autonomous chiefs, whom Māldeva had deposed, were restored to their principalities. Sher Shāh reorganized his huge army partly on tribal lines and partly on the pattern of 'Ala'u'd-Dīn's forces. He revived the system of branding horses in order to stop the fraudulent practices of the military commanders, who substituted poor-quality horses to save the good stock from destruction in time of war. His well-equipped army might have extended the Sūr empire into the Deccan and Kashmīr if he had survived.

Sher Shāh had restored peace to the country. The roads were policed by the village chiefs. From past experience of administration at the grass-roots level Sher Shāh knew that crimes were mainly committed with the connivance of the village chiefs; so, if a chief was unable to produce a thief or murderer, he was himself liable to beheading. An improved espionage system also helped curb crime. Sher Shāh's government-controlled caravanserais served both Hindus and Muslims. Brāhmans supplied water and cooked food for the Hindus, so their religious laws were not violated. New market towns grew up around these caravanserais, and the many towns named Sherpūr, from Multān to Bengal, are reminiscent of Sher Shāh's interest in the urbanization of the country. Some local trade taxes were abolished, although they did not disappear. Customs duty was levied at only two points – one in the east, the other in the west.

After Sher Shāh's death, his second son, Jalāl Khān, was crowned, adopting the title Islam Shāh. Jalāl's elder brother, 'Ādil Khān, contested his claim, and the Afghān nobles whom Sher Shāh had pacified found a golden opportunity to fish in troubled waters. Islām Khān, however, was firm and energetic and defeated his brother. Once in power he concentrated on breaking the clique of Afghān leaders whom his father had tamed and trained. He resumed the *iqtā's* previously awarded to senior Afghān commanders and transferred them to newly created junior positions. A Niyāzī Afghān uprising was totally crushed, and barbarous punishments were meted out, even to the females. A second chain of fortresses, collectively known as Mānkōt, on the upper Indus frontier was built to suppress the uprisings of the Gakkhar tribe.[15]

Islām Shāh systematically upgraded the Afghān army and artillery. He made government officials share with the local chiefs the responsibility for crimes in the villages and highways because, unlike Sher Shāh, he did not believe that only the village headmen abetted the criminals.

Islām Shāh's early death from a fistula in 1552 dislocated the administrative machinery. Before Humāyūn reconquered Delhi in 1555, three different rulers were crowned. During this time the real power lay in the hands of Hīmā, a saltpetre dealer in Rewārī belonging to the Dhāsar class, apparently a subdivision of the Gaur brāhmans.

HUMĀYŪN RECAPTURES DELHI

While Sher Shāh was approaching the Panjāb after his victory at Kanauj, Kāmrān and 'Āskarī had marched on to Kabul, and Humāyūn to Sind. At Patar, twenty miles west of the Indus, he happened to see Hamīda Bānū Begum, the fourteen-year-old daughter of his brother Hindāl's teacher, and fell in love with her. Hindāl strongly opposed Humāyūn's desire to marry her, while Hamīda herself was not prepared to marry a monarch in exile. Nevertheless Hindal's mother overcame all obstacles, and the couple were married. Accompanied by Hamīda Bānū, Humāyūn left for Jodhpur to seek Māldeva's help. On the way they passed through Amarkot, whose Rana received them warmly; there on 15 October 1542, Hamīda Bānū gave birth to Akbar.[16] Humāyūn was now warned by his ambassador at Māldeva's court of the Raja's treacherous designs to imprison him, so he abandoned his journey to Jodhpur and, wandering in Sind, set out for Qandahar in July 1543. There 'Askarī, who controlled Qandahar, also sought to imprison him. Leaving his heavy baggage and Akbar in the care of some loyal officers, Humāyūn therefore set off to seek help from Shāh Tahmāsp in Irān. In August 1544 Humāyūn joined the Shāh at Qazvīn in northern Irān. His stay at the Shāh's court was sometimes full of hope and at other times disappointing. Humāyūn's loyal supporter Bayram Khān and his wife, Hamīda Bānū, helped him overcome all crises, while Humāyūn himself diplomatically conformed to the Shī'ī way of life. In the end the Shāh gave him about 12,000 soldiers on the condition that, once Qandahār, Ghaznī, and Kabul had been captured, Qandahar would be ceded to him. No religious constraints were imposed. In September 1545 'Askarī surrendered Qandahar, and Kabul was taken from Kamran three months later. Kamran, however, continued his effort to regain Kabul. He invaded it thrice but each time was subsequently expelled by Humāyūn. 'Askarī found it difficult to accept Humāyūn's rule but finally he gave up the struggle for power and retired to Mecca, where he died. Only Hindāl remained loyal to Humāyūn but he was killed in November 1551 while fighting Kāmrān. Then Kāmrān, in a final bid to regain the throne, sought help from Islām Shāh in the Panjāb, subsequently discovering that Islām Shāh intended to imprison him instead. He escaped from the Panjāb only to be captured by the Gakkhars, whose chief, Ādam, surrendered him to Humāyūn. Pressured by his Begs, Humāyūn had him blinded in August 1553.[17] Now no family opponent was left, and the rival Sūr dynasty was disintegrating rapidly.

Leaving Kabul in November 1554, Humāyūn captured Lahore in 1555. In

Sirhind the Afghāns strongly resisted the Mughal onslaught but sustained a crushing defeat. On 23 July 1555 Humāyūn sat on the Delhi throne once more. He died only six months later while descending from the roof of his library where he had gone to observe the rising of Venus on 20 January 1556.[18]

Humāyūn's lifelong enemies were his brothers and kinsmen, but he quailed at the idea of harming them. Nothing demonstrates his keen sense of gratitude to those who helped him more than the story of his making the water-carrier, who had saved him from drowning in the Ganges, sit on his throne for half a day. He was not a good general or organizer but was courageous, optimistic, and persevering. Although he was a devout Sunnī he did not despise the Shī'īs, nor did he hesitate to seek their help and advice. Humāyūn was passionately devoted to the study of astronomy, loved painting, and wrote Persian poetry.

AKBAR THE GREAT

Before his death Humāyūn had appointed Akbar as governor of the Panjāb and made his loyal general Bayram Khān his son's guardian. While fighting the Afghāns at Kalānaur in modern Gurdāspūr district, Akbar received news of his father's death. Bayram Khān promptly crowned Akbar king on 14 February 1556.[19]

Akbar's position was still precarious. His army was small, and even the Panjāb was not completely subdued. The Afghāns drove out the Mughal governors from the Agra-Bayana region; Delhi, which was suffering from a terrible famine, had been seized by Hīmū. Akbar's nervous followers urged him to retreat to Kabul, but both he and Bayram were determined not to leave India without making every effort to regain the throne. On 5 November 1556 Hīmū's army met Akbar at Pānīpat in a fierce battle. Hīmū drove back the Mughal archers and cavalry and was about to win the day by bringing in his war elephants and reserve cavalry to scatter Akbar's centre, when an arrow pierced his eye. Consternation spread instantly among Hīmū's army, which broke and fled. Later, when Hīmū was brought before him as a prisoner, at Bayram Khān's request Akbar unwillingly struck him on the neck with his sword, and Bayram finished him off. The historian Abu'l-Fazl pays an unqualified tribute to Hīmū's administrative and military talents and suggests that, had his life been spared, Akbar's training would have made him one of the architects of the Mughal empire.[20]

After Hīmū's death, Akbar entered Delhi in triumph. Before long his rule was established from Kabul to Jaunpur and from the Panjāb hills to Ajmīr. Bayram appointed a distinguished Irānian literary scholar, 'Abdu'l Latīf, as Akbar's tutor, but like previous teachers he too was unable to arouse Akbar's interest in reading and writing. Even so, Akbar's taste in Persian sūfī poetry and liberal mystic thought was developed, although he devoted most of his time to sport. While he remained what Abu'l-Fazl calls 'behind a veil',[21] Bayram Khān, as regent and prime minister, consolidated the administration of the reconquered region. His growing pre-dominance alienated the Atkah Khail or 'foster-father battalion', consisting of the families of Akbar's nurses and their relations, while Akbar's mother resented Bayram's power. Akbar too was made to feel that Bayram unduly restrained him from organizing elephant fights. By 1560 he was eighteeen years old and wished to rule independently.

In March of that year one of his nurses, Māham Anaga, managed to have Akbar transferred from Agra to Delhi. From there Akbar wrote to Bayram ordering him to move to Gwālior and then to leave on a pilgrimage to Mecca. Bayram rejected his supporters' advice to march against Delhi and obediently left Agra, surrendering the insignia of royalty. In their bid to annihilate Bayram Khān, the Atkah Khail sent an army to pursue him. Bayram, who had by now reached Bikānīr, decided to teach them a lesson and turned towards the Panjāb. Akbar first sent an army to fight Bayram and then arrived himself. Although Bayram defeated the army near Jālandhar, he quailed at the prospect of fighting Akbar and surrendered unconditionally. Akbar ordered him to resume his pilgrimage, and on 31 January 1561 Bayram was assassinated by an Afghān at Patan in Gujarāt on his way to Mecca. His camp was plundered, but his four-year-old son, 'Abdu'r Rahim, was sent to court.

Humāyūn had considered Bayram one of his most loyal supporters. Indeed without him Humāyūn's visit to Irān would possibly have been unsuccessful. Some modern historians believe that Bayram showed favouritism to his Shī'ī co-religionists and that this was responsible for his fall. This is far from true. Bayram considered himself a defender of the Mughal interest and not the Shī'ī sect. Even fanatical Sunnīs such as Badā'ūnī considered him unmatched in wisdom, generosity, sincerity and humility. He was a deeply religious man and a great friend of the dervishes. Badā'ūnī concludes correctly that it was Bayram's strenuous efforts, bravery, and statesmanship which enabled the Mughals to found an empire in India for the second time.

Akbar's rule during the period 1560-4 has been described as a petticoat government, but this is incorrect. On the contrary, he quickly took control of the administration. By frequently changing his *wakils* or prime ministers he reduced the importance of the position and strengthened his personal power.

A new development in Akbar's career around this time was his growing interest in sūfīs, Hindu yogis, and *sannyāsīs* (hermits). In January 1562 he set off on a pilgrimage to the shrine of Khwāja Mu'īnu'd-Dīn Chishtī at Ajmīr. The region had been captured in 1557. On the way, Raja Bhārmal Kacchwāha of Amber (modern Jaipūr) waited on him. The Raja's feuds with his brother, and the enmity of Akbar's governor of Mewāt and Ajmīr, had driven him to desperate straits. In his predicament, Bharmal decided to marry his eldest daughter to Akbar in order to gain his favour. This voluntary offer was different from the former forced marriages of Muslim rulers with Hindu princesses. Akbar accepted the offer readily and, when he returned from Ajmīr, married her at Sambhar.[22] Raja Bhagavān Dās (Raja Bhārmal's heir) and Mān Singh (his nephew and adopted son), were subsequently given senior positions in the imperial hierarchy.

In March 1562 Merta, the key to Mārwār, was captured with the help of Akbar's Rājpūt supporters. This made a deep impression on Akbar's mystic mind, and after his return from the Ajmīr pilgrimage he prohibited the enslavement of prisoners of war and their forcible conversion to Islam on humanitarian grounds.[23] In 1563 he remitted pilgrim taxes throughout his dominions, although, according to Abu'l-Fazl, they yielded millions of rupees in revenue. In March 1564 Akbar lifted *jizya* (poll-tax) on Hindus. This radical departure from Islamic discriminatory laws paved the way for a more broadly based rule. None of the liberal-minded advisers who in the second half of Akbar's reign made his rule famous had yet entered his court. Akbar's mind was nevertheless filled with Islamic orthodoxy, and his liberal measures were designed merely to initiate a new state policy divorcing personal religious beliefs from the public good. Protests against the remission of poll-tax were made on economic grounds, but Akbar ignored them.

Akbar's ambitions of conquest and expansion were no different from those of other imperialists. He conquered northern India from Agra to Gujarāt and then from Agra to Bengal and the borders of Assam. Next he strengthened his north-west frontier and proceeded to subdue the Deccan. The Rājpūt states generally became his allies, but his own restless Tūrānī leaders were still a potent threat to his ambition of creating a strong centralized Mughal empire. Consequently he proceeded cautiously and established his overlordship with as little use of armed force and bloodshed as possible.

The long-awaited heir to the Mughal throne was born on 30 August 1569. The welcome birth was ascribed to the blessings of Shaykh Salīm Chishtī of Sīkrī. The infant was named Salīm after the revered sūfi saint. His mother was a Kacchwāha princess. On 7 June 1570 Akbar's second son, Murād, was also born at Sīkrī. Akbar again paid a thanksgiving visit to Ajmīr.

Akbar's remarkable conquests had filled his mind with gratitude to the Great Bestower of Victories. He spent many nights repeating the names of God and long morning hours meditating. In February or March 1575 he ordered the erection of an elegant structure near the Jāmī' mosque in his newly built town of Fathpūr-Sīkrī. It was named the 'Ibadat Khāna (House of Worship). In fact it functioned as a debating hall. On each Thursday night Akbar repaired there for religious discussions which were resumed on Friday. Only the Sunnīs were initially allowed to participate. Mulla 'Abdu'l Qādir Badā'ūnī, who had entered Akbar's court in April 1574, and Abu'l-Fazl, who joined early in 1575, were the principal debaters. Both had been trained by Abu'l-Fazl's father, Shaykh Mubārāk. Both used the same tactics to browbeat their opponents, but Badā'ūnī was left behind by Abu'l-Fazl, and he grew frustrated and disgruntled while Abu'l-Fazl progressed rapidly. The main targets of their attack were the prominent *'ulamā'* at court, such as Hājjī Ibrāhīm Sirhindī, Makhdūmu'l-Mulk, and Shaykh 'Abdu'n Nabī.[24]

Early in 1576 preparations for an expedition against Mahārāna Pratāp, the son and heir of Uday Singh of Mewār, prevented the Emperor from devoting his attention exclusively to these theological discussions. Mahārāna Pratāp posed no threat to the empire, but his continued assertions of independence were a challenge to Akbar's policy of bringing the Rājpūt princes under Mughal overlordship. In September 1572, six months after Mahārāna Pratāp's accession to his father's throne, Akbar successively sent three missions to persuade Pratāp to accept his suzerainty, but none succeeded in moving the freedom-loving Mahārāna from his ancestral path of hostility to the Mughals. Next Raja Todar Mal tried to persuade the Mahārāna to develop friendly relations with the Mughals, but to no avail. Akbar now decided to use military force. He went to Ajmīr in March 1576, commissioning Mān Singh to crush Mahārāna Pratāp and placing eminent Rājpūt and Muslim commanders under his orders. Some Muslim commanders chose not to fight under a Hindu, but the orthodox Badā'ūnī, who was only a mullah and not a warrior, joined Mān Singh's army voluntarily, to earn the merit of *jihād.* A fierce battle was fought at Haldīghātī near Kumbhalgarh on 18 June 1576. The Afghān Hakīm Sūr fought bravely in the Mahārāna's army, hoping to re-establish the Afghān contemporaries were stunned to note how gallantly the 'Hindus wielded the sword of Islam'. The Mahārāna was wounded, but his attendant turned his horse, and he withdrew to safety. Both sides lost large numbers of brave men. The exhausted Mughal soldiers failed either to capture or to kill the Mahārāna and, fearing ambush, were unable to pursue him effectively. Although the Mahārāna could no longer assemble a force large enough for a head-on confrontation, his guerrilla warfare increased in ferocity. On 12 October 1576 a disappointed Akbar left Ajmīr, although he continued trying to encircle and entrap the Mahārāna. Sirohī and Būndī were subsequently captured, and the Mahārāna's capital, Kumbhalgarh, ten miles north of Udaipūr, was taken on 3 April 1578. In 1585 the Mahārāna narrowly evaded capture, but by now Akbar was tired of the relentless chase and relaxed his pursuit. The Mahārāna continued waging guerrilla warfare until his death on 19 January 1597. He was a gallant and heroic character. Akbar was the captive of his own imperialistic ideals, which prevented him from leaving the Mahārāna in peace.

Akbar again visited Ajmīr in September 1577. At Bhīra, while returning via the Panjāb, he organized a large hunting expedition, called a *qamargha*, in which wild animals were trapped by encirclement. During this he experienced a fit of ecstasy under a tree, which revolutionized his spiritual life. He became deeply interested in learning about other religions. After his return to Fathpūr-Sīkrī he resumed the theological debates with representatives of all religious groups such as Shī'īs, Hindus, Christians, and Zoroastrians. The results were very positive. He grew convinced, as Badā'ūnī says, that all religions contained some truth and that this was not the prerogative of Islam. He believed that constant self-examination was a spiritual exercise of prime importance and that no action should be taken without sound reason.

Shaykh 'Abdu'n-Nabī meanwhile wished the Emperor to confirm the death sentence on a rich brāhman who had been imprisoned for seizing the material collected to build a mosque and also for abusing the Prophet. Akbar left the decision to him, expecting only a mild punishment to be inflicted; but the Shaykh ordered the brāhman's execution. This made Akbar angry, because he believed that according to Hanafi law, even if there were ninety-nine precedents authorizing capital punishment for a particular offence and only one allowing leniency, judgement should be based on the more merciful precedent. During this crisis Abu'l-Fazl's father, Shaykh Mubārāk, suggested the Emperor obtain the written verdict of the *'ulamā'* as to whether the Imām-i 'Ādil (Just Ruler) was empowered to decide in accordance with expediency on controversial legal questions. According to existing Sunni practices Akbar could not be denied this power, which all Muslim rulers exercised. A document dated August-September 1579, known as the *mahzar*, was consequently signed by the leading *'ulamā'* under the guidance of Shaykh Mubārāk and his sons. It was not an 'infallibility decree' as claimed by V. A. Smith, an eminent authority on Akbar.[25]

Akbar's political and military reforms, such as the branding of horses, reduction in the commanders' allowances, and the grants of the *'ulamā'* had already given rise to much dissatisfaction among the Mughal officials. The mishandling of the situation by the Bihār officials in particular sparked off a rebellion there. This spread to Bengal, where the new governor appointed in March 1579, Muzaffar Khān, was also clumsy in implementing the new revenue and military regulations and in his treatment of the Afghāns whose land had been sequestered.

The disgruntled Mughal *mansabdārs*, mainly Tūrānīs, rebelled, putting Muzaffar Khān to death on 19 April 1580. They formed their own government and declared Akbar's half-brother, Mīrzā Hakīm, their ruler. Between 1580 and 1582 the rebellion spread from Bihār and Bengal to Avadh and Katihar. The Shī'ī Mulla Muhammad Yazdī led both the Sunnī and Shī'ī groups of rebel *'ulamā'*. Akbar then ordered these *'ulamā'* to be sent to Agra by boat. Near Agra the boat was sunk, and all the *'ulamā'* in it drowned.[26] Other *'ulamā'* were either secretly killed, exiled, or imprisoned.

In February 1581 Akbar marched to Kābul against Mīrzā Hakīm. At Kābul the people received him warmly, so although he had defeated him, Akbar left Kābul in Hakim's hands and set off for Agra. The arduous journey did not prevent Akbar from entering into religious discussions. Father Monserrate, a member of the first Jesuit mission at Akbar's court (1580–3), who accompanied the Emperor, has left a lively account of these debates. When Shaykh 'Abdu'n Nabī and Makhdūmu'l-Mulk heard of the rebellion, they returned from Mecca without permission but were dismayed to find that by mid-1582 Akbar's Irāni and Rājpūt commanders had restored peace in the eastern provinces. Makhdūmu'l-Mulk died at Ahmadābād; 'Abdu'n-Nabi returned to Fathpūr-Sīkrī, where he was imprisoned while the accounts for the money given to him for Meccan charities were audited by Raja Todar Mal, Akbar's Hindu controller of finance. After some months he was strangled.

Father Daniel Bartoli, a later Jesuit author, claims that after his return from Kābul, Akbar made himself the founder and head of a new religion 'compounded out of various elements, taken partly from the Koran of Muhammad, partly from the scriptures of the Brahmans, and to a certain extent, as far as suited his purpose, from the Gospel of Christ'. This religion, Bartoli continues, was discussed by a council of learned men and commanders, from which Father Rudolf of the first Jesuit mission was excluded, where 'The men of note, especially the commandants, who had no God other than the King and no law other than his will', readily accepted Akbar as the founder of the new religion. An old shaykh, identified by V. A. Smith as Shaykh Mubārāk, was sent to proclaim to all quarters that in a short time 'the (religious) law to be professed throughout the Mughal empire would be sent from the court and that they should make themselves ready to take it for the best, and accept it with reverence, whatever it might be'.[27] This council is regarded by modern scholars as the inauguration of Akbar's alleged new faith, the Din Ilāhī (Divine Faith). The letters and reports of three Jesuit missions which visited Akbar, however, indicate that no new religion was ever promulgated. For example, Father Jerome Xavier of the third mission to Akbar's court in 1594 firmly believed that Akbar was not a Muslim but a superstitious pagan. According to him, Akbar 'aims at making a new religion, of which he himself is to be head; and it is said that he already had numerous followers; but that these are for the most part flatterers, or people who have been bribed by money'.[28] This shows that no new religion had yet been formulated even as late as 1594, although, according to the Father, 'It is more or less certain that he has a strong desire to be looked upon and esteemed as a God, or some great Prophet; and he would have people believe that he performs miracles, healing the sick with the water with which he washes his feet'.[29] Blochmann, a nineteenth-century scholar, lists eighteen people as members of the Din Ilāhī. No founder of a new faith could be proud of such a miserable following, much less a mighty emperor like Akbar. The examination of contemporary sources does not lead us to the conclusion that Akbar invented a new religion. Essentially he expected his state grandees to follow the four degrees of devotion or discipleship, denoting readiness to sacrifice their life, property, honour, and religion to promote the interest of their imperial masters. Although the high grandees of the empire were expected to renounce everything, the more junior satisfied the Emperor by expressing a readiness to sacrifice only one or two of the above.[30] Akbar had no intention of calling upon his disciples to forsake their ancestral faith; he meant only that religion should not be an obstacle to the promotion of imperial policies. It was this spirit of devotion that made Rājpūt fight Rājpūt and Muslim fight Muslim to strengthen the Mughal empire.

Akbar did believe, however, that he could offer spiritual guidance to all those who wished to sit at his feet. Some genuinely sought his help, but others were merely flatterers. There were no theological difficulties, since both Hindus and Muslims in those days believed that the king possessed supernatural spiritual powers. It was customary for the common people and great theologians and mystics to visit the graves of despotic kings like 'Ala'u'd-Dīn Khaljī in the hope that their prayers would be granted. It was even believed that Sultan Sikandar Lodī could perform miracles such as raising the dead to life. In such a credulous society Akbar's adoption of the role of spiritual guide was not naïve.

The death of his half-brother, Mirza Muhammad Hakim, on 9 August 1585 forced Akbar to leave his capital Fathpūr-Sīkrī. He moved to the north-west frontier in order to crush the ambitions of the redoubtable 'Abdu'llāh Khān Uzbek of Transoxiana to seize Kābul. He stayed there until 'Abdu'llāh Khān's death in

1598, and his thirteen years' presence firmly established Mughal rule in the area.

Akbar sent three expeditions in the middle of December from his camp at Hasan Abdāl. One left for Kashmīr, and another set out against Balūchistān. The third force went to Sawāt and Bajaur to subdue the Afghān tribes and an Afghān religious movement called the Roshanā'īs. These were followers of Bāyazīd, whose creed of 'illumination' was a pantheistic mystic-cum-political movement. Bāyazīd had died in 1580, and his son Jalāla had been captured in 1581 by Akbar's army. He had been well treated but longed for freedom and leadership and fled the imperial camp to prey upon travellers between Peshawar and Kābul. Akbar's early military operations against the Roshanā'īs and the tribes which helped them were unsuccessful, and in Feburary 1586 his trusted friend Bīrbal was ambushed by the Yūsufzā'īs and killed along with some 8,000 troops. When Akbar realized that the tribes could not be subdued by military force he decided to play the clans against each other and won some tribal chiefs over to him by promising them pensions. In 1600 Jalāla was killed; his sons lacked their father's qualities, and the Roshanā'īs ceased to be a threat to the Mughal government.

At the end of March 1586 Raja Bhagawān Dās, one of the generals of the Kashmīr expedition, succeeded in persuading Yūsuf Khān, the last ruler of Kashmīr, to surrender. Akbar, however, refused to accept his terms and instead had him and his son Ya'qub Khān arrested. Ya'qūb subsequently escaped and started preparations for resistance. The army sent by Akbar conquered Kashmīr in October 1586, and it was make a *sarkār* of Kābul province. Ya'qūb died in prison, while Yūsuf was made a minor *mansabdār* of five hundred and given a *jāgīr* in Bihār. Akbar's treatment of the ex-Sultan of Kashmīr was unjust and ungenerous.

The conquest of Kashmīr, in conjunction with Akbar's presence in the Panjāb, prompted the chiefs of the hilly regions in northern Panjāb such as Nagarkot, Jammū, Mau, Kewal, and other petty states to offer their submission. Bāltistān and Ladākh in Tibet also recognized imperial suzerainty. The army sent against Balūchistān persuaded the Baluchī chiefs to surrender. Bhakkar was already in Akbar's possession, and in 1590–1 Sind was also conquered.

Early in Akbar's reign the Shāh of Irān had captured Qandahār, but his growing preoccupation with the wars against 'Abdu'llāh Khān Uzbek gave Akbar the opportunity to regain it. He sent an army under his famous general 'Abdu'r-Rahīm Khān-i Khānan. The governor of Qandahār, Muzaffar Mīrza, surrendered and was granted a *mansab* of 5,000. One year later 'Abdu'llāh Khān Uzbek recognized the Hindu Kush as the boundary between Transoxiana and the Mughal empire.

The Mughal boundaries, extending from Sind, Baluchistān, Kābul, and Kashmīr to the Hindu Kush, were the strongest line of defence that had ever existed in India, and no other Indian ruler – not even Asoka in ancient India, nor the British in modern times – ever controlled such a formidable frontier. Akbar acquired these territories by diplomacy; his use of force was minimal.

Akbar now focused his attention on the Deccan. He was aware of the difficulties of ruling it from northern India. Consequently he intended to make the rulers his *mansabdārs*, so they could retain their ancestral lands as *watan-jāgīrs* and at the same time obtain more *jāgīrs* in the Mughal territory commensurate with their *mansab*. This was an extension of his Rājpūt policy. After Akbar's conquest of Gujarāt, Khāndesh generally had accepted his suzerainty, but its loyalty was always suspect.

In 1591, therefore, Akbar appointed his son, Prince Murād, governor of Mālwa in order to force the Deccan states into submission. The conflicts between the Habshī and the Dakhinī factions had driven the Nizām Shāhi state of Ahmadnagar into total confusion, but the differences between Prince Murād and the Khān-i Khānān were equally disastrous. The Mughals attacked Ahmadnagar, but its valiant queen, Chānd Bībī, defended it heroically. In December 1595 the Mughal forces appeared again before the walls of Ahmadnagar. They tried to detonate the five mines they had laid, but the garrison, warned by a Mughal traitor, had defused all but one. The small portions of damaged wall were repaired at once under Chānd Bībī's leadership. The Mughals fought resolutely but had to retire disappointed.[31] Nevertheless, forced by a shortage of supplies and the continuous Dakhinī feuds, Chānd Bībī made peace by ceding Berār. The Mughal forces raised the siege, although the Berār guerrillas still refused to submit. Early in 1597 Raja 'Alī Khān of Khāndesh, who had realized the futility of opposing the Mughals, died fighting in the imperial ranks. The dissension between Murād and the Khān-i Khānān continued, until the Emperor, disgusted, decided to recall them both from the Deccan. In their stead he sent his favourite, Abu'l Fazl, to use his diplomatic skills to resolve the tangled skein of Deccan politics. The Mughals believed that Raja 'Alī's son, Bahādur, would help them reduce the Deccan rulers to submission, but he decided to rebel and ignored Abu'l-Fazl's peace overtures. On 2 May 1599 Murād, who had not yet returned to court, died near Daulatābād of intemperance. Abu'l-Fazl's difficulties increased, but he began to exert pressure on both Bahādur and Chānd Bībī to surrender.

In Lahore, meanwhile, spurred on by the long struggle in the Deccan, Akbar decided to exert his personal pressure on its rulers. There was now little to keep him in the north-west, because 'Abdu'llāh Khān Uzbek had died on 4 February 1598, and he left for the Deccan in September 1599. Bahadur still refused to surrender and took refuge in Asīrgarh fort. The Mughal forces besieged him on 1 April, and Akbar arrived eight days later to direct operations. Many of Bahādur's generals accepted bribes. The subsequent assassination on 3 July 1600 of Ahmadnagar's valiant defender Chānd Bībī by one of her eunuchs, followed by the imperialist capture of Ahmadnagar, demoralized the Asīrgarh garrison. Bahādur was still not prepared to surrender unconditionally. Then Abu'l-Fazl seized Mālīgarh fort near Asirgarh at the end of November 1600, and more forts fell to the Mughals. Bahādur began to despair of success. Pestilence was now raging in the overcrowded Asīrgarh fort; the local population had fled there for safety. Bahādur finally surrendered, and Asīrgarh was captured on 17 January 1601.[32] Akbar assigned Khāndesh to his son, Dāniyal, renaming it Dāndesh. Then Prince Salīm rebelled in Allahabad, and Akbar left for the north. Daniyal was given supreme command in the Deccan, while the Khān-i Khānān controlled operations in Ahmadnagar. Abu'l-Fazl was subordinate to both. Although there was no love lost between the Ahmadnagar commanders – Malik Ambar, an Ethiopian,[33] and Rājū, a native Deccani – they remained a potent threat to the Mughals, whose leaders were unable to devise a concerted plan. In March 1602 Akbar gave Abu'l-Fazl an independent commission but, before he could implement it, recalled him to help deal with Prince Salīm's rebellion. Abu'l-Fazl rushed to the north, but Prince Salīm had him killed by the Bundela chief, Bīr Singh Deva, near Gwālior on his way to Agra. Shocked by the news, Akbar despaired of the future.

Prince Salīm, the longed-for child of many a prayer, had ignored his duties from 1591, refusing to lead an expedition either to the Deccan or to Transoxiana. He would not even venture as far as Mewār, but made his headquarters at Allahabad. Akbar's mother, Hamīda Bānū Begum, and his aunt, Gulbadan Begum, interceded for the Prince and softened Akbar's resentment. The death of Akbar's other son, Prince Dāniyal, of inebriation on 19 March was also in Salīm's favour. Those of Akbar's favourites who were friendly to Salīm, such as Mīran Sadr-i Jahān, then persuaded the Prince to visit Akbar in Agra fort. The disappointed and frustrated father gradually controlled his bitterness and allowed Salīm to stay on the opposite bank of the Jamuna. The real threat to Salīm's accession came from his own son, Khusraw, born to Mān Singh's sister on 6 August 1587, who was uncompromisingly supported by his father-in-law, Mīrzā 'Aziz Koka. Akbar did not want to pass over Salīm in favour of Khusraw but saw in him a weapon to use against Salīm. In September, Akbar fell seriously ill. Court intrigues grew increasingly brisk, but the majority of the *mansabdārs* loyal to Akbar supported Prince Salīm, although his personal followers had been dispersed by the Emperor. One of them, Shaikh Farīd Bukhārī, found Akbar breathing his last and marched out to Agra fort to congratulate Prince Salīm on his accession. He neither imposed any conditions nor sought any pledges from him, and Prince Salīm came to his father's deathbed escorted by Farīd's supporters. The dying Emperor placed his turban on his son's head and girded him with his own dagger. Akbar died on 16 October 1605. The conspiracy to set Salīm aside petered out.

Akbar's leadership ensured the loyalty to the Mughal throne of the heterogeneous religious and racial groups of the country and awakened them to the importance of coexistence, toleration, and co-operation. Although the separatist tendencies of the castes, sects, and groups could not be completely eradicated, the flexible framework of Akbar's institutions could, with a little thoughtfulness and imagination, accommodate them. He was the greatest king that India ever produced.

JAHĀNGĪR

Prince Salīm ascended the Mughal throne on 24 October 1605. He assumed the title of Jahāngīr (World-Conqueror). Throughout his life he adhered to Akbar's ideals of the coexistence of all religious communities. He remitted some local taxes on trade and the manufacture of goods. He also forbade the killing of animals for

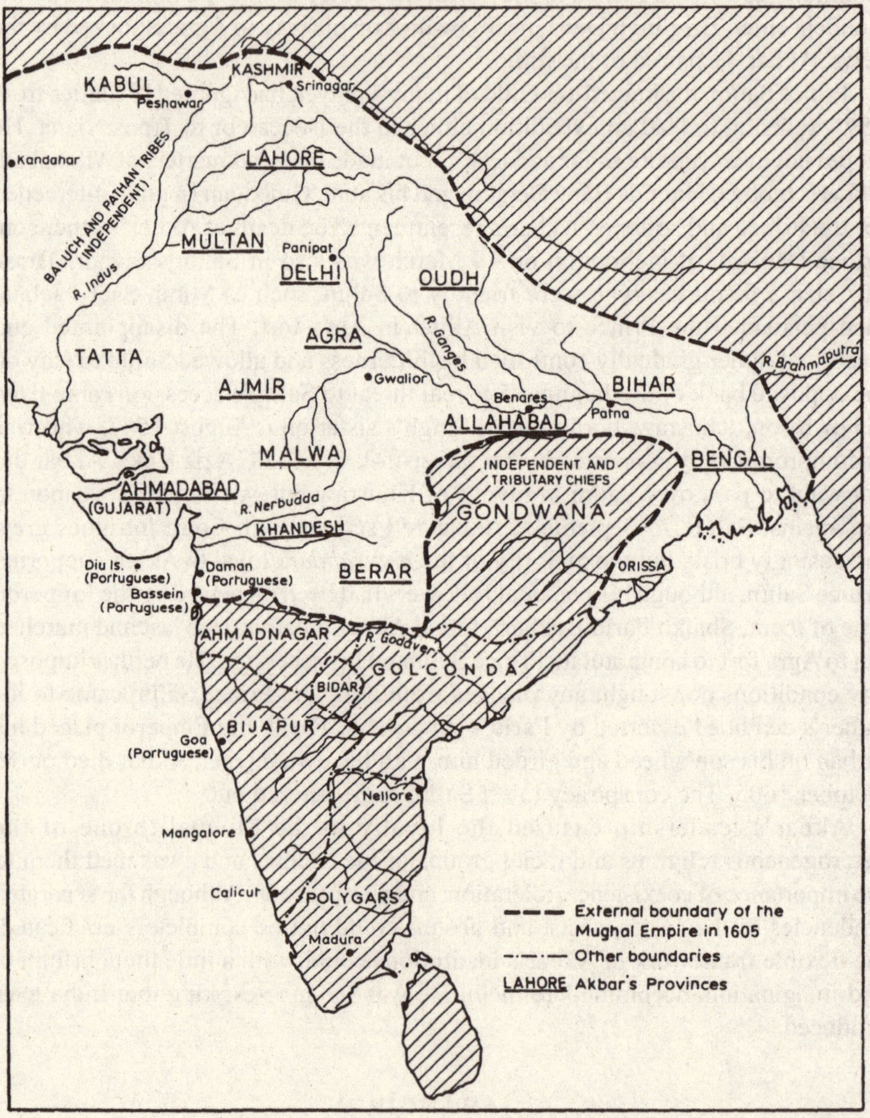

The Mughal Empire at the death of Akbar (1605)

food on Thursdays and Sundays, and no slaughtering was permitted on Jahāngīr's birthday and several other days in the year.[34]

Jahāngīr promoted to higher *mansabs* those noblemen who had helped him but he did not unduly demote the grandees of his father's reign, although he suspected some of disloyalty. On 6 April 1606 Jahāngīr's son, Prince Khusraw, fled from Agra to Lahore, gathering about 12,000 supporters on the way; even some famous sūfīs and yogīs prayed for his success. Jahāngīr pursued him personally, defeating him near Lahore. Khusraw was captured while trying to escape to Kābul; he was imprisoned, and some of his leading supporters were executed. Among the Muslim sūfīs who had blessed Khusraw was Skaykh Nizām Thaneswarī, whom Jahāngīr banished to Mecca.[35] Another of Khusraw's well-wishers, Gurū Arjan, the fifth Gurū of the Sikhs, who was greatly respected by both Hindus and Muslims, was beheaded.

From Lahore, Jahāngīr visited Kābul, where he made improvements in the road system. On his way back to Agra he ordered that Khusraw be blinded in order to disqualify him permanently from gaining the throne. The operation was not a success, however, and the Prince later regained his sight. Jahāngīr did not pursue the matter. Khusraw's personal charm and vigour were impressive, and he had been more deeply imbued with Akbar's ideals than his father. Besides the support of Mān Singh and Mīrzā 'Azīz Koka, Khusraw was loved and respected by all sections of his countrymen. These factors made a reconciliation with his father and brothers impossible.

During Akbar's reign Jahāngīr had taken no interest in subduing the Mahārāna of Mewār, but now he used both military force and diplomacy in trying to secure the surrender of Mahārāna Pratāp's successor, Amar Singh. One after the other, his leading commanders nevertheless returned unsuccessful. In 1613 Jahāngīr himself marched to Ajmīr. Villages and towns were sacked and agricultural fields burnt. New military posts were established in the inaccessible hilly regions, and Chitor was blockaded. Finally Rāna Amar Singh decided to make peace. A new phase opened in Mughal-Mewār relations, bringing to an end the war which had brought immense suffering and bloodshed to both sides. Both rulers showed understanding towards each other, but Jahāngīr cannot escape the charge of unnecessarily declaring his invasion a religious war.

After Mewar, the Deccan was Jahāngīr's main concern. In 1608 he sent the Khān-i Khānān, at his own request, to subdue it. Malik Ambar, who commanded the light Marāthā horses of Ahmadnagar, pursued his guerrilla tactics with greater vigour, however, and the Mughal invasions were repeatedly beaten back. The Mughals lost Ahmadnagar, which until then had been successfully defended. In Jahāngīr's reign the Deccan wars yielded no substantial gains, and the Mughals were unable to advance beyond northern Deccan.

In May 1611 Jahāngīr married Mihru'n-Nisā', the widow of Sher Afgan, who was killed fighting the governor of Bengal. After her marriage Mihru'n-Nisā' was given the title Nūr Mahal (Light of the Palace) and, later, Nūr Jahān (Light of the World). Although thirty-four years old, her beauty, charm, intelligence, and creative ability soon made her dominate her husband. Nūr Jahān's mother was an equally talented lady, while her father, I'timādu'd-Dawla, had been appointed joint-*dīwān* long before the wedding. Although his son Muhammad Sharīf's intrigues to free Khusraw from prison had caused I'timādu'd-Dawla considerable embarrassment, his position was not affected. After his daughter's marriage to the Emperor, his talents found recognition. His *mansab* was increased, and he was promoted as *wazīr.* His death in January 1622 was mourned as a serious loss by the Emperor.

Nūr Jahān also had an elder brother, Mīrzā Abu'l-Hasan. He was given the title I'tiqād Khān and later Āsaf Khān and was appointed Master of the Household. Both he and his father minutely controlled financial transactions and were far-sighted counsellors. In April 1612 Āsaf Khān's daughter, Arjumand Bānū Begum (later entitled Mumtāz Mahal), married Jahāngīr's third son, Prince Khurram, firmly linking Nūr Jahān's family with the Mughal household.

Nūr Jahān dictated orders and issued *farmāns.* Coins were even struck in her name, but it was not until1622 that Jahāngīr's rapidly declining health reduced him to a figure-head and made Nūr Jahān ruler in all but name.

Prince Khusraw died at Burhānpūr in August 1621 while in the custody of Prince Khurram. The official cause of death was colic, but it was generally believed that he had been strangled. Their youngest brother, Shahryār, was incompetent, although his betrothal to Ladīlī Begum, Nūr Jahān's daughter by Sher Afgan, made him the real contender to the throne. Even the news of the Irānian invasion of Qandahār did not relegate the palace intrigues to the background. Khurram, who was given the command to repel the Iranīs, urged the Emperor to grant him full control over the Panjāb. The imperial interest could be served only by invading Qandahār immediately, thus giving the Irānians no time to consolidate their recent gains there, but Khurram procrastinated. Jahāngīr was convinced that the Prince's 'brain had gone wrong' and that he was 'unworthy of all favours and cherishing'[36] he had given him. Shahryār was now elevated. His *mansab* was raised to 12,000 *zāt*, and 8,000 *sawār* (see p. 144) and some of Khurram's *jagirs* in the north were transferred to him, while Khurram was ordered to choose *jagirs* of equivalent value in the south. Shahryār was then commissioned to lead the campaign against Qandahār, which the Shāh had taken after a siege of forty-five days in 1622. Khurram sent his clever *dīwān*, Afzal Khān, to convince the Emperor of his innocence, but to no avail. Finding no way out of the impasse, Khurram rebelled and marched towards Agra. He even wrote to the Shāh of Irān requesting support. Āsaf Khān was concerned to promote Khurram's interests, and Nūr Jahān had no alternative but to seek the support of Mahābat Khān, the governor of Kābul. Although he openly condemned Jahāngīr for abandoning his independent judgement, Mahābāt Khān could not afford to miss this opportunity to increase his power. He marched to Delhi, reaching it in February 1623. Khurram did not submit, however, and the civil war lasted more than three years at great cost in money and life to both sides. Jahāngīr's grief for the loss of Qandahār and the toll of the civil war was indescribable. Khurram ultimately surrendered, having misjudged the devotion of the Mughal generals to Jahāngīr and Nūr Jahān.

The combined strength of Jahāngīr's second son, Parvīz, and Mahābāt Khān, who had exhibited considerable perseverance in crushing Khurram's rebellion, now posed a threat to Nūr Jahān and her brother, Āsaf Khān. Consequently Mahābāt was transferred to Bengal as governor, and Parvīz was ordered to stay at Burhānpūr. Jahāngīr's loyal Afghān general, Khān-i Jahān Lodī, was appointed Prince Parvīz's *wakīl* or regent. Parviz and Mahābat reluctantly submitted to the imperial orders. A second royal mandate ordered Mahābat Khān to send the elephants he had obtained during the civil war to court and to furnish an account of the large sums forfeited to the government from the dismissal of disloyal *jāgīrdārs* and *zamīndārs*. Mahābat Khān realized that ruin stared him in the face. He planned his actions coolly and cautiously. He first sent the elephants to court and then repaired there himself with 4,000 Rājpūts and 2,000 Mughals under his standard. By then the Emperor had reached Lahore from Kashmīr and was moving towards Kābul. He was camped on the bank of the Jhelam when Mahābat Khān arrived. The insults heaped upon Mahābat Khān and his son-in-law forced him to save his life and honour by militant measures. In March 1625, when the imperial cortège had crossed to the other side of the Jhelam leaving the Emperor behind, Mahābat Khān took control of the Emperor and his camp by a *coup de main.* He forgot, however, to seize Nūr Jahān, who crossed the bridge in disguise accompanied by a eunuch. She summoned Asaf Khān and the nobles and upbraided them for their negligence. They attempted to re-cross the river and free the Emperor, but the ford they selected was impassable. Āsaf Khān then fled to Attock, and the other generals took to their heels. Nūr Jahān thereupon surrendered to Mahābat Khān, who allowed her to live with the Emperor. Mahābat Khān now assumed control of the government. Initially Āsaf Khān resisted him from Attock but he too ultimately surrendered.

No real threat to Mahābat's dominance was left, but his principal objective had always been to undermine the influence of Nūr Jahān and her supporters, not to usurp the throne. Nūr Jahān, for her part, now began to foment dissatisfaction against Mahābat, while lulling him into the belief that she had no ambition to rule. Jahāngīr, under her direction, also pretended to be grateful to Mahabat Khān for freeing him from Nūr Jahān and Āsaf Khān. Towards the end of August 1626 the imperial cortège left for Kābul, and at the same river bank where six months earlier he had lost it the Emperor regained his freedom by trickery.[37] He persuaded Mahābat Khān to let him review his troops and then assumed command of them. Mahābat Khān fled to Thatta. Asaf Khān was made *wakīl*, and Nūr Jahān's supporters regained control of the government.

Mahabat Khān's success in organizing the coup was dramatic, but he could not match Nūr Jahān's tactics nor gain the Mughal nobles' confidence. Moreover Jahāngīr's rapidly declining health had diverted attention from him to his successor. In March 1627 Jahāngīr left Lahore for Kashmīr, accompanied by Nūr Jahān, Āsaf Khān, Shahryār, and other grandees. In Kashmīr his asthma took a serious turn, while Prince Shahryār contracted leprosy. The imperial cortege marched back to Lahore. The Emperor died on 29 October 1627 at Bhīmbar in Kashmīr at the age of sixty, having ruled for about twenty-two years. No important conquests were made in his reign, nor were there any remarkable administrative reforms. Although he ruthlessly persecuted any religious and Islamic sectarian leaders whom he considered a threat to his rule, his respect for the sūfī leaders and Hindu ascetics was truly sincere. He loved sūfī poetry and Vedāntic ideas. The Hindu theory of the divine incarnation of God did not appeal to him, but he celebrated all Hindu festivals with great enthusiasm. Sir Thomas Roe, the ambassador of James I at Jahāngīr's court, wrote to Prince Charles (afterwards Charles I): 'His religione is of his owne invention; for he envyes Mahomett, and wisely sees noe reason why hee should not bee as great a prophet as hee'.[38] Jahāngir aroused more hopes in the Jesuit priests that he would accept baptism than did Akbar. In his *Tuzuk*, Jahāngīr described his drinking bouts without inhibition but he did not suggest that his subjects should imitate him. His *Tuzuk* in Persian does not match Bābur's for frankness and expression, but it is nevertheless informative and reflects the author's deep appreciation of nature as well as his inherent inquisitiveness.

SHĀHJAHĀN

Jahāngīr's death made the struggle for the throne imminent. Nūr Jahān immediately alerted Shahryār, who was undergoing medical treatment, to prepare for war and she tried to arrest Āsaf Khān. He was too astute to fall into her hands and instantly sent messengers to Prince Khurram, urging him to come to Agra post-haste. Then, realizing that Khurram could not be crowned *in absentia*, Āsaf Khān played for time by proclaiming one of Jahāngīr's favourites, Khusraw's son Dāwar Bakhsh, king. The Emperor's dead body was sent from Bhīmbar to Lahore for burial in the Dilkushā garden of Shāhdara. Shahryār proclaimed himself king in Lahore and hurriedly collected an army, but Āsaf Khān easily defeated him, imprisoning him and Dāniyāl's two sons.

Khurram marched quickly from the Deccan as virtual ruler, appointing his own governors and commanders on the way. Before he reached Agra, Dāwar Bakhsh, his brother Shahryār, and Dāniyāl's two sons were beheaded. Parvīz had already died of intemperance at the end of October 1626. On 2 January 1628 near Agra, Khurram proclaimed himself emperor as Shāhjahān. Āsaf Khān was rewarded with the highest *mansab* in the Mughal military-cum-civil hierarchy and the promotion of Mahābat Khān was just as spectacular. Other supporters were also rewarded. Āsaf Khān's arrival on 26 February 1628 at Agra with Khurram's sons, the Princes Dārā, Shujā', and Aurangzīb, whom he had taken from Nūr Jahān's custody, made the imperial pageantry more colourful. The happiness of the parents was indescribable. Āsaf Khān was confirmed as *wakīl.* Nūr Jahān was awarded a pension of two lacs of rupees and retired to Lahore, where she died in 1655. She was buried near her husband's tomb.

The cold-blooded murder of all possible contenders for the throne had removed any threat from the imperial family to Shāhjahān's rule. Shāhjahān could not trust Jahāngīr's favourite, Khān-i Jahān Lodī, however, who had obtained rapid promotion under Jahāngīr and had been appointed governor of the Deccan to crush his own rebellion against the Emperor. Once Shāhjahān's rule was firmly established, Khān-i Jahān apologized to the Emperor and sent him a string of costly pearls. Initially he was made governor of Berār and Khāndesh but was soon transferred to Mālwa. He was then recalled to court and ordered to disband his forces. Finding total ruin imminent, he fled the court in October 1629 and, pursued by the relentless imperialist forces, took refuge with Murtazā Nizām Shāh of Ahmadnagar, with whom he had established friendly relations.

Shāhjahān took the field in person, leaving Agra on 3 December 1629 for Burhānpūr. A terrible famine was raging in Daulatābad, and when the Mughals invaded Ahmadnagar from different directions Murtazā was convinced of the precariousness of his position. The differences between Khān-i Jahān and Murtazā began to mount, forcing the host to move to north of the Narbada in November 1630, where the Bundelas also refused to support him. Khān-i Jahān was forced to disperse his Afghān followers, retaining only a handful for personal safety. In February 1631 he fell fighting near Bānda in modern Uttar Pradesh. His head was sent to the Emperor at Daulatabad.[39]

For sixteen months Khān-i Jahān had fought resolutely, but his defeat in the face of the vast Mughal resources was·a foregone conclusion. His supporters had dreamed of reviving Afghān rule, but Khān-i Jahān was more realistic in assessing his own strength. He could have survived longer in the Afghān tribal regions beyond Peshawar, but life as a high-ranking Mughal *mansabdār* had made him unsuited to guerrilla warfare.

Shāhjahān's war against the Bundelas was endemic. Bundelkhand, lying on the route from Agra to the Deccan, had never been peaceful; but during Jahāngīr's reign Bīr Singh Deva Bundela had become the Emperor's favourite by assassinating Abu'l-Fazl. Despite regular promotions, Bīr Singh was notorious for encroaching on both his Hindu and his Mughal neighbours' territories. After his death in 1627 his son Jujhār succeeded him. Jujhār also had a son, Vikramājit, who was greedy and cruel. While Jujhār was at Shāhjahān's court congratulating him on his accession, many reports castigating Vikramājit were received. The Emperor instituted inquiries into the administration of Bundelkhand. Although Jujhār Singh was allowed to hold a *mansab* of 4,000 *zāt* and 4,000 *sāwar* by the Emperor, he was alarmed and fled. Shāhjahān immediately ordered a massive build-up of Mughal forces. His generals besieged the whole state, and the Emperor himself moved to Gwālior, ostensibly on a hunting expedition but in reality to supervise military operations. Finding no way out of the impasse, Jujhār surrendered. A heavy fine was imposed on him, but he was confirmed in his original rank and ordered to serve in the Deccan with his own contingents. His subsequent service there earned him promotion to the rank of 5,000, but when he returned to his capital of Orcha his lawlessness revived. He arbitrarily killed the Gond chief of Chaurāgarh and seized his capital. The chief's son appealed to the Emperor, who decided to chastise Jujhār for aggrandizing himself at the expense of an imperial protectorate. Jujhār was ordered to surrender the conquered territories and stolen treasure. Before the royal orders were issued, Jujhār rebelled and recalled his son from the Deccan. The Emperor ordered Aurangzīb to attack Bundelkhand from three sides. In March 1634 Orcha was seized and a Bundela raja of a different family installed there. The imperialist forces pursued Jujhār and his son relentlessly, and eventually they were murdered and their heads sent to Shāhjahān. Jujhār's bulging treasury also fell into the Emperor's hands. The massive Orcha temple built by Bīr Singh was wantonly demolished, the idols were desecrated, and a mosque was built on the site. One of Jujhār's sons and a grandson were converted to Islam. The royal Bundela ladies were forced to serve either the imperial ladies or the Muslim nobles.[40]

Shāhjahān's punitive measures were marked by a revival of pre-Akbar vindictiveness. The wave of resentment his atrocities aroused made the rule of the imperial nominee at Orcha, Devī Singh, very difficult. Then Champat Rāy, a brave Bundela chief, crowned one of Jujhār's sons, and the Bundelas rallied around his standard. The guerrilla fighters remained as elusive as ever to the Mughal columns sent to stop Bundela incursions into Mughal territories. It was only when one of Bīr Singh Deva's sons, Pāhadh Singh, was given command of the Mughal expedition that Champat surrendered and accepted a *mansab*.

There was no resistance to the Emperor's suzerainty in Little Tibet. Kooch-Bihār had been annexed to the empire during Jahāngīr's reign and remained peaceful. In Assam the raids during 1628–39 seemed to demarcate the Mughal boundaries, enabling trade and commerce gradually to develop.

In the eastern part of Bengal the Portuguese enjoyed a monopoly of the salt trade, participated in the slave trade, and forcibly converted the local population to Christianity. They also protected the Chittagong pirates and helped the King of Arakān against the Mughals. This prompted Shāhjahān to mount an invasion, by both land and river. Huglī, the Portuguese stronghold, was besieged. After about one year the Portuguese were defeated, and the Christian prisoners were forced to embrace Islam.[41]

The north-west frontier tribes were also a source of trouble. The Roshanā'ī leader, Ahdād, was killed in 1625–6, but his successor, 'Abdu'l Qādir, made many successful raids on the Mughal army. The constant movement of troops *en route* to Transoxiana and Qandahār, however, soon intimidated the tribes, and peace was restored in the region.

The Shāh of Irān had refused to assist Shāhjahān's rebellion against his father. After his accession diplomatic relations were maintained, although the governor of Kābul was ordered to seize any opportunity to recover Qandahār. No military action was taken, but in February 1638 'Alī Mardān Khān, the Irānian governor of Qandahār, frightened by Shāh Safi's atrocities against the proteges of his father, Shāh 'Abbās, surrendered the fort to the Mughal commander of Ghaznī. He was given a *mansab* of 6,000 and appointed governor of Kashmīr. He became an asset to the Mughal empire, both as a far-sighted administrator and as an engineer. The forces of the new Qandahār governor, Qulīj Khān, quickly reconquered territory as far as Zamīndāwar. The Mughals were unable to retain Qandahār for long and

15. Bābur supervising the layout of a garden in the *Bābur-nāma* (p. 76)

16. Jahāngīr shoots a deer *c.* 1610 (p. 98)

17. The invention of the mirror under the direction of Sikandar Zu'lqarnayn (Alexander the Great) *c.* 1590 (p. 185)

18. An attractive turkey-cock painted at Jahāngir's command, attributed to Mansur, *c.* 1612 (p. 245)

19. Abu'l-Fazl, presenting the *Akbar-Nāma* to the Emperor Akbar, painted by Govardhan in the *Akbar-Nāma* (p. 87)

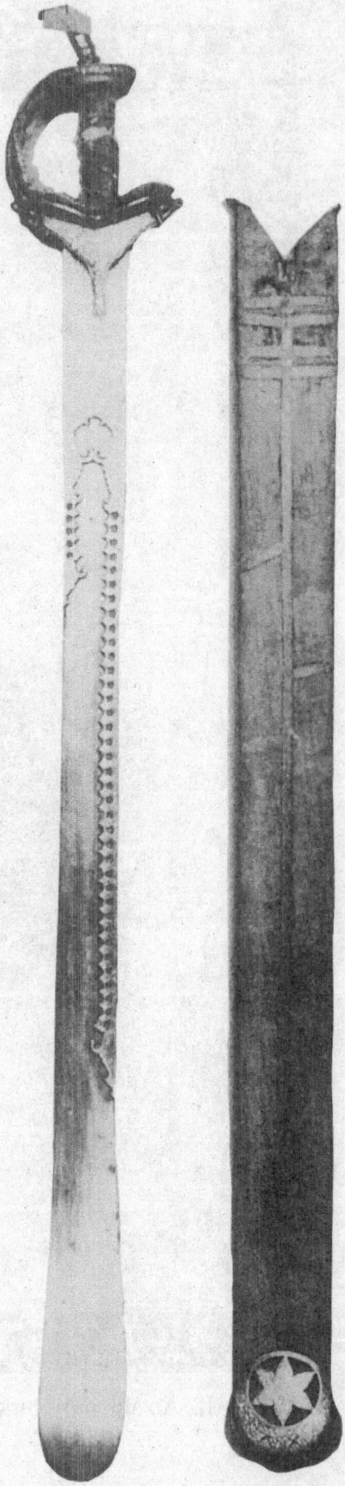

20. Sword of Sultan 'Ala 'u'd-Dīn Khaljī (p. 29)

21. Shaykh Phūl Shattārī in front of his Agra house, by Bishundās, seventeenth century (p. 214)

22. Birth of Prince Salīm in the hurriedly built house near Shaykh Salīm Chishtī's hermitage at Fathpūr-Sīkrī (p. 87)

23. The story of the unfaithful wife from *Bahāristān* of Nuru‘d-Dan ’Abdur‘ Raman Jāmī (p. 245)

24. Portrait of Shāhjahān with a halo by Bichitr (p. 245)

25. Presentation of a meal painted by Banwāri the Elder from the *Bābur-Nāma* (p. 78)

26. Portrait of Jahāngīr painted by Hāshim, below an Indian representation of John the Baptist by Nādiru'g-Zamān; on the border are Hāfiz's verses (p. 245)

had to surrender it to the Irānian army in February 1649. Both Aurangzīb and Dārā Shukoh mounted unsuccessful invasions to recover Qandahār. The Irānian artillery had grown very powerful during the wars against Turkey and remained superior to the Mughal guns. The Mughal army was trained to fight on the plains and was ignorant of siege tactics. Fighting in the hilly Qandahār region was alien to it.

The Mughal inability to fight prolonged wars in mountains and under unfavourable climatic conditions also frustrated Shāhjahān's ambitions to conquer Transoxiana. The Mughals lost more than five thousand lives during their successive invasions between 1639 and 1647. The Uzbeks suffered heavier losses and their territories were practically ruined, but they would not surrender. Shāhjahān also became more realistic and stopped dreaming of ruling over his former ancestral lands, now inhabited by hostile tribes.

Shāhjahān's imperial policies were more successful in the Deccan. Malik Ambar, the indefatigable saviour of the Nizām Shāhi kingdom of Ahmadnagar, had died in May 1626. Shāhjahān enticed some Marāthā leaders into his service. The most eminent among them was Shāhjī Bhonslē, the son-in-law of Jādhav Rāo, who had been murdered by Nizām Shāh. Malik Ambar's son, Fath Khān, whom Burhān had made his prime minister, ungratefully assassinated his patron. He subsequently placed Burhān's son, Husayn Nizām Shāh, aged ten, on the throne. The Nizām Shāhi nobles refused to co-operate with him and Fath Khān consequently surrendered to the Mughals. The Emperor would have continued fighting from his base at Burhānpūr, but the death on 7 June 1631 of his devoted wife, Mumtāz Mahal, dampened his interest in warfare. He left Burhānpūr on 6 March 1632, assigning the supreme command to Mahābat Khān, who captured Daulatabad. By this time Shāhjī was alienated from the Mughals, and his armies and those of 'Ādil Shāh of Bījāpūr fearlessly ravaged the imperial territories. Murtazā Nizām Shāh III was raised to the Ahmadnagar throne in place of Husayn Nizām Shāh, and Fath Khān's treaty with the Mughals was thrown overboard.

Mahābat Khān died of a fistula in October 1634. In February 1636 Shāhjahān again arrived in Daulatabad. He dispatched one division of his army to capture the Nizām Shāhi forts in the north-west and another to crush Shāhjī. A third division was ordered to invade Bījāpūr, and a fourth to prevent Qutb Shāh of Golkonda from helping Ahmadnagar and Bījāpūr. The Ahmadnagar kingdom was unable to resist the Mughal onslaught and lost its independence. Both Bījāpūr and Golkonda signed a treaty with the Emperor. Bījāpūr was given Konkan and some other districts of Ahmadnagar. 'Abdu'llāh Qutb Shāh of Golkonda agreed to accept the orthodox Sunnī form of the *khutba*[42] and to pay tribute to Shāhjahān.

Shāhjī was now chased by the Mughal and Bījāpūr armies from fort to fort in turn and surrendered several important strongholds. Khāndesh, Berār, Telingāna, and Daulatābād were made into four Mughal provinces. The. sixty-four hill-forts of the Deccan remained the principal centres of Mughal strength in the south.

The first viceroy, Aurangzīb, controlled all four provinces from July 1636 to June 1644. Six viceroys succeeded him, each working for a short period only. In 1652 Aurangzīb, after his dismissal from the Qandāhar expedition, was appointed viceroy of the Deccan for the second time. He made Khirkī, founded by Malik Ambar, the capital of the Mughal Deccan and named it Aurangābad. The land revenue collected was, however, insufficient to maintain the huge army necessary to control the hilly terrain. The *khālisa* revenue was reserved for expenditure at the Emperor's discretion, and the tribute paid by the rulers of Golkonda and Deogarh was not enough to balance the expenditure. Both the *mansabdārs* and the viceroy clamoured for *jāgīrs* in the fertile north in order to fulfil their obligations. The Emperor allowed the Prince to exchange his own unproductive jāgīr for more fertile ones in *mansabdār* lands, but this was no solution. The financial bickering between father and son forms a large part of Aurangzīb's correspondence known as the *Ādāb-i 'Alāmgīrī.* Murshid Qulī Khān, Aurangzīb's *dīwān* in Bālāghāt (excluding Khāndesh and Pā'īnghāt) and from 1656 onwards in the whole of the Deccan, came to the rescue by introducing Todar Mal's reforms into the Deccan. He appointed a hierarchy of village officials to improve cultivation and revenue realization. Aurangzīb also improved military efficiency and streamlined the civil administration.

Dārā's supporters, however, did not allow Shāhjahān to appreciate Aurangzīb's problems and misrepresented the steps he took to improve the administration. They ridiculed Aurangzīb's recommendations; even his minor requests were rejected. He was humiliated on insignificant issues and taken to task for acts which he never committed. Aurangzīb's persistent demands that the envoys at Bījāpūr and Golkonda should take their orders from him and that the imperial correspondence with them should be channelled through him were granted only at the close of his service and then with reservations. Aurangzīb was nevertheless keen to annex Golkonda in order to seize its fabulous wealth. The late payments of tributes and the varying exchange value of the Qutbshāhī gold coins gave him an excuse. He also took the Sultan to task for not obtaining his overlord's permission before capturing the former Vijayanagara territory of Karnātaka.

Karnātaka was conquered by 'Abdu'llāh Qutb Shāh's prime minister, Mīr Jumla, a Shī'ī adventurer from Isfahān, who was unmatched in both martial and administrative ability. Mīr Jumla's conquests in Karnātaka made him ruler of a kingdom yielding an annual revenue of 4 million rupees. His cavalry and artillery were the strongest in the region. He already possessed twenty diamond mines and he channelled the rewards from his conquests into personal commercial gains; he was not prepared to part with Karnātaka. Mīr Jumla visited Golkonda reluctantly but quickly returned to his capital Gandikota, in Karnātaka, determined never to return. From Karnātaka he sent envoys offering his services both to Bījāpūr and to Irān. Aurangzīb could not miss this opportunity to profit from Mīr Jumla's wealth and vast administrative experience. Shāhjahān promised Mīr Jumla protection, but he remained irresolute. Intrigues with three courts could not remain secret. Both the Deccan courts decided to fight Mīr Jumla when they learned of his negotiations.

The drunkenness and insolence of Mīr Jumla's son, Muhammad Amīn, while at the Qutb Shāhī court gave the Sultan a pretext to cast him and his family into prison and attach their property. Shāhjahān had appointed Mīr Jumla and

Muhammad Amīn as Mughal *mansabdārs*, however, and he wrote to Qutb Shāh ordering him to release them. The Emperor ordered Aurangzīb to seize Golkonda if the Sultan disobeyed him. Without giving Qutb Shāh time to comply, Aurangzīb ordered his son, Prince Muhammad Sultan, to invade Golkonda. He himself moved with an army to Daulatabad in order to prevent 'Adil Shāh's army from assisting Golkonda. On receipt of the Emperor's letter, Qutb Shāh sent Muhammad Amin and his family to Aurangzīb, but Muhammad Sultan remained at war. Qutb Shāh fled on 22 January 1556 from Hyderābād to Golkonda in order to save himself from total destruction. Next day the invaders entered Hyderābād, which they ransacked for two days. Qutb Shāh's entreaties and his abject obedience to the imperial command were of no avail. On 6 February Aurangzīb himself besieged Golkonda but was unable to storm the fort, because the Deccani guerrilla tactics blunted the Mughal aggression. Aurangzīb was determined to annihilate the Qutb Shāhi state in order to seize its wealth and earn religious merit for destroying a Shī'ī kingdom. Shāhjahān, however, was not prepared to take extreme measures, and Dārā Shukoh, who had been bribed by the Golkonda envoy, secured peace for them on the payment of an indemnity. Aurangzīb, considering the imperial decision fatuous, kept Shāhjahān's letter secret, until humiliating terms were accepted by Qutb Shāh.[43] On 20 March Mīr Jumla reached Aurangzīb's camp at Golkonda and gave the viceroy many valuable presents. He was immediately called to Delhi, where he again produced gifts worth several lakhs, including a large diamond. He was given a *mansab* of 6,000 and made *dīwān* in place of the lately deceased Sa'du'llāh Khān.

Aurangzīb's appropriation of the Golkonda booty increased the wrangling between him and the Emperor. The Viceroy and his officers were accused of amassing enormous wealth from the Hyderābād plunder and private gifts from Qutb Shāh. Aurangzīb complained that the war had bankrupted his treasury, that his soldier's pay was six months in arrears, and that no share of the Golkonda indemnity had been paid to him. Qutb Shāh now arranged through Dārā Shukoh to retain Karnātaka, but Aurangzīb intrigued with Mīr Jumla to prevent this. Mir Jumla had already agreed to serve Aurangzīb's interest at the imperial court, where his wealth dazzled the Emperor's eyes. Naturally he became the mouthpiece for Aurangzīb's aggressive policy, and Dārā was unable to implement his peace proposals despite his influence over the Emperor. The Emperor subsequently decided to retain Karnātaka in his own hands.

Frustrated in his aggression against Golkonda, Aurangzīb obtained an excuse to invade Bījāpūr when Muhammad 'Adil Shāh (1627–56) died. Under Muhammad 'Ādil Shāh the Bījāpūr kingdom had expanded tremendously. He was also partially successful in his invasion of the Portuguese territories of Goa and Salsette. The Sultan had lived in peace with the Emperor ever since his treaty with Shāhjahān. After his death, however, Aurangzīb refused to recognize 'Ālī 'Ādil Shāh II (1656–72), a youth of eighteen, as his successor. Instead he massed his troops at Bījāpūr, awaiting the Emperor's orders to invade the kingdom, on the plea that the new ruler was an impostor. In November 1656 Shāhjahān gave Aurangzīb a free hand against Bījāpūr. The unprovoked war violated the solemn peace agreement signed by Shāhjahān in 1636. Aurangzīb conquered Bīdar and Kalyānī, which made the fall of Bījāpūr imminent. Dārā, however, came to Bījāpūr's rescue and succeeded in persuading the Emperor to stop all further aggression against it. Besides the payment of an indemnity of 15 million rupees, Bījāpūr agreed to cede Kalyānī, Bīdar, and the fort of Parenda with its dependencies. Mīr Jumla was ordered by the Emperor to take possession of the newly ceded forts and then to return to the imperial court.[44]

While Aurangzīb was preparing to invade Bījāpūr, Shāhjī Bhonsle's son, Shivājī, seized his father's western *jāgīrs* and began capturing the Bījāpūr hill-forts. He urged Aurangzīb to allow him to seize the 'Adil Shāhi Konkan in order to gain his cooperation. Aurangzīb gave a non-committal reply. Profiting by Aurangzīb's preoccupation with Bījāpūr, Shivājī raided Junnār in south-west Mughal territory. Panic spread as far as Ahmadnagar. Aurangzīb ordered the devastation of Pūna and Chākan and ravaged other areas of Shivājī's domains, having first made sure that the imperial territory was protected against any sudden attack by the Marāthā guerrillas. After the submission of Bījāpūr, Shivājī also surrendered, asking forgiveness for his raids. Aurangzīb was still not mollified, but Shāhjahān's sudden attack of strangury in September 1657 plunged the empire into consternation.

The Emperor was more than sixty-five and had ruled with great pomp for more than thirty years. His four sons – Murād Bakhsh (b.1624), Aurangzīb (b. 1618), Shujā' (b. 1616), and Dārā Shukoh (b. 1615) – were now all mature men. The Emperor doted on Dārā and had made him viceroy of rich provinces. After he had been ill for a week Shāhjahān nominated Dārā as his successor. Susceptible to flattery and sycophancy, Dārā was devoid of Aurangzīb's shrewdness. Shāh Shujā', who had been governor of Bengal, had grown indolent, while Murād, governor of Mālwa and Gujarāt, was brave but pleasure-loving. Aurangzīb possessed a calculating mind, had developed initiative and tenacity as a result of his experience, and was a good judge of character. Of their sisters, Jahān Ārā Begum (b. 1614), called Begum Sāhiba, was Dārā's partisan, Raushan Āra (b. 1624) supported Aurangzīb, and Gawhar Āra (b. 1631) acted as a spy for Murād. In 1642 Shāh Shujā' and Aurangzīb had made a firm friendly alliance. Shujā' betrothed his daughter to Sultan Muhammad, Aurangzīb's son, and Aurangāb promised his daughter to Shujā's son. Murād also became friendly with Aurangzīb. On hearing of Shāhjahān's illness, their clandestine correspondence became more frequent, and a cipher was devised to transmit secret information.

As the Emperor's deputy, Dārā tried to stop the alarming rumours from spreading, but panic mounted.

Shāhjahān had recovered by the middle of November 1657 but the Princes refused to believe the news. Even letters from Shāhjahān and Jahān Ārā were of no avail. Then the Princes raised the battle-cry of liberating Shāhjahān from Dārā's vicious control. Early in December, Murād declared himself king, and Shāh Shujā' proclaimed his independence in his capital Rājmahal in Bengal. Shāh Shujā' reached Banāras by forced marches in January 1658. Dārā's gifted son, Sulaymān Shukoh, however, defeated him at Bahādurpūr near Banāras, and Shujā' took refuge in Patna.[45]

Aurangzīb moved cautiously. He tried to conciliate the rulers of Golkonda and Bījāpūr and wrote to Shivājī asking him not to disturb the peace there. Many disgruntled nobles at the imperial court secretly assured Aurangzīb of their support. Aurangzīb even wrote to Rāna Rāj Singh of Mewār assuring him of his determination to pursue Akbar's policy of religious harmony in order to win his favour. In the Deccan he had collected a band of able Irāni, Tūrānī, and Afghān officers. Aurangzīb had attempted to restrain Murād from acting rashly, but his brother declared himself independent and left Gujarāt.

Before he departed, Aurangzīb pledged Murād to give him one-third of any booty and conceded him the right to rule independently over the Panjāb, Kābul, Kashmīr, and Sind. Early in February 1658 Aurangzīb set off from Aurangābad. At the end of April he met Murād at Lake Dīpālpūr, near Ujjain, and the two armies camped at the village of Dharmat, on the western bank of the Gambhīra, a tributary of the Chambal.

The imperial forces under Maharājā Jaswant Singh Rāthor had already arrived at Ujjain to prevent the Princes from proceeding to Agra. Aurangzīb's men controlled the Narbada river passages so carefully, however, that no news of the Princes' movements could get through. Jaswant had expected to fight only Murād and it was not until both armies arrived near Ujjain that he learned of Aurangzīb's presence. Aurangzīb's envoy urged the Mahārāja to allow the Princes to visit his father. Jaswant was perplexed and quailed at fighting the Princes of the blood, and he was no match tactically for Aurangzīb. The Princes' refusal to return, however, forced him to give battle. He chose a narrow enclosed spot at Dharmat where he was camped. The war began on 26 April 1658. The Princes' artillery and archers soon gained the upper hand, and the Rājpūts broke and fled. Jaswant left for his home in Jodhpūr.

Shāhjahān wanted the Princes to visit him, but Dārā insisted on fighting his enemies personally, confident that he would soon rout them. He hastily collected a force of about 60,000 men, marched to Dholpār, and seized all the Chambal fords with the help of the local *zamīndārs*. The postponement of the battle until Sulaymān Shukoh joined him seemed to be in his best interest, but to his utter bewilderment Aurangzīb quickly crossed the Chambal forty miles east of Dholpur and threatened Dārā's rear. Dārā moved to Samāgarh, near Agra, to give battle. The fighting started with a heavy discharge of Dārā's artillery on 9 June. Aurangzīb retaliated cautiously at first, lulling Dārā into a false sense of superiority. Later he opened full fire and crushed Dārā's undisciplined and overconfident troops. Outmanoeuvred and despairing of victory, Dārā left his elephant and took to his horse. Aurangzīb sounded the trumpets of victory; the empty howdah of Dārā's elephant apparently proclaimed its master's death, and the imperial army fled. Dārā was left with no alternative but to hasten to Agra. More than a dozen first-ranking chiefs in Dārā's army from the Uzbek, Irānian, and Afghān tribes, as well as the Sayyids of Barba and many Rājpūts, fell fighting for their master. Aurangzīb lost only one high-ranking *mansabdār.* Although Dārā fought valiantly, his inability to direct his troops consistently destroyed his chance of victory.

Filled with shame, Dārā refused his father's request to see him. The Emperor, however, ordered the governor of Delhi to place all his resources at Dārā's disposal. Mules laden with gold coins from the Agra treasury were sent out to provide for Dārā's expenses. Aurangzīb was now camped outside Agra and rejected all Shāhjahān's invitations to visit him. Shāhjahān shut the fort gates on 16 June, fearing for his own safety. Aurangzīb found battering the fort walls too difficult so he seized another gate which opened on to the river. The supply of Jamuna water was stopped, and the fort inmates, suffering from the pangs of thirst, began to desert. Shāhjahān himself, sick of drinking the bitter well water in the fort, wrote a pathetic letter complaining to Aurangzīb:

> *Praised be the Hindus in all cases,*
> *As they ever offer water to their dead.*
> *And thou, my son, art a marvellous Musalmān,*
> *As thou causest me in life to lament for* (*lack of*) *water.*[46]

After three days Shāhjahān opened the gates, and Aurangzīb's officers took possession of the fort with its treasures and jewels. Shāhjahān was confined within the ladies' palace behind the Hall of Public Audience. Jahān Ārā's last bid to persuade Aurangzīb to agree to the partition of the kingdom, with himself as the official heir apparent, also failed. Aurangzīb refused to see his father until he had killed Dārā, whom he declared an infidel. Although himself imprisoned, Shāhjahān continued sending assistance to Dārā, thus incurring Aurangzīb's further resentment.

Aurangzīb's growing control over the administration and the desertion by many eminent nobles to his side alarmed Murād, but Aurangzīb's bribes and flattery lulled his suspicions. On 24 June they marched together from Agra towards Delhi in pursuit of Dārā. On the way Aurangzīb treacherously took Murād captive and imprisoned him in the Salīmgarh fort at Delhi. Some months later he was transferred to Gwālior fort. In the middle of December his continuing popularity and efforts to escape prompted Aurangzīb to sentence him to death. Aurangzīb then moved to Delhi, forcing Dārā to flee the Panjāb. Reaching Lahore on 14 July, Dārā recruited an army of 20,000 men. At Delhi, Aurangzīb took steps to prevent Sulaymān Shukoh from joining his father. He also resolved to formally crown himself king. The chief *qāzī* opposed this, on the ground that Shāhjahān was still alive, but Aurangzīb's favourite, Qāzī 'Abud'l-Wahhab, issued a *fatwa* enabling him to crown himself king on 1 August with the title 'Ālamgīr (Conqueror of the Universe).[47] The pursuit of Dārā was stepped up; Aurangzīb reached the river Satlaj with the main army on 25 August. Dārā abandoned Lahore for lower Sind, but the real threat to his rule came from Shujā', who was heading towards Allahabad in order to seize Agra. Aurangzīb left his commanders to harry Dārā and returned to Agra. There he dispatched a strong force under his son, Sultan Muhammad, to stop

Shuja''s onward march. On 10 January, Sultan Muhammad stood facing Shujā' near Khajwa in Allahabad. Aurangzīb also arrived, as, by forced marches, did Mīr Jumla, who had been taken captive by Aurangzīb and then released. Before the battle Jaswant Singh of Jodhpur, commanding the imperial right wing, who had made a treacherous pact with Shujā', fell on Sultan Muhammad's camp in the last night watch. He plundered it and then took off for Agra on his way to Jodhpur.

Shujā' failed to take advantage of the confusion, however, while Aurangzīb calmly stuck to his positions. At dawn he reorganized his army. Although Shujā''s battle plan was superb, he could not win the day. His army was routed, his baggage plundered, and he himself took to flight. Leaving Thatta in lower Sind, Dārā suffered great hardship in the Rann of Kacch. When he reached Ahmadābād, Shāh Nawāz Khān, the newly appointed governor of Gujarāt, joined him. They raised an army of 22,000 men and acquired an efficient artillery corps. At Jaswant Singh's invitation, Dārā set off for Ajmīr. Although Aurangzīb was furious at Jaswant's treachery, he did not wish him to join Dārā. At his instigation therefore, Raja Jai Singh, who had not shown the usual Rājpūt enthusiasm for duty when fighting Shujā' under Sulaymān Shukoh and had subsequently joined Aurangzīb, weaned Jaswant away from Dārā, promising him to have his title and *mansab* restored. Dārā was dismayed but he wisely chose to hold the pass of Deorā'ī in order to give battle, and Aurangzīb marched there to attack him. On 23 and 24 March 1659 the artillery from both sides caused considerable havoc; Dārā's guns, installed on a high position, were the more effective. Aurangzīb abandoned conventional tactics and instead launched a heavy attack on Dārā's left. He captured it, and Dārā's army turned tail. Fleeing through Gujarāt and Kacch, Dārā reached Sind. Jai Singh pursued Dārā with remarkable tenacity. Dārā reached Dadar, nine miles east of the Indian end of the Bolan Pass, on the way to the Shāh of Irān's court. There his wife died of exhaustion from the journey. Dārā lost interest in the world. He spent three days mourning her and sent her corpse with his most loyal officers to be buried near the tomb of the celebrated sūfī Miyān Mīr of Lahore. On 20 June, Dārā set off towards the Bolan Pass but was taken captive by his treacherous Afghān chief, Malik Jīwan, who handed him over to Jai Singh in the hope of obtaining a reward from Aurangzīb. Dārā, with his son and two daughters, was brought to the outskirts of Delhi on 3 September 1659. There he and his younger son, Sipihr Shukoh, were paraded in chains under the burning sun. The outbursts of public sympathy for Dārā prompted the Emperor to act quickly. The religious dignitaries gave the verdict that Dārā should be sentenced to death for stating in his *Majma'u'l-bahrayn* that Islam and Hinduism were twin brothers.[48] On 11 September both Dārā and Sipihr Shukoh were executed.

The war following Shāhjahān's illness was not a struggle between orthodoxy and heterodoxy, as many scholars suggest. The ambition of all four brothers to rule over the whole of India made a war of succession inevitable. The *mansabdārs* changed sides, not for ideological reasons but for personal reward. Dārā Shukoh, as commander of the imperial army, was served by Rājpūts more than other races. Some Rājpūts, following their martial tradition, recklessly sacrificed their lives, but others, like Raja Jai Singh, refused their support to Dārā because of personal grievances.

Murād and Shuja' were well known for their unorthodox views but they were loudest in condemning Dārā's heterodoxy and they were more full of promises to promote orthodoxy than was Aurangzīb.

Dārā's death made Aurangzīb the undisputed Emperor of Hindustan. Sulayman Shukoh marched from Allahabad to Haridvār and then took shelter with Prithvī Singh, the raja of Garhwāl. Failing to persuade the Raja to surrender Sulayman, Aurangzlb suggested to the neighbouring hill rajas that they should annex Garhwāl. Raja Jai Singh, however, weaned Prithvī's son away from Sulayman Shukoh, and in December 1660 he was surrendered to Jai Singh's son, Rām Singh. Aurangzīb sent him to Gwālior fort, where he died in May 1662 from a slow poison made from poppy seeds.

After his retreat from Khajwa, Shujā' was pursued by Prince Muhammad and Mīr Jumla as far as Bengal. Shujā''s artillery and flotilla were superior to Mīr Jumla's, and he succeeded in enticing Prince Muhammad Sultan to his side by promising to marry his daughter to him and then make him king instead of his father. Mīr Jumla's strategy of spreading out his forces in a semi-circle from Rājmahal to Mālda and his plan to attack Shuja' from an unexpected quarter, however, unnerved the latter. Prince Muhammad Sultan deserted his uncle; nevertheless Aurangzīb imprisoned him too in Gwālior fort, where he died in 1676. Moving from Rājmahal, Shujā' offered some resistance near Mālda but had to fly to Dacca. He did not receive the help he expected from the local chiefs there. On 23 May 1660 Shujā' bade farewell to Bengal, which he had ruled for twenty years, and sailed for Arakān with his family. Authentic information on their future never reached India. A Dutch report suggests that he was cut to pieces by the King of Arakān.

From his Agra prison Shāhjahān somehow managed to send letters to Dārā as long as he lived. He also wrote to his sympathizers outside the fort until Aurangzīb deprived him of writing materials. Shāhjahān nevertheless wrote often to Aurangzīb condemning his ungratefulness and irreligious behaviour and calling him a religious hypocrite. On 2 February 1666 Shāhjahān died, having been tended throughout his captivity by Jahān Ārā. His earthly remains were buried beside his dearly loved wife's grave in the Tāj Mahal.

Shāhjahān's death was deeply mourned. He was remembered as a kind ruler and a benefactor to his subjects. He strictly observed Islamic rules for prayers and fasting. Although he demolished the temples in rebel areas, he was not a bigot. The magnificence and grandeur of his court made him the greatest potentate of his time.

AURANGZĪB

Aurangzīb held his second coronation on 16 June 1659. The festivities lasted for two and a half months in the traditional extravagant manner. Initially Aurangzīb introduced few administrative changes. The senior Hindu officers in the finance ministry were retained and even promoted, although in Banāras and some other places the brāhmans were harassed, and Hindu temples were demolished by orthodox mobs. Aurangzīb stopped this desecration, but, in accordance with Islamic *sharī'a* rules no new temples could be erected. A high-powered *mansabdār* was appointed as censor of morals (*muhtasib*) to prevent drinking and to make Muslim life conform to Qur'ānic laws. The celebration of the Irānian Naw Rūz festival, which falls on the day the sun enters Aries, was banned. The *kalima*, or the confession of faith, was no longer stamped on coins, to prevent the holy words from being defiled by unbelievers or heretics.[49] These reforms in no way undermined Hindu political and economic interests.

Aurangzīb sent rich gifts to the holy men of Mecca and Medina. The Sherif of Mecca also received presents to distribute among the pious and needy, but to Aurangzīb's disappointment the funds were misused. Subhān Qulī, the Uzbek ruler of Balkh, was the first to recognize Aurangzīb as Emperor in 1658. The grand embassy sent by the Shāh of Irān was warmly received in 1660 and returned loaded with gifts. By the time the Mughal envoy, Tarbiyat Khān, reached Irān, however, Aurangzīb's atrocities against his brothers and father and his hostility to the Deccan sultans were known to the Shāh. He sent a stern reply, taunting Aurangzīb for his presumptuous title World-Conqueror when he could not control *zamīndārs* like Shivājī.

Shāhjahān had unsuccessfully tried to build up a foreign Sunnī block consisting of the Ottomans and Uzbeks to counter Shī'ī Irān and had exchanged ambassadors with the Ottoman Sultan Murād IV (1623–40). In Aurangzīb's reign no ambassadors were exchanged, although the Emperor sympathized with the Ottomans over their European defeats. After the Ottoman defeat at Vienna in 1683 Sulaymān II (1687–91) sent an ambassador to Aurangzīb to seek his help. The Emperor was too deeply involved in the Deccan wars to commit himself, and the disappointed Sultan excluded Aurangzīb's cold reply from the Ottoman records.

The first ten years of Aurangzīb's rule were militarily and politically a great success. Minor uprisings were instantly crushed, and in 1660 Rāo Karan, the Bīkānīr chieftain, submitted. Two years later the governor of Bihār annexed rocky and barren Pālāmaū in the southern limits of his province. The rebel Champat Bundela, relentlessly chased by the loyal Bundela chief Subh Karan, stabbed himself to death in October 1661. Chatrasāl, his son, remained loyal for some years but he also, like Shivājī, later became the champion of freedom in Bundelkhand.

By the end of 1661 Mīr Jumla, who was pursuing Shuja', had seized Kooch-Bihār and marched up the Brahmaputra, conquering fort after fort and establishing military outposts at strategic places. Mīr Jumla entered Garhgāon (near modern Gauhātī), the Ahom capital, at the end of March 1662. The Ahom army fled to the jungle but repeatedly tried to recapture it. Their continual depredations combined with pestilence and famine exacted a heavy toll on the Mughals. Finally, prostrated by illness, Mīr Jumla made peace with the Ahom Raja, collecting a heavy war indemnity. On 11 April 1663 Mīr Jumla died on his way to Dacca. His death deprived Aurangzīb of a wise counsellor and an indefatigable general.

The Mughal gains in the region were not permanent, however, and in 1667 they lost Garhgāon. The Arakan pirates, both Māg and Portuguese, constantly came over the water and plundered Bengal. They took both Hindus and Muslims as slaves and subjected them to harsh treatment. Not until Shayasta Khān became governor of Bengal in 1664 was an effective Bengal flotilla built and the Portuguese were defeated. Chittagong was subsequently taken from the Arakanese to the great satisfaction of the Bengalis. In 1665 the Buddhist ruler of Ladākh acknowledged the Emperor's suzerainty, under pressure from the governor of Kashmir.

Aurangzīb's early victories and triumphs pale into insignificance before later tales of woe and distress. The atrocities committed by 'Abdu'n-Nabī, the *fawjdār* of Mathura, aroused the Jāts around Mathura and Agra to rise against him. Gokula, a *zamīndār*, became the peasants' leader and killed 'Abdu'n-Nabi. Two successive *fawjdārs* failed to quell the uprising, and in December 1669 the Emperor himself leisurely marched to the area in order to strike terror into the rebels' hearts. He captured Gokula and 7,000 peasants. Gokula's limbs were hacked off in Agra police station in January 1670, and his son and daughter were converted to Islam. The region calmed down temporarily.

The Satanāmi revolt of 1672 has been given an unrealistic communal colour. The Satanāmis were a sect of Hindu devotees who maintained themselves by agriculture. They lived mostly around Narnōl, some seventy-five miles south-west of Delhi. The crisis was sparked off by a minor dispute between a Satanāmi peasant and a foot-soldier. At the same time an old prophetess appeared among them, claiming to raise invisible armies by her spells. The victorious Satanāmis plundered Narnōl, demolished mosques, and established an independent government. In response the Emperor ordered his camp to be pitched outside Delhi. He wrote charms and amulets with his own hand and ordered them to be fixed to the royal standard. The imperial army meanwhile crushed the rebellion.

Jahāngīr's treatment of their fifth Gurū had turned the Sikhs into inveterate enemies of the Mughals. Before his execution the Gurū had already established a Sikh treasury at Amritsar where tithes and offerings from the Sikhs between Kābul and Dacca were collected. Gurū Arjan's son and successor, the sixth Gurū Hargobind (1595–1644), had begun to train his disciples in self-defence, so Jahāngīr hastily imprisoned him in Gwālior fort for non-payment of his father's fines. After his release Hargobind spent his time strengthening his military resources. During Shāhjahān's reign, the Gurū came into conflict with the Emperor and fought valiantly against the Mughal army. He was forced to take refuge in Kartārpūr in the Jālandhar *doāb*, where he inflicted heavy losses on the imperial army sent to kill him. From thence he retired to Kiratpūr in the Kashmīrī hills and joined the rebel *zamīndārs.*[50] Before his death in 1644, many important Sikh centres had been established in the Panjāb. As well as artisans and merchants, militant Jāts joined the movement in large numbers.

The seventh Gurū, Har Rāy (1644–61), and Dārā Shukoh were friends. When Dārā fled from Delhi, the Gurū met him in the Panjāb. Aurangzīb summoned the Gurū to Delhi to explain the nature of this relationship. Har Rāy sent his elder son, Rāma Rāy, instead, and his manner and conduct soon won him Mughal friendship. He was given land in the Siawālik hills later known as Dehradun. After Har Rāy's death in 1661, Rāma Rāy's younger brother, Harī Krishna, who was accepted as their Gurū by the Sikhs, was summoned to Delhi to settle the question of succession, but three years later he died. To avoid outright confrontation with Rāma Rāy, who enjoyed the Emperor's support, the ninth Gurū Tegh Bahādur left for eastern India and taught Sikhism as far east as Assam. He later returned to the Panjāb, but his preachings exasperated the Mughals, who considered Rāma Rāy the Sikh leader. In November 1675, while the Emperor was at Hasan Abdal, Tegh Bahādur was beheaded on the orders of the Qāzī of Delhi. The Sikhs were angered, and two brickbats were thrown at Aurangzīb while he was returning from the Lahore Jāmi' mosque at the end of October 1676. The accused were handed over to the police, but no reprisal was made against the community.

Among the Afghāns, the Yusufza'i, Āfridi, and Khatak tribes rose against Aurangzīb one after the other. The wars against the Khatak tribe, which dominated the Peshāwar, Kohāt, and Bannū regions, were prolonged. Their leaders, Khushhāl Khān, was a *mansabdār* who had been imprisoned in Delhi during the early years of Aurangzīb's reign and later in Ranthambhor for organizing a freedom struggle in his tribe. In 1666 he was released and sent with the Mughal army to fight his traditional enemy, the Yusufza'is. He soon deserted the Mughals, however, and joined the Āfridis. Later he commanded his own guerrilla band. Khushhāl Khān revived the spirit of independence among his tribesmen through his eloquent Pashtū poetry, some of which was written during his imprisonment and condemned Aurangzīb as irreligious and anti-Islamic.[51] His poetry is still loved by the Pashtū tribesmen and it is probably the finest literature in the language.

Aurangzīb's leading generals failed to crush the Afghān uprisings, so the Emperor marched to Hasan Abdāl, between Rāwalpindi and Peshāwar. He arrived in July 1674 and stayed for a year and a half, directing military operations. Many important generals sustained severe reverses, but the Emperor's policy of setting one clan against the other, which he metaphorically defined as 'breaking two bones by knocking them together', won the day. Later Amīr Khān, as governor of Kabul from 1678 till his death in 1698, kept the tribes under control. His wife, Sahibji, noted for her tact and intelligence, was also an asset to Amir Khān's administration.[52]

Aurangzīb's most desperate crisis, however, was precipitated at the end of December 1678 by Mahārāja Jaswant Singh's death at Jamrud in the north-western tribal region. He had no heirs, but two of his pregnant queens each gave birth to a posthumous son at Lahore. One of the boys died; the other, Ajīt Singh, survived to mount the Jodhpur throne. As the paramount power, Aurangzīb escheated the Mahārāja's property upon his death and resumed the whole of Mārwār into the *khālisa.* In February 1679 the Emperor arrived in Ajmīr, ostensibly to make a pilgrimage to Khwāja Mu'īnu'd-Dīn's tomb but in reality to intimidate the Rājpūts. After his return to Delhi in April 1679, when he reimposed *jizya* despite Hindu protests, Aurangzīb brought Jodhpūr city under the imperial administration. Its temples were demolished, and the submissive Indra Singh Rāthor, the Nāgaur chieftain and a grand-nephew of Jaswant, was subsequently made Raja of Jodhpūr.

The Emperor promised to consider Ajit's claim when he came of age. The imperial office claimed that, in accordance with Mughal tradition, the *watan* could not be conferred upon ladies or servants, even though they acted as royal regents. Legally they were correct, but politically this strong adherence to rules plunged the Mughal government into chaos. A guard was placed on the house where Ajīt was staying in Delhi to prevent his servants carrying him off to Jodhpūr, but before he could be transferred to the royal palace, Durgādās, the son of one of Jaswant's ministers, kidnapped the Rānīs and Ajīt, killing the Mughal guards. Ajīt was taken to Mārwār and brought up in the lonely Abu hills.

The crisis in Mārwār offered Māharāna Raj Singh of Mewār an opportunity to realize his dreams of becoming the Māharāna Sanga of his time. He joined Jaswant's chief queen, Rāni Hādi, in pressing Ajīt's right to his father's throne. To Aurangzīb's consternation, the Rāni offered to destroy the temples in Jodhpūr and erect mosques instead, in return for Ajīt's recognition. Failing this, the Rathors of Jodhpūr preferred the resumption of Jodhpūr to the *khālisa* to the rule of Indra Singh, whom they hated bitterly.

Indra Singh failed to establish control over Mārwār and two years later he was recalled to court. In September 1679 the Emperor returned to Ajmīr and ordered his fourth son, Prince Akbar, to invade Marwar. The imperial troops advanced against Udaipur, destroying hundreds of temples. The Emperor himself visited Udaipur but, finding his presence no longer necessary, returned to Ajmīr. Prince Akbar was unable to seize any strategic Rājpūt outposts, however. Shame and fear of his father's hot temper and his brother's intrigues prompted the Prince, a youth of twenty-three, to succumb to the inducements of Mahārāna Raj Singh of Mewār and Durgādās to declare himself Emperor, thus to save the Mughal empire from the disastrous repercussions of Aurangzīb's bigoted policies. The situation was further complicated by Raj Singh's death in November 1680. Aurangzīb was appalled by the Prince's declaration of independence on 12 January 1681. Then Akbar marched upon Ajmīr. The Emperor maintained his equanimity, although his chosen troops were scattered throughout Rājasthān. He recalled his loyal generals and managed to alienate the Rājpūts from Akbar by having a counterfeit treacherous letter, addressed to Akbar, delivered to Durgādās's camp. The strategy succeeded, and the Rājpūts deserted Akbar at midnight. He escaped to Mārwār. Durgādās was soon convinced of Aurangzīb's trickery, but the opportunity for victory was lost.[53] Durgādās took Akbar under his protection and they fled to the court of Shivājī's son, Shambhājī, arriving in June 1681. Meanwhile Raj Singh's son, Jai Singh, who was devoid of his father's vigour, made peace with the Emperor. The war against the Marwar guerrillas was left to the Ajmīr governor. Aurangzīb left for the Deccan on 15 September 1681, never to return to the north.

The north Indian period of Aurangzīb's reign was marked by a gradual departure from Akbar's policy of coexistence. His early regulations were designed to offer relief to Muslims and reduce urban taxation. Customs duty on all imports was fixed in 1665 at 2½ per cent of their value in the case of Muslim traders and 5 per cent for Hindus. Two years later all customs duty for Muslims was abolished. In January 1669 the wedding of Prince A'zam to Dārā's daughter offered the Emperor a chance to show his orthodoxy by issuing innumerable puritanical ordinances. A general order to demolish temples and Hindu centres of learning was issued. The celebrated Vishvanātha temple of Banāras and the Keshava Rāī temple of Mathura, which had been presented with a stone railing by Dārā Shukoh, were reduced to ruins. This policy was implemented even in remote east Bengal, Pālāmaū, Rājasthān, and later in the Deccan. A determined effort to break Hindu *zamīndār* solidarity was initiated, and when disputes arose between them the *zamīndār* who offered to embrace Islam was favoured. Unscrupulous debtors sought to evade their debts by falsely accusing creditors of reviling the Prophet or of speaking contemptuously of Islam.

Aurangzīb's narrow legalistic approach to Akbar's administrative framework, based on toleration and broad-mindedness, made success impossible for him, even in the Deccan. Although he had been viceroy there for about ten years, in his own reign Aurangzīb failed to assess the situation realistically. The Mughal policy of penetration into the Deccan had convinced the Sultans of Bījāpūr and Golkonda, and also Shivājī, that any respite offered by the Emperor's involvement in the north would be short-lived. Shivājī meanwhile carved out an independent Marāthā state in the territories north and south of Konkan, adjoining his paternal *jāgīr* above the Ghats. Shivajl urged the Emperor to recognize his rule over the Bījāpūrī district of north Konkan, but the Emperor sent his most experienced noble, Shāyasta Khān, to crush him. Two years of ceaseless military campaigns made the Mughals master of the extreme north of Konkan, but in April 1663 Shivājī made a daring night attack on Shāyasta Khān's camp at Puna. It cost Shāyasta Khān his thumb and showed that Shivājī was still a formidable opponent. Shāyasta Khān was transferred to Bengal, but before he left, Shivājī plundered Sūrat continuously from 17 to 21 January 1664. Only the English and Dutch merchants were able to defend their factories. Prince Mu'azzam was appointed commander, but before the Mughal forces could relieve the town the Marāthās decamped with enormous booty. Jaswant Singh, who collaborated with both Shāyasta Khān and Prince Mu'azzam, was a total failure.

In October 1664 the Emperor recalled the Prince and commissioned his ablest Rājpūt general, Mīrza Raja Jai Singh, to annihilate Shivājī. Jai Singh made plans to attack from all possible directions and started fighting in the east, where he could easily threaten Bījāpūr. Marching deep into Shivājī's territory, he seized Purandar and forced Shivājī to sign a treaty in June 1665, ceding four-fifths of his territory and promising to serve the Emperor loyally. Shivājī also agreed to visit the Emperor at Agra. The prominent Mughal *mansabdārs* could not reach an understanding with Shivājī. The Mughal governors expected him to call on them as a *zamīndār*, while Shivājī expected them to treat him as undisputed ruler of the Marāthās.[54] At the imperial court the Emperor's order to stand with the *mansabdārs* behind Jaswant Singh, whom he had previously defeated, shocked him. The Mughals considered 5,000 to be a very high rank for a new entrant, but Shivājī, who had humbled both Shāyasta Khān and Jaswant Singh, expected a *mansab* of at least 7,000. The Emperor viewed the award of the *mansab* legalistically as was his wont, while Shivājī correctly related it to his political standing and prestige in the Deccan. Sensing Shivājī's reluctance to compromise, Aurangzīb placed him under house arrest, and Jai Singh's son unsuccessfully attempted to pacify him. Palace intrigue and pressure from the supporters of Shāyasta Khān and Jaswant Singh prevented Aurangzīb from resolving the misunderstandings. Before the Emperor could take further action, Shivājī escaped to the Deccan on 28 August 1666.

Jai Singh was still fighting in Bījāpūr but he was frustrated by a dearth of funds and lack of co-operation from the Muslim nobles; his Afghān colleagues openly condemned war against another Muslim state as sacrilegious. The Emperor did not understand Jai Singh's problems and recalled him. Jai Singh died on his way to court on 6 September 1667. He had won remarkable victories over Shivājī in the face of strong opposition from home. In Bījāpūr itself 'Alī' 'Ādil Shāh II (1652–72) had grown into a wise statesman and an enterprising general, who unhesitatingly crossed swords with Shivājī and his guerrillas. Only after his death was Bījāpūr plunged into civil war; even then the Mughal generals failed to penetrate it.

When he returned to the Deccan, Shivājī made peace with the new Mughal viceroy, Prince Mu'azzam. His son, Shambhājī, was given a *mansab* of 5,000 and was allowed a free hand to conquer Bījāpūr. Shivājī remained at peace with the Mughals from 1667 to 1669 while he devised laws for the Marāthā government and consolidated his power. Then, in 1670, he recovered the forts surrendered under the Purandar treaty. In the middle of October 1670 the Marāthās again attacked Sūrat and plundered it mercilessly. The English, Dutch, and French factories were spared, but the Muslim and Hindu traders were totally ruined. Not only were sixty-three lakhs of rupees lost, but trade and commerce were totally dislocated. Their conquests gave the Marāthās a safe route from Kalyāni up northern Konkan to Sūrat. In 1672 Shivajl imposed *chauth* (a levy) of four lakhs of rupees on the Mughal territories under his control, equivalent to a quarter of the Emperor's revenue from them. To Shivājī this was not blackmail but a tax on his Mughal subjects towards their country's defence. This arbitrary levy became the principal factor in the expansion of Marāthā power.

The Mughal viceroy resisted Marāthā attacks vigorously but he was unable to capture the elusive guerrilla bands. In the wake of the chaos following 'Alī 'Ādīl Shāh II's death in early December 1672, Shivājī seized Panhāla and Satāra and then burst into west Bījāpūr and Kanāra, plundering and devastating the country. Shivājī crowned himself king in his Rā'igarh fort on 17 June 1674 assuming the title Chhatrapatī (Lord of the Umbrella, or King of Kings).[55]

Two years later the new Bījāpūrī Sultan, Sikandar 'Ādil Shāh, made a treaty with Shivājī promising to pay him a heavy annual subsidy for protection against the Mughals. Shivājī also made formal peace with the Mughals, freeing himself to concentrate on his Karnātaka conquests. Early in 1677 Shivājī collected a subsidy from Abu 'l-Hasan Qutb Shāh of Golkonda to raise an army and an artillery battery.

He penetrated into Kārnataka, the Mysore plateau, and Madras, conquering Jinjī, Vellore, the adjoining districts, and some one hundred forts between 1677 and 1678. Out of the fabulous booty from that land of gold, Abu 'l-Hasan, who had borne all the expenses, received nothing. Shivājī died on 15 April 1680, leaving a vast empire covering roughly half of the Deccan.

Shivājī was a great administrator and, like his contemporaries, a despotic ruler. His central and provincial governments were based on the systems of the Deccanī sultans and Vijayanagara. *Chauth*, which was really a military tax, was already being levied in western India. An additional tax of 10 per cent, called *sardeshmukhī*, was also collected by Shivājī, as the hereditary head *deshmukh* (chief) or *sardeshmukh* of his country.

Shivājī's army drew its main supplies from neighbouring kingdoms. From July to September the troops lived in cantonments in their home territory, but from the day of Dasehra (early October) they spent eight months at war, collecting *chauth*, *sardeshmukhī* and plunder. Shivājī directed the aggression and unreliability of the Marāthā chieftains and stipend holders into fruitful channels. Neither did he neglect the navy, whose crews were recruited from among the low-caste Hindus of the Bombay coast. Shivājī was recognized as the protector of brāhmans and cows, as the architect of Hindu self-rule, and as the defender of Hindu religion and culture. Many distinguished Hindu saints blessed him and exhorted their disciples and followers to support him. The Maharashtra terrain enabled Shivājī to train his soldiers in guerrilla tactics and to encircle and annihilate his enemies.

Shivājī died without nominating a successor. An influential minister crowned his younger son, Rājarām, a boy of ten, at Rāygarh. Shivājī's elder son, Shambhājī, who had been imprisoned in Panhala fort because of his licentiousness, contested this unjust supersession. Seizing Panhāla and Rāygarh forts, he deposed Rājarām and crowned himself Marātha king on 16 January 1681.[56]

Shambhājī started his reign by sacking Burhānpūr and giving refuge to Prince Akbar. The Emperor's arrival at Aurangabad early in April 1682 frustrated his plans to fight the Mughals. Shambhājī's subsequent wars against the Siddis, descended from Ethiopian slaves, around Janjīra, his invasion of Goa in 1683–4, and minor skirmishes until 1685 gave the Emperor sufficient respite to consolidate his forces in the Deccan.

Aurangzīb decided to invade Bijapār, where the administration was deteriorating under Sikandar 'Ādil Shāh. Prince Mu'azzam did not share the Emperor's imperialistic ambitions and he and other nobles were severely reprimanded by Aurangzīb. The Emperor moved to Ahmadnagar to direct operations. Parts of Bījāpūr were annexed, and military outposts were established to facilitate the assault on Bījāpūr fort. In April 1685 the imperialists laid mines near the fort. The Emperor moved to Sholāpūr. Although provisions were scarce, Mughal reinforcements kept arriving. The defenders' numbers dwindled, and on 22 September 1686 Sikandar 'Ādil Shāh surrendered. The 'Ādil Shāhī dynasty was at an end. Bījāpūr was made the seat of the Mughal provincial governor but in a few years the city and its suburb, the fabulous Nauraspūr, were desolate.

Sikandar died in captivity in 1700, less than thirty-two years old.[57]

Now it was the turn of Abu'l-Hasan Qutb Shāh (1672–87) of Golkonda. He professed obedience to Aurangzīb but had secretly supported the Sultan of Bījāpūr. His brāhman minister, Madanna, who controlled the administration on behalf of his royal master, was pro-Marāthā. Although the Emperor used the Sultan's fraternization with Bījāpūr and the Marāthās as an excuse to annex Golkonda, his principal motive was to seize its fabulous wealth. On 28 June 1685 Aurangzīb ordered Prince Mu'azzam to march against Golkonda. Hyderābād was easily captured and the citizens mercilessly plundered. Madanna and his brother Akanna were killed by the leading Qutb Shāhi nobles, who accused them of causing Aurangzīb's invasion. At the Prince's request, the Emperor consented to pardon Abu'l-Hasan, provided he paid an enormous sum as tribute. The Emperor had no intention of honouring this agreement, however, and arriving near Golkonda at the end of January 1687, he ordered siege operations against the formidable fort. Prince Mu'azzam, who had hoped to take credit for securing Golkonda's capitulation without war, was condemned as a traitor and imprisoned with his entire family. The Turānī commanders attempted to seize the fort by an escalade but failed. Rain and famine took a heavy toll of the garrison, but the Mughal losses were appalling. At the end of June the imperialists exploded their mines; the vigilant garrison had dug a tunnel from their side leading the Mughals' trail of gunpowder back under their own camp, and a large number of Mughals were killed. Abu'l-Hasan's loyal nobles cut off supplies to Aurangzīb, but others deserted him. Famine and pestilence raged during the protracted siege. At the end of September 1687 a treacherous Afghān opened the postern gate of the fort to the Mughal army. The garrison fought bravely but was overpowered. Abu'l-Hasan was captured. The spoils taken at Golkonda amounted to nearly 70 million rupees in cash, besides masses of gold, silver, and jewels. The state revenue was 28,700,000 rupees.[58]

In February 1687 Prince Akbar left for Irān, to the Emperor's relief. Shambhājī was now sunk in debauchery and was mainly concerned with foiling the attempts of the chiefs on his own life. On 11 February 1689 he was taken captive at Sangameshwar, twenty-two miles from Ratnāgiri, by some conscientious Mughal officers. His minister Kavī-Kulash and twenty-five important commanders were also seized. They were brutally tortured and put to death. The Marāthās crowned Rājasrām as their new king at Raygarh, but the Mughals invaded it, and he fled to Jinjī. Shambhājī's family, including his son Sāhū, were captured. Aurangzīb gave Sāhū the *mansab* of 7,000 he had thoughtlessly denied his grandfather.

In seven years Aurangzīb had annihilated all his enemies. Although the Marāthā power concentrated under Rājarām at Jinjī and the consolidation of the Bījāpūr and Golkonda conquests called for serious attention, these were purely provincial problems. The prime minister, Asad Khān, urged the Emperor to move to northern India so that the world might know that nothing more remained for the Emperor to do in the south. Aurangzīb rejected the suggestion and so missed the chance to heal the wounds of the ravaged Deccan. He misjudged the strength of the

Marāthā guerrillas and mistakenly believed that he could coerce the Mughals into fighting an aggressive war indefinitely. The situation deteriorated. The plunder from Bījāpūr and Golkonda relieved the Emperor temporarily from the need to utilize his reserves, but it was not sufficient to cover the cost of the last phase of the Deccan wars.

Moreover, the Rājpūt nobility was disgusted with the absorption of the Marāthās into the Mughal *mansabdāri* system. Even the most high-ranking Bījāpūrī and Hyderābādī nobles were social misfits in the traditional Mughal hierarchy. The reputation of the Mughal war machine for invincibility was naturally undermined by the rebellions of the *zamīndārs* in northern India and the ravages of the marauding bands of Marāthās in the Deccan. Bhīm Sen, a native of Burhānpūr, who served the Mughals under the Bundela chief, Rāo Dalpat, gives a most realistic analysis of the Marāthā rise at the end of the seventeenth century. He comments that the governments of Bījāpūr and Hyderābād had stationed some 80,000 to 150,000 horsemen in their respective forts and territories. After their overthrow by the Mughals, not more than three to four thousand horsemen were permanently deployed at either place. Jahāngīr and Shāhjahān had assigned their conquered territory to eminent nobles possessing vast resources, but Aurangzīb was forced to rely on petty chieftains. The lawless elements were not to be scared by minor *fawjdārs*, who in any case preferred to make peace with them rather than fight indefinitely.

The *zamīndārs* grew increasingly powerful. They joined the Marāthās, and their combined forces made revenue collection extremely difficult for the *jāgīrdārs*. The imperial conquest of the Marāthā forts had led the homeless Marāthā soldiers to transfer their families to Mughal territories, leaving them free to fight unhampered. By the end of the seventeenth century the Marāthā guerrillas had obtained a permanent hold over the Deccan. They controlled all the roads and had grown rich from robbery and violence.[59] The two most successful Marāthā generals were Sāntājī Ghorpade and Dhanājī Jādava.

Jinji, where Rājarām had fled, withstood a Mughal siege of about eight years but it was seized in January 1688 by the Mughal general Zu'lfāqar Khān. Rājarām took shelter in Satara, where the Marāthā commanders defended the fort valiantly. Only after Rājarām's death in March 1700 was the fort surrendered. Shambhājī's son, Sāhū, was already in Aurangzīb's custody, so Rājarām's widow, Tārā Bā'ī, who had acquired considerable civil and military experience, acted as regent for her own son, Shivājī II. She was successful in stopping the internecine Marāthā wars, leaving them free to ravage the inadequately defended imperial territories. Aurangzīb was now so deeply involved in his scheme to conquer the inaccessible Marāthā forts that he could not withdraw without great loss of face.

At the end of 1699 the Marāthās crossed the Narbada for the first time. Three years later they reached the vicinity of Ujjain. The lawless Afghāns there, aroused by these events, also rebelled. In 1706 the Marāthās attacked Gujarāt and sacked Baroda. They even hovered around the Emperor's camp at Ahmadnagar.

The Marāthās appointed their own revenue collectors and road officials in their conquered regions. The merchants paid them more than three or four times the amount the oppressive imperial officials had been able to exact. They also varied their fighting techniques. Manucci says: 'At the present time they possess artillery, musketry, bows and arrows, with elephants and camels for all their baggage and tents. They carry these last to secure some repose from time to time as they find it convenient. In short, they are equipped and move about just like the armies of the Mogul.'[60]

Tempted by the regular transfer of wealth from north to south along the highway passing through their territory, the Jāts organized themselves, into fierce predatory bands. Chūrāman, Rājarām's son and successor, strengthened the Jāt fort of Sinsanī near Bharatpūr, and they fearlessly sacked regions around Agra and Delhi. Akbar's tomb at Sikandara was dug open and burnt in the hope of obtaining hidden treasure. The loyal Rājpūt chief Bishan Singh Kacchwāha seized Sinsanī in 1704, but the Jāt roving bands remained undeterred.

Gurū Tegh Bahadur's son, Gurū Gobind (1675–1708), the tenth Gurū of the Sikhs, was only nine years old when his father was executed. He grew up to excel in both martial arts and spiritual leadership. He reinterpreted the Sikh ideologies to justify military action. The Sikhs who accepted the rite of baptism which he devised were known as the Khālsa (Pure) and were given the title of Singh (Lion).

The rajas in the Panjāb hills considered Sikh military power a threat to their rule and appealed to the Emperor to overthrow them. The early attacks by the Mughal army from Lahore and Sirhind, in collaboration with the hill rajas, failed to subdue the Sikhs. A Mughal reinforcement then cut off supplies to the Sikh stronghold of Anandpur. On an assurance of safety from the Mughals, the Gurū evacuated the fort with his family, but the Hindu hillmen overtook him. A handful of Sikhs perished fighting to save the Gurū and his family. Two of his sons were killed, but the Gurū himself was saved by two Afghāns. His remaining two sons were savagely executed by Wazīr Khān, the Sirhind *fawjdār.* A pursuing Mughal column then engaged the Gurū at Khidrana but was defeated. The Gurū retired to Talwandī Sabō (now called Damadama) and repeatedly wrote to the Emperor condemning his *fawjdār's* atrocities. But the Emperor refused to interfere with his local officer's measures.

The Sikhs and the imperial troops clashed again at Chamkaur. The Sikh temple in Sirhind was demolished, but in retaliation the Sikhs pulled down mosques and killed their imāms. Prince Mu'azzam, who had been released in 1695 and appointed governor of Kabul in place of Amīr Khān, reached an understanding with the Sikhs. Large numbers of them left the Panjāb for the Peshāwar region, but the Barakza'ī Afghāns made short work of them. Prince Mu'azzam was subsequently ordered to expel the Sikhs who had taken refuge in his province. The Gurū left for the Deccan to lay his complaints against the *fawjdār* before Aurangzīb but he had reached only Rājasthān when the Emperor died.[61]

In 1686 war had also broken out between the Mughals and the English merchants. The English trade in Bengal, in raw silk, taffetas, and saltpetre, had grown tremendously. In 1668 the East India Company had exported goods worth £34,000; this rose in 1675 to £85,000, in 1677 to £100,000, and in 1680 to £150,000. Their request that duty on their imports should not exceed the annual amount fixed by Prince Shuja' was unreasonable. They also complained that illegal taxes were imposed by local officials, and the Emperor redressed this grievance. In 1684–5 a local judge in Qāsimbazaar (Bengal) decreed an award of 43,000 rupees against an Englishman, Job Charnock. The Mughal troops occupied his factory in order to collect the amount. Charnock escaped in April 1686 to Hugli, where the English forces, comprising Englishmen, Portuguese half-breeds, and Rājpūts, numbered four hundred. The Company had already decided to protect itself by force and had seized some strategic centres on the Indian coast. In Bengal, Charnock assumed control of English affairs. The *fawjdār* of Hugli, however, was not intimidated. He put the local market out of bounds to English troops and stopped the English from trading. Three English soldiers who tried to defy his orders were imprisoned. The subsequent English attempt to rescue them sparked off the war between them and the Mughal administration of Hugli. English ships seized Mughal vessels and caused serious damage to the town but they withdrew to Satanutī (modern Calcutta) when the Mughal cavalry arrived. In February 1687 the English seized the island of Hijlī, on the east coast of Medinīpūr district. They sacked Balasore, committing many atrocities. In May 1687 a Mughal army recaptured Hijlī, but the governor, Shāyasta Khān, took no further action. At the end of January 1689 Captain Heath, who had replaced Charnock, arrived in Chatgāon (now Chittagong in Bangladesh). He was determined to seize its fort and make it the base for English trading. The Company's council of war, however, refused to approve his offensive measures, and he retired to Madras.

War on the west coast between the English and the Mughals broke out later. The Mughals demanded a one per cent import duty in lieu of *jizya*. In response, in April 1687 the Company transferred its factory from Sūrat to Bombay, blockaded Mughal ports on the western coast, and seized their ships. The movement of Mughal pilgrim boats was also affected. The Collector of Customs responded by posting troops around the factory, placing the chief of the Sūrat council virtually under house arrest. The English retaliated, but the Mughals proved too strong for them. The English director was forced to surrender. The Emperor pardoned the English in February 1690 and restored their old privileges in Indian territory on payment of compensation of 150,000 rupees and the return of the captured Indian ships. English trade in Bengal was also revived. Charnock returned to Satanutī and in February 1691 laid the foundations of Calcutta. An imperial order of February 1691 allowed the English to carry on their trade in Bengal on payment of 3,000 rupees in lieu of customs and other dues.[62]

This was the only Mughal achievement before Aurangzīb's death on 3 March 1707 at the age of eighty-nine. His failures are ascribed to his bigotry and narrow-minded religious policy. Indeed, *'ulamā'* domination in forming his administrative policies gave rise to immeasurable complications. What caused the real breakdown, however, was his unrealistic estimate of the Deccan problems. His obstinate decision to stay there after 1689 made him the helpless captive of

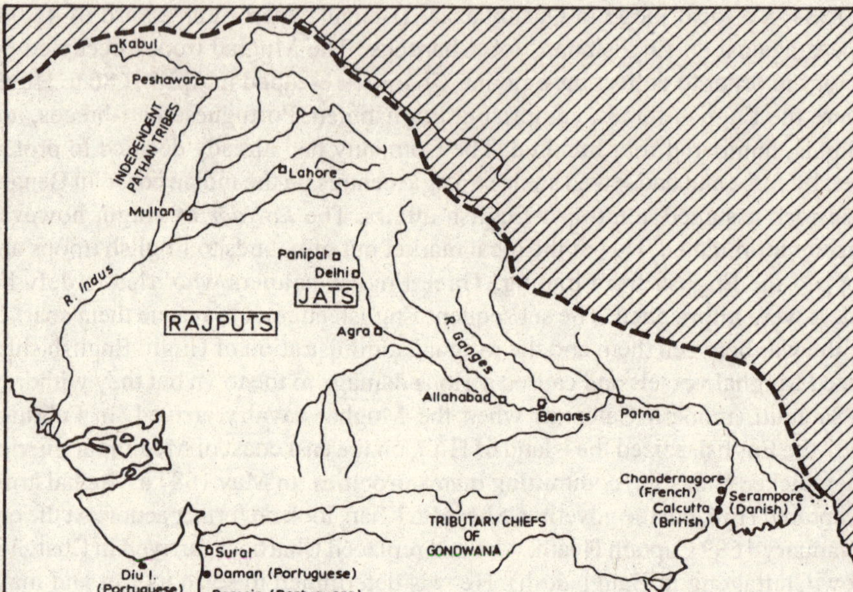

The Mughal Empire at the end of the seventeenth century

his own inflexibility. After Prince Akbar's rebellion Aurangzīb never trusted his remaining three sons and he shivered at the memory of Shāhjahān's last days. His main concern was as much to neutralize his sons' intrigues as to destroy the Marāthās.

The Emperor had denied himself any leisure and comfort in life. He presided over the court of justice twice a day, but the stream of complaints was endless. On one occasion he cried out bitterly to an intensely dissatisfied complainant, 'If you do not find your grieances redressed, pray the Almighty to grant you some other ruler!' His orthodoxy and piety evoked no enthusiasm among his nobles and sons. Sycophants ceaselessly glorified his rare ability to combine the external pomp of a lord with the soul of a mystic, while the Emperor in his turn reinforced this fusion of temporal and spiritual power by issuing amulets, which he believed would avert crises. Eminent sūfīs like Shāh Kālimu'llah of Delhi condemned him as a hypocrite.[63] The eruption of communal and sectarian conflicts at the end of his reign indicates that the wheel had come full circle and Mughal leadership was returning to the point from which Akbar had started. The Mughal imperial institutions stood in need of another Akbar – someone who was strong but also imaginative, wise and sympathetic. There was no dearth of talent among the Irāni, Tūrānī, Rājpūt, and even the Marāthā leaders. Under another Akbar, religious and communal tensions would have disappeared. Leaders such as the Irāni, Zu'lfāqar Khān, the Tūrānī, Chīn Qulīch Khān, and the Rājpūt, Sawāī Jai Singh, could have saved the Mughal government from its precipitous fall, but only under a new Akbar.

FALL OF THE MUGHAL EMPIRE

Before his death Aurangzīb is said to have left a will partitioning his vast empire among his three surviving sons, although after his victory over Dārā Shukoh he had rejected a similar suggestion made by his elder sister. The eldest, Muhammad Mu'azzam, who emerged successful in the war of succession after killing his two brothers, was sixty-four years old when he gained the throne. Unlike his father he was flexible in state politics, but his concessions to the Marāthā leaders were half-hearted, and the new boundaries were unenforceable. The Emperor, who assumed the title Bahādur Shāh, vacillated in reconciling even the Rājpūts. In October 1708 Gūru Gobind was assassinated while travelling with Bahādur Shāh's army. An obscure Sikh, Banda Bahādur, declared himself Gūru and collected a strong force. They brutally sacked Sirhind and the neighbouring regions. Many Jāt peasants converted to Sikhism to receive a share in the plunder, as did many Muslims to preserve their lives. The Emperor was busy subduing the Rājpūts and delayed taking immediate action. The imperial army, however, succeeded in bringing Banda Bahādur back to Mukhlisgarh in the Panjāb hills. Later he fled to some unknown destination. Bahādur Shāh died on 27 February 1712. During his successors' reigns the Mughal emperors lost supreme control of the administration. From 1712 to 1739, when the Irānian adventurer Nādir Shāh invaded Delhi, many ambitious Muslims from differing racial and religious groups scrambled to monopolize the highest civil and military posts. The Mughal *wazīr's* main concern was to dominate the military administration in order to appoint his own kinsmen to the governorship of important provinces and grant high *mansabs* to his favourites. Racial and religious considerations played some role in achieving group solidarity, but the struggle was not directed solely by the proverbial Irāni–Tūrānī, Sunnī–Shī'ī, or Hindu–Muslim considerations. Personal and selfish motives played the decisive role in the formation of these alliances and factions.

The period also saw the consolidation of Jāt power in the Agra region. The Kacchwaha Rājpūt bid to check the expansion of the Jāts westwards to Amber prevented them devoting whole-hearted attention to imperial interests. The Marāthās penetrated the north, undermining the strength of all the north Indian powers, Mughals, Rājpūts, and Jāts alike. Lastly, the rapid decline of the Mughal economy destroyed its political strength.

After Bahādur Shāh's death, the war of succession among his four sons was won by Jahāndār Shāh (1712–13). The repeated interference of his mistress, Lāl Kunwar, rapidly dislocated the administrative machinery, however, and he ruled for only one year. He was overthrown and killed by his nephew, Farrukhsiyar, with the help of the Sayyid brothers, Husayn 'Alī and 'Abdu'llāh of Barha, in Muzaffarnagar (western Uttar Pradesh). Farrukhsiyar's most striking achievement was the elimination of Sikh power from the Panjāb and the execution of the Sikh leader, Banda Bahadur. The Sayyid brothers were good soldiers but were not competent to act either as *wazīr* or as *Bakkshīu'l-mamālik*, the principal civil and military offices they appropriated. Their financial adviser, Lāla Ratan Chand, was incapable of preventing administrative and economic disintegration, and the financial crisis accelerated the spread of the revenue farming system. The revenue farmers, who rented land for short periods, were concerned only to make the maximum profit. Naturally the system ruined both agriculture and the law-abiding *zamīndārs.* The over-assessment of revenue prompted the peasants either to migrate to areas owned by the rebellious *zamīndārs* or to abandon farming and join the local chiefs who thrived on plunder.

Farrukhsiyar was able neither to appease the Sayyid brothers nor to neutralize the factionalism at court. His intrigues exasperated the brothers, and they dethroned, blinded, and imprisoned him. He was strangled in April 1719. The Sayyid brothers raised three kings, one after the other, in less than one and a half years. Then the dominant Tūrānī faction came to the rescue of Roshan Akhtar, one of Bahādur Shāh's grandsons, who was made king by the Sayyid brothers in September 1719. The Tūrāni faction managed to eliminate both the brothers, and Roshan reigned as Muhammad Shāh.

Nizāmu'l-Mulk, the veteran Tūrānī leader and viceroy of the Deccan, was appointed *wazīr* by Muhammad Shāh. He suggested many puritanical reforms along Aurangzlb's lines but he was out of step with the dominant court groups. Most of the nobles and the Emperor considered them unrealistic. They favoured a reversion to Akbar's policies of non-discrimination. Then Nizāmu'l-Mulk's ambitious deputy in the Deccan intrigued for independence, forcing him to move there. With Marāthā help he crushed the rebel and settled down to consolidate his administration. The Emperor awarded him the title Āsaf Jāh. An independent Āsaf Jāhī dynasty was formed in 1724. The Marāthā *peshwas* (prime ministers) virtually replaced their kings, so Nizāmu'l-Mulk made a treaty with the Marāthā *peshwa*, Bājī Rāo, granting him the right to collect *chauth* and *sardeshmukhī.*

Bājī Rāo now turned his attention to the north, sacking Gujarāt, Mālwa, Bundelkhand, and Rājasthān. In April 1737 his forces appeared at the gates of Delhi and plundered the capital for three days. The Emperor gave Bājī Rāo the governorship of Mālwa and 1,300,000 rupees in cash. Nizāmu'l-Mulk was alarmed by these concessions. Accompanied by the Rājpūts, Bundelas, and the governor of Avadh, he marched to Mālwa to crush the Marāthās. Nizāmu'l-Mulk was, however, incapable of uniting the heterogeneous groups under him. Near Bhopal the allied forces gave battle but could not overcome the Marāthās. Nizāmu'l-Mulk was forced to confirm Bājī Rāo's governorship of Mālwa and, on behalf of the Emperor, granted the Marāthās. sovereign rights over the territory between the Narbada and the Chambal.[64]

The news of the invasions of Nādir Shāh of Irān stopped the scramble for power in Delhi. The governor of Kabul had warned Muhammad Shāh of the impending attack, but the Mughal court ignored his letters. Nādir Shāh penetrated into India, accusing Muhammad Shāh of giving protection to the Afghān tribes who had earlier seized the Irānian throne. He easily overran the ill-defended cities of Ghaznī, Kābul, and Lahore. In February 1739 he routed the imperial forces at Karnāl near Pānīpat and entered Delhi. The peace negotiations were still in progress when a false rumour of Nādir Shāh's assassination prompted bands of Delhi hooligans to kill some three thousand Irānīs. Filled with rage, Nādir ordered a general massacre of the citizens of Delhi in retaliation. Twenty thousand people were killed in the bloody reprisal, and enormous treasure fell into Irānian hands. After two months' orgy of plunder and devastation, Nādir Shāh returned to Irān. The total value of spoils was estimated at 700 million rupees. Shāhjahān's famous peacock throne was also carried away. On his journey to Khurāsān, the trans-Indus province (Sind, Kabul, and the western part of the Panjāb) fell to Nādir.[65]

Akbar's formidable frontier disappeared, and the pace of Mughal decline accelerated. Before Muhammad Shāh's death in April 1748, Ahmad Shāh Durrānī, an Afghān adventurer who had accompanied Nādir Shāh when he invaded Delhi, had become a potent threat to Indian peace. After Nādir Shāh's assassination in 1747 he crowned himself king at Qandahār. He seized Ghaznī, Kābul, and Peshāwar and began to assert sovereignty over the Mughal provinces ceded to Nādir Shāh. In January 1748 he invaded India for the first time with 12,000 troops but was defeated in March near Sirhind by a Mughal army. The aged Mughal vizier who was killed on the battlefield was replaced by the Shī'ī governor of Avadh, Safdarjang, who had been the driving force behind the victory. Ahmad Shāh Durrānī, a seasoned warrior, however, duped the imperialists by prolonging the peace talks while systematically withdrawing his main force and all valuable military equipment. This was the last grand Mughal victory and was the only good news Muhammad Shāh heard before his death. The heir apparent, Ahmad Shāh, aged twenty-two, had received no literary or military education. His mother, Udham Bāī, and the harem head, Jāwīd Khān, wasted millions of rupees on coronation festivities. The holy Sunnī savant Shāh Walīullāh seems to have become their patron saint.

In October 1748 Ahmad Shāh Durrānī invaded the Panjāb again, and the defeated Tūrānī governor ceded regions west of the Indus to him. After Durrānī's third invasion in December 1751 the country as far east as Sirhind surrendered. In 1752 Safdarjang made a subsidiary alliance with the Marathās to secure their help against the Durrānī invasions, but Jāwīd Khān prevented its ratification. Jāwīd Khān was assassinated on 5 February 1753, and the growing dissatisfaction of the Tūrānīs, Afghāns, and Indian Sunnīs against the Shī'ī Safdarjang flared up openly. The Emperor dismissed Safdarjang, but he refused to step down. Instead he raised to the throne a boy of obscure origin, who was supported by Sūrajmal, the Jāt chief. The Badakhshīs, Balūchs, Marāthās, and Gūjars joined the imperialists, raising the cry of Sunni *jihād* against Shī'ī domination. Sporadic battles were fought over several months. On 17 November 1753 Safdarjang retired to Avadh. He died on 5 October 1754. His son, Shujā'u'd-Dawla, who succeeded him, strengthened the independence of Avadh. The Emperor's Rohella and Balūch commanders also gained independent control of the districts near Delhi in settlement of their outstanding salaries; the remaining imperial leaders received no financial return. Pitched battles were fought in the Delhi streets by soldiers demanding their wages. On 2 June 1754 Jahāndār Shāh's son was made Emperor and assumed the grand title 'Ālamgīr II. The deposed Ahmad Shāh and Udham Bāī were imprisoned to meet a miserable death in the dungeons. 'Ālamgīr II remitted the pilgrim tax on Hindus to appease the Marāthās and prohibited the Shī'ī mourning ceremonies of Muharram in Delhi to mollify the Sunnīs.

The Marāthās extended their control from Mālwa and Gujarāt to Bundelkhand. Their leaders carved out many independent centres of power in the region. After 1742 they burst into Orissa and Bengal, ruled by Murshid Qulī Khān's successors. 'Alī Wardī (1740–56), who then ruled Bengal, was an enterprising general. He fought resolutely against both his Afghān enemies and the Marāthās.

In the Panjāb, Ahmad Shāh Durrānī's invasions destroyed the Mughal administration, leaving the field open for the Sikhs, who had been flattened during Farrukhsiyar's reign. On 15 November 1756 Ahmad Shāh left Peshāwar to sack Delhi. There was no one left to resist him. In January 1757 he was acknowledged Emperor in Delhi but he was interested only in fleecing India of its wealth. Delhi was divided into sectors under Afghān leaders so that they might plunder it systematically. From there Durrānī marched upon Mathura and savagely looted the Hindu temples and rich merchants. The advent of summer made further Afghān advances impossible, and Ahmad Shāh returned to his country laden with treasure from his Indian invasion.

Ahmad Shāh Durrānī subsequently restored 'Ālamgīr II to the throne. On 23 June 1757 the commander of the army of the East India Company, Clive, defeated

Sirāju'd-Dawla, 'Alī Wardī's successor. To justify his aggression he wrote a long letter to the Emperor, who was now no more than a cipher.[66] 'Ālamgīr's prime minister, 'Imadu'l-Mulk, first forced Prince 'Alī Gawhar to leave and then killed his father, 'Ālamgīr II. The fugitive Prince fled to Bihār and crowned himself king, assuming the title Shāh 'Ālam II. Although 'Imadu'l-Mulk raised a puppet ruler to the throne, for all intents and purposes Delhi was controlled by the Marāthās. Then Ahmad Shāh Durrānī marched from Qandahār for the fifth time to eliminate the Marāthās, who were now virtual rulers as far as Attock.

On 14 January 1761 the Marāthās sustained a crushing defeat on the battlefield of Pānīpat. Ahmad Shāh Durrānī returned to Qandahār in March of that year. He had by now lost control of the Panjāb. He invaded it three more times to eliminate the Sikhs but died in October 1773 without having made much progress in consolidating the administration of the Panjāb. The orthodox Sunni hopes of a revival of their power through Durrānī were shattered forever. Sikh domination of the Panjāb was also short-lived. In 1803 the English conquered Delhi, although the Mughal emperors continued to rule within the four walls of the Delhi fort until 1857. But the account of the final elimination of Mughal rule and the steady advance of the British is another story.

IV

THE STATE

KINGSHIP

ACCORDING to the Qur'ān, God the Most High, Unique, and One in Himself enjoys unlimited sovereignty over His creations. Allah's undisputed power 'to give kingdom' and 'to take away kingdoms',[1] according to His will, presupposes the existence of a state whose citizens are bound to obey the divine law revealed through the Prophet Muhammad. With the Prophet's death the legislative functions which he had performed ended, and his successors, the 'rightly guided caliphs' (*ar-Rāshidūn*), inherited the Prophet's executive and judicial functions. The world-view of leadership held by the rightly guided caliphs synthesized the Arab tribal customs with those of the Meccan trading oligarchy, rejecting Irānian monarchical traditions. In subsequent centuries the image of their administrative systems was to acquire a utopian quality and to provide a norm which in theory later Muslim rulers were to strive to follow. Their successors, the Umayyads, did not enjoy the respect that the first four rightly guided caliphs had commanded, and both the 'Abbāsids, who overthrew the Umayyads, and posterity condemn their rule as *mulk* (kingdom) or irreligious kingship in contrast to the early caliphate. The 'Abbāsid caliphs strove to capitalize on their descent from al-'Abbās bin 'Abdu'l-Muttalib, the Prophet's uncle; but what impressed the multiracial society of the 'Abbāsids and left an indelible mark on posterity was the Arabic translations of the ancient Irānian *Mirror for Princes* and the Islamicized versions of this text written by scholars during their caliphate. This literary genre unequivocally asserted that rulers were divinely appointed monarchs who were accountable only to God. The jurists also maintained that God had made the caliphs the trustees of their people and that the happiest 'shepherd' before God on Judgement Day was he whose subjects had been content during his reign. Nevertheless the Muslim religious elite (*ahl al-ra'y*), while enforcing what was right and forbidding what was evil, could accuse a caliph of open violation of the *sharī'ā* and thus have him forcibly removed. This was authorized by a saying of the Prophet Muhammad: 'Do not obey a creature against the Creator.'[2] On the other hand, according to the authors of the *Mirrors*, there was no circumstance legitimizing disobedience to a ruler.

However, the completion of the *Shāhnāma* by the great Irānian epic poet Firdawsī in 1010 gave a new direction to both rulers and political theorists and was to become the most significant watershed in the history of Islamic political thought. As well as an account of the epic glory of the ancient Irānian kings, the *Shāhnāma* eloquently reminded rulers and nobles that monarchs were instruments in the execution of God's will and that their commands were therefore inviolate. The God of the *Shāhnāma* was omnipotent and omniscient, the Creator of the Zoroastrians, Jews, Christians, and Muslims, who endowed Kayūmars (the founder of the ceremonial of throne and crown) with *farr*, a supernatural effulgence or radiance, suggesting the mystique of true kingship. *Farr* symbolized the divine favour which kings possessed as long as God did not take it away from them. Thus Jamshīd, one of the greatest legendary kings of ancient Irān, is said to have asserted that he was himself endowed with this divine *farr.* He believed he was simultaneously both king and priest, who would save potential evil-doers from taking the wrong path and guide their souls towards the light. Firdawsī related that Jamshīd, by virtue of his kingly *farr*, was able to mould iron into helmets, chain-mail, armour, missile-proof vests, swords, and horse armour.

Farr or *farrah* is the *khvarenah* of the *Avesta* which held a special significance for the people of Irān. *Khvarenah* represented kingly glory or majesty, and the Shāhanshāh was not merely an emperor but the custodian of this mystical glory and charisma.

The importance of *farr* in relation to kingship was so significant that even the orthodox Abū Hāmid Muhammad al-Ghazālī (1058–1111) could not ignore it. In his *Nasīhatu 'l-mulūk* he wrote:

> It must therefore be recognized that this kingship and the divine effulgence (*farr-i Īzadī*) have been granted to them by God, and that they must accordingly be obeyed, loved and followed. To dispute with kings is improper, and to hate them is wrong; for God on High has commanded, 'Obey God and obey the Prophet and those among you who hold authority',[3] which means (in Persian) obey God and the prophets and your princes (*amīrān*). Every religious person must therefore love and obey kings and recognize that their kingship is granted by God, and given by Him to whom He wills.'[4]

Ghazālī also discussed the institution of the caliphate in a number of works, consistently demonstrating that the *sharī'a* stated that the appointment of a caliph was obligatory. To him the institution symbolized the collective unity of the Muslim community and its historical continuity, and he argued that the current situation made a change in the conditions prescribed for the election of a caliph permissible. However, he wrote:

> An evil-doing and barbarous sultan, so long as he is supported by military force, so that he can only with difficulty be deposed and the attempt to depose him would cause unendurable civil strife, must of necessity be left in possession and obedience must be rendered to him, exactly as obedience must be rendered to *amīrs*... We consider that the caliphate is contractually assumed by that person of the 'Abbāsid house who is charged with it, and

> that the function of government in the various lands is carried out by means of Sultans, who owe allegiance to the Caliph. Government in these days is a consequence solely of military power, and whosoever he may be to whom the holder of military power gives his allegiance, that person is the Caliph. And whosoever exercises independent authority, so long as he shows allegiance to the Caliph in the matter of his prerogatives of the *khutba*[5] and coinage, the same is a sultan, whose commands and judgements are valid in the several parts of the earth.[6]

Documents issued in the reign of the Seljūqs also used the terms *jahāndār* (monarch) and *jahāndārī* (monarchy) and stressed the fact that the principal duty of kings was to restore prosperity in a kingdom by dispensing justice. They stressed the interdependence of kingship and religion and emphasized the point that God had entrusted subjects to the sultan's care, it being one of the latter's principal duties to ensure their protection.

A very comprehensive Arabic *Mirror for Princes* entitled *Sirāju'l-mulūk* was compiled in 1122 by Abū Bakr Muhammad bin al-Walīd al-Turtūshī (1059–*c.* 1127), who was born in Spain and visited Irān and Irāq. Here he met the Seljūq vizier Nizāmu'l-Mulk Tūsī (1018–92) and was greatly impressed by Tūsī's scholarship and political acumen. Even the earlier *Mirror for Princes* had drawn upon the stories in *Kalīla wa Dimna*, as translated from the Pahlavī (Old Persian) by Ibnu'l-Muqaffa' (d. 756). Turtūshī's work also shows a definite debt to the same source, *Kalīla wa Dimna.* He refers also to *Muntakhabu'l-jawāhir* (*Selected Gems*), composed by the Indian, Shā-naq (Chanakya), as a guide for the monarch. This text, the *Kitāb Shānaq fi al-tadbīr*, was in fact the celebrated *Chānakya-Nīti*, a collection of political aphorisms in Sanskrit, not to be confused with the *Arthasāstra* ascribed to Kautilya or Chanakya.

Drawing on a vast range of source material available in Arabic translations, Turtūshī referred to kings by such titles as *mulūk* (rulers), *umarā'* (princes), *salātīn* (kings), and *wulāt* (lords), showing that he considered them indomitable powers. He also endorsed the view that a sultan's right to rule was of divine origin and that he was God's shadow on earth, second only in rank to prophets and angels. But a ruler was also a shepherd and in Turtūshī's world-view he was the Prophet's vicegerent, whose duty it was to promote the interests of his subjects. An eternal covenant between God and kings enforced the latter's duty to rule with impartiality and justice.[7] Turtūshī compared the benefits accruing from sultans to such natural phenomena as rain, wind, the seasons, day, and night, and described tyrants as worse than ravaging lions. However, he preferred even the latter to anarchy, maintaining that the good which emerged from a king outweighed any evil perpetrated by him. In a maxim attributed to Chānakya, Turtūshī encouraged rulers to act like the sun, moon, earth, rain, wind, fire, water, and death. From some Hindu source he presented the widespread analogy of the big fish eating smaller fish and claimed that this unstable situation was averted only by a monarchy.[8] In summary, Turtūshī confidently asserted that the relation of a monarch to his people was identical with that of the body to the soul; if the king were virtuous his people would prosper, but if he were not, evil would prevail in his territory.

By the early thirteenth century the 'Abbāsid caliphate was reduced to a mere shadow. The enterprising Turkic leaders, in order to reinforce their own positions, exhibited the caliph's sovereignty over the territories they had conquered by including his name in the *khutba* and on their coins. This enhanced their prestige as sultans and legalized their rule in the eyes of the orthodox. Mu'izzu'd-Dīn Muhammad bin Sām inscribed the caliph's names on his coins. In 1225 Iltutmish issued coins showing his close relationship with the caliph. Four years later, when this Sultan had annihilated all his rivals, the Caliph al-Mustansir (1226–42) sent his emissaries to Delhi. The occasion was celebrated with great festivity, and the Caliph's name was inscribed in Hindī on the coins in order to make the connection between the Sultan and the Caliph widely known. The name of the Caliph's successor, Must'asim (1242–58), continued to appear on Indian coins even after he had been executed and Baghdād destroyed by Hulāgū. Although Balban was fully aware of the Baghdād catastrophe, we are told by Baranī that Balban believed that ideally a sultan should obtain investiture from the 'Abbāsid caliphs. However, like his predecessors and the later Delhi sultans, Balban also considered himself a vicegerent of God and His shadow on earth. He exhibited his awareness of the doctrine of *farr* when he remarked that 'the king's heart is the mirror of the divine attributes. As long as God does not inspire the heart of kings with general decrees relating to His slaves, matters concerning them which are dependent on the heart and tongue of the rulers are not accomplished'.[9] Balban, like Iltutmish before him, claimed to be the successor of Afrāsiyāb, the ancient Tūrānian monarch. According to the *Shāhnāma*, this arch enemy of the Irāni Pīshdādian and Kayānian dynasties was defeated by the Irānian hero Rustam. Nevertheless, Balban introduced Irānian court customs and also strongly adhered to the class and racial prejudices of ancient Irān.

Balban advocated the implementation of strict justice but only for the Sunnīs. He excluded the Hindus and discriminated against the Ismā'īlīs and Muslim philosophers, thus slavishly imitating Nizāmu'l-Mulk and Ghazālī. With explicit paternalism, however, he also urged his successors to note that only such rulers deserved to be called 'king' as had not a single naked or hungry person in their territories.[10]

Balban's grandson and successor, Mu'izzu'd-Dīn Kayqubād, was a rake and a drunkard; but Amīr Khusraw, who wrote panegyrics for all the Delhi sultans from Balban to Ghiyāsu'd-Dīn Tughluq, observed that Kayqubād was endowed with the *farr* of the Kayāni dynasty.[11] Both Amir Khusraw and his friend Amir Hasan called the Khaljī Sultan 'Ala'u'd-Dīn Muhammad a *khalifa* (caliph). Describing the latter's victories in the *Khazāinu'l-futūh*, Amīr Khusraw wrote: 'Through instituting justice and the insignia of his own caliphate he once again raised the 'Abbāsid standards which grievous calamities had broken into fragments'.[12]

In 1317 'Ala'u'd-Dīn's son, Qutbu'd-Dīn Mubārāk Shāh, issued coins bearing the titles which the 'Abbāsid caliphs had adopted. In fact, from the time of Balban onwards, in Indian political terminology as elsewhere, the words 'caliph' and 'sultan' were interchangeable, but the Sultan's assumption of the title al-Wasiq Bi'llāh (Confiding in God) was a daring innovation.

When his rule became torn by internal rebellion and was dubbed irreligious and tyrannical by the *'ulamā'* and sūfīs, Sultan Muhammad bin Tughluq resorted to a unique method of silencing his opponents. To give legality to his rule he issued coins in the name of a deceased descendant of a former Baghdad 'Abbāsid caliph who had moved to Egypt. The fact that the descendant was already dead was known to the Muslim elite but the Sultan counted on the support of Muslim masses in the country. Whilst awaiting his investiture of authority from the Caliph, however, the Sultan stopped the congregational Friday and *'īd* prayers, and coins bearing the name of the dead caliph were issued only between 1342 and 1344. Finally, in 1344 Hājjī Sa'īd Sarsarī, the envoy of the 'Abbāsid Caliph in Egypt, brought to Sultan Muhammad bin Tughluq an investiture of authority, which he received with deep humility. The reception and gifts given by the Sultan to the emissary amazed Ibn Battūta, who was present at the time. The poets wrote panegyrics for the occasion; the Indian *'ulamā'* and sūfis remained unimpressed but powerless to do anything.[13]

Muhammad bin Tughluq died fighting the rebels in distant Thatta. In 1356 his successor, Sultan Fīrūz, also received his investiture and the title Sayyidu's-Salātīn (Chief of the Sultans) from the Caliph. He also gave a warm welcome to the Caliph's envoy. The Caliph's warm patronage of the *'ulamā'* and sūfis had already endeared him to them, so the investiture was merely a formality.

Baranī's *Tārīkh-i Firūz Shāhi* and the *Fatāwa-i jahāndārī* rationalized both the absolutism of kings and their use of state laws (*zawābit*). Baranī referred unhesitatingly to the Prophet Muhammad's first four successors as *jahāndārs* (worldly rulers), noting that each strictly observed Muhammad's practices. As human beings, according to Baranī, they combined the grandeur of Jamshīd with the dervishhood of mystics. After this period, caliphs and Muslim kings found themselves in the following dilemma. If they followed the practices of Muhammad, they were unable to govern; on the other hand, if they ruled vigorously and ostentatiously like pre-Islamic Irānian rulers, they were forced to violate religious law. To Baranī, spiritual life was to be attained only through humility, poverty, and self-abasement, while pride, arrogance, and self-glorification were indispensable to a king, thus rendering the coexistence of spirituality and kingship impossible. A monarch, he added, could not survive without exhibiting divinity (*rubūbiyya*), and kingship was therefore the deputyship (*niyābat*) and vicegerency (*khilāfat*) of God. In the interests of propagating God's word, enforcing the faith of Muhammad, annihilating the enemies of the faith, and their own self-preservation, Muslim *khalīfas* and kings were compelled to adopt the manners and customs of the great Irānian emperors. He compared this situation with the eating of carrion, prohibited by Islam except in extreme conditions. In the same way, Muslim kings, in the interests of Islam, were allowed to display arrogance and ruthlessness. Using this example Baranī added that even such non-Islamic customs as ceremonial prostration in the style of the Irānian court, the amassing of huge amounts of treasure, and the collection of large harems could be legalized.[14]

Baranī reaffirmed his belief that the theories on monarchy outlined in the *Mirror for Princes*, such as that 'the sultan is God's shadow on earth', 'religion and kingdom are twin brothers', and 'people follow the faith of their kings', were true. He exaggerated the importance of nobility of birth in an attempt to discourage rulers from counteracting the pressure and dominance of the aristocracy by choosing their ministers from the common people. The Hindu class and caste system strengthened the social prejudices Baranī had borrowed from the Persian *Mirrors*. Baranī agreed that as far as possible state laws should not violate the *sharī'a* and the Sunna but on questions of expediency he recommended that this should be no obstacle. After all, expiation involved only extending gifts to the *'ulamā'*.[15]

To Baranī, the ideal Muslim ruler could not satisfy his divine commission unless he deprived Hindus of all high government positions and forced the brāhmans (whom he compared with the Muslim *'ulamā'*) into bankruptcy and social misery. Those who departed from orthodox Sunnīsm, notably the Ismā'īlīs and Muslim philosophers, were to be annihilated, so as to glorify Sunnī Islam in India and make it the leading religion. According to Baranī, this validated the autocratic form of the Delhi sultans' rule and gave it a religious basis.

Modern researchers have declared that the tradition that in Cairo the 'Abbāsid Caliph formally transferred the caliphate to the Ottoman Sultan Selīm (1512–20) is mythical, since jurists recognized only a Quraysh as caliph, while, like all sultans, Selīm and his successors considered themselves both caliph and sultan. Nevertheless, Selīm did obtain the sacred relics from the 'Abbāsid family: the Prophet's robe, some hairs from his beard, and Caliph 'Umar's sword. With the conquest of Egypt, Selīm became the guardian of Mecca and Medina, a legitimate honour of which he was justly proud.[16] Inspired by these events, the Indian king Sher Shāh Sūr entertained a pious wish to annihilate the Shī'ī rulers of Irān, to resuscitate the bond of religious brotherhood with the Sultan of Turkey, and to share with him the privilege of serving one of the two holy places, Mecca and Medina.[17]

Between the reigns of Tīmūr and Akbar two major trends in political ideology crystallized, one primarily Ghazālian and the other philosophical. The latter was reinvigorated by Khwāja Nasīru'd-Dīn Tūsī (1201–74), a profound commentator on the philosopher Avicenna (980–1037). Later, the Khwāja's *Akhlāq-i Nāsīrī* was reinterpreted by the celebrated philosopher and *'ālim* Jalālu'd-Dīn Dawwānī (1427–1503) in his *Akhlāq-i Jalālī*. A new dimension was introduced when the Ghazālian doctrines and Nasīrian political philosophy were synthesized by Abu'l-Fazl 'Allā-mī (1551–1602). He was inspired by a need to rationalize the broadly based policies of peace and concord with all religious communities initiated by his patron, Akbar the Great. Besides Arabic and Persian works on kingship and government, Abu'l-Fazl had access to the Persian translations of the great Hindu epics, the *Mahābhārata* and the *Rāmayana*, to the Arabic translation of the *Chānkaya Nīti*, and to the Sanskrit works of ancient Indian *rājanīti* (polity).

Abu'l-Fazl refused to concern himself with Islamic theories legitimizing the petty military dictators who forcibly seized power and were then automatically recognized as shadows of God. To Abu'l-Fazl, the institution of kingship, rather than the individual who held the office, was endowed with *farr-i īzadī.* The word *pādshāh* (king), he observed, was a compound word – *pād* meaning stability and possession, and *shāh* denoting origin and lordship. He considered that the *padshah* was neither the sultan nor the imām of Nasīru'd-Dīn Tūsī; nor was he the Mahdī (Sahīb al-Zamān or Lord of the Age), whose prophesied appearance at the close of the first Islamic millenium (1591–2) had produced instability in the minds of many Muslims.[18] Abu'l-Fazl's *pādshāh* or *shāhanshāh* (king of kings) – another term borrowed from ancient Irānian royalty which he loved to use – was a unique personality; he was the 'perfect man' and was the real vicegerent of God on earth.

The spate of translations from Arabic and Sanskrit into Persian during Akbar's reign also included a Persian translation of the *Sirāj al-mulūk* by Turtūshī. It served to remind Indian intellectuals that Turtūshī filled an important gap in the study of political theories because he had access to the works of the sages of Persia, Byzantium, China, Hind and Sind. These were not available to his predecessors. Turtūshī asserted that an infidel king who governed his kingdom according to the right principles of kingship was preferable to a Muslim ruler who was slipshod in fulfilling his responsibilities and tardy in imposing justice.[19]

This principle, to which some earlier sultans had paid lip-service, tended to strengthen the basis on which Akbar's government was founded.

The protagonists of the Ghazālian theory of kingship under the Mughals were Shaykh 'Abdu'l-Haqq Muhaddis Dihlawī (1551–1642) and Mujaddid Alf-i Shānī. Having learnt that Jahāngīr was interested in the Prophet's traditions on kingship, Shaykh 'Abdu'l-Haqq wrote a treatise, the *Nūriyya-i Sultāniyya*, covering all the information on this subject. Although a trained scholar of *hadīs* he never questioned the authenticity of the spurious traditions which had become popular from the time of Ghazāli, and wrote:

> No rank is higher than that of a king, and all words of conventional praise are insufficient to return thanks to him... The order and arrangement of worldly affairs depends upon the king. Were every king to go into retirement, the cosmic order would be shattered. Therefore kings should so regulate their activities that their existence is not a source of disorder.[20]

Shaykh 'Abdu'l-Haqq's theory legitimizing the king was narrowed down to the exclusive benefit of Islam when he considered whether heretics and unbelievers had an equal right to justice. He thought that *kifr* (heresy) was incompatible with justice and that a *kāfir* (heretic) could never be known as an *'ādil* (just ruler). At the same time, however, when reminded of the Sasanian king Nūshīrwān, a non-Muslim renowned for his fairness, the Shaykh admitted that justice was not the sole monopoly of Islam. He therefore restrained himself from carrying the argument any further, as Akbar and Jahāngīr dispensed even-handed justice.

Returning to his favourite subject he demanded that kings act according to the laws of the *sharī'a* as interpreted by the honest *'ulamā'*.[21]

Shaykh Ahmad Sirhindī, known as Mujaddid Alf-i Sānī (1564–1624), urged the Muslim nobles in Jahāngīr's court to persuade their Emperor to enforce the *sharī'a* by state legislation, to revoke the orders prohibiting the killing of cows, and to reimpose *jizya* (poll-tax on non-Muslims), as well as to deprive Hindus and Shī'īs of all posts of responsibility and trust.[22] Nowhere does he advocate rebellion.

Designing his theory of kingship to justify his own accession to the throne and to gain the support of orthodox Sunnīs for his rule, Aurangzīb claimed that, since all actions are determined by the will of God, his victory over his brothers was a divine gift. He stated that that man was truly great who was assisted to obtain power by God. From his prison Shāhjahān accused Aurangzīb of usurpation, to which his son replied:

> Perhaps Your Majesty's *'ulamā'* have not advised Your Majesty of the correct position (about kingship) under the *sharī'a*... The treasury and property of kings and sultans are meant to satisfy the needs of the country and community; they are not private property and not an inheritance, and therefore *zakāt* is not levied on them. God most High selects someone from among the esteemed ones of His Court for the management of matters relating to the livelihood and destiny of mankind, under whose control He places the duties of binding and loosing, so that all sorts of people should lead their life on the basis of equity.[23]

LAW

In India many *fiqh* works, based on classical authorities, were written under the patronage of the rulers. Aurangzīb eventually appointed a board of *'ulamā'* to compile authoritative passages from the standard works of Hanafi *fiqh* for the guidance of the *qāzīs*. The work was completed between 1664 and 1672 and is known as the *Fatāwa al-'Ālamgīriyya.*

The Indian *fiqh* works did not ignore the importance of local customs (*'āda* or *'urf*). These were readily implemented in all cases where they did not violate the *sharī'a* laws, and in many cases even where there was a divergence they were rendered acceptable through *hiyal.*[24] A very large chapter in the *Fatāwa al-'Ālamgīriyya* explains how *hiyal* helped to overcome orthodox legal problems.

The caliphs were also empowered to make administrative regulations within *sharī'a* limits, and the *qāzīs* were bound to follow them. These regulations were intended to supplement the sacred law. The Turkic sultans of Irān and Central Asia codified administrative laws known as the laws of *jahāndārī* (worldly administration) to make their political power effective. The works of Ghazālī, particularly *Nasīhatu'l-mulūk*, and *Siyāsat-nāma* by Nizāmu'l-Mulk Tūsī, were the main source books for subsequent scholars who wrote handbooks on the sultans' legal and administrative systems. According to Ghazālī, 'necessity makes lawful what is prohibited'. Among early Indian authors Ziya' u'd-Dīn Baranī, who wrote the *Fatāwa-i jahāndārī* (legal advice on worldly rule), stated that the welfare of the state depended on state laws (*zawābit*) which did not need to be formulated in consultation with the *'ulamā'*. Although in ordinary circumstances the *zawābit* should not violate the *sharī'a*, in special circumstances when departure from it was imperative because of the vicious nature of the people, the *zawābit* should not be deemed as right and correct. The law-makers should generously give alms in expiation and be afraid of the sin which they had been forced to commit. The authority for the departure from the *sharī'a* was the precept, 'Necessity makes things forbidden lawful.'[25]

Of all the discussions on policy matters relating to the formulation of *zawābit* in the *Tārīkh-i Firūz Shāhī*, the most interesting is a dialogue between Qāzī Mughīs of Bayana and Sultan 'Ala'u'd-Dīn Khaljī. This dialogue may be fictitious; Baranī may have chosen the Sultan and his Qāzī in order to support his own theories, but the points he wished to make cannot be overemphasized. The first question the Sultan put to Qāzī Mughis related to the ordinance of the *sharī'a* concerning the Hindu *kharāj*-paying class, meaning the village leaders, *khūts*, *chawdhrīs*, and *muqaddams*. The Qāzī, quoting a part of a Qur'ānic verse – 'Until they pay the *jizya* readily, being brought low',[26] – added that the Hindus should be forced to pay their revenue in abject humility and extreme submissiveness; for the Prophet Muhammad had ordained that Hindus must either follow the true faith or else be slain or imprisoned and their wealth and property confiscated. With the exception of Abū Hanifa, who had authorized the collection *jizya* from the Hindus, the founders of the other schools of jurisprudence had ordered for them 'either death or Islam'. 'Ala'u'd-Dīn, pleading his ignorance of the laws of the *sharī'a* as stated by the Qāzī, affirmed that his ordinances were designed to reduce the rich *khāts* and *muqaddams* to poverty by forcing them to pay *kharāj*, *jiqa*, and other taxes submissively, without exploiting the poor peasants. It was by sheer chance that the Sultan's policy of impoverishing the Hindu village chiefs coincided with the Hanafi law books.

The Qāzī's views on other questions which the Sultan put to him differed widely from the *sharī'a* laws. Qāzī Mughis said that he was not aware of any rulings on punishment for embezzlement, fraudulent revenue practices, or bribery among government officials. Traditionally, only the ruler was authorized to punish them, but even then not by amputation of the hand, as the *sharī'a* prescribed for common thieves. The Sultan answered that he had fixed salaries for his officials and had ordered that if they were still found to be committing fraud, embezzlement, or bribery the loss to the treasury would justify various kinds of torture and severe punishment.

The Sultan presented the Qāzī with a list of his own harsh rules against political and criminal offences, consisting of punishments such as the imposition of a fine equivalent to three years' pay for each horseman who failed to stand muster; casting drunkards and liquor salesmen into wells dug especially for them; castration of the married male adulterer and slaying of the woman; and the infliction of the harshest possible punishment on those who rebelled or did not pay their taxes. The

Sultan asked the Qāzī whether all his laws were against the *sharī'a*, to which the Qāzī replied that the Prophet's *ahādīs* and the *'ulamā' fatwas* did not permit the ruler to impose such harsh penalties. Filled with anger, the Sultan left the court. On his return the next day, however, he had regained his composure. Although he appreciated the Qāzī's frankness, he explained, his punishments were intended to deter the rebels and the bellicose and were designed to save the lives of thousands of Muslims who were slaughtered each time a rebellion was suppressed. He was not concerned with the agreement of his laws with the *sharī'a*, he said, nor with his own punishment on Judgement Day. His main concern was the interest of the state. However, his deterrent punishments, he admitted, had so little effect on habitual criminals that mercy had become impossible.[27]

'Ala'u'd-Dīn had imagined that only the Hindus would be the leaders of insurrection and rebellion, but from the beginning of his accession Sultan Muhammad bin Tughluq was faced with Muslim rebellions which spread to all parts of the country. Around 1344 the Sultan sought Baranī's advice regarding capital punishment for the following seven offences: (1) apostasy; (2) wilful murder of the king's loyal subjects; (3) adultery by a married man with someone else's wife; (4) proven treason against the ruler; (5) leading rebellions and insurrections; (6) co-operation with the Sultan's enemies and supplying intelligence and weapons; (7) such acts of disobedience as were a threat to the kingdom. To another question Baranī answered that, according to the traditions of the Prophet, capital punishment was applicable only to apostasy, the murder of a Muslim, and adultery by a married man. The remaining four categories of offences belonged to the province of administration and were subject to the Sultan's discretion. Disagreeing even with the Irānian penal laws, the Sultan argued that the people of ancient Irān were essentially law-abiding but that he was forced by circumstances to inflict deterrent sentences, including capital punishment, merely on suspicion of a subject's guilt. Nevertheless, he was still unable to stamp out rebellions.[28] On various other occasions Baranī suggested further measures, including the Sultan's abdication and retirement in peace;[29] but the Sultan, determined as he was to eradicate rebellion, died in Sind, whilst in pursuit of a rebel.

The mild reign of his successor, Sultan Fīrūz Tughluq, saw the ostensible return to the *sharī'a.* The Sultan had inscribed on an octagonal tower near the Fīrūzabād Jāmi' mosque the *sharī'a* laws which replaced the earlier state laws.[30]

The exemption of the brāhmans from *jizya* under former sultans was attributed by Sultan Fīrūz to the negligence of their officers, who had failed to apprise their rulers of the fact that the brāhmans, being the leaders and promoters of infidelity, ought never to have been exempted. The new orders for the imposition of *jizya* on them appalled the brāhmans, and they threatened to burn themselves alive before the Sultan's palace. However, finding the Sultan unrelenting, other Hindus offered to pay *jizya* on their behalf, and a concessional rate was fixed for them.[31]

This fusion of orthodoxy and state laws was dissolved by Akbar. Bad'ūnī accuses him of annulling the statutes and ordinances of Islam: a testimony accepted unquestioningly by orthodox Muslims. According to Ghazālian polity,

Akbar, who never publicly abjured Islam, was guilty only of instituting sinful laws. According to Bada'ūnī, Akbar's laws were illegal for both religious and worldly reasons. In his opinion they were vexatious and the cause of rebellion and the destruction of the territories of the empire. For his part, Akbar argued that interference in the religious beliefs of his subjects was illegal and that Hindus forcibly converted to Islam would revert to their former religion. Hindu girls who had been made to marry Muslims should be restored to their families, and both Muslim and Hindu parents who had sold their children as slaves because of poverty could now buy them back.[32] In terms of the *sharī'a* this meant that apostasy (*irtidād* or *ridda*) was no longer punishable by death. Akbar considered the problem mainly from a humanitarian point of view. Referring to the Indian custom of preventing the woman from seeing her future husband before marriage, Abu'l-Fazl says that Akbar ruled that the consent of the bride and bridegroom and the permission of the parents were absolutely necessary in marriage contracts. This was in keeping with the *sharī'a*, but Indian custom did not require the prior consent of the bride. Akbar prohibited polygamy and allowed a second wife only in exceptional circumstances. Child marriages were forbidden on grounds of health, and the marriage of an old woman to a young husband was considered contrary to modesty. Although he appreciated that the custom was a preventive against rash divorce, Akbar nevertheless discouraged fixing heavy amounts to be met by a husband if he divorced his wife without sufficient cause (*kābīn*). To Akbar the custom was nothing more than a farce, for the money was never paid in any case. He appointed two officers called *tuī-begīs* to supervise adherence to the law and fixed a nominal amount as their fee, which could be waived in cases of hardship.[33] Akbar also prohibited the circumcision of boys below the age of twelve, making it their personal choice and not a religious obligation on the part of the parents.[34] The slaughter of animals on certain days totalling about half the year was also prohibited by Akbar; Jahāngīr reduced the number by only a few days.

Akbar ordered a considerable change in the law of evidence. According to *sharī'a* law, the plaintiff was required to present two male adult Muslims to testify orally to their direct knowledge of the truth of his claim. If in certain cases he took an oath confirming his claim, however, only one witness was necessary. The testimony of women was admissible, but two women took the place of one man. The witnesses had to be known for their extreme religious and moral probity (*'adāla*), but the cross-examination of witnesses was not allowed. Consequently, the only recourse for the defendant was to impugn the witnesses' characters. Akbar ordered the *qāzīs* to investigate all cases diligently and stated that they should not be content merely with witnesses' oral statements or oaths but should question them personally.[35]

The Mughal regulations crystallized under Akbar and became law for all government departments. They also served as the guiding principles for the different ranks of servants in military, civil, and judicial departments in their dealings with people of mixed religions and races. The laws are epitomized in the voluminous *A'īn-i Akbarī* by Abu'l-Fazl, which nevertheless suffers from some serious gaps where rules and regulations are concerned. These deficiencies are remedied only by the documents known as *dastūru 'l-'amal* and by the *farmāns* from the reigns of Akbar and his successors. Not all the diaries of the official news reporters from the provinces have survived; the few that remain suggest that the working of the laws and regulations called for changes, which in fact were quite frequent until the reign of Shāhjahān. In Aurangzīb's reign there was a reversion to the *sharī'a.* The laws and regulations instituted by Akbar had been intended to ensure the maintenance of a tolerant, dynamic, and humane leadership over heterogeneous religious and racial groups. The fomentation of factionalism, disaffection, and disintegration in Mughal society, however, were stronger than any bonds of unity. Under Akbar and Jahāngīr the state laws were under constant threat from the orthodox Sunnī elements. Shāhjahān's calm and dignified personality engendered confidence in all classes, but like his predecessors he disposed of his deceased servants' property according to his own discretion. For example, the *sharī'a* law grants equal shares to all the sons and half the sons' shares between all the daughters. However, when the celebrated Irāni *mansabdār* 'Alī Mardān Khān died in 1657, Shāhjahān transferred fifty lakhs of rupees out of his estate to the treasury in settlement of his debts to the state. Of the remaining half he gave thirty lakhs to the eldest son, Ibrahim Khān, and twenty lakhs were shared between the remaining three sons and ten daughters.[36] By the eighteenth century the customary law gave no shares in their fathers' estate to daughters.

THE ROYAL COURT AND HOUSEHOLD

As was the case with the state laws, the Umayyad and 'Abbāsid caliphs, the Turkic sultans, and Mughal *pādshāhs* also derived their court ceremonials from pre-Islamic Irānian traditions. *Sijda* (prostration), known as *zamīnbos* (kissing the ground), before the sultan had become popular even prior to the establishment of the Delhi sultanate in India. During his reign Balban made the *sijda* rules even more elaborate and pompous, while in Islam Shāh's reign prostration was made before the vacant throne.[37]

In Akbar's reign, however, his private attendants were not allowed to prostrate themselves in the hall of public audience. This was permitted only in the hall of private audience. In the hall of public audience only the *kūrnīsh* and *taslīm* were performed. *Kūrnīsh* involved placing the right hand upon the forehead and bending the head downwards. *Taslīm* was performed by placing the back of the right hand on the floor and then raising it gently till the person stood erect. In both cases the forehead did not touch the ground, and the religious sentiments of the orthodox were not hurt. The *'ulamā'* and sūfis were invariably exempted from *sijda*, although many of them performed it privately before the sultans and *pādshāhs.*[38]

Some sultans were extravagant and licentious. The more serious ones held regular public audiences where they listened to the reports from the heads of department and noted the implementation of state regulations. Ambassadors from foreign countries were also received in public audience, and the tributary chiefs and important dignitaries were accorded a formal welcome there. The princes, ministers, heads of department, and other major officials were assigned fixed places to stand. The master of ceremonies at the sultan's court was known as *amīr-i hājib* or *bārbak*, and his assistants were called *hājibs* or *nā'ib bārbak.* They stood between the sultan and his subjects. Their duty was to prevent the violation of precedence in standing in the court and to present the petitioners to the sultan. They were members of the military class and acted as commanders of military expeditions when ordered to do so. The leading *hājibs* played an active role in the war councils. The *naqību'l-nuqabā'* (chief usher) and his assistants, called *naqībs*, announced loudly the sultan's orders to the soldiers. They also proclaimed the sultan's presence in the royal cavalcade. The insignia of the *naqību'l-nuqabā'*, consisting of a gold mace and a gold tiara surmounted by peacock feathers, added pomp and lustre to the courts. A body of soldiers called *silāhdār*, commanded by the *sar-silāhdār*, also waited on the sultan during the public audiences. The sultan's bodyguards, called *jāndārs*, were loyal soldiers and wore very impressive uniforms. Their commander was known as the *sar-jāndār.*

Akbar was more accessible to his subjects than were previous rulers. After performing his morning devotions he showed himself from a window on the first floor of the palace. A large crowd of all classes of people assembled outside the palace wall and could submit their petitions to the Emperor. Some were satisfied with having merely a glimpse of him. The practice was known as *jharokha-darshan.*[39] Some Hindus neither drank nor ate until they had seen the Emperor. Known as *darshanyas*, to them the Emperor was not merely a charismatic personality, but an incarnate god. Magnificent elephants and spirited horses were also inspected during the *jharokha-darshan* ceremony. Aurangzīb abolished this institution during the eleventh year of his reign because he considered that it amounted to the worship of a human being.

Under the Mughals formal state business was transacted in the *dīwān khāna-i 'āmm wa khāss* (hall of public audience), also known simply as the *dīwān-i 'āmm.* The Mughal emperors from Akbar to Aurangzīb spent some five to six hours daily in the *dīwān-i 'āmm.* There the ministers laid their departmental reports before the emperor, and expert gladiators, wrestlers, and musicians exhibited their skills. The appointments and promotions of *mansabdārs* and other senior officers were also announced there. Commanders and governors appeared before the emperor in the *dīwān-i 'āmm* before proceeding to their assignments. Ambassadors and victorious governors were received, and defeated rebels and other prisoners were presented there.

Father Monserrate gives an interesting picture of the conduct of state business in the *dīwān-i 'āmm* and in the *dīwān khāna-i khāss* (hall of private audience). In the latter Akbar listened to the suggestions of his ministers on state matters and gave his own verdict. It was also the scene of his intellectual activity, such as listening to the reading of books and discussions. Because of its proximity to the emperor's private bath, it was also known as the *ghusl-khāna* (bathroom).

Contemporary works give a very interesting glimpse of the secret state business transacted in the *ghusl-khāna.*[40] Important ambassadors and foreign dignitaries were invited there. During Shāhjahān's reign, however, consultations with princes and leading nobles were held in a more secret chamber called the Shāh Burj.

Under the sultans the royal household was controlled by an officer of very high rank, the *wakīl-i dar.* He supervised the payment of salaries and allowances to the sultan's personal staff. The Mughals, by contrast, did not attach much importance to their household officers, and they held only minor positions.

The *kārkhānas* (manufactories) were an important part of the royal household. Their controllers bought supplies for the royal household, which were then stored in these *kārkhānas.* Objects for royal use were also manufactured there. For example, in Muhammad bin Tughluq's reign four thousand silk weavers manufactured material for the robes of honour which the sultans lavishly distributed, while five hundred craftsmen were engaged in gold embroidery.

Sultan Fīrūz divided his *kārkhānas* into thirty-six sections. Their supreme controller was a leading noble; his subordinates, who supervised each *kārkhāna* separately, were also noblemen.[41] The *kārkhānas* under the Mughals were also known as *buyūtāt.* Besides storing and manufacturing articles for the emperor's household and the court's needs, the mint, public treasury, department for construction of monuments, roads, and repairs, and artillery were also included in the *buyūtāt. Kārkhānas* were even maintained in districts far from the capital in order to manufacture articles for which local craftsmen, especially weavers, were readily available. The growing luxury of the emperor's court and the need to send gifts to foreign courts engendered a competitive spirit in these *kārkhānas;* continued efforts were made to step up production and raise the standards of manufacture. Under Akbar the *dīwān-i buyūtāt* controlled the finances and working of the *buyūtāt.* From Jahāngīr's reign the *mīr-i sāmān* was made slightly senior to the *dīwān-i buyūtāt* although both were jointly responsible for the efficient working of the system. The *mīr-i sāmān* controlled the organization of the imperial tours and the establishment which accompanied the emperor.

Each *kārkhāna* was supervised by a *dārogha* (superintendent), while its cash and materials were in the charge of a *tahwīldār* (cash keeper), and its accounts were regularly audited by the *mustawfi* (auditor). The *mushrif-i kul-o juz* was the accountant for all sections of the *buyūtāt.*[42]

MINISTERS AND THEIR DEPARTMENTS

In the Qur'ān, Aaron is referred to as the vizier (*wazīr*) of his brother Moses, so the office was not of Irānian origin as is generally believed. The vizier combined some of the functions of a prime minister with some of those of the head of the civil administration. The later jurists such as al-Māwardī (974–1058) divided viziers into two categories: one had unlimited and the other limited power. The viziers of unlimited power emerged only during the decline of the 'Abbāsids and under weak sultans.

The text *Adābu'l-harb wa'sh Shujā'a*, dedicated to Sultan Iltutmish, says that just as the body could not survive without a soul, a government could not flourish without a vizier.[43] Even those prophets who were both apostles and kings and were guided by divine revelation did not rule the country without a vizier. Under the sultanate his department was called the *dīwān-i wizārat* and dealt mainly with income and expenditure. The vizier was assisted by the *mushrif-i mamālik* and the *mustawfi-i mamālik.* The officers in the *mushrif* department supervised the collection of revenue and audited the local accounts. The *mustawfi-i mamālik* controlled state expenditure. Both the *mushrif-i mamālik* and the *mustawfi-i mamālik* had direct access to the sultan. Sultan 'Ala'u'd-Dīn Khaljī's centralization of power into his own hands made the office of vizier insignificant, and although Sultan Muhammad respected his vizier, Khwaja-i Jahān, he made major decisions independently. On the other hand, Sultan Fīrūz never interfered with the administration of his vizier, Maqbul Khān-i Jahān.

The office of *nā'ibu'l mulk* (regent) was created under Iltutmish's successors in order to reduce the importance of viziers. The sultans were mere puppets in their hands. Towards the end of 'Ala'u'd-Dīn's reign Malik Kāfūr, the *nā'ibu'l mulk*, became virtual ruler, as was Khusraw Barādū, although still legally subordinate to Mubarak Khaljī.

Bayram Khān's position in Akbar's administration was historically of exceptional importance. Initially Akbar's tutor, he was created *wakīl-i saltanat* (prime minister) and during Akbar's minority he was to all intents and purposes the Emperor. After Bayram's dismissal, Akbar reduced the power of the *wakīl* and frequently left the position vacant for long periods. Jahāngīr did not fill the position between the fifth and twentieth years of his reign. From his appointment by Jahāngīr in 1626 until his own death in 1641 Āsaf Khān Abu'l-Hasan remained *wakīl* mainly because he was instrumental in raising Shāhjahān to the throne and was his father-in-law. He was the last of the *wakīls* of the Great Mughals. After his accession Shāhjahān gave him the title Yaminu'd-Dawla (Empire's Right-Hand Man) and a very large *mansab.* He regularly attended Shāhjahān's evening *darbār* to place all important affairs before the Emperor. He kept the seal and received a copy of the reports from the provinces and of every paper filed by the *dīwān-i kull.* All warrants of appointment were sealed and signed by Āsaf Khān, and the court reporter gave him daily intelligence reports.[44]

Bahadur Shāh I appointed Asad Khān as his *wakīl* but refused to give him the power enjoyed by Āsaf Khān, reminding him that the latter's powers emanated from family relationships. Asạd Khān, in fact, remained only the governor of Delhi. In short, the Mughals did not consider the *wakīl* indispensable to the state.[45]

Under the Delhi sultans, the state departments – four in number – were deemed the four pillars of the state. Of these the *dīwān-i wizarat* was concerned with finance, the *dīwān-i risālat* with religious matters, the *dīwān-i 'arz* organized military affairs, and the *dīwān-i insha'* dealt with the royal correspondence. Although the *dīwān-i wizārat* was senior to the other three, their ministers had direct access to the sultans and enjoyed equal respect. Akbar made them interdependent and sought the counsel of a galaxy of dignitaries and nobles who remained in attendance at the court.

During the sultanate period the word *dīwān* meant a government department and was used mainly for the *wazīr*'s department, but in Akbar's reign the term was identified with the *wazīr* himself, only to be separated again in Jahāngīr's reign when the word *wazīr* was again used to describe the individual. In Shāhjahān's reign the *wazīr* was called *dīwān-i kull* (principal *dīwān*) to distinguish him from the subordinate and provincial *dīwāns.* According to Abu'l- Fazl the *dīwān* was the emperor's lieutenant in financial matters, the superintendent of the imperial treasury, and the auditor of the accounts. The *dīwān* suggested rules and regulations for the assessment and collection of revenue, allocated funds for expenditure on state activities, and supervised the work of the departmental officers. He was also responsible for stepping up agricultural production and for improving the cultivators' conditions. During his long reign Akbar had several very talented finance ministers, but posterity has ascribed all his innovations to Raja Todar Mal, who worked as *dīwān* from the twenty-second to the twenty-fourth and from the twenty-seventh to the thirty-fourth years of the Emperor's reign. Jahāngīr's *dīwān* I'timādu 'd-Dawla owed his high position to his competence and not to the marriage of his daughter Nūr Jahān to the Emperor. Shāhjahān's original *dīwan-i kull*, Afzal Khān, was a very learned man and the Emperor's favourite. Islam Khān also successfully worked as Shāhjahān's *dīwan-i kull* from the thirteenth to the nineteenth year of his reign but, realizing that the Emperor wished to make Sa'du'llah Khān the *dīwan-i kull*, he volunteered to become governor of the Deccan, and Sa'du'llah Khān replaced him. The Emperor was deeply impressed with the loyalty and efficiency of the latter and would not listen to any complaints against his *dīwān-i kull*, even from his favourite, Dārā Shukoh. Sa'du'llah's death in the thirtieth year of his reign was deeply mourned by the Emperor and deemed an irreparable loss to the empire.[46]

The assistant *dīwāns* were generally Hindus. Each of the following four branches of the *dīwān-i kull* controlled a separate department. They were the *dīwān-i khālsa* (for *khalsa* land), *dīwān-i tan* (for salaries), *mushrif* (chief accountant), and *mustawfi* (auditor). Raghunāth Rāi, the *dīwān-i khālsa* from the twenty-third to the thirtieth year of Shāhjahān's reign, was assigned the duties of the *dīwān-i tan* from the twenty-sixth to the thirtieth year of that time. He also served Aurangzīb until his own death in June 1663.

On a more senior level the ministry was responsible for the military administration, which under the Delhi sultanate was called the *dīwān-i 'arz.* Its head was referred to as the *'ārīz-i mamalik.* He directed the recruitment of soldiers and officers, maintained the muster rolls, controlled promotions and demotions, and revised salaries. The *'ārīz* also controlled the commissariat. 'Ala'u'd-Dīn Khaljī introduced the system of branding horses and maintaining a roll describing each trooper, but Fīrūz Tughluq discontinued these practices.

Under the early sultans the royal cavalry in Delhi were called *hasham-i qalb* or *ajwāj-i qalb.* They were picked troopers comprising the *jandārs* (royal bodyguards) and sultans' slaves. *Hasham-i atrāf* was the name given to the troops posted in the provincial head-quarters and the garrisons. According to Thomas, 'the form of the saddle, the seat of the horseman, the *chanfrein* or head armour of the steed and his erect tail' as portrayed on Iltutmish's coins 'seem to point to the Turki ideals of a best in horsemen'. Barbosa's description of the Gujarāti and Deccani troops in the fifteenth century is also very impressive. The army was organized on the basis of a decimal system. Although Bughra Khān's classification of military grades did not necessarily represent the true state of military command,[47] al-'Ūmarī, an important authority, says that a *khān* commanded ten thousand horsemen or more, a *malik* commanded a thousand, an *amīr* a hundred, and a *sipah sālār* less than one hundred.[48] Amir Khusraw also confirms this decimal gradation.

Although the Turks dominated the army of the early sultans, troopers of other races, including Hindus, were not ignored. The practice of employing Hindu troops had started as early as the reign of Qutbu'd-Dīn Aybak, and they served the sultans with loyalty and devotion.

According to the *Ādabu'l-harb*, bows were the troopers' most prized weapons, followed by the sword. The short spear, the short lance, the mace, and the lasso were also used. The finest horses were found in the sultan's stables, as he exercised a monopoly over their purchase. Many horses were imported from Hazramawt and the Persian Gulf region, although the Panjāb hills were also fine horse-breeding grounds. Horses were also bought from the Himalayas and north-eastern regions.

Elephants were effectively used from the days of Mahmūd of Ghaznī, who developed an impressive stable which contained 1,000 elephants, tended by a Hindu staff. The elephants were lined up in the front and centre of the armies. When out of control they played havoc with the ranks, but their advantages were believed to outweigh the disadvantages, and they were always present.

Before 'Ala'u'd-Dīn Khaljī's reign the sultans assigned *iqtā's*, the revenues from different territorial units, to their military commanders for their personal maintenance and that of their troops. These *iqtā's* were frequently transferred and were not identical with the fiefs of the European feudal age. The yield of each *iqtā'* was roughly estimated, and the assignees were given more than was needed for their maintenance. The *iqtā'* holders or *muqta's* were expected to remit the surplus, or *fawāzil* to the sultan, but this was occasionally withheld by adventurers such as 'Ala'u'd-Dīn Khaljī.

During Iltutmish's reign *iqtā's* were also distributed to some two to three thousand Delhi troopers in the *doāb* and around Delhi. By Balban's reign most of the troopers had died, and the remainder were now invalids. Their *iqtā's*, however, with the connivance of the military department, had become incorporated into their family estates. Balban initially decided to resume all *iqtā's* belonging to those who could not render military service but desisted on the recommendation of his *kotwāl*, Malik Fakhru'd-Dīn.

'Ala'u'd-Dīn Khaljī abolished the system of assigning *iqtā's* to his standing army and paid them a cash salary. The valuation of the *iqtā'* he gave to the commanders in provinces was calculated exactly and was equivalent to the commander's salary plus the pay for his troopers. This was deemed a direct charge on the state treasury and not left to the commander's discretion.[49] Sultan Muhammad bin Tughluq was also strict in assigning *iqtā's* and in some cases rescinded the commander's power to collect reven ue. Under Fīrūz the practice of assigning revenue to the standing army was restored, and the transfer of *iqtā's* became rare.[50] To all intents and purposes the *iqtā'* system as it was before the time of 'Ala'u'd-Dīn continued to be followed until the sixteenth century. The Afghāns divided the empire into large areas, assigned to the tribal leaders.

The infantry was mainly composed of Hindus and slaves called *pāyak.* They were efficient archers (*dhānuk*). Barbosa found the bows of the Deccan foot-soldiers as long as those in England. As bodyguards they were most trustworthy. Not only did they save the sultans' lives on many occasions but they also thwarted various rebel conspiracies.

Under the Mughals the duties of the *mīr bakhshī* were complex. He was responsible for presenting the candidates for *mansabs* (grant of ranks) to the emperor, although the princes, governors, and commanders of various military expeditions could also, on the basis of their knowledge, introduce prospective *mansabdārs* to the emperor. The papers regarding the rank and salary of the *mansabdārs* approved by the emperor were prepared mainly in the offices of the *dīwān-i tan* and the *bakhshīs.* The formalities were tedious. The *mansabdārs* had to furnish surety, and according to Manucci even the princes 'had to conform to the customs'.[51] Bankers and money-lenders were readily accepted as guarantors for the good behaviour and character of the candidates, although eminent *mansabdārs* also acted as guarantors.

The *mir bakhshī* or his assistants inspected the soldiers, the horses, the beasts of burden, and other accoutrements which the *mansabdārs* were required to maintain. The horses approved by the *mīr bakhshī* were branded (*dāgh*), and a roll describing the soldiers (*tashiha*) was compiled. Not only the appointment papers of the *mansabdārs* but even those of other ministers passed through the *mīr bakhshī.* The *mīr bakhshī* asssigned to different *mansabdārs* the duty of mounting guard on the royal palace. This practice enabled Shaykh Farid, the *mīr bakhshī* during the last years of Akbar's reign, to foil the attempts by Khān-i A'zam, the *wakīl*, and Raja Man Singh to raise Khusraw, in supersession of Prince Salīm, to the throne.

News reports from the provinces were first received by the *mīr bakhshī* and then presented to the emperor, either directly or through the *wakīl.* The *mīr bakhshī* accompanied the emperor on his tours, hunting expeditions, and pleasure trips. When the emperor personally commanded the army on the battle-front, the *mīr bakhshī* accompanied him. He was also ordered to go on all important military campaigns led by the princes. Sometimes the *mīr bakhshī* were given independent commands in battle, when they were assisted by two other *bakhshīs* deployed at the centre of the army.

THE MANSABDĀRS AND THE ARMY

Mansab means literally a rank or a position. It also meant a function, prerogative, or duty. The *mansabdārs*, or holders of *mansabs*, were required to perform either military or civil duties or both, but all of them were placed on the military payroll. This was the most significant feature of the system. According to the *Akbar-nāma*, in 1573 Akbar introduced regulations concerning the branding of horses (*dāgh*) and fixing the grades of the officers of the state (*marātib*), despite the nobles' stubborn resistance. Two years later, when Akbar returned from his Bihār expedition, the *dāgh* regulations were completely implemented, and the officers' *mansabs* were fixed according to their merit and the contingents they maintained. A cash payment had been substituted for the assignment of territories (*jāgīr*). According to the *Ā'in-i Akbarī*, the ranks (*mansabs*) of *mansabdārs* ranged from the *dahbāshi* (commander of ten) to the *dah hazārī* (commander of 10,000), but *mansabs* above 5,000 were reserved for the princes. Following the numerical value of the letters in the name Allah, sixty-six *mansabs* were established, although only thirty-three feature in the *A'in.* It would seem that some *mansabs* were not assigned and that others were dropped to simplify the system.

Until 1595 each *mansabdār* had to keep in his pay the number of troopers indicated by his rank. He also maintained a fixed number of horses, elephants, camels, and carts. However, many *mansabdārs* were unable to fulfil their obligations. For example, the historian Mulla Badā'ūnī, who was a *mansabdār* of twenty, should have maintained twenty horsemen but could not afford to do so. Other *mansabdārs* were in the same position. Realizing the hardships suffered by many *mansabdārs*, in 1595 Akbar divided them into three categories: first, those who had troopers equal in number to their *mansab;* second, those who had half or more; third, those who had less than half. In the table of *mansabdārs*, the *A'in-i Akbari*, compiled that same year, gives only single-number *mansabs* and mentions the number of horses of different categories, elephants, camels, and carts that that grade of *mansabdār* was required to maintain. It does not list the number of horsemen. The dual ranks of *zāt* and *sawār* occur from early 1597, and the first important *mansabdār* mentioned with both was Mīrza Shāhrukh with 5,000 *zāt* and 2,000 *sawār.* The number of horsemen which a *mansabdār* had to maintain was indicated in his *sawār* rank, while the *zāt* rank indicated his personal pay in the pay schedules. Sūrviving pay schedules from Shāhjahān's reign show that the salary against *zāt* and *sawār* ranks was different. The salary paid to a *mansabdār* against the *zāt* rank included his personal pay and the cost of the horses, elephants, camels, and carts which were his responsiblity according to the schedule. By Aurangzlb's time, the *mansabdār*'s *sawār* rank was generally higher than his *zāt* rank. Consequently the pay against *sawār* ranks, or the troops maintained by him, was generally more than double the *zāt* rank. The *zāt* rank was not symbolic nor intended to decide precedence among the *mansabdārs.* Both the *zāt* and *sawār* ranks were meant to show particular obligations and salaries.[52]

Some *mansabdārs* were paid in cash from the imperial treasury, but generally they were assigned a territory known as *jāgīr*, whose estimated revenue (*jama'*) was equal to the pay due for their *zāt* and *sawār maruabs.* The *jāgīrs* were the same as *iqtā's;* sometimes these terms were interchangeable. The word *tuyūl* was also used for *jāgīr.* Those who were granted *jāgīrs* were known *jāgīrdārs.* The *jāgīr* assigned in lieu of salary were known as *tankhwāh jāgīr.* The territorial chiefs were also granted *mansābs*, and their salary was equivalent to the *jama'* (revenue) from their dominions, known as the *watān jāgīr.* Beside the latter, some territorial chiefs were also granted *tankhwāh jāgīr* in the imperial territory, depending upon their merit and service. The *tankhwāh jāgīr* was one of the major inducements to the territorial chiefs to remain loyal to the Mughal throne.

Jāgīrs, like *iqtā's*, were transferable, and ordinarily no *mansabdār* held a *jāgīr* in one place for more than three to four years. In fact, the *jāgīrdārs* and their officers were generally not sure of keeping the same holding for more than one year. The *jāgīrs* did not correspond necessarily with the revenue divisions in the empire. These were administered by the imperial officers and not by the *jāgīrdārs'* employees, and their tax collectors were not allowed to violate the emperor's revenue and tax regulations. In 1647 about 60 per cent of the estimated revenue (*jama'*) of the empire was assigned to 445 *mansabdārs* of 500 rank and above.[53] This accounts for the concentration of the bulk of the country's wealth among less than five hundred families in the empire. A *mansabdār's* salary was calculated on the basis of very complex schedules, but even top commanders like 'Abdu'r-Rahīm Khān-i Khānān in Akbar's reign, or princes such as Dārā Shukoh under Shāhjahān, were not satisfied with their respective grants and transfers. All the *mansabdārs* pressured the *dīwān-i kull* to give them the most easily manageable villages as their *jāgīrs*, although it was government policy to assign them the *jāgīrs* nearest the stations where they were posted.

The trooper's salary varied according to the number and type of horses he possessed. Additionally, in 1595, by an imperial order, the Rājpūt soldiers drew a slightly lower wage than the Mughal, Afghān, and Indian Muslim troopers. It would seem that the supply of Rājpūt soldiers exceeded demand.[54]

Some particularly efficient troops were taken under the emperor's control by Akbar and his successors. They were ordinarily not placed under the *mansabdārs.* They were named *ahadīs* (from *ahad* or 'one'), as a reminder that Akbar believed in divine unity. Their equipment was of a very high standard, and their salary was 500 rupees. Each had to muster five horses. They were placed under a separate *dīwān* and *bakhshī* and were mustered every four months. When recruited they had to bring their own horses, but these were later on supplied by the government.[55] In the Mughal decline of the eighteenth century the term *ahadī* came to mean 'idler'. The crack troops had lost their vitality and energy.

According to de Laet, Jahāngīr inherited from his father 2,941 *mansabdārs*, ranging from the rank of 10 to 5,000. In the twentieth year of Shāhjahān's reign there were 8,000 *mansabdārs* and 7,000 *ahadīs* and mounted artillerymen, paid by the imperial treasury.[56]

The Mughal infantry was also divided into several categories. These included the *darbāns* (porters) and the *khidmatiyyas* (palace guards). According to Abu 'l-Fazl, the *khidmatiyya* caste were originally notorious highway robbers whom the earlier sultans had been unable to control. Akbar, however, took them into his service and tamed them. He also recruited the natives of Mewāt, known as *mewras*, who made excellent spies. Even several kinds of gladiator were incorporated into part of the infantry, while Irāni and Tūrānī boxers and wrestlers, some of whom became celebrities in their day, were employed as infantrymen. Slaves were also included in the infantry. Akbar called them *chelas* or disciples because he disliked using the word 'slave'. He detested the custom of Muslims buying Hindus for slaves and vice versa. Palanquin bearers, and others who carried heavy loads on their shoulders, also belonged to the infantry.[57]

Some recent scholars, such as Abū Zafar Nadvī and Muhammad Akram Makhdoomee, assert that the Delhi sultans introduced artillery into India. It would seem, however, that they wrongly confused the naphtha- and missile-throwing engines such as mangonels with gunpowder and cannon. The literary evidence from the sultanate period suggests that it was in the mid-fourteenth century that gunpowder became known in northern India and explosive devices were introduced, possibly through Turkey. In the second half of the fifteenth century sultans such as Zaynu'l-'Ābidīn of Kashmīr, Mahmūd Begarha of Gujarāt, and Mahmūd Shāh Bahmanī are known to have possessed guns, and the last two used them on military expeditions.[58]

Bābur was the first to use cannon effectively in battle and he gives a vivid description of making a cannon at Agra. In Humāyūn's reign the number of guns in the Emperor's arsenal increased considerably. According to Abu'l-Fazl, only Turkey could compete with India in the manufacture of guns. Bābur's gunners were from Turkey. The number of Portuguese and other European gunners in India increased as a result of Akbar's conquest of Gujarāt and Bengal, but Akbar himself remained the major innovator in gun manufacture. Although firearms were mainly used in siege operations, Akbar made both light and very heavy guns. Those known as *narnāls* could be carried by a single person; others, such as *gajnāls*, were carried on elephants. Some guns could be taken to pieces for easy handling during marches and reassembled later.[59] In Akbar's reign Hakīm Fathu'llah Shīrāzī invented the multi-barrelled cannon.

At the end of the Thirty Years War in Europe (1618–48) many European adventurers with considerable experience of firearms came to India and obtained service under the Mughals. For example, Niccolao Manucci, an Italian boy of fourteen, reached India as a stowaway in 1646. Despite this, the cannon manufacturing techniques did not improve. Thévenot says: 'They have Cannon also in their Towns, but since they melt the Metal in diverse Furnaces, so that some of it must needs be better melted than others when they mingle together, their Cannon is commonly good for nothing.'[60]

A matchlock contingent was also included in the infantry. According to Abu'l-Fazl, earlier matchlocks could not be filled for more than a quarter of the barrel without bursting when fired, but Akbar's matchlocks were so strong that they did not explode though filled to the top. Some of Akbar's guns were two yards long, others only nine inches in length. Improved barrels were submitted to Akbar for inspection, and the modifications he suggested were implemented in the design.[61]

Akbar also profitably used elephants on the battlefield, and there are many examples of his chivalry in controlling them when they were enraged. Akbar had no navy and did not possess any sea-going ships. The *Ā'in-i Akbarī* suggests, however, that shipbuilding was not altogether neglected. Vessels were constructed on the west, south, and east coasts of India. Those ships built in Allahabad and Lahore were sent to the coast, while vessels for pilgrimage and commerce were constructed by the Mughal artisans. Larger boats, for the transport of troops and military stores, were built in Bengal, Kashmīr, and Sind.

FINANCE

Charity in general and the payment of *zakāt* (alms tax) in particular are obligatory duties for Muslims. As a rule the property assessable for *zakāt* should have been in the owner's possession for at least one year. This law, however, enabled some property owners to evade payment with impunity. For example, Makhdūmu'l-Mulk used to transfer all his property to his wife towards the end of the year and then repossess it before the year had run out.[62] Similar tricks are ascribed to several Muslim dignitaries. *Zakāt* money is paid specifically to different categories of poor people and was not a source of revenue for the rulers. It was Fīrūz Shāh Tughluq who included *zakāt* on his list of regular state demands and established a separate treasury for it.

The 2½ per cent *zakāt* on Muslim traders' imports and exports was levied under both the sultans and the Mughals. Pious merchants conscientiously paid *zakāt*. Some of them believed that the blessings obtained from this payment protected them from the loss of their merchandise, although it was known that many dishonest Muslim merchants evaded paying it.

No records of customs rates under the Delhi sultans are available. Abu'l-Fazl confirms that 2¼ per cent was the maximum under Akbar. Finch says that the charges at Sūrat were 2½ per cent on goods and 3 per cent on provisions. In Jahāngīr's reign customs duties were 3½ per cent on all imports and exports of goods and 2 per cent on money, either gold or silver. According to Pelsaert, these duties were collected for the king by the governor of Gujarāt but formerly 'they were assigned to various lords as salary'.[63] In Thévenot's time, customs duties ranged from 4 to 5 per cent. Aurangzīb fixed a higher rate for non-Muslims, but the order was not effective, because Muslim merchants smuggled goods belonging to Hindus, thus paying a lower rate of 2½ per cent.[64]

Transit dues were also realized, although Akbar remitted them on at least two occasions. The river toll, however, was always levied under Akbar. Jahāngir remitted both road and river dues. According to travellers such as Mundy, Thévenot, and Tavernier, transit dues were in force throughout large areas of the country. Father Manrique tells how the passport granted to him as an ecclesiastic to travel from Lahore to the mouth of the Indus was used by a merchant in his party to evade many demands during the journey. [65]

Innumerable articles, mainly vegetables, betel-leaves, meat, and fish, were subject to octroi levies. Cesses were imposed on trades such as cotton carding, soap-, rope-, oil- and brick-making, and maintaining gambling houses and centres of amusement, probably brothels. Sultan Fīrūz remitted these cesses, finding them not sanctioned by the *sharī'a.* According to Father Monserrate, the low prices prevailing in Akbar's camp were due to goods being exempted from tax.[66] Although after their accession Akbar's successors also reissued orders to stop the cesses on merchandise and trades, they had become so deeply rooted in the normal trade practices of the times that the orders were never fully implemented.

Presents were often another source of income at court. The presentation of gifts to the court and noblemen was an important custom. The more valuable gifts were presented by foreign visitors and officials of all ranks. Under the Mughals the emperor received presents on all festive occasions, birthdays and accession anniversaries, and even after recovering from an illness. The *mansabdārs* also made gifts on occasions such as their promotion and reinstatement. The rulers reciprocated by giving robes of honour, precious jewels, and rare objects to show honour to their noblemen and visitors.

Foreign observers condemned the Mughal emperors for enriching their treasury by confiscating the property of their deceased *mansabdārs.* For example, Pelsaert says:

> Immediately on the death of a lord who has enjoyed the King's *jāgīr*, be he great or small, without any exception – even before the breath is out of the body – the King's officers are ready on the spot, and make an inventory of the entire estate, recording everything down to the value of a single pice, even to the dresses and jewels of the ladies, provided they have not concealed them. The King takes back the whole estate absolutely for himself, except in a case where the deceased has done good service in his lifetime, when the women and children are given enough to live on, but no more.[67]

The literature on the subject shows that the Mughal *mansabdārs* in fact borrowed enormous sums from the state for their military expeditions and invariably died in debt. The Mughal confiscation system simply offered the state first claim on their estate. When disposing of the rest of the deceased's property, the Mughal emperors violated *sharī'a* laws by granting larger shares to the elder sons or to their favourites.

In the early centuries of the Arab and Turkish conquests, booty (*ghanīma*) was an important source of state finance. According to the *sharī'a* one-fifth is set apart for the state, and the remaining four-fifths are distributed among the soldiers, although mounted troopers receive one or two shares more. On the other hand, the Indian sultans generally appropriated four-fifths themselves and distributed one-fifth to the soldiers. Since the army consisted of paid soldiers, the sultans did not consider this policy illegal. Fīrūz, however, restored the early Islamic rules, although the booty acquired in his reign was almost negligible. But for petty campaigns, the Mughals did not distribute booty to their soldiers, for their army was organized on a non-religious basis.

Jizya (poll-tax) formed an important source of the Muslim rulers' finances. It was sanctioned by the Qur'ān. *Jizya* was levied on Jews, Christians, and Zoroastrians, who were known as protected subjects (*zimmīs*). Both taxes were prevalent in the Sassanian and Roman-Byzantine empires conquered by the Arabs. Those who embraced Islam were exempted from paying *jizya* but then became liable to pay *zakāt.* Islamicization neither undermined state finances nor helped the convert financially.

As mentioned earlier, Muhammad bin Qasim accorded both Hindus and Buddhists *zimmī* status and imposed *jizya* on them. According to Imām Malik, *jizya* could be collected from 'faithless Turks and Indians'. The same view was held by Imām Abū Hanīfa. It would appear that the Ghaznavids and Delhi sultans collected *jizya* from Hindus according to the *shari'ā* law.

Western historians such as Hardy,[68] because of an incorrect interpretation of the historical texts, and some Muslim historians, in order to demonstrate Islamic liberalism, try to prove that under the Delhi sultans *jizya* meant land revenue. In fact, under the Delhi sultans the imposition of *jizya* was not disputed. The moot question was the legality of giving *zimmī* status to Hindus. A section of *'ulamā'* urged that Hindus should either be converted to Islam or be slaughtered. The sultans and their viziers had to perform the uphill task of convincing the unrealistic *'ulamā'* of the impracticability of their demand. The earlier Turkic sultans correctly exempted brāhmans from the payment of *jizya*, but Sultan Fīrūz wrongly imposed it on them, blaming the earlier sultans for incorrectly interpreting the *sharī'a* law. The brāhmans protested and resorted to hunger strikes, but the Sultan did not relent. Ultimately, the rich Hindus offered to pay *jizya* on their behalf; as a concession the Sultan reduced the prevalent rate in the case of brāhmans. Sultan Fīrūz could also boast that his orders to remit *jizya* made a deep impact upon the Hindus, and a large number of them embraced Islam.[69] The collection of *jizya* from the Hindus in towns posed no problem, but in the villages, like early land-revenue collections, it was assessed as a collective tax.

In 1564 Akbar remitted the collection of *jizya.* According to Abu'l-Fazl, it was imposed both from contempt for the rival faith and to facilitate the accumulation of wealth by the rulers. Abu'l- Fazl goes on to say that Akbar found no justification for collecting *jizya;* for not only had men of all other religions become his devoted servants, but his treasury was already full.[70] Although Akbar's advisers, the *'ulamā'*, and the revenue experts opposed him, he rejected their representations. For the rest of Akbar's reign and the reigns of Jahāngīr and Shāhjahān no *jizya* was collected.

Aurangzīb also did not collect *jizya* during the first twenty years of his reign· but he reimposed this tax on non-Muslims in April 1679. According to a contemporary historian, the Emperor's principal aim was to spread the law of Islam and to overthrow infidel practices. Khāfī Khān, another historian, says that the new law was designed to reduce the Hindus to poverty. [71] The Satnāmī rebellions of 1672 had already upset the Delhi Muslims, and the Emperor may have believed that Hindu affluence was the root cause of the local uprisings. For the imposition of *jizya* the population was divided into rich, middle, and poor classes. Those who owned property worth ten thousand *dirhams* or more were classed as rich, those with property valued at two hundred *dirhams* or more as the middle class, and those with property at less than two hundred *dirhams* as poor[72] Since the *dirham* was not current, the collection was made in silver. According to J. N. Sarkar's calculations, the rates for the three classes respectively were 13⅓, 6⅔, and 3⅓ rupees; i.e. 6 per cent of the gross income of the poor, 6¼ per cent on the middle class and 2½ per thousand on the rich. The tax naturally hit the poorest section. Government officials and the priestly classes were exempt. In commercial centres such as Gujarāt, *jizya* yielded 3½ per cent per annum of the total gross revenue of the province and was quite sufficient to provide the *'ulamā'* with a holy source of livelihood.[73]

The outcry and demonstrations by the Hindus of Delhi, particularly the artisans, money-lenders, and cloth merchants, were of no avail. Several Hindu demonstrators were trampled to death under the feet of the elephants and horses, and ultimately they surrendered. The literary evidence suggests that the Muslim *jizya* collectors were generally harsh, but it is difficult to believe Manucci's report that 'many Hindus who were unable to pay turned Muhammadan'.[74]

The principal financial source of both the Delhi sultans and the Mughals was, however, land revenue (*kharāj*). The administrative framework of this tax before the thirteenth century is not known, but it would seem that in India the traditions from the Arab rulers of Sind and the Ghaznavid rulers were followed. The owners of cultivated land were not dispossessed, but any land, particularly that near the capital, whose owner had been killed in battle or was not traceable was allotted to Muslims. The Muslim owners paid one-tenth (*'ushr*) of their produce in tax on land watered by rain, but on land dependent for irrigation with buckets or wheels only one-twentieth of the produce was paid as a levy. These blocks of land were known as *'ushri.* The land left with its known Hindu owners and that allotted to Hindus was known as *kharājī* or *kharāj*-paying (land-revenue-paying) land. Other terms used for *kharāj*, especially under the Mughals, were *hāsil* or *māl.* In the thirteenth century a collective assessment of revenue was made on the villages. Their chiefs, known as *rānas*, *rā'is* and *rāwats*, paid revenue to the *iqtā'* holders.

Those villages where revenue was reserved for the sultan's treasury were known as *khālisas.* They also paid revenue on the basis of collective assessment. The sultan's *muhassils* (revenue collectors) realized the demands through the village headmen known as *chawdhrīs*, *muqaddams*, and *khūts.* These headmen were often very rich, for they did not themselves pay *kharaj*, *jizya*, and other taxes but collected the perquisites due to them for working as a headman from their own villages. Sultan 'Ala'u'd-Dīn had all the land under cultivation measured, and the revenue was fixed on the basis of a standard yield. No concessions or perquisites were granted to the chiefs, who were assessed on a par with the *balāhars* or ordinary peasants. The standard *kharāj* (revenue demand) was fixed at one-half of the produce, and a tax was also imposed on the pastures. An army of revenue collectors (*'āmils*), accountants, and auditors was recruited to collect the land revenue, which was realized in kind, although there was also cash payment in some areas. The collectors' vigilance made the *chawdhrīs*, *muqaddams*, and *khūts* subservient.[75] The new system of taxation was enforced in all areas easily accessible from Delhi, but these did not include eastern Uttar Pradesh, Bihār, lower Panjāb, and Gujarāt.

The structure of 'Ala'u'd-Dīn's innovations crumbled before his death. His successor, Ghiyāsu'd-Dīn Tughluq, was a moderate. He does not seem to have reduced the state demand for one-half of the produce but he prevented any further increases and removed the levy on pastures. He also replaced the crop-sharing system with the measurement system inaugurated by 'Ala'u'd-Dīn in the *khālisas.* The headmen's perquisites were restored, but they were encouraged to co-operate with the government towards the improvement of cultivation and collection of revenue. The *iqtā'* holders in charge of the *kharāj* land had always been under pressure to remit more, but Ghiyāsu'd-Dīn Tughluq fixed the increase between 10 and 11 per cent.

The next ruler, Sultan Muhammad bin Tughluq, enhanced revenue in the Gangetic *doāb.* He also sought to increase the government's power by collecting revenue through his own collectors, or farming out the *iqtā'* revenue to the highest bidder.

His successor, Sultan Fīrūz, instituted a six-year survey of crop production, enabling him to fix permanently the estimated revenue (*jama'*) of the sultanate at 67,500,000 *tankas.* The entire revenue of the country was assigned to the army and civil officers, and these assignments were made hereditary. However, only 50 per cent of the amount mentioned in these orders was paid to the troopers or *iqtā'* holders by the village officers; apparently the rest was appropriated as collection charges. These assignments could also be sold for 30 per cent of their face value to city brokers. Under the rebellious governors of Fīrūz's successor, however, it proved impossible for the assignment holders to collect anything at all.

The Lodīs and Sūrs assigned hereditary *iqtā's* to the Afghān tribal leaders. Sultan Sikandar Lodī introduced the *gaz-i Sikandarī* (Sikandar's yard) of 32 digits for measuring cultivated fields, but the revenue based on this was confined to the *khālisas.* The principal *iqtā'* holders could assign parts of territory to their subordinates for raising troops. In Sher Shāh's reign also the systems of crop sharing and imposition of fixed revenue demand were given up. Revenue was fixed on the basis of measurements; the only exceptions were those regions which were not completely subdued, such as Multān and Rājasthān. Schedules for crop rates were prepared on the basis of the quality of the land, but his reign was too short to crystallize the system.

In the early years of Akbar's reign the crop schedules and *jama'* (assessed revenue) schedules of the Sūr rulers were made the basis of the revenue administration, although new experiments were constantly made to find a sound revenue policy. Between 1567 and 1571 the Sūr schedules of crop rates were replaced by separate schedules for seasonal harvests. In 1575 the old method of measuring the land with hemp ropes was discarded, and a measure consisting of bamboo poles linked together with iron rings was adopted. By 1576 the empire was greatly expanded, and a new survey and assessment had to be undertaken. The year 1580 was a watershed in Akbar's revenue reforms because of the introduction of the *ā'īn-i dahsāla*. This did not mean the 'laws for ten years' as the term implies, but laid down the *dastūrs* or annual demand rates in cash per area unit. Each area unit was a different assessment circle and consisted of smaller circles of the same type of soil fertility. The price, crop, and revenue over the previous ten years was the principal basis for the new assessment.[76]

In June 1588 the *gaz-i Ilāhī*, or new yard for land measurement, consisting of forty-one digits (approximately 33 inches) was introduced. The *gaz-i Ilāhī* helped to standardize the land survey. Farmers were allowed the option of paying their land tax through various systems such as the *kankūt* (a rough estimate of the produce in a field), or crop sharing, called *batā'ī*, *bhaulī*, or *ghalla-bakhshī*, but the state's share was calculated in cash before collection.[77]

The system's success depended upon the efficiency, competence, and resourcefulness of the *amalguzār* or the *pargana* revenue collectors, who were obliged to act in a friendly fashion to the peasants. They were required to advance loans to needy farmers and recover them in easy instalments. The collectors were assisted by the village headmen, who received 2½ per cent of the tax as remuneration after the realization of the full rental. The farmers were encouraged to pay their dues direct to the *pargana* treasury, however, and the collectors were warned not to depend on the headmen for the survey and assessment of land. The collection of the winter harvest (*rabī'*) commenced on the day of the Hindu festival of Holi (in March), while that of the harvest of the rainy season (*kharīf*) started from the Hindu Dasehra day (in October).

The collectors' main duty was to extend the areas of crop production by encouraging the cultivation of former waste-lands. If no unused land was left in a village, the farmers could be given any surplus in the neighbouring villages. The collectors were also required to encourage the planting of more valuable crops such as sugar-cane, oil-seed, spices, and poppies. They were responsible for supervising the land surveyors, assessors, and other revenue officials.

In the reign of Akbar's successors the revenue rates were revised from time to time, but the broad framework evolved under Akbar remained the same. The surviving revenue guidebooks compiled in Aurangzīb's reign also urged the Mughal officers to be friendly towards the farmers and to reclaim any waste-land.. In no case was more than one-half of the produce to be taken as land revenue. It was stressed that the survey papers, *jama'* schedules, and other revenue records had to be compiled carefully and punctually.

JUSTICE

As we have seen, the *'ulamā'* endeavoured to transform Islam into a religion of law, but, as custodians of justice, the rulers made the *sharī'a* courts subservient to their sovereign power. Theoretically the rulers had to be obedient to the *sharī'a*, and history has preserved cases where sovereigns unhesitatingly submitted to the *qazīs* decision. However, as the supreme authority who appointed judges and ministers, the rulers sat in a court known as *mazālim* (complaints). According to Ibn Battūta, Muhammad bin Tughluq heard complaints each Monday and Thursday. Baranī says that Muhammad bin Tughluq founded a special court called *dīwān-i siyāsat*, presided over by tyrannical judges, in order to ruthlessly kill his Muslim opponents.[78] This is a gross misrepresentation of the Sultan's efforts to establish his system of justice on a broader basis.

From the thirteenth century onwards, an officer known as the *amīr-i dād* presided over the secular court in the sultan's absence. He was also responsible for implementing the *qāzīs'* decisions and for drawing their attention to cases which, in his opinion, constituted miscarriages of justice.

The *muftīs* were the experts on *sharī'a* law and gave *fatwas* (formal legal rulings) on disputes referred to them by members of the public or by *qāzīs*. Their rulings were binding in matters of marriage, divorce, and inheritance, but other legal questions were either decided by the *qāzīs* or were left to the ruler's discretion. The chief judge of the sultanate was known as the *qāzī-i mamālik*, also known as the *qāzīu 'l-quzāt*. *Qāzīs* were also appointed to the army and in the towns.

Discord could nevertheless erupt between the *qāzīs* and the sovereign, and after the rebellion in the eastern provinces in 1580 Akbar ordered a large number of *qāzīs* to be killed or exiled for inciting disaffection and revolt. For all that, many *qāzīs* were efficient and honest; Shaykh Mu'īn (d. 1587), the *qāzī* of Lahore, was described by Mulla Badā'ūnī as 'an angel in human form'. His successor was Shī'ī, Sayyid Nūru'llāh Shustarī (1549–1610), although Lahore was predominantly Sunnī. Badā'ūnī, a Sunnī fanatic himself, praised Shustarī in glowing terms: 'In truth he has reduced the insolent *muftīs* and crafty and subtle *muhtasibs* of Lahore, who ventured to give lessons to the teacher of the angels, to order and has closed to them the avenues of bribery, and restrained them within due bounds as closely as a nut is enclosed in its shell, and to such a degree that stricter discipline could not be imagined.'[79]

The counterpart of the secular judge (*amīr-i dād*) of the Delhi sultans was the *mīr 'adl* of the Mughals. He acted as a judge on the emperor's behalf. He was not allowed to depend solely on witnesses' oaths and testimony but was required to make impartial and diligent personal inquiries. The *mīr 'adl* was also responsible for implementing the *qāzīs*' decisions. The Emperor Jahāngīr considered himself finally responsible for justice in his realm and sought to enhance the importance of the *mazālim* court.

Under the Mughals the *qāzīs* continued as registrars of surety bonds, bail bonds, contracts, and title deeds. In 1591–2 Qazi Nūru'llah Shustarī was appointed by

Akbar to the commission examining the maladministration of the revenue from Kashmīr. He was also sent to Agra five years later to investigate the tenures of the *madad-i ma'āsh* grants.[80]

A growing acceptance of the *qāzīs*' authority in civil cases was manifested in the provinces and districts when provincial governors and local officers consulted them. The fundamental conflict of interests remained, however, and, according to the records surviving from Aurangzīb's reign, disagreements between the *qāzīs* and the civil and military authorities were still frequent.

The size of the Mughal empire made it difficult to recruit talented and honest *qāzīs*. Naturally in India these posts in the smaller towns became hereditary. During Aurangzīb's reign the *qāzī* of Jodhpūr was an uneducated man. These *qāzīs* were forced to depend upon the local chiefs' recommendations and they usually advised them to base their decisions on local customs, which were sometimes contrary to the sharī'a. Shāh Nawāz Khān's remarks about the *qāzīs* in Aurangzīb's reign are most revealing. He says:

> Those who sell religion for worldliness (*dīn ba dunyā*) regard this noble office as a very easy one and spend money in bribes (to obtain it), in order that by doing away with the rights of men they may extort a hundred times more. They regard *nikāhāna* (fees on marriages) and *mahrāna* (fees on dowers) as more their due than their mother's milk. What shall be said of the hereditary *qāzīs* of the townships, for to be in touch with knowledge is the lot of their enemies [i.e. they arc ignorant], and the registers of the *deshpāndya* (village accountants) and the words of *zamīndārs* are their holy book and *sharī'a*.[81]

In the *Ā'īn-i Akbarī*, Abu'l-Fazl does not discuss the appointments of the *muhtasibs* and *muftīs*, and both continued as subordinate officers of the *qāzīs*. However, the *muhtasibs* became low-ranking officers under Akbar's administrative regulations, once their more important duties had been incorporated into the *kotwāl's* jurisdiction. The *muhtasibs'* responsibilities had traditionally included the control of sale and purchase transactions in the bazaars, weights and measures, and genuineness of coins, and the suppression of prostitution and other immoral offences. Akbar's reduction of their status was not really an innovation, because the early Muslim administration also did not strictly separate the duties of the *muhtasib*, *qāzī*, and chief of *shurta* (police).

In the second year of his reign (1659) Aurangzīb enhanced the prestige of the *muhtasib*'s department by appointing as chief *muhtasib* a distinguished scholar from Tūrān, 'Iwaz Wajīh. He was given a high salary and a high *mansab*, and lower-ranking *mansabdārs* were appointed to assist him. His jurisdiction encompassed the prevention of forbidden and unlawful deeds, particularly drinking intoxicating liquor, taking *bhang* (Indian hemp) and other drugs, and committing shameful acts such as adultery. Khafi Khān comments that the *muhtasibs* were ordered to eradicate brothels, gambling houses, and idol worship. Their previous duties, such

27. Chār Mīnār in Hyderābād Deccan (p. 235)

28. The Qutb Mīnār in Delhi (p. 227)

29. The temple pillars in the cloisters of the Qūwwatu'l-Islam mosque near Qutb Mīnār (p. 227)

30. Qutb Mīnār, details of carvings (p. 228)

31. The tomb chamber in the Tāj Mahal in Agra (p. 240)

32. The upper domes in the Bīrbal's house at Fathpūr-Sīkri (p. 239)

33. Atāla Mosque, Jaunpūr (p. 230)

34. The Buland Darwāzā (Gate of Victory) in Fathpūr-Sīkrī (p. 238)

35. Interior of Iltutmish's tomb, near Qutb Mīnār (p. 228)

36. Alā'ī Darwāza, near the Qutb Mīnār, Delhi (p. 228)

37. The Qūwwatu'l Islam Mosque screen, Delhi (p. 227)

38. Elaborately carved pillar in one of the chambers of Fathpūr-Sīkrī (p. 238)

as supervising weights and measures and market rates (*nirkh*), were not returned to them until some years later. Subsequently, the enforcement of Sunnī laws, the suppression of all Shī'ī practices, and the introduction of moral reforms were also reincorporated into their duties, and in 1699 they were allotted the task of destroying Hindu temples.[82]

Another senior position was that of the principal *sadr* or the *sadru's sudūr*. He was the main link between the *'ulamā'* and the ruler, and the highest ambition of the *'ulamā'* class was to attain this rank. The *sadru's sudūr*'s importance was derived from his power to grant revenue-free subsistence land known as *madad-i ma'āsh*, *amlāk*, *a'imma*, or *suyurghāl*. According to Abu'l-Fazl, the person appointed to the 'lofty position of *sadr'* should be wise and perspicacious, so that poor and deserving people might be intrduced to the emperor in order to receive stipends and grants. The *Ā'īn-i Akbarī* divides the recipients of those qualifying for *madad-i ma'āsh* into four categories:

(1) Dispassionate seekers after knowledge.
(2) Ascetics.
(3) The illiterate weak and poor.
(4) Uneducated men of noble birth who could not earn their living as tradesmen or professionals.[83]

Not all the members of this class were necessarily parasites, as some Marxist historians think. A considerable number of the *madad-i ma'āsh* recipients ran seminaries and schools out of their grants. Many Mughal *madad-i ma'āsh* documents show that a large number of these blocks of land had not been previously cultivated, although they were arable and they were not included in the *jama'*. In fact, the assignees performed a useful state service by extending cultivation and planting orchards, etc.

Even before Akbar's reign, *madad-i ma'āsh* land had been granted to non-Muslims, but from his rule onwards grants to them were increasingly frequent. Some *madad-i ma'āsh* recipients, however, occupied unauthorized land. Sher Shāh considered it necessary to send his *farmāns* (royal decrees) on *madad-i ma'āsh* in a sealed bag. The village officials, upon receiving such an order, would first have the land to be granted to the recipients measured and then hand over the *farmān* to them. The Mughal emperors possibly took similar precautions. The revenue authorities were ordered to make sure that the *madad-i ma'āsh* holder did not expel the peasants from their revenue-paying land. These grants were not hereditary. The sons were generally allowed to inherit, but the emperors reserved the right to review the case afresh and to make new grants, which might be reduced. In 1690 Aurangzīb made *madad-i ma'āsh* grants hereditary, but the *farmān* insisted that since *madad-i ma'āsh* was an article of loan (*'ārīyat*), not property, its inheritance was to be governed by imperial orders and not by the sharī'a.

THE POLICE

The principal police officer in the cities was the *kotwāl.* The term is of Hindi origin. Because the towns were enclosed by fortified walls and gates, their officers came to be known as the guardians of forts (*kotpāl* or *kotwāl*). *Kotwāls* were not military officers but they worked in collaboration with the military commandant. Some *kotwāls* in the thirteenth and early fourteenth centuries, such as Balban's *kotwāl* Fakru'd-Dīn and 'Ala'u'd-Dīn's *kotwāl* 'Ala'u'l-Mulk, played a major role in influencing events, but this was a result of their personal competence and character, not of their position.

During Akbar's reign the *kotwāls* were ordered to compile a census of all towns and large villages, giving details of the inhabitants' professions and activities. The towns were divided into *mohallas* (quarters), and each was placed under a *mīr-i mohalla* (officer of the *mohalla*). Spies obtained reports of daily events from the *mīr-i mohalla* and forwarded them to their superiors. Information concerning the movements of both residents and visitors was also given to the *kotwāl* through the *mīr-i mohalla.* The *kotwāls* controlled the bazaars, merchants, artisan guilds, brokers, prices, and weights and measures. They were required to ensure that no unauthorized imposts were levied in towns and were also responsible for supervising mints and the gold and silver content of coins. Their duties included eradicating unemployment and investigating the sources of income of those who spent money extravagantly. Prohibitions were also enforced through the *kotwāls.* They were responsible for recovering stolen property and had to make recompense themselves if they failed to catch the thieves. The growth in urbanization increased the area of roads over which they were responsible for safety.

Kotwāls were also required to prevent unwilling widows from being incinerated on their dead husband's funeral pyre. Another of their duties was to stop boys under twelve being circumcised. They had to expel religious impostors and charlatans and see that no oxen, buffaloes, horses, or camels were slaughtered. The *kotwāls* were required to allot separate quarters to butchers, animal hunters, sweepers, and people who prepared dead bodies for cremation.[84] Many of these provisions seem to echo the practices of the ancient Hindu kingdoms, as reflected in such texts as the *Arthasāstra* attributed to Kautilya. It is possible that Akbar was influenced to some extent by Hindu advisers.

THE PROVINCIAL ADMINISTRATION

The Delhi sultans divided their empire into small units. A province was known as *wilāyat* or *iqlīm.* The names of governors in Baranī's history show that under 'Ala'u'd-Dīn's reign there were twelve provinces: (1) Multān and Siwistān, (2) Dīpālpūr and Lahore, (3) Gujarāt, (4) Sāmāna and Sunām, (5) Dhār and Ujjain, (6) Jhā'in, (7) Chittor, (8) Chanderī and Iraj, (9) Badā'ūn and Kol, (10) Avadh, (11) Karā, (12) Bihār and Bengal. To facilitate the fiscal administration, these were subdivided into *shiqqs* or *sarkārs.* In 1580 Akbar divided the empire into twelve *sūbas* (provinces): Kabūl, Multān, Lahore, Delhi, Agra, Allahabad, Avadh, Bihār, Bengal, Ajmīr, Mālwa, and Gujarāt. When Berār, Khāndesh, and Ahmadnagar were conquered, the number of *sūbas* increased to fifteen. Later, Kashmīr and Qandahar were included in Kabul, Thatta or Sind in Multān, and Orissa in Bengal. Each *sūba* was divided into a number of *sarkārs* and each *sarkār* into *parganas*. *Parganas* and *sarkārs* had earlier formed the basis of Sher Shāh's administration. Chittor, Jodhpūr, Bīkānīr, and the autonomous Rājpūt chiefs' *watan jāgīrs* were the *sarkārs* of Ajmīr province; Amber was a mere *pargana* of Ajmīr *sarkār* in the province of the same name.

Qutbu'd-Dīn Aybak's directives to a governor (*wālī*) show that the governor was responsible for the implementation of both the *sharī'a* and the sultan's laws. He controlled the *'ulamā'*, the military commanders, and the civil servants. It was his duty to extend cultivation, reduce imposts where possible, guard highways and roads, and promote trade and commerce. Fīrūz Tughluq's instructions to the governor of Sind were similar.[85] The governors under the Delhi sultans were supreme executive officers; they were not responsible for the recruitment of army personnel and could not interfere with the judicial authorities. The sultans also appointed a principal revenue administrator (*sāhib-i dīwān*) called a *khwāja*. The *khwāja* maintained the revenue accounts and helped the sultan to settle the account.

The Mughal governor was called a *sipahsālar* (military commander), but the tities *sūbadār* and *nāzim-i sāba* were also used. Very influential *mansabdārs* or princes were appointed as governors. All the provinces of the Deccan were generally placed under one governor, but in other areas not more than two contiguous provinces were combined thus. The Mughal governors were the emperor's vicegerents. They commanded the provincial troops and were responsible for the maintenance of peace and prosperity in their provinces. Normally death sentences were passed only by the emperor, but a governor could impose capital punishment on rebels to suppress an uprising. The governors were required to distribute loans (*tāqāwī*) in order to increase cultivation and had to ensure that soldiers were not billeted in houses without their owner's consent. Akbar's *farmān* peremptorily asked governors to prevent any interference in people's faith and creed. Governors were duty-bound to obtain intelligence reports from independent sources and to examine them thoroughly in order to arrive at a sound conclusion. The promotion of education and military skills were also the governor's responsibility.[86]

From 1595 the imperial *diwān* began to appoint the provincial *diwāns* himself, in order to make the provincial revenue administration subordinate to the centre. The provincial *bakhshī* recruited the local troops and maintained their descriptive rolls and salary records. He assisted the governors in conducting military expeditions against rebels. The provincial *bakhshī* issued certificates to the *mansabdārs* confirming the fulfilment of their duties. There was also a provincial newswriter (*wāqi'a-nawīs*) who reported directly to the emperor important events in the provinces, including the progress of the revenue collections. Another independent reporter called the *sawānih nawīs* or *khufiyanawīs* (secret reporter) also sent intelligence to the central government. An additional source of news was provided by the independent spies known as *harkāras*.

Both horsemen and dispatch runners transmitted news and reports expeditiously. Even under the Delhi sultans the human runner travelled faster than the horseman. According to Ibn Battūta, the horse-post, called *ūlāq*, used royal horses stationed at four-mile intervals. The foot-post, which was called *dāwa*, had three stations per mile. Ibn Battūta goes on to say:

> The postal service of India is of two kinds. The horse-post, which they call *ūlāq*, consists of horses belonging to the Sultan (with relays) every four miles. The service of couriers on foot has within the space of each mile three relays, which they call *dāwa*, the *dāwa* being a third of a mile, and a mile itself is called by them *kurūh.* The manner of its organization is as follows. At every third of a mile there is an inhabited village, outside which there are three pavilions. In these sit men girded up ready to move off, each of whom has a rod two cubits long with copper bells at the top. When a courier leaves the town he takes the letter in the fingers of one hand and the rod with the bells in the other, and runs with all his might. The men in the pavilions, on hearing the sound of the bells, get ready to meet him and when he reaches them one of them takes the letter in his hand and passes on, running with all his might and shaking his rod until he reaches the next *dāwa*, and so they continue until the letter reaches its destination. This post is quicker than the mounted post, and they often use it to transport fruits from Khurāsān which are regarded as great luxuries in India; the couriers put them on (woven baskets like) plates and carry them with great speed to the Sultan. In the same way they transport the principal criminals; they place each man on a stretcher and run carrying the stretcher on their heads.[87]

The speed of the foot-runners was equally surprising to Pelsaert. In his note he recorded the distance from one post to another as being much greater than Ibn Battuta said it was. He wrote:

> The King's letters or farmāns to the chief lords or princes are transmitted with incredible speed, because royal runners are posted in the villages 4 or 5 kos apart, taking their turns of duty throughout the day and night, and they take over a letter immediately on its arrival, run with it to the next village in a breath, and hand it over to another messenger. So the letter goes steadily on, and will travel 80 kos between night and day. Further the King has pigeons kept everywhere, to carry letters in time of need or great urgency. No doubt this is done at home [Holland], also in the case of sieges, but only for short distances, whereas this King possesses the largest area of all the kingdoms of the world.[88]

The provincial *sadrs*, *qāzīs*, *mīr 'adls*, and *kotwāls*, although theoretically subordinate to the governor, were in direct contact with their superiors at the centre. The close system of checks and balances made the administration effective at all levels and kept the Mughals in power for more than two centuries.

DISTRICT ADMINISTRATION

The provinces were divided into districts both for revenue and for general administration. For fiscal purposes the province was divided into *sarkārs*, the latter being subdivided into *parganas*. Each *pargana* contained a number of villages and formed a territorial unit; groups of villages which had been combined for fiscal purposes only were known as *mahāls*. The *'āmil* or *karōrī*, who was the head of the land administration for the *parganas* was chiefly responsible for collecting revenue and promoting agriculture.

Occasionally the same person acted both as *diwān* and *amīn*, but the positions were generally kept separate. Shāhjahān and his successors appointed *amīns* in each *mahāl* in order that all arable land should be cultivated. The *amīn's* duties included the issue of lease deeds (*patta*) and obtaining deeds of acceptance (*qabūliyat*). He was also required to ensure that unauthorized cesses were not realized and that the *'āmils* and other officers did not act dishonestly. The *qānūngos'* offices were hereditary, and they were responsible for keeping a record of the land belonging to the villages and *parganas* and the revenue assessments.

To facilitate civil administration, the provinces were also subdivided into units known *fawjdārī*. A *fawjdār*, during Akbar's reign, was responsible for a number of *parganas* but not usually an entire *sarkār*. The *fawjdārs* were composed of smaller units known as *thānas*, or military outposts. These were controlled by a *thānadār*, who had to maintain a specified number of *sawars* to support the administration. The emperor appointed the *fawjdārs* himself, and they were controlled by the *bakhshīu'l mamalik*. The more senior *thānadārs* were also nominated by the central government.

The *fawjdārs* were very senior officials. They performed military, police, and judicial functions and also helped in revenue administration. They were required to deal with any rebellions by the *zamīndārs*, *jagīrdars*, and *'āmils*, using as little force as possible. Initially they had to try persuasive methods but, if these failed, could resort to intimidation by putting on a display of strength in the hope that the rebels would surrender without any fighting. The next step was to use the infantry; the cavalry were used only in the event of continued rebellion. The *fawjdārs* were also under orders to sever the rebels' communication lines before attacking their forts; this was looked upon as the last resort. Once the rebel camp was taken, the government due was first deducted, and the rest of the booty was distributed equally among the men.[89]

The *fawjdār* was also apparently expected to maintain law and order on the roads, although this is not mentioned in the *Ā'in-i Akbarī*. Originally an authority who helped the revenue officials, he was later associated directly with land revenue administration. In fact, the *fawjdār* had continually to exert military pressure on the unruly *zamīndārs* in order to make them pay their taxes. Regarding the imposition of the imperial regulations the *fawjdār* had sole authority, but in cases concerning *sharī'a* law he acted in collaboration with the *qazīs*.

V

SOCIAL AND ECONOMIC CONDITIONS

SOCIAL STRUCTURE

MUSLIM society in India was ridden by racial prejudices. Political and economic pressures kept the Qur'ānic demands that all believers be treated as brothers at a low key. The gradual weakening of the *sharī'a* influence on political institutions – in other words, the influence of *dīn* (faith) over *dawla* (political domain) – facilitated the assimilation of ancient Irānian political institutions and social customs into the body politic of Islam.

The Turks as a race were imbued with a sense of a divinely ordained mission. The historians under the Turkic dynasties preached that Allah had promised Abū Hanīfa in the Ka'ba at Mecca that, as long as the sword was in the hands of the Turks, the Hanafiyya doctrines would not die.[1] However, the Turks who made up the thirteenth-century governing class were not themselves a monolithic group. They belonged to different tribes, and tribal rivalries and jealousies were frequently manifested politically. They were also divided into slave and free-born classes. The free-born Khaljīs played an important role in the Ghūrīd army and had conquered Bengal. Until the Khaljīs ascended the throne, all the Delhi sultans had been either slave commanders or their descendants. Both the Khaljīs and the Tughluqs, however, had acquired a large number of Turkic slaves. Sultan Muhammad bin Tughluq had 20,000 Turkic slaves of whom 10,000 were eunuchs.[2]

By the time of the Lodīs' the Turks were merged into the Indian Muslim professional and religious groups. On the other hand, many racial groups such as the Habshīs and the Afghāns retained their distinctive identity.

The Habshīs were slaves from Ethiopia and the Horn of Africa and their descendants. They rose to prominence through their position as bodyguards. Queen Raziyya's favourite, Jamālu'd-Dīn Yāqūt, was a Habshī slave. Even the much-travelled Ibn Battūta was struck by the prominence of the Habshīs throughout India. Habshīs, who had arrived by sea, obtained important positions in the local courts of both Gujarāt and Bengal. They were also successful in the Bengal army, where they played the role of king-makers.

In the Deccan, under the Bahmanī sultans, the Habshīs even acted as governors and as *diwāns.* They forged alliances with the local Deccani Muslim groups in order to subvert the Turkic and Irānian factions, and in the fifteenth and sixteenth centuries the kingdoms of Ahmadnagar and Bījāpūr were dominated by them.

Their most prominent leader was Malik Ambar. They also controlled the Gujarāt and the Deccan sultans' navies and were virtual masters on the Konkan coast. The Mughals too recruited Habshī slaves into their service; some served as *kotwāls*, and a few acted as governors.

The Afghāns, according to al-Bīrūnī, lived in the western frontier mountains or the Sulaymān ranges. A group of them living between Lamghān and Peshāwar were subjugated by the Turkic leader Subuktigīn. There were Afghāns in both the Ghaznavid and Ghūrid armies. Ulugh Khān (the future Emperor Balban) was the first ruler to make them prominent. In 1260 he recruited some 3,000 Afghāns into his army, and they crushed the Mewāti rebellion around Delhi. When Ulugh Khān became sultan, he placed the newly created military outposts near Delhi such as Patyālī, Kampil, and Bhōjpur under Afghān control, and in Sultan 'Ala'u'd-Dīn's reign an Afghān, Ikhtiyāru'd-Dīn, was created a leading noble. Muhammad bin Tughluq appointed several Afghāns as governors, although some of them rebelled against him later. Their influence increased under Fīrūz and his successor, and Gujarāt, Mālwa, the Deccan, Bihār, and Bengal became major centres of Afghān power. The Afghān, Lodī, and Sūr kingdoms became a haven not only for Afghān military adventurers but also for their holy men and merchants. Akbar, however, was faced with several Afghān rebellions, but this did not affect his recognition of those leaders who remained loyal to him. Towards the end of his reign, a most promising young Afghān, Pīr Khān or Pīru, rose to prominence. Jahāngīr awarded him the title of Khān-i Jahān Lodī, and his influence over the Emperor increased the number of Afghāns in Mughal service. Khān-i Jahān subsequently led a rebellion against Shāhjahān, and the Emperor lost faith in Afghāns. In the first half of Aurangzīb's reign they did not gain prominent positions, although they had supported him loyally in the war of succession. The Deccan wars in the later half of Aurangzīb's rule brought a number of Afghān leaders into the limelight, and eventually the Emperor became more favourable.

From the mid-thirteenth century the native Muslims emerged as the largest distinctive group of Muslims but they were debarred from holding important positions, which were monopolized by the Turkic governing classes. Some of these Indian Muslims were descended from Arab or Turkic conquerors, their mothers being Islamicized Hindus. As early as 1253 their leader 'Imādu'd-Dīn Rayhān's rise to power not only showed his ability to unite Indian leaders but also lent his ability to obtain the support of the Turkic *iqtā'dārs*.

After his accession, Balban crushed both the Turkic and Indian factions, but under 'Ala'u'd-Dīn they again rose to power. In 1305 a Hindu who may have been Islamicized, Malik Nā'ib, acted with outstanding courage whilst repelling the Mongol invaders 'Alī Beg and Tartāq. His bravery so impressed 'Ala'u'd-Dīn that he began to appoint more Indian Muslims to higher positions. The Turkic monopoly of senior government positions was at last broken – initially by 'Ala'u'd-Dīn's favourite, Malik Kafūr, and then by Qutu'd-Dīn Mubārāk Shāh's protege, Khusraw Khān Barādū.

Baranī abused those members of the Muslim artisan groups such as the vintners, cooks, barbers, gardeners and their descendants whom Muhammad bin Tughluq had promoted to high positions. Nevertheless one cannot fail to marvel at the fact that this class produced such a large number of talented administrators.

The Mongol captives who had been converted to Islam, and settled down in Delhi and in other towns, married Indian Muslim or Hindu girls and after a generation or two became members of Indian Muslim society. Arab, Syrian, Egyptian, and Irānian migrants were also Indianized through marriage. On the western and eastern coasts, however, and in the Deccan they established their own separate settlements.

The military aristocracy of Bābur and Humāyūn was also imbued with a sense of imperial mission but it was less united than its earlier thirteenth-century counterpart. Its members belonged to Irānian and Central Asian groups. Those who traced their origin from the areas north of the Oxus were known as Tūrānīs; those whose ancestors had lived south of the Oxus were styled Iranis.

Bābur kept his nobles under strict control, and they co-operated with him to found an empire. Humāyūn, however, although impelled by a high conception of monarchy, lacked the qualities of a leader and could not discipline his nobles and the members of the Tīmūrīd family. Their aim was purely mundane. They intended to retain their own freedom of action even if it meant conquering only small areas of Kābul under one of his relations, rather than governing a whole Indian province under Humāyūn. Their individualism cost Humāyūn his empire. They even thwarted his attempts to regain it by their disloyalty and intrigued with his family and enemies during his wanderings in the Panjāb and Sind.

In 1545 Humāyūn reconquered Kābul, but the nobles upon whom he could rely were few, and he twice lost Kābul again. Finally, in 1550, in an attempt to consolidate his authority before crushing his brother Kāmrān, he took political decisions in consultation with the leaders of various groups. When he reconquered India, Humāyūn had decided to divide his kingdom into several regions and to assign each of these to one of his nobles. It was planned to place an independent army at their disposal, while Humāyūn's personal cavalry would consist of only 12,000 horses.[3] This was an admission of his failure to forward a centralized empire and was designed to conciliate his ambitious Tīmūrīd princes and nobles, but Humāyūn died before the scheme could be implemented. To cement his relations with the Afghāns, like Bābur, Humāyūn established matrimonial relations with the Afghān chiefs. In the early years of his reign Akbar perceived that neither Tūranī support nor that of the Irānīs was sufficient to realize his ambitious schemes of conquest and the centralization of the empire. Indigenous support was indispensable. The Afghāns were untrustworthy, although some of them had surrendered; Akbar's only alternative was to ally himself with the martial Rājpūt race. About this time also, a brāhman, Bīrbal, and a khattrī, Todar Mal, entered the imperial service. Thereafter the door of Mughal service was opened to all Hindus. The introduction of the *mansabdār* system also changed the structure of the Mughal governing classes. The new *mansabdārs* were appointed from a variety of classes and ethnic groups of both foreigners and Indians. Their mutual contacts and dependence on the Indian troopers had transformed them into a multicultural society, but the dominant groups were proud of their own social customs and prejudices. By the end of the sixteenth century class divisions among the Muslims became very pronounced. In his statistics on Muslim *zamīndārs* in different provinces, Abu'l-Fazl not only mentions the Afghāns as a separate class but considers Sayyids, Shaykhs, and Shaykhzādas as castes such as Rājpūts and brāhmans.[4]

The conversion to Islam of Rājpūts, Jāts, and other tribal groups, even in areas predominantly Muslim such as western Panjāb and eastern Bengal, was a slow process. Even today, families in the same tribal group have both Hindu and Muslim members. Islamic converts, according to *sharī'a* law, must disown and renounce their earlier worship, cultural identity, and traditions. Although the new Muslims strictly followed *sharī'a* religious practices, it proved impossible to sever social links with their Hindu families until many centuries later. Local customs, common taboos regarding marriage and childbirth, and the rites for various stages of a child's progress also continued to be observed. Then, as now, the offering and distribution of food to bring merit to the soul of the dead were performed according to local traditions.

The women were generally blamed by the orthodox Indian Muslim men for their adherence to pre-Islamic customs, but the men themselves retained many Hindu traditions. Although widows were permitted to remarry under *sharī'a* laws, this was taboo in accordance with local Hindu ideas.[5] It soon became obvious that even those who recommended widow remarriage were not prepared to practise it themselves.[6]

WOMEN

Islamic society was polygamous, although there was a limit of four to the number of wives permitted at any time. It was so hard to satisfy the conditions for marrying more than one woman, however, that the Qur'ān advised monogamy. There was no limit on the number of concubines. In his youth, Akbar, who at that time was completely under orthodox influence, is known to have exceeded the limit on wives. The *'ulamā'* in his court admitted that the same Qur'ānic verse which stipulated four wives could also be interpreted to authorize nine or even eighteen. The consensus of the *'ulamā'* was that not more than four wives could be taken in *nikāh* (permanent marriage), but under *mut'a* (marriage for a fixed temporary period) any number of women could be married. The controversy was prolonged. Summing up the conflicting opinions, the historian Badā'ūnī asserted that, although Imām Abū Hanīfa and Imām Shafi'ī considered *mut'a* marriages unlawful, Imām Mālik and the Shī'īs accepted them as legal. However, a *fatwa* from a Mālikī *qāzī* permitting *mut'a* marriage was also valid for both the Hanafis and the Shafi'īs. Akbar therefore dismissed the Hanafi *qāzīs* and replaced him with a Mālikī *qāzī* who subsequently legalized *mut'a*. Akbar's four wives were deemed wedded under *nikah*, and the rest under *mut'a*.[7] This was an exceptional case, for licentious men normally remained within the law by continuously divorcing one or two wives and then taking new ones. In later life Akbar prohibited polygamy, although the ordinance was ignored.

From the time of their earliest settlement, Muslims had married Hindu girls, although from the thirteenth century onwards many immigrants either came with their families or summoned them when they had settled down. The Muslims preferred girls from the higher classes as wives. For example, when Khwāja Mu'īnu'd-Dīn Chishtī settled at Ajmīr he took two wives, although he was then aged sixty-five. One of them was a Sayyid's daughter, and the other was a Hindu raja's daughter who had been seized during a raid on the Hindus by the local Muslim commander.[8] Sultan 'Ala'u'd-Dīn Khaljī married Kamlā Devī, the widow of Raja Karan of Gujarāt, who had been taken captive after the Raja's defeat. 'Ala'u'd-Dīn's son, Khizr Khān, married Kamlā Devī's daughter by Raja Karan, Deval Devī. During 'Ala'u'd-Dīn's reign, Ghiyāsu'd-Dīn Tughluq, whom the Sultan had made governor of Dīpālpūr, had wished to marry his brother Rajah to one of the Raja of Dīpālpūr's daughters. Then, upon hearing of the beauty of Rāna Mal Bhattī's daughter, he made the Rāna's life unbearable until the girl was married to Rajah. Fīrūz Shāh Tughluq was their son. During Muhammad bin Tughluq's reign, Fīrūz himself married the pretty sister of a Gūjar, Saharan.

It is significant that the Shaykhzādas (descendants of the sūfī leaders) married brāhman girls. In the sixteenth century Mīran Sadr-i Jahān and Shaykh 'Abdu'r-Rahīm, who hailed from Avadh, married brāhman wives whom they have obviously chosen themselves.[9]

Women played a significant historical role. Turkān Khātūn, Raziya's mother, was the most prominent among Iltutmish's queens. Qāzī Minhāj was deeply impressed by her munificence to the *'ulamā'*, holy men, Sayyids, and Muslim ascetics. Raziya herself not only commanded the army against rebel *iqtā'dārs* but was also a brilliant administrator. Her successors' mothers were arch-intriguers. Malika-i Jahān, Sultan Nāsīru'd-Dīn's mother, was the principal instrument behind her son's rise to the throne. According to Baranī, Jalālu'd-Dīn's wife paved the way for 'Ala'u'd-Dīn's accession by preventing her elder son from assuming his father's crown immediately after Jalālu'd-Dīn's assassination. Ibn Battuta was deeply impressed by the generosity to the sūfīs and *'ulamā'* of Makhdūma-i Jahān, Muhammad bin Tughluq's mother.

The ladies of the Mughal palace were proficient in both horsemanship and social etiquette and were also often astute politicians and artists. Akbar's mother, Hamīda Bānū Begum, was a capable adviser to both her husband and her son. Indeed, Humāyūn owed much of his success at Shāh Tahmasp's court in Irān to her astute diplomacy. Akbar's wife, Salīma Sultāna Begum, was also endowed with superb mental powers and natural ability. The woman writer Gulbadan Begum has been immortalized by her facile pen, while Nūr Jahān's role as the power behind Jahāngir's throne need not be repeated here. Mumtaz Mahal, Shāhjahān's wife, was the Emperor's leading counsellor, and after her death her place was taken by their daughter, Jahān Āra. Jahān Āra was also Dārā Shukoh's principal supporter;

but despite this, Aurangzīb took her into his confidence after Shāhjahān's death.

Father Monserrate reports that the imperial *farmāns* (royal decrees) were sealed, eight days after they were received from the *wazīr*, 'by one of the queens, in whose keeping is the royal signet ring and also the great seal of the realm'.[10] The small signet ring (*uzuk*) was affixed to *farmāns* granting senior appointments, titles, *jāgīrs*, and the payment of large sums of money. During Shāhjājān's reign the *uzuk* was kept in Mumtāz Mahal's custody. On the queen's request it was handed over for some years to her father, Āsaf Khān, the *wakīl.* After Mumtāz Mahal's death it was controlled by her daughter, Jahān Āra.

The veiling of women was strictly observed by higher-class Muslim families, and the Hindus imitated the Muslim governing classes by keeping their women at home. Both Muslim and Hindu women travelled in closed litters. However, in Rājasthān the Rājpūt women merely covered their heads with a scarf. Females labouring on building sites and in the fields did not even cover their heads.

The birth of a son was deemed a blessing by both Hindus and Muslims; girls were unwelcome. Although the Rājpūts took many wives, they considered girl babies a curse, and female infanticide was widespread. Both Muslims and Hindus married off their children at an early age without their consent. Dowries were essential for girls and were a great strain on a family. Many Muslims with several daughters were full of praise for *satī* (the Hindu custom of incinerating widows on their husbands' funeral pyres). However, others, like Ibn Battūta, were shocked to see the enthusiasm at these *satī* scenes. Akbar's ordinance forbidding the forcible burning of Hindu widows was not strictly obeyed.

SLAVERY

Slavery in Islam is a legacy from pre-Islamic traditions. Islam did not peremptorily abolish slavery but urged believers to treat slaves humbly and, where possible, to free them. Strict obedience to the Qur'ānic injunctions would have led to the gradual demise of the system, but instead Islamic monarchic traditions strengthened it. The 'Abbāsid Caliph al-Mu'tasim (833–42) had Turkic slaves brought from Transoxiana as his guards. Slaves soon comprised the majority of the bodyguards for both the sultans and the caliphs. An intelligent newly bought slave was initially trained as a foot-soldier; a year later he was allowed to mount a horse with a plain saddle. In the fifth year of training he obtained a better saddle and a mace and in the seventh year was promoted to the position of tent commander. From there the doors of promotion were opened wide; talented slaves rose rapidly. They were often employed by the sultans, or their governors, in positions of trust in the royal household, such as keeper of the stables, wardrobes, or armoury, or bearers of the ceremonial parasol (*chatr*). They were loyal to their original masters alone. Like any other chattel they could be inherited, sold, or given away, and usually they felt no loyalty to their original master's family. Even though many leading military slaves had been freed, they often opposed their former master's children.

From the fourteenth century, Islamicized Hindu slaves rose to senior positions.

Malik Kāfūr, Khusraw Khān Barādū, and Fīrūz Shafi's *wazīr*, Khān-i Jahān Maqbūl, were all Islamicized slave leaders. Fīrūz also accepted young boys from the *iqtā's* in lieu of their annual tax. Fīrūz kept 180,000 slaves. They were generally trained in Delhi and in the *iqtā's* in various arts, crafts, and literary skills. Of the trained slaves, 12,000 became artisans, and 40,000 served the Sultan in the palace and imperial cavalcade. All the imperial *kārkhānas* were manned by them. They were also sent to the provinces. According to 'Afif, their rise brought disaster to the Tughluqs. They ruthlessly slaughtered Fīrūz's sons and destroyed the dynasty.

Slaves also served as military commanders under the sultans of provincial dynasties and were a source of both strength and weakness to these different rulers. None of the important military commanders under the Mughals were slaves. Akbar employed a slave contingent called *chelas*, but they were only foot-soldiers.

The majority of slaves, both male and female, were employed in domestic and agricultural duties. They had in the main been taken captive in wars and raids against Hindu chiefs and were then sold in the local market. We are told by Baranī that in Mu'izzu'd-Dīn Kayqubād's reign slave boys and girls were specially trained in music, dancing, and the intricacies of wooing, courting, flirtation, love-making, and coquetry.[11] They were also taught horse-riding, polo, and lance-throwing. The Sultan's death did not put an end to the demand for pretty and charming slave girls. The aristocrats bought them for their harems. According to Ibn Battūta, ordinary Indian captive girls were very cheap, and even the skilled ones were comparatively inexpensive. The *Masālik al-absār* also confirms this fact and adds that their price was normally very low. However, exceptionally pretty and talented Indian slave girls were sold at a very high price.[12]

The number of slaves in a nobleman's household was limitless. 'Imadu'l-Mulk Rāwat-i'Arz, the maternal grandfather of Amīr Khusraw, who was not a particularly extravagant man, kept an enormous number. Some fifty to sixty of them prepared betel leaf for him and his visitors. Without slaves they could not maintain their grandiose establishments. Each Mughal *mansabdār* had to maintain an army of slaves. Two or three slaves were needed to look after each horse, and about eight of them pitched the tents in the fore-camp and rear; they also managed the kitchen and transport and worked as torch bearers and guards.

During famines both Hindu and Muslim families sold their children. This sparked off a controversy among the *'ulamā'*, whose leaders did not approve of selling Muslim children into slavery. In 1562 Akbar abolished the practice of taking the wives and children of defeated rebels as captives,[13] although rebellion itself was still of course strongly condemned. After Akbar's death, however, this new law was apparently largely ignored. The Mughal economic documents do not, like those of earlier periods, mention the price of slaves; evidently the trade had declined. It was stepped up in east Bengal by the Arakan pirates, both Māg and European.

VILLAGES

Ibn Battūta states that there were 1,500 villages in Amroha, now a small town. Nizāmu'd-Dīn Ahmad, who seems to have had access to Akbar's 1581 census records containing the number and occupation of the inhabitants of each village, is more realistic. He reports that Akbar's empire contained 120 large cities and 3,200 small towns (*qasbas*), each controlling one hundred to one thousand villages. According to another source, the total number of villages in Aurangzīb's empire, excluding Bījāpūr and Hyderābād, was 401,567. Villages were in a state of flux, however. They were frequently deserted, and their land was then incorporated into neighbouring settlements. The population moved frequently between villages. Bābur notices that 'In Hindustan hamlets and villages, towns indeed, are depopulated and set up in a moment! If the people of a large town, one inhabited for years even, flee from it, they do it in such a way that not a sign or trace of them remains in a day, or a day and a half.'[14]

Villages were founded by both *zamīndārs* and *madad-i ma'āsh* holders. In northern India wandering tribes, Jāts and Gūjars were induced to settle in them. One such village was Shaykhupura near Delhi, founded by Shaykh Faridu'd-Dīn (d. 1579). He built a mosque and a *khānqāh* (hospice); artisans and peasants from surrounding villages, attracted by the Shaykh's personality, moved to the new village. A group of Hindu Jāts, previously habitual thieves, settled there and abandoned crime for agriculture. The village also developed into a rendezvous for homeless Afghāns.[15] New villages were founded by the Sayyids, brāhmans, and high-caste Hindus. Some were inhabited by mixed castes, while others belonged exclusively to a particular group. Villages of lower castes were also founded in order to obtain cheap labour.

Such villages were no more than a cluster of huts with arable and waste-land, groves, and pastures. Their products were marketed in the neighbouring towns. They were an asset to the developing cities of the Delhi sultans and the Mughals. The peasants used buckets to irrigate their land, but Bābur considered this laborious and filthy. He says:

> At the well-edge they set up a fork of wood, having a roller adjusted between the forks, tie a rope to a large bucket, put the rope over the roller, and tie its other end to the bullock. One person must drive the bullock, another empty the bucket. Every time the bullock turns after having drawn the bucket out of the well that rope lies on the bullock-track, in pollution of urine and dung, before it descends again into the well.'[15]

Bābur's description of Persian wheels, which he saw in Lahore and Dīpālpūr, is interesting:

> They make two circles of ropes long enough to suit the depth of the well, fix strips of wood between them, and on these fasten pitchers. The ropes with

> the wood and attached pitchers are put over the well-wheel. At one end of the wheel-axle a second wheel is fixed, and close (*qash*) to it another on an upright axle. This last wheel the bullock turns; its teeth catch in the teeth of the second, and thus the wheel with the pitchers is turned. A trough is set where the water empties from the pitchers and from this the water is conveyed everywhere.[16]

Rivers, streams, and reservoirs were also an important source of water for irrigation. Fīrūz Shāh constructed a double system of canals whose headwaters were drawn from the Jamuna and Satlaj. The Satlaj section joined the main stream at Karnāl. The original course of the Jamuna may be followed from its emergence in the outer ranges of the Himalayas, through the Chitang river to Hansī and Hisār.

Fīrūz Shāh's Jamuna canal was repaired during Akbar's reign. In Shāhjahān's time it was reopened from its mouth at Khizrābād, nearly 72 miles in length, to serve Delhi. It was known as the Nahr-i Bihisht (Channel of Heaven); its modern successor is the West Jamuna Canal. It always served to irrigate a considerable area of land.

The observations of foreign travellers, read in conjunction with the account of crops in the *A'īn-i Akbarī*, show that cereals, millets, pulses, oil-seeds, both the common and thick variety of sugar-cane, cotton, hemp, indigo, poppies, and betel were grown for sale to merchants from neighbouring towns and elsewhere. Vegetables were also cultivated. Bengal produced rice in such abundance that it was transported up the Ganges as far as Patna and exported by sea to Masulipatam and many other ports on the Coromandel coast. It was also exported to Srī Lanka and the Maldives. Bengal was equally rich in sugar-cane. It exported sugar to Golkonda and Karnātak, also to Arabia, Irāq, and Irān, through Mocha, Basra, and Bandar 'Abbas. Ajmīr sugar-cane was perhaps the best in quality in the sixteenth century. In the seventeenth century sugar-cane cultivation spread to many places in Bihār and the region around Aurangabad.

Indigo was increasingly in demand in the sixteenth century. It was used for washing and dyeing cotton cloth. Towards the close of the century, the European woollen industry replaced woad with indigo. This resulted in a tremendous increase in indigo production in India, centred in Sarkhīj (Gujarāt) and Bayāna (near Agra). Bayāna indigo was made up in balls and was known as Lāhorī in the Aleppo market, because the caravans bringing it came from Lahore. Sarkhīj indigo, formed into cakes, contained an admixture of sand, so that about 1.30 kilos of Sarkhīj were equivalent to 0.90 kilos of Lāhori. It was exported mainly through the Persian Gulf. Indigo from Sehwān (Sind) and Telingāna (Deccan) was of better quality. By the beginning of the seventeenth century other north Indian towns had also grown into important indigo production centres.

At the end of Akbar's reign an imperial envoy returning from Bījāpūr brought a hookah to court. Jahāngīr prohibited the use of tobacco, and some addicts were severely punished, but smoking spread rapidly to all classes. Many puritanical *'ulamā'* wrote *fatwas* condemning tobacco, and heated debates were held between its supporters and opponents. The Muslims did not give it up; only the Sikhs totally abandoned it in obedience to Gurū Gobind, while the Jāts became strongly addicted. Tobacco became a very valuable crop, extensively cultivated. Coffee was grown in Maharashtra. Tea was still unknown. Chilli was introduced by the Portuguese via Goa. *Pan* (betel leaf) was extensively grown. Saffron cultivation was confined to Kashmīr. Both sweet and ordinary potatoes were introduced by the Portuguese. Bābur had introduced many Central Asian fruits, and a variety of rare fruits were grown in the imperial gardens. The aristocracy also produced fruit, both for their own consumption and for sale.

In the villages white and brown sugar and indigo dyes were manufactured, and oil was extracted from oil-seeds. Cotton was also cleaned and carded there. After the fourteenth century Bengal villages became centres for the rearing of the mulberry silkworm.

Food grains were distributed by *banjāras* or wandering grain dealers. They bought grain in the villages and then transported it to the towns on their bullocks. In 'Ala'u'd-Dīn's reign, food grain was sold to the *banjāras* under government supervision immediately after the harvest. In other times the sale was free, although the army and townships depended upon the grain traders for their survival. The peasants were compelled to sell their produce, since they needed money to pay their taxes and to buy ornaments and clothes, while the evil of hoarding grain had always been condemned by the *'ulamā'*. A surviving *farman* from Aurangzīb says that in Ahmadābād the local officers, *seths* (bankers), and *desāīs* (headmen) were buying all the newly harvested grain, and only the rotting produce was left for the traders, although they had to pay the full price. The *farman* urged the *diwān* to stop this illegal trade.

The peasants' scanty clothing, primitive straw huts, and poor belongings shocked European observers, who also vividly described the famines and droughts. Their comments in the sixteenth and seventeenth centuries hold good even today. However, the occasional references to village life in contemporary Persian sources indicate that the villages were composed of both rich peasants and landless labourers. The rulers' fiscal policy considerably affected peasant life. For example, 'Afif says that Fīrūz Shāh's policies made the villages exceedingly prosperous, and the peasants had accumulated large amounts of gold and silver. They even possessed many luxuries such as fine bed sheets, pretty cots, and other household items, while no woman was without ornaments.[17] Possibly this affluence was confined to villages in the neighbourhood of Delhi and those benefiting from the new canal system. Nevertheless, most of the peasants owned the land they tilled on a hereditary basis. They could sell, transfer, or bequeath their land and, as long as they paid their taxes, could not be evicted. Some of them had lived in the same village for many generations and owned their own bullocks and implements. They were known as the *khudkāsht* peasants or the 'resident cultivators'.

The brāhmans *zamīndārs* and *khudkāsht* ordinarily did not put their own hands to the plough. They employed a group of farm-hands known as *pāhīs* who moved from village to village offering their services to the *zamīndārs* and the *khudkāsht* peasants. Some *pāhīs* had their own bullocks and ploughs; others used those belonging to the *zamīndārs* or *khudkāsht.* Some lived in one village and worked in another. The *pāhīs* were in great demand for turning 'cultivable waste' into productive land. They were also given some land rights. The landless labourers who worked for wages were in the minority. The peasants would have been better off financially if then, as now, they had not wasted their savings on weddings, parties, and festivals.[18]

THE ZAMĪNDĀRS

The Muslim governing classes, religious aristocracy, and converts formed only a very small percentage of the Indian population, even by the end of the seventeenth century. The bulk consisted of Hindu peasants, labourers, tribal groups and their leaders, village chieftains, and indigenous rulers. After the establishment of the Delhi sultanate the village hereditary chieftains, known as *rānas*, *rāys*, and *rāwats*, paid tribute only at the point of a sword. Frequent military expeditions had also to be mounted to exact revenue from the *chawdhrīs*, *khūts*, and *muqaddams.* Muslim rule changed neither the Hindu class structure nor its social ethics.

From Akbar's reign onwards, all those who possessed rights superior to those of ordinary peasants were called *zamīndārs.* Although the term had been in use since the fourteenth century, under Akbar it was extended to include all classes of chiefs. The *madad-i ma'āsh* holders, and the Turko-Afghān *iqtā'* holders who had settled down in villages and small towns, also acquired *zamīndārī* rights. They had now become dependent for their livelihood, like the hereditary village headmen, upon receiving a share of the revenue paid by the peasants. From the seventeenth century a small section of Mughal *mansabdārs* and cavalry troopers began to invest their savings in acquiring *zamīndārī* rights.

The *zamīndārs* might be divided into three categories:

Chieftains who were the hereditary, autonomous rulers of their territories and enjoyed practically sovereign power. Akbar made most of them *mansabdārs.* Accordingly, in the second half of Aurangzīb's reign, 15 per cent of the total number of the one thousand or more *mansabdārs* belonged to the ruling chieftain houses. Their income as *mansabdārs* was several times higher than the income from their ancestral territories. The Mughals converted the hereditary dominions of the autonomous chieftains into *watan jāgīrs.* These were usually inherited by the chief's heirs, but the emperor had the right to 'recognize' a younger son or even a distant relation as successor. If the ancestral territory's assessed land tax fell short of the salary commensurate with the *mansab* rank granted to the chief, he was assigned *jāgīr* as salary elsewhere. This not only added to. his income but also enhanced his prestige, making loyalty to the Mughal throne more rewarding than rebellion. On their part, the chieftains introduced the Mughal pattern of provincial government into their territories unless it clashed with their own interests. This contributed to the uniformity of rules and regulations throughout the empire.

The primary *zamīndārs* held proprietary rights over agricultural as well as inhabited land. This included both the peasant proprietors, who themselves worked with the help of hired labour, and the larger proprietors, who owned one or two villages. Their rights were hereditary but alienable. These terms were given to all those who undertook to extend cultivation or who qualified for the *madad-i ma'āsh* grants. These rights could also be bought. The primary *zamīndārs* collected revenue from the peasants and deposited it with the appropriate authorities.

The intermediary *zamīndārs* were the counterparts of the *chawdhrīs*, *khūts*, and *muqaddams* of the pre-Mughal period. They collected revenue from the primary *zamīndārs* and paid it to the *jagīrdārs*, chieftains, or the imperial treasury.[19]

The primary and intermediary *zamīndārs* were entitled to a share in the land's produce and other perquisites. They also taxed merchants and travellers. The *zamīndārs* helped the Mughal administration in various ways. The *zamīndār* troops, according to Abu'l-Fazl, numbered more than 4,400,000 men.[20] They were never used in imperial battles but helped to maintain law and order in the country.

The *zamīndārs* either inherited or built fortresses to protect themselves from their rivals and from the high-handed government officials. In the more inaccessible areas where hills, ravines, or jungles formed natural obstacles, the *zamīndārs* were unruly and rebellious. The whole country was dotted with these areas, particularly in Katihar, Mewāt, the Panjāb, and the hills and jungles of Bundelkhand and Bihār; and, close to the capital, Agra, to the north and west, lay the wild domain of the unruly Jāts. These districts were known as *mawās.*

A dominant caste or class would usually own the *zamīndārī* rights over a single village or group of villages. Large regions were often controlled in this way by a particular caste group, mainly Hindus, and caste and clan interests increasingly dominated the *zamīndārs'* decisions. As Abu'l-Fazl reports: 'The custom of the majority of the *zamīndārs* of Hindustan is to leave the path of single-mindedness and to look to every side and to join anyone who is powerful or who is making an increasing stir.'[21] The Mughals resorted to threats, intimidation, force, and rewards to control the *zamīndārs.* In an attempt to break the caste monopolies in certain areas, Aurangzīb, by a mixture of force and economic temptations, converted the more obdurate *zamīndārs.*

The advent of Rājpūt nobles to the Mughal courts also increased the *zamīndārs'* confidence and loyalty. They became more co-operative, and those in peaceful areas were incorporated into the Mughal elite. However, the rebellious *zamīndārs* in the *mawās* were influenced only by the ability of the local Mughal officers to assert their authority.

In the peaceful areas many Hindu *zamīndārs* imitated Mughal manners, dress, and life-style. Some even read Persian poetry. The majority, however, preferred the local poets, who composed epics which exaggerated their petty exploits to read like the *Mahābhārata.* The *zamīndārs* were represented as the defenders of *dharma*, whose wars were intended to fill the world with Hindu values of justice and righteousness. The *zamīndārs* also attempted to organize their administration on the Mughal pattern, although from the second half of the seventeenth century the Jāts, Bundelas, and Sikhs fought against Mughal rule.

TOWNS AND CITIES

Many of the larger villages, *parganas*, and *thāna* headquarters were gradually transformed into towns, known as *qasbas*. Although they generally presented a village skyline, from the fourteenth century they were significant centres for various crafts and mercantile and commercial transactions. By the seventeenth century the members of the occupational caste groups, such as weavers, goldsmiths, carpenters, blacksmiths, dyers, potters, and shoemakers, had grown so large that in many towns they lived and worked in separate streets. There were even different Muslim graveyards for the various classes and occupational castes, although theoretically Islam is classless.

Villages and *qasbas* in different regions by this time specialized in local products, which they exported to other parts of the country. Sind specialized in cotton textiles, silk, wooden articles, ivory bangles, and saltpetre; Kashmīr was the centre of silk materials, paper, and woollen articles such as shawls, and blankets. The introduction of the Irānian vertical loom into Kashmīr and elsewhere in the fourteenth century stepped up both the quality and quantity of carpet production. Gujarāt excelled in the art of weaving gold and silk threads into brocade, velvet, gauze, needle-work, and embroidery in a variety of textures and dyes. Medicinal products, jewellery, furniture, and weapons were also produced in Gujarāt. The Panjāb was a centre for cotton textiles, blankets, and paper. Delhi and the Agra region were known for their paper manufacture, glassware, and copper and brass utensils. Jaunpūr was famous for cloth-weaving and wooden articles; Avdah produced saltpetre; Bihār was known for its glass vessels and wooden articles; and Bengal specialized in muslin, cotton textiles, and silk-weaving.

The secret of perfection in art and crafts resided in individuals and was never widely publicized. Master-craftsmen trained their apprentices from a very tender age but they did not teach them the more subtle aspects of their craft. Neither did they write books revealing the secrets of their perfection. These points were revealed by the master-craftsman only towards the end of his life and only to a favoured apprentice. Their secrets often died with them.

New towns were founded by the Delhi sultans, their noblemen, and the rulers of provincial dynasties. Delhi itself underwent many changes. Its earliest site was known as Indraprastha. Between the ninth and tenth centuries the Delhi of the former Rājpūt rulers developed near the town now known as Sūrajkund. Prithvīrāja's Delhi was near Anangpal's citadel, Lālkot, built in about 1052. In 1192 Qutbu'd-Dīn Aybak built the Qūwwatu'l-Islam mosque near the citadel and started to construct the adjoining minaret to call the faithful to prayer. It was also intended as a memorial to the eastern Turkic conquests. The first Muslim Delhi was formed when the area was fortified. Outside the fortification, south of Mihraulī village, Iltutmish dug a reservoir to collect rainwater for the use of the growing Delhi population. Ibn Battūta found this reservoir to be about two miles long and one mile broad. On its west bank were steps and a stone pavilion. In its centre was a double-storeyed pavilion of dressed stone.

About the year 1289 Mu'izzu'd-Dīn Kayqubād built his palace at Kilokhrī, then on the banks of the Jamuna. Although this did not develop into a city, all classes of people visited it daily, which made it very crowded. It was the village of Sīrī, built as a bulwark against the Mongol invasions by 'Ala'u'd-Dīn Khaljī, that became the second Delhi. It is now the modern village of Shāhpūr, and the remains of the Khaljī palace described by Ibn Battūta have not survived. About two miles west of Sīrī, 'Ala'u'd-Dīn Khaljī constructed the famous Hawz-i Khāss (Royal Reservoir). Along its sides there were forty pavilions surrounded by houses for male and female musicians, a most extensive bazaar, a Jāmi' mosque, and various minor mosques.[22]

The most ambitious construction was Tughluqābād, built by Sultan Ghiyāsu'd-Dīn Tughluq, some five miles to the east of the first city. The layout of the streets and houses and the remains of the citadel and a mosque indicate that it was designed as an extensive and fortified town. The Sultan's tomb, in an artificial lake, was connected by a fortified passage to the citadel. The lake water was held by embankments. Muhammad bin Tughluq built his fort 'Ādilābād south-east of Tughluqābād and connected it with a causeway.

Sultan Muhammad bin Tughluq fortified the suburbs outside the first Delhi and named it Jahānpanāh. According to Ibn Battūta, its walls were twelve metres thick and contained rooms for nightwatchmen, granaries, and war equipment, including mangonels and other military machines.[23] The level of the lake within the walls was regulated by a sluice of seven spans decorated with subsidiary arches and towers. Fīrūz Shāh Tughluq's Fīrūzabād was located near the citadel known as Fīrūz Shāh Kotla. Near his palace complex and the mosque Fīrūz built a three-storey pyramidal structure in order to form a base for an Asokan column brought from near Ambala. During his reign Delhi covered an extensive area and contained an enormous population. Tīmūr's invasion, however, destroyed its glory. The Sayyid sultans built Khizrābād and Mubārākabad on the Jamuna. Humāyūn left Dīnpanāh near lndraprastha unfinished. It was completed by Sher Shāh, but only its northern gate, near Fīrūz Shāh Kotla, and the southern gate opposite the citadel survive. In 1550 Islam Shāh built Salīmgarh. Delhi was revived by Shāhjahān, who built his new fort, known as the Red Fort, near. Salīmgarh. Commenced in 1639, it was completed nine years later. In 1650 work on Delhi Jāmi' Masjid began. New monuments connecting the Jāmi' mosque and the shopping complex known as Chandni Chawk transformed Shāhjahān's New Delhi or Shāhjahānābād into the most imposing capital in the East.

Both Muslim rulers and governors founded new towns at strategic centres. The ancient town of Manayach, between Avadh and Banāras, was destroyed by Mahmūd of Ghaznī in 1018. On its site Zafar Khān, one of 'Ala'u'd-Dīn Khaljī's commanders, founded Zafarābād. The planning of Daulatābād, built by Muhammad bin Tughluq in 1327, is vividly described Shaykh Mubārāk told the author of *Masālik al-absār:*

> When I left it six years ago it was not yet completed. And I do not think it is yet complete on account of the vast extent of the area of the city and hugeness of its buildings. The Sultan had divided it in such a wise that separate quarters were built for every class of people; a quarter for the troops, a quarter for the *wazīrs*, a quarter for the secretaries, a quarter for the judges and the learned men, a quarter for the Shaykhs *and faqīrs* and a quarter for merchants and handicraftsmen. In every quarter there were found, according to the needs of every class, mosques, minarets, bazaars, public baths, ovens for (baking) flour; so that the people of that quarter did not depend upon the other quarter for selling and buying and exchanging things and that each quarter was in the position of a separate self-contained city and not dependent on others for anything.[24]

In 1359 Fīrūz Tughluq founded Jaunpūr near Zafarabad, which later became the capital of the Jaunpūr Sharqī dynasty. Besides Fīrūzābād, near Delhi, Fīrūz Shāh Kotla, and Jaunpūr, Fīrūz Shāh built a large number of other cities.[25]

Many of the independent sultans also created large numbers of new towns. Most noteworthy is Ahmadābād in Gujarāt founded by Sultan Ahmad Shāh I in 1411, which grew rapidly under both the Gujarāt sultans and the Mughals. The sultans and their nobles chose blocks of land in the suburbs, known as *puras*, for their residences. There were 360 to 380 *puras*. In Akbar's time most of these had grown into separate villages. Further population spirals transformed them into independent towns.[26]

In 1505 Sultan Bahlul Lodī rebuilt Agra. Bābur added baths and gardens to it. The Lodīs built many towns between Agra and their homeland in the north-west. Akbar made Agra his capital, added Fathpūr-Sīkrī as a satellite town, and founded Allahābad near Prayga.

Many new towns were built by reconstructing old towns or important villages. They were designed to serve both strategic and commercial needs, and the leading government officials and merchants built stately houses in them. The thirteenth- and fourteenth-century aristocracy favoured three-storey mansions. For example, Rāwat-i 'Arz, Amīr Khusraw's maternal grandfather, built a three-storeyed house near Delhi which included one of the fort's bastions. It contained spacious verandas and rooms, although nearby were many small thatched houses and even some thatched mosques. Fires were frequent in the fortified areas because of congestion. By 1285 Rāwat-i 'Arz's house had been reduced to ashes.[27] Even in Shāhjahān's Delhi fires frequently consumed the houses inhabited by petty *mansabdārs* and merchants. According to Bernier their houses were made only of clay. The walls were covered with a fine white lime, the thatched roofs supported by a layer of long, strong canes. The dwellings of the noblemen and leading *mansabdārs* in Shāhjahān's Delhi were scattered in every direction along the banks of the river and in the suburbs. They were airy and exposed to the breeze on all sides, especially to the northern winds. Bernier says:

A good house has its courtyards, gardens, trees, basins of water, small *jets d'eau* in the hall or at the entrance, and handsome subterraneous apartments which are furnished with large fans, and on account of their coolness are fit places for repose from noon until four or five o'clock, when the air becomes suffocatingly warm. Instead of these cellars many persons prefer *Kas-kanays*, that is, small and neat houses made of straw or odiferous roots placed commonly in the middle of a parterre, so near to a reservoir of water that the servants may easily moisten the outside by means of water brought in skins. They consider that a house, to be greatly admired, ought to be situated in the middle of a large flower-garden, and should have four large divan-apartments raised to the height of a man from the ground, and exposed to the four winds, so that the coolness may be felt from any quarter. Indeed no handsome dwelling is ever seen without terraces on which the family may sleep during the night. They always open into a large chamber into which the bedstead is easily moved, in case of rain, when thick clouds of dust arise, when the cold air is felt at break of day, or when it is found necessary to guard against those light but penetrating dews which frequently cause a numbness in the limbs and induce a species of paralysis.

The interior of a good house has the whole floor covered with a cotton mattress four inches in thickness, over which a fine white cloth is spread during the summer, and a silk carpet in the winter. At the most conspicuous side of the chamber are one or two mattresses with fine coverings quilted in the form of flowers and ornamented with delicate silk embroidery, interspersed with gold and silver. These are intended for the master of the house, or any person of quality who may happen to call. Each mattress has a large cushion of brocade to lean upon, and there are other cushions placed round the room, covered with brocade, velvet or flowered satin, for the rest of the company. Five or six feet from the floor, the sides of the room are full of niches, cut in a variety of shapes, tasteful and well proportioned, in which are seen porcelain vases and flowerpots. The ceiling is gilt and painted, but without pictures of man or beast, such representations being forbidden by the religion of the country.[28]

The Muslim aristocracy, in both the *qasbas* and the cities, was extravagant and prodigal, and the common Muslims imitated them. Childbirth, *'aqīqah* (shaving of an infant's hair), circumcision, *bismīllāh* (a party when a child starts his education), weddings, and death ceremonies were ostentatiously celebrated. Public festivals, such as Shab-ibarāt (the fifteenth night of the eighth month, Sha'bān), 'Idu'l-fitr (the feast of alms), on the first day of the tenth month, and 'Idu'l-azha (the feast when a lamb, cow, or camel was sacrificed), were also occasions of great extravagance. Any words advising restraint were deeply resented. For example, when Bābā Farīd's brother,[29] Shaykh Najību'd-Dīn Mutawakkil, urged his patron to make better use of the money he intended to spend on his daughter's wedding, he was expelled from the house his patron had given him.[30]

Like the Tūrānī, Irānī, and Indian Muslims, the Rājpūt aristocracy was lavish and prodigal. Only the Afghāns were frugal. Manucci comments:

> They are very avaricious and foolhardy. When they come to court they are well clad and well armed, caracoling on fine horses richly caparisoned, posing as persons of some consideration, and followed by several servants borrowed or hired for the day. On reaching their house they divest themselves of all this finery, and, tying a scanty cloth round their loins and wrapping a rag round their head, they take their seat on a mat, and live on *quichire* (*khichri*, i.e. rice and lentils) or badly cooked cow's flesh of low quality, which is very abundant in the Mogul country and very cheap. In this manner they put by money and grow into merchants.[31]

Naturally, as Baranī says, from the very beginning of the thirteenth century the Delhi sultans' aristocracy could save nothing and was always in debt. The Multānīs (Hindu merchants) and Sāhs (Hindu money-lenders), who advanced loans to the nobles against drafts on their *iqtā'* revenue, grew exceedingly rich. Besides charging exorbitant rates of interest, the money-lenders also received gifts from the debt-ridden aristocracy, in order to keep them quiet.

The service conditions of the *iqtā'-dārs* and *mansabdārs* increased their debts. They had to go to war at short notice, which involved raising large amounts of cash for salary advances to their soldiers, because they, like their masters, were always short of money. Even the horses were neglected, as Baranī's biographical notice on Rawat-i 'Arz suggests.[32] Only the Hindu money-lenders came to their rescue. When 'Abdu'r-Rahīm Khān-i Khānan was ordered to seize Qandahār, Abu'l-Fazl wrote that he should take loans at the rate of 50 or 100 per cent in order to make every effort to seize the fort.[33] Akbar introduced the practice of lending money from the imperial treasury. He appointed a separate treasurer and a military officer to advance loans on interest. The system was given the honorific title of *musā'adat.* In the first year the loan could be returned without interest; in the second year the repayment total was increased by one-sixteenth; in the third year, by one-eighth; in the fourth, by one-fourth; from the fifth to the seventh, by one-half; from the eighth to the tenth year, by three-quarters; and from the tenth year onwards, double the original loan was charged.[34]

Contemporary historical works do not give much information about the plight of the common people in Delhi or in other towns. It is only from the sūfī literature that we learn that the population of rural labourers had migrated from the villages to Delhi in search of work. Petty grocers and merchants set up their thatched stalls wherever a suitable patch of vacant land was available. Only the influential and rich merchants owned warehouses, shops, and houses in the fashionable shopping streets or arcades. In the early centuries of the Turkic sultans' rule the *iqtā'dārs'* vacant houses could be temporarily occupied by dignitaries known to them. Since they were not rented, however, they had to be vacated at short notice, and disputes between the parties concerned were common.

The poor, many of whom would otherwise have starved to death, received food from the almshouses (*langars*) which were scattered all over Delhi and other towns. The *langars* either were attached to the sūfī *khanqahs* or had been founded by rich men hoping to obtain divine mercy or worldly fame. Low-caste Hindus who could eat food cooked by Muslims were also benefited by *langars*. Shaykh Nizāmu'd-Dīn Awliyā claimed that the thought of the numbers of starving people, forced to sleep in the corners of mosques and in the streets, made it difficult for him to swallow food.[35]

EDUCATION

Both Hindu and Muslim children normally received their primary education at home. The Muslim aristocracy engaged male and female tutors for their boys and girls. These tutors lived in the aristocrats' houses and supervised their offspring. The children belonging to other members of the family or family friends were also allowed to attend the lessons.

Higher education was available at the *madrasas*. These institutions were established by the sultans, their noblemen, and their more influential ladies. Their principal aim was to produce students for the *'ulamā'* class who would qualify for the civil service and judiciary. Iltutmish founded the Nāsiriyya College of Delhi in memory of his son, Nasīru'd-Dīn Mahmūd. His daughter, Raziyya, appointed the historian Qāzī Minhāj Sirāj as its principal. The main endowments of the leading colleges were supervised by influential scholars; Minhāj Sirāj was one. The Mu'izzī Madrasa, named after Sultan Mu'izzu'd-Dīn Muhammad bin Sām, near the congregational mosques (Jāmi' Masjid) and the cloth-merchants' market (Bazaar-i Bazāzān) in Delhi, was a large mosque-like structure.[36]

Subsequently the number of seminaries multiplied rapidly. In Muhammad bin Tughluq's reign they are said to have numbered 1,000 in Delhi alone, but this seems to be an exaggeration. The Fīrūz-Shāhī Madrasa, founded by Sultan Fīrūz Shāh on the southern bank of the Hawz-i Khāss in Delhi, was an imposing structure. It consisted of a double-storeyed building in front, facing the Hawz-i Khāss, and a single storey at the back. Its sweeping colonnades and square, domed halls were eloquently praised by the contemporary poet Mutahar of Karā.[37] *Madrasas* were also built, both by the sultans and by their nobles, so that the famous scholars who came to Delhi would have their own establishments. The cities and towns each had their seminaries, but those in the cities were staffed by more competent teachers. The grant of *madad-i ma'āsh* land to scholars helped to increase the number of *madrasas*. The sūfi *khānqāhs* also served as institutions of higher training for their own disciples.

Although the early *madrasas* specialized in teaching *fiqh*, this involved a thorough study of *hadīs*, Qur'ānic exegesis, logic, *kalām* (dialectics), and Arabic literature. The *Hidāya* by Marghinānī (d. 1196) and *Usūl-Bazūdī* by Bazūdī (d. 1089) were the chief textbooks. The study of *hadīs* gained momentum in India only during the fifteenth century. Philosophy was studied in India in the thirteenth and fourteenth centuries, but its full flowering was the result of Sultan Sikandar Lodī's patronage.

Books were rare. Scholars had either to transcribe them personally or to have them copied by professional scribes. Rich men could have books transcribed and illuminated with gold, and sometimes illustrated. A personal library was indispensable for scholars, even poor ones. In the thirteenth and fourteenth centuries it was an uphill task for the poor scholars to procure correct copies of important works and even more difficult to find the money to pay for the paper and wages of the scribe. By the end of the sixteenth century bookshops had also set up, and the sale of undesirable books could now be banned. Experiments in printing in Arabic had been made in the West, and Jesuit missionaries in south India had begun to adopt Tamil and Malyalam script to printing; but other than this there was no printing in India.

Akbar compiled a code of education regulations, although they seem to have been ignored by the *madrasas* in his empire. They suggest drastic innovations in both teaching methods and syllabus, from the elementary to the highest stage. According to these regulations every boy should read books on morals, arithmetic, agriculture, household matters, the rules of government, medicine, logic, mathematical and religious sciences, and history. When studying Sanskrit, students should learn the Vyākaran (grammar), Nyāya (logic, one of the six systems of Hindu philosophy), and Patanjali's *Yoga-Sūtra* on yoga philosophy.

Abu'l-Fazl emptily claims that 'These regulations shed a new light on schooling and cast a bright light over *madrasas*' – Akbar's regulations in fact brought about no actual changes. The government in medieval times did not control the educational institutions, They were run by the *'ulamā'*, who were not interested in Akbar's syllabus. However, the changes initiated by Hakīm Fathu'llāh Shīrāzī (d. 1589) and his disciples, who founded seminaries all over India, were far-reaching. Fathu'llāh Shīrāzī was a philosopher, mathematician, and scientist. He combined these specialized subjects with a knowledge of *hadīs* and *fiqh.* His system was developed by Mullā Nizāmu'd-Dīn of Firangī Mahal Lucknow (d. 1748), who had been trained in the Fathu'llāh's traditions. The Mulla's syllabus, known as the Dars-i Nizāmī, is still regarded in conservative Muslim circles as the best training for *'ulamā'*.[38] Its important feature is its combination of Greek philosophy with religious sciences.

The syllabus adopted by the medical practitioners was different. Starting with Arabic rhetoric, grammar, and philosophy, it laid great emphasis on Avicenna's *Qānūn fi't-tibb* (*Canon of Medicine*) and *Kitāb al-Shifa'* (*Book of Healing*).

By the end of Akbar's reign a special syllabus had been devised for accountants and secretaries. A letter written by a Hindu secretary, Chandrabhān Brāhman, to his son gives a fair idea of the contemporary educational requirements. Their mastery over the syllabus included works on the history of Islam, particularly the history of the Mongols and Tīmūrīds of Irān. The study of Persian ethico-political works in the syllabus was intended to acquaint students with the philosophy of Avicenna and Shaykh Shihābu'd-Din Suhrawardī Maqtūl (d. 1191) and his followers, known as Ishrāqīs (Masters of the Philosophy of Illumination). Persian poetry was prescribed for stylistic reasons. *Siyāq* (accountancy) is not included in Chandrabhan's list, but books on this subject were also written. The growing interest among all castes in this study is decried by Chandrabhān, claiming that any success in the secretary's profession depended upon a deep understanding of all departments of the Mughal administration.[39]

Abu'l-Fazl advised the nobles to study the works of al-Ghāzalī, as well as historical and ethico-political works. However, he considered that, being practical people, they should prefer historical works to ethico-political and sūfi literature.

INLAND TRADE

Inland trade increased in the thirteenth and fourteenth centuries as a result of growing urbanization. The old trade and pilgrim routes were cleared of the encroaching jungle and opened up. An old road was reopened connecting Delhi with Daulatābad, Telingāna, and Ma'bar. Postal stations were built along these new roads, and travellers were also allowed to stay there. In the fifteenth century the network of local roads radiating out from the provincial capitals increased considerably. Sher Shāh built four roads from Sonārgāon (near Dacca) via Agra and Delhi to the Indus; from Agra to Jodhpūr and the fort of Chitor; from Agra to Burhānpūr; and from Lahore to Multān. Trees were planted on both sides of these roads. Caravanserais with wells and surrounded by trees were established at four-mile intervals. They had separate food areas for Hindus and Muslims. They replaced the old postal stations and facilitated the rapid transmission of news. In Akbar's reign a network of roads like these covered the land. It was possible to travel with comparative ease between any two cities of the empire. According to a Central Asian history written in 1584, caravans arrived in Peshāwar with goods from the Deccan, Gujarāt, Multān, and other parts of India which were destined for Khurāsān and Transoxiana. The routes from Lahore and Kābul and from Multān to Qandahār made Kābul the leading entrepot for trade with Irān and Central Asia. The vigilance of the Mughal governors and the payment of pensions to the unruly Afghān tribal chiefs ensured that the Khaybar route was reasonably safe.

Merchandise from the Panjāb was sent to markets in Kābul, Ghaznī, Khurāsān, and Central Asia. River-borne traffic from the Panjāb connected the region with the Sind ports. Horn Burnford, an employee of the East India Company who travelled from Agra to Thatta in 1639, says that the white cloth woven in Panīpat was sent to Sirhind or Lahore for sale. He also noted that the products from the famous calico town of Sāmānā were directly exported to Isfahān and its adjacent markets by the Persian and Armenian merchants through Qandahār. He found Lahore 'the prime city of traffic in India', from whence 'all commodities of the adjacent places being brought hither and are brought by the Wonsbecks [Uzbeks] or Tartars and so transported by Cabull into those parts'.[40]

In 1590-l Akbar abolished a number of tolls and imposts on goods for urban consumption. Jahāngīr also removed many taxes on similar goods.

More caravanserais were built both in the *jāgīrs* and *khālisas*, some of which subsequently developed into towns. The *zamīndārs* were responsible for safety on the roads and in return were allowed various privileges such as charging commission and tax. They were also granted revenue-free land (*nānkār* or *bānth*).

The river systems were more convenient for transporting goods, because the land routes were expensive and not always safe. The Indus river system connected the cities and villages of Kashmīr, Panjāb, and Sind, and the Jamuna-Ganges system ran through cities and villages from Delhi to Bengal. The Brahmaputra connected cities and villages in Assam. The responsibility for supplying boats for the army and for the transport of government goods fell on the local chieftains under the Delhi sultans and on the *zamīndārs* under the Mughals. They also supplied boats and escorts to ordinary merchants and travellers. In the sixteenth century inter-provincial land trade was accelerated mainly to avoid European control. The Malābarīs sent their pepper overland to evade the Portuguese.

COASTAL TRADE

From ancient times Indian merchandise had been exported to the Persian Gulf and thence overland through Mesopotamia to the Mediterranean coast. Another sea route carried goods to the Red Sea ports, and then through Egypt to the Mediterranean. Merchandise was distributed from there to Western Europe by Venetian and other Italian merchants. Wares from India and Sind for Irāq and Khurāsān were dispatched via Hurmuz, to the east of the entrance to the Persian Gulf. Jādda and Aden, where a large colony of Indian merchants lived, were the main trading ports on the Red Sea route. The neighbouring port of Dhofiu exported horses to India.

In India, Debal or Dewal in Sind was the main early Arab port, but by the end of the fifteenth century Lahrī Bandar in lower Sind had gained predominance. The leading port of Gujarāt was Cambay. Div, with a good harbour, was also busy since it was free from the dangerous tides in the Gulf of Cambay. Sūrat on the left bank of the Tāptī, and Rānder, on its right, were other large ports in Gujarāt. Ships sailed from Gujarātī harbours to the Red Sea, Hurmuz, East Africa, and Malabār (now Kerala). Ibn Battūta's account shows that the Malabār coast was studded with harbours where small coastal boats anchored. According to him Cālīcut and Quilon were, as ports, the equal of Alexandria, the best he had seen in the world. Barbosa also gives a vivid picture of early sixteenth-century commerce.

Malabār was a half-way house between Sri Lanka, Malacca, and the Spice Islands on the one hand and the Persian Gulf, the Red Sea, and the ports of East Africa on the other. Arab and Persian merchants basked in the patronage of the local rajas. India exported spices, sandalwood, sugar, rice, coconut, precious stones, coral, beads, drugs and seed pearls. Goods carried to India on the return voyage included Arabian horses, gold, silver, lead, quicksilver, coral, vermilion, rose-water, saffron, and opium. The Arab and Irāni merchants of Cālīcut visited the Persian Gulf and Red Sea ports annually. The Arab settlements on the African coast such as Zeila, Makdashau, Mombasa, and Kiwa promoted trade between Gujarāt and East Africa. Ships carrying Indian cloth, beads, and spices brought back gold, ivory, and wax from Africa.

Malacca, situated in the straits between Sumātra and the Malay peninsula, was the most important international port in South-east Asia. Ships from Cambay, Rānder, Cālīcut, Srī Lanka, Coromandel, Bengal, and Thailand sailed to Malacca. Natives from Jāva, the adjacent islands, and Gujarāt (both Muslims and Hindus) had settled in Malacca. Gold from Sumātra, cloves from the Moluccas, white sandalwood from Timor, mace and nutmeg from Banda, camphor from Borneo, and aloe-wood from China were exchanged there for Cambay cloth, white cotton cloth from Bengal, incense, pepper, saffron, coral, quicksilver, and opium. Albuquerque wrote that 'the Guzerates understand the navigation of those parts much more thoroughly than any other nations, on account of the great commerce they carry on in those places'.[41] Next in importance was the port of Pegu. Burmese lac of a superior quality, cloves, musk, and rubies were imported in exchange for different varieties of cloth, drugs, coral, and vermilion. Silk, coloured taffetas, satin, blue and white porcelain, gold, silver, copper, iron, and quicksilver from China were bartered for Indian cloth, drugs, and other products.

Before the development of Malacca as a commercial centre, the Chinese had taken their ships as far as the entrance to the Red Sea and the head of the Persian Gulf but after the fourteenth century they rarely went as far as the Coromandel coast: Following the Chinese, the Indians also stopped at Malacca. This resulted in a rapid decline in Indian coastal enterprise.

The trade with Srī Lanka was in the hands of merchants from Coromandel, Malabār, Vijayanagara, and Gujarāt. Sri Lanka exported cinnamon and some precious stones, while India supplied it with foodstuffs and clothing.

Trade between Cālīcut and the Red Sea was dominated by the Arabs and Irānians, but Gujarāti Muslims, Irānians, Turks, and Gujarāti Hindus, known as *vanias*, handled the trade on other routes. The sailors were largely Muslims, although ships were owned by both Hindus and Muslims. Hurmuz and Aden were dominated by Muslims, but Malacca was controlled by Gujarāti merchants.

In the thirteenth and fourteenth centuries Muslim sailors and merchants were deeply devoted to the Irānian sūfī saint Shaykh Abū Ishāq Gāzirūnī (d. 1035), who had become a sort of patron saint of seafarers. Ibn Battūta says:

> This Shaykh Abū lshāq is highly venerated by the people of India and China. Travellers on the Sea of China make a practice, when the wind turns against them and they fear pirates, of making vows to Abū Ishāq, and each one of them sets down in writing the obligation he has undertaken in his vow. Then when they come safely to land, the servitors of the hospice go on board the ship, take the inventory, and exact (the amount of) his vow from each person who has pledged himself. There is not a ship that comes from China or India but has thousands of *dīnārs* in it (vowed to the saint), and the agents, on behalf of the intendant of the hospice, come to take delivery of that sum. The king

of India (probably Muhammad bin Tughluq) once vowed ten thousand *dīnārs* to Shaykh Abū Ishāq, and when the news of this reached the poor brethren of the hospice, one of them came to India, took delivery of the money, and went back with it to the hospice.

The chain of Abū Ishāq's *khānqāhs* started from Gāzirūn near the Persian Gulf and ended at Zaytūn (Ts'wan-chow-fu), a port in China. The Gāzīrūnī *khānqāhs* in Cālīcut and Quilon collected the gifts promised to the Shaykh and also offered hospitality to guests. According to Ibn Battūta, the Gāzīrūnī *khanqah* in Zaytūn was situated outside the town and received sums of money from merchants vowed in gratitude for their protection.[42]

In the first quarter of the sixteenth century Portuguese naval dominance gave them sovereignty over the sea, which had until then been free to all. No Indian ship could sail to East Africa, China, Japan, or the Spice Islands without Portuguese permission. They had to obtain *cartaz* or passes for safe conduct and had to call at a Portuguese fort to pay duty on their cargo before proceeding to their destination. No ship was allowed to carry munitions, spices, pepper, iron, copper, or wood to the Turks and Ethiopian Muslims. The Portuguese fleet of warships prevented any violation of the *cartaz* system and kept the local coastal powers under control. From the middle of the sixteenth century, the Portuguese made it compulsory for all merchant ships to travel in small convoys. They were escorted by Portuguese war-frigates and could not evade their control. Free *cartaz* were given to the Indian rulers, and even the Emperor Akbar obtained one from the Viceroy of Goa. The Portuguese had no territorial settlements in Sūrat but they ruled over Div and Daman, from where they controlled the convoys. The rise of Div undermined the flourishing trade of Cambay and gave a death-blow to Rānder, the centre for Chinese and Far Eastern goods in Gujarāt. Those merchants who did not live in Div had to pay duty both at their home Gujarāt port and to the Portuguese at Div or Daman. However, pirates frequently challenged Portuguese supremacy, and sea voyages became very dangerous.[43]

Portuguese sovereignty over the Indian Ocean was destroyed by the Dutch and English. In 1595 the first Dutch fleet rounded the Cape of Good Hope in defiance of the Portuguese. From 1596 various groups of Dutch merchants began trading with Sumātra and Jāva and the Dutch had fitted out as many as fifteen voyages by 1601. In 1602 the merchants united to form the Dutch East India Company, which successfully defeated the Portuguese maritime force in Asia. Between 1638 and 1658 the Dutch expelled the Portuguese from Sri Lanka and they seized Malacca in 1641. In 1652 they obtained possession of the Cape of Good Hope.

The local rulers also had begun to attack the Portuguese. In 1632 the Mughal governor of Dacca dealt a crushing blow to Portuguese power at Hugli. The King of Arakān defeated both the Portuguese and the half-caste pirates who had established themselves at Chittagong and had raided the coasts of Bengal and Arakan. Round about 1665 the Mughal governor swept the Portuguese out of Bengal.

Dutch traders entered Gujarāt in 1601 and two years later appeared on the

Coromandel coast. They opened a factory at Masulipatam, the principal seaport for Golkonda, in 1606. Four years later they established a factory at Pulicat, twenty miles north of Madras, where the weavers specialized in the type of clothes worn in the Spice Islands. In Gujarāt the Sūrat factory, which had not been a success, improved rapidly between 1620 and 1629 under the management of Pieter van der Brocke. Thus the period between 1624 and 1660 saw a sharp rise in Dutch commercial success.

In 1600 Queen Elizabeth of England chartered the English East India Company to undertake trade with all countries, as well as with the Cape of Good Hope and India. Captain William Hawkins travelled to Agra in 1608, but the Jesuit missionaries in Jahāngīr's court frustrated his plans. Three years later Captain Middleton was permitted by the Mughal governor to trade from Swally near Sūrat. The Portuguese failure to defeat the English Captain Best led to the founding of an English factory at Sūrat in 1611. By 1616 the English had established factories at Ahmadābād, Burhanpār, Ajmīr, and Agra.

Sir Thomas Roe, the ambassador from King James I to the Mughal court from 1615 to 1619, obtained *farmāns* from the Emperor Jahāngīr and his son Prince Khurram, granting the English favourable terms. In 1616 the English established a factory at Masulipatam, and ten years later in Amrgaon, some distance north of Pulicat. Six years after that the English joined the Irānians in a successful attack on the Portuguese port of Hurmuz, and its trade was diverted to the port of Gombroo, called Bandar 'Abbās. The growing Mughal-Irānian conflict prompted both the English and Gujarāti merchants to make Basra the trade centre for the region from the mid-seventeenth century. After 1623 the Dutch were also given a share in the Gulf trade. The English merchants made Thatta another centre for their trade, exporting goods from its port, Lahrī Bandar, to the Persian Gulf and southwards along the coast to Gujarāt and Goa. However, the Bengal trade was more profitable. In 1630 both the Dutch and English began trading from Piplī and Balasore.

As well as establishing new direct trade routes between India and Western Europe, Dutch and English merchants successfully modified aspects of the old-fashioned Indian commerce with other parts of Asia and the east coast of Africa. For example, the export of silk to Japan was accelerated from 1653. From the Coromandel ports, the Dutch sent to Batavia a large variety of goods, such as iron and steel, sacks, leather, salt, and even roofing tiles, which were not readily obtainable in Java. They also bought slaves in Pulicat and Arakān for their families who had settled in the Spice Islands. Food grain also began to be exported from India, and the export of saltpetre was a new feature in Indian commerce; it was an essential constituent of the gunpowder of that period. This trade was initiated by the Dutch shortly after settling down on the Coromandel coast; a little later, Gujarāt, Agra, the Konkan ports, and Patna also exported saltpetre. In 1646 Prince Aurangzīb, then viceroy of Gujarāt, stopped the export of saltpetre on the grounds that the Europeans would use their gunpowder against Turkey.[44] After his transfer from Gujarāt, however, the export was resumed. Because the Mughal artillery also used vast quantities of gunpowder, the export of saltpetre naturally declined.

The development of a European demand for Indian cloth goods, particularly Indian calico, increased with remarkable rapidity from 1619. Gujarāt was unable to meet the orders, and the English factors began to buy calico in bulk from Patan, Avadh, Agra, and Sāmānā. In 1640 some English merchants opened a factory in Lucknow to buy calico from Daryābād, east of Lucknow, and Khayrābād in the north, The export of yarn for European weavers also commenced. The European beet-sugar industry had not yet come into existence, and the principal sources of cane sugar were China and India in the East and Brazil and the Caribbean islands in the West.

These increased exports were paid for almost entirely in gold and silver. The only new feature – the import of copper from Japan into northern India – appears to represent not an increase in copper consumption. but an attempt to make good the failure of some local sources.

European novelties, described by the English merchants as 'toys', were very popular with the Mughal aristocracy. European drinking glasses, platters for dainty sweets, a variety of looking-glasses, and paintings were much in demand.[45] The aristocracy took little interest in European mechanical inventions because of their aesthetic deficiencies. However, most interesting was the request by the East India Company's broker, Bhimji Parik, for a printing press, possibly to print his bills in order to save on the enormous quantity of 'papers and quills' that traditional commercial practices consumed. A printer was sent by the East India Company in 1671. Despite the considerable expense borne by Bhimji and the printer's efforts, they were nevertheless unsuccessful 'in contriving ways to cast the Banian (Gujarāti) characters in the English manner'. The Sūrat council blamed the printer's lack of experience in casting, and it was suggested that a type-caster should be sent out at Bhimji's expense.[46] The plan seems to have petered out, for no further information on Parik's pioneering efforts at printing in India are available.

Western clocks could easily have been made in India, but since other means of knowing the time such as sun dials were easily available little interest was displayed in either using or manufacturing them. Western labour-saving devices were also considered irrelevant in a country with an abundant population.[47]

COMMERCIAL PRACTICES

Even in the thirteenth century the Hindu merchants in Gujarāt impressed the Muslims with their fair dealing. They quoted correct prices and did not bargain. The Lahore merchants, possibly Muslims, quoted double the correct price. This practice was so abhorrent to the Gujarāti merchants that, according to Shaykh Nizāmu'd-Dīn Awliyā', they questioned how a city with such commercial practices could survive. Shortly afterwards, says the Shaykh, Lahore was devastated by the Mongols. To the Shaykh, the Lahore merchants' malpractices were responsible for their town's destruction.[48]

The ruler's dependence on the merchants for the import of overseas goods, particularly horses and slaves, had forced the Delhi sultans to allow them to act independently and in their own interests. For example, Lahore was invaded by the Mongols in 1241. It was inhabited by many merchants and traders who travelled to Khurāsān and Turkistān in connection with their business. Because they had obtained passes from the Mongols they refused to help defend the city, and the Mongol invaders seized Lahore. When the city was liberated, no action was taken against these merchants because of their influence.[49]

No organized Muslim merchant guilds or groups appear to have existed, but the leading business men were known as the *maliku 't-tujjār* (merchant princes) and they exercised some influence over the rulers. According to Shaykh Nasīru'd-Dīn Chirāgh-i Dihlī, the *maliku 't- tujjār* Qazi Himīdu'd-Dīn was Sultan 'Ala'u'd-Dīn's favourite and could enter the Sultan's private apartments without notice.[50] It is not unlikely that Sultan 'Ala'u'd-Dīn Khaljī discussed his price control system with the *maliku 't-tujjār*, but the belief that the Sultan introduced this control for philanthropic reasons is naive. The leader of the Muslim merchants continued to be called the *maliku 't-tujjār* until Mughal rule ended. For example, Hājjī Zāhid was the *maliku 't-tujjār* until his death some time after 1664.

Even the Hindu merchants enjoyed considerable autonomy under the Delhi sultans and Mughal rule. The Hindu bankers and money-lenders called *multānīs* and *sāhs* (title indicating a privileged status) and *mahājans* freely indulged in usury. The *sarrāf* money-changers (Anglicized version: *sharoff*) monopolized all monetary transactions. Tavernier observes: 'In India a village must be very small if it has not a money-changer, whom they call sharoff, who acts as banker to make remittances of money and issues letters of exchange'.[51] They issued bills of exchange called *hundīs* and organized the insurance (*bīma*) of goods. Muslim merchants do not seem to have become involved in usury and frequently made interest-free loans to the sūfīs, who did not receive their *futūh* (unsolicited gifts on which they depended for their livelihood) regularly.[52] The bankers, on the other hand, made no exceptions, even for the Emperor Aurangzīb. A news report in 1702 from Aurangzīb's court shows that the Emperor requested the bankers of the imperial camp to advance him half a million rupees as an interest-free loan (*qarz-i hasana*). The bankers refused, declaring that if reports of such a loan reached the provinces the governors would also start demanding interest-free loans, and they would be ruined.[53]

The European factory records give the exact amount of loan repayments and the interest charged by the bankers. English merchants generally financed their trade with loans raised in India. In 1646 the English had received 80,000 rupees in loans from Agra. By 1670 the English Company's debt in Sūrat was 200,000 rupees. The Dutch Company also took Indian loans, which amounted in 1639 to 800,000 rupees at the rate of 1¼ and 1 ½ per cent per month.

Some Indian business men were very rich and influential. Vīrjī Vohra, who frequently made loans to the English, was a Jain merchant who lent money to promote his commercial interest. He was a very well-known and powerful man, and in 1639 Shāhjahān invited him to court to explain the Sūrat merchants' grievances against their governor. The English also recognized his unique position and requested the governor of Sūrat to issue passes for maritime trade only to those who were known to Vīrjī Vohra in order to prevent the passes falling into pirate hands.[54]

When Shāhjahān's son Prince Murād rebelled in Gujarāt after his father became sick, he asked the Sūrat merchants to lend him 10 million rupees. Vīrjī Vohra and Hājjī Zāhid paid the amount as an interest-free loan on behalf of the Sūrat merchants and obtained a written bond from the *mutsaddī* (administrator) guaranteeing repayment.[55]

When Shivājī invaded Sūrat in January 1664 he initially invited the Sūrat *mutsaddī*, Vīrjī Vohra, Hājjī Zāhid, and Hājjī Qāsim to negotiate terms with him. When the merchants refused to pay the ransom for the town, Shivājī set it on fire and killed its inhabitants. He seized pearls, valuable jewels, rubies, emeralds, and an incredible amount of money, from Vīrjī Vohra's house. Hājjī Zāhid's house was likewise ransacked.[56]

In 1671 the sons of Vīrjī Vohra and Hājjī Zāhid laid the Sūrat merchants' complaints about the administrator's extortions before Aurangzīb's court. When they heard of the Emperor's proclamation inviting people to file any complaints they had against him, the sons of Vīrjī and Hājjī Zāhid also petitioned the Emperor to repay the loan previously advanced to Prince Murād Bakhsh. The Emperor told them to prove their case. When they asked whether they should use the civil (*dīwanī*) or *sharī'a* procedures, the Emperor replied that both were admissible for redressing grievances. They proved their claim on the basis of a ruling from the *Fatāwa al-'Ālmgīriyya*, which had recently been compiled. The imperial treasurer then reported that the sealed chest of money, which had been borrowed by the Prince, lay still unopened in the treasury. Before the Emperor could order its return, Hājjī Zāhid's son told him that they were interested only in proving their case and not in receiving any money. The chest and its contents were a humble gift to the Emperor from them. The Emperor was pleased, gave them robes of honour, and recalled the Sūrat *mutsaddī*.[57] The story demonstrates both the wealth of the merchants and their influence at court.

Shāntīdās Jawharī, the leading Jain jeweller and banker in Ahmadābād, also had great influence at the Mughal court. He was a very devout Jain, and in 1629 Shāhjahān granted land to the *poshālas* (places for a Jain to stay when fulfilling a vow) built by Shāntīdās. He also built a very beautiful Jain temple near Ahmadābad. In 1654, however, Aurangzīb, who was then governor of Gujarāt, converted it into a mosque by building a *mihrāb* (niche) for prayer in it. Shāntīdās complained to Shāhjahān. Mulla 'Abdu'l-Hakīm, the great scholar and philosopher, declared that Aurangzīb had flagrantly violated the *sharī'a* in usurping Shāntīdās's property. Consequently the mosque had no sanctity. Shāhjahān ordered that a screen be erected in front of the *mihrāb* and the temple be restored to Shāntīdās. The imperial *farmān* also commanded that any material taken from the temple be restored and compensation paid for any material lost.

In November 1656 Prince Murād Bakhsh, who was then governor of Gujarāt, granted the village Palitana to Shāntīdās for the use of Jain pilgrims. Shāhjahān confirmed the grant. Before leaving Ahmadābād, Murād borrowed 550,000 rupees from Shāntīdās and his family. On 30 January 1658 Murād reconfirmed the Palitana grant to Shāntīdās, who had followed him to his camp at Mathura. Two days later Murād issued another *farmān* ordering the repayment of the loan from the Gujarāt revenue. Aurangzīb imprisoned Murād on 1 July. However, after his coronation in Delhi, Aurangzīb issued two *farmāns* dated August 1658. The first confirmed Murād's arrangements for repaying the loan; the second ordered Shāntīdās 'to conciliate all the merchants, *mahājans* and common inhabitants and general residents of the Ahmadābad region to his rule' and to urge them to carry on peacefully with their normal daily activities. He also ordered the regional officers to help Shāntīdās in his business. Aurangzīb issued another *farmān* in 1659 in favour of Shāntīdās's son, ordering the government officers in Gujarāt to help him realize his outstanding debts. On 22 March 1660 the Emperor issued yet another *farmān* acknowledging Shāntīdās's help in providing the army with provisions for its march during the war of succession. He also confirmed the grant of Palitana.[58]

Brokers arranged for the supply of goods as middlemen between customers and small-scale producers. They also acted as clearing agents for their clients, paid customs duty, transported merchants' goods to warehouses, and arranged their sale. They obtained samples of cloth and other manufactured goods for their clients, paid advances to the manufacturers, and were helpful in many other ways. They controlled prices and the sale and purchase of commodities, exacting commission from both buyers and sellers. Baranī called them profiteers and considered them responsible for rising prices. Sultan 'Ala'u'd-Dīn effectively stopped their profiteering and seems to have obtained their co-operation in fixing prices in relation to production costs. Sultan Fīrūz abolished the tax which brokers were required to pay. In Akbar's reign the *kotwāls* appointed and supervised the broker for each occupational group.

During the seventeenth century the brokers proved indispensable to the European merchants, who knew neither the language nor the local craftsmen and constantly demanded loans from the local bankers. According to Pelsaert, the Hindus were very clever brokers and were employed throughout the country, 'except for the sale of horses, oxen, camels, elephants, or any living creatures, which they will not handle as the Moslems do'.[59] Tavernier says, 'The members of this caste are so subtle and skilful in trade that, as I have elsewhere said, they could give lessons to the most cunning Jews.'[60] Although there were Muslim and Parsi brokers, the Hindu brokers of the Vaishīa class were preferred even by Muslim merchants.

VI

RELIGION

PHILOSOPHICAL MOVEMENTS

ISLAMIC religious movements generally arose out of controversies about Allāh's attributes and decrees and their impact on the universe. Such movements did not emphasize the dichotomy between the secular and religious or temporal and spiritual. Muhammad, unlike Christ, did not urge his followers to 'render unto Caesar the things that are Caesar's and to God the things that are God's'. Islamic religious and spiritual movements consequently have major political implications and repercussions. The founders of various religious movements sought state support to strengthen their ideologies, but this often recoiled upon the leaders' own heads.

It was in the wake of the battle of Siffin in June-July 657, between 'Alī and Mu'āwiya, that a new movement, the *'ilm al-kalām* (the science of defending orthodoxy by rational arguments), crystallized. One of the most important controversies within this movement concerned free will. One section, Jabriyya, denied man's freedom and claimed that human actions were subordinate to divine compulsion. Conversely another section, the Qadariyya, rejected predestination and believed that man produced his own actions; the word 'created' was never used. Their position was modified by the Mu'tazila, who founded the speculative dogmatics of Islam. According to them men are endowed with free will and are therefore rewarded for good deeds and punished for evil ones. God is aware of evil actions but He does not create them. He is just, neither desiring evil or ordaining it. His will and His commands are identical. The Mu'tazila recognize the divine attributes of knowledge, power, and speech but assert that they are not distinct from God's essence. They do not believe that there is an uncreated Word within God. 'Word of God' signifies that God gave the power of language to contingent beings so that He could communicate His law to man. The Qur'ān, as the 'Word of God', according to the Mu'tazila refers to what God wants man to know.

The Mu'tazila were a pro-'Abbāsid group but they were rejected by the 'Abbāsid Caliph al-Mutawakkil (847–61). Several leading Mu'tazila, who left the movement and founded their own schools, became pioneers of the defence of Sunnī orthodoxy. The most prominent among them was Abu'l-Hasan al-Ash'arī (873–936), who attracted a large number of disciples. He opposed the Mu'tazila by asserting that God knows, sees, and speaks by His knowledge, sight, and speech, and that Qur'ānic expressions such as 'God's hand and face' do not refer to corporeal attributes but denote His 'grace' and 'essence'. According to the Ash'arites, the Qur'ān is the word of God, eternal and uncreated. Whereas the Mu'tazila rejected belief in the possibility of a human vision of God, because this implied that He is corporeal and limited, al-Ash'arī preached the reality of the beatific vision after death, although its nature cannot be explained. The Ash'arites believe that the same matter assumes different forms and that the world consists of atoms which are united, disconnected, and reunited again. Al-Ash'arī's contemporary, Abū Mansūr al-Māturīdī, also fostered the development of orthodox Sunnīsm although he differed from the Asha'rites on many significant points. To the Māturīdīs predestination and free will stand side by side. Both systems flourished in India and provided the basis for orthodox Sunnī intellectuals and *kalām.*

The 'Abbasid Caliph al-Ma'mūn (813–33) set up an institution called the Baytu'l-hikma (House of Wisdom) where Greek scientific and philosophical literature of the late Hellenistic schools was translated into Arabic from Greek and Syriac. Some of the translators brought their conclusions into line with Islamic doctrines. Al-Kindī (*c.* 800–70), known as Faylsūfu'l-'Arab (Philosopher of the Arabs), pioneered this strategy. Ar-Rāzī, known in Europe as Rhazes (d. 932) of Rayy (near Tehrān), made original contributions to both philosophy and medicine. Al-Fārābī (875–950), known as 'the second teacher' (Aristotle was the first), improved on al-Kindi's interpretations. His philosophy combined Aristotle and Plato's *Republic* and *Laws* with Neoplatonism. In the centre of Fārābī's philosophy is the First Being or Absolute One, identified with Allāh. Following Plato, Fārābī identifies God with Absolute Good, while thinking and thought coincide in Being. Ibn Miskawayh's (d. 1030) *Tahdhīb al-akhlāq* added a new dimension of deep ethical sensitivity to the understanding of Being. It was, however, Avicenna (Ibn Sīna, 980–1037) who suggested that the entire knowledge of the physical world is subordinate to the knowledge of Being. He advocated an ontological distinction between essence (*māhiya*) or nature, and existence (*wujūd*) or experience on the one hand, and a division between the necessary (*wājib*), the possible (*mumkin*), and the impossible (*mumtani'*) on the other Unity and existence are only accidents which may or may not be added to essence for contingent humanity; but in the Necessary Being (Wājibu'l-Wujūd) or God, essence and existence are inseparably united. The orthodox Islamic *kalām* preached that the world began at some point in time. They rejected the Greek system of the eternal heavens or any other order of reality which violated the notion of the transcendence of God. They believed that the entire creation is dependent upon the transcendence of the divine principle. Consequently the orthodox did not approve of the cosmological doctrines of Fārābī and Avicenna, asserting that creation is the manifestation (*ta'aqqul*) by God of His own Essence. Ghazālī (1058–1111) took both Fārābī and Avicenna to task for advocating the eternity of the world and denying a specific act of creation. He contended that to state that earlier philosophers had believed that God was the maker or agent who created the world was to distort their philosophical writings. In fact, he claimed, according to the philosophers, God has no will or attributes, and whatever proceeds from Him is a necessary consequence of His nature. About a century later, Fakhru'd-Dīn Rāzī (1149–1209) carved out a new defence of Sunnī Ash'arite doctrine. He neither totally rejected Greek philosophy nor, like Avicenna's peripatetic followers, adhered strictly to it. He wrote critical commentaries on Avicenna's best-known works, such as *al-Ishārāt wa'l-tanbīhāt* and the *Qānān.* Rāzī completely rejected the Muslim philosophers' theory that only unity can follow from unity, claiming that multiplicity is also possible.

The influence of Ghazālī and Rāzī provided a firm basis for the Sunnī intellectual system, but the generation following Rāzī depended mainly on the state for the defence of Sunnī orthodoxy. The Sunnīs expected the state to annihilate their opponents, particularly the philosophers. For example, Sayyid Nūru'd-Dīn Mubārāk Ghazanawī (d. 1234–5), who was a highly respected scholar in Delhi, claimed that kings could not obtain salvation unless they banished philosophers and stopped the teaching of philosophy.[1] According to Baranī, if Avicenna, who had revived Greek philosophy and was the philosophical leader in Muslim countries, had fallen into the hands of Sultan Mahmūd of Ghaznī, his contemporary, the Sultan would have ordered him to be cut into pieces and his flesh given to vultures.[2] However, to Baranī's utter disappointment, it proved impossible either to stop the study of philosophy or to bring about the expulsion of philosophers from India. The *Qānūn* (*Canon of Medicine*) and the *Kitāb al-Shifā'* (*Book of Healing*) by Avicenna were indispensable for physicians, whose numbers were rapidly increasing. The *Kitāb al-Shifā'* fascinated the Sultan Muhammad bin Tughluq who was a great patron of philosophy. According to Baranī, it was the study of philosophy that had made Sultan Muhammad ruthless, stone-hearted, cruel, and irreligious; that study ought therefore to be taboo for rulers and their noblemen.[3]

In the fifteenth century Gujarāt became the centre for Muslim intellectuals, the most prominent among whom was Abu'l-Fazl Gāzirūni. Shaykh Abu'l-Fazl's father, Shaykh Mubārāk, was Gāzirūni's disciple and had studied the *Kitab al-Shifā'* and *al-Ishārāt wa'l-tanbīhāt* under him. From Sultan Sikandar Lodī's reign the study of Avicenna's philosophy grew increasingly popular in Delhi. The pioneers in Delhi were Shaykh 'Abu'llah Tulambī (d. 1516) and Shaykh 'Azizu'llāh Tulambī of Multan. When Shaykh Mubārak arrived in Agra in 1543 the study of philosophy and *kalām* was further increased. Abu'l-Fazl's mastery of philosophy and *kalām* enabled him to defeat the orthodox *'ulamā'* in the religious discussions at Akbar's court. The interest in philosophy and science was accelerated in northern India by Mir Fathu'llāh Shirāzī, who moved from 'Adil Shāh's court in Bījāpūr to Akbar's court in 1582. Fathu'llāh Shirāzī remained at court until he died in 1589 while accompanying Akbar on his tour to Kashmīr.

We learn from the Sunnī puritan revivalist, the Mujaddid,[4] that the philosophers at Akbar's court were inspired by Greek philosophy and by Persian translations of Sanskrit works by ancient Hindu sages. One of these philosophers was the famous Abu'l-Fazl, who referred to himself as 'the perfect and accomplished': *al-fāzilah wa'l-fazl.* He claimed that the main aim of the institution of prophethood was to promote knowledge and public welfare and to reform people's lives. Prophets were supposed to prevent strife, lawlessness, and licentiousness. They had nothing to do with ultimate salvation but were concerned merely with ethical regeneration and the promotion of the virtues contained in works of philosophy. According to him physical acts of worship did not affect salvation, since they did not influence the spiritual world. The Mujaddid wrote the *Isbāt al-Nubūwwa* to strengthen the general belief in the prophets and to prove that Muhammad was the 'seal of the prophets'. In their defence the philosophers at Akbar's court asserted that they rejected neither the pophets nor Muhammad. They sought to emphasize the prophets' ethical mission and glossed over their miracles. Consequently the orthodox puritanical literature failed to undermine the study of philosophy. Both Jahāngīr and Shāhjahān patronized philosophers. In Shāhjahān's reign there flourished Mulla Mahmūd Farūqī Jaunpūrī (d. 1652), whose scholarship and learning had made a very deep impact even on Irānian philosophers. Prince Shāh Shujā' and Shāyista Khān were his disciples. The *Shams al-bāzigha*, by Mullā Mahmūd, is an outstanding contribution to physics and metaphysics. It is even now an important text in the traditional Indian seminaries.

The most interesting philosopher in the courts of Shāhjahān and Aurangzīb was Dānishmand Khān. He was a native of Yazd and entered Shāhjahān's court in 1651. He resigned because of differences with Dārā Shukoh, but Aurangzīb re-employed him in the second year of his reign, awarded him a high *mansab*, and reappointed him governor of Delhi. In consideration of his studious habits, Aurangzīb exempted him 'from the ancient ceremony of repairing twice a day to the assembly, for the purpose of saluting the king'. Dānishmand employed Dārā Shukoh's principal Sanskrit scholar to explain Hindu philosophy to him. The French doctor Bernier taught him the medical discoveries of William Harvey (1578–1657) and Jean Pecquet (1622–74) and the philosophy of Pierre Gassendi (1592–1655) and Descartes (1596–1650).[5] The *Dabistān-i Mazāhib*, the seventeenth-century encyclopaedia of religions, discusses the important and original philosophers of Shāhjahān's reign in great length. They, however, drew mainly on Hindu and Islamic sources and were not interested in the Western philosophy which so fascinated Dānishmand Khān.

SŪFI MOVEMENTS

The philosophers' objective was to rationalize the nature of Necessary Being, while the *kalām* scholars were principally concerned to defend divine transcendence (God as above His creation and not one with it). Sūfism, on the other hand, strove to achieve the inner realization of divine unity by arousing intuitive and spiritual faculties. Rejecting rational argument, the sūfīs plunged into contemplation and meditation. Some of them were overpowered by ecstasy and frenzy, but sobriety was generally considered essential to sūfism.

Such a system is bound to be studded with controversial judgements and marred by personal prejudices. We shall therefore follow the historical analysis of the eighteenth-century Indian scholar Shāh Walīu'llāh, who combined in himself both the sūfī and *kalām* traditions. He contends, when outlining the history of sūfism, that Islam is endowed with two aspects: the exoteric and esoteric. Islam's exoteric aspect is concerned with public good, while its esoteric one involves the purification of the heart through ethical regeneration. The Shāh identifies the esoteric aspects with *ihsān*, the doctrine that Allāh should be worshipped with the certainty that either the worshipper is watching Allāh or He is watching the worshipper. The holy men who were known as *awliyā' Allāh* (proteges of God) or sūfīs upheld *ihsān*.

The Shāh divides sūfism into four epochs. The first began with the prophet Muhammad and his companions and extended until the time of Junayd of Baghdād (d. 910). The sūfīs of the first period devoted themselves to prayer, fasting, and *zikr* (invoking one of God's names). They were sometimes transported into spiritual ecstasy, but this was not considered necessary for spiritual life. The second epoch started during Junayd's time. Many sūfīs of the period lived in a state of continued meditation and contemplation. This resulted in intuitive insights and intense spiritual experiences which could be expressed only symbolically or in unusual phrases. These sūfīs were so emotionally affected by *samā'* (religious music) that they swooned or tore their clothes in ecstasy. Their spiritual illumination enabled the sūfīs to see into people's hearts. To protect themselves from material desires or thoughts and from the devil's temptings, the sūfīs practised self-mortification. Many ate only grass and leaves, wore rags, and lived an isolated existence in the mountains and jungles.

From the advent of Shaykh Abū Sa'īd bin Abu'l Khayr (d. 1049) and Shaykh Abu'l-Hasan Kharaqānī (d. 1034), sūfism entered upon its third stage. The emphasis among the sūfī elite of this epoch was to live in a state of ecstasy which led to *tawajjuh* (spiritual telepathy), although many perfect sūfīs still followed earlier beliefs and practices. The sūfīs in *tawajjuh* overcame worldly constraints. The veils separating them from the divine dispersed, and they could see existence issuing from Being. In contemplating the union of temporal and eternal their individuality dissolved, and they even ignored their regular religious practices such as prayers and fasting.

The fourth epoch dates from just before the birth of Shaykh al-Akbar Muhīyu'd-Dīn Ibnu'l 'Arabi (1165-1240), when the sūfīs discovered the theory of the five stages of the descent from Wājibu'l-Wujūd (Necessary Being). The first stage is Ahadiyya (Essence of the Primal One). The second stage is Wahdāniyya (Unity of God); the third descent is the sphere of Arwāh (Sphere of Infinite Forms), the fourth is the sphere of Misāl (Similitude or Angelic Forms), and the fifth the sphere of Ajsām (Bodies of the Physical World). The problems of the Wahdat al-Wujūd lie in the perception of the steps of the descent of Being.[6] The important question is whether these stages are really One or merely give this impression.

The Shāh does not claim that the four historical epochs were mutually exclusive. There was a considerable overlap; some of the sūfīs of the fourth epoch exhibited the characteristics found in the first. What is remarkable is that the contributions from the sūfīs of each epoch helped to make sūfism a unique movement in the history of Islamic spiritual development.

The Shāh says that sūfism began with the Prophet Muhammad. Some of his companions, who led a retired life in the Medina mosque, given to poverty and self-mortification, are counted as sūfī leaders. Among them were the Ethiopian Bilāl, the Irānian Salmān, Abu 'Ubaydah, 'Ammār bin Yāsir, and Abū Dharr Ghifārī. Although the first three successors to the Prophet are deeply respected by the sūfīs, 'Alī is regarded by them as their Shaykh (leader). Hasan Basrī (642–728) is believed to be the link between 'Alī and the sūfī sects. Hasaṇ was both a Qadariyya and an ascetic. The word 'sūfī' was not applied to the Prophet's companions, who were known as *sahāba* (companions), *tābi'ūn* (those who had seen one or more of the Prophet's associates), or *tabatābi'ūn* (those who had seen one or more of the *tābi'ān*). The word 'sūfī' – which is derived from *sūf* meaning 'wool' – appeared before Hasan Basrī's death, in reference to those ascetics who wore woollen garments in place of finer ones of silk or cotton as a mark of asceticism and self-denial. Hasan Basrī asserted: 'He who wears wool out of humility towards God increases the illumination of his insight and his heart, but he who wears it out of pride and arrogance will be thrust down to hell with the devil.'[7] The greatest threat to sūfism came from the impostors and charlatans who were innumerable even in the first century of Islam. In subsequent centuries their number became enormous.

Among the leading sūfīs of the first epoch was one of the greatest sūfī women of all time. She was Rābi'a (d. 752) of Basra. Many famous sūfīs called on her in her lonely hermitage and even visited her when she had withdrawn into the wilderness. Her disinterested love of God added a major dimension to the sūfī devotional attitudes.

Before the end of the first epoch, a sūfī home, known as a *khānqāh* (hospice), was built by a Christian dignitary in Ramla near Jerusalem. This enabled the sūfīs to share their ideas, but individual mystical experience is the true hallmark of sūfism.

Towards the end of the first epoch, Bayāzīd or Abū Yazīd Tayfūr of Bistam in Irān (d. 874 or 877–8) became famous. According to Junayd, he occupied the highest rank among the sūfīs, as Gabriel did amongst the angels. He believed that he had shed his 'I' in mystical annihilation (*fanā'*) 'as snakes their skin' and in that state of changed consciousness he shocked the orthodox by declaring: 'Glory be to me! How great is my majesty! Thy obedience to me is greater than my obedience to thee.'[8] Some hagiologists suggest that Bayāzīd learnt the doctrine of *fanā'* from his teacher, Abū 'Alī Sindī. From his surname it seems that the latter teacher came from Sind, and thus his ideas may have been influenced by Hindu or Buddhist mysticism. This very probable theory is supported by some Western scholars, although others reject it.[9] The controversy is misplaced, however. Ancient Indian thought and mysticism were a source of continual interest to religious people of the eastern and central Irānian regions, and this knowledge naturally fused with Bayāzīd's expression of his own mystical experience.

Bayāzīd's utterance, in what is known as mystical intoxication (*sukr*), was matched by those of al-Hallāj. He was born at Tūr in Fārs in eastern Irān in

857–8. In 913 he was imprisoned after his theopatic cry, 'Ana'l-Haqq' ('I am the Truth or God'). While in prison, Hallāj wrote his famous work on the case of Iblīs, the Devil, *Tā Sīn al-Azal.* Hallāj believed Iblīs's monotheism had prevented him from prostrating before Adam. After nine years in prison Hallāj was cruelly tortured and hung on a gibbet. Junayd, who had supported Bayāzīd, repudiated his contemporary, Hallāj. Now entering its second epoch, sūfism was divided into two groups: those who expressed themselves uninhibitedly (*sukr*) and those who restrained their expressions (*sahw*). The sūfīs of both schools believed that just as a raindrop is not annihilated in the ocean, although it ceases to exist individually, the sūfī soul, in the unitive state, is indistinguishable from the universal divinity.

In the second epoch the sūfīs were better organized and were divided into sects according to the distinctive ideologies and practices evolved by their founders. Sūfi literature on doctrine, practice, and history was written in both poetry and prose. Sūfi masters now began to send their disciples to distant lands to disseminate their teachings. This tendency increased in the third epoch. Many eminent sūfīs also moved to India.

Of these migrants, Shaykh Safiu'd-Dīn Gāzirūnī, the nephew of Shaykh Abū lshāq Gāzirūni, settled at Uch. It was apparently Mahmūd of Ghaznī's conquest of the Panjāb that prompted many notable sūfīs to settle there. The sūfī who left an indelible mark both on India and on the history of sūfism was Abu'l-Hasan 'Ali bin 'Usmān al-Hujwirī, known as Dātā Ganj Bakhsh (Distributor of Unlimited Treasure). He seems to have reached Lahore in *c.* 1035 and died some time after 1089. His *Kashfu'l-mahjūb*, in Persian, gives the biographies, thought, and practices of sūfīs from Prophet Muhammad's days to his own time.

The *'Awārifu'l-ma'ārif* by Shaykh Shihābu'd-Dīn Suhrawardī (1234–5) was the second important sūfi textbook on which the early Indian sūfi doctrines and practices were based. Both works denounce those who believe that gnosis (spiritual knowledge) absolved sūfis from the need to obey the *sharī'a.* To them, *sharī'a* (law), *ma'rifa* (gnosis), and *haqīqa* (reality) were interdependent. The achievement of particular states (*hāl*) in sūfism involved a changing psychological condition, while *maqām* (position in time and space) was relatively permanent. It was not essential that mystics lose all consciousness in a state of *fanā'* (annihilation), since when the state of *baqā'* (abiding in God) was achieved a sūfi regained his power of action. The section on sūfi ethics and mystic ways of life in the *'Awārif* is a marked improvement upon the corresponding discussion in Hujwirī's *Kashfu'l-mahjūb.*

By the thirteenth century the division of sūfis into fourteen orders or *silsilas* had already crystallized. The sūfis of each *silsila* guarded their traditions strictly and urged their disciples to refrain from entering more than one order. Some of Shaykh Shihābu'd-Dīn's disciples migrated to India, but the real founder of the Suhrawardiyya *silsila* was Shaykh Bahā'u'd-Dīn Zakariyya. He was born at Kot Karor, near Multān, in about 1182-3. After completing his education he went on a pilgrimage to Mecca. Travelling through Jerusalem, he reached Baghdad and was initiated into the Suhrawardiyya order by Shaykh Shihābu'd-Dīn, who appointed him his *khalīfa* (deputy) in Multān, although it was already full of leading holy men and sūfis. Bahā'u'd-Dīn's scholarship and acute spiritual perception made a deep impact upon the people in Multān and neighbouring towns. It would seem that many merchants from Irāq and Irān admired him, and their gifts enabled him to build an enormous *khānqāh* with granaries and stores. He did not mix with the common people, and the wandering dervishes, known as Qalandārs, were not welcome in his *khānqāh.* They were bitterly opposed to him. He invited Sultan Iltutmish to invade Multān and topple its ruler, Qabācha. After his annexation of Multān in 1228, Iltutmish appointed Bahā'u'd-Dīn the Shaykhu'l-Islam (leader of the Muslim community). In his case this was not an administrative office, but it enhanced his prestige among the people. During the continued Mongol invasions of Multān the Shaykh raised public morale and once succeeded in negotiating peace between the invaders and the Muslim army, through the Muslim dignitaries serving with the Mongols. He died in 1262.[10] His disciple and son-in-law, Shaykh Fakhru'd-Dīn Ibrāhim 'Irāqī, was a born poet. At Qūnya (Koniq in Turkey) he attended lectures given by Shaykh Sadru'd-Dīn on the *Fusūs al-hikam* of Ibnu'l-'Arabi. Iraqi composed a treatise, called *Lam'āt* (*Flashes*). This work constitutes a very impressive commentary on the Unity of Being (Wahdat al-Wujūd) around which the ideologies of the fourth epoch of sūfism revolve. Before his death 'Iraqi sent a copy of his *Lam'āt* to Bahā'u'd-Dīn's son and successor, Shaykh Sadru'd-Dīn 'Ārif. Shaykh 'Ārif's disciple, Amīr Husayn, the author of *Zādu 'l-musāfirīn*, wrote several works comprising thoughtful commentaries on the doctrine of Wahdat al-Wujūd.

Shaykh 'Ārif's son, Shaykh Ruknu'd-Dīn, was highly respected by the Delhi sultans from 'Ala'u'd-Dīn Khaljī to Muhammad bin Tughluq; his fame spread as far as Alexandria, and Ibn Battūta was advised to call on him. According to Shaykh Ruknu'd-Dīn the leaders of the sūfi community should possess three attributes. Property was essential in order that the sūfi leaders could satisfy the Qalandars' demands for sherbet. Otherwise the disappointed Qalandars would commit the sin of abusing their sūfi leaders and would be punished on resurrection day. Knowledge was the second requirement for a leader so that he could discuss scholarly questions with the *'ulamā'. Hāl* (mystical enlightenment) was also necessary, or else the leaders would not be able to impress other sūfis.'[11] Shayk Ruknu'd-Dīn died in 1334–5. After his death the Suhrawardiyya *silsila* declined in Multān, but the order became very popular in other provinces and spread from Uch to Gujarāt, the Panjāb, Kashmīr, and even Delhi. It was revitalized by the sūfi Sayyid Jalālu'd-Dīn Bukhari, popularly known as Makhdūm-i Jahāniyān (Lord of the World's People). So widely travelled was he that he was called Jahāngasht (World Traveller). During Fīrūz's reign he lived in Uch but frequently visited Delhi. He was an ardent puritan and strongly objected to the Hindu accretions to Muslim social and religious practices – for example, the celebration of the Shab-i barāt festival which is held in the evening of the middle of Sha'bān, the eighth month in the Muslim calendar, when fireworks are let off and lighted lamps are placed on the newly whitewashed graves, in obvious imitation of the Hindu Diwāli. Only in India, he commented, was there such a blatant disregard of the *sharī'a*, for such customs were not found in Ghaznī, Irān, or Arabia.[12]

Qutb-i 'Ālam (d. 1553), a grandson of Makhdūm-i Jahāniyān, settled near Ahmadābād, the new capital of Gujarāt founded by Sultān Ahmad (1411–42). His son, Sayyid Muhammad, known as Shāh Mahjhan, was also very famous. He was given the title Shāh-i 'Ālam (King of the Universe). Many leading Gujarāti noblemen were among his disciples. One of them collected from his *iqtā'* only those taxes sanctioned by the *sharī'a.* Consequently all the peasants wished to move there, and his *iqtā'* grew very prosperous.[13]

In the fourteenth century a collateral line of the Suhrawardiyyas, known as the Firdawsiyya, emerged. The outstanding sūfi of this order was Shaykh Sharafu'd-Dīn Ahmad Yaha Munyarī, whose ancestors had settled in Bihār in the early thirteenth century. He practised arduous ascetic exercises in the forests. Throughout the reigns of both Muhammad bin Tughluq and Fīrūz Tughluq, Shaykh Sharafu'd-Dīn's *khānqāh* in Munayr was the rendezvous for many seeking a spiritual life. The Shaykh's letters to his disciples, which have been compiled in several volumes, exhibit his real talent as a teacher. The Shaykh was deeply disappointed in Sultan Fīrūz, who had mercilessly executed his friends and fellow-sūfis, such as Shaykh 'Izz Kaku'ī and Shaykh Ahmad Bihārī, at the instigation of the bigoted *'ulamā'*. Shaykh Sharafu'd-Dīn expressed surprise that a town in which such killings were tolerated still remained standing and had escaped destruction at God's hands. The Shaykh was saved from execution by the intervention of Makhdām Jahāniyan. The sūfi hagiologists ascribe the destruction of Delhi during Tīmūr's invasion to the execution of two sūfis there.[14]

The Shaykh believed in the Wahdat al-Wujūd and drew heavily on the ideas of the exponents of this ideology such as the Persian poets Farīdu'd-Dīn 'Attār (d. 1220), 'Irāqī, and Jalālu'd-Dīn Rūmī (d. 1273). Shaykh Sharafu'd-Dīn died in 1381. His spiritual descendants were also influential, and their surviving letters epitomize the Firdawsiyya devotion to the Wahdat al-Wujūd doctrine.

The fifteenth- and sixteenth-century Suhrawardiyya Delhi centres owed their reputation to the scholarship and impressive personality of Shaykh Samā'u'd-Dīn, who died in 1496. His disciple, known by his *nom de plume* Jamālī, was an eminent poet who travelled throughout the Islamic world. Sultan Sikandar Lodī admired Jamālī greatly, but after Bābur's conquest Jamālī wrote a panegryric to the new ruler. Later Jamālī accompanied on his expedition to Gujarāt, dying there in 1536.[15] Of Jamālī's two sons, Shaykh 'Abdu'l Hayy (d. 1551–2) was a member of Sher Shāh's court, but his elder son, Shaykh Gadā'ī, remained loyal to the Emperor Humāyūn and his prime minister, Bayram Khān. After Akbar's restoration, Bayram Khān repaid Gadā'ī's services to the Mughal cause by appointing him the Sadru's-Sudūr. Gadā'ī revoked the innumerable *madad-i m'āsh* grants recklessly given by Sher Shāh and the Lodīs to the Afghān *'ulamā'* and dignitaries, so naturally the dispossessed Sunnī orthodoxy turned against him. After Bayram's fall from power in 1560 Gadā'ī retired into obscurity and died in 1569 or a year later.[16] The rise of new *silsilas* with influential friends at court undermined the Suhrawardiyya *silsila.* Of the old *silsilas*, only the Chishtiyyas, who had never depended on court patronage, retained their popularity.

The Chishtiyya *silsila* is essentially an Indian one. The branches which were developed in Chisht or Khwāja Chisht about sixty miles east of Hirat have not survived. In India the Chishtiyya *silsila* was founded by Khwāja Mu'inu'd-Dīn. Unfortunately for us the records of his early career are legendary and arose from apocryphal literature written in the names of famous sūfis. He was born in Sijistān (Sīstān) in about 1142 and was educated at leading intellectual centres in eastern Irān. After travelling through many parts of the Islamic East, the Khwāja reached Lahore and arrived in Delhi after Sultan Mu'izzu'd-Dīn's death in 1206. He eventually settled in Ajmīr. The stories of his encounter with Prithvīrāja's yogis, telling how the Khwāja's slippers brought a flying yogi down to the ground, are among the stock-in-trade of sūfi legends. The surviving sayings of the Khwāja show that his life's mission was to inculcate piety, humility, and devotion to God. According to him those who know God avoid unduly mixing with other people and keep silent on matters relating to divine knowledge. Some of his sayings are no different from those of Abā Yazīd, the ninth-century sūfi known for his ecstatic utterances. For example, he says: 'Like a snake we cast off our slough and look attentively. We did not find any distinction between lover, beloved and love. In the realm of divine unity they are identical.' He also comments: 'For years I used to go around the Ka'ba; now the Ka'ba goes around me.'[17]

Khwāja Mu'īnu'd-Dīn died in 1236 at Ajmīr. His tomb was at first tended by the sultans of Mālwa, but from Akbar's reign it came under state management. The Mughal emperors' devotion to the Khwāja's tomb and their frequent visits for both political and spiritual reasons made Ajmīr the leading Muslim pilgrim centre in India.

The Khwāja's young disciple, Shaykh Hamīdu'd-Dīn, made Nagaur (Rājasthān), containing a predominantly Hindu population, the chief Chishtiyya centre. His father, Ahmad, had migrated from Lahore to Delhi, where Hamīdu'd-Dīn was born after its conquest in 1192 by Mu'izzu'd-Dīn. Shaykh Hamīdu'd-Dīn had in Nagaur a small plot of land which he worked himself. He and his wife lived in a hut and supported themselves on the produce of the land. He refused to accept gifts of either land or money from the rulers, although he had barely enough to keep body and soul together. A Muslim merchant took his letters to the Suhrawardiyva leader Shaykh Bahā'u'd-Dīn in Multān. Baha'u'd-Dīn was wealthy, but his justifications of his affluence did not convince Hamīdu'd-Dīn. Both stuck to their own principles; Bahā'u'd-Dīn lived prosperously, while Hamīdu'd-Dīn chose to remain poor. Shaykh Hamīdu'd-Dīn died in November 1274 and was succeeded by his grandson, Shaykh Farīdu'd-Dīn Mahmūd.[18] Sultan Muhammad bin Tughluq was deeply devoted to Shaykh Farīd's family and married his daughter to Shaykh Farīd's grandson. One of Shaykh Farīd's disciples, Khwāja Ziyā'u'd-Dīn Nahkashabi (d. 1350–1), was a famous scholar. He translated Chintamani Bhatta's *Suka-saptati* into Persian from Sanskrit and gave it the title *Tūtī-nāma* (*Stories from a Parrot*). He also translated the *Rati-rahasya* (*Mysteries of Passion*) of Kokapandita, containing a classification of female physical types, into Persian poetry. To Nakhashābī, Islam was the religion of moderation, which trod a middle path between asceticism and extravagance.[19] The Chishtiyyas' work in Delhi was organized by Khwāja Qutbu'd-Dīn Bakhtiyār Kākī, the most important disciple of Khwāja Mu'īnu'd-Dīn. Khwāja Qutbu'd-Dīn had arrived in Delhi some time after 1221. The Emperor lltutmish was deeply devoted to the Khwāja, but the sūfīs' indulgence in *samā'* (audition; sūfī music and dancing) to arouse mystical ecstasy caused trouble with the *'ulamā'*, who were hostile to the sūfīs in general and to *samā'* in particular. However, the Shaykh's towering personality popularized *samā'*. In 1235 he died in a state of ecstasy aroused by a verse in *samā'*.[20]

Of the Khwāja's disciples, Shaykh Farīdu'd-Dīn, or Bābā Farīd, was very celebrated. The Shaykh's father was a scholar, but it was his mother, an exceedingly pious lady who spent her nightly vigils in lengthy prayers, who exerted the greatest influence on the future sūfī saint. Bābā Farīd, however, decided to leave Delhi when his fame became an obstacle to his prayers and he finally settled at Ajodhan. In Adjodhan he built his *jamā'at-khāna* – a thatched hall for communal living, with a separate cell for his own meditations. It had no furniture, and everyone slept on the floor. On special occasions a cot was provided for distinguished visitors. Among his few possessions Bābā Farīd had a small rug which he used by night as a blanket but which barely covered him. Khwāja Qutbu'd-Dīn's wooden staff lay behind his head as a pillow. His food consisted of wild fruit and millet bread. Abstaining from nourishment during the day, in the evening he broke his fast by taking sherbet, often mixed with dried grapes. After prayers, two pieces of bread smeared with *ghī* (clarified butter) were given to him. One he gave away to his visitors, the other he ate himself, sharing it with his favourite disciples. Because his *jamā'at-khāna* was situated on a main trade route, men from all classes and sections of Indian society thronged there. The Qalandars were shockingly rude and insolent, but the Bābā would not forbid them entry into his communal hall. Towards the end of his life the local governor's hostility towards him scared off the common people, and their gifts to him stopped. His family suffered considerable deprivation, but he remained indifferent to these difficulties, concentrating on God alone.[21] In 1265 he died.

The Bābā's successor was Shaykh Nizāmu'd-Dīn Awilyā'. He came originally from Badā'ūn but had settled in Delhi. The stories of his own apprenticeship in *jamā'at-khāna* at Ajodhan show that the Bābā trained him in a very vigorous environment so that he could make the Chishtiyya order the dominant sūfī *silsila* in India. The ethical influence radiating from Ghiyāspūr, where the Shaykh resided, seems to have made a considerable impact upon the people of Delhi. The Shaykh was, however, completely estranged from Sultan Qutbu'd-Dīn Mubārāk and Ghiyāsu'd-Dīn Tughluq, although Nasīru'd-Dīn Khusraw had befriended him. When the future Sultan Ghiyāsu'd-Dīn Tughluq invaded Delhi, Khusraw offered huge gifts to the holy men in Delhi to seek their blessing for his success. Three of the sūfīs rejected the gifts; others accepted them, intending to return them to the next ruler if Khusraw lost.

Shaykh Nizāmu'd-Dīn accepted the gifts, but then, according to his custom, instantly distributed them among the needy. Naturally he could not return the gifts to the new Sultan. The *'ulamā'* and some other sūfis, who were envious of the Shaykh, poured oil on the fire of growing enmity and reopened the old question of *samā'*, accusing the Shaykh of frivolity and sin. More than two hundred and fifty scholars gathered to oppose the Shaykh at an assembly organized by the Sultan to settle the dispute. The Shaykh was accompanied only by his disciples. A heated discussion took place, but the Sultan refused to yield to *'ulamā'* pressure to deliver judgement against the Shaykh. The Shaykh died in April 1325, while the Sultan was away on his Tirhut expedition. They were still estranged. The Sultan died three months later, in July.

According to the Shaykh, the first lesson in sūfism was not related to prayers or meditational exercises but began with the practice of the maxim: 'Do unto others what you would they do unto you; wish for yourself what you wish for them also.' Defining renunciation, the Shaykh said that it was not wearing a loincloth in a state of asceticism, for one should wear clothes and continue to eat, but rather the distribution of all unnecessary items to the poor. He was impressed by those people who fed all the hungry indiscriminately, ignoring caste and class distinctions. Like the contemporary *'ulamā'* and sūfīs, the Shaykh was hostile to the Muslim philosophers' cosmological theories and loved to relate anecdotes from Shaykh Abū Sa'īd and Shihābu'd-Dīn Suhrawardi, condemning Avicenna and other philosophers.[23]

Shaykh Nizāmu'd-Dīn Awliyā' was succeeded in Delhi by his talented disciple Shaykh Nasīru'd-Dīn Mahmūd, later known as Chiragh (the Lamp) of Delhi. Both he and some leading Chishtiyya saints were reluctant to serve the state, and this brought them into conflict with Sultan Muhammad bin Tughluq, who wished the sūfīs to help him realize his political ambitions. During Sultan Fīrūz's reign many sūfī *khānqāhs* prospered as a result of state grants, although the Shaykh himself never abandoned his ascetic life. One of the Qalandars tried to assassinate him, but the Shaykh stopped his disciples taking revenge. He died in 1356. Because he considered none of his disciples worthy of receiving the relics bequeathed to him by Shaykh Nizāmu'd-Dīn Awliyā' they were buried with him in his grave.[24]

Shaykh Nasīru'd-Dīn's teachings were embodied in the *Khayru'l-majālis*, compiled by one of his disciples. They represent a peak in the Chishtiyya philosophy which had evolved in India during the course of the thirteenth and fourteenth centuries. Following the tradition of his spiritual ancestors, the Shaykh emphasized the necessity for associating with the common people but simultaneously withdrawing from them. Shaykh Nasīru'd-Dīn was deeply distressed at the degeneration of Delhi sūfism into mere formalism. Many of his disciples wisely decided to start new centres in the provinces rather than remain in the capital. This did not result in the disintegration of the centre, for other important Chishtiyyas stayed on in Delhi.

By the end of the fourteenth century the doctrine of Wahdat al-Wujūd had become firmly rooted in India. Its principal Chishtiyya exponent was Mas'ūd-i

Bakk. Although he was related to Sultan Fīrūz, pressure from the *'ulamā'* compelled the Sultan to behead him. In a verse he cried out:

> *From Mas'ūd-i Bakk there disappeared all human qualities.*
> *Since he in reality was Essence, he ultimately became Essence.*[25]

Another follower of this doctrine was Sayyid Muhammad Husayni bin Ja'far al-Makkī. His long life extended from the reign of Sultan Muhammad bin Tughluq to that of Sultan Bahlūl Lodī. He travelled widely. According to him the ecstatic cries of Bāyāzīd and Hallāj did not emanate from themselves; their spiritual absorption had converted them into the same form as the Absolute Being.[26]

Another sūfī, Mawlānā Burhānu'd-Dīn Gharīb, an aged *khalīfa* of Nizāmu'd-Dīn Awliya', was forced by Muhammad bin Tughluq to leave Delhi for Daulatābād in the Deccan. The sūfi who did most to make the Chishtiyya *silsila* popular in the Deccan, however, was Sayyid Muhammad bin Yūsuf al-Husaynī, commonly known as Khwāja Banda Nawāz or Mīr Gīsū Darāz. He was Shaykh Nasīru'd-Dīn's leading disciple. Apparently the news of Timur's invasion of Delhi prompted Gīsū Darāz to move to a safer place. He went first to Gujarāt and later to Gulbarga on the western border of the Deccan. Mīr Gīsū Darāz was a prolific writer. His earlier works are based on the Wahdat al-Wujūd philosophy, but he was later converted to the Wahdat al-Shuhūd doctrines. He was influenced by the works of 'Alā'u'd-Dawla Simnānī (d. 1336), the founder of the Wahdat al-Shuhūd movement, who was violently hostile to the Wahdat al-Wujūd beliefs. The Wahdat al-Wujūd followers held that there cannot be two orders of reality (Creator and created), independent of each other, while the Wahdat al-Shuhūd considered that ideas undermining the divine transcendence were heretical. Mīr Gīsū Darāz was amazed that Ibnu'l-'Arabi's followers should call themselves sūfis, when they did not recognize God's true transcendental form. Condemning the works of Ibnu'l-'Arabi and the sūfi poets, such as 'Attār and Rūmī, who ardently supported the Wahdat al-Wujūd philosophy, Mīr Gīsū Darāz denounced them as enemies of Islam. He died in November 1422, having lived for about 101 years.[27]

In Bengal the Chishtiyya centre was established by Shaykh Nizāmu'd-Dīn Awliya's disciple, Shaykh Akhī Sīrāju'd-Dīn 'Usmān. At Pandua he made Shaykh 'Ala'u'l-Haqq, who held a high position in the government, his *khalīfa.* Shaykh 'Ala'u'l-Haqq renounced the world. He died in 1398, and his spiritual descendants established Chishtiyya *khanqāhs* in many parts of Bengal. In the fourteenth and fifteenth centuries, the Chishtiyya *khānqahs* in Jaunpūr, Rudawli (near Lucknow), Lucknow, Kālpī, and Gangoh (east of Delhi) exerted a considerable influence on the spiritual life in their respective regions. In the sixteenth century Thaneswar became an important Chishtiyya centre. Shaykh Jalāl Thāneswari and his disciple, Shaykh Nizām Thāneswarī, were famous Chishtiyya sūfis; but in May 1606 Jahāngīr banished Shaykh Nizām to Mecca for blessing the rebel Prince Khusraw. The Shaykh died in Balkh in modern Afghānistan, having utterly condemned the Mughals as irreligious. The sixteenth- and seventeenth-century Chishtiyya centres in Delhi were also well known, although they could not compete with the popular Shaykh Salīm Chishtī, whose prayers, Akbar believed, were responsible for the birth of his son Prince Salīm in August 1569. Akbar built Fathpūr-Sīkrī to show his gratitude to the Shaykh. At the same time the intellectually challenging Gujarāt Chishtiyya centre pushed the Suhrawardiyyas even further into the background. The Chishtiyya centres in Burhānpūr, Jaunpūr, and Lucknow were also famous, but the outstanding Chishtiyya sūfi. Scholar was Shaykh Muhibbu'llah Mubāriz Ilāhābādi. He was pitted against Mullā Mahmūd Jaunpūri, one of the greatest Muslim philosophers India has produced. The Shaykh tried to undermine the importance of both philosophy and *kalām.* He also waged a battle royal against the opponents of the Wahdat al-Wujūd doctrine and did not even spare 'Ala'u'd-Dawla Simnānī and Gisū Darāz.

THE KUBRAWIYYA

The principal centre of the Kubrawiyyas was Kashmīr. The order was introduced there by Mīr Sayyid 'Alī Hamadānī, who had been initiated by one of Shaykh 'Ala'u'd-Dawla Simnānī's disciples. After travelling through different parts of the Islamic world, the Mīr arrived in Uch, but Makhdūm Jahāniyān, the Suhrawardiyya leader, took no notice of him. The Mīr then proceeded to Kashmīr, where preliminary propaganda in his favour had already been disseminated by his cousin. Apparently he reached Srinagar in 1381. The miracles allegedly performed by the Sayyid in order to convert the brāhman priest of the Kālī temple are reminiscent of those attributed to Khwāja Mu'īnu'd-Dīn Chishtī and many other sūfis. It is claimed that when the priest flew in the air, the Sayyid threw his slippers at him and brought him down. Ibn Battūta also states that he saw the yogis at Sultan Muhammad bin Tughluq's court fly. The Kālī temple was demolished, and a prayer platform was built there for the Sayyid. Like 'Ala'u'd-Dawla Simnāni, the Mīr was a zealous missionary and encouraged his followers to demolish Hindu temples and convert the Hindus to Islam. After staying three years in Kashmīr, he left Srinagar but fell ill while travelling, dying in January 1385. His dead body was taken to Khuttalān (now in Tājikistān, USSR) and buried. However, a number of his disciples remained in Kashmīr. They had been trained in the *futāwwa* (chivalric) Irāni sūfi tradition and resorted to forcible conversion. They also introduced the *akhi* (brotherhood) spirit of the Anatolian and Irānian dervishes who were either members of or associated with merchant and artisan guilds (*isnāf*). In Kashmīr they appear to have found new avenues for promoting their commercial interests. They also ransacked Hindu temples in order to enrich themselves and their local followers.[28]

The arrival of Sayyid 'Alī's son, Mīr Muhammad, in Srīnagar in 1393 revived the evangelical spirit of the earlier Irāni settlers. Sultan Sikandar (1389–1413) became a disciple of the young migrant and built a *khānqāh* on the site where his father had first constructed a prayer platform. One of Sikandar's powerful and influential nobles, Suhā Bhatta,[29] became Mīr Muhammad's disciple, adopted

Sayfu'd-Dīn as his Muslim name, and married his daughter to his young teacher.

Under the influence of Mīr and Suhā, Sultan Sikandar demolished many ancient temples in Kashmīr. Many puritanical and discriminatory laws were implemented, and *jijya* was introduced for the first time in Kashmīr. The persecution of brāhmans, their exclusion from the top tiers of government, and their replacement by Irāni migrants hastened the conversion of the brāhman elite, because they were unwilling to give up their superior positions in the administration. Before long, however, Sultan Sikandar realized the effects of his bigoted policy and, according to the brāhman historian Jonarāja, 'fixed with some difficulty a limit to the advance of the great sea of the Yavanas (Muslims)' and abolished *turush-kadanda* (*jizya*).[30] This change in state policy seems to have so disappointed Mīr Muhammad that, after staying twelve years, he left Kashmīr like his father before him. However, more than a dozen major disciples stayed behind and strengthened the already increasing predominance of Persian officers in the administration.

Another group of Irāni immigrants, known as the Bayhaqī Sayyids, were also Kubrawiyyas; Sultan Zaynu'l-'Ābidin (1420–70) became their patron. Paradoxically, they supported the Sultan's policy of crushing the fanatical Sunnī elements in the administration and worked towards reconciling the Hindus and integrating the two.

In 1481 the Tīmūrid Sultan, Husayn Mīrzā (1469–1506) of Hirāt, sent Mīr Shamsu'd-Dīn 'Irāqī to Kashmīr as his envoy. The Mīr preached the Nūr Bakhshiyya sūfi doctrines of Irān in Kashmīr and became a fast friend of the leading Kubrawiyyas. After going back to Hirāt he again returned to Kashmīr in 1501 but this time he tried to convert the Kashmīris to Isnā 'Ashari Shī'īsm. Many of the Sultan's leading nobles became his disciples. The spread of Shī'īsm, however, was energetically checked by the well-known Kashmīri Suhrawardiyya, Shaykh Hamza Makhdūm, and his disciple, Bābā Dāwud. After Akbar's annexation of Kashmīr in 1586 the religious atmosphere stabilized, and the Shī'ī faith was contained.[31]

THE QALANDARS

The development of the Qalandariyya is shrouded in obscurity. The movement had ripened in the eleventh and twelfth centuries, and the Persian verses of this period glorify the Qalandars' (wandering dervishes') attainments. The movement flourished in Syria, eastern Irān, and Transoxiania. Early glimpses of their order in India are preserved in the Chishtiyya records. According to these works, the Qalandars hated the *khānqāh* life of the sūfīs, considering it sacrilegious, and accused the sūfīs of transforming themselves into idols. They also refused to obey the *sharī'a* laws. They used Indian hemp and other drugs, shaved their heads, moustaches, beards and eyebrows, and always kept a razor handy. They wore iron rings through their ears, on their hands, and on other parts of their bodies. Authentic sūfī records recount some incredible miracles performed by them. Leading sūfīs like Shaykh Bahā'u'd-Dīn Zakariyya and Bābā Farīd were always the targets of the Qalandars' attacks. The Qalandars travelled widely and went as far east as Bengal. In Balban's reign, his rebel governor, Tughril, was so deeply devoted to a Qalandar that he gave enough gold for him and his Qalandars to wear gold necklaces, bangles, and earrings instead of iron ones.

The Qalandars belonged to different groups. The more famous *jwālqīs* wrapped themselves in blankets;[32] others went naked except for a loincloth. The founder of the Haydari Qalandars belonged to Turbat-i Haydar near Mashhad in Irān. Jamālī says that the Haydarīs passed round iron rods through their genitals and called them *sīkh-i muhr* (rod of the seal). This custom, acquired from the Hindu Naga *sannyāsīs*, indicated their determination to remain celibate. The Haydarīs, and other Qalandars too, pierced their ears and wore iron rings. This practice was borrowed from the *kanphata* (split-ear) yogis.

Shaykh Abū Bakr Tūsī Haydarī settled on the banks of the Jamuna in Delhi and built a *khānqāh* there. Many important sūfīs, including Shaykh Nizāmu'd-Dīn Awliyā', used to call on him. Abū Bakr often visited the court and, at Sultan Jalālu'd-Dīn's instigation, mortally wounded the powerful dervish Sīdī Mawla. The leading princes and noblemen were deeply devoted to the Sīdī, but the Sultan considered him an arch-conspirator and a threat to his rule. In about 1342 Ibn Battūta also met a party of Haydarīs at Amroha. Describing their feats, he records:

> Their chief asked me to supply him with firewood that they might light it for their dance, so I charged the governor of that district, who was 'Azīz known as al-Khammār, to furnish it. He sent about ten loads of it, and after the night prayer they kindled it, and at length, when it was a mass of glowing coals, they began their musical recital and went into that fire, still dancing and rolling about in it. Their chief asked me for a shirt and I gave him one of the finest texture; he put it on and began to roll about in the fire with it on and to beat the fire with his sleeves until it was extinguished and dead. He then brought me the shirt showing not a single trace of burning on it, at which I was greatly astonished.[33]

A most prominent Qalandar, Abū (Bū) 'Alī Qalandar (d. 1324), lived in Panīpat. Like others of his kind he had previously been a trained religious scholar but, in a fit of ecstasy, gave away his books and became a Qalandar, though he kept using the *sharī'a* laws. Although some of the sūfī letters and verses ascribed to him are not genuine, the authentic ones are deeply impregnated with spirituality. A seventeenth-century Chishtiyya believed that Abū 'Alī had been initiated into the Chishtiyya order by Khwaja Qutbu'd-Dīn Bakhtiyār Kākī's spirit. This gave rise to a Chishtiyya-Qalandariyya *silsila.*[34]

Although Shaykh Bahā'u'd-Dīn Zakariyya was at war with the Qalandars, his son-in-law, Shaykh Fakhru'd-Dīn 'Irāqī, had followed their practices during his youth. In his old age 'Irāqī adopted the settled life of the *khānqāh*, but he never gave up his independent thinking. La'l Shahbāz, another prominent Qalandar, was also a disciple of Shaykh Bahā'u'd-Dīn Zakariyya. Many incredible miracles are ascribed to his tomb in Sihwan in Sind.

THE MUSLIM INTELLECTUAL PERCEPTION OF HINDUISM

The establishment of Turkic rule in India opened up many opportunities for contact between Hinduism and Islam. Only al-Bīrūnī (d. after 1050), however, took the trouble to translate Sanskrit classics into Arabic. He then wrote his monumental *Kitāb fi tahqīq mā li'l-Hind* in order to acquaint his Ghaznavid rulers with Hinduism. He admitted that there were many barriers separating Hindus from Muslims but claimed that they were based either on political reasons or on language barriers. The Sanskrit scientific and religious texts were composed in verse form; consequently many errors and interpolations had entered into them. This made it difficult to authenticate books without painstaking research.[35] Al-Bīrūnī's task was made even more difficult because he never visited centres of brāhmanic scholarship such as Kanauj, Vārānasī, and Kashmīr. He stayed in Ghaznī, where his assistants were a few Sanskrit scholars and educated merchants. He mentions a man from Somnath, some people from Kanauj, and a man who had travelled through Nepal as his informants. He found the contemporary Hindus were full of religious prejudices, insularity, exclusiveness, national pride, and conceit.[36] Al-Bīrūnī admits that previous generations of Hindus were more liberal but stresses that prejudices against foreigners were universal. He also acknowledges the fact that, although the Hindus he met refused to enter into religious arguments, many Muslims forbade any discussion at all on religious matters.

In the *Kitāb fi tahqīq rna li'l-Hind*, Al-Bīrūnī's main thesis is that 'the beliefs of educated and uneducated people differ in every nation' and that the educated 'strive to conceive abstract ideas and to define general principles', while the uneducated submit to derived rules and regulations. This dichotomy applied to both religion and science. Discussing the Hindu concept of God, Al-Bīrūnī says that Hindus believe that 'He is eternal, without beginning and end, acting by free will, almighty, all wise, living, giving life, ruling, preserving, one who in His sovereignty is unique, beyond all likeness and unlikeness.'[37] Al-Bīrūnī quotes from Patanjali's *Yoga-Sūtra*, the *Bhagavad Gītā*, and the *Sānkhya-Karika* to substantiate this assertion. He contends that, at the level of the common people, anthropomorphism is found in Hinduism, Islam, Jewry, and Christianity. He goes on to say that Caliph Mu'āwiya, the founder of the Umayyad dynasty, thought idols 'were only memorials'. When his army brought back golden idols adorned with jewels after sacking Sicily in 672–3, the Caliph ordered their sale in Sind.[38] He considered the matter from an economic not a religious point of view and had no scruples about their use in 'abominable idolatry'. Al-Bīrūnī upheld Mu'āwiya's practical approach as meaningful, and suggested that Mahmūd's policy of indiscriminate destruction of idols was malevolent.

Although al-Bīrūnī, like other scholars, does not attempt to define Hinduism, he identifies it in relation to other religious communities. He says:

> As the word of confession, 'There is no god but God, Muhammad is His prophet', is the shibboleth of Islam, the Trinity that of Christianity, and the institute of the Sabbath that of Judaism, so metempsychosis is the shibboleth of the Hindu religion. Therefore he who does not believe in it does not belong to them, and is not reckoned as one of them.[39]

Al-Bīrūnī's distinction between the religions of the masses and those of the élite is extended to differentiate scientific and legendary theories. He says that the Purānic version of the world's shape and other geographic details and the scientific truths discovered by the astronomers are contradictory. He contends, however, that the astronomers allowed religious prejudices to influence their own interpretation of their discoveries, so that the theory that the earth was a rotating ball and other natural scientific laws were glossed over by the scientists to conform to Hindu mythology.[40] The common people who depended on the astronomers for their knowledge therefore received mainly religious explanations instead of scientific truths, an unscientific mixture of fact and fiction.

Proud of his mathematical and scientific heritage, al-Bīrūnī was hostile to mystical ideas. He condemned sūfī irrationalism and compared Muslim alchemy and Hindu *rasāyana* (chemistry) with witchcraft. In his *Kitāb fi tahqīq* he provides a penetrating study of human relationships and cultural complexities in various faiths. Although he concentrates mainly on Hindu society, he relates it to the social behaviour and psychology of other religious communities and investigates the intimate relationship between belief, religious philosophy, and social organization. Al-Bīrūnī concludes that the strangeness of others' customs is essentially relative, and gives a historical explanation of cultural and social behaviour. He does not specifically defend the social customs and manners of the Hindus but explains their caste, class, and family organization, their cultural attitudes, folk customs, mores, and prejudices in a historical context. His analysis shows that a historical perspective and a knowledge of the history of ideas are required to understand society.

Al-Bīrūnī defines the Hindu colour divisions as *tabaqāt* (classes) and the castes (*jāti*) as birth divisions (*nasab*). The brāhmans were created from the head of Brahma, the Kshatriya from his shoulders and hands, the Vaishiya from Brahma's thigh, and the Sudra from his feet. Below the Sudra were the Antyaja or casteless. They were divided into eight guilds: fullers, shoemakers, jugglers, basket- and shield-makers, sailors, fishermen, hunters of wild animals and birds, and weavers. The villages and towns were inhabited by the superior classes, while the Antyaja lived just outside them. The Hādī, Doma, and Chāndāla, who did the cleaning and scavenging, were outcasts. It was claimed that they were the result of an illegal act of fornication between a Sudra father and a brāhman mother and were therefore excluded from the recognized Hindu community. Foreigners were also regarded as 'unclean ' or *mleccha*, and Hindus were forbidden any contact, either matrimonial or social, with them.[41] Al-Bīrūnī asserts that, since the whole Hindu system had no parallel in Islam, contact and understanding between Hindus

39. Akbar controlling the elephants who cross the Jamuna, *Akbar-Nāma* (p. 86)

40. Political lessons through animal behaviour, from the *Anwār Suhaylī* by Kāshifī (p. 127)

41. Black buck painted by Manohar with beautiful caligraphy on the borders (p. 245)

42. Dārā Shukoh with Miyān Mir, Mullā Shāh and the *khānqāh* servants (p. 217–18)

43. Jahāngīr weighing Prince Khurram; the Khān-i Khānān holds the balance (p. 96)

44. Shāhjahān with two princes, possibly Dārā and Shujā, watching Samā' (Sufi music) c. 1650 (p. 198)

45. Jahāngīr riding, painted by Manohar (p. 245)

46. Integration of Sūfi music with Bhaktas; Kabīr is in the front on the left (p. 297–99)

47. Bābur visiting Gorakhtarī from the *Bābur-Nāma* (p. 209)

48. The heroine being served by a maid from *Lor Chanda* (p. 246)

49. Captivity of Hīmū, painted by Shankar, *Akbār-Nāmā* (p. 86)

50. News of the birth of Akbar communicated to Humāyūn, *Akbār-Nāmā* (p. 84)

51. Workmen building Agra fort, *Akbār-Nāmā* (p. 236)

52. Village life from *Anwār Suhaylī* by Kāshifī (p. 170)

and Muslims was very limited. He contends, however, that Muslim and Hindu class divisions had a common ancestor in the ancient Aryan class distinctions.

Al-Bīrūnī claimed that the Hindus considered sodomy, which was prevalent among the Turks, as revolting as eating beef. They permitted prostitution, but this was due to the laxity of their rulers. Prostitution had also existed in Muslim society. Both the Buwayhid Prince 'Azu'd-Dawla (949–83)[42] of Irān and Nūru'd-Dīn Mubārāk Ghaznavī justified it as a means of protecting the honour of Muslim women.[43]

We might say that, at least until the eighteenth century, no non-Indian anywhere in the world understood so much about the religion and customs of the Hindus as this learned Central Asian scholar, whose knowledge was, for its time, universal and whose thought is characterized by tolerance, benevolence, and sound common sense.

Amīr Khusraw was deeply impressed by India, but his studies of Hinduism were not based on Sanskrit sources. He was impressed by the depth of learning among Indians and their ability to speak any language. He also greatly admired the brāhmans, who could teach all subjects without having to study overseas and who had devised the numerical system, written *Kalīla wa Dimna* on the art of government, and invented chess. In considering that Hindus were metaphysically confused, Amīr Khusraw was a Muslim chauvinist. He admitted, however, that they believed in the unity and eternity of God and were superior to materialists, star worshippers, and Christians. Although the Hindus worshipped stones, animals, plants, and the sun, they believed that these things were God's creations and they only imitated their ancestors.[44]

As mentioned earlier, Nakhshabī, who had translated two Sanskrit works, had a better understanding of Sanskrit. Mīr Gīsū Darāz also studied Sanskrit, thereby intending to defeat the brāhmans' arguments and convert them to Islam.[45] Following his conquest of Nagarkot in 1362 Fīrūz Shāh Tughluq acquired some 1,300 books from the Jwālāmukhī temple. He commissioned Sanskrit scholars to translate some of them into Persian. On the basis of the translations of works on physics and astronomy, 'Izzu'd-Dīn Khālid Khān compiled the *Dalā'il-i Fīrūz Shāhī*, a work that is not now available. One of the surviving Persian translations from Sanskrit is the *Brhatsamhita*, by the celebrated Indian astronomer Varahamihira. It had been translated earlier by al-Bīrūnī, but the new translator, 'Abdu'l 'Azīz Shams Bahā-i Nūrī, does not seem to have had access to this work. Sultan Zaynu'l-'Ābidīn of Kashmīr, Sultan Sikandar Lodī, and several other Muslim rulers also ordered the translation of various Sanskrit works into Persian in order both to satisfy their own intellectual curiosity and to increase Muslim understanding of Hinduism.

Akbar's translation bureau (the Maktab Khāna) also helped considerably to change the Muslim perception of Hinduism. Its most remarkable productions were the translations of the *Mahābhārata*, the *Rāmāyana*, and the *Yoga Vashishta.* Abu'l-Fazl wrote the preface to the *Mahābhārata.* Discussing Akbar's motives for ordering the translations, he claimed that the Emperor sought to heal the religious differences amongst his subjects. Akbar did not discriminate between Hindu and Muslim, friend and foe. He felt that reliably translated texts from both religions would form a basis for a united search for truth. He had also discovered that often the common people among the Hindus were forced to rely on distorted interpretations of texts, while the theologians kept the standard works to themselves. Akbar therefore concluded that the translation of these texts into simple language would enable the people to understand the true spirit of their religion.

Abu'l-Fazl continually censured the ignorance and short-sightedness of his contemporaries. He was convinced that the Hindus followed their faith uncritically and were prey to superstition. Their fantastic beliefs shocked the Muslims, who had no means of learning the more profound Hindu doctrines. For their part, most Muslims had never studied their own great books, such as those by Imām Ja'far al-Sādiq (702–765) and Ibn al-'Arabī.[46]

In the third volume of the *A 'īn-i Akbarī*, Abu'l-Fazl gave a detailed description of Hinduism, although he was aware that his work was not the equal of al-Bīrūnī's *Tahqīq* in depth of analysis. He urged his Muslim readers to study his account of Hindu learning with open minds. He suggested that 'putting aside the estrangements of ignorance' they compare it with the religious teachings of the sūfīs and philosophers. The *A 'īn-i Akbarī* includes some discussion on contemporary Hindu and Jain philosophy. Abu'l-Fazl was amazed at the flexibility of yogic postures and interestedly described the Hindu knowledge of *sakuna* (augury).

Yet more Sanskrit works were translated into Persian during Jahāngīr's reign. Dārā Shukoh undertook to translate the *Upanishads* in order to discover any Wahdat al-Wujūd doctrines hidden in them, and not as a linguistic exercise. He accused the Hindu pandits (teachers) of hiding the Upanishadic truth from both Muslims and Hindus in order to keep their teachings on the Wahdat al-Wujūd doctrine secret. Dārā Shukoh believed that his translation would help mystics of both faiths, although he stressed the primacy of the Qur'ān, and the translation in fact proved to be of universal interest. Although he died before it was circulated, many copies are still extant throughout India; during Nawwāb Shujā'u'd-Dawla's reign in Avadh (1754–75) the French Resident sent a copy to a Parisian scholar of ancient religions, Anquetil Duperron, who translated it into Latin and French. The French edition was never published, but the Latin version, published in 1801–2, was of particular interest to the German philosopher Schopenhauer, who found its study 'the solace of my life' and 'the solace of my death'.[47]

The Muslim intellectuals believed that some prophets had been sent to India, but a fierce controversy raged as to their identification. Later, during the sixteenth and seventeenth centuries, the Mujaddid (Shaykh Ahmad Sirhindī, 1564–1624) also considered that prophets had come to India, although the Indians generally had ignored their teachings. According to him, the Hindu works on divine being had been plagiarized from the works of ancient prophets. He asserted that the terms 'prophet' and 'apostle' occurred only in Arabic and Persian and had no Indian equivalents. Consequently, the Indians had no perception concerning prophets.[48] The Mujaddid did not believe that Rāma and Krishna were prophets and could not tolerate the suggestion that they were divine names. Mīrzā Mazhar Jān-i Jānān (d. 1781), however, a distinguished sūfī scholar of the Mujaddis's sūfic order, accepted both Rāma and Krishna as prophets.[49] He also glossed over Hindu idol-worship, although he considered any Hindus who persisted in their faith in Rāma and Krishna after the advent of Islam to be infidels who had departed from the right path.

THE HINDU IMPACT ON SŪFĪSM

According to al-Bīrūnī, the sūfī theories of the soul were similar to those in Patanjali's *Yoga Sutra.* Like the *Yoga Sutra*, sūfī works also stated that 'the bodies are the snares of the souls for the purpose of acquiring recompense'. Al-Bīrūnī also identifies the sūfī doctrine of divine love as self-annihilation with parallel passages from the *Bhāgavad Gītā.*[50] Hujwirī comments that before he settled in Lahore some sūfīs believed in theories that he calls brāhmanical. According to Hujwirī they wrongly believed that 'annihilation (*fanā'*) signifies loss of essence and destruction of the personality, and that subsistence (*baqā'*) indicates the subsistence of God in man'. Condemning the views as misguided, Hujwirī says that 'real annihilation from anything involves consciousness of its imperfection and the absence of desire for it', and subsistence means 'subsistence of the remembrance of God'.[51] Sūfi views on this question always remained divided, and arguments over annihilation and subsistence were endemic.

By the thirteenth century the Indian sūfīs were confronted with the *kanphatā* (split-eared) yogis or the Nāth followers of Gorakhnāth. Shaykh Nizāmu'd-Dīn Awliyā''s description of his conversation with yogis shows that he was impresssed with their theory of the division of the human body into the regions of Siva and Saktī. The area from the head to the navel, associated with Siva, was spiritual; the area below the navel, associated with Saktī, was profane.[52] Shaykh Nizāmu'd-Dīn Awliyā' was also impressed with the yogic theory that a child's moral character was determined by the day of the month on which he was conceived.[53] Some sūfīs also learned from the yogis medicines to grow long hair.[54] The Hatha yogic treatise *Amrita-Kunda*, which had been translated into Arabic and Persian in the thirteenth century, had a lasting effect on sūfīsm.

Shaykh Nasīru'd-Dīn Chirāgh-i Dihlī observed that controlled breathing is the essence of sūfīsm. Controlled breathing is initially a deliberate action but later becomes automatic. He urged practising articulated breathing like the perfect yogis, known as *siddhas.* Yogic postures and breath control became an integral part of Chishtiyya sūfic practice, and controlled breathing was incorporated finally as a vital aspect in all the sūfī orders except the Indian Naqshbandiyyas.

The sūfī theory of Wahdat al-Wujūd and sūfī analogies for it were remarkably similar to those of the yogīs. Shaykh Hamīdud-Dīn Nāgaurī's Hindī verses reflect this yogic influence.[55] The Nāth doctrines had a far-reaching influence on the Chishtiyya Shaykh 'Abdu'l Quddūs Gangōhī (d. 1537). His Hindī *nom de plume* was Alakh (Imperceptible). His *Rushd-nāma* contains Hindī verses composed by himself and his spiritual guides and is designed to support the truth of the Wahdat al-Wujūd doctrine. The Imperceptible Lord (Alakh Niranjana), he says, is unseeable, but those who are able to perceive Him are lost to themselves. In another verse the Shaykh identifies Niranjana (the Imperceptible) with God (Khuda).[56] References to the yogi saint Gorakhnāth in the *Rushd-nāma* equate him with Ultimate Reality or Absolute Truth. Some references to these names imply 'perfect man' or 'perfect *Siddha*'.[57] The union of Saktī, the sun, and Siva, the moon, is according to the Shaykh symbolized by prayers performed hanging upside down with the legs suspended from a roof or the branch of a tree. Here we find very clear evidence of the practices of Hindu tantricism influencing sūfī beliefs.

The cross-fertilization of sūfī beliefs with those expressed by the Kashmīrī Saivite woman yogi Lalla or Lāl Ded (Lalla Yogesvarī) is reflected in the Rishi movement of Shaykh Nūru'd-Dīn Rishī (d. 1439) of Kashmīr. The Shaykh's teachings are embodied in his Kashmīrī verses, some of which are almost identical with those composed by Lalla. Through them the Shaykh emerges as an ardent devotee of God trying to reach the Unknowable in the heart by lighting the lamp of love. Nūru'd-Dīn and his disciples preferred to call themselves Rishīs, using the well-known term for the Hindu sages, not sūfīs. Their main theme was universal love. They served the people without considering caste and class distinctions, planted trees to shade travellers, and tried to turn Kashmīr into a haven for the neglected sections of society. Shaykh Nūru'd-Dīn believed that, although eating meat was permitted by the *sharī'a*, it entailed cruelty to animals, and he became a vegetarian.[58]

The Nāth ideas found great popularity in fifteenth-century Bengal. The *Amritakunda*, a text on Hatha yoga, was first translated into Arabic in Bengal in the early thirteenth century. In 1498–9 Shaykh Zāhid wrote a book in Bengali entitled the *Ādya-Parichaya*, based on the *Amritakunda.* Sayyid Murtazā (d. 1662) later wrote the *Yoga-Qalandar*, identifying the Qalandariyya discipline of Abū 'Alī Qalandar with yoga practices. Sayyid Sultan (d. 1668) of Chittagong also composed a number of Bengali works on Muslim themes of absorption into God, with Hindu and yogic overtones. The *Haqā'iq-i Hindī* by 'Abdu'l-Wāhid (d. 1608) of Bilgrām (near Lucknow) was intended to crush orthodox opposition to the use of Vaishnavite themes in the Hindī poetry recited by the Chishtiyya sūfīs to arouse ecstasy. To Gīsū Darāz, Hindī poetry was more subtle and elegant and transported the sūfīs to higher planes of mystical ecstasy than Persian verses did.[59]

The sixteenth century saw a tremendous increase in the volume of Hindī poetry. Naturally its recitation at sūfī gatherings required some defence. Mīr 'Abdu'l Wāhid sought to justify this practice by giving Islamic equivalents for features of the Krishna legend such as Krishna, Rādha, Gopī, Braj, Gokul, Jamuna, Gangā, Mathurā, and the flute in his *Haqaā'iq-i Hindī.* He pleads that this identification renders unobjectionable the transport of sūfīs into ecstasy on hearing Hindu Vaishnavite poetry.

The translation of Sanskrit works into Persian at Akbar's court had made

Muslims aware of the Vedanta School of Hindu philosophy. Jahāngīr identified the highest form of sūfīsm with the Vedanta. According to him the following lines by Bābā Fighānī (d. 1516 or 1519) embodied the essence of both the Vedanta and sūfism.

There is one lamp in this house, by whose rays,
Wherever I look there is an assembly.[60]

THE MAHDAWĪ MOVEMENT

In Islam messianic movements emerged shortly after the Prophet Muhammad's death. The idea was borrowed from the Zoroastrian and Christian faiths. The Muslim messiah is known as the Mahdī. Mahdī means 'guided one' or the 'directed one' – he who is fit to direct others. Except for the collection of *ahādīs* compiled by Bukhāri and Muslim all the important works of Sunnī *ahādīs* refer to prophecies concerning the Mahdī and state that all the Prophet's leading companions are in one way or the other associated with these stories. There are serious discrepancies among the traditions concerning the Mahdī; the signs preceding his appearance and the descriptions of his features also differ. Ibn Khaldūn says:

> It has been well known (and generally accepted), by all Muslims in every epoch, that at the end of time a man from the family (of the Prophet) will without fail make his appearance, one who will strengthen the religion and make justice triumph. The Muslims will follow him, and he will gain domination over the Muslim realm. He will be called the Mahdī. Following him, the Antichrist will appear, together with all the subsequent signs of the Hour (the Day of Judgement), as established in (the sound tradition of) the *Sahīh.* After (the Mahdī), 'Īsa (Jesus) will descend and kill the Antichrist. Or Jesus will descend together with the Mahdī, and help him kill (the Antichrist), and have him as the leader in his prayers.[61]

The Isnā' 'Asharī Shī'ī traditions, however, differ markedly from those of the Sunnī sect. According to them the twelfth Imām, Muhammad son of Imām Hasan 'Askarī, who disappeared from human sight after his occultation in 873, is still alive and will reappear before Judgement Day. This belief in the Mahdī is an indispensable part of the Isnā' 'Asharī Shī'ī faith, but the Sunnīs attach much less importance to the Mahdī traditions.

According to some Sunnī authorities, even the first four successors to the Prophet were known as *mahdīyīn* ('guided ones'). From that time to the end of the nineteenth century a large number of Sunnī adventurers declared themselves the Mahdī. The end of some of them was tragic; during Fīrūz Shāh's reign, one Rukn declared himself the Mahdī, with the result that he was beheaded.[62]

Sayyid Muhammad of Jaunpūr left an indelible mark on the Mahdawī movement in India. He was born in September 1443, during Sultan Mahmūd

Shāh Sharqi's reign. The Mahdawī sources, compiled within one hundred years of Sayyid Muhammad's lifetime, recount miracles at his birth reminiscent of those at the Prophet Muhammad's nativity. According to the Mahdawī traditions, he started his education when he was four years, four months, and four days old. He proved a prodigy by completing it when he was only twelve years old. The legends say that, accompanied by Sultan Husayn Sharqi, Sayyid Muhammad marched against Rāy Dalpat of Gaur and defeated him. The histories of the period do not mention such a battle, which seems to be a later myth created to make the Sayyid a leader in both war and peace, as was the Prophet. In *c.* 1489 the Sayyid, accompanied by 360 companions, travelled to Mecca. Although his followers had always believed him to be the promised Mahdī, it was only after reaching Mecca in 1495–6 that he formally proclaimed his mission. After staying a few months in Mecca he returned to India, where he visited Ahmadābād. A considerable number of the local residents became the Sayyid's disciples. Even Sultan Mahmūd I Begra wished to visit him, but the Sultan's nobles, concerned with maintaining peace in Gujarāt, prevented him. In Gujarāt the Sayyid twice publicly declared himself the promised Mahdī, thus arousing deep hostility among the orthodox *'ulamā'*. The Sayyid was not intimidated; he wrote letters to the neighbouring rulers, inviting them to recognize him as the Mahdī, but the *'ulamā'* proved too powerful for him, and he was banished from Gujarāt. He moved to Thatta and from thence to Farah in Afghānistān, where he died in 1505. His disciples belonged to all classes: soldiers, commanders, *'ulamā'*, sūfīs, artisans, and ordinary men. They believed that the Mahdī had appeared and died and that no other Mahdī would arise. This united them into a group separate from the other Sunnīs, who did not believe that Sayyid Muhammad was the Mahdī. Some important Sunnī *'ulamā'* recognized him as a scholar and an infallible guide but they glossed over his claims to be the Mahdī. They admitted to being deeply impressed by both the Sayyid and his followers, but that was as far as they would go.

Sayyid Muhammad was succeeded by his son, Sayyid Mahmūd, who died in 1512. Mahmūd's successor, Khwandamīr, was also his brother-in-law. He fought many pitched battles against the Gujarāt troops and was killed in August 1524. Khwandamīr was a scholar. Seven treatises that he wrote in Hindī and Persian, giving an authentic picture of the Sayyid's teachings, have survived.

As Mahdī, Sayyid Muhammad claimed that Allah had commissioned him to restore Islam to its original purity. He urged his followers to devote themselves whole-heartedly to the remembrance of God (*zikr*) and not to waste time in earning a living or other worldly pursuits. Unlike earlier Mahdīs and subsequent claimants, the Sayyid was not interested in politics. Although he believed that non-Mahdawīs were infidels he did not collect poll-tax from them, for he had not been ordered by Allah to do so. However, Mahdawīs were not allowed to offer prayers behind a non-Mahdawi. Consequently they never travelled alone, in case they missed congregational prayers. They lived in their own settlements called *dā'iras* which contained small huts for the women and a community hall with mud walls and a thatched roof, called the *jamā'at khāna*, for the men. There the Mahdawīs practised only those laws which were sanctioned by the *sharī'a.* They depended generally for their living on unsolicited gifts (*futūh*). Those who worked at some profession or trade contributed one tenth of their daily income to the *dā'ira.* Each evening the entire *futūh* collection, and the wage contributions were distributed equally to the *dā'ira* members. None was allowed more than the others. The distributor was also forbidden to look at the recipients' faces in case this should influence the division. Nothing was kept for the next day; saving was considered contrary to dependence on God. 'Many a one,' says Mulla Badā'ūnī, 'thought it was his duty to empty his cooking vessel at a nightfall of all the necessities of life, even his salt and flour and water, and let them remain upside down, and they kept nothing in the way of means of existence by them, from their extreme faith in the providence of Almighty God, and the saying "Each day brings a new provision" was the basis of their practice.'[63]

Dā'ira members were not allowed to mix with their non-Mahdawī relations. New entrants could not marry the daughters of senior *dā'ira* members without first serving one year's probation. As a precondition to their marriage they had to give an undertaking to leave their wives in the *dā'ira* if they had to leave it. The *dā'ira* members were not all equally dedicated; there were hypocrites and opportunists among them. At the end of each week the Mahdawīs assembled to confess their sins publicly. Those who had violated any *sharī'a* laws went to the *dā'ira* leader to receive the punishment prescribed by the *sharī'a.* The Mahdawīs carried arms and forcibly stopped non *sharī'a* practices in their locality.[64]

The *dā'iras* in Gujarāt, Sind, Rājasthān, and the Deccan rose to great prominence, but the most important Mahdawī leaders in Islam Shāh Sūr's reign were Shaykh 'Abdu'llāh Niyāzī and his disciple, Shaykh 'Alā'ī Makhdūmu'l Mulk, the leading Sunnī divine, convinced Islam Shāh that Shaykh 'Alā'ī was a revolutionary who laid claim to being the Mahdī, and that the Mahdī himself would be king of the whole world: consequently as he presumed to revolt he was deserving of death.' The military commanders were confused; pointing to Shaykh 'Alā'ī, one of them remarked: 'This fellow, in this condition and with this miserable appearance, wishes to take away the kingdom from us. Does he imagine that we Afghāns are all corpses!' Nevertheless Islam Shāh was greatly concerned at the growing conversion of the Afghān commanders to the Mahdawī movement. In religious discussions the *'ulamā'* failed to subdue Shaykh 'Alā'ī. In 1550, however, he was beaten to death at Makhdūmu'l-Mulk's orders for holding Mahdawī beliefs.[65] This made him a Mahdawī martyr, and the movement was far from crushed. In Gujarāt the Mahdawī scholars made life impossible for Shaykh 'Alī Muttaqī (d. 1567), one of the most famous Indian *hadīs* scholars, and he moved permanently to Mecca. Shaykh 'Alī Muttaqī's talented disciple Shaykh Muhammad bin Tāhir also failed to remove the Mahdawī influence from Gujarāt.

After Akbar conquered Ahmadābād, he promised to crush the Mahdawī movement but he took no steps to persecute them. Although Mīrzā 'Azīz Koka, Akbar's governor in Gujarāt, seems to have offered to help Shaykh Tāhir, he left to seek further assistance from Akbar. He was assassinated on his way to Agra.

In Akbar's reign the Mahdawīs, like other religious communities, were also free to convert people to their faith but they were more successful farther south.[66] Aurangzīb did not succeed in destroying the Mahdawīs, and they are still an important Muslim minority in Hyderābād and Mysore.

THE NEW SŪFĪ ORDERS (THE SHATTĀRIYYAS)

The fifteenth and sixteenth centuries in India saw the development of some new sūfī orders which quickly became popular. Of these the Shattariyyas were the spiritual successors to Shaykh Bāyazīd Bistāmī. In Central Asia and Irān the order was known as 'Ishqiyya (successors to Shaykh Abu Yazīd 'Ishqī) and in Turkey as the Bistāmiyya, after Abu Yazīd Bistāmī. The order's Indian founder, Shāh 'Abdu'llāh, earned the name Shattār (Fast Runner) when he claimed to make his disciples perfect by the shortest and quickest means.

Leaving his homeland in Transoxiana, Shāh 'Abdu'llāh reached India during the first half of the fifteenth century. He travelled in style through northern India, dressed like a king, while his dervishes marched wearing soldiers' uniforms, beating drums, and displaying their banners. He challenged all the sūfīs either to learn the principles of Wahdat al-Wujūd from him and become his disciples or to teach them to him and make him their disciple. No sūfī, the Shattariyya literature asserts, accepted the challenge. He went as far as Bengal and converted the leading sūfī Shaykh Muhammad 'Alī, known as Shaykh Qāzin of Hājjīpur, to his order. From Bengal he travelled to Mandu, where Sultan Ghiyāsu'd-Dīn Shāh (1469–1500) also became his disciple. In Jaunpūr, Shaykh Buddhan Shattārī, a disciple of Shāh 'Abdu'llāh's *khalīfa* Shaykh Hāfiz, acquired several eminent sūfīs as his followers. Shāh 'Abdu'llāh died at Mandu in 1485.

The outstanding Shattariyya sūfī, however, was Ghaws Shattārī. His elder brother, Shaykh Phūl, Emperor Humāyūn's great favourite, was killed by Humāyūm's rebel brother, Mīrzā Hindal, in 1539. For a long time before settling down at Gwālior, Shaykh Ghaws had been practising rigorous mystical ascetic exercises in the Chunar caves near the Ganges. When Sher Shāh moved to Agra in 1540 Shaykh Ghaws fled to Gujarāt for fear of persecution. Nevertheless he managed to keep in touch with Humāyūn. After Akbar took the throne the Shaykh returned to Gwālior; the young Emperor ignored him, but the Shaykh owned vast tracts of land and livestock and was able to live affluently until he died in 1563.

His books were controversial. In one of them he claimed that he had made a mystical ascent and had been close to God, like the Prophet Muhammad. He also re-translated the yogic *Bahru'l hayāt*, but his most famous work is the *Jawāhir-i khamsa*, which deals with mystical and magical practices, techniques in exorcism, and invoking the great names of Allah for material benefits. These mystical Shattariyya exercises were borrowed mainly from yogic practices and deeply impressed both Hindus and Muslims.

Many eminent sūfīs became Shaykh Ghaws's disciples. The most prominent among them was Shaykh Wajīhu'd-Dīn Ahmad of Gujarāt (d. 1589–90), who was celebrated for his profound learning and scholarly works on *hadīs* and *fiqh*. His conversion to the Shattariyya order made it very popular from Gujarāt to Burhānpūr. Shaykh Wajīhu'd-Dīn's disciples introduced the Shattariyya order into Mecca and Medina, from where seventeenth-century pilgrims carried it to Syria, Indonesia, and Malaya.

In the reigns of Shāhjahān and Aurangzīb, Gujarāt, Gwālior, Mandu, and Burhānpūr were the principal Shattāriyya centres. The Burhānpār Shattāriyyas became prominent because Shaykh 'Isā, the well-known commentator on Ibnu'l Arabī, and his disciple, Shaykh Burhānu'd-Dīn, lived there. Shaykh Burhānu'd-Dīn would not see rich men and princes and even refused to allow the orthodox Prince Aurangzīb, who was viceroy of the Deccan from 1636 to 1644 and 1652 to 1657, to visit him. Aurangzīb again tried to obtain his blessing before leaving to march against Dārā Shukoh, but the Shaykh refused to see him. Later, however, the Shaykh relented, agreeing to meet the Prince outside his *khānqāh* when he went to pray and to bless him.[67] The Shaykh died in 1678–9, mourned by a large number of followers. The Shattāriyya sūfīs attracted both scholars and common men as disciples and were eagerly sought as teachers of sūfīc mysteries outlined in the *Jāwahir-i khamsa*.

THE QĀDIRIYYA ORDER

The Qādiriyyas originated from the great sūfī Muhyīu'd-Dīn 'Abdul-Qādir Jīlānī (d. 1166). One of his descendants, Shaykh Muhammad al-Husaynī, settled in Uch, and his son, Shaykh 'Abdu'l-Qādir (d. 1533), made the Qādiriyya order famous throughout the Panjāb and Sind. 'Abdu'l-Qādir's son, Shaykh Hāmid, was also very well known. After his death in 1571 his two sons, Shaykh 'Abdu'l-Qādir and Shaykh Mūsa, sought Akbar's decision on who should inherit their father's position. Shaykh 'Abdu'l-Qādir annoyed Akbar by offering prayers in the hall of audience at Fathpūr instead of the mosque. The Emperor therefore favoured Shaykh Mūsā, who accepted a *mansab* and remained a lifelong supporter of Akbar and a friend to Abu'l-Fazl and his associates. Shaykh Mūsā, in his capacity as a *mansabdār*, was killed when suppressing a rebellion against Akbar in 1602.[68] Shaykh 'Abdu'l-Qādir retired to Uch, where he ran the *silsila* until he died.

Shaykh Hāmid's disciple, Shaykh Dāwud, became a great celebrity at Chātī in Lahore because of his devoted followers. According to Badā'ūnī, each day the Shaykh converted fifty to one hundred Hindus and their families to Islam. The number is grossly exaggerated, for at this rate the whole of the Panjāb would have been Islamicized in a short time. The story proves only the Shaykh's enthusiasm for proselytism.

In the fifteenth and sixteenth centuries the Qādiriyya order became famous for its teaching of the Wahdat al-Wujūd doctrine in Delhi and its neighbourhood. Shāh 'Abdu'r Razzāq (d. 1542) of Jhanjhāna, not far from Delhi, was a very successful teacher of this doctrine. His disciple Shaykh Amān Pānīpatī (d. 1550), wrote several treatises on the Wahdat al-Wujūd. Although this was an advanced mystical philosophy not usually publicly discussed, Shaykh Amān claimed that he could convince anyone who was not prejudiced of its truth.[69] Among his favourite disciples was Shaykh Sayfu'd-Dīn, the father of Shaykh 'Abdu'l-Haqq Muhaddis Dihlawī.

Shaykh 'Abdu'l-Haqq was born in 1551. He received his early education from his father and was initiated into the Qādiriyya order by Shaykh Mūsā in 1577. Although Shaykh Mūsā was friendly to Akbar and his favourites, Shaykh 'Abdu'l-Haqq despised them, considering them enemies of Islam. However, 'Abdu'l-Haqq's respect for Shaykh Mūsā did not wane, and he always praised his teacher. In 1586 the Shaykh left for Mecca for pilgrimage, returning in 1592. Dissociating himself from the court, he lived in Delhi. After Akbar's death he hoped that Jahāngīr would start a new policy by reinvigorating the *sharī'a.* He wrote a short treatise, the *Nūrīya-i Syltānīya*, in order to show Jahāngīr some aspects of Sunnī polity. In 1619–20 Jahāngīr honoured him with an audience, and the Shaykh presented him with his biographical dictionary of Indian sūfīs, entitled the *Akhbāru 'l-akhyār.*[70] Before his death, however, the Emperor turned against the Shaykh and his son, Nūru'l-Haqq, suspecting them of being friends with Prince Khurram, who was trying to seize the throne. Nūru'l-Haqq was banished to Kābul. The Shaykh was summoned to Kashmīr, but, while he was in Lahore, the Emperor died. After Khurram's accession as Shāhjahān, both father and son were allowed to return to Delhi. Nūru'l-Haqq was reappointed Qāzī of Agra, and Shaykh 'Abdu'l-Haqq lived in Delhi until he died in 1642. The Shaykh's fame rests on his works on *hadīs.* His *Madāriju 'n-Nubūwwah* is designed to satisfy both the mystics and the rationalists who misunderstood the holy and exalted status of the Prophet and minimized the importance of his miracles.

Shaykh 'Abdu'l-Haqq's sūfīsm was expressed as an unceasing wish to reconcile the exoteric with the esoteric, the *sharī'a* with the sūfī path, and *fiqh* with sūfīsm. In his mystical writings he tried to cut across differences in sūfīc beliefs and practices and reminded sūfīs that dogmatism was alien to mysticism. To him a judicious combination of scholarship, sūfīc ecstasy, and *ma'rifa* (gnosis) was indispensable for a sūfī, although he admitted that this ideal was rarely achieved. The Qādirī idea of a perfect life in the world, according to the Shaykh, was to follow first the *sharī'a* laws and the jurists' teachings and then the sūfi path. Those who chose to become mystics without first obtaining mastery over *fiqh* had strayed from the safe path. It was possible for a scholar and an *'ālim* to obtain initiation into sūfism and to achieve perfection in that realm, but after ecstasy and mystic illumination had filled a student, a return to scholarship was impossible.

To the Shaykh both the Jabriyya and Qadariyya were extremists. The former reduced men to inanimate stones by believing humanity was helpless and God was responsible for all their actions; while the Qadariyya maintained that men were completely responsible for their own actions, ignoring the divine will. Both, asserted the Shaykh, had strayed from the middle path.

The Shaykh also rejected the idea that rules of worship, prayers, and obedience to the *sharī'a* laws were meant only for externalists and widows and that dervishes were naturally exempt. He asserted that these misguided sūfis failed to remember that the laws had initially been laid down by the prophets and came in their final form from Muhammad, who by God's will had perfected human ethics.

Shaykh 'Abdu'l-Haqq fiercely criticized those who lived dissolutely and ignored the *sharī'a* laws in the name of Wahdat al-Wujūd. He called them hypocrites who cried 'Hama Ūst!' ('All is He!') when their souls were foul and vicious. They used the Unity of Being as an excuse for licentious behaviour and grounds for abusing those sūfis who lived virtuously.

In his famous letter to the Mujaddid, 'Abdu'l-Haqq wrote that Ibnu'l-'Arabi's explanation of the Wahdat al-Wujūd doctrine was not based on revelation, since it was a subjective statement of his own convictions. The Shaykh believed that only the intelligible parts of Ibnu'l-'Arabi's books should be accepted by true Muslims, and these should be taken at their face value only, because God alone knew the author's true intentions.[71]

Shaykh 'Abdu'l-Haqq's sons and disciples were both sūfis and *'ulamā'* and followed the teachings in his *khānqāh* closely. A mystical strand was nevertheless introduced into the Qādiriyya discipline by Miyan Mīr and his disciples. They favoured a more emotional stance and many of them eventually left their careers as theologians and scholars to live as ascetics and hermits. Miyān Mir's ancestors came from Siwistān in Sind. The Mīr completed his formal education in Lahore and then turned to practical sūfism. Accompanied by some disciples, he began to visit the graves of eminent sūfis in Lahore. They would afterwards walk far into the jungle, where each would sit alone under a tree to meditate. At the prescribed hours of obligatory prayer they would assemble for congregational prayers. Miyān Mīr became very popular but in 1607–8, finding fame a burden, he left for a secluded life in Sirhind. There he fell ill and developed a chronic pain in his knee. He returned quietly to Lahore a year after leaving it, and although he moved to the quarter occupied by the gardeners, his presence soon became known. Miyān Mīr tried to avoid his numerous admirers and returned any gifts, commenting that the giver had mistaken him for a beggar while in fact he was rich with God. Miyān Mīr trusted God completely and even on hot Lahore evenings threw out all his water so that none remained for the next day. In 1620 the Emperor Jahāngīr, *en route* to Kashmīr, invited Miyān Mīr to visit his camp. Although he was greatly impressed with the Mīr's mystical discourse, out of regard for his asceticism the Emperor dared present him with only the skin of a white antelope to pray on.[72] He died in 1635.[73]

The most renowned of Miyān Mīr's disciples was Mullā Shāh. He was born in a village near Rūstāq in Badakhshān and settled down in India in 1614–15. He was a distinguished scholar and wrote very perceptive sūfic literature. His most controversial work is a commentary on the Qur'ān composed in 1647–8. Defining the infidel, he wrote:

Oh believer! The infidel who has perceived the Reality and recognized it

> [which is the acme of faith] is a believer. Conversely the believer who has not perceived the Reality and has not recognized it is an infidel. This shows that the spiritual elite see a believer and an unbeliever differently. The blessed are they who have seen the believer-infidel and have obtained the essence of faith through such an infidelity; the loser is one who has not met this type of *kāfir.* Whatever is general knowledge and belief is commonplace and imperfect. Perfection is something different. Similarly *'ishq* (love) and *'irfān* (gnosticism) differ; everyone is found submerged in the ocean of love but love undoubtedly reminds one of dualism. *'Irfān* involves a transcendence of the dichotomy between 'I' and 'You'. It is easy for iconoclasts to smash idols but the destruction of the ego depends on a deeply rooted spirituality. This attribute is not acquired through personal effort but by divine grace.[74]

In 1639–40 both Prince Dārā Shukoh and his sister Jahān Āra became Mullā Shāh's disciples. The Emperor Shāhjahān was also deeply devoted to him. Mullā Shāh lived during the summer in Srinagar and in winter in Lahore. After Dārā Shukoh was defeated by Aurangzīb, the new Emperor sought to imprison Mullā Shāh. He could find no excuse and had to be content with ordering him to reside permanently in Lahore, where he died in October 1661.

Aurangzīb continually condemned Mullā Shāh for discussing such an inflammatory theory of sūfism as the Wahdat al-Wujud with his father and elder brother instead of keeping his mystical ideas for sūfī ears only.[75] Dārā Shukoh, Shāhjahān's eldest son, was also his father's favourite, and the Emperor believed that he could make him his successor without much difficulty. Dārā Shukoh therefore received a specialized literary education and military training, but he was no match for his brothers in political intrigue and far-sightedness.

Prince Dārā Shukoh's interest in sūfism aroused the attention of the Qādiriyya and Chishtiyya sūfīs. This in turn stimulated him further, and he became obsessed with the idea that the Indian sūfī orders were the pivot on which all worldly and spiritual matters depended. Accepting the impossibility of a Muslim attaining his spiritual goal and final salvation without their aid, Dārā Shukoh argued that all Muslims should be brought within the sūfī discipline.[76] He attributed his own well-being to the Qādiriyyas.

From 1640 Dārā Shukoh began to write sūfi treatises. The *Sakīnatu'l-awliyā'*, completed in 1642, includes a detailed biography of Mīyān Mīr and his disciples. He also wrote short sūfi tracts, of which the *Hasanātu'l-'ārifīn* is devoted to the ecstatic sūfī sayings. His growing interest in Hindu mysticism upset the orthodox. In his *Majma'u'l-bahrayn* (The Mingling of Two Oceans) he tried to prove that an appreciation of the deeper elements in sūfism and Hindu mysticism could be achieved only by the elite of both religions. Comparing the Islamic sūfi concepts and terminology with those of the Hindus, he proved they were identical.

The *Majma'u'l-bahrayn* was singled out by the *'ulamā'* as justification for condemning Dārā Shukoh to death. They accused him of calling infidelity and Islam 'twin brothers', even though the work in fact lies strictly within Ibnu'l-

'Arabī's ideological framework. It asserts that the stage of universality and perfection was reserved for the Prophet Muhammad, and that divine transcendence was harmoniously blended with immanence. The Hindu equivalents are intended merely to reinforce the Muslim sūfi beliefs. Dārā's most important contribution was the Persian translation of the *Upanisads*, which, he said, contained subtle hints relating to the Wahdat al-Wujūd doctrines.[77]

Dārā Shukoh's sister, Jahān Āra Begum, sometimes known as Begum Sāhiba, was also devoted to Mullā Shāh. In her early career she was interested in Chishtiyya sūfism and she wrote a biography of Khwāja Mu'īnu'd-Dīn Chishtī and some of his disciples. She completed her biographical account of Mullā Shāh, entitled the *Sāhibīya*, in 1641. It was a major contribution to sūfī literature. Jahān Āra served her father devotedly during his captivity and tried to allay his hatred of Aurangzīb.[78] Aurangzīb admired her and, after Shāhjahān's death, sought her advice on state matters. She died unmarried in 1681. During Aurangzīb's reign the Qādiriyya order lost the patronage of the court, but its general popularity did not wane.

THE NAQSHBANDIYYA ORDER

The Naqshbandiyya order, or the order of the Khwājas, originated in Transoxiana. Its distinctive features were formed by Khwāja 'Abdu'l-Khāliq (d. 1220) of Ghujduwān or modern Gizduvan, near Bukhāra. The main principles of the order were controlled breathing and mental *zikr*, although strict observance of the *sharī'a* was also strongly stressed. The order of the Khwājas came to be called the Naqshbandiyya following Khwāja Bahā'u'd-Dīn Naqshband (d. 1389).

The Naqshbandiyya order was popularized in India by Bābur, the first Mughal Emperor. Following in his father's footsteps, Bābur was deeply devoted to the Naqshbandiyya leader Khwāja 'Ubaydu'llāh Ahrār (d. 1490). The Khwāja was both a scholar and a political leader. His spiritual descendants supported Bābur in his fight for the throne against Uzbeks. Some of them subsequently moved to India.

An important migrant to India was Khwāja Khāwand Mahmūd. He lived in Kashmīr and visited the courts of Akbar and Jahāngīr. Later Jahāngīr stopped the Khwāja's anti-Shī'ī and puritanically orthodox activities, and he moved from Kashmīr to Kābul. The Khwāja returned to Kashmīr during Shāhjahān's reign, but the Emperor found his anti-Shī'ī sermons a threat to law and order and expelled him. The Khwāja settled in Lahore, dying there in 1642. His son, Mu'inu'd-Dīn, was a scholar of both jurisprudence and sūfīsm.[79]

The sūfī who did most to make the Naqshbandiyya order outstanding in India was Khwāja Bāqī Bi'llāh of Kābul. He was born in 1563 or 1564 and was initiated into Khwāja 'Ubaydu'llah Ahrār's Naqshbandiyya branch near Samarqand by a local leader. In 1599 he moved to Delhi and settled there. Many leading nobles from Akbar's court became his devotees. He died in 1603. Although he lived in India for only four years he left an indelible mark on its spiritual and intellectual life.

Two of his spiritual descendants, Shaykh Ilahdad and Shaykh Tāju'd-Dīn Sambhalī, left India when they failed to wrest the leadership from Shaykh Ahmad

Sirhindī, the most talented disciple of Khwāja Bāqī Bi'llāh. Shaykh Ahmad was born at Sirhind in 1564. His father, Shaykh 'Abdul-Ahad, taught him when he was young and initiated him into the Chishtiyya and Qādiriyya orders. He seems to have visited Fathpūr-Sīkrī some time before the imperial court left for the Panjāb in August 1585. Shaykh Ahmad was shocked by the dominance of rational and philosophical thinking at the court. In a discussion with Abu'l-Fazl he is said to have remarked that Imām Ghazālī had written in the *Munqiz min al-zalal* that useful sciences which the philosophers claimed as their invention were astronomy and medicine, but these were in fact plagiarized from the books of the former prophets. The remaining sciences, such as mathematics, were of no use to religion. Abu'l- Fazl was annoyed at these remarks and declared that Ghazālī was unreasonable. Each disliked the other. Like Shaykh 'Abdu'l-Haqq, Shaykh Ahmad also believed that Akbar's supporters were hostile to the idea of prophethood. He therefore wrote several short treatises on the subject. The *Isbāt al-Nubūwwa* asserts the importance of miracles and the prophets, particularly of Muhammad. Another treatise discusses the importance of the first clause of the Islamic credo, 'There is no God but Allah', while a third, *Radd-i Rawāfiz*,[80] condemning the Shī'īs, also became very popular. This treatise refutes the letter written by the Shī'ī *'ulamā'* of Mash had in response to the argument of the Transoxianan *'ulamā'* in about 1587 concerning the infidelity of the Shī'īs.

In 1599 Shaykh Ahmad's father died, and he decided to leave for Mecca. He halted at Delhi and visited Khwāja Bāqī Bi'llāh, who initiated him into the Naqshbandiyya order. He revisited Delhi twice during the Khwāja's lifetime. Like his father, Shaykh Ahmad at first followed the Wahdat al-Wujūd doctrines, but his sūfi exercises under the Khwāja made him expert in the Wahdat al-Shuhūd system. He wrote to the Khwāja discussing his mystical progress, and the Khwāja encouraged him to take an independent line.

The Shaykh also wrote to his contemporaries, particularly Shaykh Nizām Thāneswarī, urging him to abandon the Wahdat al-Wujūd beliefs. After Akbar's death he wrote to various leading noblemen, urging them to persuade Jahāngīr to reverse Akbar's political and religious policies. He urged that *jizya* should be reimposed, that cow-slaughter should be resumed, and that positions in the finance department should no longer be offered to Shī'īs and Hindus. Muslims should avoid infidels as they did dogs. In another letter he wrote that Shī'īs were worse than infidels and.that showing them honour amounted to destroying Islam. Shaykh Ahmad vehemently condemned the worldly *'ulamā'* and sūfis, considering them responsible for the rulers' departure from Sunnī orthodoxy. He believed that he was the renewer (*mujaddid*) of the first millennium of Islam and had been sent by God to restore Sunnī orthodoxy to its pristine purity.

The first volume of the Shaykh's correspondence, containing 313 epistles, was published in 1616–17. His short treatise on the Wahdat al-Shuhūd theories, entitled the *Mabda'wa ma'ād*, had already been published. His political and social ideas and the account he gave of his mystical achievements created a considerable sensation. In 1619–20 Jahāngīr summoned him to court and ordered him to justify his claim of a mystical ascent to heaven, as mentioned in one of his letters to Khwāja Bāqī Bi'llāh.[81] Finding his answers unconvincing, the Emperor imprisoned Shaykh Ahmad in Gwālior fort. He was released after twelve months and allowed to stay either in the imperial camp or at Sirhind. The Shaykh, to whom we shall henceforth refer by his title of Mujaddid, chose the imperial camp.

The Mujaddid lived there for about three years, considering that camp life suited his mission and was no different from life in a monastery. He delivered sermons and wrote letters to his sons and disciples. The second volume of his correspondence, consisting of 99 letters, was published in 1618–19, and the third volume, of 122 letters, in 1621–2. In letter No. 87 in this third volume the Mujaddid claimed that he was both the disciple of God and His desire. To Shaykh 'Abdu'I-Haqq, already concerned at the extravagant claims of the Mujaddid and his disciples, it seemed that he claimed to be equal to the Prophet. 'Abdu'l-Haqq wrote a long letter to the Mujaddid, calling him presumptuous and accusing him of making self-contradictory statements.[82]

Opposition to the Mujaddid mounted quickly, but he and his sons and disciples defended his teachings and continued to preach. In December 1624 the Mujaddid died. He was succeeded by his third son, to whom he had previously written stating that God had inspired him to declare him (his son) Muhammad Ma'sūm, the Qaiyūm or Eternal, on whom the existence of the universe depended.

The Mujaddid's second son, Khwāja Muhammad Sa'īd, collaborated with his brother in furthering their father's mission. Their eldest brother, Muhammad Sadiq, had died during their father's lifetime. In Shāhjahān's reign both Muhammad Ma'sūm and Muhammad Sa'īd wrote letters to Prince Aurangzīb in an attempt to foster the development of the Mujaddid's teachings. They realized that Prince Dārā Shukoh would not help them. Muhammad Sa'īd declared that Prince Aurangzīb was the only hope for Muslims in the days of Islam's decline.[83]

In 1656–7 Khwāja Ma'sūm, Khwāja Sa'īd, and a party of sūfīs left on a pilgrimage to Mecca, returning home after Aurangzīb's accession. Aurangzīb received them cordially, filling them with high hopes for the consummation of the Mujaddid's political programme. They wrote letters urging the Emperor to promote puritanically orthodox Sunnī practices and to eliminate all sinful innovations. Military victories over the Shī'īs and Hindus provided them with opportunities to congratulate the Emperor on his success and to remind him that any unorthodox Sunnī practices which still remained should be eradicated. They hoped to gain maximum support from the imperial family and nobility for the promotion of the Mujaddid's political, social, and religious projects. Despite the political support, it was an uphill task fighting a powerful section of the *'ulamā'* and sūfīs, whose hostility to the Mujaddid's teachings was growing.

Muhammad Ma'sūm died in 1668. His brother had died earlier. Their sons also wrote to Aurangzīb, the princes, and leading *mansabdārs*, hoping to persuade them to promote the Mujaddid's mission. In 1665 Aurangzīb was initiated into the Naqshbandiyya order, but even he could not overcome the orthodox opposition to the Mujaddid. At the end of 1679 the Emperor was forced to ban the teaching of the Mujaddid's letters in Aurangabad, which seems to have been the principle centre of the anti-Mujaddidiyya movement.[84] Many *'ulamā'* in the Panjāb and other places even wrote *fatwas* declaring the Mujaddid's letters sacrilegious. Another anti-Mujaddid movement arose in Mecca and Medina as a result of the sermons preached by the Mujaddid's disciple Shaykh Ādam Banūrī. Shaykh Ādam was banished from India by Shāhjahān in 1642 and died in Medina at the end of 1643. Khwāja Muhammad Ma'sūm and his party also failed to convince the *'ulamā'* in Mecca and Medina of the truth of the Mujaddid's mystical claims. In 1682–3, the Sherif of Mecca wrote to Aurangzīb saying that the *'ulamā'* there were agreed that Shaykh Ahmad was an infidel.[85] The views of the Mujaddid's supporters were ignored. Towards the end of Aurangzīb's reign the Mujaddidī movement was undermined by the organized Chishtiyya and Qādiriyya opposition. It revived in the eighteenth century, however, through the leadership of such devoted Naqshbandiyyas as Mīzrā Mazhar[86] and Khwāja Mīr Dard.[87]

The sons of Bāqī Bi'llāh, Khwāja Kalān and Khwāja Khwurd, were a potent threat to the Mujaddid's movement. They had been trained by the Khwāja's talented disciple Khwāja Husāmu'd-Dīn and by the Mujaddid himself, but they chose to follow Khwāja Bāqī Bi'llāh's Wahdat al-Wujūd beliefs. Both Khwāja Kalān and Khwāja Khwurd wrote a number of short treatises in a bid to convert Khwāja Ma'sūm and other Mujaddidiyyas to the Wahdat al-Wujūd doctrines.[88] They did not oppose the use of sūfī music, which the Mujaddid had strongly condemned. The eighteenth-century Shāh Walīu'llah Dihlawī (d. 1762) was a devoted follower of Khwāja Khwurd's school of thought.

THE SHĪ'ĪS

The Shī'ī sect was first established in India in Sind. Many Shī'īs who had been persecuted by the Umayyad and 'Abbāsid caliphate moved there. Around 982 the Sind governors, who had owed allegiance to the 'Abbāsid caliphate, were replaced by governors whose allegiance was to the Egyptian Fātimid caliphs. The Fātimid were Ismā'ilī Shī'īs and had introduced the hierarchical *dā'īs* missionary system, which preached Ismā'īlī Shī'ism secretly.[89] In Sind they appear to have converted both Hindus and Sunnīs. Their missionaries had the gift of recognizing a promising candidate who would easily be converted. Initially they shook the potential convert's faith in his own religion and then taught him only as much Ismā'īlī doctrine as he would accept. 'All was presented to both Sunnīs and Hindus as the perfect ideal for all mankind. It was not difficult to convince the Hindus that 'Alī was an incarnation of Vishnu. The Ismā'īlīs interpreted their teachings esoterically and never bothered to change their Hindu converts' names, ancestral social customs, or laws of inheritance and succession.

In 1010 Sultan Mahmūd of Ghaznī tried ruthlessly to annihilate the Ismā'īlīs in Multān; they nevertheless emerged later as a powerful community. Mu'izzu'd-Dīn Muhammad of Ghur also fought them but was apparently killed himself by an Ismā'īlī assassin. In Raziyya's reign, a certain leader named Nūr Turk, who had established a reputation for learning and piety, started a campaign against the Sunnī *'ulamā'*, condemning them as hostile to 'Alī. In 1237 he collected his devotees from Sind and Gujarāt and attempted to seize power, but his *coup d'etat* was foiled by Raziyya.

Nūr Turk moved to Mecca and died there. The Ismā'īlī missionaries retired to Gujarāt and Sind, where they continued preaching their religion. The south-eastern half of lower Sind remained Ismā'īlī, however, and the Sūmra rulers of Sind practised the Ismā'īlī faith until the fourteenth century before gradually changing to Sunnīsm.

The Bohra community of Gujarāt was apparently converted to the Ismā'īlī sect in the thirteenth century. The stories of this conversion are legendary. As their main occupation was in trade and commerce, they maintained cordial relations with the Hindus and found no difficulty in trading in Gujarāt and western India. A sub-sect of the Ismā'īlīs was known as the Khojas. Their *dā'īs* were also active missionaries who promoted cohesion within the sect.

The Isnā' 'Asharī Shī'īs[90] believed in the twelve Imāms, the last being the hidden Imām Mahdi. The sect seems to have been introduced into India after the conversion of the Īl-Khānid Mongol, Uljaytu Khudābanda (1304–14), to Shī'īsm. Istikhān al-Dihlawī, the author of *Basātinu 'l-Uns*, a collection of Hindu tales compiled in 1326, credited Sultan Muhammad bin Tughluq with making the Ja'frī faith (Isnā' 'Asharī Shī'īsm) strong in India. Its introduction brought to India Muharram, the mourning ceremonies commemorating Imām Husayn's martyrdom, which were initiated by the Shī'ī immigrants and their converts. Sultan Fīrūz stated that the Rawāfiz (Shī'īs) produced their own religious books and treatises and continually sought converts. They also 'openly reviled and foully abused' the first three caliphs who succeeded the Prophet, the Prophet's beloved wife, 'Ā'isha Siddiqa, and all the respected sūfīs.[91] According to Fīrūz the Shī'īs also doubted the Qur'ān's authenticity, claiming that the third Caliph, 'Usmān, had included many baseless interpolations.[92] Fīrūz tried unsuccessfully to crush Shī'īsm by executing its partisans, burning Shī'ī books, and censuring and threatening possible converts.

After Tīmūr's invasion, the Shī'īs and Sunnīs with Shī'ī leanings moved from Irān to the provincial courts in India, particularly to the Deccan. A leading Irānian sūfī, Sayyid Muhammad Ashraf Jahāngīr Simnānī (d. *c.* 1436), in an attempt to convert the Shī'īs, arranged several debates against them. Yūsuf 'Ādil Shāh of Bījāpūr (1490–1510) took the unprecedented step of making Isnā' 'Asharī Shī'īsm the official religion of the sultanate. He may have been encouraged to do so by Shāh Ismā'il Safavi of Irān's (1501–24) decision to make Isnā' 'Ashari Shī'ī faith the state religion. Although 'Ādil Shāh replaced the names of Muhammad's successors with those of the twelve imāms in the *khutba*,[93] he refused to allow the extremists to insult the Prophet's companions.

The Isnā' 'Asharī Shī'ī faith entered a new phase when Shāh Tāhir, son of Shāh Raziu'd-Dīn, arrived in the Deccan from Irān. He converted Burhan Nizām Shāh (1508–54) of Ahmadnagar to the Shī'ī faith. Burhan sent Shāh Tāhir as an envoy to Bahādur Shāh's court in Gujarāt. The Shāh's reputation as an *'ālim* and his diplomatic ability greatly impressed Sultan Bahādur. He also succeeded in establishing relations with the Gujarāt *'ulamā'*, thereby preparing the way for the spread of Isnā' 'Asharī Shī'īsm there. Subsequently other scholars moved from Irān to the Deccan, where they were warmly welcomed by Shāh Tāhir. He died in 1549. The Shī'ī immigrants from Irān were also favoured by the Shī'ī Qutb Shāhi rulers in Golkonda. Their prime minister, Mīr Muhammad Mu'min (d. 1625), established Shī'ī religious ceremonies in the newly founded city of Hyderābād.

In Kashmīr the Shī'ī faith was established by Mīr Shamsu'd-Dīn 'Irāqī, a former Nūrbakhshiyya sūfī. This order had strong Shī'ī overtones. The Mīr converted Mūsa Rayna, one of Sultan Fath Shāh's (1493–1514) leading nobles, to Shī'ism. Although Rayna provided funds for a monastery at Jaddībal in Srinagar, the strong Sunnī *'ulamā'* opposition forced the Mīr to leave for Bāltistān, where many Buddhists were converted to Shī'īsm. The Mīr soon returned to Kashmīr at the invitation of Rayna, who was now prime minister. Many Chak nobles professed Shī'īsm before the Mīr died around 1533. During Mīrza Haydar Dughlāt's reign (1540–1) the Shī'īs were mercilessly persecuted. Mīr Shamsu'd-Din's tomb was desecrated, and his son, Shaykh Dāniyāl, was first imprisoned and then beheaded. After Mīrza's death the Shī'īs regained their former position, but in the early part of Akbar's reign many acrimonious disputes arose between them and the Sunnīs in Srinagar.[94]

Although Bābur, the founder of the Mughal empire in India, was a Sunnī, he had no objection to professing Shī'īsm when seeking Shāh Ismā'il's support against the Uzbeks. Bābur's son, Humāyūn, who had an Irāni mother, also favoured the Irānīs and was believed to be a Shī'ī convert. Some of Humāyūn's Persian allies on the Qandahār and Kābul expeditions were Shī'īs and they immigrated to India despite orthodox Sunnī opposition.

Apart from Kashmīr, the Shī'īs avoided any confrontation with the Sunnīs during the early part of Akbar's reign. Bayram Khān, who had supported Humāyūn so loyally, was a Shī'ī but he soon lost his position as prime minister. This, however, did not affect the Shī'ī immigrations to India even under the domination of the orthodox Sunnī *'ulamā'* Makhdūmu'l Mulk and Shaykh 'Abdu'n-Nabī. Often posing as sūfīs, the Shī'īs would first go to the Shī'ī states of the Deccan; the other Irānis at court would help them, and eventually they progressed to Delhi. They were also protected by the Tafzīlīa Sunnīs, who believed that 'Alī was superior to all the Prophet's companions. Both the Tafzilia and the Nūrbakhshiyya doctrines served as a stage in the transition from Sunnīsm to Isnā' 'Asharī Shī'īsm.

Mullā Badā'ūnī incorrectly gives us the impression that all the Irānīs in Akbar's reign were Shī'īs.[95] Among the leading nobles at Akbar's court who openly practised the Shī'ī faith were Hakim Abu'l-Fath Gīlānī, Hakīm Humām, and Hakim Fathu'llāh Shirāzī. All three were great scholars. Fathu'llāh Shirāzī's interest in mathematics and science has already been mentioned. Mullā Ahmad of Thatta, another famous Shī'ī, was a historian and wrote a large portion of the *Tār'ikh-i Alfi.* He was assassinated in 1588 by a Sunnī fanatic, Mīrzā Fawlād, in Lahore.

After the Emperor Akbar had left for Kashmīr, the Sunnīs in Lahore exhumed his dead body and burnt it.[96] It is interesting that an important Shī'ī leader, Mullā Muhammad Yazdī, combined with the Sunnī *'ulamā'* to spearhead the movement to overthrow Akbar because of those ordinances that were heretical to them.[97]

The most learned Shī'ī of Akbar's reign was Qāzī Nūru'llāh Shustarī. Mullā Badā'ūnī, who usually never mentions any Shī'ī without abusing him, pays glowing tribute to the Qāzi's piety and scholarship. As a *qāzī*, Nūru'llāh was impartial and just,[98] and as a revenue administrator he was conscientious.[99] Nevertheless in September 1610 he was flogged to death on Jahāngīr's orders. The contemporary authorities give different reasons for his execution.[100] Since he had always been a well-known Shī'ī, his faith could not have been the cause. The orthodox Sunnī *'ulamā'* apparently claimed that his potential work, the *Ihqāqu'l-Haqq*, was subversive and posed a threat to Sunnīsm. The Qāzī was undoubtedly executed solely to please the Sunnī *'ulamā'*. Far more serious threats to Jahāngīr had been treated less drastically; Shaykh Nizām Thāneswarī, who had blessed the rebel Prince Khusraw, was merely banished to Mecca.[101] The Shī'īs consider the Qāzī a martyr and a victim of the Emperor's bigotry. However, Jahāngīr did not subsequently adopt any anti-Shī'ī policy and never even mentions the tragic incident in his Memoirs. Neither the Qāzī's family nor the Shī'īs were persecuted by Jahāngīr. Shāhjahān appointed 'Ala'u'l-Mulk Husaynī, one of the Qāzī's sons, as tutor to Prince Shāh Shujā' and sent him to Bengal with the Prince.[102] Shujā's Shī'ī leanings may be ascribed to 'Ala'u'l-Mulk's teachings.

Most of the Irānian *mansabdārs* during the reigns of Jahāngīr, Shāhjahān, and Aurangzīb were Shī'īs. However, they never exhibited their faith publicly and ran the Mughal administration on the basis of its recognized rules and traditions. Despite his Sunnī orthodoxy and puritanism, even Aurangzib did not appoint *mansabdārs* or award promotions on sectarian or religious considerations.[103] Shī'ī and Sunnī conflicts frequently arose in Kashmīr, but in other parts of the Mughal empire there were no sectarian tensions or riots. It was only in the wake of the disintegration of the empire in the eighteenth century that Shī'ī proselytization was stepped up, and Shī'ī-Sunnī polemics and tensions increased. Shāh Walīu'llāh and his son, Shāh 'Abdu'l 'Azīz, played a leading role in fomenting such sectarian conflicts.

VII

FINE ARTS

PRE-MUGHAL ARCHITECTURE: THE FIRST PHASE

THE excavations of Mansūra-Brahmanābād and the ruins of Thatta in southern Sind tell us of the early mosque-building activity of the Arab rulers there. The palaces of Mahmūd of Ghaznī and of Mas'ud III (1099–1115) in Ghaznī are largely Irānian in style, but the lavish use of marble in Ghaznī palaces indicates an Indian influence. Parts of a minaret named after Mas'ud III and another called after Bahrām Shāh (1118–52) still survive. In the tenth and early eleventh centuries similar minarets with a polygon base and cylindrical shaft were built with great skill in north-west Irān. Nothing built by the Ghaznavid rulers in the Panjāb province survives; possibly everything was destroyed by the Mongols.

The literary sources tell us that a variety of arts flourished under the Delhi sultans, but only architectural monuments are extant. Even in this sphere, the palaces and houses were grossly neglected after their original owners died. Their descendants chose different sites for their houses and sometimes demolished the earlier edifices for building materials. Only the mosques and mausoleums have been preserved – mainly out of religious sentiment.

Muslims can pray individually, but congregational prayers are preferred. When the Prophet moved from Mecca to Medina he built a mosque consisting of a hall with pillars of palm tree trunks and a roof of branches. It was extended, renovated, and he built many times. After conquering a country, therefore, the first step the Muslim rulers took was to build a mosque there. Besides congregational prayers, mosques were used as assembly halls for religious and social needs, also serving as schools. Their structural plan was radically different from the Hindu temples. Each mosque contained a *mihrāb* or niche indicating the direction for prayers or *qibla.* In India it is west, towards the Ka'ba, the cube-like ancient sanctuary in Mecca. On the right-hand side of the *mihrāb* is the stepped pulpit or *minbar* (or *mimbar*) from which the *khutba* (sermon) is recited. Unlike in Christian churches, the covered area or hall is wider than it is deep. It is preceded by an open area, containing a water tank for ablution, and enclosed by walls whose main entrance in India is towards the east. There are cloisters along the sides of the larger mosques. A tall slender tower known as a minaret (*ma'zana*), from where the faithful are called to prayers, is erected near the hall. The principal mosque, where the midday congregational prayers on Fridays are held, is known as the Jāmi' Masjid.

In Delhi the Jāmi' Masjid, later known as the Qubbatu'l-Islam mosque (Mosque of the Cupola of Islam, i.e. Delhi) or Quwwatu'l Islam (Might of Islam) mosque, was begun immediately after Delhi's conquest in 1192, on the orders of Mu'izzu 'd-Dīn Muhammad's commander, Qutbu'd-Dīn Aybak. In a desperate hurry, Qutbu'd-Dīn Aybak did not wish to send to Irān for engineers, where arches and domes were highly developed, but ordered the local Hindu architects to follow their trabeate system. This involved erecting the edifice on pillars with the help of supporting brackets and spanning the roof with horizontal beams. Some twenty-seven temples were destroyed, the plinth of one of the original Hindu temples was converted into a courtyard, and a new plinth was constructed. This was enclosed by pillared cloisters, three bays deep on the east and two bays on the north and south. The original short temple pillars were placed one above the other to achieve the desired height. The idols were disfigured or destroyed, and the corbelled ceilings and lintels were rearranged to form the new ceiling. In 1199 an Islamic character was given to the western pillared cloisters by building an imposing screen in front of the courtyard. The screen's central arch is flanked on either side by two lesser arches; the two other flanking arches do not survive. All the arches in the screen were corbelled out like the ogees in the Buddhist rock-cut caves. The true arch with radiating voussoirs, in which the Muslims specialized, could not be built because of the want of competent architects. The calligraphy from the Qur'ānic verses which dominates the sinuous tendrils, curling leaves, and geometric traceries of the arabesque, however, compensates for the absence of a true arch. The iron pillar from the Gupta age facing the central arch was retained. Ibn Battūta describes it as an 'awe-inspiring column of which (it is said) nobody knows of what metal it is constructed'.[1]

In the south-east corner of the mosque Aybak started building the world-famous tapering minaret of red sandstone now known as the Qutb Mīnār, although until 'Ala'u'd-Dīn Khaljī's reign it was known simply as Mīnāra or Mīnār-i Shamsī (Shamsu'd-Dīn Iltutmish's Mīnāret). It was designed on the pattern of Irānian minarets, with round and triangular spurs connected by balconies. The bottom storey, consisting of alternately rounded and angular flutes, was built by Aybak. Some three metres from the plinth, however, the looped bell and garland and the lotus borders of the ancient Hindu tradition have been carved. The first storey leads up to a bracketed gallery, supported by a stalactite of the honeycomb work commonly used in Islamic pendentives. The second, third, and fourth storeys were built by Iltutmish. The fourth storey was struck by lightning in 1370, after which Sultan Fīrūz Tughluq replaced it with two more storeys. The first three storeys are constructed of grey quartzite faced with red sandstone, while the fourth and fifth storeys, which do not harmonize with the first three, are built of red sandstone faced largely with marble. This last stage raised the mosque's height to 72.59 metres.

Although the Qutb Mīnār is exclusively Islamic in conception, its execution was the work of Hindus. Again the Qur'ānic verses dominate, but their ornamentation consists of spiralling bands of arabesques, floral designs, and festooned strips of the kind used in Indian jewellery. Nāgarī writing on some stones suggest that they were part of larger inscribed panels. Some masons have signed the stones. Twice on the basement *samvat*, 1256 (AD 1199) is inscribed in Nāgarī, indicating when construction commenced.

Aybak demolished the gigantic Vaishnava temple at Ajmīr and built a mosque which is known as Arhā'i-din kā jhūnpra or 'the Hut of two and a half days', as it was called later. The mosque was built on high ground, and this time the architects used material from a Hindu temple more carefully and imaginatively. The two corners of the eastern facade banded circular bastions, and a single broad aisle was built around the three sides of the open court. The prayer chamber stands on richly carved pillars, each consisting of three Hindu shafts placed on top of each other to make a ceiling 6.10 metres high. It is covered with diagonally laid beams and stone slabs decorated with concentric circles. What gives the sanctuary the character of a mosque is the exquisitely carved *mihrāb* made from a single slab of white marble with a cusped arch, and the screen shaped like a tall painted arch flanked by two cusped arches and one plain, smaller arch. The prayer chamber was constructed in 1199–1200. The screen was built by Shamsu'd-Dīn Iltutmish, but he could not compete with the ornamentation of the Qūwwatu'l-Islam screen, although the carving and relief on the Ajmīr screen are perfect.

In 1230 Iltutmish more than doubled the area of the Qūwwatu'l-Islam mosque by adding wings to the prayer chamber and screen. Here too the delicacy and beauty of the earlier ornamentation are lacking, and the reliefs are flat and lifeless. About three miles from the Qutb Mīnār, Iltutmish constructed a mausoleum for his eldest son, Nāsiru'd-Dīn Mahmūd. Built in 1231–2, it is known as the Sultan Ghārī (Sultan of the Cave), for the cenotaph is in an underground chamber. The roof is an octagonal platform; no trace remains of the pillared pavilion which it might have contained. The material for its fluted pillars, capitals, architraves, and corbelled pyramidal roof was taken from Hindu monuments, but the process of remodelling them to suit Muslim needs had already begun.

In the north-west corner of the Qūwwatu'l-Islam mosque stands Iltutmish's mausoleum, built by himself before his death in 1235. The most interesting innovation is the use of squinches to transform the square base into the circular diameter of the corbelled dome. As the dome no longer exists, the richly sculptured motifs of both Islamic and ancient Indian origin on its walls and polylobed arches can easily be seen – they are open to the full daylight. The mausoleum is built of red and grey sandstone, the cenotaph of marble.

Balban's tomb, not far from the Qutb Mīnār, is in ruins, but it deserves mention for its unusual arches. These are not constructed by using horizontal courses after the ancient Indian structural technique but were built by means of voussoirs. This development opened up a new era in Indo-Islamic architecture.

'Ala'u'd-Dīn Khaljī made some ambitious plans for enlarging the Qutb area. He wished to extend the mosque enclosure towards the north and east. He started building a rival Qutb Mīnār whose inner diameter was 27.43 metres; it was intended to rise to 145 metres, but he died before it was completed. The southern gateway to the Qūwwatu'l-Islam mosque, known as 'Alā'ī Darwāza (Gateway of

'Ala'u'd-Dīn), built in 1311, is a real monument to his glory. Undoubtedly he had heard of the celebrated Tāq-i Kisra, the archway built by the Sasanid King Kisra Nūshīrwān at Ctesiphon in Iraq, and apparently some Irānian architects, who had moved to Delhi, translated his dreams into stone with the aid of Hindu stone-cutters and masons. The material used is red sandstone and white marble, with inlays of black marble and blue schist, indicating the contributions of Gujarāt artisans.

The gateway is a cubical structure of 15.25 metres each side, covered by a flat dome. The three large pointed horseshoe arches supporting the dome are of dressed stone. They are true arches. On each side of the doorway there are two windows containing marble grilles one-third of their size. The façade on the north contains a semi-circular doorway of an ancient Indian pattern. The pendentives in the interior, which consist of simple inset arches, are remarkably beautiful. The adaptation of different styles in the 'Alā'ī Darwāza has in no way undermined the proportion and harmony of the structure.

During the reign of the Tughluqs, ornamentation was replaced by lineaments and masses. The immense walls of Tughluqābād, built by Ghiyāsu'd-Dīn Tughluq, are protected by circular bastions and crenellated parapets. The rough-hewn boulders used in the city's construction seem to have been quarried on the site. The Sultan's mausoleum, built in an artificial lake and connected with the citadel by an elevated causeway, looks like a fortress. Its plan is square, the walls rise upwards at acute angles, and lintels are set across the base of the three entrance archways to strengthen them. The hemispherical marble dome and the marble inlays running in broad bands around the building relieve the monotony of the grey and red sandstone structure.

The tomb was built by the Sultan himself, the angled walls inspired by the Perso-Arabian traditions of the Multān tombs. When Ghiyāsu'd-Dīn Tughluq was governor of Dīpālpūr, or shortly after his accession to the throne of Delhi, he ordered the construction of a tomb for the remains of his patron sūfī saint, Shaykh Ruknu'd-Dīn. This octagonal, double-storeyed brick structure stands on a terrace. The first storey is 15.25 metres high, and the second is 7.62 metres, while the dome rises 15.25 metres inside. Sunk into its walls are bricks inlaid with glazed tiles. Chiselled coloured bricks, carved timber, and terracotta make the walls shimmer and shine.

Many fulsome panegyrics praising Muhammad bin Tughluq's monuments were written, but because his edifices have not survived no comments can now be made. Fīrūz Tughluq's *madrasa* (seminary) reflects his scholarly ideals. The combination of Hindu columns, arch and lintel arcades, and kiosks is most striking. Sultan Fīrūz's tomb, however, has lost all its stucco and glazed tiles. On the whole, the structure is unpretentious and dignified.

Sultan Fīrūz was an indefatigable builder. Many of his citadels, mosques, and towns still stand, although now derelict. Most of them were built of rubble and plaster, with pillars, architraves, and brackets of local grey granite. The vigour and simplicity of these monuments with their tapering buttresses are a legacy from the early Tughluq architecture. Nevertheless, they are not entirely devoid of innovation. For example, the machicolations in the fortification at Kotla Fīrūz Shāh and the pyramidal structure crowning the Asokan pillar demonstrate the Sultan's ingenuity. The mausoleum for Khān-i Jahān Maqbūl, built by his son Jaunā Shāh in 1368, deserves mention for its structural innovations. Its outer enclosure contains the usual Tughluq strong walls and corner towers, but it is built on an octagonal plan instead of the usual square. Although the tomb at Sultan Ghārī, already discussed, is also octagonal, the precursor of Khān-i Jahān's tomb was Shaykh Ruknu'd-Dīn Multānī's mausoleum. Possibly, therefore, the architects were not inspired by the Dome of the Rock in Jerusalem or the octagonal Irānian tombs, as modern scholars suggest. The octagonal chamber of the tomb, surmounted by a central squat dome and eight dome-like cupolas, one over each face, is surrounded by a low-arched veranda. The structure suffers from innumerable defects of proportion, which the later Sayyid and Afghān octagonal tomb designers corrected, but the architects of Khān-i Jahān's tomb were pioneers.

ARCHITECTURE OF THE REGIONAL KINGDOMS

Fīrūz Shāh's death marked the end of the first major phase of architectural development in India. The second era began with the establishment of the new regional dynasties, whose founders adorned their capitals with distinctive and imposing structures. Although the Sharqī dynasty of Jaunpūr was short-lived, one of its rulers, Ibrāhīm Shāh Sharqī (1401–40), was a great builder. In 1408 he completed the Atala mosque. This was built on the site of a temple at Atala Devi, demolished by Fīrūz in 1376, reusing the original Hindu pillars, lintels, brackets, and ceilings. The screen before the prayer chamber is dominated by a massive façade sloping sides, over 22.87 metres high. It is 16.77 metres wide at the base and resembles the propylons in some ancient Egyptian temples. Tier upon tier of arched niches within rectangular frames relieves its huge bulk. The façade nevertheless looks like like a triumphal gateway. The prayer chamber is surmounted by a hemispherical dome which is partly concealed by the pyramidal double-storeyed arch. On the north, south, and east are double-storeyed colonnaded cloisters, each five aisles deep, with flat ceilings. The intricate ornamentation in the prayer chamber, however, gives the Atala mosque the effect of a Hindu temple.

Other mosques in Jaunpūr largely follow the Atāla pattern. The Khālis-Mukhlis mosque is plain, but the name Jhanjhrī (Perforated) is given to another mosque because of its fine stone tracery. The Lāl Darwāza (Red Gate) mosque contains vermilion-painted gates and a propylon smaller than that of the Atala. The largest mosque in Jaunpūr is the Jāmi', built by Husayn Shāh Sharqī (1458–79) in *c.* 1470. Like Sultan Fīrūz's mosques in Delhi, the Jami' mosque is raised over a basement terrace, and the propylon in the middle of the prayer chamber façade and equally imposing. The barrel vaults replacing the flat roofs are a failure, however, and make the Jami' mosque inferior to the Atala.

Building stone is scarce in Bengal. Bamboo is the traditional building material, but bricks, being easy to make, were used by both the Buddhists and the

Muslims. Although Muslim architectural activity started immediately after the conquest of Bengal, the surviving monuments date from 1338. The Adina or the Jāmi' mosque, built by Sultan Sikandar Shāh (1358–90), was at Pandua, a most ambitious structure. Enclosed by a high brick wall, it had cloisters on three sides. These have now crumbled, and the roof has fallen in, but the nave retains some of its original stately appearance. The pillars were taken from Hindu temples and palaces in Lakhnauti. The tomb of Sultan Jalālu'd-Dīn Mahmūd Shāh (1414–32), known as Eklakhī, is the prototype of subsequent Islamic architecture in Bengal. Its plain hemispherical dome and octagonal turrets projecting from each corner of the square structure introduced Fīrūzian techniques into Bengal. The Dakhil Darwaza at Gaur, a massive triumphal arch, was built on the orders of Bārbak Shāh (1459–74). Its projection and recesses are both angular and circular.

The Tāntīpura mosque in Gaur was built about 1475. Its prayer chamber is divided into two aisles by stone pillars of the square and chamfered variety used in Hindu temples. The Tāntīpura was the precursor of seven important mosques built at Gaur. The Barā Sona Masjid (Great Golden Mosque), the largest mosque in Gaur, was erected in 1526 and marks the culmination of the Bengal style. Constructed in brick, faced throughout with black basalt, its severe and massive bulk is pierced by eleven narrow pointed arches, and its austerity is relieved only by a few courses of plain moulding. The Chota Sona Masjid (Small Golden Mosque), built in 1510, has a cusp which imitates the Arhā'ī-Din Ka Jhūnpra cusp at Ajmīr, while the terracotta patterns of the Daras Bārī Masjid are similar to the foliage of the Sīdī Sayyid mosque screen at Ahmadābād. Much smaller than the Qutb Mīnār is the Fīrūz Mīnār at Gaur, built in *c.* 1488. It is 25.62 metres high, with three twelve-sided storeys, topped by two upper round ones. Besides brick and terracotta ornamentation it is decorated with blue and white glazed tiles.

In the first decades of the fifteenth century the sultans of Mālwa demolished Hindu temples and used the materials to build two mosques at Dhār and two at Mandu. The stones were recarved and redressed in an effort to disguise their origin. In the buildings in Mandu, which they made their capital, the Mālwa sultans successfully translated their sense of vigour and imagination into architecture. Sultan Hūshang commenced the Jāmi' mosque in Mandu which his successor, Sultan Mahmūd I, completed in 1440. It is built on a high plinth; the front is composed of rows of arched chambers. These arcades, the sculptured *mihrāb*, and the imposing *minbar* with canopy in the columned hall of the prayer chamber create a majestic aura.

Near the Jāmi' mosque is the complex known as the Ashrafi Mahal (Gold Mohur Palace). It was hurriedly built of roughly prepared rubble, and a royal mausoleum was built projecting from the front of the seminary near the palace. Some time after 1443 Sultan Mahmūd (1439) built a tower at Māndū to commemorate his victory over the Rānā of Chitor. The Rānā had earlier erected the Jaya Stambha (Victory Column) at Chitor to celebrate his defeat of Mahmūd. The Rana's Jaya Stambha still stands, but only the basement of Mahmūd's tower survives.Hūshang's (1405–35) mausoleum, which he had begun to build before he died, was finished by Sultan Mahmūd (1439) around 1440. This square structure stands on a high plinth of about 30 metres and is faced with white marble, A cupola rests on each corner, and the roof is formed by a large central dome. Of all the monuments in Mālwa the most bizarre is the Hindola Mahal. It consists of a long hall whose arches are supported by sloping buttresses. The resulting optical illusion led to its being called the 'Swinging Palace'. A marked contrast to it is the double-storeyed Jahāz Mahal (Ship Palace), which has an arcaded front, pillared inner rooms, and luxurious bathing-halls. The open pavilions, kiosks, and corridors shed their reflection in two lakes near the palace. The palaces and pavilions associated with the romance of Bāz Bahādur and Rupmati are delicately built, but they do not have any architectural or ornamental importance. The monuments in Chanderi broadly follow the Mandu traditions. The stilted domes and arches of the Jāmi' mosque there repeat the Mandu pattern, but the convoluted brackets supporting the eaves are predominantly local Hindu.

Raja Mān Singh (1486–1517) built a famous palace in his capital, Gwālior. The entrance, or Elephant Gateway, is protected by two rounded bastions and consists of a circular archway surmounted by a guard room with a projecting balcony. The main palace has two storeys, but the rooms are small and dark with only low openings for light. The intricately moulded pillars, finely perforated lattices, and profuse carvings, however, make it a piece of decorative architecture.

The Gujarāt monuments are known for their distinctive decorative features. The fourteenth-century edifices in Gujarāt were built from materials from Hindu and Jain monuments. Shaykh Farīd's mausoleum at Patan is simply a Hindu temple with some additions and alterations. In Broach the pillared halls of three temples were rearranged to make a mosque. Beneath the lintel a pointed Islamic arch has been introduced. Its arched windows were fretted with stone tracery.

In the Jāmi' mosque in Cambay some structural improvements were made. As in the Arhā'ī Din Kā Jhūnpra of Ajmīr, the cloisters and entrance porches are relics from sacked Hindu shrines. The alternating narrow and broad courses of masonry seem to have been contributed by the Delhi architect. The mosque was built in 1235. The Jāmi' mosque built at Dholka eight years later is similar to the Cambay, but its turrets are the precursors of the tall slender minarets of the later Gujarāt mosques.

The Cambay mosque also served as a model for that built by Ahmad Shāh (1411–42) in the citadel of his newly founded capital, Ahmadābād. Here the mosque of Haybat Khān contains bastions similar to those in Sultan Fīrūz Tughluq's monuments, and the Sayyid 'Alam mosque anticipates some features of the celebrated Jāmi' mosque built in 1423 in Ahmadābād. On either side of the central arch of the latter stand lesser pointed arches flanked by colonnades, supported by round arches. The great pillars immediately within the central arch reach up to the massive architrave from which the central dome springs. The stylized trees on the niches, the hanging lamp and bell ornament, and the semi-geometrical decoration of the pierced and relief panels harmoniously blend Hindu and Jain features with Islamic ones.

Nearby stands a gateway of three elegant arches of equal height: the Tin Darwāza, built in Ahmad Shāh's reign. The buttresses projecting from the piers are richly carved. The tomb of Ahmad Shāh is in an enclosure to the east of the Jāmi' mosque, and the contours of its arches are similar to those of the Tin Darwaza. The arrangement of its parapets is most elegant. Farther east is the Rānī Kā Hujra, or the Tomb of the Queens, consisting of an open court enclosed by an arched screen with columned cloisters both inside and out. The marble cenotaphs are richly carved and inlaid with metal and mother-of-pearl. Some nine kilometres south-west in Sarkhīj are the mausoleum and mosque built in memory of the great sūfi Shaykh Ahmad-i Khattū Maghribī (d. 1446). The complex was completed in about five years, and many palaces, a pavilion, and gateways were subsequently added by various religious people. The earlier mosque is marked by elegant pillars arranged in groups of unending variety. The central chamber is surmounted by an imposing dome.

The greatest builder in Gujarāt was Sultan Mahmūd Begarha (1459–1511). He founded three major cities: Batwa, Mahmūdābād, and Champānīr. He adorned all of them, and Ahmadābād as well, with mosques, tombs, and palaces. The arrangement of arches in the mausoleums of the period make them distinctive monuments. The Rānī Sīprī mosque, built in Ahmadābād in 1514, is an exquisite gem in both plan and detail. Although not large, its matchless beauty lies in its symmetry and decorative rhythm. The most famous of all the Gujarāt monuments are the perforated screens which fill in the tympanums of the arches of the small mosque of Sīdī Sayyid. The mosque has a unique feature pierced stonework depicting patterns of natural trees and foliage, normally found only on brass and silver.

The Muslims built mosques and tombs out of the rubble, brick, and stone from Hindu temples in Kashmīr also. From time immemorial, however, wood was the principal building material in Kashmīr, which it still is. The Muslims in Kashmīr, as in other places, also incorporated many ancient Hindu architectural features into their monuments. The double-storeyed wooden mosque of Mīr Sayyid 'Alī Hamadāni stands on the masonry foundation of an ancient temple on the right bank of the Jhelam river in Srīnagar. Its low pyramidal roof is surmounted by an open pavilion from where the faithful are still called to prayer and over which rises the steeple with its finial. The Jāmi' mosque, founded by Sultan Sikandar, was built three times – in 1479, 1620, and 1674. It was rebuilt each time without changing the plan. The lofty colonnades around the court are screened by an arched façade, and each of the 378 pillars in the colonnades is made from a single deodar trunk.

The buildings in the Deccan are equally impressive. The Daulatābād mosque, built in 1318, is the earliest surviving specimen of its kind in the region. Its prayer chamber stands on 106 pillars and is roofed by a flattish corbelled dome. A few Irānī architects moved to Gulbarga and in collaboration with some Delhi and local architects created the Bahmanīd school of architecture, which concentrated on mass and ornamentation. The remains of Gulbarga fort show that it was a massive structure. The Jāmi' mosque in the fort, which has escaped destruction, is unique in many respects. In it the Indian and Irānian elements are so intertwined as to be indistinguishable. Unlike other Indian mosques, the whole structure is a vast pillared hall covered by a roof. There is no open courtyard. Large domes overhang each corner, while a central dome, raised on a clerestory, covers the *mirhāb* on the west side. The entire roof is covered by small domes arranged in seven rows. The tombs of the Bahmanīd kings largely follow the Tughluq style. Many mosques built in the Bahmanīd region are still intact.

The fort and palaces in Bīdar were built on the edge of the lateral scarp, overlooking the plain. They are also in a dilapidated condition, and only the rough cast remains; but they were finished in lime plaster and polished. The Irānian frescoes and the gold, red, and blue inscriptions, painted by Ahmad Shāh Wali (d. 1436), are most elegant. The most prominent monument is the *madrasa* (seminary) of Mahmūd Gāwān, built in 1472. It contains four three-storeyed wings enclosing an open court; at each corner of the façade stood two imposing minarets in three stages. Despite the magnitude of the elevation, the homogeneity and proportion of the structure is remarkable. The surface was decorated with brightly coloured encaustic tiles of geometrical, floral, and calligraphic patterns, only a few of which now survive.

The chevron patterning on the encaustic tilework and bold bands of Qur'ānic verses in the Chand Mīnār, built at Daulatabad in 1435, make it a typically Irānian monument. It is slightly tapered and rises in four stages to 30.50 metres.

In Amhadnagar the octagonal tomb of Salābat Khān, a minister under Sultan Murtazā I (1565–88), known as Chānd Bībī's palace, stands at the centre of an octagonal terrace on a picturesque hill site. The grandeur and elegance of the later Bahmanīd style were also repeated in the 'Adil Shāhi monuments in Bījāpūr. Their arches are flattened, like those of the Tudor style in England, and their domes emerge from a band of conventional petals, bulging slightly as they rise. The most remarkable is the Gol Gumbad (Round Dome) built by Muhammad 'Adil Shāh (1627-56) for his mausoleum. The plain outlines of the square structure, which supports the gigantic central dome, are broken by an enclosing row of small arches all around. Crowned with crenellations at the corners, and attached to the structure, stand six-sided towers with seven storeys of little arches, surmounted by bulbous domes. All these elements, however, are relegated to the background by the enormous hemispherical dome whose external diameter is about 44 metres – the largest dome in India.

The Qubt-Shāhī monuments in Golkonda also incorporate Indo-Irānian features from the Bahmanī and Bījāpūrī kingdoms. They are distinguished by large arches, ornamental façades, corner minarets, and bulbous domes. They are generally built of ashlar stone and brick-and-lime masonry. The foliage and entwining creepers of the Qutb-Shāhī stucco decorations exhibit considerable ingenuity, while the encaustic tiles and mother-of-pearl inlay in the stones are exquisite. Some of the Golkonda tombs are double-storeyed; 'Abdu'llāh Qutb Shāh's (d. 1672) mausoleum is a huge two-storeyed monument. The profusion of little minarets and cupolas suggests Hindu influence. The archway in Hyderābād called the Char

Mīnār (Four Mīnārets), however, is designed to symbolize the Shī'ī faith of the Qutb-Shāhi rulers. The four stately minarets, about 49 metres high, balance the four archways, one on each side of the square structure. A double screen of arcades of diminishing size helps to make the Char Mīnār more a piece of sculpture than of architecture. The mosque on the western end of the open roof is the embodiment of tranquillity and repose; it was completed about 1595. To the north of the Char Mīnār are four monumental portals measuring double the height of its arches. They are known as Chār Kamān.

Vijayanagara, on the south bank of the river Tungabhadra, is now in ruins, but the literary descriptions from both Irānī and European visitors are impressive. It was 'as large as Rome'; the king's palace enclosed 'a greater space than all the castles of Lisbon'. The city was surrounded by seven fortifications. The hall of audience comprised three spacious stages at different levels and was reached by elaborate flights of steps.[2] Although the halls and palaces no longer survive, some palace remains suggest the architectural glory of Vijayanagara. In a building known as the Elephant Stables, the Hindu and Muslim styles blend harmoniously. Its Islamic arches and façades projected balconies on brackets. The Hindu resurgence of the period is reflected in the large number of temples that are built. The continuous panels of sculpture on the walls illustrate various myths and legends, while the carved pillars constitute a major architectural scheme in the temple complex. In many pillars the shafts are merely the central core of involved groups of statues, chiselled entirely in the round, with a horse as the most conspicuous element. Varieties of lotuses with large seed-pods dominate the ceiling slab. The temple of Hazāra Rāma is an exquisitely carved small building and seems to have been the private chapel of the Vijayanagara kings. A group of exuberantly carved and highly polished squat stone pillars support the roof. Even the brackets, beams, and undersides of the ceilings are elaborately ornamented. In 1513 the Vitthalasvāmī temple was planned on a grandiose scale of about three times the size of Hazara Rama but it could not be completed. The main complex of this unfinished temple is a long rectangular structure, and the entire scheme, raised over a profusely ornamented stylobate, ends in deep roll cornices surmounted by parapets and pyramidal rootlets in brick and plaster. The *mandapas* or the halls in some of the Vijayanagara temples are very large. The Kalyāna *mandapa* at Vellore is the richest and most beautiful structure of its kind. Its piers not only exhibit the exuberance and ingenuity of the sculpture but also demonstrate the vigour and forcefulness of the kingdom.

THE LODĪ AND SŪR MONUMENTS

Returning again to north India, we find that Khān-i Jahān Maqbūl's tomb spired the Sayyid rulers (Mubārāk and Muhammad) and Sikandar Lodī to build octagonal tombs for their earthly remains. Sikandar's tomb stands in an extensive walled enclosure with an ornamental gateway. The inner and outer shell of the masonry, with a space left between the two in the dome of Sikandar's tomb, marks the beginning of the double dome. The technique was perfected by the Mughals. During the reigns of the Sayyids and Lodīs also many square-plan tombs were erected, but the Sūr family tombs at Sahasram in the Shāhabad district of Bihār are all octagonal. The architectural defects in early Sūr tombs were remedied in Sher Shāh's own mausoleum, which was built on a large lake and connected by a causeway to the guard rooms on the northern shore. The high plinth over which the massive octagonal tomb rises in three diminishing levels contains double stairways framed by corner pavilions and recessed windows. The crenellated parapet continuing the projecting eave of the arched first stage of the mausoleum has pillared kiosks of open pavilions in the corners. This serves to balance the magnitude and dimensions of the structure. The second storey is a plain wall with a pillared kiosk in each right angle, and the sixteen-sided drum of the dome forms the third level. The imposing dome and artistic finial give this ponderous structure a unique fascination. The interior of the mausoleum is simple; the ascending rows of arches diminish in height but increase in number, and the decoration is confined to the inscriptions on the western wall

Sher Shāh died before he could complete the capital he planned at Delhi, now known as the Purānā Qal'a (Old Fort). The gateways of the bastioned walls are built of red sandstone, picked out with white marble and tastefully embellished with blue glaze. Only the mosque built by Sher Shāh and the bastion-type structure known as the Sher Mandal survive. The flatness in the curve towards the crown of the arches in the mosque's façade and the co-ordination of the archway's members are very artistic and pleasing.

THE MUGHAL MONUMENTS

Bābur mentions his continued interest in erecting mosques and planting gardens in his autobiography. He built a mosque at Panipat and another at Sambhal, east of Delhi, but he was dissatisfied with the one he built in the old Lodī fort at Agra.[3] Humāyūn, in the first years of his reign, also erected many new buildings, but Sher Shāh destroyed Humāyūn's monuments.

The history of Mughal architecture therefore starts with Akbar. In 1564 Humāyūn's widow, Hajji Begum, settled in Delhi. There she built a tomb for her husband, under the supervision of Irānian architects, which synthesized Irānian and Indian architectural characteristics. In a large square garden, protected by high walls, an extensive sandstone square terrace, 6.71 metres in height, with arcaded sides, was built. In its centre stands Humāyūn's tomb, square in plan and faced with red sandstone picked out with marble. In the middle, facing each side, are four great arches, behind which open the tomb entrances. The space between each arch and the wall behind it is filled with Irānian conventional dappled work. Inside the tomb each corner is cut off and provided with an arch; and overall rises a magnificent dome, clad in white marble, dipping sharply to culminate in a delicate point. The vaulted ceiling of the main hall is covered by a second marble shell, making it a double dome. This device allows the ceiling to be hemispherical, whatever the outer shape of the dome.

In 1565 Akbar ordered the construction of a fort at Agra, containing several palaces. The north-western escarpment of the Sīkrī ridge was quarried for these works. Two massive octagonal towers flank the main entrance of the fort's walls on the west. It is known as the Delhi Gate. The front consists of an archway; at the back are arcaded terraces. The guard rooms are inside the gate. It is an improved model of the Elephant Gateway in Gwālior fort. Unfortunately the two free-standing stone elephants, which Akbar installed at the gate, were removed by Aurangzīb in 1669. He was unable, however, to interfere with the inlay panels above the second storey depleting fabulous animals – partly lion, partly horse, partly elephant, and some partly bird and duck. Other animal motifs were too prominent to be ignored but were also not destroyed. In fact, in previous centuries, a large number of monuments in Iraq and Irān were adorned with animal and human figures, yet the orthodox Muslims did not object. Aurangzīb finally bowed before cultural realities and left the animal forms in decorations untouched.

None of the 'five hundred buildings of masonry, after the beautiful designs of Bengal and Gujarāt', which according to Abu'l-Fazl were built in the fort, survive.[4] They were doubtless swept away by Shāhjahān, when he too altered the Delhi gate. The early Turkic conquerors had resorted to the trabeate style for want of master-masons trained in constructing arches and domes, but Akbar deliberately chose it, hoping to inject a Hindu atmosphere into his architectural enterprises. The Jahāngīrī Mahal in the Agra fort is the only surviving monument there from Akbar's reign. It is an uneasy blending of the design of the Mān Mandir with a Muslim palace, and the halls and rooms are irregular and confused. The carvings on the red sandstone brackets and balconies are largely patterned after wood chiselling. The brackets on the oblong top-storey chamber, which is surrounded by verandas, passages, and staircases and stands to the west of the central quadrangle, are, however, exquisitely carved with peacock and serpent motifs. The repetitions of geese, flamingos, and lotuses in the carvings throughout this storey make it a predominantly Hindu living-room. Early in his reign Akbar built a palace fortress at Lahore. In 1570 he constructed another at Ajmīr and in 1583 he completed a massive fort at Allahabad. In Fathpūr-Sīkrī, where Akbar lived for about twelve years, most of his important buildings have survived. The Jāmi' mosque there was completed in 1571–2. It was supervised by Akbar's patron saint, Shaykh Salīm Chishti, and it took five years to build. It is the principal and largest monument at Fathpūr. Towards the rear of the vast courtyard is the majestic arch of the central prayer chamber with three *mirhābs* in each of its seven bays. In 1580–1 Shaykh Salīm Chishti's tomb was completed, constructed on the spot where the Shaykh had prayed. The tomb was partly faced with marble. In the early years of Jahāngīr's reign, the outer marble screens were added, and the walkway was paved also with marble. In the south-east corner is a particularly fine marble screen, offering a sober yet delicate pattern of hexagons enclosed within an interlacing eight-foil ornament and, in turn, enclosing elaborate eight-pointed stars. The hollow brackets supporting the steeply sloping stone eaves are so finely worked that they suggest a supple yet stylized snake, a rare achievement in stonework. Over the cenotaph in the interior rises a most remarkable and beautiful catafalque. It has a framework made of or, at any rate, veneered thickly with ebony, supported at the four corners by elaborate capitals and surmounted by a domed roof.

In 1573 Akbar added the Buland Darwāza (Lofty Gateway) to the mosque, to commemorate his Gujarāt conquests. It was completed two years later. From the pavement in front of it, to the apex of the central pinnacle screening it, the arch of the Buland Darwāza is 40.84 metres high. The pavement itself is raised on vaulting 13.52 metres above the level of the road below; so the total height of the Buland Darwāza from the ground is 53.63 metres. It has few equals in size in Islamic architecture. Its large arched recesses in the centre, and its range of kiosks and cupolas, partly screened by perforated parapets, ensure the archway's artistic success, even from the decorational viewpoint.

The complex of palaces, offices, and halls of audience in Fathpūr-Sikrī also contains innumerable gems of structural and decorational ingenuity. The Anup Talao (Peerless Pool) was completed in 1575. At its north-east angle is a small but very decorative structure. Unfortunately, only the principal room and the 'lean-to' stone roof of the veranda survive. It has often been described as a 'superb casket'; the elaborate carvings on its brackets, friezes, coupled columns, pillars, pilasters, and piers make it appear the work of woodcarvers from Kashmīr rather than of stone-cutters. The luxuriant vegetation and the Chinese cloud forms on the dado panels were inspired by miniature paintings. In fact many stone-cutters at Akbar's court were also accomplished miniature artists. The structure itself is popularly known as the Turkish Sultāna's palace, but no lady could ever live in the neighbourhood of the halls meant for imperial use, since they were so public. Most of the identifications at Fathpūr-Sīkrī, as at other palaces, are figments of the ignorant guide's imagination. Although many structures towards the end of the vast courtyard have disappeared, two elegant chambers survive. One of the chambers is dominated by a massive and richly carved pillar which supports one of the most fantastic red stone capitals ever conceived. Possibly it was one of the treasuries built, according to Abu'l-Fazl, by Akbar, and not the 'Ibādat-Khāna or the Dīwān-i khāss.[5]

The ladies' palaces also occupy a vast area. The principal *haram sarā*, or ladies' palace, is known as Jodh Bā'i's palace. Its exterior is solemn and massive, and the entrance, once guarded by eunuchs, is double-storeyed. The passage leading to the harem passes through a dark vestibule, and turns sharply to the right, and then left, to prevent anyone seeing straight into the spacious quadrangle. The bases, columns, and capitals of the pillars in the central rooms are carved in the Hindu manner with small lozenges, pellets, semi-lotus rosettes, and bell-and-chain ornaments; the columns, first square in section, become octagonal, then sixteen-sided, and finally circular. However, there are marked differences in style and execution, despite a strong family resemblance in all of them.

A five-storeyed structure known as Panch Mahal (Five-Storeyed Palace) was originally connected with the principal ladies' palace. It seems to have been designed to allow the ladies to take the cool air unseen. It is also a unique structure, entirely columnar, consisting of four storeys of decreasing size disposed asymmetrically upon a ground floor, which contains eighty-four columns. The carvings on each of these columns, representing different mythological stories, are still unexplained. To the north-east of the principal ladies' palace stands an elegant house which was splendidly decorated throughout with paintings glowing with gold. It is now known as Maryam's Palace, after Akbar's mother, Maryam Makānī, but the golden paintings are commemorated in its other name – the Golden Palace. The carvings on the north side bracket show Rāma being worshipped by Hanūmān; another shows a pair of fat geese, while yet others depict elephants, geese, and rosettes.[6]

Although many other structures in the complex are also attractive, they cannot match the double-storeyed northern palace for the imperial harem, wrongly called Bīrbal's house. Its central core consists of four square rooms, of which the north-western and south-eastern ones have a domed upper room above, placed corner to corner. Each pilaster is finely carved in low relief with a pleasant geometrical pattern. The bases are cut with a deep double semi-circle enclosed in a fan-like halo. A Hindī inscription on a pier at the western side of the house says that the building was erected in Samvat 1629 to 1572. Few visitors notice this Hindu mason's pride in his work.

Before his death Akbar began to build his own tomb at Sikandara, near Agra. In 1607 Jahāngīr visited the site and decided that the work was not 'unique in the world'.[7] He therefore ordered some experienced architects to make a new plan, which he finally approved. It was finished in 1613 and, out of respect for Akbar's cultural ideals, it deliberately departed from the prevalent domed structures. Upon a high foundation rests an edifice of three diminishing arcaded galleries furnished with small pavilions, some of which are roofed with oblong pyramids. The fourth storey is open to the air and paved with white marble; in the middle stands the Emperor's cenotaph. The enclosure is walled with perforated marble screens surmounted by a frieze upon which the ninety-nine names of Allāh are carved. The Emperor's corpse was buried in a vault deep in the ground. The inlay on the main gateway contained Christian motifs, but Aurangzīb had them plastered over. The present gateway is an early twentieth-century structure.

In 1628 Nūr Jahān, Emperor Jahāngīr's wife, completed a tomb for her father, I'timādu'd-Dawla, by the Jamuna at Agra. In form it is not unlike a Turkish kiosk, being a double-storeyed and square marble structure. The central chamber, containing the cenotaph, is surrounded by a series of rooms and passages corresponding to an enclosed veranda. It is finished with four short but elegant minarets, standing on each corner of the mausoleum platform. Earlier Mughal monuments were adorned with white and black marble, but the art called *pietra dura*, the technique of inlaying mosaic with hard and precious stones such as lapis, onyx, jasper, topaz, and carnelian, commenced with I'timādu'd-Dawla's mausoleum. The profusion of wine-vessels, cups, flower vases, and scent bottles depicted on the walls offered many opportunities to the designer to display his ingenuity. The handles of some wine-vessels are serpents with birds' beaks, some are dragon-shaped, others depict a lion motif, and some are plain. Animal motifs on the inlays of flower vases include dancing peacocks, peacocks accompanied by peahens, fish, and even mice. Geometrical patterns and floral designs, however, predominate. The excessive decoration on the dados in the interior reflects the designer's immaturity in planning. Later on the Mughal designers learned to restrain themselves. Indeed, I'timādu'd-Dawla's tomb marks the transition from Jahāngīr's ornamental extravagance to Shāhjahān's finesse.

At Shāhadra near Lahore, the elegant octagonal minarets in five stages, on the corners of the lofty platform of Jahāngīr's tomb, hide the mausoleum's structural defects. The marble pavilion in the middle of its terraced roof was a graceful addition but it no longer survives. Near Jahāngīr's tomb stands the mausoleum of Shāhjahān's father-in-law, Āsaf Khān, who died in 1641. Its marble facing has disappeared, but the surviving ornamentation of tile-work on the exterior walls indicates the intended contrast with the marble. The grandeur of the monument has not waned.

Shāhjahān greatly admired white marble and he destroyed earlier buildings in Agra fort to make way for his own monuments, which used it more extensively. He built a broad marble-paved embankment between some rocky hills at Ajmīr to hold an artificial lake which he decorated with a series of elegant kiosks. He also constructed various palaces at Ajmīr and Delhi. The Dīwān-i 'Āmm (Hall of Public Audience), which he built in Agra fort on his accession in 1627, set a model for posterity, and his own subsequent buildings are also derived from it. Its square pillars support ornate arches edged with small projections which incline into small ogees. The surface of the pillars and the walls is panelled with shallow arches in the same style. The hall itself has elegant double columns and a Bengal-style curved roof covered in copper. The roof is finished, rather artificially, with bronze finials projecting at right angles from the curve. The design was repeated in the curved overhanging eaves on the pavilion on the top of the Musamman Būrj or 'Eight-Sided Bastion'. The Būrj's dados are framed by inlays which resemble the Mughal painted borders. On the dados themselves the carved plants merge naturally with each other. The effect of a stylized garden is reinforced by the fountain in the lotus basin on one of the verandas.

Shāhjahān's most celebrated building is the Tāj Mahal on the left bank of the Jamuna in Agra. Built as a tomb for his wife, Mumtāz Mahal (d. 1631), it marks the culmination of the evolving garden tombs. The three-storeyed gate of the Tāj, opening to the south, has a massive archway. The upper lines in the ornamental inscriptions decorating the archway, which one would expect to appear smaller, seem just the same size as the lower ones.

The tomb itself, set in a lovely garden and clad in glistening white marble from Makrān in Jodhpūr, is reflected in a long narrow pool of water in front. On the other side it overlooks the flowing river Jamuna. To the west rises a contrasting red sandstone mosque, and opposite stands its duplicate, a hall known as a *jawāb* (answer). Framing the tomb are four graceful minarets crowned with eight-windowed cupolas, their white marble revetment picked out with black stone in imitation of mortar. The dome, bulging gently before dipping towards its gilded bronze finial and rising from a plain broad band fringed with conventional petals, dominates the tomb. The square tomb has chamfered corners, framed by two broad arches. The Tāj's magnificent recessed central arch leads into a smaller arch containing an entrance door and filled with marble screens. This opens into the dark octagonal tomb chamber, lit only by the light filtering through the screens and the high glazed windows. Another elegant marble screen encloses the finely cut marble cenotaphs of the Emperor and Empress. The chamber's hemispherical ceiling is the low face of the second dome enclosed within the outer shell. The conventional foliage on the outer walls of the cenotaph and their surrounding screen is depicted in the finest *pietra dura* work and bas-relief. The impression of richness, surpassing that of I'timādu'd-Dawla's tomb, derives from the increased use of semi-precious stones such as lapis lazuli and carnelian, although the work is in fact not so ornate.

This is the most famous building in India and is known throughout the world. Its glory springs from a perfection of balance and proportion such as few other buildings anywhere possess. On passing through the gateway the first sight of this great white tomb, reflected in the pool and surrounded by a beautiful garden, produces an intense aesthetic thrill that no other building can give. This is not the ordinary world; rather, it reflects the heaven of the Islamic mystic, a perfection and security beyond space and time. Most other tombs are earthbound by comparison.

Shāhjahān next concentrated on devising the palace buildings which would overlook the Jamuna and run along the eastern wall of his new fort at Shāhjahānābād (Delhi). He built an elegant Dīwān-i 'Āmm which contains a two-storeyed pavilion studded with semi-precious stones. The Peacock Throne stood on its upper storey. The restrained decoration was intended to create an atmosphere of awe and grandeur so that the *mansabdārs*, standing with bated breath, would concentrate their gaze on the glittering throne and the *pietra dura* glowing in the alcove above it.

The adjacent Dīwan-i Khāss (Hall of Private Audience) has an arcaded façade of five arches. It contains an exquisite marble screen surmounted by a black inlay depiction of the scales of justice. It is extremely well proportioned, and its massive piers, supporting foliated arches, harmonize with the flat roof they carry. Both the walls and ceilings were decorated with gold, and *pietra dura* inlays added to the brilliance of its walls. This unique structure, where gold ran riot, was nevertheless relegated to the background by the Rang Mahal (Delightful Palace), the Emperor's private apartment. Unfortunately all traces of the beautiful ornamentation in the Rang Mahal have long since disappeared. A marble water-channel connected with the Nahr-i Bihisht (Canal of Paradise), which entered the fort through a sluice, runs through the central apartment of the Rang Mahal. Its dry fountains, enclosed in lotus-shaped basins, earlier sprinkled water in the shape of a flower. Little remains of this lost glory, but the literary sources pay glowing tribute to the splendour of the Rang Mahal.

In 1644 work commenced on the Jāmi‘ Masjid. It dominates the landscape, rising on a lofty terraced base on sloping ground, with three majestic flights of steps leading to the gates of its great courtyard. A row of little kiosks, finished with white marble cupolas, edge the gateway parapets. The prayer chamber rests on massive piers and is covered by three large white domes. Although they look most impressive from behind, rising above the plain red wall with engrailed arches in low relief, from the front they become confused with the surrounding parapets, because the band at their base is too narrow.

The Moti Masjid (Pearl Mosque) in Agra fort, built in white marble by Shāhjahān in 1654, is also disproportionate, and so is Aurangzīb's marble mosque built in Delhi fort in 1659, although it is a charming miniature. Its slightly exaggerated round domes and the awkward disparity between height and breadth hint at an impending decline in aesthetic standards. The Bādshāhī mosque at Lahore, despite its grandeur, illustrates the final degeneration of Mughal architecture. The row of foliated arches seems too small to support the vast façade of the prayer chamber, while the three mediocre bulbous domes hover uncertainly, too small to be ignored and not large enough to merit attention. The corner minarets, recently restored, however, have helped to integrate the building.

MUGHAL GARDENS

Gardens were very popular in Irān, and Bābur transplanted his love for them into Indian soil. Remnants of his Ārām Bāgh, or Garden of Repose, can still be seen in Agra. The Mughal formal square garden is divided into quarters by paved paths radiating from a central square on which a pavilion usually stood; hence the name 'fourfold plot' or *chār bāgh.* Gardens were included in all Mughal palaces and tombs, and many were laid out purely for enjoyment. Shāhjahān completed the Shalīmār Gardens in Lahore in 1637, and Jahāngīr cultivated many in his favourite summer retreat, the Vale of Kashmīr. Fountains normally featured in these gardens; one can imagine how delightful and fresh they must have appeared to the Mughals seeking shelter from the heat and dust of Hindustan.

PAINTING

The art of painting was condemned by orthodox Muslim opinion, which considered that it blasphemously imitated God's creativity. It was therefore not fostered by religion, but depended upon royal patronage. In Irān, which had a long artistic heritage in this sphere, it developed rapidly.

The invasion of Irān by the nomadic Mongols, in the first quarter of the thirteenth century, resulted in the introduction of a strong Chinese influence. In the fourteenth century Irānian painters merely imitated the Chinese landscapes and confined their art to illustrating history, epic, and romance. They had no sense of perspective or depth. Their figures were two-dimensional stereotypes, and their settings were formal and stylized.

Shirāz (in southern Irān) was an important artistic centre in the fifteenth century. Many painters moved first there and then on to the Indian Muslim courts in Gujarāt, Mālwa, Jaunpūr, and the Deccan. This movement brought about the cross-fertilization of Shīrāzī and Indian art techniques which upset the rigid application of theoretical rules to contemporary Indian painting. A major watershed in Perso-Islamic painting is the *Ni'mat-nāma*, or *Cookery Book*, illustrated in Mālwa in the early sixteenth century. In it the Indian rounded body contours are displayed against a background of Shirazi formalized leaves and luxuriant vegetation.

The stiff Irānian forms also underwent considerable change. Bihzād (1450–1536), a painter at the Tīūrid court of Sultan Husayn Mīrzā of Hirat, after studying human and animal life, fostered a naturalistic approach. The conventional stereotypes gave way to lively expressive figures in spatially organized groups. Bihzād was gifted with skill and originality in line drawing. His painting was distinctive in the frequency of low-toned browns and the lively combination of blues and greens with touches of bright red. His colour schemes were conventional, however, and the skies remained unchanged. His techniques were developed by his disciples, but none of them attained his mastery. Although he signed his miniatures, forgeries still appeared.

Bihzād's school remained influential, and a considerable number of talented Irānian painters, representing its best trends, gathered around Humāyūn during his exile in Irān, although his resources were slender. They included Sayyid 'Alī, Mullā 'Abdu's-Samad, and Mullā Dūst Muhammad. 'Abdu's-Samad was appointed tutor to the young Prince Akbar by Humāyūn. Akbar enjoyed painting although he neglected his more formal lessons.

In about 1567 Akbar ordered the preparation of a lavishly illustrated manuscript of the Persian translation of the *Hamza-nāma*, the celebrated Arab epic about a legendary Hamza (not the Prophet's uncle, Hamza bin 'Abdu'l-Muttalib). Sayyid 'Alī and 'Abdu's-Samad were appointed to lead a group of roughly one hundred painters. The project took fifteen years to complete, and most of the Indian painters who founded the Mughal school were trained during that period. By the end of the sixteenth century they had successfully synthesized ancient Indian plasticity with the Bihzad school's symmetry and proportion.

The *Hamza-nāma* had 1,004 illustrated pages in its twelve volumes. The extant pages in Eastern and Western libraries provide a fascinating study of early Mughal painting in India, which initially followed the Bihzād school. Paintings made in the second half of Akbar's reign exhibit elements peculiar to India in costumes, buildings, and plant life, and a Mughal-Rājpūt colouring pervades the Irānian-Arab environment. The *Tūtī-nāma* (in the Chester Beatty Library, Dublin), illustrated in the 1580s, also contains vivid representations of plants, flowers, animals, and men.

Mughal miniature painting, although based on the Irānian style, derives its distinctive character from indigenous painters whom Akbar employed. Until recently, apart from the *N'imat-nāma*, some Jain paintings, and the continuation of Pāla and Kashmīr art in Nepal and Tibet, no specimens of Indian painting between the thirteenth and sixteenth centuries were available. Now, however, some illustrated manuscripts by the court painters to the provincial rulers in Mālwa and Jaunpūr have been discovered. These show how painting has always been part of Indian culture. As soon as Akbar offered his patronage, many local artists thronged the imperial court. According to Abu'l-Fazl, 'Few, indeed, in the whole world are found equal to them.'[8]

One of the leading painters at Akbar's court was a potter's son, Daswanth. He used to paint figures on walls, and Akbar, impressed by his talent, sent him to 'Abdu's-Samad around 1575. His illustrations of the Persian translation of the *Mahābhārata* now belong to the Raja of Jaipur. Another painter, Basāwan, was equally talented. Abu'l-Fazl claims that he excelled in 'preparing backgrounds, drawing of features, distribution of colours, portrait painting and in several other branches'. Abu'l-Fazl refers by name to only thirteen Hindu and five Muslim painters, although Akbar employed more than one hundred artists. Many signatures on the 112 large miniatures from the *Tārīkh-i Khāndān-i Tīmūriyya* in the Khudābakhsh Library in Patna have been cut off by the careless binders.[9] Out of the fifty-one legible names, only nine are Muslims, of whom three are Kashmīris. Of the six Hindus, one originated in Gwālior, four others came from Gujarāt, while another was also a stone-cutter.

The *Tārīkh-i Khāndān-i Tīmūriyya* is not an original work, because it contains extracts relating to Indian history taken from the *Tarīkh-i Alfī*, completed around 1592. These extracts were probably lifted from an earlier draft of the *Tarīkh-i Alfī* in order to start the illustrations as soon as possible. Thus the paintings were prepared in the 1590s. A study of the signatures shows that in some instances the drawing was done by one artist and the colouring by another. In rare cases the outline was sketched in by one artist, the features were delineated by a second, and the faces were modelled in depth by a third. The work was designed to form a Tīmūrīd album covering the reign of Tīmūr and his successors down to Akbar's time. The first miniature depicts Tīmūr as a child playing with his younger comrades and assuming the position of a king. Of the Indian themes, the most interesting are Bābur's rejoicing at Humāyūn's birth, when the Emperor invites his chiefs and nobles to a grand feast. Another miniature presents Humāyūn's accession to the throne. The miniature depicting his campaign against Champānīr shows Humāyūn, followed by Bayram Khān and thirty-nine commanders, ascending the fort at night, and also the slaughter of the garrison. The scene of Akbar's birth is a masterpiece; Akbar's mother, dressed in a green robe, lies exhausted on a couch, and the baby Akbar is seen in the arms of a nurse with a high conical Tātār cap. The background shows rejoicing throughout the palace. The lower part of the painting shows how the news is transmitted to Humāyūn.

Abu'l-Fazl mentioned the titles of nine works which Akbar's court painters illustrated. Except for one, all have been saved from destruction. Of these the *Bābur-nāma*, dated 1597, is in the National Museum, New Delhi. Another illustrated copy, in the British Museum, was completed about the same time. The *Akbar-nāma*, a copy of which is in the Victoria and Albert Museum, London, and the Chester Beatty Library, Dublin, and the *Razm-nāma* (the Persian translation of the *Mahābhārata*) in the personal collection of the Raja of Jaipur, provide the best specimens of sixteenth- and early seventeenth-century miniature painting.

The scenes in the *Bābur-nāma* are a living memorial to Mughal vigour in battle and siege. They explicitly portray Bābur's dynamic leadership. Some miniatures vividly highlight Bābur's keen interest in everyday life; Indian animals are painted on the basis of his own descriptions. The exuberance of details in figure and animal drawing in the *Razm-nāma* is also remarkable. Among other things this text portrays the colourful Rājpūt costumes and ornaments. The 117 miniatures in the *Akbar-nāma* in the Victoria and Albert Museum present an exciting panorama of the many facets of Akbar's age.

The court painters had become aware of European miniature painting by the last years of Akbar's reign. In 1607 Father Jerome Xavier presented the Emperor Jahāngīr with an Irānian version of the Lives of the Apostles, *Dāstān-i Ahwāl-i Hawāriyān*, which had been painted in India in the Italian style. Jahāngir's artistic interests inspired his artists to draw upon European paintings for inspiration, and many copies were made of the miniature portrait by the famous and talented Isaac Oliver which King James I of England presented to the Emperor, through the ambassador Sir Thomas Roe, in 1615. Gradually the flat and clear-cut Irānian figures were abandoned for European line shading and chiaroscuro. In the late sixteenth and early seventeenth centuries a clear sense of realism emerges in Mughal painting. The sixteenth-century Italian style of painting particularly influenced Miskīn, who in 1595 illustrated the story of 'the unfaithful wife' in the *Bahāristān* of Jāmī.

The works of painters during Jahāngīr's reign, such as Abu'l-Hasan, Manohar, Bishun Dās, Goverdhan, Mansūr, and Dawlat, show the crystallization of European, Indian, and Irānian artistic trends. This combination provided the ground for individuality and distinctive characteristics in late Mughal painting. Jahāngīr himself particularly admired portraits. Individuals were usually presented either in profile or in a three-quarter stance, against a turquoise or dark-green background. Two fine examples of group portraits are the scene of an audience (*c.* 1619), now in the Boston Museum of Fine Arts, and the scenes of the weighing ceremony of Prince Khurram (later Shāhjahān), now in the British Museum.

One of the imperial artists, Mansūr, specialized in painting rare animals and birds, while Pidārath and 'Ināyat also skilfully depicted subjects from the animal and vegetable worlds. Many court painters captured scenes of Jahāngīr's hunting prowess. The animals are in characteristic poses and stand amidst distant hills. After 1615 Jahāngīr is represented in some miniatures as superhuman, shown surrounded by the halo reminiscent rather of Italian paintings of Christian saints than of the haloes of gods.

Most of Jahāngīr's well-known artists remained at Shāhjahān's court. The most important painters in hiṣ reign were Kalyān Das (alias Chaturman), Anūp Chitr, Rāi Anūp, Manohar, Muhammad Nādir Samarqandī, Mīr Hāshim, and Muhammad Faqīru'llah Khān. They improved colour techniques and used more subtle shades. Their subjects were realistic scenes from everyday life, such as dancers, concerts, and firework displays, although themes illustrating emotional tensions and noble sentiments were also popular. The Emperor's son, Dārā Shukoh, also displayed an interest in European art, and his artists were strongly influenced by European techniques. His album is preserved in the India Office Library in London.

Aurangzīb's rule, however, heralded a period of decline. He withdrew imperial patronage, and many artists were forced to work for the nobles, who did not pay well. A sense of stagnation developed. A surviving painting of Aurangzīb shows him as a haloed, mounted figure receiving a sword from a saint. An orthodox Muslim, he ordered that all the wall paintings be plastered over. After his death, the dynasty also began to decline. His successors were interested in fine art but they lacked the resources to maintain peace and order, let alone to patronize artists. Most artists migrated to the west Himalayas bordering the Panjāb and worked in the more peaceful dominions of the hill chieftains.

The Mughal court frequently left the capital city, either for military reasons or on hunting expeditions. Jahāngīr in particular periodically visited his Kashmīr retreat. This led to a productive mingling of the Mughal court style with that of the local artists, and interesting provincial styles developed. The most notable were the Rājasthān schools, whose paintings are the work of indigenous artists. The painters at the courts of the chieftains in Bundelkand, Rājasthān, and the Himalayan foothills were also stimulated by the changing artistic trends in the Mughal court. Their themes were inspired by both literature, such as the *Purānas*, the *Rāmāyana*, and the *Mahābhārata* and daily life in the towns and villages. The legends of Krishna were a most popular subject, and Shiva's dance was also often portrayed. Greater contact with the Mughal court resulted in new themes of court life and the relations between the Rājpūt princes and the Mughal rulers.

A unique and interesting synthesis was the symbolic representation of musical modes in Rājpūt painting. *Rāgas* are a series of notes on which a melody is based. Grammatically and symbolically they are masculine, and the *rāginīs* or lesser modes are feminine, looked on as the wives of the *rāgas.* They were personified and associated with particular scenes from Hindu mythology. Many of these were obtained from romantic-devotional literature, especially the stories of Krishna. The *Rāgamāla* (*Garland of Song*) paintings depict *rāgas* and *rāginīs* in their emotive settings, usually in a series of thirty-six scenes. Each melodic root form was symbolically assigned a specific colour, which remained constant in all compositions. The functions and qualities of the melodic roots determined the mood of their representation. The Rājpūt court painters improved upon earlier traditions, as shown by a comparison of figures in their *Rāgamāla* paintings with those in the *Laur Chanda* or *Chandāyan* (an eastern Hindī ballad by Mullā Dāwūd). The synthesis of the Mughal and Rājpūt way of life pervades customs, manners and fashions. The *rāginīs* were portrayed as Mughal ladies sitting under blossom-covered branches, but these are invariably the branches of Indian trees. Different Rājpūt states, such as Jaipur, Jodhpūr, Mewar, Būndī, and Kishangarh, developed schools of miniature painting with specific characteristics.

Medieval wall paintings are also interesting. In south India attempts at perspective are noticeable in the fragments in remote temples and in some frescoes from the Chola period in the great temple at Tanjore. Perspective was abandoned in the Vijayanagara period (1336–1565), in whose wall paintings the naturally hidden further eye protrudes from the profiles of the vigorous, richly dressed figures. Similar figures were painted in the nineteenth century under royal patronage on the walls of the maharajas' palaces in Trivandrum and Cochin. A cruder version appears on the ceiling of a Jain temple near Kānchīpuram, on the walls of some of the courtyards of the Mīnākshi temple at Madurai and even in Tīpū Sultan's summer pavilion at Seringapatam, where the outer walls are covered with scenes of his war against the British. There is no real development, however, and the work is indistinguishable from contemporary folk art. In fact, it bears a close resemblance to the soldiers and maidens, and lions and elephants, nowadays painted in vivid colours on white-walled Rājpūt houses. Unfortunately little is known of the history of wall painting under the Deccan Muslim rulers. The frescoes on the palaces of the Qutb-Shāhī sultans of Golkonda fell to Aurangzīb's fierce orthodoxy, leaving no trace.

MUSIC

In writing about medieval Indian music we are at a disadvantage in that there was no system of musical notation capable of recording anything more than the bare structure of a piece of music. From the sixteenth century onwards European musical compositions were regularly written down, but even here many of the finer points in their execution are lost. The situation in India was much worse. Only the basic notes of a melody could be recorded, and the subtle ornamentation and variations of the basic theme are lost forever. We can separate performances of Bach and Scarlatti approximately as they were intended. The music of such a great performer and composer as Tansen is completely lost to us.

Unlike architecture and painting, pre-Islamic music in Arabia was relatively advanced. As a result of their conquests, the music of the Arabs was rapidly impregnated with Byzantine and Irānian musical influences. Books on musical theory and performance, including works by the philosophers al-Kindī, al-Fārābī, and Avicenna, were written in Arabic. At the end of the twelfth century two books in Persian are said to have been produced for Mu'izzu'd-Din Muhammad Sām. Dancing was also a recognized art form, as Baranī's description of the revelries at Sultan Mu'izzu'd-Dīn Kayqabād's court suggests. The mere memory of the musicians and dancers at Sultan Jalālu'd-Dīn Khaljī's court was sufficient to transport the aged Baranī to the realm of youthful passions. According to Amīr Khusraw, however, it was Indian music that burnt the heart and soul and was superior to that of all other. He claimed that it was so difficult that foreigners, even after a stay of thirty or forty years in the country, could not play a single Indian tune correctly.[10]

The cross-fertilization of Perso-Arab and Indian music had started even before the conquest of Irān by the Arabs. It is said that the Sasanid monarch Bahrām Gūr

(421–39) established colonies of 10,000 singers and dancers from Hindustan all over his country.[11] They may have been the ancestors of the gypsies who later spread to Byzantium and Europe. In the thirteenth century many Hindu musicians and artisans were converted to Islam. Although the courts offered them patronage and livelihood, many musicians preferred to serve the sūfis, who were also connoisseurs of music, and who sharpened the talents of the musicians. Many distinguished musicians thronged sūfi gatherings both to earn a livelihood and to gain religious merit.

Even as early as the thirteen century, the sūfis considered Indian classical music and poetry more effective than Persian.[12] The latter was not neglected, however, and the flood-gates of opportunity were opened for the development of a new form of music, pioneered by Amīr Khusraw, which may be called Indo-Persian. Amīr Khusraw was a favourite of both Shaykh Nizāmu'd-Dīn Awliya' and the Delhi sultans. After Sultan 'Ala'u'd-Dīn Khaljī's conquest of the Deccan, many distinguished musicians from that region moved to Delhi. Amīr Khusraw seized the opportunity to study the Deccanī music of the Karnātaka school, which preserved the musical tradition of ancient India with greatest purity. Among the Deccanī migrants, the most prominent was Naīk Gopāl. The literary sources recount several stories of the encounter between him and Amīr Khusraw. What emerges is the fact that Amīr Khusraw could successfully copy and adapt the most difficult Deccanī classical music to his own technique and style. Amīr Khusraw is said to have written several treatises on music. In his third volume of poems, entitled *Ghurrat al-kamāl* and completed in 1294, Khusraw wrote that he had already produced three volumes of poetry and could easily write three more on music.[13] Unfortunately, none of them was written, although he frequently refers to melodies and musical instruments in his other works. Rather surprisingly, he never mentions the *sitār* (a long-necked lute, now the most popular instrument of north India), which is popularly regarded as his invention. Later works credit him with inventing about nineteen melodic forms, of which *khyāl*, *tarāna*, and *qawl* are the most noteworthy.

Khyāl in Arabic means 'imagination', 'reflection', or 'meditation'. The musical rhythms (*tālas*) in *khyāl* allow considerable variation and manipulation, so a *khyāl* musician is able to project his own personality effectively. *Tarāna* is a form of singing which uses meaningless syllables to escape the bonds of language and treats the voice purely as a musical instrument. It is usually sung in fast tempo and is similar to the south Indian *tillana*. *Qawl* is the precursor of the Muslim sūfī music called *qawwālī*. It was designed to adapt ancient Indian musical rhythms to Persian or Arabic verses.

The continued interest in both Indian and Persian music is reflected in two important works written by an anonymous author during Fīrūz Shāh's reign. Both works were dedicated to the author's patron, Malik Abū Raja, the governor of Gujarāt from 1374 to 1375. Abū Raja, according to his protege, was a connoisseur of both Persian and Indian music and organized discussions between the expert musicians at his court. The author, who was elderly, had already translated into

Persian and Arabic book on music entitled *Kitāb Fārighu'z-zamān fi ma'rifat al-ilhān.* The only known copy of this work is the *Ghunyatu 'l-munya*, which is in the India Office Library, London. It is based on seven Sanskrit works, three of which must have been destroyed.[14] Of the surviving books, *Sangītaratnakara* by Sārngadeva (1210–47), a musician to the Yadava kings of Devagirī, is a monumental study which stimulated many experts to write commentaries on it. Besides drawing upon these and various other sources, the author of *Ghunyatu 'l-munya* makes valuable comments on contemporary musical trends and informs us of some important developments in his own time. For example, he says that the finger-board of the *bīn* or *vīna* (the form of lute still current in south India) was enlarged to accommodate twenty-one note-points marked over it at larger intervals than before. This, he contended, radically promoted musical development.

The rulers of the regional kingdoms in the fifteenth and sixteenth centuries were also great patrons of music. In 1420 a musical treatise, *Sangītaśiromanī*, was dedicated to Ibrāhim Shāh Sharqī of Jaunpūr. Husayn Shāh Sharqī (1458–79) was a musical expert and devised many notes, scales, and melodies, of which Husaynī or Jaunpūrī is very famous. He composed an Arabic air known as 'Zangula' or 'Jangla' and is credited with making improvements to 'Khyal'. In Kashmīr, Sultan Zaynu'l-'Ābidīn's patronage of musicians was responsible for the compilation of a commentary on the *Sangītaratnākara.*

Raja Mān Singh Tomar of Gwālior (1450–1528) was himself a skilled musician as well as a patron of musicians. He transposed the dassical material form known as *dhrupad* (Sanskrit: *dhruvapada*) into Hindī. The musical rhythms of *dhrupad* are analogous to the poetic rhythm of Greek and Latin hexameter. The typical musical rhythm of this style is known as *chawtāla* because four of its six bars (*padas*) are strongly accented. At his instigation his court musicians researched the rules governing *rāgas* and enunciated them with greater precision. Their work was put into book form and entitled the *Mān Kautuhal* (*Curiosities of Raja Mān*). Mān Singh's musicians publicized their results in various other Indian courts. One of the musicians, Baijū, known as Bāora (Crazy), moved to the Court of Bahādur Shāh of Gujarāt and is said to have composed the melody 'Bahādurī' to commemorate his patron's name.

The fifteenth century is marked by even more significant de-velopments in the realm of devotional music. A classical melodic form emerged for the songs of Kabīr which was known as Kabīra'ī. Another development was the invention of a special vocal form for the Vaishnavite songs, known as Bishunpad. Changes were also made to various notes and airs to harmonize them with the hymns of Bāba Nānak, the founder of Sikhism, who was always accompanied by his Muslim minstrel Mardāna, a specialist in devotional music.

The last Delhi sultans and the Mughals were also great patrons of music. The *Lahjāt-i Sikandarī*, written under Sultan Sikandar's patronage, is a notable contribution to classical music. Akbar's court musicians were both male and female, Hindus, Iranīs, Tūranīs, and Kashmīris. Abu'l-Fazl names thirty-six musicians who played vocal and instrumental music at Akbar's court; of these ten were from Gwālior. They were divided into seven ranks. The leading singer was Miyān Tān Sen of Gwālior (1555–1610), and according to Abu'l-Fazl, India had not seen a singer of his talent for the last thousand years.[15] The literary sources recount fantastic anecdotes of the effects of his *dīpaka* (lamp) *rāga*. It was believed that Tan Sen's melodies could make rain fall out of season, while his *rāgas* were supposed to set candles alight. He is, however, blamed for introducing a Persian influence into Hindu music.

Shāhjahān cultivated music in his court and himself acquired considerable proficiency in the art. For the first ten years of his reign Aurangzīb generously rewarded his musicians and appeared to be devoted to music. From 1668, however, he tried to suppress it, although his sons and nobles continued their patronage.[16] The greatest contribution to musical theory during this period was the *Tuhfatu 'l-Hind*, written by Mirza Muhammad ibn Fakru'd-Dīn Muhammad for Aurangzīb's grandson, Prince Muhammad Mu'izzu'd-Dīn Jahāndar Shāh, who reigned from 1712 to 1713. During Muhammad Shāh's reign (1719–48) Mughal military and political glory declined rapidly, but music reached a new peak. The Emperor often performed himself, being expert in both singing and dancing.

The Deccan courts also cultivated music and dancing. Ibrāhīm 'Ādil Shāh II of Bījāpūr was both poet and musician. His poems, collected in the *Kitāb-i Nawras* (The Sanskrit *Navarasa – The Nine Emotions*), were designed to be sung in different *ragas* which are identified as *maqāms* (modes) in the Perso-Arabic system. Perso-Arabic music seems also to have considerably influenced the Deccanī Karnātaka music at the Vijayanagara court. Kallina acknowledges its influence in his commentary on the *Sangītaratnākara* in the mid-fifteenth century – as does Rāmāmāya, a minister of the Vijayanagara King Rāma Raya, in his well-known treatise, *Svaramelakalānidhi*, written in 1550.

The continued devotion of the musicians to the sūfīs, particularly the Chishtiyya sūfīs, stimulated the classical style of music. Famous musicians were proud to play before Shaykh Bahā'u'd-Dīn of Barnāwa (d. 1628) and frequently visited him. In his old age Tān Sen is also said to have performed before the Shaykh and to have sent his son to sit at the Shaykh's feet. According to the Shaykh, *dhrupad*, invented by Raja Mān Singh, was a disservice to the classical forms of music and was designed to cheapen the art. The Shaykh, accompanied by his carpenters, would personally select the wood from local forests for musical instruments, which were made to his own specifications and under his supervision. Of all his inventions the most interesting was a musical instrument in the shape of a pen case (*qalamdān*) which opened to reveal a series of strings and pegs. This instrument; which the Shaykh called a *sāzkhyāl*, soon became popular. Unfortunately, none of the instruments described in his biography survive. The accounts of his contributions to the development of music, together with those of Hindu mystics and other sūfīs, are culturally very revealing, however. It is also remarkable that the Shaykh succeeded in establishing contact with Hindu devotees in the Deccan who were expert in Karnātaka music.[17]

CONCLUSION

THE history of the eighth to twelfth centuries in northern India is, in the words of *The Wonder That Was India*, Volume I,

> a rather drab story of endemic warfare between rival dynasties.... In the 9th and 10th centuries the Gurjara-Pratihāras, who probably originated in Rājasthān, were masters of Kānyakubja, and the most powerful kings of northern India. They successfully resisted the Arabs, who, in 712, had occupied Sind, and who, for over a century, made frequent attacks on their eastern neighbours.*

Except during the Mauryan period, political unity was unknown, and the highly organized and tightly controlled administration of the ancient Indian state had no counterpart in inter-state relations, where endemic anarchy was only mitigated by a tradition of fair play in warfare, which was by no means always followed.

> Akbar was the greatest ruler ever to have governed India.... This is written advisedly with Asoka in mind. We know only the 'public image' which Asoka chose to present and thus we have no valid means of comparing Asoka's moral greatness with that of Akbar. Judged by results, however, Akbar was a far greater ruler than Asoka, since Asoka's reforms ended and his empire disintegrated with his death, while Akbar established a regime which lasted in full force for over a century after him and laid down principles of government which are still more or less valid in contemporary India.†

The ground was prepared for Akbar, however, by the Delhi sultans. Iltutmish carved out the north-west boundary of the Delhi sultanate, which he consolidated as far as Bengal and Assam in the east. Although the Mongols devastated the Muslim lands west of the Indus, the peace and prosperity of Iltutmish's reign made India a rendezvous for intellectuals, military leaders, and holy men from Irān and Central Asia. After his death, the religious classes supported Iltutmish's daughter, Raziyya, but the Turkic clique overthrew her. The subsequent scramble for power among this group plunged the country into anarchy. Balban, who emerged triumphant, destroyed the strength of the other Turkic leaders. His understanding of the problems of foreign rule on Indian soil was realistic. Thus, although he shed

* *The Wonder That Was India*, London, 1954, pp. 670; Ibid, p. 77.

† A. L. Basham, Foreword to *Fathpūr· Sīkrī* by S.A. A. Rizvi and V. J. A. Flynn, Bombay 1975, p. VII.

some crocodile tears at his inability to govern the country by orthodox Islamic principles, he evolved firm administrative laws on the basis of expediency, and the *sharī'a* (Islamic law) was not allowed to override considerations of *jahāndārī* (worldly administration) and *jahāngīrī* (world conquest).

Balban's ideals were firmly implemented by 'Ala'u'd-Dīn Khaljī, who ascended the throne by treacherously assassinating his uncle and father-in-law, after amassing vast riches from his conquest of Devagiri in western Deccan. He subsequently conquered Rājasthān and Gujarāt and extended his rule in the Deccan to Madurai. The revenue reforms and price-control system he introduced made the rural areas and the capital interdependent.

The next great ruler, Muhammad bin Tughluq, wished to assert his authority over the regions under the Mongols, but his schemes were misunderstood and unimaginatively implemented by his officials. His energies and resources were needlessly frittered away in suppressing rebellions. An independent Muslim kingdom consequently arose at Madurai, lasting till it was overthrown by the newly established Hindu kingdom of Vijayanagara. In central Deccan the Muslim Bahmanīd kingdom which came into being lasted for about 170 years. After its dismemberment, five independent sultanates were established in the Deccan. Of these, Ahmadnagar, Bījāpūr, and Golkonda remained autonomous for more than 150 years, and before long their capitals became prosperous towns, attracting merchants and adventurers from Arabia, Ethiopia, Irān, and Transoxiana.

Muhammad bin Tughluq's successor, Fīrūz Shāh, restored the authority of the Delhi sultanate over Bengal and Sind, but Tīmūr's invasion in 1398–9 again fragmented India. Innumerable Muslim provincial dynasties emerged; the Rājpūt rajas of Rājasthān in particular became very powerful.

In 1526 Bābur, who was descended from Tīmūr on his father's side and from Chingīz through his mother, founded the Mughal empire, but his son and successor, Humāyūn, was driven out of India by an able Afghān leader, Sher Shāh Sūr. Sher Shāh founded a second Afghān empire in Delhi; the first one, ruled by the Lodīs, had been overthrown by Bābur. Sher Shāh united the restless Afghān leaders into a powerful force. He introduced fiscal and land reforms of far-reaching importance. His network of roads, dotted with caravanserais in close proximity to each other, restored peace and prosperity to the regions he had conquered. His successors, however, were unable to retain control when Bābur's son, Humāyūn, reconquered India ten years later.

Humāyūn died after a few months, leaving the throne to his thirteen-year-old son, Akbar, who was the real architect of the Mughal empire, for which some foundations had thus been laid. Akbar's vast conquests convinced him that kingship was a divinely ordained institution which did not exist solely for the benefit of Muslims. His two immediate successors adhered to his policy, but his great-grandson, Aurangzīb, gave preferment to Muslim religious law, to the detriment of the empire. Aurganzib's heirs tried to revert to Akbar's policies but they were unable to inject his dynamism into the government system, although there was no dearth of gifted Muslim and Hindu political leaders in eighteenth century India. A prevailing apathy weakened Mughal rule to such an extent that the empire became vulnerable to local rebellions and foreign domination.

Hindu polity was governed by the concept of the *chakravartin* raja, or the overlord emperor. That position was achieved by 'Ala'u'd-Din Khaljī through brute force, but Akbar invested his kingship with an additional mystical aura in order to make his dignitaries sacrifice life, religion, honour, and wealth to help him gain his political ambitions. He made these four stringent requirements of discipleship an intrinsic element of his system of rule, and his descendants retained this mystical dimension. Even Aurangzīb, as a prince, always addressed Shāhjahān as a *pīr wa murshid* (spiritual guide), and Aurangzīb's sons spoke to him in the same manner.

The Delhi sultans had introduced a decimal chain of military command and had granted their commanders *iqtā's*, or the right to collect land revenues from the peasants in their assigned areas through a hierarchy of local leaders. In return they maintained troops to extend and consolidate their conquests and placed these at the sultan's disposal as and when ordered. Akbar's *mansabdarī* system was based on the same principle, with an *iqtā'* called a *jāgīr;* but the Mughal system of classification was more complex and stratified than that of the Delhi sultans. Muslims of different racial groups, and even Hindus, were admitted to the rank of *mansabdār.* Akbar and his successors opened government positions to talent and awarded *mansabs* to competent candidates of all races and religions. Among the more successful and prominent groups were the Tūrānis from the Mughal Sunnī ancestral lands, Irānis from the Shī'ī regions, Hindu Rājpūts, Indian Muslims, and Afghāns. Even Aurangzīb was not influenced by religious and sectarian considerations when granting the most important *mansabs* and senior government positions. By the eighteenth century, however, the emperors were unable to harness religious and racial interests to consolidate and unite the empire.

During the reigns of the early Delhi sultans, village leaders were known as *rānas* and *rāwats.* From the reign of Akbar, however, all those who were invested with higher rights and duties than the peasantry were known as *zamīndārs.* The hereditary rulers of Rājasthān were given the more respectful title of *zamīndār* rajas. The process of integrating the rajas into the administration was further augmented under the Mughals. Loyalty became more profitable to them than rebellion. They helped graft Mughal urban culture upon villages, and the entire administration, from the capital to the villages, was unified. The presence of Muslim *zamīndārs* and Muslim *madad-i ma'āsh* (subsistence grant-holders) in villages promoted cultural *rapprochement* between religious communities there.

Muslim rule also stimulated urbanization. Even the Arab rulers of Sind had founded new towns and had added an Islamic character to those already existing, by establishing mosques, schools, and bazaars where the Hindu caste and class taboos were shaken. From the thirteenth century the pace of urbanization, which had been retarded by the feudal Rājpūts of ancient India, gained impetus. The jungles were cleared, facilitating military movement and trade and breaking the isolation of villages from the towns. In ancient times, pilgrimage centres and trade settlements had developed into new towns; now the headquarters of leading *iqtā'* holders, strategic fortifications, and military cantonments gave rise to a proliferation of new towns. The growing number of sūfī *khānqāhs* and tombs transformed many villages into towns. Many caravanserais also developed into towns due to the escalation of trade and commerce. As they grew in size near the rural hinterlands from which they obtained food and materials, the harmony between government, artisans, craftsmen, merchants, and villagers intensified. Most important was the role of the Hindu money-lender, who dominated the economic life of both village and town. *Iqta'* holders and *mansabdārs* alike paid money-lenders high rates of interest in order to borrow funds to raise troops at short notice and to meet the wasteful needs of their luxurious way of life. In the sixteenth and seventeenth centuries, villages such as Khairābād and Daryābād in Avadh developed into towns, mainly through the fame of their textiles. The urban sprawl, in many cases vast, beyond the ramparts of the capital towns led to the growth of prosperous suburbs and satellite towns.

In the technological and industrial fields there was much development. The Muslims improved the ancient Indian *araghatt*, the precursor of the Persian wheel, for irrigation purposes. By the time Bābur arrived in India, it was mechanically more sophisticated. The growing demand for different varieties of cloth stepped up the use of the bow-string for carding cotton and of the spinning-wheel. Refined sugar was also much in demand. Mulberry trees, silk worms, and cocoons were introduced into Bengal, and silk weaving, which had earlier depended upon imported raw materials, thus made rapid progress. Sericulture was commenced in Kashmīr. Fīrūz Tughluq's orchards in the vicinity of Delhi produced grapes in abundance, while Bābur introduced new varieties of fruit trees and planted orchards and Mughal gardens known as *chārbāghs*.

In 1508 the Portuguese introduced tobacco cultivation into the Deccan. Early in the seventeenth century Asad Beg Qazwīnī, Akbar's envoy to Bījāpūr, brought some tobacco and a pipe back to Agra. Akbar himself smoked it and asked his foster-brother, the Khān-i A'zam Mīrzā. 'Azīz Koka, to try it. The royal physician refused to copy European customs blindly, wishing to test it himself. Akbar supported Asad Beg, observing that it was not advisable to reject a popular innovation on the grounds that Muslim books did not mention it. Even so, Akbar himself did not smoke again, although he did not prohibit it. Jahāngīr forbade the use of tobacco, and the *'ulamā'* issued *fatwas* (legal decrees) condemning it. But the habit was too firmly entrenched; by the end of Aurangzīb's reign, tobacco was widely cultivated in the Sūrat and Agra regions. The Portuguese also introduced cashew nuts (*bādām-i farangī*) and pineapples.

Before the rise of Islam, Indian merchants had settled in the Yemen, and the Jāt population in the Persian Gulf ports was substantial. After the Arab conquest of Sind and the establishment of the Delhi sultanate, a phenomenal expansion occurred in both maritime and overland trade and communication. The Delhi sultans exchanged gifts, luxuries, and novelties with West Asian and Central Asian courts; Muhammad bin Tughluq sent Ibn Battūta as his envoy to China; horses from Arabia were exported to India from all the southern ports on the Persian Gulf and were bought by both Hindu rajas and Muslim sultans. The sultans and the Hindu rulers owned ships on the western coast of India, as did rich Hindu and Muslim merchants and the Mughal emperors and dignitaries. Although Portuguese control over the west coast ports was politically disastrous, the Indians learnt improved shipbuilding techniques from them and other Europeans. According to Ovington, in 1689 the Indian ships' carpenters at Sūrat could build a ship after the 'Model of any English Vessel, in all curiosity of its building... as exactly as if they had been the first contrivers'.*

Under the Mughals the demand for luxury goods to meet the extravagance of the court and nobles improved the quality and quantity of manufactured commodities. The enormous variety of cotton fabrics mentioned in the English factory records emerged in response to the escalation of export demands; the same was true of the production and export of silk from Bengal. Indigo was now extensively produced to meet the needs of European merchants. Both the court dignitaries and members of the middle income group acquired valuable jewellery and used silver and gold utensils. The imperial *kārkhānās* employed a variety of meticulous craftsmen, and there was an equal degree of talent and specialization among the local artists. The mining of diamonds developed, due to demand from both the imperial court and Europeans. European labour-saving devices were not used in Indian mining, however, and, although the Indians cut and polished the diamonds skilfully, they could not compete with the more sophisticated European finish. According to Tavernier, had the Indians possessed iron wheels like those used in Europe they 'could give the stones a better finish than they do'.† No wonder that in 1584 Akbar took the English gem expert William Leeds into his service. Jahāngir also employed European jewellers, including a Venetian. Mīr Jumla contributed a great deal to the refinement of lapidary works in India.

The superiority of Indian manufactured goods resulted from the skill and workmanship of the artisans and not from the tools, which remain primitive even to the present day. Mughal *kārkhānās* employed highly skilled craftsmen, while Europeans sometimes hired an entire village of weavers to mass-produce textiles for export purposes. The Mughal rulers and dignitaries were so confident of the competence of their artists and craftsmen that they believed any rare commodity imported from Europe could be easily imitated in India. European travel narratives suggest that they were not wrong.

It was the Mughal indifference to improvements in artillery manufacture that proved disastrous for their rule. Akbar himself took a keen interest in the development of guns, and Mīr Fatu'llāh Shīrāzī produced valuable inventions at his court. As Manrique points out, however, matchlockmen, known as *tufangis* in the Mughal army, were without rank‡; it was skill with the sword that Mughals

* Ovington, *A Voyage to Sūral in the year 1689*. ed. H. C. Rawlinson, London, 1929, p. 166.

† Tavernier, *Travels in India, 1640-67*, tr. V. Ball, 2 vols., London, 1949, II, p. 58.

‡ Manrique, *Travels, 1629-43*, tr. C. L. Luard, 2 vols., London. 1927, II, p. 125.

and Rājpūts valued. The strength of their enormous manpower resources allowed Akbar's successors to neglect the new techniques of warfare. Even Shāhjahān's repeated failure to seize Qandahār did not open his eyes in this respect, while Aurangzīb plunged himself into the thick of the war against Shivājī's hill-forts and guerrillas without improving his artillery.

The most fascinating aspect of Muslim history in India is Indo-Islamic architecture. This is characterized by the adaptation of Indian resources, expertise, design, and motifs to the needs of Islam. The unique stalactite bracketing beneath the balconies of the tapering cylindrical Qutb Mīnār was executed by Hindu workmen under the direction of their Muslim masters. The horseshoe shape of the central opening of the 'Alā'ī Darwaza was never imitated, but its grace and charm cannot be questioned. Tughluq architecture, with its heavy, severe lines, influenced monuments in Mālwa and the Deccan. Irānian curvilinear architecture is juxtaposed with traditional Hindu ornamentation in mosques at Cambay, Ahmadābād, and Champānir.

Although Akbar deliberately chose to follow Hindu architectural styles, what emerged was an eclectic pattern. In the Fathpūr-Sīkrī palaces, Hindu imagination was superimposed on Irānian simplicity. The niches and false windows give a unique lightness and airiness to Humāyūn's tomb. The kiosks, or *chatrīs*, at its corners make the mausoleum typically Indo-Islamic. The terraced structure of Akbar's tomb at Sikandra, near Agra, reminds one of Buddhist monuments. It seems that the imposing Panch Mahal (the five-storeyed palace) of Fathpūr-Sīkrī was transferred to Sikandra in a new form. The elegant mausoleum of Jahāngīr's father-in-law, I'timadu'd-Dawla, marks the transition from the pre-Shāhjahān era to the phase of Shāhjahān's imperial structures. Its delicate inlay work, in hard stone, foreshadows the ornamentation of Shāhjahān's monuments in Delhi and Agra. The elegance and majesty of the Tāj Mahal, which Shāhjahān built to immortalize his queen, Mumtāz Mahal, ensured its place as one of the wonders of the world; the imagination and sensitivity of its designer made it the unparalleled flower of Indo-Islamic civilization.

The Mughal miniature was another important aspect of the blossoming of Indo-Islamic civilization. It offered an opportunity for the blending of influences from European figurative art, particularly Flemish and Belgian, with the art of the East.

Indian influence on Islam was markedly chequered. The puritanically orthodox Muslim leaders of the thirteenth and fourteenth centuries exhibited deep hostility towards the brāhmans and pleaded with their rulers to annihilate them or reduce them to abject poverty. The Chishtiyya sūfī leader Shaykh Nizāmu'd-Dīn Awliyā', however, urged his own disciples to learn a lesson from the brāhmans' devotion to their faith, which Muslim persecution could not destroy. The sight of Hindus bathing in the Jamuna transported the Shaykh into a state of ecstatic joy. As early as the thirteenth century Nāth yogis visited the *khānqāhs* of Chishtiyya sūfīs, who had adapted such important Nāth yogi practices as breath control to their own meditational exercises.

The death anniversaries and other celebrations in sūfī monasteries developed into significant cultural institutions eagerly awaited by the whole population, rich and poor alike. Sūfis began to write Hindī poetry for their *samā'* (musical) parties from the very beginning of the thirteenth century. The subtle refinement of Hindī music, combined with Persian conventions and artistry, gave fresh meaning and depth to Indian sūfī *samā'*. A knowledge of the local dialect offered sūfīs a spiritual satisfaction they could then share with Hindu *bhaktas*, whose spirit equally thirsted for the higher reaches of reality. Hindī sūfī poets and *bhaktas* rebelled against all forms of religious orthodoxy, hypocrisy, and stupidity, and tried to create a new world in which spiritual bliss was the all-consuming goal. They were unconcerned with converting each other to their respective religious beliefs, and their main desire was to promote spiritual consciousness and the understanding of different religious symbols. The followers of the philosophy of Ibn al-'Arabī (1165–1240) were not confined to mystics; they founded a religious and social movement seeking to eradicate religious differences and disputes. Akbar incorporated these ideals into politics and made them the corner-stone of his policy of universalism, aimed at promoting peace and concord between all religious communities. In Jahāngīr's reign, Shaykh Ahmad Sirhindi, the Mujaddid, reinterpreted the Wahdat al-Shuhjūd (Unity of Appearances) doctrines of 'Alā'u'd-Dawla Simnānī (1261–1336) in order to influence Jahāngīr's dignitaries to reverse Akbar's broadly based policies; but the Mujaddid's ideology made little impact during the reigns of Jahāngīr and Shāhjahān. Although Aurangzīb respected the Mujaddid's descendants, he never gave them unqualified support either. The *'ulamā'* of Aurangzīb's time, particularly those from the Panjāb, declared the Mujaddid's theology to be sacrilegious, and the Emperor banned the teaching of the Mujaddid's letters at Aurangabad.

In the eighteenth century the conflict between the two groups gained further momentum. The Sunnī and Shī'ī polemics at the end of the century, and the impact of the Wahhābī ideologies from the Arabian peninsula in the nineteenth century, almost resulted in open religious and sectarian warfare. Nevertheless, despite their inanity and loss of power, Aurangzīb's successors to the Mughal throne in the eighteenth and nineteenth centuries never changed their policy of peace and friendship with all religious communities. Religious polarization did not take effect until the end of the nineteenth century, when competition for positions in the newly constituted British civil service was one of the major factors in exacerbating the differences which eventually led to the partition of India at Independence in 1947.

BIBLIOGRAPHY AND REFERENCES

The following standard abbreviations are used:

b.	Born.
ed.	Edited by.
edn	Edition.
Encyclopaedia of Islam[2]	*The Encyclopaedia of Islam*, ed. by H. A. R. Gibb *et al.*, new edition (Leiden and London, 1960).
Ethé	Manuscript in the India Office Library, London, in the *Catalogue of the Persian Manuscripts in the Library of the India Office*, by H. E. Ethe (Oxford, 1902, 1937).
JASB	*Journal of the Asiatic Society of Bengal.*
JRAS	*Journal of the Royal Asiatic Society.*
M.	Muhammad.
n.d.	Manuscript undated.
Rieu	Manuscript in the British Library, London, described in the *Catalogue of the Persian Manuscripts in the British Museum*, but C. R. Rieu (London, 1879–83).
s.	Sayyid.
Sh.	Shaykh.
Storey	Manuscript mentioned in the *Persian Literature: A Bio-Bibliographical Sūrvey*, by C. A. Storey (London, 1953, 1970).
r.	Translated by.
I, II, III	Volume numbers.

A NOTE FOR THE READER WHO WISHES TO READ FURTHER

The present work is based on contemporary Persian and Arabic sources; sources in regional languages have also been used. Since the book is intended primarily for those who know no Arabic or Persian, reference is made to English translations wherever possible. In the notes to each chapter, the names of authors and books are only briefly mentioned if their full names, titles, and publishing details appear in any section of the bibliography.

The following general histories deal mainly with political events but also discuss matters of social, economic, and cultural interest. The histories on dynasties and monarchs mentioned in relation to Chapters I, II, and III also consider social, economic, and cultural topics. But neither the general histories nor the works listed for Chapters I, II, and III have been repeated in the bibliographies for Chapters IV to VII. Similarly, works cited for Chapters IV to VII also refer to political events although they have not been mentioned in the bibliographies of Chapters I, II, and III.

GENERAL BIBLIOGRAPHY

General Histories in Persian

Bada'uni, Mulla 'Abdu'l-Qādir, *Muntakhabu't-tawārzkh*, Calcutta, 1864; Engl. Tr. I, G. S. A. Ranking, Calcutta, 1885–9; II, W. H. Lowe, Calcutta 1884–98; III, T. W. Haig, Calcutta, 1899–1925.

Firishta, M. Qasim Hindu Shāh, *Gulshan-i Ibrāhzmz* or *Tārikh-I Firishta*, Kanpur, 1884; Engl. tr. J. Briggs, Calcutta, 1908–10, reprint.

Khafi Khān, Muhammad Hashim, *Muntakhabu'l-lubāb*, Calcutta, 1860–74; Engl. tr. summarized Annees Jahān Syed, *Aurangzīb*, Bombay, 1977.

Nizāmu'd-Dīn Ahmad, Khwaja, *Tabaqāt-i Akbar!*, Calcutta, 1913–31; Engl. tr. B. De, Calcutta, 1913–40.

Sujān Rāy Bhandārī, Munshī, *Khulāsatu't-tawārīkh*, Delhi, 1918.

Modern Works in English

Ahmad, Aziz, *Studies in Islamic Culture in the Indian Environment*, Oxford, 1964.

Elliot, H. M. and Dawson, J., *History of India as Told by its Own Historians* (*the Muhammedan Period*), 8 vols., London, 1866–77; Allahabad, 1964, reprint.

Hodivala, S. H., *Studies in Indo-Muslim History- Critical Commentary on Elliot and Dows.on's 'History of India as Told by its Own Historians'*, I, Bombay, 1939; II (Supplement), Bombay, 1957.

Ikram Sh. M., *Muslim Civilization*, ed. T. Embree Ainslie, New York, 1969.

_____, and Rashid, Sh. A., *History of Muslim Civilization in India and Pakistan*, Lahore, 1962.

Mujeeb, M., *The Indian Muslims*, London, 1969.

Bibliographical Works

Blochet, E., *Catalogue des manuscrits persans de la Bibliotheque Nationale*, Paris, 1905–12.

Brockelmann, C. B., *Geschichte der arabischen litteratur*, Weimar-Berlin, 1898–1902.

Ethe, H. E., *Catalogue of the Persian Manuscripts in the Library of the India Office*, Oxford, 1902, 1937.

Morley, W. H. M., *A Descriptive Catalogue of the Historical Manuscripts in the Arabic and Persian Languages Preserved in the Library of the Royal Asiatic*

Society, London, 1854.

Muqtadir, Maulavi 'Abdu'I, *Catalogue of the Arabic and Persian Manuscripts in the Oriental Public Library at Bankipore*, Patna, 1903, 1937.

Rieu, C. R., *Catalogue of the Persian Manuscripts in the British Museum*, London, 1879–83.

_____, *Supplement to the Catalogue of the Persian Manuscripts in the British Museum*, London, 1895.

Sachau, C. E., and Ethe, H. E.,*Catalogue of the Persian Manuscripts in the Bodleian Library*, Oxford, 1889.

Storey, C. A., *Persian Literature: A Bio-Bibliographical Sūrvey*, London, 1953, 1970.

I: THE ARABS AND THE TURKS

BIBLIOGRAPHY

Contemporary Persian Sources

'Afif, Shams-i Siraj, *Tārīkh-i Firūz Shāhī.*, Calcutta, 1888–91; Engl. tr. Elliot and Dowson, III, pp. 271–373, abridged.

Amīr Khusraw Dihlawl, *Qirānu's-sa'dayn*, Aligarh, 1918; Engl. abstract.

_____, E. B. Cowell, *JASB*, 1860, pp. 225–39.

_____, *Mifhāiu'l-futāh*, Alīgarh, n.d.

_____, *Khazā'inu'l-futāh*, Calcutta, 1953; Eng. tr. Muhammad Habib, Bombay, 1931, abstract.

_____, *Diwal Rani. Khizr Khān*, Aligarh, 1917; Engl. tr. Elliot and
Dowson, III, pp. 544–57, abstract.

_____, *Nuh Sipihr*, Bombay, 1931, Engl. tr. Elliot and Dowson, III, pp. 557–66, abstract.

_____, *Tughluq-nāma*, Hyderabad, 1933.

Baranī, Ziya'u'd-Dīn, *Tārikh-i Firūz Shāhī*, Calcutta, 1860–2; Eng. tr. A. R. Fuller, *JASB*, 1869, pp. 181-220; P. Whalley, *JASB*, 1870, pp. 1–51; 1871, pp. 185–216; Auckland Colvin, *JASB*, 1871, pp. 217–47. Incomplete.

al-Bayhaqī, Abu'l-Fazl, *Tārīkh-i Bayhaqz*, Calcutta, 1861–62; Engl. tr. Elliot and Dawson, II, pp. 53–154, extracts.

Fīruz Shāh Tughluq, *Futāhāt-i Firūz Shāhī*, Aligarh, n.d.; Engl. tr. Elliot and Dawson II, pp. 374–88.

Hasan Nizāmi, *Tāju'l-ma'āsir*, MS. British Library; Rieu, I, 239a; Engl. tr. Elliot and Dawson II, pp. 204–43

'Isāmī, *Futāhu's-salātīn*, Madras, 1948; Engl. tr. Mahdi Husain, 3 vols., Bombay, 1967, 1976, 1977.

Juwaynī, 'Alā 'u'd-Dīn 'Ata' Malik, *Tārīkh-i jahān-gushāy-i Juwaynī*, Leiden and London, 1912, 1916; Engl. tr. J. Boyle, Manchester, 1958.

Kufi, 'Alī b. Hamid, *Chach-nāma*, Hyderābād, n.d.; Engl. tr. Mirza Kalichbeg

Fredunbeg, Karachi, 1900; Delhi, 1979, reprint. Minahj, Siraj, *Tabaqāt-i Nāsirt*, Calcutta, 1863–4; Engl. tr. H. G. Raverty, Calcutta, 1873–81.

Ni'matu'llāh al-Harawī, *Tārikh-i Khān-jahānī u Makhzan-i Afghāni*, Dacca, 1960; Engl. tr. B. Darn, London, 1829–36.

Timur, *Malfūzāt-i Timūrī*, Oxford, 1783; Engl. tr. Major C. Stewart, London, 1830.

al-'Utbī, Abū Nasr, *al-Yamīnī* (Arabic); Persian tr. *Tarjama-i Yamī-nī*, after 1205–6, Tehran, 1856; Engl. tr. J. Reynolds, London, 1858.

Yahya, Sirhindī, *Tārīkh-i Mubārak Shāhī*, Calcutta, 1931; Engl. tr. K. K. Basu, Baroda, 1932.

Yazdī, Sharafu'd-Dīn 'Alī, *Zafar-nāma*, Calcutta, 1885–6; Engl. tr. from French tr., incomplete, Paris, 1722.

Anonymous, *Sīrat-i Firūz Shāhī*, MS. Bankipur, Patna; Engl. tr. (Jajnagar expedition), *JASB*, 1942, pp. 58–77.

Modern Works in English

Ahmad, M. A., *Political History and Institutions of the Early Turkish Empire of Delhi*, Lahore, 1949; New Delhi, 1972, reprint.

Banerjee, J. M., *History of Firāz Shāh Tughluq*, Delhi, 1967. Bosworth, C. E., *The Ghaznavids*, Edinburgh, 1977.

Digby, S., *War-Horse and Elephant in the Delhi Sultanate*, Oxford, 1971.

Habib, M., *Hazrat Amīr Khusrau of Delhi*, Bombay, 1927.

_____, *Sultan Mahmūd of Ghaznīn*, Delhi, 1951.

_____ and Nizāmī, K. A. (eds.), A *Comprehensive History of India*, V, Delhi, 1970.

Habibullah, A. B. M., *The Foundation of Muslim Rule in India*, Allahabad, 1961, 2nd rev. edn.

Haig, W. (ed.), *The Cambridge History of India*, III, New York, 1928.

Halim, A., *History of the Lodī Sultans of Delhi and Agra*, Dacca, 1961. Haq, S. M., *Baranī's History of the Tughluqs*, Karachi, 1959.

Hardy, P., *Historians of Medieval India*, London, 1960.

Husain, Mahdi, *Tughluq Dynasty*, Calcutta, 1963.

Jauhari, T. C., *Firāz Tughluq*, Agra, 1968.

Lal, K. S., *Twilight of the Sultanate*, Bombay, 1963; New Delhi, 1980, rev. edn.

_____, *History of the Khalfis*, Bombay, 1967; New Delhi, 1980, rev. edn.

_____, *Growth of Muslim Population in India*, Delhi, 1973.

Majumdar, R. C., *The Struggle for Empire*, Bombay, 1957.

_____ and Pusalker, A. E., (eds.), *The Delhi Sultanate*, Bombay, 1967, 2nd edn.

Nazim, M., *The Life and Times of Sultan Mahmūd of Ghazna*, Cambridge, 1931; New Delhi 1971, reprint.

Nigam, S. B. P., *Nobility under the Sultans of Delhi*, Delhi, 1968.

Nizāmi, K. A., *Studies in Medieval Indian History and Culture*, Allahabad, 1966.

_____ (ed.), *Politics and Society during the Early Medieval Period*, New Delhi, 1974.

Prasad, I., *A History of the Qaraunah Turks in India*, Allahabad, 1936. Qureshi, I.

H., *The Muslim Community of the Indo-Pakistan Subcontinent*, The Hague, 1962.
Siddiqi, I. H., *Some Aspects of Afghān Despotism in India*, Aligarh, 1969.
Srivastava, A. L., *The Sultanate of Delhi*, Agra, 1953, 2nd rev. edn.
Thomas, E., *The Chronicles of the Pathān Kings of Delhi*, reprint, Delhi, 1967.
Venkataramanayya, N., *Early Muslim Expansion in South India*, Madras, 1942.

REFERENCES

1. *Qur'ān*, Engl. tr. M. Pickthall, Chapter II, verse 136.
2. C. L. Cohen, 'Kharadj' in *The Encyclopaedia of Islam*², IV, pp. 1030–4; A. K. S. Lambton, 'Kharadj in Persia', ibid., pp. 1034–52.
3. Qureshi, *The Muslim Community*, p. 35.
4. The copper or silver unit of the Arab monetary system, which is still prevalent in some countries. It weighed around three to four grams of silver, copper, or brass.
5. Fredunbeg (tr.), *Chach-nama* p. 165.
6. Ibid., p. 166.
7. Ibid., pp. 168–9.
8. Ibid., pp. 171.
9. The dynasty which ruled in North Africa, and later in Egypt from 909 until 1171; M. Canard, 'Fatimids', in *The Encyclopaedia of Islam*², II, pp. 850–62
10. Qureshi, *The Muslim Community*, pp. 40–2.
11. Nazim, *Mahmūd of Ghazna*, pp. 96–101.
12. Ibid., pp. 98–9.
13. Ibid., pp. 49, 88, 89, 91, 97, 98, 195.
14. Ibid., pp. 104–5.
15. Ibid., pp. 107–8.
16. Ibid., pp. 209–10.
17. Ibid., pp. 209–24.
18. C. E. Bosworth, *Mahmūd of Ghazna in Contemporary Eyes and in Later Persian Literature*, pp. 85–92; Rizvi, *Shāh Walī Allāh and his Times*, pp. 293–4.
19. Nazim, *Mahmūd of Ghazna*, p.124.
20. Bosworth, *The Ghaznavids*, pp. 98–128.
21. Ibid., pp. 77–82.
22. Ibid., p. 110.
23. Ibid., pp. 210–18.
24. Ibid., p. 128.
25. Abu'l-Qasim al-Junayd (d. 910) strongly opposed the growing eclectic tendencies among the sūfīs.
26. Habibullah, *The Foundation of Muslim Rule in India*, pp. 53–7.
27. *Tāju'l-ma'asir*, in Elliot and Dowson, II, p. 215.
28. Minhaj, tr. Raverty, *Tabaqat-i Nasīri*, I, pp. 512–14.

29. Ibid., I, pp. 515–19; *Tāju'l-ma'asir*, in Elliot and Dowson, II, pp. 219–21.
30. *Ttiju'l-ma'tisir*, in Elliot and Dowson, II, pp. 227–8.
31. Minhaj, tr. Raverty, I, pp. 518–22.
32. *Tāju'l-ma'asir*, in Elliot and Dowson, II, pp. 231–2.
33. Minhaj, tr. Raverty, I, pp. 548–51.
34. Ibid., I, pp. 552–95.
35. Ibid., I, pp. 472–86.
36. A. L. Srivastava, *The Sultanate of Delhi*, Agra, 1964, 4th edn, pp. 84–7.
37. K. A. Nizāmī, 'Foundation of the Delhi Sultanate', in Habib and Nizāmā (eds.), *A Comprehensive History of India*, V, p. 185.
38. Ibid., p. 182.
39. Minhaj, tr. Raverty, I, pp. 511–51.
40. Ibid., pp. 496–507.
41. Ibid., I, pp. 530–8.
42. Ibid., I, pp. 285–99.
43. Ibid., I, pp. 538–44.
44. Ibid., I, pp. 540–1.
45. Ibid., I, pp. 628–9.
46. S. Rizvi, *History of Sūfism in India*, I, pp. 135–6.
47. Minhaj, tr. Raverty, I, p. 638.
48. Ibid., I, pp. 631–3.
49. Ibid., I, pp. 635–7.
50. Ibid., I, pp. 637–8.
51. Ibid., I, pp. 639–48.
52. Baranī, *Tārīkh-i Firūz Shāhī*, p. 25.
53. Minhaj, tr. Raverty, I. pp. 649–51.
54. Ibid., I, pp. 655–60.
55. Ibid., I, pp. 660–4.
56. Ibid., I, pp. 666–9.
57. Ibid., I, pp. 675–82.
58. Ibid., I, pp. 683–6.
59. Ibid., II, pp. 825–40.
60. Habibullah, *Foundation of Muslim Rule*, pp. 210–11, 213, 215, 216, 220.
61. 'Isami, *Futuhu's-salātin*, pp. 161–6.
62. Habibullah, *'Foundation of Muslim Rule'*, pp. 161–4.
63. Baranī, pp. 65–6.
64. Ibid., pp. 50–l.
65. Ibid., p. 56.
66. Ibid., pp. 57–8.
67. Ibid., pp. 54–5.
68. Ibid., pp. 81–6.
69. Yahya Sirhindi, *Tārīkh-i Mubārak Shāhī*, pp. 42–3.
70. Baranī, pp. 89–107.
71. Ibid., pp. 109–10.

72. Ibid., pp. 120–3.
73. Ibid., pp. 130–56; Amīr Khusraw, *Qirānu's-sa'dayn*, pp. 11–15.
74. Amir Khusraw, *Qirānu's-sa'dayn*, pp. 158–73.
75. Ibid., pp. 175–80.
76. Ibid., pp. 183–7; Khusraw, *Miftāhu'l-futūh*, pp. 35–9.
77. Khusraw, *Miftāhu'l-futūh*, p. 189.
78. Baranī, p. 218.
79. Ibid., p. 213.
80. Ibid., pp. 208–12; Rizvi, *History of Sūfism*, I, pp. 308–9.
81. Baranī, pp. 221–36.
82. Ibid., pp. 237–40, 242–50.
83. Amīr Khusraw, *Khazā'inu'l-futuh*, pp. 36–44.
84. Baranī, pp. 300–1.
85. *Khazā'inu'l-futūh*, pp. 49–54; Baranī, pp. 251–2.
86. *Khazā'inu'l-futūh*, pp. 59–64; Baranī, pp. 272–3.
87. Ibid., pp. 264–72.
88. Ibid., pp. 282–7.
89. Ibid., pp. 288–90.
90. Coins of high value mainly of silver, but gold *tankas* were also minted.
91. Baranī, pp. 305–11.
92. Ibid., pp. 312–17.
93. Ibid., pp. 318–19.
94. Rizvi, *A History of Sūfism*, I, p. 189.
95. Baranī, p. 300.
96. *Khazā'inu'l-futūh*, pp. 60–1.
97. 'Isamī, *Futūhu's-salatin*, pp. 273–81.
98. *Khazā'inu'l-futūh*, pp. 113–21.
99. Ibid., pp. 128–32; Baranī, pp. 325–34.
100. Amir Khusraw, *Diwal Rānī Khizr Khān*, pp. 233–64.
101. Baranī, pp. 372–87.
102. The territories directly under the administration of the sultans or the emperors were known as *khālisa.*
103. Amir Khusraw, *Tughluq-nama*, p. 19.
104. Ibid., pp. 20–1; Baranī, pp. 389-409.
105. Ibid., pp. 432–3; Rizvi, *History of Sūfism*, I, p. 161.
106. Baranī, pp. 446–9.
107. Ibid., p. 450.
108. 'Isami, *Futuhu's-salatin*, pp. 417–20.
109. Gibb (tr.), *The Travels of Ibn Battuta*, III, pp. 654–6.
110. Baranī, p. 452.
111. Yahya, Sirhindi, *Tarikh-i Mubārāk-Shāhi*, pp. 36–7; Abu'l-Fazl, tr. Jarret, *A'in-i Akbarī*, III, p. 275.
112. Baranī, p. 505.
113. 'Isami, *Futuhu's-salatin*, pp. 423–4.

114. Rizvi, *History of Sūfism*, I, pp. 175–6.
115. Ibid., p. 182.
116. Baranī, pp. 476–7.
117. Ibid., pp. 477–8.
118. Badr-i Chach, *Qasa'id*, Lucknow, n.d., pp. 27–8.
119. Baranī, pp. 475–6.
120. K. A. Nizāmi, 'Sultan Muhammad bin Tughluq', in Habib and Nizāmi (eds.), *Comprehensive History*, V, p. 539.
121. Mahdi Husain (tr.), *The Rehla of Ibn Battūta*, Baroda, 1976, pp. 189–91.
122. Gibb (tr.), *Travels of Ibn Battūta*, III, pp. 720–7.
123. Baranī, pp. 498–9.
124. Ibid., pp. 500–5.
125. 'Isami, *Futāhu's-salātin*, pp. 550–7.
126. Baranī, pp. 509–14.
127. Bada'uni, tr. Ranking, *Muntakhabu't-tawārīkh*, I, p. 317.
128. Rizvi, *History of Sūfism*, I, p. 186.
129. B. P. Saksena, 'Firūz Shāh Tughluq', in Habib and Nizāmi (eds.), *Comprehensive History*, V, pp. 566–7.
130. Firāz Shāh, *Futāhat-i Fīrūz Shāhī*, pp. 18, 24; Baranī, pp. 555–8; 'Afif, *Tārīkh-i Fīrūz Shāhi*, pp. 178–84.
131. 'Afif, *Tārīkh-i Fīrūz Shahī*, pp. 109–24, 145–72.
132. Ibid., pp. 183–250.
133. Yazdi, *Zafar-nāma*, II, pp. 99–125.
134. Ibid., pp. 126–82.
135. See below, p. 240.

II: THE INDEPENDENT RULING DYNASTIES

BIBLIOGRAPHY

Contemporary Persian Sources

'Abdu'r-Razzaq Samarqandī (d. 1446–7), *Matla'u's-Sa'dayn*, Lahore, 1933; Engl. tr. (a small portion) R. H. Major, London. (Hakluyt Society), 1859.

'Alī bin Mahmūd al-Kirmani, *Ma'asir-i Mahmūd Shāhī*, MS. Cambridge, Browne Supplement 249.

_____, *Mir'āt-i Ahmadi*, supplement; tr. Syed Nawab 'Alī, Baroda, 1928.

Dughlat, Mirza Haydar, *Tārīkh-i Rashīd*, Engl. tr. E. D. Ross and N. Elias, London, 1895.

Ghulam Murtaza, *Basātznu's-salātzn*, Hyderābād, n.d.

Mahmūd Gawan, *Riyāzu'l-insha'*, Hyderābād, 1948.

Nami, Mir Muhammad Ma'sum, *Tārīkh-i Sind*, Poona, 1938.

Sikandar bin Muhammad Manjhu, *Mir'āt-i Sikandarī*, Bombay, 1890; Engl. tr. Fazlu'llah Lutfu'llah Faridi, Bombay, 1899.

Tabataba, Sayyid 'Alī bin 'Azīz, *Burhān-i Ma'āsir*, Hyderābād, 1936.

Portuguese Sources

Albuquerque, Alfonso de, *The Commentaries of Albuquerque*, ed. and tr. Walter de Gray Birch, 4 vols., London, 1875–84.

Gama, Vasco da, *Journal of the First Voyage*, tr. E. G. Ravenstein, London, 1898.

Modern Works in English

Acharya, N. N. *The History of Medieval Assam*, Gauhati, 1966.

Commissariat, M. S., *A History of Gujarāt*, 2 vols., Bombay, 1938-57.

Danvers, F. C., *The Portuguese in India*, 2 vols., London, 1894.

Hasan, M., *Kashmīr under the Sultans*, Calcutta, 1959.

Husaini, A. Q., *Bahman Shāh*, Calcutta, 1959.

Nuniz, Fernao, *Chronicle;* tr. R. Sewell in *A Forgotten Empire*, London, 1900.

Pannikkar, K. M. *A History of Kerala*, Annama1ai University, 1960.

Radhey Shyam, *The Kingdom of Ahmadnagar*, Delhi, 1966.

Saeed, Mian M., *The Sharqī Sultans of Jaunpur*, Karachi, 1972.

Sharma, G. N., *Mewār and the Mughal Emperors*, Agra, 1962.

_____, *Social Life in Medieval Rājasthān*, Agra, n.d.

Sherwani, H. K., *The Bahmanzs of the Deccan*, Hyderābād, 1953.

_____, *Muhammad Quiz Qutb Shāh*, Bombay, 1968.

_____, *History of the Qutb-Shāhl Dynasty*, Delhi, 1974.

_____ and Joshi, P. M.(eds.), *History of Medieval Deccan*, 2 vo1s., Hyderabad, 1973–4.

Sūfi, G. M.D., *Kashīr*, Lahore, 1948–9.

Tarafdar, M. R., *Husain Shāhī Bengal*, Dacca, 1965.

Tod, J., *Annals and Antiquities of Rājasthān*, Oxford, 1920.

Venkataramanayya, N., *Early Muslim Expansion in South India*, Madras, 1942.

REFERENCES

1. See below, p. 65.
2. Tarafdar, *Husain Shāhī Bengal*, pp. 1–32.
3. Barbosa, tr. Dames, *The Book of Duarte Barbosa*, II, pp. 147–8.
4. Acharya, *The History of Medieval Assam*, pp. 41, 87, 100.
5. Tarafdar, *Husain Shāhī Bengal*, pp. 69, 74.
6. S. Dutta, 'Rājpūt States', in R. C. Majumdar (ed.), *Delhi Sultanate*, Bombay, 1960, VI, pp. 331–2.
7. Shyamal Das, *Vir Vinod*, I, in Hindī, Udaipur, n.d., p. 308; G. H. Ojha, *Udaipur rajya k itihās*, Ajmīr, 1938, I, pp. 260–2.
8. Nizāmu'd-Dīn, tr. De, *Tabaqāt-i Akban*, III, pp. 131–3.
9. Dutta, Majunder (ed.), *Delhi Sultanate*, pp. 332–4.
10. Bābur, tr. Beveridge, *Bābur-nāma*, II, pp. 426–529; Sharma, *Mewār and the Mughal Emperors*, pp. 7–20.
11. G. N. Sharma, 'The Rathors of Marwar', in Habib and Nizāmi (eds.), *A Comprehensive History of India*, III, pp. 812–14.

12. Rizvi, *History of Sūfism*, I, pp. 289–90.
13. J. C. Dutt (tr.), *Kings of Kashmīr*, Bombay, 1896, pp. 15, 22, 26, 28.
14. Hasan, *Kashmīr under the Sultans*, pp. 48-53.
15. Dutt, *Kings of Kashmīr*, pp. 59-60, 112.
16. Dughlat, tr. Ross and Elias, *Tārīkh-i Rashīdī*, pp. 3–4, 434; R. K. Parmu, 'Kashmīr', in Habib and Nizāmi (eds.), *Comprehensive History*, V, pp. 754–5.
17. Hasan, *Kashmzr under the Sultans*, pp. 79–90.
18. *Tabaqāt-i Akbarī*, III, p. 273.
19. Yahya Sirhindi, *Tārikh-i Mubārak Shāhī*, pp. 153–5, 159.
20. Ram Babu Saksena, *Kzrti Lata* (Hindī), Allahabad, 1929, pp. 14–18; *Tabaqāt-i Akbarī*, III, pp. 275–8.
21. *Tabaqāt-i Akbarī*, III, pp. 279–83.
22. Ibid., III, pp. 284–7.
23. Ibid., III, pp. 310–12, 318–19.
24. Ibid., III, p. 288.
25. Ibid., III, pp. 161–2.
26. Tabataba, *Burhān-i Ma'āsir*, p. 68.
27. *Tabaqāt-i Akbarī*, III, pp. 312–49.
28. Ibid., III, p. 35.
29. Ibid., III, pp. 351–6.
30. Ibid., III, p. 357.
31. Ibid., III, p. 384–92.
32. Ibid., III, p. 403.
33. Hajjiu'd-Dablr, *Zafaru'l-Wālih*, p. 52.
34. Tabataba, *Burhān-i Ma'āsir*, p. 68.
35. Sikandar bin Muhammad, *Mir'āt-i Sikandarī*, pp. 5–18.
36. Ibid., pp. 19–21.
37. Ibid., pp. 33–6.
38. Ibid., pp. 44–6.
39. A. K. Forbes, *Ras Mala*, ed. H. G. Rawlinson, London, 1924, I, pp. 318–25.
40. *Tabaqāt-i Akbarī*, II I, p. 147.
41. Ibid., III, pp. 152–68.
42. Albuquerque, *The Commentaries*, II, pp. 208–14; R. S. Whiteway, *The Rise of Portuguese Power in India 1497–1550*, London, 1916, II, pp. 114–20.
43. Varthema, *Travels*, pp. 109–10.
44. *Tabaqāt-i Akbarī*, III, p. 173.
45. *Zafaru'l-Walih*, I, p. 230.
46. Danvers, *The Portuguese in India*, I, p. 406.
47. Mahdi Husain (tr.), *The Rehla of Ibn Battuta*, Baroda, 1976, pp. 189–91.
48. Danvers, *Portuguese in India*, I, pp. 50–69.
49. Ibid., I, pp. 77–116.
50. Pearson, *Merchants and Rulers in Gujarāt*, pp. 67–73.
51. Ibid., pp. 73–77.

52. Husain (tr.) *The Rehla of Ibn Battūta*, pp. 226–7.
53. See above, p. 49.
54. J. Briggs (tr.), *History of the Rise of the Mahomedan Power in India*, Calcutta, 1966, reprint, II, pp. 175–6.
55. *Burhān-i Ma'asir*, pp. 43–52.
56. Ibid., pp. 56–61.
57. Briggs (tr.), *Mahomedan Power*, II, p. 279.
58. R.J. Major (tr.), *India in the Fifteenth Century*, New York (Hakluyt Society), 'The Travels of Nicolo Conti', reprint from first series, 1857, p. 14.
59. Briggs (tr.), *Mahomedan Power*, II, pp. 300–2.
60. Mahmūd Gawan, *Riyāzu'l-inshā'*, pp. 122, 163, 170, 181, 233, 238, 244, 249.
61. Briggs (tr.), *Mahomedan Power*, II, pp. 309–18.
62. Sherwani and Joshi (eds.), *History of Medieval Deccan*, I, pp. 285–7.
63. Fuzāni Astarabadi, *Tazkiratu'l-muluk*, British Library, Rieu, I, 317a, ff. 36b-40b.
64. Sherwani, *Qutb-Shāhī Dynasty*, pp. 119–75.
65. *Tazkiratu'l-mulāk*, ff. 41b–46b.
66. Briggs (tr.), *Mahomedan Power*, III, pp. 250–5.
67. Danvers, *Portuguese in India*, I, pp. 551–7.
68. Gurty Venkat Rao, 'The Vijayanagara Empire', in Habib and Nizāmi (eds.), *Comprehensive History*, V, pp. 1031–43.
69. Ibid., pp. 1044–5.
70. Ibid., pp. 1049–50.
71. Major (tr.), *India in the Fifteenth Century*, pp. 23–32 (Journey of Abd-er-Razzak).
72. Briggs (tr.), *Mahomedan Power*, II, pp. 265–6.
73. Gurty Venkat Rao, 'The Vijayanagara Empire', in Habib and Nizāmi (eds.), *Comprehensive History*, V, pp. 1062–3.
74. R. Sewell, *Forgotten Empire*, Madras, 1932, pp. 236-90.
75. Habib and Nizāmi (eds.), *Comprehensive History*, V, pp. 1074–84.
76. Ibid., V, pp. 1087–9.
77. See above, p. 83.

III: THE AFGHANS AND THE MUGHALS

BIBLIOGRAPHY

Contemporary Persian Sources

'Abbas Khān Sarwani, *Tuhfa-i Akbar Shāhī*, Dacca, 1964.

'Abdu'I-Hamid Lahauri, *Bādshāh-nāma*, Calcutta, 1866–72.

Abu'l-Fazl 'Allamī, *Akbar-nāma*, Calcutta 1873–87; Engl. tr. H. Beveridge, Calcutta, 1897-1921.

'Arif Qandahari, *Tārzkh-i Akbarī*, Rampur, 1962.

Asad Beg, *Hālat-i Asad Beg*, MS. British Library, Rieu, III, 979b.

Bābur, Zahiru'd-Dīn Muhammad, *Bābur-nāma* (Turkī text), Leiden and London, 1905; Engl. tr. A. S. Beveridge, London, 1921.

Bayazid Biyat, *Tārīkh-i Humāyān*, Calcutta, 1941.

Bhim Sen, *Dilkushā*, MS. British Library, Rieu, I, 271a; Engl. tr. in V. G. Khobrekar (ed.), *Sir Jadunath Sarkar Birth Centenary Volume*, Bombay, 1972.

Gulbaden Begam, *Humāyūn-nāma*, text and Engl. tr. A. S. Beveridge, London, 1902.

Isar Das Nagar, *Futāhāt-i 'Alamgīrī*, MS. British Library, Rieu, I, 269a.

Jahāngīr, Emperor, *Tuzuk-i Jahāngīrī*, Alīgarh, 1863–4; Engl. tr. A. Rogers and H. Beveridge, London, 1909–14.

Jawhar Aftabchi, *Tazkirātu'l-wāqi'āt*, MS. British Library, Rieu, I, 246; Engl. tr. C. Stewart, London, 1832.

Kazim, Munshi M., *'Alamgīr-nāma*, Calcutta, 1865-73.

Khāfi Khān, M. Hashim, *Muntakhabu 'l-lubāb*, Calcutta, 1860–76; Engl. tr. Anees Jahan Syed, *Aurangzeb*, Bombay, 1977.

Khwand-Amir, *Humāyān-nāma*, Calcutta, 1940; Engl. tr. Baini Prasad, Calcutta, 1940.

Muhammad Salih Kanbo Lahauri, *'Amal-i Sālih*, Calcutta, 1912.

Musta'id Khān, Muhammad Saqi, *Ma'āsir-i 'Alamgīrī*, Calcutta, 1870–3; Engl. tr. J. N. Sarkar, Calcutta, 1947.

Mu'tamad Khān, *lqbāl-nāma-i Jahāngīrī*, Lucknow, 1870.

Razi, 'Aqil Khān, *Waqi'āt-i 'Alamgīrī*, Lahore, 1936.

Sadiq Khān, M., and Abu'l-Fazl Ma'mūrī, *Shāhjahān-nāma*, MS. British Library, Rieu, I, 262.

Sujan Ray Bhandari, *Khulasatu't-tawārīkh*, Delhi, 1918; Engl. tr. (a part) J. N. Sarkar, *The India of Aurangīb*, Calcutta, 1901.

Talish, Shihabu'd-Dīn, *Fathiya-i 'ibrīya*, Calcutta, 1847; Engl. tr. H. Blockmann, *JASB*, 1872, pp. 49–101; J. N. *Sarkar*, *Journal of the Bihār and Orissa Research Society*, 1915, pp. 179–95 (incomplete).

European Sources

Broughton, T. D., *Letters Written in a Mahratta Camp*, Constable, London, 1892, rev. edn.

Camps, A., *Jerome Xavier, SJ, and the Muslims of the Mogul Empire*, Schoneck-Beckenried, 1957.

Correla-Allfonso; J., *Jesuit Letters and Indian History*, Bombay, 1955.

Dar, Harihar, *The Norris Embassy to Aurangzīb*, Calcutta, 1959.

Monserrate, A., *The Commentary of Father Monserrate*, tr. and ed. J. S. Hoyland and S. N. Banerji, London, 1922.

Payne, C. H. (tr. and ed.), *Akbar and the Jesuits*, London, 1926.

____, *Jahāngīr and the Jesuits*, London, 1930.

Modern Works in English

'Alī, Athar, *The Mughal Nobility under Aurangzīb*, Bombay, 1968.

Bangerjee, S. K., *Humāyun Bādshāh*, 2 vols., London, 1938.

Chandra, S., *Parties dnd Politics at the Mughal Court*, Alīgarh, 1959.
Commissariat, M. S., *Studies in the History of Gujarāt*, Bombay, 1935.
Duff, James G., *History of the Mahrattās*, ed. S. M. Edwards, 2 vols., London, 1921.
Faruki, Z., *Aurangzīb and his Times*, Bombay, 1935.
Gokhale, Kamal, *Chatrapati Sambhājī*, Pune, 1978.
Haig, Wolseley (ed.), *The Cambridge History of India*, IV, Cambridge, 1937.
Irwin, W., *Later Mughuls*, 2 vols., Calcutta, 1921-2; New Delhi, 1971, reprint.
Islam, R., *Indo-Persian Relations*, Tehran and Lahore, 1970.
Khān, I. A., *Political Biography of a Mughal Noble*, New Delhi, 1973.
Kincaid, C. A., and Parasnis, R. B., *A History of the Marāthā Power*, 3 vols., London, 1931, 2nd ed.
Kulkarni, A. R., *Mahārāshtra in the Age of Shivājī*, Poona, 1969.
MacKenzie, D. N., *Poems from the Diwan of Khushhal Khān Khattak*, London, 1965.
Maclagan, E. D., *The Jesuits and the Great Mogul*, London, 1932.
Majumdar, R. C., and Pusalker, A. D., (eds.), *The Mughal Empire*, Bombay, 1974.
Malik, Z., *The Reign of Muhammad Shāh*, Bombay, 1977.
Malleson, G. B., *History of the French in India*, London, 1893, 2nd edn.
Modi, J. J., *The Parsees at the Court of Akbar and Dastār Mehergee Rāna*, Bombay, 1903.
Moreland, W. H. (ed.), *Relations of Golconda in the Early 17th Century*, London, 1931.
Owen, S. J., *The Fall of the Mogul Empire*, Varanasi, 1960, 2nd edn.
Polier, A. L. *Shāh 'Alam II and his Court*, Calcutta, 1947.
Prasad, B., *History of jahangzr*, Allahabad, 1940, 3rd edn.
Prasad, 1., *The Life and Times of Humāyān*, Bombay, 1956, rev. edn.
Qanungo, K. R., *Dārā Shukoh*, Calcutta, 1935.
____, *Sher Shāh and his Times*, Bombay, 1965.
Rahim, M., *History of the Afghāns in India*, Karachi, 1961.
Rizvi, S. A. A., *Muslim Revivalist Movements in Northern India in the Sixteenth and Seventeenth Centuries*, Agra, 1965.
____, *Religious and Intellectual History if the Muslims in Akbar's Reign*, Delhi, 1975.
____, *Shāh Wali-Allāh and his Times*, Canberra, 1980.
____, *Shāh 'Abd al-'Azīz*, Canberra, 1982.
Saksena, B. P., *History of Shāhjahan of Delhi*, Allahabad, 1959.
Sardesai, G. S., *A New History of the Marāthas*, 3 vols., Bombay, 1948-56.
____, *Main Currents if Marātha History*, Bombay, 1959.
Sarkar, Jadunath, *The India of Aurangzīb*, Calcutta, 1901.
____, *History of Aurangzīb*, 5 vols., Calcutta, 1925–34.
____, *Bihār and Orissa during the Fall of the Mughal Empire*, Patna, 1932.
____, *Fall of the Mughal Empire*, 4 vols., Calcutta, 1932–50.

____, *Studies in Aurangzīb's Reign*, Calcutta, 1933.
____ (ed.), *The History of Bengal*, II, Calcutta, 1948.
____, *The Persian Sources of Marātha History*, Bombay, 1953.
____, *House of Shivājī*, Calcutta, 1955, 3rd rev. edn.
____, *Shivājī and his Times*, Calcutta, 1961, 6th rev. ed.
____, *A Short History of Aurangzīb*, Calcutta, 1962, 3rd rev. edn.
____, *Anecdotes of Aurangzīb*, Calcutta, 1963, 4th edn.
____, *Nādir Shāh in India*, Calcutta, 1973, reprint.
Sarkar, Jagdish, *Islam in Bengal*, Calcutta, 1972.
____, *Some Aspects of Military Thinking and Practice in Medieval India*, Calcutta, 1974.
Sarkar, Jagdish, *History of History Writing in Medieval India*, Calcutta, 1977.
____, *The Life of Mīr Jumla*, New Delhi, 1979, rev. edn.
Singh, Khushwant, *A History of the Sikhs*, 2 vols., Princeton, 1963.
Smith, V. A., *Akbar, the Great Mogul*, Delhi, 1958, reprint.
Spear, T. G. P., *Twilight of the Mughuls*, Cambridge, 1951; New Delhi, 1970, reprint.
Srivastav, A. L., *A Short History of Akbar the Great*, Agra, 1957.
____, *The Mughal Empire*, Agra, 1957, 2nd rev. edn.
____, *Akbar the Great*, 2 vols., Agra, 1962, 1967.
____, *Studies in Indian History*, Agra, 1974.
Williams, L. F. R., *An Empire Builder of the Sixteenth Century*, reprint, Delhi, 1962, reprint.

REFERENCES

1. Baranī, *Tārīkh-i Firūz Shāhī*, p. 483.
2. Shaykh Rizqu'llah Mushtaqi, *Wāqi'āt-i Mushtāqī*, British Library, Rieu, II, 802b, ff. 14–81.
3. Ibid., ff. 81–207.
4. Bābur, tr. Beveridge, *Bābur-nāma*, pp. 456–74.
5. Ibid., pp. 553.
6. Ibid., pp. 554–74.
7. Ibid., pp. 531–3, 543–4, 548, 616–34.
8. Ibid., pp. 132, 604, 619–20.
9. Abu'1-Fazl, tr. Beveridge, *Akbar-nāma*, I, Delhi, 1972, reprint, pp. 30 3.
10. Qanungo, *Sher Shāh and his Times*, pp. 154–62.
11. *Akbar-nāma*, I, pp. 337–9.
12. Ibid., pp. 349–97.
13. Qanungo, *Sher Shāh*, pp. 330, 343–4.
14. Ibid., pp. 395–418.
15. Ibid., pp. 270–302.
16. *Akbar-nāma*, I, pp. 364, 50–68.
17. Ibid., I, pp. 600–8.

18. Ibid., I, pp. 652–8.
19. Ibid., II, pp. 4–12.
20. Ibid., II, pp. 67–8.
21. Ibid., II, pp. 111–16.
22. Ibid., II, pp. 240–3.
23. Ibid., II, pp. 246–7, 294–5.
24. Rizvi, *Religious and Intellectual History of the Muslims in Akbar's Reign*, pp. 107–20.
25. Smith, *Akbar, the Great Mogul*, pp. 178-81; see also Rizvi, *Religious and Intellectual History of the Muslims in Akbar's Reign*, pp. 141–60.
26. Ibid., pp. 161–5.
27. Smith, *Akbar, the Great Mogul*, pp. 210–15; Rizvi, *Religious and Intellectual History*, pp. 374–418.
28. Payne (tr.), *Akbar and the Jesuits*, p. 68.
29. Ibid., p. 68.
30. Rizvi, *Religious and Intellectual History*, pp. 394–403.
31. *Akbar-nāma*, III, p. 1043.
32. Rizvi, *Religious and Intellectual History*, pp. 472–81.
33. Ibid., pp. 482–5.
34. Jahāngīr, tr. Rogers and Beveridge, *The Tuzuk-i Jahāngīrī*, I, pp. 5–10.
35. Ibid., I, p. 60.
36. Ibid., II, pp. 247–99.
37. Prasad, *History of Jahāngīr*, pp. 337–59.
38. Roe, ed. Foster, *The Embassy of Sir Thomas Roe to India*, p. 270.
39. Saksena, *History of Shāhjahān of Delhi*, pp. 66–78.
40. Ibid., pp. 80–90.
41. Manrique, tr. and ed. Luard and Holsen, *Travels of Fray Sebastian Manrique*, II, pp. 325–39;'Abdu'l-Hamid Lahauri, *Bādshāh-nāma*, I, pp. 435–6.
42. The oration delivered on Fridays at the time of meridian prayer and after the two *'id* prayers. The Sunnīs in their *khutba* eulogize the first four successors to the Prophet; the Shī'īs extol the virtue of the Prophet's cousin and son-in-law (the fourth Caliph in order of succession) and his eleven successors.
43. Rizvi, *A Socio-Intellectual History of the Isnā 'Asharz Shī'īs in India*, I, pp. 328–34.
44. Ibid., I, pp. 280–1.
45. Jadunath Sarkar, *History of Aurangzīb*, I, pp. 265–346.
46. Ibid., II, pp. 348–420.
47. Rizvi, *Muslim Revivalist Movements in Northern India*, pp. 393–4.
48. Ibid., pp. 362–4; Sarkar, *History of Aurangzīb*, II, pp. 440–550.
49. Khafi Khān, *Muntakhabu'l-lubāb*, tr. Anees Jahān Syed, *Aurangzīb*, pp. 135–6.
50. Singh, *A History of the Sikhs*, I, pp. 89–94.
51. MacKenzie, *Poems from the Diwān of Khushāl Khān Khattak*, pp. 215–16.
52. H. Beveridge and Baini Prasad (trs.), *The Ma'āthir-ul-umarā'*, Patna, 1979, I, pp. 247–53.

53. Satish Chandra *et al*, *Mārwār under Jaswant Singh*, Meerut, 1976, pp. 255–68.
54. Jagdish Sarkar, *The Military Despatches of a Seventeenth-Century Indian General*, Calcutta, 1969; Jadunath Sarkar and Raghubir Singh, *Shivājī's Visit to Aurangzīb at Agra*, Calcutta, 1963, pp. 1–27.
55. Jadunath Sarkar, *Shivājī and his Times*, Calcutta, 1961, pp. 201–15.
56. Gokhale, *Chatrapatī Sambhājī*, pp. 33–50.
57. Jadunath Sarkar, *History of Aurangzīb*, IV, pp. 362–94.
58. Ibid., IV, pp. 395–456.
59. Bhīm Sen, *Dilkushā*, in Rizvi, *Shāh Walī-Allāh and His Times*, pp. 99–100; Engl. tr. Khobrekar, *Tarīkh-i Dilkushā*, pp. 230–2.
60. Manucci, *Storia de Mogor*, II, p. 505.
61. Singh, *History of the Sikhs*, I, pp. 94–5.
62. Jadunath Sarkar, *History of Aurangzīb*, V, pp. 232–91.
63. Rizvi, *Shāh Walī-Allah and his Times*, p. 108.
64. Ibid., pp. 120–41.
65. Ibid., pp. 142–6.
66. S.C. Hill (ed.), 'Bengal in 1756-57', *Indian Record Series*, II, pp. 459–63.

IV: THE STATE

BIBLIOGRAPHY

Basic Arabic and Persian Sources

'Abdu'l-Haqq Muhaddis Dihlawi, *Nāriyya-i Sultaniyya*, India Office, Delhi, Persian 659b.

Abu'l-Fazl, *A'in-i Akbarī*, 3 vols., Lucknow, 1892: Engl. trs. H. F. Blochmann, rev. D.C. Phillot, Calcutta, 1939, 2nd edn.; II and III, H. S. Jarrett, rev. Jadunath Sarkar, Calcutta, 1948. Baranī, *Fatāw-i jahāndārī*, Lahore, 1972; Engl. tr. Mohammad Habib and Mrs Afsar Umar Salīm Khān, Allahabad, n.d.

Ghazali, Abu Hamid, *Naszhatu'l-mulāk*, Tehran, n.d.; Engl. tr. F. R. C. Bagley, *Ghazālī's Book of Counsel for Kings*, Oxford, 1964.

Hamadānī, Mir Sayyid 'Alī, *Zakhīratu'l-mulūk*, Lucknow, n.d.

Ibn Khaldun, *The Muqaddimah* (Arabic); Engl. tr. F. Rosenthal, 3 vols., New York, 1958.

Nizāmu'l-Mulk, *Siyasat-nama*, Tehran, 1956; Engl. tr. H. Darke, *The Book of Government or Rules for Kings*, London, 1960.

Qabil Khān (ed.), *Adab-i 'Alamgīrī*, Lahore, 1971.

al-Turtushi, Muhammad b., al Walid, *Sirāju'l-mulūk*, Alexandria, 1872–4 (Arabic); Persian tr. MS. in Oriental Institute, Dushanbe.

Modern Works in English

Ahmad, M. B., *The Administration of Justice in Medieval India*, Alīgarh, 1941.

Arnold, T. W., *The Caliphate*, London, 1965, 2nd rev. edn.

Aziz, Abdul, *The Mansabdārī System and the Mughal Army*, London, 1946; Delhi, 1972, reprint.

____, *Arms and Jewellery of the Indian Mughals*, London, 1947.
Day, U. B., *Administrative Systems of Delhi Sultanate*, Allahabad, 1959.
Habib, I., *The Agrarian System of Mughal India*, Bombay, 1963.
Hasan, S. N., *Thoughts on Agrarian Relations in Mughal India*, New Delhi, 1973.
Ibn Hasan, *The Central Structure of the Mughal Empire*, Karachi, 1967, reprint.
Irvine, W., *The Army of the Indian Moguls*, New Delhi, 1962, reprint.
Lambton, A. K. S., *Landlord and Peasant in Persia*, London, 1953.
Qureshi, I. B., *The Administration of the Sultanate of Delhi*, Lahore, 1944, 2nd edn.; Karachi, 1958, rev. edn.
____, *The Administration of the Mughal Empire*, Karachi, 1966.
Richards, J. F., *Mughal Administration of Golconda*, Oxford and London, 1975.
Saran P., *The Provincial Government of the Mughals*, Allahabad, 1941.
____, *Studies in Medieval Indian History*, Delhi, 1952.
Sarkar Jadunath, *Mughal Administration*, Calcutta, 1952, 4th edn.
Sen, S.B., *Administrative System of the Marāthas*, Calcutta, 1925, rev. edn.
Sharma, Sri Ram, *Mughal Government and Administration*, Lahore, 1959, 3rd rev. edn.
Topa, I., *Politics in Pre-Mughal Times*, Delhi, 1976, reprint. Tripathi, R. P., *Some Aspects of Muslim Administration*, Allahabad, 1956, rev. edn.

REFERENCES

I. Qur‘ān, Chapter III, verse 25.
2. Abu'l ‘Ala' Maududi, Abu Hanīfah and Abu Yusuf, in M. M.Sharif (ed.), *A History of Muslim Philosophy*, Wiesbaden, 1963, I, pp. 687-8.
3. Qur‘ān, Chapter IV, verse_ 62.
4. Ghazali, tr. Bagley, *Ghazāll's Book of Counselfor Kings*, pp. 45-6.
5. See above, p. 333.
6. Ghazali, ‘*Ihyā‘ ’ulūm al-dīn*’, in H. A. R. Gibb, *Islamic Society and the West*, London, 1960, reprint, I, p. 31.
7. Al-Turtūshi, *Sijāj al-mulūk*, pp. 88, 92.
8. Ibid., p. 12.
9. Baranī, *Tār’ikh-i Firūz Shāhī*, pp. 70–l.
10. Ibid., p. 147.
11. Amir Khusraw, *Qirānu‘s-s’dayn*, Alīgarh, 1918, pp. 21–2.
12. Amir Khusraw, *Khazā‘inu‘l-futūh*, p. 6.
13. Badr-i Chach, *Qasā‘id-i Badr-i Chāch*, pp. 14–16.
14. Mohammad Habib and Mrs Afsar Umar Salīm Khān, *The Political Theory of the Delhi Sultanate*, Allahabad, pp. 39–40.
15. Ibid., pp. 64-5.
16. Arnold, *The Caliphate*, pp. 140–1.
17. Bada’uni, tr. Ranking, *Muntakhabu’t-tawār’ikh*, I, p. 480.
18. Rizvi, *Religious and Intellectual History of the Muslims in Akbar’s Reign*, p. 360.

19. Turtāshi, *Sirāju'l-mulāk*, Persian tr. Dushanke, USSR, f. 3a.
20. 'Abdu'l-Haqq, *Nāriyya-i Sultāniyya*, ff. 6–11a, 14a.
21. Ibid., ff. 10b-11a.
22. Rizvi, *Muslim Revivalist Movements in Northern India*, pp. 223–32.
23. Qabil Khān (ed.), *Abāb-i 'Alamg'ir'i*, Lahore, 1971, II, pp. 1146–7.
24. *Encyclopaedia of Islam*², III, pp. 510–13.
25. Habib and Salīm Khān, *Political Theory of the Delhi Sultanate*, p. 65.
26. Qur'ān, Chapter IX, verse 29.
27. Baranī, *Tārīkh-i Fīrūz Shāhī*, p. 97.
28. Ibid., pp. 509–11.
29. Ibid., p. 522.
30. Nizāmu'd-Dīn, tr. De, *Tabaqāt-i Akbarī*, I, p. 239.
31. 'Afif, *Tār'ikh-i Fīrūz Shāhī*, pp. 382–4.
32. Bada'uni, tr. Lowe, *Muntakhabu't-tawārīkh*, II, pp. 367–8.
33. Abu'l-Fazl, tr. Blochmann, *A'īn-i Akbarī*, I, pp. 287–8.
34. Bada'uni, tr. Lowe, II, p. 388.
35. Abu'l-Fazl, tr. Jarrett, *A'īn-i Akbarī*, II, pp. 42–3.
36. Muhammad Salih Kamboh, *'Amal-i Sālih*, Calcutta, 1923–46, III, pp. 246–8.
37. Bada'uni, tr. Ranking, *Muntakhabu't-tawārikh*, I, p. 497.
38. Abu'l-Fazl, tr. Jarrett, I, pp. 166–9.
39. Ibid., I, p. 165.
40. Manucci, *Storia do Mogor*, II, pp. 361, 400.
41. Qureshi, *The Administration of the Sultanate of Delhi*, 1958, IV, pp. 69–71.
42. Monserrate, *Commentary*, p. 201; Manucci, *Storia do Mogor*, II, p. 419.
43. *Adābu'l-harb wa'sh-Shujā'a*, India Office, London, Ethe, I, 2767, f. 52a.
44. Ibn Hasan, *The Central Structure of the Mughal Empire*, pp. 173–87.
45. Chandra, *Parties and Politics at the Mughal Court*, pp. 25–6.
46. Ibn Hasan, *Central Structure*, pp. 188–209.
47. Baranī, *Tārik-i Firūz Shāhī*, p. 145.
48. 'Umari, tr. Spies, *Masālik al-absār fi mamālik al-amsār*, p. 29.
49. Irfan Habib, 'Agrarian Economy', in Raychaudhuri and Habib (eds.), *The Cambridge Economic History of India*, I, pp. 70–1.
50. 'Afif, *Tārikh-i Firūz Shāhī*, pp. 296–7.
51. Manucci, *Storia do Mogor*, II, p. 377.
52. Aziz, *The Mansabdārī System and the Mughal Army*, pp. 46–93; 'Alī, *The Mughal Nobility under Aurangzīb*, pp. 40–7.
53. 'Abdu'l-Hamīd Lahauri, *Bādshāh-nāma*, II, pp. 715–16.
54. Abu'l-Fazl, tr. Beveridge, *Akbar-nāma*, III, p. 1032.
55. Abu'l-Fazl, tr. Blochmann, I, p. 259–60.
56. De Laet, tr. Hoyland and Banerjee, *The Empire of the Great Mogal*, Bombay, 1928, pp. 113–14.
57. Abu'l-Fazl, tr. Blochmann, I, pp. 261–4.
58. I. A. Khān, 'Early Use of Cannon and Musket in India', *Journal of the Economic and Social History of the Orient*, 1981, pp. 146–64.

59. Abu'l-Fazl, tr. Blochmann, I, pp. 119–21.
60. Thévenot, ed. Sen, *Indian Travels of Thivenot and Careri*, New Delhi, 1949, p. 62.
61. Abu'l-Fazl, tr. Blochmann, I, p. 121.
62. Bada'uni, tr. Lowe, *Muntakhabu't-tawār'ikh*, II, p. 206.
63. Pelsaert, tr. Moreland and Geyl, *Jahāngīr's India: The Remonstrantie of Francisco Pelsaert*, p. 42.
64. Jadunath Sarkar, *History of Aurangzīb*, III, pp. 275–8.
65. Manrique, tr. and ed. Luard and Holsen, *Travels*, pp. 224–5, 236.
66. Monserrate, *Commentary* p. 214.
67. Pelsaert, tr. Moreland and Geyl, *The Remonstrantie*, pp. 54–5.
68. *Encyclopaedia of Islam*[2], II, p. 566–7.
69. Fīrūz Shāh, *Futāhāt-i Firūz Shāh-ī*, p. 21.
70. Abu'l-Fazl, tr. Beveridge, II, pp. 316-7; Rizvi, *Muslim Revivalist Movements in Northern India*, pp. 69–70.
71. Khafi Khān, tr. Anees Jahān, *Muntakhabu'l-lubāb*, pp. 275–6.
72. See above, note 4, Chapter 1, p. 321.
73. Jadunath Sarkar, *History of Aurangzīb*, III, pp. 268–75; S. Chandra, 'Jizyah and the State in India during the 17th Century', *Journal of Economic and Social History of the Orient*, 1969, pp. 322–40.
74. Manucci, *Storia do Mogor*, II, p. 234.
75. Baranī, p. 287.
76. Habib, *The Agrarian System of Mughal India*, pp. 204–14.
77. Ibid., pp. 301, 353–63.
78. Baranī, *Tārlkh-i Firūz Shāhī*, p. 497.
79. Bada'uni, tr. Haig, *Muntakhabu't-taswārīkh*, III, p. 194.
80. Abu'l-Fazl, tr. Beveridge, III, p. 1063.
81. *Ma'āthir al-umarā'*, I, p. 77.
82. Jadunath Sarkar, *History of Aurangzīb*, III, pp. 82-92.
83. Abu'l-Fazl, tr. Blochmann, I, p. 278.
84. Abu'l-Fazl, tr. Jarrett, II, pp. 43–5.
85. Qureshi, *The Administration of the Sultanate of Delhi*, pp. 197–9.
86. Abu'l-Fazl, tr. Jarrett, II, pp. 37-41.
87. Ibn Battuta, tr. Gibb, *The Travels of Ibn Battūta*, p. 594.
88. Pelsaert, tr. Moreland and Geyl, *The Remonstrantie*, p. 58.
89. Abu'l-Fazl, tr. Jarrett, II, pp. 41–2.

V: SOCIAL AND ECONOMIC CONDITIONS

BIBLIOGRAPHY

Travels and Geography: Arabic

Abu Zayd, *Relation des voyages faits par les Arabes et les Persans dans l'Inde eta La Chine* (*Silsilat al-tawānkh*)*; The Account of Sulaymān the Merchant*, written in AD 851 and compiled by Abu Zayd Hasan towards AD 916 (Arabic text), Langles (1811); French tr. and commentary, M. Reinaud, 2 vols., Paris, 1845.

Ibn Battuta, *Voyages d'Ibn Batoutah*, ed. C. Defremery and B. R. Sanguinetti, 4 vols., Paris 1853–8; Engl. tr. and selected, H. A. R. Gibb, London, 1953; Engl. tr. H. A. R. Gibb, 3 vols., Cambridge 1958–71 (Hakluyt Society), tr. Mahdi Husain, *Rehla*, Baroda, 1976.

Ibn Khurradazbih, *Kitāb al masālik wa'l-mamālik.* Leiden, 1889.

al-Idrisi, al-Sharif, *Kitāb Nuzhat al-Mushtāqfi'Khtirāq al'Afoq;* Engl. tr. and commentary, S. Maqbul Ahmad, Leiden, 1960. Khwarizmi, Abu Ja'far Muhammad, *Kitāb Sūrat al-Arz*, Leipzig, 1926.

Marvazi, Tahir, *Sharaf al-zamān Tāhir Marvazi on China, the Turks and India;* Arabic text with Engl. tr. and commentary, V. Minorsky, London, 1942.

Mas'udi, *Kitāb Murāj al-Zahab wa ma'adin al-jawhar;* Arabic text with French tr. C. Barbier de Meynard and Pavet de Courteille, *Les Prairies d'Or*, Paris, 1861–77.

al-Qalqashandi, Shihabu'd-Dīn, *Subh al-A'sha*, Cairo; Engl. tr. of chapters on India, Otto Spies, *Muslim University Journal*, Aligarh, June 1935, pp. 1–77.

al-'Umari, Shihabu'd-Dīn, *Masālik al-absār fi mamālik al-amsār;* Engl. tr. of Indian portion, Otto Spies, *Muslim University Journal*, Alīgarh, March 1943, pp. 1–63.

Travels: Chinese

Ma Huan, *Ying-yai Sheng-lan* 1433; Engl. tr. J. V. G. Mills, *The Over-All Sūrvey of the Ocean's Shores*, Cambridge (Hakluyt Society), 1970.

Travels: Europeans

Barbosa, Duarte, *The Book of Duarte Barbosa: An Acount of the Countries Bordering on the Indian Ocean and their Inhabitants;* Engl. tr. M. L. Dames, 2 vols., London (Hakluyt Society), 1918, 1921.

Bernier, François, *Travels in the Mogul Empire, 1656–68;* Engl. tr. Irving Brock; rev. and annotated, A. Constable, London, 1891; rev. and annotated, V. A. Smith, London, 1914, 1916.

Birch, Walter de Gray, *The Commentaries of the Great Alfonso D'Alboquerque*,

4 vols., London (Hakluyt Society), 1880.

Cabral, Pedro Alvares, *The Voyage of Pedro Alvares Cabral to Brazil and India;* Engl. tr. W. N. Greenlee, London, 1938.

Foster, W., *Early Travels in India*, London, 1921.

Fryer, John, *A New Account of East India and Persia, Being Nine Years' Travels 1672–81*, ed. W. Crooke, 3 vols., London (Hakluyt Society), 1909, 1912, 1915.

Jourdain, John, *The Journal of John Jourdain 1608-17*, ed. W. Foster, Cambridge (Hakluyt Society), 1905.

de Laet, John, *De Imperio Magni Mogolis, Sive India Veri Commentarius e Varius Sactoribus Congestes*, Amsterdam, 1631; Engl. tr. *J.* S. Hoyland and S. N. Banerjee, Bombay, 1928.

Locke, John C. (ed.), *The First Englishmen in India*, London, 1930. Major, R. H., *India in the Fifteenth Century*, London (Hakluyt Society), 1857.

Manrique, F. S., *The Travels of Fray Sebastian Manrique;* 2 vols., Engl. tr. and ed. C. E. Luard and H. Holsten, London (Hakluyt Society), 1927.

Manucci, N., *Storia do Mogor;* Engl. tr. W. Irvine, 4 vols., London, 1908.

Moreland, W. H. (ed. and tr.), *Relations of Golconda in the Early Seventeenth Century*, London (Hakluyt Society), 1931.

Mundy, P., *The Travels of Peter Mundy*, ed. R. C. Temple, 5 vols., Cambridge (Hakluyt Society), 1914.

Oaten, E. F., *European Travellers in India during the 15th, 16th and 17th Centuries*, London, 1909.

Ovington J., *A Voyage to Sūral in the Year 1689*, ed. H. G. Rawlinson, London, 1929.

Pelsaert, *F.*, *Jahāng'ir's India: The Remonstrantie of F. Pelsaert;* Engl. tr. W. H. Moreland and P. Geyl, Cambridge, 1925, Delhi, 1972, reprint.

Pinkerton, T., (compiler), *A General Collection of the Best and Most Interesting Voyages and Travels in All Parts of the World*, 17 vols., London, 1908–14.

Polo, Marco, *Marco Polo: The Description of the World*, Engl. tr. A. C. Moule and P. Pelliot, 2 vols., London, 1938.

Purchas, S. (compiler), *Purchas, his Pilgrimes*, 20 vols., Glasgow, 1905–7.

Rawlinson, H. G. (ed.), *Narratives from Purchas, his Pilgrimes*, Cambridge, 1931.

Roe, Sir Thomas, *The Embassy of Sir Thomas Roe to the Court of the Great Mogul*, ed. W. Foster; London, 1926, rev. edn; 1970, reprint.

Tavernier, J. B., *Tavernier's Travels in India;* Engl. tr. V. Ball, ed. W. Crooke, 2 vols., London, 1889; 2nd edn. 1925, New Delhi, 1977, reprint.

Thévenot, Jean de,. *Indian Travels of Careri and Thivenot*, ed. S. N. Sen, Delhi, 1949.

Valle, Pierto della, *The Travels of Pietro della Valle in India*, ed. E. Grey, 2 vo1s., London, 1892.

Varthema, Lodovic de, *Travels in Egypt, Syria, Persia, India, Ethiopia*, tr. J. W. James, ed. G. P. Badger, London (Hakluyt Society), 1863.

Wheeler, J. T. and Macmillan, M., *European Travellers in India*, Calcutta, 1956.

Modern Works on Numismatics

Agarwala, V. S., 'A Unique Treatise on Medieval Indian Coins' in H. K. Sherwani (ed.), *Ghulām Yazdāni Commemoration Volume*, Hyderābād, 1936.

Ahmad, S., *Supplement to Volume III of the Catalogue of Coins in the Indian Museum, Calcutta* (Mughal Emperors of India), Calcutta, 1939.

Husain, M. K., *The Catalogue of Coins of the Mughal Emperors*, (Treasure trove collection, Bombay), Bombay, 1968.

Lane-Poole, S., *The Coins of the Mughal Emperors of Hindustan in the British Museum*, ed. R. Stuart Poole, London, 1892.

Rodgers, C. J., *Catalogue of Coins in the Government Museum*, Lahore, 1891.

____, *Coins of the Mughal Emperors of India*, Calcutta, 1893.

Wright, H. N., *Catalogue of Coins in the Indian Museum, Calcutta*, II (sultans of Delhi and contemporary dynasties), III (Mughal emperors), Oxford, 1907, 1908.

____, *Coinage and Metrology of the Sultans of Delhi*, incorporating 'The Catalogue of Coins in the Author's Cabinet now in the Delhi Museum ', Delhi, 1936; Delhi, 1974, reprint.

General Modem Works in English

Alvi, M. A., and Rahman, A., *Fathullāh Shirazi-A Sixteenth Century Indian Scientist*, New Delhi, 1968. Appadorai, A., *Economic Conditions in Southern India (1000–1500 AD)*, Madras, 1936.

Baden-Powell, B. H, *Land Systems of British India*, 3 vols., Oxford, 1892.

Buchanan, F., *A Journey from Madras through the Countries of Mysore, Cavara and Malabar*, Madras, 1807.

Chaudhuri, K. N., *The Trading World of Asia and the English East India Company, 1660–1760*, Cambridge, 1978.

Chicherov, A.I., *India, Economic Development in the 16th-18th Centuries: Outline History of Crafts and Trade*, Moscow, 1971.

Chopra, P. N., *Some Aspects of Social Life during the Mughal Age (1526–1707)*, Jaipur, 1963.

Datta, K. K., *Survey of India's Social Life and Economic Conditions in the Eighteenth Century, 1707–1813*), Calcutta, 1961.

Goiten, S. D., *Studies in Islamic History and Institutions*, Leiden, 1966.

Gokhale, B. G., *Sūral in the Seventeenth Century*, London, 1979.

Gopal, S., *Commerce and Craft in Gujarāt: 16th and 17th Centuries*, New Delhi, 1975.

Gupta, A. Das, *Malabar in Asian Trade, 1740–1800*, Cambridge, 1967. Haque, Ziaul, *Landlord and Peasant in Early Islam: A Study of the Legal Doctrine of Muzāra'a/Share Cropping*, Islamabad, 1977.

Hourani, G., *Arab Seafaring in the Indian Ocean*, Princeton, 1951.

Khān, Ahsan Raza, *Chieftains in the Mughal Empire during the Reign of Akbar*,

Simla, 1979.
Kurz, Otto, *European Clocks and Watches in the Near East*, London, 1975.
Lambton, A. K. S., *Islamic Society in Persia*, London, 1954.
____, *Landlord and Peasant in Persia*, London, 1954.
Maddison, Angus, *Class Structure and Economic Growth – India and Pakistan since the Mughals*, London, 1971.
Mookerji, K K., *Indian Shipping*, Bombay, 1912.
Moreland, W. H., *India at the Death of Akbar*, London, 1920.
____, *From Akbar to Aurangzeb, a Study in Indian Economic History*, London, 1923.
____, *Agrarian Systems of Moslem India*, Cambridge, 1929.
Naqvi, H. K., *Urban Centres and Industries in Upper India, 1556–1803*, Bombay, 1968.
____, *Urbanization and Urban Centres under the Great Mughals*, Simla, 1972.
Ojha, P. N., *Some Aspects of North Indian Social Life, 1556-1707*, Patna, 1961.
Pearson, M. N., *Merchants and Rulers in Gujarāt*, Berkeley, Calif., 1976.
Qaisar, A. J., *The Indian Response to European Technology and Culture* (*1498–1707*), Delhi, 1982.
Rashid, A., *Society and Culture in Medieval India*, Calcutta, 1969.
Raychaudhuri, T., *Bengal under Akbar and Jahangīr*, Calcutta, 1953; New Delhi, 1969, reprint.
____ and Habib, I. (eds.), *The Cambridge Economic History of India*, I (*c.* 1200–*c.* 1750), Cambridge, 1982.
Richards, D. S. (ed.), *Islam and the Trade of Asia*, Oxford and Pennsylvania, 1970.
Saletore, B. A., *Social and Political Life.in the Vijayanagara Empire*, Madras, 1934.
Serjeant, R. B., *The Portuguese of the South Arabian Coast*, Oxford, 1963.
Siddiqi, N. A., *Land Revenue Administration under the Mughals*, Bombay, 1970.
White, Lynn Jnr., *Medieval Technology and Social Change*, New York, 1964.
Wolf, E., *Peasants*, Englewood Cliffs, N.J., 1960.

REFERENCES

1. Ar-Rāwandi, Muhammad ibn 'Alī ibn Sulayman, *The Rāhatu's sudār*, London, 1921, p. 17.
2. 'Umari, tr. Spies, *Masālik al-absār*, p. 28.
3. Abu'l-Fazl, tr. Beveridge, *Akbar-nāma*, I, p. 642.
4. Abu'l-Fazl, tr. Jarrett, *A'in-i Akbari*, II, tables of *Sarkārs.*
5. Rizvi, *Shāh 'Abd al-'Aziz*, pp. 182–3.
6. Rizvi, *Muslim Revivalist Movements in Northern India*, p. 142.
7. Bada'uni, tr. Lowe, *Muntakhabu't-tawār'ikh*, II, pp. 211–13.
8. Rizvi, *A History of Sūfism in India*, I, p. 124.
9. Rizvi, *Religious and. Intellectual History of the Muslims in Akbar's Reign*, pp. 183–4.

10. Monserrate, *The Commentary*, p. 209.
11. Baranī, *Tarzkh-i Firāz Shāhz*, pp. 156–8.
12. 'Umari, tr. Spies, *Masālik al-absār*, pp. 45–6.
13. See above, p. 106.
14. Bābur, tr. Beveridge, *Bābur-nāma*, p. 487.
15. Rizvi, *History of Sūfism*, II, p. 276.
16. Bābur, tr. Beveridge, pp. 486–7.
17. 'Afif, *Tārzkh-i Firāz Shāhz*, pp. 99–100, 1078–84.
18. Satish Chandra, 'Standard of Living', in Raychaudhuri and Habib (eds.), *The Cambridge Economic History of India*, I, pp. 458–60.
19. Hasan, Nūrul, 'Zamīndārs under the Mughals', in R. E. Frykenberg (ed.), *Land Control and Social Structure in Indian History*, Wisconsin, 1969, pp. 17–28.
20. Habib, *The Agrarian System of Mughal India*, p. 164.
21. Jadunath Sarkar, *History of Aurangzīb*, V, pp. 333–4.
22. Gibb (tr.), *The Travels of Ibn Battuta*, III, pp. 624–5.
23. Ibid., III, pp. 619–22.
24. 'Umari, tr. Spies, *Masālik al-absār*, pp. 18–19.
25. 'Afif, *Tarzkh-i Fīrūz Shāhz*, pp. 124–6, 148.
26. 'Alī bin Mahmūd, tr. Syed Nawab'Alī, *Mir'āt-i Ahmadi*, supplement, pp. 8–17.
27. Rizvi, *History of Sūfism*, I, p. 158.
28. Bernier, ed. Constable, *Travels in the Mogul Empire*, pp. 247–8.
29. See below, p. 243.
30. Rizvi, *History of Sūfism*, I, p. 153.
31. Manucci, *Storia do Mogor*, II, p. 453.
32. Baranī, *Tānkh-i Fīrūz Shāhl*, pp. 116–7.
33. Rizvi, *Religious and Intellectual History*, p. 322.
34. Abu'l-Fazl, tr. Blochmann, *A'in-i Akban*, I, pp. 275–6.
35. Rizvi, *History of Sūfism*, I, p. 164.
36. Minhaj, tr. Raverty, *Tabaqat-i Nasin*, I, p. 646.
37. K. A. Nizāmi, *Studies in Medieval Indian History and Culture*, Allahabad, 1966, pp. 73–9.
38. Rizvi, *A Socio-Intellectual History of the Isnā 'Ashan Shī'īs in India*, II, pp. 203–11.
39. Rizvi, *Religious and Intellectual History*, pp. 196–7.
40. W. Foster (ed.), *The English Factories in India,1637–1641*, Oxford, 1912, p. 134; K. N. Chaudhuri, 'The Structure of Indian Textile Industry in the Seventeenth and Eighteenth Centuries', *Indian Economic and Social History Review*, New Delhi, 1974, XI, Nos. 2–3, p. 136.
41. Birch, *The Commentaries of the Great Alfonso D'Alboquerque*, III, p. 58.
42. Gibb (tr.), *Travels of Ibn Battūta*, III, p. 288.
43. Pearson, *Merchants and Rulers in Gujarāt*, pp. 40–4, 76–7, 83–4, 93–5, 99–100.

44. W. Foster (ed.), *The English Factories in India 1646–50*, Oxford, 1914, p. 34.
45. Qaisar, *The Indian Response to European Technology and Culture*, pp. 70–104.
46. Ibid., pp. 60–4.
47. Ibid., pp. 64–9.
48. Hasan Sijzi, *Fawā'idu'l-fu'ād*, pp. 130–l.
49. Minhaj, tr. Raverty, *Tabaqāt-i Nāsiri*, II, p. 1133.
50. Hamid Qalandar, *Khayru'l-majālis*, p. 241.
51. Tavernier, *Travels in India*, 1889 edn., I, p. 28.
52. Anecdote of Khwaja Qutbu'd-Dīn Bakhtiyār Kaki in Rizvi, *History of Sūfism*, I, p. 137.
53. Irfan Habib, 'Usury in Medieval India', *Comparative Studies in Society and History* (The Hague), VI, 1964, p. 413.
54. Pearson, *Merchants and Rulers in Gujarāt*, pp. 125–7, 135, 149–50.
55. M.F. Lokhandwala (tr.), *Mir'āt-i Ahmadi*, pp. 210–11.
56. Jadunath Sarkar, *Shivājl and his Times*, pp. 96-8, 171–5.
57. Khafi Khān, tr. Anees Jahān, *Muntakhabu'l-lubāb*, pp. 271-2.
58. M. S. Commissariat, *Studies in the History of Gujarāt*, Bombay, 1935, pp. 54–76.
59. Pelsaert, tr. Moreland and Geyl, *The Remonstrantie of Francisco Pelsaert*, p. 78.
60. Tavernier, *Travels in India*, II, p. 183.

VI: RELIGION

BIBLIOGRAPHY

Primary Sources in Persian

'Abdu'I-Haqq Muhaddis Dihlawi, *Akhbāru'l-akhyār*, Delhi, 1914. Amir Hasan Sijzi, *Fawā'idu'l-fu'ād*, Bulandshahr, 1855–6.

Amir Khwurd, *Siyaru'l-awliyā'*, Delhi, 1882.

Ardistani, Zu'lfaqar, *Dabistān-i Mazāhib*, Lucknow, n.d.; Engl. tr. David Shea and Anthony Troyer, *The Dabistān or the School of Manners*, Paris, 1843.

-Biruni, *Kitāb fi tahqzq mā li'l-Hind*, Hyderābād, 1958 (Arabic); Engl. tr. E. C. Sachau, *Alberānz's India*, London, 1887; Delhi, 1964, reprint.

Dara Shukoh, *Sakznat'ul-awliyā'*, Tehran, n.d.

____, *Safinatu'l-awliyā'*, Kanpur, 1900.

Ghulam Sarwar, Mufti, *Khazznatu'l-asfzyā'*, Kanpur, 1894.

Hamid Qalandar, *Khayru'l-majālis*, Alīgarh, 1959.

Hashim Badakhshani, Muhammad, *Zubdatu'l-maqāmāt*, Kanpur, 1890.

Hujwiri, 'Alī b., 'Usman, *Kashfu'l-mahjāb*, Lahore, 1923; Engl. tr. R. A. Nicholson, London, 1959, reprint.

Jamali, Kanboh Dihlawi, *Siyaru'l-'ārifin*, Delhi, 1893.

____, *Lawā'ih*, ed. and tr. E. H. Whinfield and Mirza Muhammad Qazwini, London, 1906.

Jami, Maulana 'Abdu'r-Rahman, *Nafahatu'l-uns*, Tehran, 1947.

Mujaddid Alf-i Sani, Shaykh Ahmad Sirhindi, *Maktābāt-i lmam-i Rabbānz*, Karachi, 1972.

Qasuri, 'Abdull'ah, Khweshgi, *Ma'āriju'l-wilāyat*, MS. Azar Collection, Panjāb University.

Rumi, Jalalu'd-Dīn, *The Mathnavz*, ed. R. A. Nicholson, 8 vols., London, 1925–40.

____, *Tales of Mystic Meaning;* Engl. tr. R. A. Nicholson, London,1931.

____, *Selections (from the Masnavī, Dīvān and Fīhi mā fih)*, Engl. tr. R. A. Nicholson, ed. A. J. Arberry, London, 1950.

____, *Discourses of Rāmi*, Engl. tr. A. J. Arberry, London, 1961.

____, *Tales fromthe Masnavi*, Engl. tr.J. A. Arberry, London, 1961.

Waliu'llah Dihlawi, Shāh, *Anfāsu'l-'ārifin*, Delhi, 1897.

____, *Hama'āt*, Hyderābād Sind, n.d.; Urdu tr. Lahore, n.d.

Modern Works in English

Abdel-Kader, A. H., *The Life, Personaliry and Writings of al-Junayd*, London, 1962.

Afifi, A. A., *The Mystical Philosophy of Muhyi'd-Dīn Ibnu'l-'Arabī*, Cambridge, 1939.

Ahmad, Aziz, *Studies in Islamic Culture in the Indian Environment*, Oxford, 1964.

____ and von Grunebaum, G. E., *Muslim Self-Statement in India and Pakistan, 1857-1968*, Wiesbaden, 1970.

Ahmad Shāh, *The Bijak of Kabīr*, Hamirpur, 1917.

Arberry, A. G., *An Introduction to the History of Sūfism*, Oxford, 1962.

____, *Muslim Saints and Mystics*, London, 1966. Arnold, T. W., *The Preaching of Islam*, London, 1896.

Burkhardt, T., *An Introduction to Sūfi Doctrine*, tr. D. M. Matheson, Lahore, 1963.

Carpenter, J., *Theism in Medieval India*, London, 1921; New Delhi, 1977, reprint.

Cunningham, J. D., *A History of the Sikhs*, ed. H. L. 0. Garrett and R. R. Sethi, Delhi, 1955.

Dasgupta, S., *Obscure Religious Cults*, Calcutta, 1962.

Faruqi, Burhan Ahmad, *The Mujaddid's Conception of Tauhld*, Lahore, 1940.

Friedmann, Johanan, *Shaykh Ahmad Sirhindi: An Outline of his Thought and a Study of His Image in the Eyes of Posterity*, Montreal, 1971.

Gibb, H. A. R., *Mohammedanism*, New York, 1958.

Grewal, J. S., *The Mughals and the Jogīs of Jakhbār*, Simla, 1967.

____, *Gurū Nānak in History*, Chandigarh, 1969.

Halepota, *A.J.*, *Philosophy of Shāh Wallu'llāh*, Lahore, n.d.
Haqq, Enamul, *Muslim Bengali Literature*, Karachi, 1957.
Hasrat, B. J., *Dārā Shikoh*, (*sic*) Santiniketan, 1953; New Delhi, 1982, rev. edn.
Hodgson, G. S., *The Order of Assassins*, The Haque, 1955.
Hourani, G. F., *Essays on Islamic Philosophy and Science*, New York, 1975.
Husain, Y., *Glimpses of Medieval Indian Culture*, Bombay, 1957.
Izutsu, T., *A Comparative Study of the Key Philosophical Concepts in Sūfism and Taoism*, Tokyo, 1966.
____, *Ethico-Religious Concepts in the Qur'ān*, Montreal, 1966, rev. edn.
Landau, R., *The Philosophy of Ibn 'Arabī*, London, 1960. Macauliffe, M.A., *The Sikh Religion*, Oxford, 1909.
Mcleod, W., *Gurū Nānak and the Sikh Religion*, Oxford, 1968.
Mirza, M. W., *The Life and Works of Amīr Khusrau*, Calcutta, 1935.
Misra, S.C., *Muslim Communities in Gujarāt*, Bombay, 1964.
Nicholson, R. H. A., *The Mystics of Islam*, London, 1914.
____, *The Idea of Personality in Sūfism*, Cambridge, 1923.
____, *Studies in Islamic Mysticism*, Cambridge, 1967, reprint.
Nizāmi, K. A., *The Life and Times of Shaikh Farīd al-Dīn Ganj-i Shakar*, Alīgarh, 1955.
____, *Religion and Politics in India during the Thirteenth Century*, Bombay, 1961.
Oddie, G. A. (ed.), *Religion in South Asia*, Delhi, 1977.
Oman, J. C., *The Mystics, Ascetics and Saints of India*, London, 1903.
____, *The Brahmans, Theists and Muslims of India*, London, 1907.
Orr, W. G., *A Sixteenth-Century Indian Mystic*, London, 1947. Qureshi, I. H., *The Muslim Community of the Indo-Pakistan Subcontinent*, The Hague, 1962.
Rafiqi, A. Q., *Sūfism in Kashmīr*, Varanasi, n.d.
Rizvi, S. A. A., *Muslim Revivalist Movements in Northern India in the Sixteenth and Seventeenth Centuries*, Agra, 1965.
____, *Religious and Intellectual History of the Muslims in Akbar's Reign*, Delhi, 1975.
____, *A History of Sūfism in India*, 2 vols., Delhi, 1978, 1982.
____, *Shāh Wali Allah and his Times*, Canberra, 1980.
____, *Shāh 'Abd al-'Aziz*, Canberra, 1982.
____, *A Socio-Intellectual History of the Isna' 'Ashari Shī'īs in India*, Canberra and Delhi, 1986.
Roy, Asim, *The Islamic Syncretistic Tradition in Bengal*, Princeton, 1983.
Sarkar, Jadunath, *Anecdotes of Aurangzīb*, Calcutta, 1963, 4th edn.
Schimmel, A., *Gabriel's Wing*, Leiden, 1963.
____, 'Islamic Literatures of India, Sindhi Literature, Classical Urdu Literature', in J. Gonda (ed.), *History of Indian Literature*, Wiesbaden, 1973-5.
____, *Mystical Dimensions of Islam*, Chapel Hill, 1975.
____, *Pain and Grace*, Leiden, 1976.
____, *The Triumphal Sun*, London, 1978.

Sharif, Jafar, *Islam in India*, tr. G. A. Herklots, London, 1921, rev. edn.; New Delhi, 1972, reprint.

Singh, D., *Indian Bhakti Tradition and Sikh Gurūs*, Ludhiana, 1968.

Singh, Mohan, *Kabīr and the Bhakti Movement*, Lahore, 1934.

____, *A History of the Punjābi Literature*, Amritsar, 1956.

Subhan, J. A., *Sūfism, its Saints and Shrines*, Lucknow, 1960, reprint.

Tara Chand, *Influence of Islam on Indian Culture*, Allahabad, 1963, 2nd edn.

Titus, M. T., *Islam in India and Pakistan*, Calcutta, 1959, rev. edn. Trilochan Singh, *Gurū Nānak's Religion*, Delhi, 1968.

Trimingham, J. S., *The Sāfi Orders in Islam*, Oxford, 1971.

Vaudeville, Charlotte, *Kablr*, I, Oxford, 1974.

Watt, M., *The Faith and Practice of al-Ghazali*, London, 1953.

____, *Muslim Intellectual: A Study of al-Ghazali*, Edinburgh, 1963. Wescott, G. H., *Kabīr and the Kabzr Panth*, Calcutta, 1953, 2nd edn. Zaehner, R. C., *Hindu and Muslim Mysticism*, London, 1960.

REFERENCES

1. Baranī, *Tarikh-i Fīrūz Shāhī*, pp. 41–4.
2. M. Habib, *The Political Theory of the Delhi Sultanate*, Allahabad, 1961, p. 5.
3. Baranī, *Tankh-i Fīrūz Shāhi*, p. 465.
4. See below, pp. 269–70.
5. Bernier, ed. Constable, *Travels in the Mogul Empire*, pp. 324-5.
6. Rizvi, *A History of Sūfism in India*, I, pp. 103-8; II, pp. 36–53; see below, pp. 245, 265.
7. Rizvi, *History of Sūfism*, I, p. 28.
8. *Encyclopaedia of Islam2*, I, pp. 162–3.
9. Zaehner, *Hindu and Muslim Mysticism*, pp. 93-134, 198–218.
10. Rizvi, *History of Sūfism*, I, pp. 190-4.
11. Ibid., I, pp. 210–14.
12. Ibid., I, pp. 277–82.
13. Ibid., I, pp. 283–4.
14. Ibid., I, pp. 228–40.
15. Ibid., I, pp. 285–8.
16. Rizvi, *A Socio-Intellectual History of the Isna' 'Ashan Shī'īs in India*, I, pp. 202–5.
17. Amir Khwurd, *Siyaru'l-awliya'*, pp. 55–6.
18. Rizvi, *History of Sūfism*, I, pp. 127–31.
19. Ibid., I, pp. 131–3.
20. Ibid., I, pp. l33–8.
21. Ibid., I, pp. 139–54.
22. Ibid., I, pp. 154–64.
23. Ibid.; I, pp. 165–8.

24. Ibid., I, pp. 184–90.
25. Ibid., I, pp. 242–3.
26. Ibid., I, pp. 244–7.
27. Ibid., I, pp. 251–6.
28. Ibid., I, pp. 289–96.
29. Ibid., I, p. 297.
30. Jonaraja, *Rajatarangini*, p. 112.
31. Rizvi, *Socio-Intellectual History*, I, p. 167–76, 183–5.
32. Rizvi, *History of Sūfism*, I, pp. 300–3.
33. Gibb (tr.), *Travels of Ibn Battūta*, II, pp. 273–4.
34. Rizvi, *History of Sūfism*, II, p. 289.
35. Al-Biruni, tr. Sachau, *Alberānī's India*, I, pp. 7–8.
36. Ibid., I, pp. 19–23.
37. Ibid., I, p. 31.
38. Ibid., I, p. 124.
39. Ibid., I, p. 50.
40. Ibid., I, p. 233.
41. Ibid., I, pp. 19-20, 101-2; II, pp. 76, 137.
42. Ibid., II, p. 157.
43. Baranī, *Tarikh-i Firāz Shāhz*, pp. 42-3.
44. Mirza, *The Life and Works of Amzr Khusrau*, pp. 143-4.
45. Rizvi, *History of Sūfism*, I, p. 254.
46. Rizvi, *Religious and Intellectual History of the Muslims in Akbar's Reign*, pp. 207–9.
47. Rizvi, *History of Sūfism*, II, pp. 423–4.
48. Ibid., II, pp. 398–9.
49. Rizvi, *Shāh Walī Allah and his Times*, pp. 329–35.
50. *Alberunī's India*, I, p. 55.
51. Hujwiri, tr. Nicholson, *The Kashju'l-mahjub*, pp. 236, 243, 260–6, 271.
52. Amir Hasan Sijzi, *Fawa'idu'l-fu'ad*, p. 97; Rizvi, *History of Sūfism*, I, p. 143.
53. *F'awa'idu'l-ju'ad*, pp. 257–8; Rizvi, *History of Sūfism*, I, p. 144.
54. *Fawa'idu'l-ju'ad*, p. 250; Rizvi, *History of Sūfism*, I, p. 143.
55. Rizvi, *History of Sūfism*, I, pp. 327–8.
56. Ibid., I, p. 337.
57. Ibid., I, pp. 339–40.
58. Ibid., I, pp. 350–l.
59. Rizvi, *Muslim Revivalist Movements in Northern India*, p. 57.
60. Jahāngīr, tr. Rogers and Beveridge, *Tuzuk-i jahangīrī*, I, p. 359.
61. Ibn Khaldān, tr. Rosenthal, *The Muqaddimah*, II, p. 156.
62. Fīrūz Shāh, *Futuhat-i Fīrūz Shāhī*, p. 8.
63. Badā'āni, tr. Ranking, *Muntakhabu't-tawarīkh*, I, p. 511.
64. Rizvi, *Muslim Revivalist Movements*, pp. 104–10.
65. Bada'āni. tr. Ranking, I, pp. 523–5.
66. Rizvi, *Muslim Revivalist Movements*, pp. 133-4.

67. Rizvi, *History of Sufism*, II, pp. 151–73.
68. Ibid., II, pp. 58–61.
69. Ibid., II, pp. 76–80.
70. Jahāngīr, tr. Rogers and Beveridge, II, p. 111.
71. Rizvi, *History of Sūfism*, II, pp. 94–6.
72. Jahāngīr, tr. Rogers and Beveridge, II, p. 119.
73. Rizvi, *History of Sūfism*, II, pp. 103–6.
74. Ibid., II, p. 121.
75. Ibid., II, pp. 122–5.
76. Ibid., II, pp. 133–4.
77. Ibid., II, pp. 413–24.
78. Ibid., II, 480–1.
79. Ibid., II, pp. 181–5.
80. Ibid., II, p. 198.
81. Mujaddid, *Maktubat-i Imām-i Rabbani*, I, No. 11.
82. Rizvi, *History of Sūfism*, II, p. 218.
83. Ibid., II, pp. 242-3.
84. Ibid., II, p. 223.
85. Ibid., II, p. 339–42.
86. Rizvi, *Shāh Wall Allah*, pp. 317–53.
87. Ibid., pp. 343-58; Schimmel, *Pain and Grace.*
88. Rizvi, *History of Sūfism*, II, pp. 249–51.
89. Rizvi, *Socio-Intellectual History*, I, pp. 142–8.
90. Ibid., I, pp. 8–12.
91. Fīrūz Shāh, *Futuhat-i Fīrūz Shāhī*, p. 7.
92. Rizvi, *Socio-Intellectual History*, I, pp. 157–8.
93. Ibid., I, pp. 262–4.
94. Ibid., I, pp. 166–86.
95. Badā'uni, tr. Lowe, II, p. 337.
96. Rizvi, *Socio-Intellectual History*, I, pp. 227–35.
97. Ibid., I, pp. 215, 218, 219.
98. Ibid., I, pp. 348, 349.
99. Ibid., I, p. 350.
100. Ibid., I, pp. 376–84.
101. Jahāngīr, tr. Rogers.and Beveridge, I, p. 60.
102. Rizvi, *Socio-Intellectual History*, II, pp. 3–4.
103. Sarkar, *Anecdotes of Aurangzīb*, 4th edn. p. 88.

VII: FINE ARTS

BIBLIOGRAPHY

Architecture

Batley, C., *Indian Architecture*, Bombay, 1965.

Brown, P., *Indian Architecture* (*Islamic Period*), Bombay, 1975, 2nd rev. edn.

Briggs, Martin S., *Everyman's Concise Encyclopaedia of Architecture*, London, 1959.

Fergusson, James, *History of Indian Art and Architecture*, 1876; Delhi, 1967, reprint.

Ghurye, G. S, *Rājpūt Architecture*, Bombay, 1968.

Havell, E. B., *Indian Architecture*, London, 1919.

____, *A Handbook.to Agra and the Tāj*, Calcutta, 1924. Hurlimann, M., *Delhi, Agra, Fathpūr-Sikr'i*, London, 1963.

Husain, A. B. M., *Fathpūr-Sīkrī and its Architecture*, Dacca, 1970.

Kittoe, M., *Illustrations of Indian Architecture from the Muhammadan Conquest downwards*, Calcutta, 1838.

Kuhnel, E., *Islamic Art and Architecture*, New York, 1962. Latif, S. M., *Agra Historical and Descriptive*, Calcutta, 1896. Lockwood, de Forest, *Indian Domestic Architecture*, New York, 1885.

Nath, R., *The Immemorial Tāj Mahal*, Bombay, 1972.

____, *Some Aspects of Mughal Architecture*, New Delhi, 1976. Rizvi, S. A. A., and Flynn, V.J., *Fathpūr-Sikr'i*, Bombay, 1975. Smith, V. A., *A History of Fine Art in India and Ceylon*, rev.

K. de B. Codrington, Oxford, 1930; third edn enlarged and rev.

Karl Khāndalavala, Bombay, 1969.

Terry, J., *The Charm of Indo-Islamic Architecture*, London, 1955.

Toye, Sydney, *The Strongholds of India*, London, 1957.

Painting and Music

Archer, W. G., *Indian Miniatures*, Greenwich, 1960. Arnold, T. W., *Painting in Islam*, London, 1928.

___ and Wilkinson, J. V. S., *The Library of Chester Beatty; Catalogue of the Indian miniatures*, 3 vols., Bloomsbury, London, 1936.

Barrett, D., *Painting of the Deccan, XVI-XVII Century*, London, n.d.

___ and Gray, Basil, *Painting in India*, Skira, 1963.

Binyon, L., and Arnold, T. W., *The Court Painters of the Grand Moguls*, Oxford, 1921.

Brown, P., *Indian Painting under the Mughals, A.D. 1550 to 1750*, New York, 1975, reprint.

Clarke, C. Stanley, *Mughal Painting: The School of Jahangir*, New Delhi, 1983.

Coomaraswamy, A. K., *Indian Drawings*, London, 1910–12.

____, *Catalogue of the Indian Collections in the Museum of Fine Arts, Boston*, Cambridge, Mass., 1930.

Das, A. K., *Mughal Painting duringjahang'ir's Time*, Calcutta, 1978. Ettinghausen, R., *Paintings of Sultans and Emperors of India*, New Delhi, 1961.

Goeshuis, M., *Indian Painting*, London, 1978.

Gray, Basil, *Treasures of Indian Miniatures in the Bikaner Palace Collection*, Oxford, 1951.

____, *Persian Painting*, Skira, 1961.

Ha'jek Lubor, *Indian Miniatures of the Moghul School*, Prague, 1960.

____, *Miniatures from the East*, London, 1960.

Jones, William, and Willard, N.A., *Music of India*, Calcutta, 1962. Khāndelala, K., *Pahari Miniature Painting*, Bombay, 1958.

____ and Chandra, M., *Miniatures and Sculptures from the Collection of the Late Sir Cowasji Jehangir, Bart.*, Bombay, 1965.

____ and ___, *New Documents of Indian Painting: A Reappraisal, Prince of Wales Museum of Western India*, Bombay, 1969. Krishnadasa, Rai, *Muglzal Miniatures*, New Delhi, 1953.

Kuehnel, E., and Goetz, H., *Indian Book Paintings from Jahāngīr's Album in Berlin*, London, 1926.

Raiff, R., *Indian Miniatures: The Rājpūt Painters*, Tokyo, 1959. Randhawa, M.S., *Basohli Painting*, New Delhi, 1956.

____, *The Krishna Legend*, New Delhi, 1956.

____, *Kāngra Paintings of the Bhāgavata Purana*, New Delhi, 1960.

Rawson, P. S., *The Indian Sword*, London, 1968.

Ray, Niharranjan, *Mughal Court Paintings: A Study in Social and Formal Analysis*, Calcutta, 1975.

Robinson, B and W., *et al.*, *Islamic Painting and the Arts of the Book*, London, 1976.

Stchoukine, I., *Miniatures indiennes du musie du Louvre*, Paris, 1919.

____, *La peinture indienne a l'ipoque des grand moghols*, Paris, 1929.

Stuart, C. M. Villiers, *Gardens of the Great Mughals*, London, 1913. Verma, S. P., *Art and Material Culture in the Paintings of Akbar's Court*, New Delhi, 1978.

Welch, S.C., *The Art of Mughal India*, New York, 1963.

____, *Imperial Mughal Painting*, London, 1978.

Wellesz, E., *Akbar's Religious Thought Reflected in Mogul Painting*, London, 1952.

REFERENCES

1. Gibb (tr.), *The Travels of Ibn Battūta*, p. 622.
2. R. H. Major (tr.), *India in the Fifteenth Century* (*Journey of Abd er-Razzak*), New York (Hakluyt Society), 19, pp. 23–35.

3. Brown, *Indian Architecutre (Islamic Period)*, p. 89.
4. Ibid., p. 93.
5. Rizvi and Flynn, *Fathpūr-Slkn*, pp. 37–8.
6. Ibid., pp. 53-4.
7. Jahāngīr, tr. Rogers and Beveridge, *Tuzuk-i Jahāngīrī*, I, p. 152.
8. Abu'l-Faz1, tr. Blochmann, *A'in-i Akbari*, I, p. 114.
9. A. Muqtadir, *Catalogue of the Arabic and Persian Manuscripts in the Oriental Public Library at Bankipore*, Patna, 1921, VII, pp. 40–9.
10. Mohammad Wahid Mirza, *The Life and Times of Amir Khusrau*, Calcutta, 1935, pp. 237–9.
11. Firdawsi, *Shāhnama*, Tehran, n.d., IV, pp. 1961–2.
12. Rizvi, *History of Sūfism in India*, I, pp. 326–7.
13. *The Life and Times of Amir Khusrau*, pp. 164–6.
14. Ethe (*Catalogue of Persian Manuscripts in the Library of the India Office*), No. 2005. For a paper on the work, see Mrs K. N. Hasan, *Proceedings of the Indian History Congress*, Delhi session, 1961, pp. 177–9.
15. Abu'l-Fazl, tr. Blochmann, *A'in-i Akbarī*, I, p. 681.
16. Jadunath Sarkar (tr.), *Ma'asir-i 'Alamgīrī*, Calcutta, 1947, p. 45.
17. Rizvi, *History of Sūfism in India*, II, pp. 468–70.

APPENDIX

MEDIEVAL INDIAN LITERATURE AND THE *BHAKTI* MOVEMENT

In ancient times the enormous body of sacred Hindu literature written in Sanskrit, comprising the *Vedas*, the *Brahmanas* (meaning texts of sacrificial rituals; not to be confused with the highest Hindu priestly class, the brāhmans or Anglicized brahmins), and the *Upanishads*, were the exclusive preserve of the learned brāhmans, who in succeeding centuries interpreted and reinterpreted them in the light of new challenges and demands. The two epics, the *Mahābhārata* and the *Rāmāyana*, the compendia of legends and religious instructions, of which there are eighteen main ones, in the *Purānas*, and the books of sacred law and numerous hymns and religious poems, although in Sanskrit, were available to all, including men of low caste and women.

At least a century before the birth of Christ, the influence of the *Bhagavad Gitā* from Book VI of the *Mahābhārata*, comprising the ethical sermons of Lord Krishna to Arjuna on the battlefield when the Kurus were drawn up against the Pandavas, changed Hindu religious attitudes. They moved away from sacrifice and mystical techniques based on the ascetic virtues of renunciation and self-forgetfulness towards the impassioned religion of self-abandonment in God. The three paths to the Absolute whereby spiritual fulfilment was attained, as spelled out in the *Bhagavad Gitā*, are the path of knowledge (*jnāna*), the path of action (*karma*), and the path of deep adoration (*bhakti*). The goal of the paths of knowledge and action is for the soul to realize itself by its own efforts; but according to the path of *bhakti*, God actively helps the soul to liberation by the exercise of His grace. *Bhakti* does not recognize Hindu class and caste distinctions. Referring to Krishna's teachings on the subject, al-Birāni says:

> All these things originate in the difference of the classes or castes, one set of people treating the others as fools. This apart, all men are equal to each other, as Vasudeva says regarding him who seeks salvation: 'In the judgement of the intelligent man, the brāhman and the Candala are equal, the friend and the foe, the faithful and the deceitful, nay, even the serpent and the weasel. If to the eyes of intelligence all things are equal, to ignorance they appear as separated and different.'[1]

In the face of attacks from the materialists, the Buddhists, and Jainas, and the indifference of their own members towards the ossified ceremonies, the more enlightened brāhmans elevated Vishnu from his role of sun deity in the *Rig-Veda* to the state of supreme spirit. They identified him with Bhagavan, Vasudeva, Krishna, Narayana, and other less widely known divine figures. Similarly, the worship of the *Rig-Vedic* deity, Rudra, was transformed into Shaivism or Shiva worship.

Much of the vernacular sacred poetry was produced in the Peninsula. Some is of great value, and is considered to be very holy. A beautiful collection of moral aphorisms in Tamil verse, the *Tirukkural* (*Sacred Couplets*), attributed to Tiruvalluvar, perhaps dates from the fourth or fifth century AD, though some authorities would put it much earlier. Later, from the seventh to the tenth centuries, the eleven sacred books (*Tirumurai*) of the Tamil Shaivites were composed, anthologies of hymns by the sixty-three Nayanārs, or Teachers. Chief of these eleven works are the *Tevaram*, containing songs by the three poets Appar, Nānasambandar, and Sundaramurti, and the *Tiruvasagam* of Manikka Vasagar. The Tamil Vaishnavites produced at about the same period the *Nalāyiram* (*Four Thousand*), a collection of stanzas attributed to the twelve Alvars or saints of the sect.[2]

The Alvar hymns in Tamil were composed in honour of the god Vishnu and his *avatars* (incarnations) Rama and Krishna, particularly Krishna. They proposed *bhakti* (fervent devotion) as a path for all – outcaste and caste Hindu alike. The name Alvar, based on a Tamil root meaning 'be immersed', epitomizes the intuitive mystical content of their devotionalism. Rebelling against the superior caste claims of the brāhmans, the greatest of the Alvars was Nammalvar (*c.* AD 800), himself a lowly Shudra. In the hymns of Antal, a female Alvar, both the childhood of the incarnate god Krishna and his youthful days are lyrically depicted.

In the realm of philosophy, the influence of the south Indian Shaivite brāhman, Shankara (?788–820), strengthened the classical Vedanta, which is one of the six systems of salvation in Hinduism. Shankara's greatness lies in his brilliant dialectic. By able use of logical argument – and, we must admit, by interpreting some phrases very figuratively – he reduced all the apparently self-contradictory passages of the *Upanishads* to a consistent system which, though not unchallenged, has remained the standard philosophy of intellectual Hinduism to this day. The comparison of Shankara in Hinduism with St Thomas Aquinas in the Roman Catholic Church is a very fair one. The doctrine of Shankara is often known as *advaita* ('allowing no second', i.e. 'monism') or *kevalādvaita* ('strict monism'). On the everyday level of truth, the world was produced by Brahma, and went through an evolutionary process similar to that taught by the Sankhya school, from which Shankara took over the doctrine of the three *gunas* (constituent qualities, causing virtues *[sattva]*, passion *[rajas]* and dullness *[tamas]*). On the highest level of truth the whole phenomenal universe, including the gods themselves, was unreal; the world was *māya*, illusion, a dream, a mirage, a figment of the imagination. Ultimately the only reality was Brahman, the impersonal world – soul of the *Upanishads*, with which the individual soul was identical.[3]

Despite his rigid *Upanishadic* doctrine of salvation of knowledge, Shankara was the reputed author of some fine devotional poems in Sanskrit. In fact the Tamil country was absorbed in impassioned devotionalism, and Shankara could not remain unaffected. Hinduism remains indebted, however, to Ramanuja (?1017–1137), who was also a south Indian brāhman. He taught in the great temple of Srirangam. Although he admitted Shankara's doctrine of salvation by knowledge, he declared 'that those so saved would find a state of bliss inferior to the highest'. The best means of salvation was devotion, and the best yoga (mystical training) was *bhakti-yoga* such intense devotion to Vishnu that the worshipper realized that he was but a fragment of God, and wholly dependent on Him. Another means of salvation was. *prapatti*, the abandonment of self, putting one's soul completely in the hands of God, trusting in His will, and waiting confidently for His grace.

Ramanuja's god was a personal being, full of grace and love for his creation. He could even override the power of *karma* to draw repentant sinners to him. Unlike the impersonal world-soul of Shankara, which made the illusory universe in a sort of sport (*lila*), Ramanuja's God needed man, as man needed God. By forcing the sense, Ramanuja interpreted the words of Krishan, 'the wise man "I" deem my very self, to imply that just as man cannot live without God, so God cannot live without man. The individual soul, made by God out of His own essence, returned to its maker and lived for ever in full communion with Him, but was always distinct. It shared the divine nature of omniscience and bliss, and evil could not touch it, but it was always conscious ofitselfas an '1', for it was eternal by virtue of its being a part of godhead, and if it lost consciousness it would cease to exist. It was one with God, but yet separate, and for this reason the system of Ramanuja was called *visistādvaita* ('qualified monism').[4]

It was the compilation of the *Bhāgavata Purana* by some Bhagavata brāhman community in the Tamil country between 850 and 950, however, that made *bhakti* popular with both intellectuals and non-intellectuals. The tenth book of the *Bhāgavata Purāna*, describing the life and achievements of Krishna, highlights important Hindu cosmological and philosophical theories. The ecstatic and passionate love of the *gops* for Krishna, and his reciprocal love for them, went a long way to making *bhakti-yoga* predominant in the Hindu ways of salvation. In the *Bhāgavata Purāna*, the Supreme Being is predominantly qualified (*saguna*) and is conceived of as personal. Although the achievements of the cowherd god as an *avatar* (incarnation of a god, especially of Vishnu) satisfy the intense spiritual cravings of the devotee, the *Bhāgavata Purāna* also emphasizes the *nirguna* (unqualified) approach to the deity. In a very remarkable manner the great work blends devotionalism with non-dualism by focusing its attention on the worship of Krishna as the transcendent and supreme deity of the Vaishnavites.

The translation of the *Bhāgavata Purāna* from Sanskrit into Indian regional languages (some forty in Bengali alone) made the *bhakti* movement predominant in Hinduism. In short, the deification of Krishna, Rama, or Shiva and the devotional religion of the saints of the *bhakti* movement shook the foundation of brāhmanical dominance of Hinduism. *Bhaktas* ('devotees') adopted Gurūs or spiritual directors, many from the lower castes, as their supreme authority. The

Gurū was not necessarily a living being or an historical personality; legendary figures or abstract ideas of divinity were elevated to the position of Gurū. The devotees, or *bhaktas*, reverently treasured the hymns composed by Gurūs or ascribed to them, although interpolations were frequently made as they passed from generation to generation. Supernatural feats were freely credited to these Gurūs and were gullibly accepted as historical facts by the devotees.

The twelfth- and thirteenth-century Hindu mystics, such as Mādhva (1197–1276), a Kanarese brāhman and the founder of the Madhavasect, and theTelegu brāhman Nimbarka (c. 1130–1200), who settled near Mathura, also greatly influenced the *bhakti* movement. In northern India the cumulative impact of the Buddhist Sahajiyas,[5] Tantrics,[6] and Nath yogis led to the development of the north Indian *sant* (saintly) traditions, whose followers organized themselves into spiritual orders known as *panths*.

Bhakti devotion was not confined to a simplistic, singular attitude, or the *bhāva* to god or gods. It could assume the form of a servant's attitude to his master, such as the monkey god Hanuman's devotion to Rama (*dāsya-bhāva*)*;* that of a friend to a friend (*sakhya-bhāva*), such as that of Arjuna to Krishna; a parent's attitude to his or her child, as that of Kausalya to Rama (*vātsalya-bhāva*)*;* a child's attitude to his or her parent, such as Dhurva to Suniti (*sānta-bhāva*)*;* a wife's attitude to her husband, such as Sita's to Rama (*kānta-bhāva*)*;* the beloved's attitude to her lover, such as Radha's to Krishna; or even the attitude of hatred, such as that of an atheist or god-hater towards God, as Sisupala's to Krishna. The overriding feature of the attitudes in the *bhakti* movement is self-abandonment to a personal God, and this tends to be highly emotional.

These *bhāvas* were aroused by hymns and songs in regional dialects of the twelfth century onwards and helped to fill the heart of devotees from all classes with warmth and ecstasy. They gave rise to a rich corpus of devotional literature in these languages.

The tenth- and eleventh-century mystic songs, in the north Indian dialects known as *charyapadas*, are a curious mixture of a decadent Mahayana Buddhism and Tantric and Nath cult beliefs, but the devotional elements in them are deeply appealing. The most valuable contribution to the *bhakti* movement in Maharashtra was made, however, by the Marathi commentary on the *Bhagavad Gītā* entitled the *Bhāvārthdīpikā*, popularly known as *Jnanesvarī*, by Jnanesvara (1271–96), also known as Jnanadeva.

Jnanesvara's contemporary, Nāmdev (1270–1350), belonged to a low-caste family of Pandharpur tailors. Although his hymns are predominantly Vaishnavite, the notes of devotion to the invisible and formless God of the *nirguna* (unqualified) *bhakti* are obvious. There is a story that Nāmdev once fell into a trance and believed himself to be playing the cymbals in God's honour. God finally appeared and took the instrument from him. On awakening, Nāmdev composed the following hymn:

Come, God, the Qalandar
Wearing the dress of an Abdālī.

Nama's Lord is the searcher of all hearts,
And wandereth in every land.[7]

The sūfī terminologies such as 'Qalandar' and 'Abdal' in these verses suggest that, even before the conquest of the region by Sultan 'Ala 'u'd-Dīn Khaljī, sūfī ideas were already strongly entrenched there.

The most remarkable feature of Namdev's leadership was his indomitable courage in abolishing class and caste distinctions. This was decidedly an Alvar legacy, but the sūfī traditions also contributed to the opening of the doors of devotion to the Lord of all classes. A galaxy of hymnodist saints of low caste – such as Gora the potter, Samvata the gardener, Chokha the untouchable, Sena the barber, and janaba'i the maid – were Namdev's friends. Even though the low-caste Chokha was forbidden access to the temple, the god Vitthal carried him into the *sanctum sanctorum* and, according to the legend, gave him his own necklace. The townspeople refused to believe Chokha's story, however, and along with other untouchables he died a miserable death whilst performing labour. In a touching *abhang* (hymn), his friend Namdev describes how he was asked by Vitthal to go and find Chokha's remains in order to erect a monument over them.

The mystic Eknath (?1533–99) was a brāhman but he made *kīrtan* (group singing) in Marathi into the highest form of worship to the Lord. He published a reliable edition of the *Jnānesvan* and wrote a commentary on the *Rāmāyana* entitled the *Bhāvārtha Rāmāyana.* He also made no distinction between a brāhman and a *mahār* (outcaste) and frequently ate with untouchables.

Tukaram (1598–1650), the greatest *bhakti* poet in the Marathi language, was the son of a grocer. He would never have succeeded in life, because he gave away whatever he possessed or earned to the needy. He wrote emotional *abhanga* (hymns) in order to arouse devotion to Krishna. The great Marāthā ruler Shivājī respected him greatly, but Tukaram did not attend his court.

The Marathi poet and saint Ramdas (1608–81) exerted a strong influence on Shivājī. He was the son of a Nasik brāhman. When the priest who was officiating at his wedding uttered the word *'svadhan'* ('be constant'), Ramdas interpreted it as a divine command to serve God and left the place. He began to wander through the Marāthā region as a devotee of Rama and gathered a considerable following. He rebuilt dilapidated temples, established *mathas* (monasteries), and wrote several works to reinvigorate Hindu devotion to Rama.

The Bengali movement was inspired both by Vaishnavite and Sahajiya sources. The *Bhāgavata Purāna* gave a new form and meaning to the *Gīta Govind* (1199), a poet at the court of Lakshman Sena of Bengal, which features the love stories of Krishna and his celestial consort, Radha, who in later Krishna *bhakti* themes assumes the form of the supreme *hladini shakti* or joy giving Even uninitiates are fascinated by the romance of Krishna, Radha, and the *gopīs;* to the *bhaktas* it is an allegory of the soul's love and craving for the divine. It has been suggested that Jayadeva's Sanskrit version is based on the *apabrahmsa* (traditional vernacular or archaic Bengali) and that the Krishna cult was predominant in Bengal much earlier than the twelfth century. Chandidas (*c.* 1350–1430) and other Vaishnavite poets identified themselves with Krishna's female companions. Chaitanya (1485–1533) proved even more radical by personally identifying himself with Radha and her love for Krishna, which symbolized the soul's search for God. Chaitanya's emotional attachment to Krishna immersed him in long spells of ecstasy and epileptic fits. His favourite form of worship as a *bhakta* was *kīrtan* or *samkīrtan* (group singing and dancing) accompanied by drums, cymbals, or a one-stringed fiddle, during which the words 'Hari' and 'Krishna' were constantly chanted. The singing sessions were not confined to private homes and temples, but spilled over into the streets. For three centuries hymns, ballads, legends, and dramas centring around Chaitanya's interpretations of Krishna multiplied in Bengali literature. In the seventeenth century Govind Dās reinvigorated the Chaitanya traditions.

A unique offshoot of the Chaitanya tradition was the *bāul* movement. This began in Nadia and spread all over Bengal.

Although Hindus and Muslims adapted their own version, they both wrote their rapturous songs in Bengali. The Muslim *bāuls* followed the sūfī tradition, while the Hindu *bāuls* were Vaishnavites. They are both regarded as 'men of the heart'. The *bāuls* were non-dualistic, conceiving the body as the microcosm of the universe. A *bāul* poet wrote: 'The man of the house is dwelling in the house – in vain have you become mad by searching for Him outside.'[8]

The Indo-Aryan dialects, such as Bhojpuri, Magadhī, and Maithili of modern Bihār, Avadhi, of the Avadh region, Braj Bhasha of the Mathura region, and Rājasthānī, Panjābi, Kashmīri, Sindī, and Gujarāti; also assumed new forms and meaning through *bhakti* poetry. The love ballads on Radha and Krishna by Vidyapati (fourteenth to fifteenth centuries), in Maithilī, are a legacy from Chandidas. Their vigour and refined diction made them popular even in Bengal, Assam, and Nepal.

In the fifteenth century the area which may loosely be called 'the land of Hindī' saw a new turn in the *bhakti* movement under the influence of Ramananda (*c.* 1360–1470). In his early days, Ramananda probably lived in South India and was initiated into Ramānuja's Srivaishnava sect. Later he travelled all over India, spending some time teaching in Banāras and Agra. He advocated devotion to the incarnation of Vishnu in the form of Rama and his consort Sita, and worshipped their close companion, the monkey god Hanuman. His *Adhyatmā-Rāmāyana* in Sanskrit is a remarkable literary achievement which re-aligns the *saguna* and *nirguna* forms into parallel currents. His disciples belonged to both the Vaishnavite and *nirguna bhakti* north Indian *sant* (Hindu saints) traditions. Ramananda firmly repudiated the injustices of caste, and among his twelve outstanding disciples were an outcaste, a woman, and a Muslim. Raidas, the *chamar* (shoemaker) disciple of Ramananda, wrote songs condemning brāhmanical rituals and caste prejudices.

The famous *bhakti* poet Kabīr was also one of Ramananda's disciples, but he reorientated the prevailing north Indian *nirguna bhakti* traditions. He uninhibitedly declared:

I am not Hindu nor Muslim
Allah-Ram is the breath of my body!

Kabīr's history is shrouded with myths. Some legends state that Kabīr was the illegitimate son of a brāhman widow. One version claims that he was conceived by a widow because of Ramananda's blessings, and that, as with Christ, this occurred without a natural father. In order to protect herself from public slander, the widow left her baby near a pond some way out of the city. A Muslim weaver called 'Alī, popularly known as Nirā, saw the baby; being childless, he and his wife Nima decided to adopt it as their own. This story is reminiscent of the adoption of Moses by the Pharaoh's daughter after she had found him abandoned in the bulrushes. The local *qāzī* gave the child the name Kabīr. This story was an obvious invention and was an attempt to associate Kabīr's parentage with Hinduism. What is more probable is that Kabīr was born into a Muslim family, the members of which were deeply imbued with Nath beliefs. That his parents' ancestors were yogis is not impossible. Of various dates for his birth, 1425 is the most likely.

Kabīr constantly travelled around the Banāras area and was directly in touch with a number of Hindu *sants* and sūfis. It is not unlikely that he exchanged ideas with eminent sūfis in Kara, Manikpār, and Rudawli. Their views on the Wahdat al-Wujād ('unity of being' doctrine), expressed in Hindī, revolutionized Kabīr's spiritual sensitivity. Although Kabīr's mythology was predominantly Hindu, Muslim equivalents are commonplace and laboured. His verses were generally memorized by his disciples after they had been uttered, and then written down immediately or soon afterwards. This process gave rise to considerable interpolation, and naturally many inauthentic verses are included. Those in the *Adi Granth*, the *Kabīr Granthāwali*, and the *Bijak* (*Treasury*) are the most reliable.

Kabīr was married and although he was unhappy with his role as a husband and a father he preached neither renunciation nor celibacy. Throughout his life, when he was not travelling he lived the traditional life of a married man. Before his death he is said to have migrated from Banāras to Maghar. Some authors suggest that Maghar was close to Banāras; others believe it was in the district of Basti near Gorakhpur in Uttar Pradesh. The decision was deliberately taken by Kabīr in order to belie the Hindu superstition that one who died in Maghar would return in a following life as an ass. Of the many dates given for Kabīr's death, 1505 is the most probable.

The earliest sūfī traditions refer to Kabīr as *muwahhid* (unitarian, or a follower of the Wahdat al-Wujud), who could not be called either an orthodox Hindu or an orthodox Muslim.[9] According to the seventeenth-century *Mir'ātu'l-asrār*, he was a Firdawsiyya sūfī, but the Irāni author of the *Dabistān-i Mazāhib* places Kabīr against the background of the legend of the Vaishnavite *vairāgis* (mendicants). 'Abdu'llāh Khweshgi, the author of the early eighteenth-century *Ma'āriju'l-wilāyat*, says:

Shaykh Kabīr *Julāha* [weaver] is the disciple of Shaykh Taqi.[10] Kabīr was one of the perfect *awliyā'* (sūfīs) and the most famous gnostic of his age, but he chose for himself the path of the *malāmatiyya.*[11] He adopted this technique in order to remain unknown. His Hindī poetry is sublime and is a proof of the greatness of the author. If his poetry is carefully examined it is found full of ideas of unification (*wisāl*), with little mention of separation. He was a pioneer in expressing spiritual truth and gnosis through the medium of Hindī. He wrote a great variety of Hindī poetry, and his *Bishunpads* and *sākhīs* (forms of Hindī poetry) are very famous. Those who do proper justice to Kabīr's poetry are convinced that no other poetry can match it in the ex pression of divine secrets and spiritual truth. Muhaqqiq-i Hindī (Malik Muhammad Ja'isi) imitated the style of Kabīr but he chose the *soratha* and *dohas* (forms of Hindī poetry) through which to express his thoughts. Kabīr's spiritual eminence attracted both Muslims and Hindus to his discipleship. Each religious group considered him to be a member of its own religion, but in reality he transcended all such distinctions. Were someone to assert that Kabīr had only Hindu followers, this claim would still not undermine his *wilāyat* (position as an eminent sūfī). An earlier example of a similar situation was the devotion of the Rafizis (Shī'īs) to the fourth Caliph, 'Alī; this did not undermine the reputation of the latter, but on the contrary established the greatness of 'Alī, to whom even the irreligious (Shī'īs) were drawn.[12]

'Abdu'llāh Khweshgi concludes his obituary of Kabīr by quoting about twenty of Kabīr's verses with sūfic explanations.

Modern scholars overemphasize the Hindu aspect of Kabīr and Nanak, but both sages mirror the spiritual movement which relentlessly fought against simple-minded Hindu and Muslim ritualism, die-hard fanaticism, and religious, sectarian, class, and colour distinctions. They were the devotees of an omnipotent and omniscient God and intensely loved all living beings.

Kabīr's *nirguna* Brahma (Supreme Being) has both a transcendental and an immanent nature. He is the God of gods, Supreme Lord, primal and omnipotent. Kabīr's notion of the void, referred to as *sānya*, is based on Mahayana Buddhism and on Hindu esoteric philosophy. It represents his concept of the 'ultimate reality'. Although he refers to 'reality' by more commonly used Hindu and Muslim names, the word he most frequently uses is 'Rama' who, as he himself explains, is *nirguna* Rama. He reminds us:

Kabīr, call Him Rām who is omnipresent;
We must discriminate in mentioning the two Rāms;
The one Rām (God) is contained in all things;
The other (Ram Chandra) is only contained in one thing, himself[13]

Kabīr equated Ram with Rahim (the Merciful), Hari with Hazrat, and Krishna with Karim, but it was his frequent identification of Ram with Rahim that went a long way to make the *bhakti* movement a unique religious experience in the Indian subcontinent. Denouncing idolatry, Kabīr wrote that if God were found worshipping stone, he would worship it in a hand-mill, which 'grindeth corn for the world to eat'. To him, the prayers, pilgrimages, and fasting of the Muslims were equally mechanical. Essentially a *bhakta* (devotee), Kabīr was totally absorbed in his devotion to the Supreme. But he was also deeply upset by Hindu and Muslim intolerance and religious chauvinism. Ironically, after his death, his Hindu and Muslim disciples could not even agree on the disposal of his corpse. The Hindus wished to cremate him; the Muslims fought to bury him. There are two *samādhis* (graves) of Kabīr at Maghar; one is venerated by Hindus, the other by Muslims. The Hindu *Kabīr Panthīs* and their branches are more prominent than the Muslim ones, although his verses were frequently quoted by Muslims, *even* by the puritan Naqshbandiyya leaders such as the Mujaddid Alf-i Sani and his descendants. The *rawza* (tomb) of Kabīr is maintained by a Muslim keeper who collects the offerings, but the modern politicized Muslim of the subcontinent is indifferent to Kabīr.

Unlike that of Kabīr, the broad outline of Gurū Nānak's life is reasonably clear. He was born in the village of Talwandi, later known as Nankāna Sāhib, south-west of Lahore, now in Pakistan, in 1469. His father, Kalil, a *khattīz* (member of the Hindu commercial classes), was a village accountant and, as was customary with members of that profession, supplemented his income through agriculture. Attempts were made to give Nanak lessons in Hinduism and the official Persian language, but Nanak was interested in meditation, not in formal learning. When Nanak was sixteen, his parents arranged his marriage, and under pressure from his family he later became a merchant and a farmer. Nevertheless, most of his time was spent with yogis who lived in the surrounding jungles.

Gurū Nānak's brother-in-law, Jai Ram, a steward of Dawlat Khān of Sultanpur, the Lodī governor of the region lying between Sirhind and Dipalpur, secured a position for him in the Khān's commissariat. There, the minstrel Bha'i Mardana joined him, and they became lifelong friends. While at Sultanpur, the Gurū shocked both Muslims and Hindus by declaring that there was neither a (true) Hindu nor a (true) Muslim. His spiritual sensitivity had reached its climax. Soon afterwards, accompanied by Bha'i Mardana, Nanak travelled from Panipat to Assam, visiting Hindu and sūfī pilgrim centres. According to the Sikh hagiological literature, he conversed with sūfīs and *bhaktas* who had died long ago, but these dialogues in fact took place spiritually in Nana's vision. By 1520 the Gurū and his friend were back in the Panjāb to witness the carnage during Bābur's third invasion of India. Nanak's sensitive heart was poured into the verses known as *Bābur-Vāni.* They are invaluable as an historical document.

Gurū Nānak's second journey took him down south, as far as Ceylon. Returning from there he visited Kashmīr. It is not unlikely that later on he travelled as far as Mecca and Baghdad; such travels were customary with Muslim wandering dervishes and yogis who did not bind t.hemselves with religious forms and taboos. In later life, Gurū Nānak lived mainly in the Panjāb, occasionally visiting Ajodhan,

Multān, and Gorakhtāri in Peshawar. On 22 September 1539 he died at Kartarpur. Before his death he had appointed his disciple Lihna as his successor.

Although Lihna came from a rich family, in keeping with the traditions of sūfī *khānqāhs*, he had previously been made to perform such humiliating duties as carrying loads of wet grass. As the first Gurū he was known as Gurū Angad (1539–42). This title, meaning 'of my own limb', was bestowed on him by Gurū Nānak himself. Although the word 'Gurū' in Nanak's teachings stood for the voice of God, and not necessarily for an individual, posterity recognizes him as the personification of the light of God. The Hindu incarnation theories became the cardinal feature of Gurū Nānak's movement. The sūfī idea of the transmission of a *pir's* light to his successor was also emphasized. The disciples of Gurū Nānak and his successors formed themselves into a *panth* or the order of Gurmats, the followers of the Gurū's doctrine. During the lifetime of the third Gurū, Amar Dās (1552–74), the hymns of the first three Gurūs, and those of the *sants* and sūfīs whose teachings were compatible with the Gurū's aphorisms, were compiled. In 1603–4 the fifth Gurū, Arjan Deva (1581–1606), added his own compilation and that of his father to the earlier collection. The volume was entitled the *Adi Granth*, later known as *Gurū Granth Sahib.* It became the divine scripture of the *panth*, and the followers of the Gurū's teachings, as recorded in it or expressed in the corporate will of the community, were known as Sikhs.

The execution of Gurū Arjan by Jahāngīr, for blessing the rebel Prince Khusraw, transformed the Sikhs into a martial race. Although the Gurūs themselves belonged to the urban mercantile community of *khattris*, their followers, who were rural Jāts, are the backbone of the Sikh community. Before his death the tenth Gurū, Gobind Singh (1675–1708), closed the line of personal Gurūs; henceforth the scripture, or the *Gurū Granth Sāhib*, and the corporate will of the community, the *panth* or Khalsa Panth of Gurū Gobind Singh, *were* to be recognized as their sole guide. Their political struggles made the followers of Gurmat – the Sikhs – radically different from the *panths* or orders of earlier *bhaktas* or saints.

Gurū Nānak's doctrine of salvation through the divine name (*nām*) was similar to the teachings of the *sants*, but it was more consistently sūfic. Their *Upanishadic* interpretations are also equally valid. In His primal aspect, Gurū Nānak's Lord is fhe eternally unchanging formless one (*nirankār*), inscrutable (*agam*), boundless (*apār*), beyond time (*akāl*), ineffable (*alakh*), with divine will (*qudrat*) in the technical sense of sūfīsm, beyond comprehension. Nānak's loving devotion to God is expressed in the forms of address he uses, such as Pita (Father), Pritam (Lover), and Khasam (Husband or Master). According to the nature of the occasion and mood, Gurū Nānak selected traditional terms used by Hindus and Muslims to invoke God, such as Allah, Khuda, Rabb, Rama, Govinda, Hari, and Murari. But it is *Gurū Kā Sabad*, or the Gurū's word (a divine voice mystically heard within the human heart), that reinvigorates the spiritual sensitivity of the devotee. This is the mysterious Ism-i A'zam (the Great Name) of the sūfīs. A meditation upon the essence of the *nām* (divine name) is the real *nām simaran* (holding the divine name in remembrance) or *nāmjapan* (repetition of the divine name) and not mechanical repetition of the name of God. This is sūfī *zikr par excellence.* The creative activity of the Supreme is His *hukam* (the divine 'order'), the counterpart of *rizā* (divine will) in sūfī terminology.

Nanak's teachings infused a stern ethical tone and a practical approach into the problems of life. He advocated living a normal life accompanied by piety and righteousness. He envisaged a society in which cultivators prepared the soil for sowing properly, and merchants were honest. Income earned from dishonest means included the sale of the forbidden products of pork and beef to Muslims and Hindus respectively. He condemned the social prejudices surrounding the concepts of high and low castes, believing that only those who considered themselves *n'ich* (low) before God attained salvation.

Like those of Kabīr, Dado's biographical details are shrouded with myths and legends. There are many other similarities. It is generally agreed that he was born in 1544, but that his birthplace was Ahmadābād is disputed. His father, Lodī Ram, was said to have been a merchant but possibly he was a converted Muslim cotton-carder, and Dado's name was also Dawud with interchangeable Persian letters in the words 'Dado' and 'Dawud'. Dado's life was spent at Sambhar in Rājasthān, and it is not improbable that he was even born in one of the villages of the region. The teacher who revolutionized Dado's ideas belonged to the Ramanandi tradition; Dadu's Hindu disciple, Sundar Das, refers to him as Vriddhananda. In the Muslim tradition he is called Buddhan. Both names suggest that he was an elderly sage. The traditions also relate that the Supreme Being appeared to Dado in the character of an old ascetic and initiated him into divine truth. His growing fame in Rājasthān resulted in the Emperor Akbar's leading dignitary, Raja Bhagavan Das, becoming his disciple. The Raja introduced him to the Emperor before Akbar's departure from Fathpur-Sīkrī for Kābul in 1584. After a short stay at the capital, Dado left for Rājasthān. In the last days of his life he left for Nara'ina in Rājasthān, where he died in 1603.[14]

Dadu's eldest son, Carib Das, performed his father's last rites and was accepted by his father's disciples as his successor. Before long, however, Carib Das resigned from this position, and the responsibility for the direction of the *panth* was assumed by his disciples. Dado's hymns and poems, known as *Bān'i* (inspired utterances or oracles), were compiled by his favourite disciples such as Tila (a Jat), Mohan Daftari, Rajjab Das, and Sundar Das the younger. The eighteenth-century decline of the Mughals and Rājpūts transformed the Dadu Panthis into *nāgas* or prpfessional fighters.

Dado was deeply influenced by Kabīr, who is frequently mentioned in his *Bani.* In his hymns Dado reiterates that Ram, Govind, and Allah are his spiritual teachers and he occupies a distinctive place in the galaxy of the saints such as Nāmdev, Pipa, Sena, Raidas, and Kabīr. Dadu's cosmology and the stages of the soul's pilgrimage are markedly sūfic. Like later Kabīr Panthis, Dadā Panthis also became predominantly Hindu.

The Hindu traditions treasure the memory of the *sants* and *bhaktas* for their subtle mystical thought and lyrical verses in regional languages; but Hindu spiritual devotion was, and is, satisfied only by accepting the son of Dasratha, or Krishna, as the human incarnation (*avatara*) of the Absolute. Their *saguna*, rather *nirguna*, form is dear to the Hindu heart. It was this spiritual yearning that made the sixteenth-century Mirabal, Sūrdās, and Tulsidās the greatest poets of the *bhakti* movement in Hindī, although their imagery and terminology are impregnated with *sant* traditions.

Mirabaī, the only daughter of Ratna Singh, a Rājpūt noble of the House of Rathor, was born in *c.* 1498 in a village in Merta near Ajmīr. In 1516 she was married to Bhoja Raj, the heir apparent of Rana Sanga of Mewar. Her husband died before his father, however, and she had no children. In her poems Mira speaks of herself as a virgin. She invited *sadhās* (Hindu mendicants) to the women's quarters in the palace and mingled with Hindu holy men in the temples in her town. The members of her royal household could not tolerate her devotion to these ascetics; in order to discipline her they frequently chastised her, locked her up, and even tried to poison her. Such stories are, however, discounted by many authorities. What her poems suggest is that her fervent devotion to Lord Krishna had made her totally indifferent to worldly life. She seems to have died around 1546.

Mirabal's extraordinarily brilliant poetry, known as *Padāvalī* (a series of poems), portrays a feeling of deep personal association with the Lord Krishna and a yearning to dissolve herself in Him. Her Lord is not *nirguna*, nor totally indescribable, but is interchangeable with her beloved Shyama (Krishna). She advocates image worship and the observance of special fasts and takes delight in describing Vishnu's descent to earth. Like Chaitanya, she is transported to the heights of ecstasy and bliss by singing and dancing. She had no hesitation in saying:

My Beloved dwells in my heart,
I have actually seen that Abode of Joy.
Mira's Lord is Han, the Indestructible.
My Lord, I have taken refuge with Thee,
Thy slave.[15]

Vallabhacharya (1479–1530), of the Telugū-speaking region of south India, reinvigorated the Krishna *bhakti* traditions with his Sanskrit works. Besides the *Vedanta* and *Bhagavad Gita*, they are greatly influenced by the *Bhagavata Purāna.* In them Krishna is *sat-cit ananda* (existence, intelligence, and bliss) personified. When the devotee's soul is dissolved in Krishna, he is transported into the Lord's own ineffable bliss. The Lord's grace is attainable by singing hymns praising Krishna, listening to His legends, worshipping His image, and making pilgrimages to Vaishnava shrines. Vallabha established the Srinath temple on Goverdhan hill, west of Mathura. He almost ignored Radha, who was later made predominant in Vallabha's system by his son Vitthalnath (1515–88?).

In 1571 Vitthalnath established his centre at Gokul near Mathura and gathered together a group of singers and poets known as *asht chap* (the eight seals or insignia). They believed themselves to be Krishna's favourites and wrote in the Braj Bhasha dialect with great refinement and ecstasy. Nanddās and Sūrdas were the most venerated poets among them.

Nanddas's (?1533–85) *padas* (poems for singing) have been rendered into English by R. S. McGregor under the title *The Round Dance of Krishna and Uddhav's Message.* They portray the soul's love and longing for God, matched by God's perfect love and grace, through the symbolism of the herd-girls' revels with Krishna on the bank of the Jamuna.[16]

Nanddas's contemporary, the blind poet Sūrdas (*c.* 1478–1583), vividly deals with all the details of Krishna's life, from His birth, and His activities as a child, including the theft of butter, to the herd-girls' love for Him and His for them. He portrays Radha with great devotion in his *magnum opus*, the *Sūr Sagar* (*Sūr's Ocean*), as well as in other poems. The melody of Krishna's defence in the poem 'I Didn't Eat the Butter *Ma*' transports the listener to the realm of spiritual ecstasy. But all Sūr's poetry symbolizes the truth that social duties and even the universe and life itself are meaningless without the love of the Lord.

Sūrdas's contemporary, Tulsidas (1532–1623), identifies Lord Rama with the Absolute, although he does not reject the *nirguna* Absolute. His *magnum opus*, the *Ram-charit-mānas* (*The Lake of the Story of Rama*), or the *Ramayana* in Hindī, is the bible of north Indian Hindus. Tulsīdas is believed to be a reincarnation of Valmīkī, the author of the Sanskrit *Rāmāyana.* Its lyrical fervour and devotional sensitivity are miraculous. In Tulsidas's *Vinaya-patrika* and the *Kavitavalī* there are references to some details of his own life and his political, social, and economic environment, but it is misleading to interpret them literally. They are designed to remind his readers of the sinful condition of Kal-yuga (the Dark Age), beginning from the Christian era, when alien kings ruled much of India and plunged the country into a progressive decline of piety and ethical values. Akbar's rule is not necessarily the target of Tulsidas's attack. In his world-view, hypocrisy and tyranny were common to all temporal rulers, whom he compares with *Rāvana* (the Demon); and he invokes Rama to kill them in order to restore the environment in which devotion to the Lord could be promoted uninterruptedly. The messianic hopes of Muslim mystics are similar to those of Tulsidas.

The *Rām-charit-mānas* idealizes all forms of human relationships, but the most impressive is the devotion of Hanuman to Rama. Not only does the monkey devotee imprint 'Rama's lotus feet upon his heart', Rama's affection for his devotee is also deep and warm. Indeed human beings and God are indispensable to each other. The only counterpart of the lyrical idealization of Hanuman by Tulsidas is the visionary treatment of the *gopis* by Krishna. Both open the doors of *bhakti* (devotion) to men and women of all classes and reinvigorate touching streaks of tender human relations between all fellow-beings and their Lord.

BIBLIOGRAPHY

Ahmad Shāh, *The Bijak of Kabīr*, Hamirpur, 1917.

____, *Hindu Religious Poetry*, Cawnpore, 1925.

Ajwani, L. H., *History of Sindhi Literature*, New Delhi, 1970.

Allchin, F. R. (tr.), *Kavitāvali*, New York, 1964.

____, *Tulsi Dās' Petition to Rām*, London, 1966.

Alston, A. J., *The Devotional Poems of Mirābaī*, Delhi, 1980.

Archer, W. G., *The Loves of Krishna*, London, 1957.

Babineau, E. J., *Love of God and Social Duty in the Rāmcaritmānas*, Delhi, 1979.

Barua, B. K., *History of Assamese Literature*, New Delhi, 1964.

Barz, R., *The Bhakti Sect of Vallabhāchārya*, Faridabad, 1976.

Bhandarkar, R. G., *Vaisnavism, Saivism and Minor Religious Systems*, Strasbourg, 1913.

Bharadwaj, K. D., *Philosophy of Rāmānuja*, New Delhi, 1958.

Bhārati, A., *The Tāntric Tradition*, London, 1965.

Bhattacharya, S. K., *Krsna-Cult*, New Delhi, 1978.

Carpenter, J. E., *Theism in Medieval India*, London, 1921. Carpenter, J. N., *The Theology rif Tulsz Dās*, Edinburgh, 1930.

Chatterji, S. K., *Language and Literature of Modem India*, Calcutta, 1963.

Dasgupta, S. B., *An Introduction to Tāntric Buddhism*, Calcutta, 1958, 2nd edn.

____, *Obscure Religious Cults*, Calcutta, 1962.

Dasgupta, S. N., *Hindu Mysticism*, New York, 1927.

____, *A History of Indian Philosophy*, 5 vols., London, 1966--9, 2nd edn.

Dutt, M. N. (tr.), *A Prose English Translation of Harīvamsha*, Calcutta, 1897.

Farquhar, J. N., *An Outline of the Religious Literature of India*, Delhi, 1967.

Goetz, H., *Mīrābaī*, Bombay, 1966.

Grewal, J. S., *Gurū Nānak in History*, Chandigarh, 1969.

Growse, F. S. (tr.), *The Rāmāyana of Tulsīdās*, Allahabad, 1966.

Gupta, M.P., *Gosvāmī Tulsī Dās*, Allahabad, 1946.

Handoo, C. K., *Tulsī Dās, Poet, Saint and Philosopher of the Sixteenth Century*, New Delhi, 1964.

Hawley, J. S., *Krishna, The Butter-Thief*, Princeton, 1983.

___, *Sūr Dās, Poet, Singer, Saint*, Washington, 1983.

Hooper, J. S.M. (tr.), *Hymns of the Alvārs*, Calcutta, 1929.

Hopkins, E. W., *The Great Epic of India*, New York, 1901.

Jaiswal, S., *The Origin and Development of Vaisnavism*, Delhi, 1967. Jesudasan, C. and H., *A History of Tamil Literature*, Calcutta, 1964.

Jhaveri, K. M., *Milestones in Gujarātz Literature*, Bombay, 1914.

Jindal, K. B., *A History of Hindl Literature*, Allahabad, 1955.
Keay, F. E., *A History of Hindī Literature*, Calcutta, 1960, 2nd edn.
Lorenzen, D. N. (ed.), *Religious Change and Cultural Domination*, Mexico, 1981.
Macauliffe, M. A, *The Sikh Religion*, 6 vols., Oxford, 1909.
Macfie, J. M., *The Rāmāyana of Tulsī Dās*, Edinburgh, 1930.
Macnicol, N., *Indian Theism*, Oxford, 1915.
Majumdar, A. K., *Bhakti Renaissance*, Bombay, 1965.
Mansinha, M., *History of Orrya Literature*, New Delhi, 1962.
Marfatia, M., *The Philosophy of Vallabhāchārya*, Delhi, 1967.
McGregor, R. S., *Nanddās, the Round Dance of Krishna and Uddhav's Message*, London, 1973.
McLeod, W. H., *Gurū Nānak and the Sikh Religion*, Oxford, 1968.
Misra, A. P., *The Development and Place of Bhakti in Sankara Vedanta*, Allahabad, 1967.
Misra, J., *The Religious Poetry of Sūr Das*, Patna, 1934.
Morgan, K. (ed.), *The Religion of the Hindus*, New York, 1953.
O'Flaherry, W. D., *Asceticism and Eroticism in the Mythology of Siva*, Delhi, 1975.
Orr, W. G., *A Sixteenth-Century Indian Mystic*, London, 1947. Parameswaram, P. K., *History of Malayalam Literature*, New Delhi, 1967.
Ranade, R. D., *Pathway to God in Hindī Literature*, Bombay, 1961.
____, *Pathway to God in Marathī Literature*, Bombay, 1961.
Rukmani, T. S., *A Critical Study of the Bhagavata Purana*, Varanasi, 1970.
Sen, Sukumar, *History of Bengali Literature*, New Delhi, 1960.
Singh, Khushwant, *A History of the Sikhs*, Princeton, 1963, 1966.
Sukla, R. C., *Gosvamī Tulsī Das*, Prayag (Allahabad), 1935.
Varadachari, K. C., *Alvars of South India*, Bombay, 1966.
Vaudeville, Ch, *Granthavali* (French trans.), Pondichery, 1957; *Pastorales par Sour-Das*, Paris, 1971.
____, *Kabīr*, I, Oxford, 1974.
Westcott, G. H., *Kabīr and Kabīr Panth*, Calcutta, 1953.
Zaehner, R. C., *Hinduism*, Oxford, 1966, 2nd edn.
____, *The Bhagavad Gīta*, Oxford, 1969.
Zvelebil, K., *Tamil Literature*, Wiesbaden, 1974.

REFERENCES

1. *Alberūnī's India*, II, pp. 137–8.
2. *The Wonder That Was India*, Volume I, pp. 299–300.
3. Ibid., p. 328.
4. Ibid., p. 332.

5. *Sahaja* means 'that which is inborn or the quintessence which all the animate and inanimate possess by virtue of their very existence; the realization of this sahaja was regarded by the Sahijiyas (those who yearned for sahaja) as the highest attainment of spiritual yearning. They condemned, in the strongest language they could command, all kinds of insincerity and artificiality in life and religion and, at the same time, recommended the most natural path for the attainment of truth'. – S. B. Dasgupta, *Obscure Religious Cults*, pp. 164–5. There were both Vaishnavite and Buddhist Sahajiyas.
6. 'Tantrism is followed by certain left-hand sects of Hindus and Buddhists. Shaivites (sects like the Saktas, Siddhas, Nathas, Kapalikas, and the Vaishnavite Sahajiyas) practise Tantrism. In common parlance, *tantra* means an esoteric literature of a religious and practical nature. In Buddhism it includes a mass of heterogeneous elements, the chanting and muttering of *mantr(ls* (syllables or sacred verses from the scriptures), describing various mystic diagrams, making postures and gestures, worshipping various types of gods and goddesses including a host of demi-gods and other such beings, meditation and salutation of various types, and, last but not least, yogic practices, sometimes involving sex relations.' S. B. Dasgupta, *An Introduction to Tāntric Buddhism*, p. 2.
7. M.A. Macauliffe, *The Sikh Religion*, VI, pp. 69–70.
8. Dasgupta, *Obscure Hindu Cults*, p. 124.
9. Rizvi, *A History of Sūfism in India*, I, p. 373.
10. According to the *Ma'āriju'l-wilāyat*, Shaykh Taqi, the *pir* of Kabīr, was also a weaver and lived in Kara Manikpār. *Ma'āriju'1-wilāyat*, Shirani collection, Panjāb University Library, ff. 344b–45a.
11. Sūfis who outwardly behave outrageously in order to make themselves appear disgusting to the Muslims.
12. *Ma'āriju'l-wilāyat*, ff. 345–47a; Rizvi, *A History of Sūfism in India*, II, p. 413.
13. Macauliffe, *The Sikh Religion*, VI, p. 413.
14. W. G. Orr, *A Sixteenth-Century Indian Mystic*, pp. 44–58.
15. A.J. Alston, *The Devotional Poems of Mirābaz*, pp. 1–8, No. 116.
16. R. S. McGregor, *Nanddās, the Round Dance of Krishna and Uddhav's Message*, London, 1973, pp. 29–54.

INDEX WITH GLOSSARY

Note: Delhi and India have not been included

D

J